Helping Children Learn Mathematics

Sixth Edition

Robert E. Reys
University of Missouri

Mary M. Lindquist
Columbus State University

Diana V. Lambdin
Indiana University

Nancy L. Smith
Emporia State University

Marilyn N. Suydam
The Ohio State University

John Wiley & Sons, Inc.

New York   Chichester   Weinheim   Brisbane   Singapore   Toronto

Acquisitions Editor: Maureen E. Prado Roberts
Developmental Editor: Marian Provenzano
Marketing Managers: Catherine Beckham/Allison Fichter
Production Services Manager: Jeanine Furino
Production Editor: Sandra Russell
Senior Designer: Karin G. Kincheloe
Cover Designer: Carol C. Grobe
Cover Credit: *Accolades,* 1993 by Libby Lehman
Photo Editors: Nicole Horlacher/Sara Wight
Illustration Editor: Anna Melhorn
Production Management Services: Omegatype Typography, Inc.

Permission is granted by the publisher to reproduce the forms on pages 382–405.

This book was typeset in 9.5/12 Stone Serif by Omegatype Typography, Inc., and
printed and bound by R.R. Donnelley & Sons, Inc. (Willard). The cover was printed
by Phoenix Color Corp.

The paper in this book was manufactured by a mill whose forest management programs include
sustained yield harvesting of its timberlands. Sustained yield harvesting principles ensure that the
number of trees cut each year does not exceed the amount of new growth.

This book is printed on acid-free paper. ∞

Library of Congress Cataloging-in-Publication Data

Helping children learn mathematics / Robert E. Reys . . . [et al.].— 6th ed.
  p.   cm.
   Rev. ed. of: Helping children learn mathematics / Robert E. Reys, Marilyn N. Suydam,
Mary Montgomery Lindquist. 4th ed. c1995.
   Includes bibliographical references and index.
   ISBN 0-471-36785-0 (paper : alk. paper)
   1. Mathematics—Study and teaching (Elementary)   I. Reys, Robert E.   II. Reys, Robert
E. Helping children learn mathematics.
   QA135.5 .R49 2001
   372.7'044—dc21
                                                          00-027637

Printed in the United States of America

10 9 8 7 6 5 4 3 2 1

About the Authors

Robert E. Reys is professor of mathematics education at the University of Missouri–Columbia. He is a former mathematics teacher and district mathematics coordinator. His research interests are in the areas of calculators, mental computation, estimation, and number sense. He has authored more than 150 articles in professional journals, and was general editor for five yearbooks of the National Council of Teachers of Mathematics.

Mary M. Lindquist is the Fuller E. Callaway Professor of Mathematics Education, Columbus State University (Georgia). She works with undergraduate and graduate students in early childhood, middle grades, and secondary mathematics education. Mary was president of the National Council of Teachers of Mathematics and chair of the Commission on the Future of the Standards, the oversight committee for *Principles and Standards of School Mathematics* (NCTM 2000). She has served on many national and international committees, including those involved with the National Assessment of Education Progress (NAEP) and the Third International Mathematics and Science Study (TIMSS). Recently Mary was awarded the Lifetime Achievement Award for her service, leadership, and research by the Mathematics Education Trust.

Diana V. Lambdin is an associate professor of mathematics education at Indiana University in Bloomington, where she teaches undergraduate courses for prospective elementary teachers, supervises students' field experience, and works with masters and doctoral students in mathematics education. Prior to entering the field of teacher education, she was a mathematics teacher in Massachusetts, Michigan, and Iowa. Diana has been active as an author, editor, project evaluator, and workshop leader, and was a member of the writing team for *Principles and Standards for School Mathematics* (NCTM 2000).

Nancy L. Smith, Ph.D., has been an educator for twenty years. She taught elementary school and middle school mathematics for ten years in Richmond, Missouri. She is currently an associate professor in the Division of Early Childhood/Elementary Teacher Education at Emporia State University in Emporia, Kansas. At ESU she teaches elementary mathematics education courses for preservice and inservice teachers, teaches general elementary education courses, and supervises student teachers.

Marilyn N. Suydam is professor emeritus at Ohio State University. She was an elementary school teacher prior to becoming a faculty member at Penn State University and later at Ohio State University. Marilyn made significant contributions in her pioneering efforts to review, analyze, synthesize, and interpret research in mathematics education for elementary school teachers and administrators. In recognition of her many contributions to mathematics education, Dr. Suydam received the prestigious Lifetime Achievement Award from the National Council of Teachers of Mathematics.

Preface

The sixth edition of *Helping Children Learn Mathematics* coincides with one of the most exciting times in the history of mathematics education. Change is everywhere. Over ten years ago the release of the *Curriculum and Evaluation Standards for School Mathematics, Professional Standards for Teaching Mathematics,* and *Assessment Standards for School Mathematics* by the National Council of Teachers of Mathematics stimulated unprecedented activity in all levels of mathematics education through the 1990s and into the new millennium. These publications have orchestrated major changes affecting the K–12 school mathematics curriculum, standardized tests, and teacher education. As a teacher of mathematics in elementary school, you not only experience these changes but, more important, you also have an opportunity to help lead the way.

In an effort to continue the momentum, the NCTM prepared the *Principles and Standards for School Mathematics* (PSSM) to help focus change into the new millennium. This new edition of *Helping Children Learn Mathematics* reflects the spirit and major ideas detailed in the PSSM.

This book is intended for those of you who are or who will be teachers of mathematics in elementary school. It is designed to help you help children learn mathematical concepts and skills, as well as important problem-solving techniques. In the process it will challenge your thinking and further stimulate your interest in mathematics.

Helping Children Learn Mathematics is divided into two main parts. The first part (Chapters 1–5) provides a base for understanding the changing mathematics curriculum and how children learn mathematics. It offers some guidelines for planning and evaluating instruction. Attention is directed to problem solving and assessment, both of which have profound implications for mathematics teaching at all levels. Their importance is reflected throughout the book as they are integrated into various chapters.

The second part (Chapters 6–16) discusses teaching strategies, techniques, and learning activities related to specific mathematical topics. Emphasis is on using models and materials to develop concepts and understanding so that mathematics learning is indeed meaningful. We believe that meaning is most effectively established by helping students discuss mathematics as they move from concrete materials and examples to generalizations and abstractions.

Helping Children Learn Mathematics is a unique resource. Following are thirteen (a baker's dozen) features designed to make this book particularly useful.

FEATURES OF THIS TEXT

1. **Mathematical Processes.** The five mathematical processes, problem solving, communication, connections, representations, and reasoning and proof, identified by the PSSM are addressed in a separate chapter (Chapter 5). The development of student competence with these processes must be a goal of every school mathematics program. These processes and the links among them are often established in rich problem-solving activities. Therefore this chapter discusses various problem-solving strategies and also presents a wide variety of problems with which the strategies are useful. You will also find a problem-solving spirit reflected in the Lesson Ideas and In the Classroom activities, as well as in many of the discussions throughout the book.

2. **Snapshots of a Lesson.** Snapshots of a Lesson provide a brief look into a variety of mathematical lessons at different grade levels. All of the content-specific chapters (Chapters 6–16) open with one of these Snapshots to remind you of the realities of

teaching. The Snapshots both demonstrate many effective classroom practices and illustrate the vital role that you play as the teacher in leading and promoting students to talk and learn about mathematics.

3. **Lesson Ideas and In the Classroom activities.** Lesson Ideas and In the Classroom activities are used to highlight a wide variety of instructional topics. Lesson Ideas are designed to provide a skeletal outline for a lesson. In the Classroom activities focus on specific mathematical topics, and an objective accompanies each activity. These In the Classroom activities are designed to be used with children. Some activities shown in *Helping Children Learn Mathematics* are enlarged and duplicated in *Teaching Elementary Mathematics: A Resource for Field Experiences.* The larger format enables teachers and children to work effectively with each exercise. Below is a sample In the Classroom activity.

In The Classroom 8–5

Multig

Objective: Using a game to practice basic multiplication facts.

▼ Use the playing board here or make a larger one on heavy construction paper. Each player needs some buttons, macaroni, or chips for markers.

Don't forget the spinner. You can't play this game without it!

1. Take turns. Spin twice. Multiply the 2 numbers. Find the answer on the board. Put a marker on it.

56 25 40
36 49 20 81
30 64 35 48 32
56 42 63 28 54 45
32 48 54 72 24 16 35
16 24 28 36 40 30 25 20
63 45 81 56 49 42 64
20 25 72 45 24 36
40 49 32 28 54
30 16 72 48
42 35 63

2. Score 1 point for each covered ◇ that touches a side or corner of the ◇ you cover.

3. If you can't find an uncovered ◇ to cover, you lose your turn.

4. Opponents may challenge any time before the next player spins.

5. The winner is the player with the most points at the end of 10 rounds.

---

4. **Research Base.** A research base has been threaded throughout. As a teacher, you are often called on to provide a rationale for curricular or instructional decisions, and we think you will find this integration of relevant research, along with its implications, useful.

5. **Technology.** Technology, such as calculators and the Internet, is widely available to everyone—including young students. Calculators are powerful tools, and we have included calculator activities throughout the book. Other tools, such as spreadsheets, simulation packages, and the Internet, can enhance mathematics learning; we have made a conscious effort to integrate a wide variety of uses.

6. **Computational Alternatives.** Computational alternatives—mental computation, estimation, written techniques, as well as calculators—are explicitly discussed in Chapter 9. Technology has increased the importance of students' making wise choices among the computational alternatives, and we have dedicated a chapter to provide a balanced discussion of them.

7. **Encouraging Children to Construct Meaning.** As written techniques are developed, attention has been given to the value of encouraging young students to create, invent, construct, or use written methods that are meaningful for them. Much learning and understanding can be gained from exploring alternative algorithms, including some of the traditional algorithms that are part of our culture. However, tedious computational algorithms, such as long division, are de-emphasized. We believe that meaningful operations with numbers must be established, but our development focuses on understanding and facility with the computational alternatives and pays less attention to the painfully laborious task of crunching large numbers.

8. **Cultural and Gender Equity.** Equity—treating students of different sexes as well as different ethnic and cultural backgrounds similarly, with equal expectations—is an important issue in mathematics classes. We have reflected equity and provisions for individual differences in many ways—from the wide range of student abilities portrayed in the Snapshots of a Lesson to the Lesson Ideas and In the Classroom activities. Our use of calculators and our integration and discussion of research findings provide further insight into equity issues as well as other individual differences. We think such discussions will be helpful in implementing a mathematical environment that is positive and productive for everyone.

9. **Use of Children's Literature.** Literature is a powerful ally in learning and one that has often

been underused in mathematics classes. We have made direct efforts to identify books that might be effectively used to complement and supplement mathematics learning. In some cases, we have cited and discussed specific books within the text. In others, we have identified titles of books we have found useful in the Book Nook for Children sections, which appear at the end of many chapters.

10. **Things to Do.** Things to Do are found near the end of each chapter. These sections have been divided into two parts. One section relates directly to this book and is subtitled "From What You've Read." The other section is subtitled "Going Beyond This Book" and often includes explorations into other resources and references as well as some microteaching with children. Some of these activities are linked to *Teaching Elementary Mathematics: A Resource for Field Experiences.* All of the Things to Do embody our active learning and teaching approach to mathematics. These experiences are designed to engage you in inquiring and thinking about mathematics—investigations that will provide the greater understanding and insight that is needed to be a successful teacher.

11. **References.** Many helpful references (some new, some old, but all relevant) are listed at the end of each chapter to document research, as well as further illustrate ideas and other points made within the chapter. Some of these works discuss ideas that have been mentioned, but space did not allow us to develop them to the extent we would like. Others elaborate and extend ideas that will promote greater insight and understanding.

12. **Resources.** We have provided a Web site for *Helping Children Learn Mathematics* that is available at www.wiley.com/college/reys. This site includes addresses and phone numbers of major publishers and distributors of mathematics materials. It also includes copies of the master pages in Appendix B.

13. **Blackline Masters.** In our teaching, we have found certain materials to be frequently useful in a variety of ways. A number of these materials are included as blackline masters in Appendix B. These pages can be used as masters to make multiple copies for your students or to make a transparency for an overhead projector. As you teach and use these materials, we welcome feedback from you about other masters you would like to see in future editions.

NEW IN THIS EDITION

Chapter 1, School Mathematics. This chapter is an introduction to the profession and the current issues important to today's teachers. Exciting changes are taking place that will affect mathematics education. This chapter introduces the *Principles and Standards for School Mathematics;* a new highlighted appendix details the NCTM Standards 2000.

Chapter 2, Learning Mathematics with Understanding. Both behaviorism and constructivism are developed with increased attention to principles that should guide teaching toward helping children make sense of mathematics. Research-based ideas related to equity—both gender and ethnic—are discussed, and their implications are integrated into practical instructional ideas.

Chapter 3, Teaching: Your Role. A new introduction to this chapter ties recommendations for teachers' roles to what is known about how students learn mathematics with understanding. A new section on different types of lesson plans contrasts teacher roles in investigative lessons, direct instruction lessons, and review-teach-practice lessons. There are new sections on adapting textbook-based lessons, using children's literature to motivate mathematics lessons, and incorporating technology in mathematics instruction.

Chapter 4, Assessment: Enhanced Learning and Teaching. The basic structure of this chapter is the same, but the chapter has been expanded and updated by adding more examples of assessment devices such as scoring rubrics, observation schedules, attitude inventories, writing prompts, and suggestions for math portfolios.

Chapter 5, Five Mathematical Processes. This chapter (which previously focused solely on problem solving) has been expanded by adding sections on each of the five key mathematical processes identified in *Principles and Standards for School Mathematics:* problem solving, reasoning and proof, communication, connections, and representation. In addition, much of the material on problem solving from the fifth edition has been retained with minor changes.

Chapter 6, Beginning Number Sense: Counting and Early Benchmarks. This chapter retains its strong development of different aspects of early number sense. Updates are provided that integrate newly reported research, such as subitizing, with a long-established knowledge base about counting and early number development.

Chapter 7, Extending Number Sense: Place Value. New Lesson Ideas illustrating ways to engage children in exploring arithmetic and algebraic patterns and talking about what they are doing, thereby establishing a firm foundation for the later development of written computation, have been added.

Chapter 8, Operations: Meanings and Basic Facts. The structure of this chapter remains the same, but the section discussing strategies for learning basic facts has been reorganized and streamlined.

Chapter 9, Operation Sense: Mental Computation, Calculators, and Estimation. The discussion of technology is expanded and strengthened. Several continuing calculator myths (such as "Computations with calculators are always faster" and "Calculators are only useful for calculation") are dispelled. Also, recent research documenting that computational proficiency is not necessarily accompanied by good number sense is discussed with specific implications for teaching.

Chapter 10, Operations: Standards and Alternative Algorithms. Emphasis is placed on having students make sense of computational algorithms. Increased attention is given to alternative algorithms, in particular, low-stress algorithms that can serve as transitions to standard algorithms (for example, the partial-products algorithm for multiplication and the subtractive algorithm for division).

Chapter 11, Fractions and Decimals: Meanings and Operations. This chapter retains the conceptual development of fractions and decimals, but major changes have been made in the approach to addition and subtraction algorithms and the division algorithm for fractions.

Chapter 12, Ratio, Proportion, and Percent: Meanings and Applications. The structure of this chapter remains the same, but it now includes increased attention to technology.

Chapter 13, Patterns, Relationships, and Algebra. This chapter has been revised substantially to include more algebraic thinking. It uses some of the previous number theory ideas as a way to generalize and represent ideas algebraically. It is moved earlier in the book to complement the recommendations in *Principles and Standards for School Mathematics*.

Chapter 14, Geometry. The van Hiele levels have been added and are discussed within the context of learning and teaching geometry.

Chapter 15, Measurement. Measurement is one of the ten NCTM Standards, and this chapter exemplifies how the process standards, especially problem solving, communications, and reasoning, are central to learning measurement skills and using measurement.

Chapter 16, Data Analysis, Statistics, and Probability. Aligned with Standards 2000, this chapter increases the focus on engaging children in the data analysis process. Children are encouraged to develop questions, collect data to answer those questions, analyze the data in a variety of ways, and use their results to answer their questions.

SUPPLEMENTS

The sixth edition of *Helping Children Learn Mathematics* is accompanied by the following Instructor and Student Supplements.

Instructor's Manual and Test Bank

The Instructor's Manual (ISBN 0-471-38920-X) is a useful resource for both veteran and new elementary methods instructors. Each chapter includes:

- Chapter overview, student objectives, and key vocabulary
- Supplemental lecture ideas, textbook extension ideas, and class and field activity suggestions
- Extensive resource list (both print and media)
- Extensive transparency masters highlighting key textbook ideas, NCTM Standards 2000 summaries, and children's work samples
- A test bank featuring both objective and open-ended questions, classified by Bloom's taxonomy

Teaching Elementary Mathematics: A Resource for Field Experiences

This accompanying student resource (ISBN 0-471-38921-8) is designed to be used by students when they participate in field experiences such as practicums, observations, and professional development school (PDS) experiences in K–8 classrooms. This resource is aligned with and designed to support *Helping Children Learn Mathematics* but may also be used as a stand-alone resource. Activities engage preservice elementary teachers in collecting information about the school and school resources, observing and interviewing teachers and children, and doing mathematics with children in the form of games, technology activities, and minilessons. Students not only learn more about elementary schools and teaching elementary mathematics but are also encouraged to reflect on their experiences.

Helping Children Learn Mathematics is an ideabook. We believe that you will learn much from reading and talking about what you have read. The

NCTM Standards have identified communication as an important part of mathematics learning, and this book is designed to encourage and facilitate communication.

It is not possible—or desirable—to establish exact steps to follow in teaching mathematics. Too much depends on what is being taught, to whom, and at what levels. In your classroom, it is you who will ultimately decide what to teach, to whom to teach it, how to teach it, and the amount of time to spend. This book will not answer all of these questions for you, but we think you will find it very helpful in making wise decisions as you guide elementary school students in their learning of mathematics. We believe this book will be a valuable teaching resource that can be used again and again in your classroom long after the course has been completed.

ACKNOWLEDGMENTS

As we complete this sixth edition of *Helping Children Learn Mathematics,* we welcome Diana Lambdin to the author team. Diana is an experienced classroom teacher who now specializes in working with preservice elementary teachers. She also served as one of the writers for the PSSM.

We wish to acknowledge the many colleagues, friends, and students who have contributed in various ways to the development of this book over the years. In particular, we thank Barbara Reys and Gay Ragan, University of Missouri; Frank Lester, Indiana University; Douglas Grouws, University of Iowa; and Bob Glasgow, Southwest Baptist University.

We acknowledge the help of specific reviewers for this sixth edition, including Christine Browning, Western Michigan University; Elsa L. Geskus, Kutztown University; Kim Harris, University of North Carolina, Charlotte; Ruth M. Heaton, University of Nebraska, Lincoln; Todd Johnson, Eastern Washington University; Eula Ewing Monroe, Brigham Young University; Jamar Pickreign, Rhode Island College; Thomas E. Rowan, University of Maryland, College Park; Frances Stern, New York University; David L. Stout, University of West Florida; and Dorothy Y. White, University of Georgia.

We also wish to recognize the help of reviewers for previous editions, including Roda Amaria, Salem State College; Tom Bassarear, Keene State College; Daniel Brahier, Bowling Green State University; Grace Burton, University of North Carolina, Wilmington; Bob Drake, University of Cincinnati; Marvel Froemming, Moorhead State University; Claire Graham, Framingham State College; Janet Handler, Mount Mercy College; Ellen Hines, Northern Illinois University; Robert Jackson, University of Minnesota; Susan Johnson, Northwestern College; Mary Kabiri, Lincoln University; Rick Kruschinsky, University of St. Thomas; Vena Long, University of Tennessee; Robert Matulis, Millersville University; William Merrill, Central Michigan University; Don Ploger, Florida Atlantic University; Jacelyn Marie Rees, McNeese State University; Tom Romberg, University of Wisconsin; Mary Ellen Schmidt, Ohio State University–Mansfield; Juan Vazquez, Missouri Southern State College; Margaret Wyckoff, University of Maine–Farmington; and Bernard Yvon, University of Maine.

R.E.R.
M.M.L.
D.V.L.
N.L.S.
M.N.S.

Contents

4   Assessment: Enhanced Learning and Teaching   50

5   Five Mathematical Processes   76

6   Beginning Number Sense: Counting and Early Benchmarks   107

16 ▶ Data Analysis, Statistics, and Probability   344

1 ▶ *School Mathematics*

Introduction

Soon you will be in your own classroom, responsible for helping children learn mathematics. What mathematics will you be teaching? How will you teach children mathematics? This book will help you gain a clearer understanding of the answers to those two questions.

You will also be asking other questions, as all teachers must, including these:

- What mathematical knowledge and understandings will each student bring to the class?
- What mathematics do they need to learn?
- How can each child, different in many ways from the others, be taught so that he or she will learn?
- How important is my own attitude toward mathematics?

The answers to such questions provide the framework for the elementary school mathematics program; your own answers will influence what you do when teaching. No matter what age children you teach, you will probably have several general goals:

- To help children make sense of specific mathematical content, including both procedures and concepts
- To help children learn how to apply mathematical ideas to solve problems
- To foster positive dispositions such as persistence, flexibility, willingness to learn, and valuing mathematics

Developing ways to help children learn a range of mathematical content will be considered in later chapters of this book. Our focus in this chapter is an overall look at the mathematics program that has evolved through the years and is continuing to change. It is a place to begin thinking about your own perceptions of mathematics and the role mathematics plays in elementary and middle schools. What influences the curriculum? How do your beliefs influence what you will teach?

You are entering the teaching field at a particularly exciting time. The curriculum in mathematics, as well as many other subject areas, is being adapted to the changing needs of our society, changing knowledge about how children learn, and changing viewpoints of mathematics. Before we examine these changes, let us think about the subject itself.

WHAT IS MATHEMATICS?

Which of the following five views of mathematics is closest to your perception of mathematics? How will your view of mathematics affect how you help children learn?

1. Mathematics is a *study of patterns and relationships*. Children need to become aware of recurring ideas and of relationships between and among mathematical ideas. These relationships and ideas provide a unifying thread throughout the curriculum. Children must come to see how one idea is like or unlike others already learned. For instance, children in first grade can consider how one basic fact (say, $3 + 2 = 5$) is related to another basic fact (say, $5 - 3 = 2$). Or children in later grades can consider the effect that changing the perimeter of a figure has on its area.

2. Mathematics is a *way of thinking*. It provides us with strategies for organizing, analyzing, and synthesizing information. People who are comfortable with mathematics use it to solve everyday problems.

For example, some people write an equation, others form tables to record information.

3. Mathematics is an *art,* characterized by order and internal consistency. Many children think of mathematics as a confusing set of discrete facts and skills that must be memorized. Because teachers tend to focus on developing the skills required to "do" mathematics, they may forget that children need to be guided to recognize and appreciate the underlying orderliness and consistency as they construct their own understanding of mathematics.

4. Mathematics is a *language* that uses carefully defined terms and symbols. These terms and symbols enhance our ability to communicate about science, real-life situations, and mathematics itself.

5. Mathematics is a *tool.* It is what mathematicians use, but it is also used by everyone in the course of daily life. Thus, children can come to appreciate why they are learning the facts, skills, and concepts that the school program involves. They, too, can use mathematics to solve both abstract and practical problems, just as mathematicians do. Mathematics has become an essential part of the technological world, both in everyday life and in the workplace.

WHAT DETERMINES THE MATHEMATICS BEING TAUGHT?

Mathematics plays a prominent role in the elementary school program. It is second only to reading in the amount of time devoted to it and in the amount of money spent for curricular materials. Its importance is reflected in the degree of concern intermittingly voiced by parents and other members of the public.

The federal government has not specified a national curriculum for school mathematics as is the practice in most other countries. The National Council of Teachers of Mathematics (NCTM), the largest professional organization of prekindergarten through high school teachers of mathematics in the world, has developed standards for curriculum, teaching, and assessment (NCTM 1989, 1991, 1995). Because states and localities in the United States hold the rights to determine school policies, none of these standards documents are prescriptive, but they do provide vision and direction for school mathematics. In 2000, the NCTM published an update of the standards in a document named *Principles and Standards for School Mathematics* (NCTM 2000). As we updated this book, we turned to this document and will bring to you its main messages.

Three general factors—the needs of the subject, the needs of the child, and the needs of society—

Equity Principle Excellence in mathematics education requires equity—high expectations and strong support for all students.

Curriculum Principle A curriculum is more than a collection of activities: it must be coherent, focused on important mathematics, and well articulated across the grades.

Teaching Principle Effective mathematics teaching requires understanding what students know and need to learn and then challenging and supporting them to learn it well.

Learning Principle Students must learn mathematics with understanding, actively building new knowledge from experience and prior knowledge.

Assessment Principle Assessment should support the learning of important mathematics and furnish useful information to both teachers and students.

Technology Principle Technology is essential in teaching and learning mathematics; it influences the mathematics that is taught and enhances students' learning.

Figure 1–1 ● **Principles for school mathematics** (Reprinted with permission from "Principles and Standards for School Mathematics," pp. 12, 14, 16, 20, 22, 24, copyright 2000 by the National Council of Teachers of Mathematics. All rights reserved.)

have influenced the mathematics programs of schools. As we discuss the evolution of these factors, we will interweave the underlying principles of school mathematics (NCTM 2000), shown in Figure 1–1, and discuss some of the current issues.

Needs of the Subject

The nature of mathematics has helped to determine what is taught and when it is taught in elementary grades. Whole numbers are the basis for many mathematical ideas; moreover, experiences with them arise long before children come to school. Thus, whole-number work is stressed first. Work with rational numbers logically follows work with whole numbers. Such seemingly "natural" sequences are the result of long years of curricular evolution. This process has involved much analysis of what constitutes a progression from easy to difficult, based in part on what is deemed necessary at one level for the development of ideas at later levels.

Once a curriculum is in place for a long time, however, people tend to consider it the only proper sequence. Thus, to omit a topic or to change the sequence of topics often involves a struggle for acceptance.

Sometimes the process of change is aided by an event, such as when the Soviet Union sent the first Sputnik into orbit. The shock of this evidence of another country's technological superiority sped curriculum change in the United States. The "new math" of the 1950s and 1960s was the result, and millions of dollars were channeled into mathematics and science education to strengthen school programs.

Mathematicians became integrally involved, and because of their interests and the perceived weaknesses of previous curricula, they developed curricula based on the needs of the subject. Emphasis was shifted from social usefulness to such unifying themes as the structure of mathematics, operations and their inverses, systems of notation, properties of numbers, and set language. Not only was new content added at the elementary school level but some older topics were introduced at lower grade levels.

Mathematics continues to change; new mathematics is created and new uses of mathematics are discovered. Technology has made some mathematics obsolete and has opened the door for other mathematics. You will teach in a time that technology dominates much of what we do, in school and out of school. The Technology Principle (see Figure 1–1) acknowledges the centrality of technology in teaching and learning mathematics as long as it enhances what is being learned and how it is being taught. It is the tool of today that can help us in our teaching and learning of mathematics. You should keep asking three questions: (1) How can I help children use technology appropriately? (2) What mathematics do children need to use technology wisely? and (3) What mathematics is no longer necessary?

Some parents are concerned about the use of calculators in elementary schools. An examination of all research prior to early 1980s on calculator use (Hembree and Dessart 1986) strongly suggested that using calculators did not harm students. We support the position that children need to learn to use this tool appropriately as they do any other tool. As you study the remainder of this text, we will return to what is meant by *appropriate*. At this point, begin to think about the issue.

No one knows exactly what mathematics will be needed for the twenty-first century, but it is clear that students will need to know how to reason mathematically and how to apply mathematical thinking to a wide range of situations. They need to be afforded the opportunity to experience a curriculum that is more than a collection of isolated skills or fun activities. They need to have a curriculum (see the Curriculum Principle in Figure 1–1) that focuses on the important mathematics topics at each grade, that fits together in a meaningful way, and grows across the grades. The ten content and process standards in *Principles and Standards for School Mathematics* (NCTM 2000) give guidance to judging whether or not your curriculum is coherent, focused, and well-articulated across the grades.

Needs of the Child

Clearly, the mathematics curriculum has been influenced by beliefs about how children learn. Until the early years of this century, mathematics was taught to train "mental faculties" or provide "mental discipline." Struggling with mathematical procedures was thought to exercise the mind, helping it work more effectively.

Around the turn of the century, mental discipline was replaced by *connectionism*, dominated by the thinking of Edward Thorndike. The stimulus-response theory, which deemed it necessary to establish strong bonds or connections, resulted in an emphasis on speed and accuracy, attained by repeated drill. Much stress was placed on identifying specific skills to be mastered and on the relative difficulty of the various topics. Precise placement of topics seemed vital, leading to such practices as introducing 7 × 3 a full year before introducing 3 × 7. Standardized tests were developed and normed so that children could be graded according to their attainment of mathematical skills. In turn, teachers resorted to endless drill in an attempt to ensure high scores on the tests.

In reaction to the strictures of a drill-based program, and under the influence of writers such as John Dewey, the Progressive Movement of the 1920s advocated *incidental learning*. It was believed that children would learn as much arithmetic as they needed and would learn it better if it was not systematically taught. The teacher was to make use of situations as they occurred and to create situations in which arithmetic would arise.

During the late 1920s, a committee of school superintendents and principals from midwestern cities surveyed pupils to find out when topics were mastered (Washburne 1931). They then suggested the mental age at which each topic should be taught. Thus, subtraction facts under 10 were to be taught to children with a mental age of 6 years 7 months, and facts over 10 at 7 years 8 months; subtraction with borrowing or carrying was to be taught at 8 years 9 months. The Committee of Seven had a strong impact on the sequencing of the curriculum for years to come.

Another change in thinking occurred in the mid-1930s, as *field*, or *Gestalt, theory* was advanced. Greater emphasis was placed on a planned program to encourage the development of insight and the understanding of relationships, structure, patterns, interpretations, and principles. This contributed to a shift to concern for *meaning and understanding,* with William Brownell as a prominent spokesperson. Learning was seen as a meaningful process. The value of drill was noted, but it was placed after understanding; drill no longer was the major means of sequencing the curriculum and providing instruction.

The roles of drill and understanding are still debated today. Drill is necessary to build speed and accuracy and to make skills more automatic. Think about whether you would get through the day if you did not do some things automatically; but also think about whether you still need the same skills that your grandparents needed.

Often people juxtapose understanding and skill learning; it is not an either-or situation. You need to know *why* as well as *how.* Our position is that both must be developed and that they can be developed together.

Changes in psychology have continued to evolve. Educators during the latter part of the twentieth century believed that the developmental level of the child is a factor in determining the sequence of the curriculum. Topics cannot be taught until a child is developmentally ready to learn them. Or, from another point of view, topics must be taught in such a way that children at a given developmental level are ready to learn them.

Increasingly, educators' attention is drawn to the evidence that children *construct* their own knowledge; to help children learn mathematics, teachers must be aware of how the children have constructed mathematics from their experiences both in and out of school. Such ideas and inferences have been taken into consideration as the curriculum has evolved.

These factors will be considered in more depth in Chapter 2, but the Teaching Principle and the Learning Principle (see Figure 1–1) should trigger some beginning questions for you. What does it mean to learn mathematics with understanding? How did you learn mathematics? How do you learn to understand what children know? Where do you turn to find what mathematics children need to learn and how to challenge and support them to learn it?

Needs of Society

The practicality and usefulness of mathematics in everyday situations and in many vocations has also affected what is taught and when it is taught. This has been true since colonial times, when mathematics was considered necessary primarily for clerks and bookkeepers. The curriculum was limited to counting, the simpler procedures for addition, subtraction, and multiplication, and some knowledge of measures and of fractions. Much of the computation was with denominate numbers involving measures in commercial use (such as 3 feet 5 inches).

By the late nineteenth century, business and commerce had increased to the point that mathematics was considered important for everyone. The arithmetic curriculum expanded to include such topics as percentage, ratio and proportion, powers, roots, and series.

The emphasis on teaching what was needed for use in occupations continued into the twentieth century. One of the most vocal advocates of *social utility* was Guy Wilson. He and his students conducted numerous surveys to determine what arithmetic was actually used by carpenters, shopkeepers, and other workers. He believed that the "dominating" aim of the school mathematics program should be to teach those skills, and only those skills.

We have already noted the outburst of public concern in the 1950s, when the desire to improve the curriculum so that the United States wouldn't fall behind in the "space race" resulted in a wave of curriculum development and research in mathematics. Much of this effort was focused on the mathematically talented student. In the mid-1960s, however, concern was also expressed for the disadvantaged student as U.S. society renewed its search for equality of opportunity. With these changes—in fact, with *each* change—more and better mathematical achievement was promised.

In the 1970s, when it became apparent that once again the promise had not fully materialized, another swing in the curricular emphasis occurred. Renewed emphasis was placed on skills needed for "survival" in the real world. The minimal-competency movement stressed the basics. As embodied in sets of objectives and in tests, the basics were considered to be primarily addition, subtraction, multiplication, and division with whole numbers and fractions. Thus, the skills needed by children in colonial times were again considered by many to be the sole necessities even though children were now living in a world with calculators and computers.

By the 1980s, it was acknowledged that no one knew exactly what skills were needed for the future but that everyone needed to be able to solve problems. The emphasis on problem solving matured through the last twenty years of the century to the point where problem solving was not seen as a separate topic but a way to learn and to use mathematics.

As we enter the twenty-first century, we see dramatic changes in the needs of society. No longer does it suffice for only a few to be mathematically literate. The Equity Principle (Figure 1–1) states clearly that to have excellence in mathematics education, we must have high expectations for all students. This cannot be accomplished unless each person involved with education believes that all children can learn mathematics and without providing each child the opportunity to learn worthwhile mathematics. Certainly, this means designing our instructional programs to meet differences such as interest, strengths, needs, cultures, and mathematical backgrounds of our students. This is a challenge, but we have evidence that our all our students can learn mathematics if we rise to that challenge and if we expect them to rise to that challenge.

Our society needs a citizenry and a work force that can solve problems, reason mathematically, process and interpret data, and communicate in a technological world. We need to continue to improve our mathematics programs in order to prepare students for life in today's society.

WHERE CAN YOU TURN?

There are many places you can turn for help with the curriculum, with helping students learn, and to continue developing your knowledge of mathematics and of mathematics learning and teaching. We present a few suggestions here, introducing some of the resources we will use throughout this book.

National Guidelines for School Mathematics

We have already mentioned the latest update of the NCTM Standards, *Principles and Standards for School Mathematics* (NCTM 2000) and will refer to it throughout this book. The five content standards are specified in more detail at the various grade bands (Pre-K–2, 3–5, 6–8, and 9–12). For your reference, we have included these expectations for Pre-K through Grade 8 in Appendix A. The five process standards also can be found in Appendix A. The entire document is available, both in print and electronically from NCTM (http://www.nctm.org). These expectations will help you as you determine what children at different ages are expected to learn.

State Guidelines

Almost every state and province has standards, guidelines, or frameworks for school mathematics. Most are more specific than the national standards and specify content grade by grade. Many states are in the process of aligning their state assessments with their standards. You should check to see what is available for your state and what emphasis is placed on these guidelines.

Research

The body of research in mathematics education, both about children's learning and about teaching, is substantial. The recommendations made by the National Council of Teachers of Mathematics (NCTM 2000) have a strong research base. We will use research references through the book to illustrate information about children's learning. There are several references that we will use often and with which you should become familiar.

The first is the National Assessment of Educational Progress, better known as NAEP (pronounced "nape"). This is the nation's measure of students' achievement and trends in achievement in the academic subjects. The mathematics assessments began in 1973 and now are given every four years to fourth-, eighth-, and twelfth-grade students. The assessments are updated to reflect the trends you have read about. A set of secured items from the 1973 battery is given periodically, and the results are shown in Figure 1–2. We often hear the public say, "students cannot do math like they used to do"; this graph paints a different picture of student performance on basic-skill items.

Although we are not declining in performance, we should not be satisfied. The comparison of our students with others around the world clearly shows that we could do better. We will reference the Third International Study in Science and Mathematics (TIMSS). This was a massive study that examined curriculum, instruction, and achievement at grades 3–4, 7–8, and end of schooling. We can learn much from knowing how other countries teach mathematics.

There are reports of research in many journals; we sometimes refer to the *Journal for Research in Mathematics Education* (JRME). Many times articles from this journal are interpreted with a classroom flavor in the other journals from the National Council of Teachers of Mathematics.

History

If you want a fun exploration, find some textbooks from the 1800s and early 1900s. Did you realize that arithmetic was a college and then high school subject before the 1900s? Read the prefaces of the books, examine the size, and find some activities that are appropriate for children today. If you are in early childhood education, you may particularly enjoy the books from the 1920s.

If you are a student of history, you may want to examine the trends in mathematics education. This chapter includes a list of historical references to start you on this task.

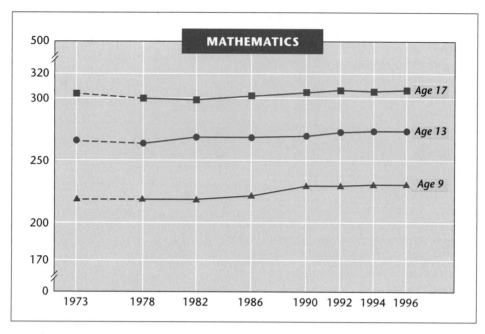

Figure 1–2 ● Trends in student performance: NAEP

Textbooks and Other Materials

Most teachers use a textbook when teaching elementary and middle school mathematics. Today's textbooks provide many supplementary materials such as assessment, problems to solve, and extra practice. Teacher's manuals also provide a wealth of materials and suggestions. Additionally, many supplementary materials are provided in the manual and in other books.

There are many different types of textbooks. Some provide a great amount of drill and practice but offer little help in developing the understanding and using mathematics. Others may provide more help in developing the understanding but are short on practice of necessary skills. As you become experienced, you will be able to better judge the quality of the textbook. Unless you have had experience, you may want to follow the textbook until you become more comfortable with teaching. Keep questioning why you need to teach a given lesson. Does it help children develop the mathematics that they need? Does it do it in a way that makes sense to children?

Electronic Materials

The opportunity to have materials at your fingertips is increasing every day. The Web provides immediate access to lesson plans, help with the mathematics itself, assessment items, and information that can be used in teaching mathematics. Because of the rapid change, we have not listed sites here. A simple search of mathematics for elementary or middle school students and teachers will lead you to many places. Again, a caution: Availability does not always mean quality. Just recently, a perspective teacher brought to class an activity that she had found on the Web. It involved young children finding the capacity of their mouths by filling them with marshmallows. Not only was the mathematics questionable since the unit of measurement was not firm, it was dangerous for children. Teaching involves making good judgments on many fronts.

Testing

The Assessment Principle (Figure 1–1) is an indication of the importance of assessment. You will learn more about assessment in Chapter 4, especially about assessment that will help you plan instruction and monitor children's progress.

We all need to be responsible for helping children learn, and the public is demanding accountability measures. A plethora of tests are required by many states and localities. These are often standardized norm-referenced tests or criterion-reference tests. Often, the results of these tests are published in papers for the community to see.

You can use these tests to help you in your quest to provide a sound mathematics education for your students. If the test is reasonable and aligned with your guidelines, then you can see how your students are doing in comparison to a standard or to other students or which mathematical topics are presenting difficulty. However, do not be driven foolishly by a test that does not measure what is important. If you teach children to "do test items" but do not allow them to develop understanding, then any gains will likely be only for the short term.

Professional Organizations

Being a part of a profession opens many opportunities and responsibilities. Your teaching career will be enhanced by the professional association you have with others and the support you can find from being a part of a professional organization. Often the journals, conferences, and other materials of a professional organization are available to schools or to nonmembers.

For example, the National Council of Teachers of Mathematics (NCTM) has many publications as well as a journal for elementary teachers of mathematics (*Teaching Children Mathematics,* formerly the *Arithmetic Teacher*) and one for middle school teachers (*Teaching Mathematics in Middle Grades*). You will find many references in this book to these journals. Additionally, NCTM offers conferences, workshops, and other support activities. There are also over 260 affiliated groups, both state and local, that offer many programs.

Professional Development

Begin to take advantage of the professional development opportunities that are available. Some of these are formal such as workshops, college courses, and conferences, and others are informal study groups. Some will be provided for you by your school, district, or state. Others will be commercially sponsored or sponsored by a professional organization. There will be increasingly many opportunities on the Web designed so you can participate in your own time at home.

Often your school or district has funds set aside for professional development that are available on request. Other districts have teachers design their own professional development plans and support you in carrying out that plan.

Other Teachers

All of us in teaching have learned much from our colleagues. You will learn from your school experiences, but do not let it stop there. Look for a school where sharing ideas about helping students learn mathematics and sharing teaching tips and materials is the norm. Look for teachers in other schools near you or far away but connected electronically who are willing to discuss and to share.

WHAT IS YOUR ROLE NOW?

In many ways, you have been preparing for teaching mathematics throughout your life. As you look more closely at this task, we challenge you to do three things.

- Examine your own disposition toward mathematics and who can learn mathematics. Be ready to question your beliefs, to evaluate proposed changes, and to make a difference in helping children learn mathematics.

- As you begin working with children, stop and listen to them, individually and collectively. Reflect on what you are hearing and learn with the children.

- Realize that you may feel that you know less about teaching mathematics because you will understand how much there is to know. If you come to this realization and take action, you are well on your way to becoming a teacher.

A Glance at Where We've Been

The mathematics curriculum is continually changing to reflect the needs of the subject, the child, and society. This chapter gave a very brief history of the changing curriculum as well as recommendations for today. Additionally, it introduced resources that you should be familiar with as you study the rest of this book but, more importantly, as you teach. It challenged you to keep an open mind and continue your own learning about teaching children mathematics.

Things to Do: From What You've Read

1. What are the three general goals mentioned in the introduction? Which do you think is the most important? Explain why.

2. Give an illustration (in addition to those in this chapter) of how mathematics is a study of patterns and relationships, a way of thinking, an art, and a language.

3. Several educators have noted that the curriculum is in a continuous process of change in order to maintain balance as the needs of the subject, the child, and society pull it first one way and then another. Discuss this comment.

4. Explain in your own words the six principles that underpin the standards presented in *Principles and Standards for School Mathematics*.

5. Which of the resources discussed in this chapter have you already used? Which ones do you think will be the most helpful to you?

6. React to the three challenges presented in the close of the chapter.

Things to Do: Going Beyond This Book

field Additional activities, suggestions, and questions are provided in *Teaching Elementary Mathematics: A Resource for Field Experiences.*

1. *field* Math Focus. As you observe in a school, look for signs of the role mathematics plays in that school. Does it differ from class to class?

2. Read Chapter 2 of *Principles and Standards for School Mathematics*. Choose the principle that you think is the most important; critique the discussion of that principle.

3. *field* All Children. Interview a teacher (or some students) about their belief that all children can learn mathematics and what it would take to make this happen.

4. Examine some aspect of the history of mathematics education, beginning by reading one of the articles or books listed in the historical references or by examining old textbooks.

5. *field* Curriculum Guide. Examine a copy of a state or district curriculum guide. How does the scope and sequence of topics align with the expectations for Pre-K–2, Grades 3–5, and Grades 6–8 in the *Principles and Standards for School Mathematics* (see Appendix A)?

Selected References

Campbell, Jay R.; Voelkl, Kristin E.; and Donahue, Particia L. *NAEP 1996 Trends in Academic Progress.* Washington, D.C.: U.S. Government Printing Office, 1997.

Hembree, Ray, and Dessart, Donald J. "Effects of Hand-held Calculators in Precollege Mathematics Education: A Meta-Analysis." *Journal for Research in Mathematics Education,* 17 (March 1986), pp. 83–99.

National Council of Teachers of Mathematics. *Curriculum and Evaluation Standards for School Mathematics.* Reston, Va.: NCTM, 1989.

National Council of Teachers of Mathematics. *Professional Standards for Teaching Mathematics.* Reston, Va.: NCTM, 1991.

National Council of Teachers of Mathematics. *Assessment Standards for School Mathematics.* Reston, Va.: NCTM, 1995.

National Council of Teachers of Mathematics. *Principles and Standards for School Mathematics.* Reston, Va.: NCTM, 2000.

Silver, Edward A., and Kenney, Patricia Ann (eds.). *Results from the Seventh Mathematics Assessment of the National Assessment of Educational Progress.* Reston, Va.: NCTM, 2000

U.S. Department of Education. *Pursuing Excellence: A Study of U.S. Eighth-Grade Mathematics and Science Teaching, Learning, Curriculum, and Achievement in International Context.* Washington, D.C.: U.S. Government Printing Office, 1996.

U.S. Department of Education. *Pursuing Excellence: A Study of U.S. Fourth-Grade Mathematics and Science Achievement in International Context.* Washington, D.C.: U.S. Government Printing Office, 1997.

Washburne, Carleton. "Mental Age and the Arithmetic Curriculum: A Summary of the Committee of Seven Grade Placement Investigation to Date." *Journal of Educational Research,* 23 (March 1931), pp. 210–231.

Historical References

Commission on Post-War Plans of the NCTM. "Guidance Report of the Commission on Post-War Plans." *Mathematics Teacher,* 40 (July 1947), pp. 315–339.

DeVault, M. Vere, and Weaver, J. Fred. "Forces and Issues Related to Curriculum and Instruction, K-6." In *A History of Mathematics Education in the United States and Canada,* Thirty-Second Yearbook (ed. Phillip S. Jones). Washington, D.C.: NCTM, 1970.

Edwards, E. L., Jr.; Nichols, Eugene D.; and Sharpe, Glyn H. "Mathematical Competencies and Skills Essential for Enlightened Citizens." *Arithmetic Teacher,* 19 (November 1972), pp. 601–607.

National Advisory Committee on Mathematical Education. *Overview and Analysis of School Mathematics Grades K-12.* Washington, D.C.: Conference Board of the Mathematical Sciences, 1975.

National Commission on Excellence in Education. *A Nation at Risk: The Imperative for Educational Reform.* Washington, D.C.: U.S. Government Printing Office, 1983.

National Council of Supervisors of Mathematics. "Position Paper on Basic Mathematical Skills." *Arithmetic Teacher,* 25 (October 1977), pp. 18–22.

National Council of Supervisors of Mathematics. "Essential Mathematics for the 21st Century." *Arithmetic Teacher,* 37 (September 1989), pp. 44–46.

National Council of Teachers of Mathematics. *An Agenda for Action: Recommendations for School Mathematics of the 1980s.* Reston, Va.: NCTM, 1980.

Washburne, Carleton. "Mental Age and the Arithmetic Curriculum: A Summary of the Committee of Seven Grade Placement Investigations to Date." *Journal of Educational Research,* 23 (March 1931), pp. 210–231.

Wilson, Guy M. "The Social Utility Theory as Applied to Arithmetic, Its Research Basis, and Some of Its Implications." *Journal of Educational Research,* 41 (January 1948), pp. 321–337.

2 ▶ *Learning Mathematics with Understanding*

Introduction

How is mathematics learned? This important question has no simple answer. Teachers provide their "answers" through classroom practices. In fact, every instructional activity within the classroom expresses the teacher's view of learning. The way in which lessons are planned, topics presented, and questions handled reflects how learning is perceived and influences what happens in classrooms.

Consider this exchange about the amount of homework needed:

> STUDENT: Do we have to do all thirty exercises on this page?
>
> TEACHER: Yes, do every one of them. Why do you think they are there if we are not supposed to do them?

A common pitfall in assignments is too much practice too soon. Research confirms that students rarely need all the practice provided in a textbook. Far more important than the quantity of exercises done is the developmental instruction that precedes them and the distribution of practice that follows (Koehler and Grouws 1992).

Because teachers' beliefs about the learning process make such a difference in the classroom, a thoughtful study and understanding of how mathematics is learned should have high priority for every elementary teacher. The purpose of this chapter is to build on your previous knowledge from educational psychology and stimulate your thinking about how children learn mathematics.

HOW DO CHILDREN LEARN MATHEMATICS?

Although many unanswered questions remain about how children learn mathematics, it is generally agreed that "students must learn mathematics with understanding, actively building new knowledge from experience and prior knowledge" (NCTM 2000, p. 20). Discussion within the Learning Principle of the *Principles and Standards for School Mathematics* (PSSM) states that "Learning with understanding is essential to enable students to solve the new kinds of problems they will inevitably face in the future" (NCTM 2000, p. 21). This premise for mathematical learning is based on research that has been accumulating for many years, and reflects advances in mathematics education, psychology, and medicine. For example, in medicine, it has been reported that learning changes the physical structure of the brain, and different parts of the brain may be ready to learn at different times (National Research Council 1999).

Early in the twentieth century, John Dewey asserted that learning comes from experience and active involvement by the learner. Much has been discovered since then about how children learn mathematics, but the importance of meaningful experience remains unchallenged. More recently, Jean Piaget argued that learners actively construct their own knowledge. This view of learning, known as *constructivism*, suggests that rather than simply accepting new information, students interpret what they see, hear, or do in relation to what they already know.

Thus a middle-grade child who concludes that 0.285 is greater than 0.4 because "0.285 has more digits" is building on what he or she already knows about whole numbers and interprets the information about decimals in light of this previous knowledge. The student had constructed knowledge, but this example is a reminder that the constructed knowledge is not always correct.

More will be said about constructivism later, but first let's examine key elements of two major theories of how children think and learn. Each view holds implications for learning and teaching mathematics. One of these views has long been associated with mathematics learning (behaviorism), and the other has been shown to be helpful in promoting meaningful learning (constructivism).

Building Behavior

Behaviorism has its roots in stimulus-response and conditioned learning. This theory asserts that behavior can be shaped through rewards and punishments. Over the years, it has marshaled a number of distinguished advocates, including Edward L. Thorndike, B. F. Skinner, and Robert Gagné. However, no learning theorists today argue for an exclusively behaviorist approach to mathematics learning. Behaviorism has had a significant impact on mathematics programs, but the strict adherence to a behaviorist approach to mathematics learning in elementary school is clearly inappropriate.

One of the major tenets of behaviorism is reinforcement, which is practice promoting the desired behavior. The value and power of meaningful practice are well documented; however, research has reported negative effects associated with excessive practice, premature practice, or practice without understanding (Koehler and Grouws 1992). Such practice often leads to a fear or dislike of mathematics and an attitude that mathematics doesn't need to make sense when, in fact, sense making of mathematics is a major goal of mathematics learning. In our judgment, behaviorist psychology must be considered by teachers, but used wisely. Keeping this point in mind, let's examine behaviorism a bit more closely to see why.

The hierarchical nature of mathematics makes it a popular candidate for a behaviorist approach. The first step in such an approach is to state precisely the objective, or goal, of instruction. This statement gives teachers direction in planning instruction and gives the student clear expectations—both valuable outcomes that are consistently supported by research. Once an objective has been clearly stated, behaviorists recommend that the prerequisites for achieving that goal be identified and used as building blocks in planning instruction.

Consider the following example.

Objective:
Correctly use the formula $A = \frac{1}{2}ba$ to find the area of a triangle.

Some prerequisite questions are:

What is area?
What is base?
What is altitude?
What is a triangle?

Clear answers to these prerequisite questions are necessary if the objective is to be reached. However, this particular task analysis could be extended to include these questions:

How do you multiply by a fraction?
How do you multiply by whole numbers?

Thus it is hard to imagine constructing a complete task analysis for any objective, no matter how simple it may seem. It is obvious that important prerequisites must be considered in preparing lessons, but teachers must be guided by common sense, not by zeal to construct "the definitive task analysis."

Behaviorism is useful in clarifying goals and focusing learning outcomes. Although forming behaviorally oriented objectives may be useful, such objectives often focus on low-level knowledge that may involve virtually no mathematical thinking. Behaviorism can be good or bad—the key is balance. As teachers, we must maintain a balanced focus that attends to cognitive processes and important skills.

An examination of mathematics programs discloses a heavy influence of behaviorism as students are "shown" algorithms and mathematical relationships are "illustrated" on the textbook pages. The influence of a behaviorist orientation can also be found in daily, unit, grade, and program objectives.

The behaviorist approach does have some attractive features: it provides instructional guidelines, allows for short-term progress, and lends itself well to accountability pressures. However, a real and constant danger in using a behaviorist approach is to focus on simple, short-term objectives that are easily measured. This approach can produce mastery of specific objectives, but it lacks the critical connections that make the so-called knowledge meaningful and useful. Often the emphasis on short-term objectives results in other things being deemphasized, and these other things generally include long-term goals and higher-level cognitive processes such as problem solving.

Behaviorism needs to be refocused to have a positive effect on mathematics learning. It is possible for behaviorism to provide more learner involvement and promote higher-level thinking in mathematics. This possibility is illustrated by the use of many behaviorally oriented verbs—such as *explore, justify, represent, solve, construct, discuss, use, investigate, describe, develop,* and *predict.* Each of these verbs encourages critical thinking and requires an active role for children in doing and eventually learning mathematics.

Behaviorism does need to be refocused, but even then, it is indefensible to rely exclusively on behaviorism to guide mathematics instruction. For this reason, we now turn to a different interpretation of how children learn.

Constructing Understanding

The notion of meaningful learning advanced by William Brownell during the first half of the twentieth century was a forerunner of constructivism. Brownell conceived of mathematics as a closely knit system of ideas, principles, and processes—a structure that should be the cornerstone for learning mathematics. Connections among concepts should be established so that "arithmetic is less a challenge to the pupil's memory and more a challenge to his [or her] intelligence" (Brownell 1935, p. 32).

In recent years, research has consistently confirmed that isolated "learnings" are not retained (Hiebert and Carpenter 1992). Mathematics can and should make sense. If it does, it has meaning and is understood as a discipline with order, structure, and numerous relationships—and it is likely to be called upon in a variety of problem-solving situations. Meaningful learning provides the base for mathematical connections, and it is also an integral part of constructivism.

In addition to Brownell, Jean Piaget, Jerome Bruner, and Zoltan Dienes have each contributed to the growth of constructivism. Many of the major recommendations for teaching mathematics advocated by the *Professional Standards for Teaching Mathematics* (NCTM 1991) and more recently in the PSSM are based on how children learn mathematics. Both documents provide strong support for change from the traditional behavioralist approach to constructivism. In fact, "educational research offers compelling evidence that students learn mathematics well only when they *construct* their own mathematical understanding" (National Research Council 1989, p. 58).

What does it mean for students to construct their mathematical knowledge? It means different things to different people, and some of the myths associated with constructivism—such as "constructivist learners work alone" or "cooperative learning is constructivist"—continue to linger (Clements 1997). Although definitions vary, three basic tenets on which constructivism rests provide an answer to this question.

1. Knowledge is not passively received; rather, knowledge is actively created or invented (constructed) by students. Piaget (1972) suggested that mathematics is made (constructed) by children, not found like a rock nor received from others as a gift.

2. Students create (construct) new mathematical knowledge by reflecting on their physical and mental actions. They observe relationships, recognize patterns, and make generalizations and abstractions as they integrate new knowledge into their existing mental structure (Dienes 1960).

3. Learning reflects a social process in which children engage in dialogue and discussion with themselves as well as others (including teachers) as they develop intellectually (Bruner 1986). This tenet suggests that students are involved not only in manipulating materials, discovering patterns, inventing their own algorithms, and generating different solutions, but also in sharing their observations, describing their relationships, explaining their procedures, and defending the processes they followed.

Clearly, these tenets have significant implications for learning and teaching mathematics. The tenets also suggest that constructivism is a process that takes time and reflects several developmental stages.

Research has documented that children's level of mathematical development provides a window of opportunity for a range of learning activities. At each stage of development, the lower limit of this window of opportunity rests on previous concepts and skills that have been established, and the upper limit is determined by tasks that can be successfully completed only with step-by-step instruction. Learning activities and experiences that fall within this range, or window of opportunity, have been identified by the Russian psychologist Lev Vygotsky as being within a child's "zone of proximal development" (Steele 1999).

Research suggests that learning activities that fall within a child's zone of proximal development have a high probability of success, whereas engaging in activities outside of the zone have much less likelihood of success. The challenge provided by Vygotsky is to know our students well and to have a reasonably good understanding of these zones.

Theories of learning suggest that it is a natural process. Learning is active and internally monitored; it is a process of acquiring, discovering, and constructing meaning from experience. The process results in learning that is filtered through the student's unique knowledge base, thoughts, perceptions, and feelings.

Although the levels of development are characterized differently by Piaget, Bruner, and Dienes, as outlined in Figure 2–1, the frameworks proposed by each are remarkably similar. A careful examination of these frameworks reveals that:

- Children are actively involved in the learning process, and opportunities for talking about (communicating) their ideas are essential.

- Several characteristic and identifiable stages of thinking exist, and children progress through these as they grow and mature.

- Learning proceeds from the concrete to the abstract. Here we need to keep in mind that *concrete* is a relative term. To one child, joining two blocks and four blocks is concrete, but 2 + 4 is not; another child may view 2 + 4 as concrete and *x* + *y* as abstract.

- Symbols and formal representation of mathematical ideas follow naturally from the concrete level, but only after conceptualization and meaningful understanding have been established.

Taken collectively, theories about how children learn help considerably in planning instruction and developing curricula. They provide a strong argument for using appropriate models and concrete materials to illustrate mathematical concepts and for actively in-

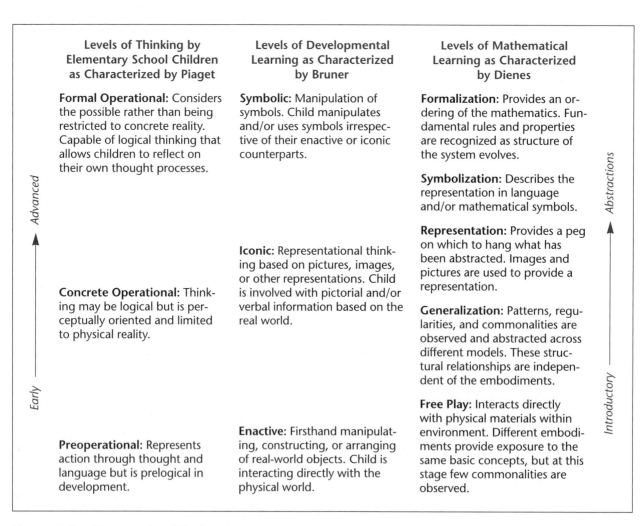

Figure 2–1 • Frameworks of the learning process

volving students in the learning process. A major instructional implication is that teachers should explain new information in terms of knowledge students already possess. This idea raises a critical question—what mathematics do students need?

WHAT MATHEMATICAL KNOWLEDGE SHOULD BE LEARNED?

The importance of skills versus concepts in mathematics learning has long been debated. Such debates create a false dichotomy that plays one against the other. The truth is that skills (procedural knowledge) and concepts (conceptual knowledge) are both necessary for expertise in mathematics. As teachers, we need to understand what constitutes procedural and conceptual knowledge and the importance of helping students make connections and establish meaningful relationships between them.

Procedural knowledge is based on a sequence of actions, often involving rules and algorithms; *conceptual knowledge,* on the other hand, is based on connected networks that link relationships and discrete pieces of information (Hiebert and Carpenter 1992). Computation provides the setting for much procedural knowledge, since algorithms can be acquired through a prescribed, step-by-step sequence of procedures. These procedures can be acquired with understanding or can be applied by rote. For example, to compute 23 + 49, one might use a series of regroupings to apply a written algorithm and produce a sum of 72; or one might add 20 and 40 to get 60 and then add 12 more to get 72; or one could use the related mental computation of 23 + 50 = 73, and then subtract 1 to get 72. Each of these "algorithms" illustrate procedural knowledge, and each can be developed with meaning and understanding.

However, it is also possible to learn the same algorithms as a series of steps devoid of meaning. For example, 23 + 49 could be memorized as "add the 3 and the 9 to get 12. Bring down the 2 and carry the 1. . . ." Such rote learning has no place in school mathematics, yet it highlights one of the ever-present dangers associated with algorithms. Research suggests that students with highly developed rules for manipulating symbols are reluctant to connect these rules to other representations that might give them meaning (Hiebert, Carpenter, et al. 1997). Other research reports that once elementary students learn procedures to do written computation, they are more likely to use the written rather than mental procedures (Reys and Barger 1994). These

studies remind us that once particular procedures are established and practiced, they become fixed, and the process makes later acquisition of understanding using the procedures less likely.

Although procedural knowledge may provide a rule or definition to answer a specific question, the resulting knowledge might be limited or devoid of important connections. For example, in response to a question—what is a square?—a student might respond correctly—"a square has four congruent sides and four right angles"—but without further probing, we don't know if other relationships—such as a square is a rectangle, a parallelogram, a regular polygon, or an equilateral quadrilateral—also exist. Awareness of these relationships requires conceptual knowledge that may not be evident from the initial response.

Conceptual and procedural knowledge can and should be developed with meaning and understanding. Although the nature of conceptual knowledge requires the establishment of meaningful relationships and connections, it is possible to develop procedural knowledge without regard for meaning. For example, "invert the divisor and multiply" will produce a correct result for the quotient of two fractions. A student may be able to apply this procedure but have no way to explain why it works. If only the answer is important, then the student has no desire to learn why the algorithm works.

Conceptual knowledge requires the learner to be active in thinking about relationships and making connections, along with making adjustments to accommodate the new learning with previous mental structures. On the other hand, procedural knowledge can be acquired in a more passive mode, as when a certain procedure is demonstrated or illustrated and the student is required only to imitate the technique. Later, the consequence of such rote learning is observed as the student grasps for a set of steps, a rule, or a formula to apply in some algorithmic manner. The student's ability to properly use procedural knowledge relies completely on memory, which may be inadequate to make the necessary recall due to a lack of connections and networks between conceptual and procedural knowledge. When this happens, errors occur. Students possessing only procedural knowledge have limited means of detecting and correcting errors and unreasonable answers.

As teachers, we need to acknowledge the importance of procedural and conceptual knowledge in mathematics learning. The need to help students establish connections and relationships between conceptual and procedural knowledge is great, and current research (Hiebert and Carpenter 1992) suggests that understanding and connections (conceptual knowledge) should come before proficiency in skills (procedural knowledge). Any discussion of what mathematics should be learned must include discussion of the way it is taught. This fact is elegantly captured in the statement, "What students learn is fundamentally connected with how they learn it" (NCTM 1991, p. 21).

Now let's turn to some specific instructional implications to help students build connections and learning bridges as they explore and learn mathematics.

IMPLICATIONS OF WHAT WE KNOW ABOUT LEARNING MATHEMATICS

Teaching occurs only to the extent that learning occurs. Therefore, effective teaching of mathematics rests heavily on considerations about how children learn. The process of building bridges from the concrete to the symbolic and helping children cross them is at the heart of good teaching—and it is a continual challenge.

The practical principles for teaching mathematics are consistent with the Learning Principle outlined in *Principles and Standards* (NCTM 2000) and reflect a blend of research, teaching experience, and thinking about how children learn mathematics. Because each principle addresses a specific issue, they are presented separately, and no priority of importance is suggested by the order in which they are listed.

Principle 1: Actively Involve Students

This principle is based on the conviction that active involvement will encourage students to make sense out of what they are doing and thereby develop greater understanding of mathematics. Recall the ancient Chinese proverb:

> I hear and I forget;
> I see and I remember;
> I do and I understand.

It reflects the importance of active involvement as a cornerstone on which students construct their own mathematical meaning. Active involvement may provide for physical activity but always demands mental activity. It takes many forms, including interaction of children and teachers, hands-on experience with manipulatives, and use of special learning materials such as textbooks or technology. One of the daily challenges of teaching is to provide experiences that will encourage, promote, and reward active involvement.

Suppose, for example, you were developing a lesson on volume. One approach might be to provide a formula for finding the volume of a right prism: $V = bhl$. You could show students drawings of various right prisms and then ask them to use the formula to compute the volume for each.

An active approach to developing volume is shown in In the Classroom 2–1. Here children are provided with some blocks and asked to build different boxes (right prisms). As they build the boxes, they begin to relate the dimensions of the boxes to their volumes. Finding the volume of boxes is a primary objective for this activity. However, as students find the volume of the boxes in In the Classroom 2–1, they also learn that different boxes may have the same volume. Furthermore, the need to multiply the dimensions becomes clear, so the formula for the volume of a box evolves naturally from this active involvement. Children are involved in using models, making decisions, and thinking about mathematics, rather than methodically applying a formula. They are also experiencing important mathematical properties, such as $4 \times (2 \times 2) = (4 \times 2) \times 2$, or $4 \times (2 \times 2) = (2 \times 2) \times 4$, which provide practice in arithmetic and develop algebraic thinking.

Principle 2: Learning Is Developmental

Effective and efficient learning of mathematics doesn't just happen. Children learn best when mathematical topics are appropriate for their developmental level and are presented in an enjoyable and interesting way that challenges their intellectual development.

It takes time to extract mathematics from real-life experiences and concrete materials. It takes time to search for patterns, observe relationships, and make connections, as errors naturally occur along the way. Yet this time is well spent, since it helps develop a lasting facility not only to think about mathematics, but also to think mathematically.

The theory of the zone of proximal development suggests that students vary greatly in their development and readiness for learning. Thus some first

In The Classroom 2–1

Patterns with Blocks

Objective: Finding the volume of rectangular prisms and connecting it to factors.

▼ Each of these boxes holds 16 blocks:

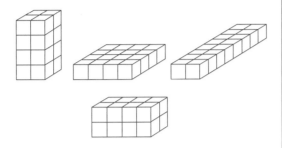

▼ Take 24 blocks. Make as many different boxes as you can.

- How many different boxes did you make?
- Tell how many layers each box had.
- Tell how many blocks are in each layer.

▼ Suppose that you have 4 piles of blocks and that all the blocks in the pile must be used:

Pile A has 16 blocks.   Pile B has 25 blocks.

Pile C has 36 blocks.   Pile D has 50 blocks.

- Which pile of blocks would you choose to build the most different boxes? Tell why.
- Which pile would you choose to build the fewest different boxes? Tell why.

graders will understand addition and develop fluency with basic facts before some third graders. Likewise, some middle-grade students may have difficulty visualizing the blocks shown in In the Classroom 2–1, and they may need to "build" these boxes before the task becomes meaningful.

Teachers play a critical role in judging the developmental stage, and subsequently determining zones of proximal development. The decisions reached allow teachers to establish rich environments for students to explore mathematics at an appropriate developmental level. Teachers must not only provide a rich classroom environment for learning mathematics but must provide the necessary direction to help children recognize relationships, make connections, and talk about mathematics.

Principle 3: Build on Previous Learning

Mathematics must be organized so that it is appropriate and understandable to students. Because mathematics includes both conceptual and procedural knowledge, the challenge is not only to develop these types of knowledge but to establish relational understanding between them. In no other discipline is previous knowledge and learning more critical. For example, it is fruitless to try to estimate a distance in kilometers if you don't know what a kilometer is.

Quality mathematics programs are organized both to provide continuous development and to help students to understand the basic structure of mathematics. Scope-and-sequence charts provide an overview of how a particular program is arranged. A careful examination of such a chart will reveal how a sequence of activities is organized in a spiral approach.

Ideally, the *spiral approach* provides many opportunities over time to develop and broaden concepts. More specifically, it incorporates and builds on earlier learning to help guide the child through continued but increasingly more intricate study of related topics. Angle measurement, for example, is informally introduced in primary grades and returned to many times. When the concept of "angle" reappears in later grades, greater levels of sophistication are required. The diagram in Figure 2–2 shows how previous experience is used to develop the concept.

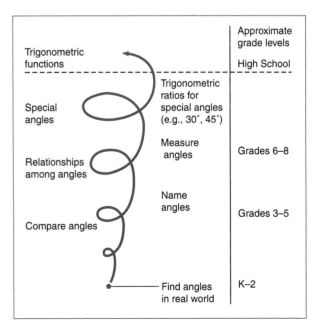

Figure 2–2 • Spiral approach toward developing angles

There is, however, a danger associated with the spiral approach to curriculum that should be recognized. Although in theory the spiral mathematics curriculum provides for continuous growth and development, in reality many topics are revisited each year without appreciable change in the intellectual level of treatment. Consequently, much valuable time is spent each year treading water, merely reviewing topics rather than continuing an exploration that builds on prior learning or introduces new topics. For example, the Third International Mathematics and Science Study (TIMSS) reported that mathematics programs in the United States reflect more review of topics from year to year than other countries, such as Germany and Japan (TIMSS 1996). Such repetition is detrimental because it turns students off. It robs both teachers and students of the excitement inherent in exploring fresh and new mathematics. It also diverts large amounts of instructional time from new learning to reviewing familiar concepts, which means that fewer new ideas can be experienced each year.

The spiral approach holds profound implications for learning and teaching. Instructional planning must consider the prerequisites for success on the current lesson, and the teacher must check to see if students have them. It is not unusual to find students who have skipped, never learned, forgotten, or incorrectly learned prerequisite topics. Detecting these weaknesses early and quickly allows the inclusion of reviews, so that later lesson development is not hampered by students' lack of prerequisites.

Just as we must know what has happened in earlier grades, we must look ahead to what will be expected of our students tomorrow, next month, and next year. Third-grade teachers must know what has happened in kindergarten, first grade, and second grade, as well as what will be expected of their students in later years. This broad perspective helps each of us to better understand and appreciate the importance of our role. It also demands that we guard against learning gaps in mathematics and, whenever they are detected, do our best to fill them.

Principle 4: Communication Contributes Significantly to Understanding

Models, manipulatives, and real-world examples provide many opportunities for thinking, talking, and listening. The importance of communication in mathematics learning is demonstrated by the fact that communication is one of the key process standards in the *Principles and Standards* (NCTM 2000). Opportunities to explain, talk about mathematics, make conjectures, and defend one's thinking orally as well as in writing stimulate deeper understanding, and talking and writing about mathematics are essential parts of learning mathematics.

Although precision is valued in mathematics, precision in mathematical language is a product of learning; it is not necessarily a tool for the learning of mathematics. As teachers, we must be careful about pushing for too much precision in language too soon. Students at all levels should talk about mathematics before they are expected to communicate mathematics symbolically. Just as speaking precedes writing for children, so should the oral language of mathematics precede symbolization. Both student-to-student communication and student-to-teacher communication are important in the learning process.

In talking about mathematics, students are likely to provide valuable insights into their thinking and understanding. This talk may take different forms. For example, consider two second graders who are responding to the following question:

> Today is February 9—how many days are left in the month?

Student-to-Student Communication

WILLIAM: The answer is 21.

WHITNEY: I got 19.

WILLIAM: How did you get that?

WHITNEY: I said 9 plus 10 is 19 and 10 more is 29. That is one too many days, so it is 19. How did you get 21?

WILLIAM: I subtracted . . . [he proceeds to write

$$\begin{array}{r} 28 \\ -\ 9 \\ \hline \end{array}$$

and then says] I messed up. I subtracted 8 from 9 instead of 9 from 28. You're right, it is 19.

This kind of talking between students is natural and provides many opportunities for explanations, justifications, and sharing of methods. As teachers, we may often be unaware of such conversations, but we should do all we can to stimulate and encourage student-to-student communication.

Consider now the following student-teacher interaction as a fourth-grade class is exploring primes and composite numbers by building rectangles with tiles.

Student-to-Teacher Communication

BOB: So every even number is composite.

TEACHER: What about two?

This question stimulates additional thinking and will encourage Bob to justify this overgeneralization.

Raising questions and challenging answers that have been proposed by students are excellent ways to stimulate thinking and talking about mathematics and create a classroom that encourages students to engage in communication. Such interaction allows students opportunities to talk about their ideas, get feedback for their thinking, and hear other points of view. Thus, students learn from one another as well as from teachers.

In writing about mathematics, students provide insight into what they are thinking and what they understand. It may be helpful to write prompts to help students get started. For example,

I think the answer is . . .

Another way to do it is . . .

The thing I liked best was . . .

I still don't understand . . .

Children can and will tell us much about what they know and don't know. In the process, they are developing some important communication skills. Talking and writing about mathematics make it more alive and more personal, thus heightening student interest. Reading and listening carefully to what is being said, as well as noticing what is not being said, allow us to better tailor our teaching.

Principle 5: Good Questions Facilitate Learning

Students can and should ask questions of each other. Students can and should ask questions of teachers, and teachers can and should ask questions of students. Questions are a vital element of the learning process. Teachers need to know when to ask a question and what kinds of questions to ask. The teacher also needs to know when to answer a question and when to ask another question that will facilitate the answering of the original question.

In theory, there are no bad questions. Some that are raised may be unnecessary because they have just been answered, but the person asking was not paying attention. Some questions may be stated poorly and may be misunderstood. Some questions may be more appropriate at another time. There may be times, for example, when low-level questions with a unique answer are appropriate (for example, "What is seven times six?"), but at other times, more open-ended questions are most effective ("About how many tennis balls will fit in our room?"). Our attention here (and in further discussion of questions in Chapter 3) is to focus on the need for good questions that stimulate thinking and learning.

What are good questions? Good questions take a variety of different forms but are generally characterized by their potential to encourage critical thinking, establish relationships, and promote meaningful connections.

Here are some examples of several different types of good generic questions that need to be an integral part of mathematics learning:

What would be a reasonable estimate for the answer?

How did you solve that problem?

Can you solve that a different way?

What is different about these solutions?

What pattern do you see?

Can you explain that a different way?

Explain how . . . ?

Explain why . . . ?

What are some possible solutions for . . . ?

What is another example of . . . ?

Are there other patterns . . . ?

What do you think would happen if . . . ?

What do you still not understand about . . . ?

How would you help someone else understand?

How is . . . related to . . . ?

How is this . . . related to . . . that we studied earlier?

How would you use this . . . to . . . ?

How does . . . affect . . . ?

How are . . . and . . . similar?

How are . . . and . . . different?

All of these questions are appropriate for either students or teachers to ask. It is important that, as teachers, we be sensitive to the need to raise good questions and encourage our students to do so as well.

Principle 6: Manipulatives Aid Learning

Manipulative materials and models assume a critical role in helping students learn mathematics throughout elementary school. By their very nature, mathematical thoughts are abstract, so any model that embodies them is imperfect and has limitations. Even though the model is not the mathematics, the model provides a context for the mathematical concept under consideration. Research shows that learning occurs best when students have a meaningful context for the mathematical knowledge and understand fundamental relationships associated with the knowledge (National Research Council 1999).

Helping children link, connect, or establish meaningful bridges from the model (context) to the mathematics is a challenge, but it is a rewarding struggle.

Suppose you were developing the concept of a circle. A plate could be used to illustrate this concept, but it would also illustrate many other mathematical concepts: area, boundary, circumference, and diameter, to name but a few. When a concept is being formed, the learner has no way of knowing which attributes characterize it. Thus, irrelevant variables (design on the plate, its attractive finish, a chip or crack) may be the only things "seen." It will not be clear exactly what characterizes a circle.

Other models, such as coins or jar lids, could be introduced, but the focus might still be on the interior rather than the boundary of these models. Additional models, such as a rim of a wheel, a bike tire, a ring, and the core from a roll of paper towels, would reinforce the roundness associated with a circle but would also make it clear that a circle is associated with the outer edge or boundary of the models (see Figure 2–3). Research has shown that mildly attracting attention to the important attributes will enhance learning, so one might take a piece of chalk or a water-soluble pen and mark around the outer part of the coin or plate to highlight the circle.

The use of perceptually different models, such as those shown in Figure 2–3, is called multiple embodiment, or *multi-embodiment*. Research has shown that transfer across contexts is difficult when the concept appears in only a single context rather than in multiple contexts (National Research Council 1999). The more different the models or contexts, the more likely the students are to extract only the common characteristics and make abstractions. It is foolhardy to make abstractions from a single model in mathematics. Multi-embodiment encourages students to abstract but to do so with discretion. It also decreases the likelihood of a mathematical concept being uniquely associated with a particular model. Such associative learning can occur whenever a single model is used to illustrate a mathematical concept.

Although research has documented the value of providing multi-embodiments, important questions remain. For example, how long should a model be used? The length of time that a model is used depends on both the student and the content. It is, however, safe to say that, in general, too little time is spent with a model. That is, students are rushed (or dragged) too quickly through firsthand experiences with models and then confronted with symbolizations. Students need to feel comfortable with a model and both observe and talk about the key mathematical features it embodies. Even at this stage, leaving a model doesn't mean that it will never be used again. In fact, the same model may be used at various levels throughout elementary school to develop new and/or more sophisticated concepts.

Mathematical learning depends heavily on abstraction and generalization. The multi-embodiment principle rests on the value of experiencing a mathematical concept in a variety of different physical settings. Within each embodiment, many attributes or characteristics appear. The use of *mathematical variability* ensures that, within a given embodiment, various mathematical features are allowed to change. Many different examples and nonexamples are needed before generalizations can be made.

Let's reconsider one of the embodiments of a circle—the plate shown in Figure 2–3—to develop the concept of a circle. In order to dispel the attention given to physical features, such as size, design, or chips, several different kinds of plates could be used. Hopefully, this experience with variability would refocus attention on the plate's roundness. The model is unchanged, but examples within it are varied. These changes within a given model enhance the prospects of the learner's focusing on only the significant mathematical attributes.

Similarly, if rings are used, different designs, styles, and materials will provide a reminder that the rings model a circle. It is also advisable to point out that some rings don't model a circle.

For example, consider this "adjustable ring":

Although it is a ring, it does not model a circle. Such *nonexamples* play an important role in concept formulation. An oval serving platter could be used with the plates to provide a nonexample within that multi-embodiment.

Plate   Coin   Ring   Bike tire

Figure 2–3 • Some models of a circle

Research confirms that students learn more when presented with a combination of examples and nonexamples of a mathematical concept than with examples alone (Hiebert and Carpenter 1992). Implementation of mathematical variability provides opportunities to vary examples and include nonexamples.

Principle 7: Metacognition Affects Learning

Metacognition refers to what one knows or believes about oneself as a learner and how one controls and adjusts one's behavior. Students need to become aware of their strengths, weaknesses, and typical behaviors and of the repertoire of procedures and strategies that they use to learn and do mathematics and, more specifically, solve problems.

Metacognition is a form of looking over your own shoulder—observing yourself as you work and thinking about what you are thinking. Students who monitor their mathematical thinking search for understanding and strive to make sense of the mathematics being learned. Competent problem solvers are efficient at keeping track of what they know and of how well or poorly their attempt to solve a problem is proceeding. They continuously ask,

What am I doing?

Why am I doing it?

How will it help me?

A growing research base suggests that what students know or believe about themselves as mathematics learners not only greatly affects their performance but also influences their behavior as they do mathematics (Renga and Dalla 1993).

Examples of metacognitive knowledge range from knowing that practice improves task proficiency and that drawing a picture often helps in understanding a problem to knowing that "I get scared when I see a word problem." Metacognitive knowledge often helps students control and adjust behavior. Thus if Sheena knows that she has frequently made keystroking errors with her calculator, she is more likely to work slowly and to check on the reasonableness of her calculator's answers.

The development of metacognition requires that children observe what they know and what they do and reflect on what they observe. Encouraging students to "think about their thinking" is an important ingredient of mathematics learning. Teachers can do several things to help students develop this metacognitive awareness:

- Be explicit about how they themselves work when solving problems. Teachers often present complete polished solutions to students, which may hide many critical decisions made while planning the lesson. For example, consider the following questions:

Why did you do that?

How did you know not to use that information?

Why did you decide to estimate?

Such questions are routinely addressed by teachers in preparing lessons, but students are not often made aware of this background. There is value in sharing some of the behind-the-scenes decision making with students.

- Point out to students various aspects of problem solving, such as the following:

Some problems take a long time to solve.

There may be more than one right answer to a problem.

Some problems can be solved several different ways.

You don't have to solve problems the way the teacher does.

- Students should also be encouraged to become more aware of metacognition and the need to think about their mathematical thinking. For example, teachers might ask students to discuss the following:

What mathematics problems do you like best? Tell why.

What mathematics problems are most difficult?

What can you do to improve as a solver of these problems?

What do you do when you find a mathematics problem that you don't know how to do?

What errors do you make most often in mathematics? Why do you think you make them?

Principle 8: Teacher Attitudes Are Vital

Students' attitudes toward mathematics are a by-product of learning and are linked to both motivation and success in mathematics. Students' values, including attitudes, are greatly influenced by teachers. Teachers who enjoy teaching mathematics and share their interest and enthusiasm for the subject tend to produce students who like mathematics (Fennema et al. 1990).

Thus if teachers' words or actions suggest that boys or students of Asian background, for example, are likely to excel in mathematics, then a message of differentiated expectation has been sent to girls or to students who are from a different ethnic background. However, if it is made clear that mathematics exists in every culture and that high achievement is expected of all students regardless of race or gender, then a different message is sent. The power of this message of "mathematics is for everyone" is documented by research consistently confirming that teacher expectations greatly affect student performance (Koehler and Grouws 1992).

Similarly, if the mathematics instruction places heavy emphasis on computational skills, students will view computation as very important. However, if teachers reward creative solutions or approaches to problems, then students will develop respect for divergent thinking. Furthermore, if teachers make it clear that critical thinking and problem solving are valued and respected, then critical thinking and problem solving will be viewed as important by students. Establishing what is important and valued within each mathematics classroom greatly influ-

ences not only what is learned and how it is learned but students' attitudes toward mathematics as well.

Principle 9: Experiences Influence Anxiety

Mathematics anxiety, or "mathophobia," is a fear of mathematics or an intense negative feeling about mathematics. Some classic symptoms of mathematics anxiety (such as poor performance, misunderstandings, and dislike of mathematics) are shown in Figure 2–4. Other negative emotions may be reflected by insecurity, as well as fears of failure, punishment, ridicule, or stigmatizing labels. In some students, mathematics anxiety may be reflected as a negative attitude toward mathematics or as a negative emotional reaction to mathematics.

Mathematics anxiety is often associated with how mathematics is learned. Research suggests that primary-grade children are generally positive about mathematics, yet the likelihood of mathematics anxiety increases as children move into middle school

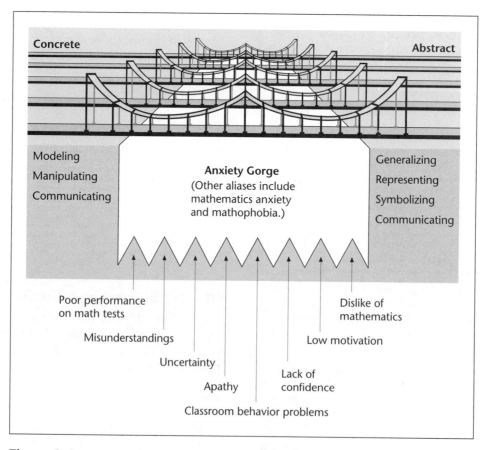

Figure 2–4 • Bridges linking meaning to mathematics

and junior high school (Renga and Dalla 1993). Students who experience mathematics anxiety tend to take less mathematics during secondary school, thereby blocking their access to many careers.

What can be done about mathematics anxiety? The following suggestions address ways to help students cope with the problem of mathematics anxiety:

- Emphasize meaning and understanding rather than memorization. Our brains do not easily learn isolated facts, things that are not logical or that have no meaning (Caine and Caine 1995). Mathematics learning must be characterized by sense making—that is, the mathematics learned must make sense to the learner. Children attempting to memorize mathematics without understanding are likely to fall into the "anxiety gorge" in Figure 2–4. Helping students make connections between concrete models and either conceptual or procedural knowledge facilitates understanding and promotes greater learning success.

- Model problem-solving strategies rather than presenting a finished solution. Encourage students to offer suggestions and try their ideas, and see what happens. Help students realize that incorrect strategies and steps are a natural part of problem solving. Remind students that in the long run the problem-solving journey is more important than the resulting answer. This focus on the process rather than the answer helps reduce anxiety associated with "wrong" answers.

- Provide mathematical experiences that are interesting and challenging but that allow children to be successful. Self-confidence results from successful experiences in learning mathematics.

- Help all students appreciate the power, usefulness, and importance of mathematics. Make it clear that success in mathematics is for everybody, and avoid any suggestion that different mathematics expectations are associated with race or gender.

- Show an enjoyment for mathematics.

- Maintain and project a positive attitude toward mathematics and students.

- Encourage students to tell you how they feel about mathematics. What do they like? Why do they like it? This self-reflective (or metacognitive) diagnosis can help you detect symptoms of mathematics anxiety.

- Be careful not to overemphasize speed tests or drills in your classroom. Some children enjoy the challenge of competition. Others are uncomfortable with timed pressure; for these students, timed races breed apprehension and fear of mathematics.

- Use diagnostic techniques to identify students who are experiencing particular difficulty or need special help, and provide this help quickly to get them back on track.

Research indicates that unless action is taken or help provided, the level of anxiety does not lessen on its own (Hart and Walker 1993), so the best strategy is prevention, and the second best is early detection followed by some of the specific actions highlighted above.

Principle 10: Gender Aptitudes Are Equal

A complex assortment of social forces produces or influences gender inequities related to mathematics. For example, parents of young children may express different expectations in mathematics classes for their sons than for their daughters. School counselors may subtly discourage girls from pursuing mathematical careers. Such factors may contribute to fewer girls taking advanced mathematics courses, which may prematurely foreclose, or at least delay, options for careers in mathematics, science, and technical fields.

Research suggests that teachers may actually treat boys differently from girls in the classroom. For example, teachers may call on boys more often in mathematics classes than girls, and teachers may be less likely to praise girls than boys for correct responses and less willing to prompt girls who give wrong answers (Ansel and Doerr 2000). Teachers also are more likely to attribute boys' failure to a lack of motivation than they are girls' failure. Girls may take such criticism to heart and think this is a true indicator of their talent in mathematics.

Risk taking, or the willingness of students to take a chance in answering a question they are not certain of, may influence gender differences on tests. Research suggests that the format of the test may produce gender differences. Numerous studies have reported that boys gamble more than girls in choosing answers to questions that they are not sure of, and this may be rewarded by higher scores (Ramos and Lambating 1996). More specifically, multiple-choice tests tend to favor males because these objective tests often focus on small bits of knowledge, require a choice of one right answer with no chance to explain the choice, and exist in a competitive environment that girls find more stressful, whereas more open-ended responses favor girls because they are less stressful and allow for more creative, complex answers.

Although both boys and girls experience *learned helplessness,* girls are particularly susceptible to this syndrome. Learned helplessness is the belief that the individual cannot control outcomes and is destined to fail without the existence of a strong safety net. Learned helplessness includes feelings of incompetence, lack of motivation, and low self-esteem. It usually develops from what is perceived as failure or lack of success in learning, and it is often associated with mathematics. Students feel there is little sense in trying because the opportunity for success is beyond their control.

Strong efforts to confront and eliminate gender biases are reflected in the Equity Principle of the *Principles and Standards* (see Figure 1–1). Among successful actions taken by teachers to address gender inequities are:

- Dispelling myths (such as "mathematicians work in complete isolation" or "only white males do mathematics") that discourage women and some minorities from pursuing careers in mathematics (Henrion 1998)

- Having equally high expectations for both boys and girls, and clearly communicating these expectations to both students and their parents.

- Engaging both boys and girls in answering difficult questions, raising questions and communicating their mathematical thinking, and making sure boys don't dominate the class discussion or the teacher's time.

- Calling attention to female role models in mathematics and science, as well as helping students become increasingly aware of the career opportunities for people with strong mathematics backgrounds.

- Communicating to parents the importance of encouraging and supporting their daughters to aspire to and persist in nontraditional fields, such as mathematics.

- Discussing learned helplessness with people having problems, and developing ways to prevent or help remedy the situation (Renga and Dalla 1993).

- Providing a variety of ways (different testing formats, interviews, and portfolios) to assess student performance.

Principle 11: Retention Can Improve

A very important aspect of learning is *retention*. For example, if students can read a clock in class but not when they get home, their retention of this skill is so limited that it is virtually useless. Retention reflects the amount of knowledge kept, skill maintained, or problem-solving behaviors consistently exhibited.

Forgetting is a problem in all disciplines, but the cumulative nature of mathematics increases its importance. Forgetting occurs over a summer, a spring vacation, a weekend, a day, or even shorter periods. The graph in Figure 2–5 shows that skills and specific knowledge are subject to dramatic changes. Factual knowledge, such as the answers to the following questions, is quickly forgotten when it isn't used regularly.

What is a prime number?

State the transitive property.

Skills, such as how to do the following exercises, are also quickly lost without regular maintenance.

What is the quotient of $\frac{2}{3}$ and $\frac{1}{5}$?

Use the formula for a trapezoid.

Thus, classroom and achievement tests often report very volatile levels of performance on mathematical skills and knowledge.

The skill of problem solving, on the other hand, is less susceptible to big declines, and performance is more stable over time. One reason is that problem solving is a complex behavior requiring a number of higher-level thinking processes. Such processes take time to develop, but once established, they are retained longer than other skills and often improve as time goes by.

Retention is an important goal in mathematics education. Instructional efforts must recognize the importance of retention and try to maximize it.

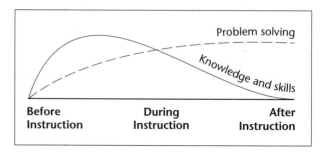

Figure 2–5 • **Typical learning retention curve**

How can retention be improved? Research suggests several ways:

1. Meaningful learning is the best way to shore up retention. All phases of mathematics (knowledge, skills, and problem solving) that have been developed with meaning and learned with understanding are retained longer.

2. The context in which a concept is learned provides useful links to long-term retention (National Research Council 1999). For example, the exploration of the perimeter or circumference of a circle will be facilitated by measuring the diameter and perimeter of many different circles. Physically measuring them and recording and observing patterns provides a link to remembering the ratio of the circumference and diameter is constant.

3. Establishing connections in the spirit of the *Principles and Standards* aids long-term retention. Connections help children see how mathematical ideas are related to each other and to the real world. Mathematical topics must not be taught in isolation as discrete topics, but they must be developed in conjunction with problem solving and applications in meaningful contexts. For example, in the previous discussion of the perimeter (circumference) of a circle, alerting students that the word *rim* is contained within the word *perimeter* and then connecting *rim* to a bicycle tire can facilitate retention of the notion of perimeter. Research documents the value of establishing connections to not only gain better understanding but also to promote greater retention and recall.

4. Periodic reviews of key ideas help anchor knowledge and can contribute substantially to the retention of mathematical knowledge of children at any age. Such maintenance is provided in the spiral development of high-quality mathematics programs. These reviews may be overt or subtle. In either case, they will help remove rustiness, provide important reinforcement and refreshers that improve immediate performance, and contribute to higher levels of learning and improve retention.

A Glance at Where We've Been

Mathematics learning can and must have meaning. This statement is the cornerstone of all instructional planning and teaching.

Conceptual and procedural knowledge are essential elements of mathematics learning, but decades of research have revealed no single best path to their development. There is, however, a strong and growing research base from learning theories to guide the learning process. These theories recognize the importance of the concrete level and offer effective ways to help children learn mathematics with meaning and understanding.

Research and experience suggest that there is significant value in children constructing their own knowledge and that the teacher plays an important role in facilitating such construction. In addition to hands-on experiences, children learn from telling, explaining, clarifying, making conjectures, and reflecting on what they have done. They also learn from watching, listening, reading, following directions, imitating, and practicing. All of these experiences contribute to learning mathematics; teachers have the responsibility of deciding the proper balance of these experiences.

We know that mathematics learning is influenced by factors specific to the individual, such as previous experience, environmental influences, maturation, ability, and motivation. Consequently, no single comprehensive learning theory can be unequivocally applied to all students at all levels for all mathematical knowledge. We also know that mathematics learning is a slow process that requires years of development. We know that many individual differences exist and that the rate of learning varies greatly among children. Given these variables, the essential role of teachers is to help children construct mathematical knowledge that is meaningful to them. In performing this role, teachers must make countless decisions to plan appropriate learning activities, establish an inviting classroom environment, and organize the classroom to ensure that all children are actively participating in experiencing, learning, abstracting, and constructing mathematics that is meaningful to them.

Things to Do: From What You've Read

1. List some characteristics of mathematics anxiety. Discuss how the use of learning bridges can save victims from the "anxiety gorge."

2. Provide some examples to help distinguish between procedural and conceptual knowledge in mathematics.

3. Give an example of meaningful learning in mathematics. Then give an example of nonmeaningful learning. State in your own words what distinguishes them.

4. Examine the learning frameworks in Figure 2–1. Tell how the models proposed by Piaget, Bruner, and Dienes are alike. How are they different?

5. Identify the three tenets on which constructivism is based.

6. State in your own words what the zone of proximal development is. Do you think it is important? Tell why.

7. What is metacognition? Examine In the Classroom 2–1. Describe how metacognition might be used to think about your thinking during that activity.

8. What are some specific actions an elementary teacher can take to better ensure gender equity?

9. Do you think the learning principles are equally appropriate for elementary and middle school students? Tell why or why not.

10. Describe some specific steps that teachers can take to improve retention of mathematics learning.

Things to Do: Going Beyond This Book

field Additional activities, suggestions, and questions are provided in *Teaching Elementary Mathematics: A Resource for Field Experiences.*

1. *field* Use In the Classroom 2–1 with a child. Did the child realize that two of the pictured boxes are the same box, just in a different position? Would it make sense to try this activity with children if blocks were not available? Why?

2. *field* *Classroom Manipulatives.* Identify models and manipulatives that are available to use in a mathematics classroom that you visit. Did you see them being used? If so, what models and manipulatives were being used and how?

3. Examine an article discussing gender/race as related to learning mathematics, such as Renga and Dalla (1993), Ramos and Lambating (1996), or Sumrall (1995). Describe significant issues raised, and implications for you as a teacher.

4. *field* *Equity in Whole-Class Lessons.* Observe a mathematics class and be sensitive to the verbal and physical clues that suggest boys are treated differently from girls. Did you see evidence that boys were treated differently from girls? If so, discuss some examples.

5. Check the Women's Educational Equity Act (WEEA) Equity Resource Center Web site, http://www.edu.org/womensequity/ for a history of Title IX, a list of publications, current articles, and other Web site links. Report on something related to equity and mathematics that you find at this site.

6. *field* *Equity for Students with Special Needs.* Observe a *mainstreamed* mathematics class. How many children were physically impaired? Behaviorally disordered? Had IEPs? What types of adaptations were made to support these student's learning of mathematics? Were they successful? Why or why not?

7. Examine one of the vignettes from the *Professional Standards for Teaching Mathematics* (NCTM 1991). Present this vignette to your classmates, and discuss its value in helping you help children learn mathematics.

8. Obtain a publication from the Math/Science Network (Lawrence Hall of Science, University of California, Berkeley, Calif. 94720), such as *Math for Girls and Other Problem Solvers* or *Use Equals To Promote the Participation of Women in Mathematics.* Review one of their publications and share your reactions.

9. Examine the Learning Principle in the *Principles and Standards for School Mathematics* (NCTM 2000). Describe some specific ideas that would be useful in planning instruction and helping children learn mathematics.

10. Examine the book *Gender Equity: Sources and Resources for Education* by Sanders, Koch, and Urso, 1997. Describe some things you can do in your teaching to help encourage girls to study mathematics.

11. *field* *Student Attitudes.* Ask a child some questions to learn about their attitudes and perceptions about mathematics. For example:

    If I say, "Let's do some mathematics," what would you do?

    What school subject do you like most? Are you good at it?

    Do you think knowing mathematics will help you when you grow up? Tell why.

    Do you think your teacher liked to teach mathematics? Tell why.

    Summarize what you learned about this child's feelings about mathematics.

12. Examine the NCTM Yearbook *Multicultural and Gender Equity in the Mathematics Classroom* (Trentacosta and Kenney 1997). Read one of the articles, and then identify and discuss several specific implications for mathematics teaching.

13. Examine the books by Edeen et al. or Reimer and Reimer in Book Nook for Children and report how you might use these resources. Do you think this personalization helps promote more interest in learning mathematics? Do you think helping children learn more about women's contributions in mathematics is an important instructional goal? Tell why.

BOOK NOOK FOR CHILDREN

Edeen, Susan; Edeen, John; and Slachman, Virginia. *Portraits for Classroom Bulletin Boards: Women Mathematicans.* Palo Alto, Calif: Dale Seymour Publications, 1990.

Perl, T. *Women and Numbers: Lives of Women Mathematicans Plus Discovery Activities.* San Carlow, Calif: Worldwide, 1993.

Reimer, Luetta, and Reimer, Wilbert. *Mathematicians Are People, Too,* 2 vols. Palo Alto, Calif: Dale Seymour Publications, 1990.

Selected References

Ansel, Ellen & Doerr, Helen. "NAEP Findings Regarding Gender: Achievement, Affect, and Instructional Experiences." In *Results from the Seventh Mathematics Assessment of the National Assessment of Educational Progress* (eds. E. A. Silver and P. A. Kenney). Reston, Va.: National Council of Teachers of Mathematics, 2000.

Boling, Ann Neaves. "They Don't Like Math? Well, Let's Do Something." *Arithmetic Teacher,* 38 (March 1991), pp. 17–19.

Brownell, William A. "Psychological Considerations in the Learning and the Teaching of Arithmetic." In *The Teaching of Arithmetic,* Tenth Yearbook (ed. W. D. Reeves). Reston, Va.: NCTM, 1935, pp. 1–31.

Bruner, Jerome. *Actual Minds, Possible Worlds.* Cambridge, Mass.: Harvard University Press, 1986.

Buxton, Laurie. *Math Panic.* Portsmouth, N. H.: Heineman and Boynton/Cook, 1991.

Caine, Renate, and Caine, Geoffrey. "Reinventing Schools through Brain-Based Learning." *Educational Leadership* (April 1995), pp. 43–47.

Clements, Douglas H. "(Mis?)Constructing Constructivism." *Teaching Children Mathematics* (December 1997), pp. 198–200.

Dienes, Zoltan P. *Building Up Mathematics.* London: Hutchinson Education, 1960.

Feldt, Constance Curley. "Becoming a Teacher of Mathematics: A Constructive, Interactive Process." *Mathematics Teacher,* 86 (May 1993), pp. 400–403.

Fennema, Elizabeth; Peterson, Penelope L.; Carpenter, Thomas P.; and Lubinski, Cheryl. "Teacher Attributions and Beliefs about Girls, Boys and Mathematics." *Educational Studies in Mathematics,* 21 (February 1990), pp. 55–69.

Ginsburg, Herbert P., and Baron, Joyce. "Cognition: Young Children's Construction of Mathematics." In *Research Ideas for the Classroom: Early Childhood Mathematics* (ed. Robert J. Jensen). Reston, Va.: NCTM, and New York: Macmillan, 1993, pp. 3–21.

Hart, Laurie E., and Walker, Jamie. "The Role of Affect in Teaching and Learning Mathematics." In *Research Ideas for the Classroom: Middle Grades Mathematics* (ed. Douglas T. Owens). Reston, Va.: NCTM, and New York: Macmillan, 1993, pp. 22–38.

Henrion, Claudia. *Women in Mathematics: The Addition of Difference.* Bloomington, Ind.: Indiana University Press, 1998.

Hiebert, James, and Carpenter, Thomas P. "Learning and Teaching with Understanding." In *Handbook of Research on Mathematics Teaching and Learning* (ed. Douglas Grouws). New York: Macmillan, 1992, pp. 65–97.

Hiebert, James; Carpenter, Thomas; Fuson, Karen; Murray, A.; Oliver, P. Human; and Wearne, Diane. *Designing Classrooms for Learning Mathematics with Understanding.* Portsmouth, N.H.: Heinemann Educational Books, 1997.

Kamii, Constance, and Lewis, Barbara A. "Constructivism and First-Grade Arithmetic." *Arithmetic Teacher,* 38 (September 1990), pp. 36–37.

Kloosterman, Peter, and Gainey, Patricia Haynes. "Students' Thinking: Middle Grade Mathematics." In *Research Ideas for the Classroom: Middle Grades Mathematics* (ed. Douglas T. Owens). Reston, Va.: NCTM, and New York: Macmillan, 1993, pp. 3–21.

Koehler, Mary S. "Classroom, Teachers and Gender Issues in Mathematics." In *Mathematics and Gender* (eds. Elizabeth Fennema and Gilah C. Leder). New York: Teachers College Press, 1990, pp. 128–148.

Koehler, Mary S., and Grouws, Douglas A. "Mathematics Teaching Practices and Their Effects." In *Handbook of Research on Mathematics Teaching and Learning* (ed. Douglas Grouws). New York: Macmillan, 1992, pp. 115–126.

Morrow, Jean; Schrock, Connie; and Buchman, Debbie. "'Real People': A Fifth-Grade Class Investigates the Lives of Mathematicians." *Mathematics Teaching in the Middle School,* 1(4) (January–March 1995), pp. 274–282.

National Council of Teachers of Mathematics. *Principles and Standards for School Mathematics.* Reston, Va.: NCTM, 2000.

National Council of Teachers of Mathematics. *Professional Standards for Teaching Mathematics.* Reston, Va.: NCTM, 1991.

National Research Council. *Everybody Counts: A Report to the Nation on the Future of Mathematics Education.* Washington, D.C.: National Academy Press, 1989.

National Research Council. *How People Learn: Brain, Mind, Experience, and School.* Washington, D.C.: National Academy Press, 1999.

Nichols, Rosalie S., and Kurtz, V. Ray. "Gender and Mathematics Contests." *Arithmetic Teacher,* 41 (January 1994), pp. 238–239.

Piaget, Jean. *To Understand Is to Invent.* New York: Grossman, 1972.

Ramos, Ismael, and Lambating, Julia. "Risk Taking: Gender Differences and Educational Opportunity." *School Science and Mathematics,* 96(2) (February 1996), 94–98.

Renga, Sherry, and Dalla, Lidwins. "Affect: A Critical Component of Mathematical Learning in Early Childhood." In *Research Ideas for the Classroom: Early Childhood Mathematics* (ed. Robert J. Jensen). Reston, Va.: NCTM, and New York: Macmillan, 1993, pp. 22–39.

Reys, Barbara J., and Barger, Rita. "Mental Computation: Issues from the United States Perspective." In *Computational Alternatives for the 21st Century: Cross Cultural Perspectives from Japan and the United States* (ed. Robert E. Reys and Nobuhiko Nohda). Reston, Va.: NCTM, 1994, pp. 31–47.

Sanders, Jo; Koch, Janice; and Urso, Josephine. *Gender Equity Sources and Resources for Education Students.* Mahwah, N.J.: Lawrence Erlbaum, 1997.

Steele, Diana. "Learning Mathematical Language in the Zone of Proximal Development. *Teaching Children Mathematics,* 4 (September 1999), pp. 38–42.

Sumrall, William J. "Reasons for the Perceived Images of Scientists by Race and Gender of Students in Grades 1–7." *School Science and Mathematics*, 95(2) (February 1995), 83–90.

Third International Mathematics and Science Study (TIMSS). *U.S. National Research Center Report No. 7*. East Lansing, Mich.: TIMSS U.S. National Research Center, Michigan State University, December 1996. http://ustimss.msu.edu/

Trentacosta, Janet, and Kenney, Margaret J. (eds.). *Multicultural and Gender Equity in the Mathematics Classroom*. 1997 Yearbook. Reston, Va.: NCTM, 1997.

Wheatley, Grayson H. "Constructivist Perspectives on Science and Mathematics Learning." *Science Education*, 75 (1991), pp. 9–21.

Snapshot of a Lesson Plan

(Copyright © 1970 by Arnold Lobel. Used by permission of HarperCollins Publishers.)

Topic

Primary early number

Objective

Students will classify and describe objects by their attributes

Theme

Book: *Frog and Toad Are Friends: A Lost Button*

Materials

Frog and Toad Are Friends, buttons of various colors, shapes, and sizes (or paper buttons or attribute blocks)

Introduction

Ask children to tell about some times when they lost something. Discuss how they find things they have lost. Tell children to listen to a story about how Toad knew which button was his. Read *A Lost Button.*

Class Activities

Whole-Class Discussion

Initiate discussion about the story. How did Toad identify his button? Bring out the fact that attributes (characteristics) of objects help us describe something. Examples: a person—tall/short, brown/blond/black hair, male/female; a book—blue cover, paperback/hardback, small/large. Ask students to contribute similar ideas.

Talk about the buttons children are wearing on their clothing. Have them describe those buttons using 4 attributes: size (for example, large, small), color, shape (for example, round, square), and number of holes.

Modeling

Place a handful of buttons (or attribute blocks) in a pile on the overhead. Tell students to pretend Toad wants to sort the buttons into piles by their attributes. Hold up some buttons from the piles and discuss how we would describe them using the four attributes. Then show how the buttons can be sorted by size, color, shape, or number of holes. Regroup the buttons and show how they could be sorted another way.

Small-Group Work

1. A sorting game (collaborative small-group work).

   Divide the class into groups of four. Give each group a collection of buttons (in a cup). Two members of the group should pretend to be Frog and sort the buttons. The other two members will pretend to be Toad and guess what attribute was used to sort. Then allow the pairs to change roles.

Circulate while the children work and check for understanding by telling students Toad is looking for a particular button (for example, large, round, white, with two holes). Have students find buttons fitting various descriptions in their piles.

2. A hiding game (independent practice)

Tell students they are going to play a Frog and Toad guessing game. Model how to play the game before they begin in their groups. One person in the group is Toad and removes a button from the pile. The other group members may ask yes/no questions to try to find what kind of button was hidden (for example, Is it big? Round? Red?) Group members should take turns hiding buttons and guessing.

Assessment

While students are playing both games, walk around and observe their participation. Identify and make notes about students who can successfully identify buttons by their attributes and students who have difficulties.

Gearing Up

If the sorting task seems too difficult for some students, reduce the number of attributes to three or even just two (for example, take away all the buttons that are not round, so that shape is no longer a distinguishing attribute).

If the sorting task seems too simple for some students, place two intersecting circles of yarn on the desk (forming a Venn diagram). Have students collaborate to sort the buttons so everything in one circle has a certain attribute (for example, large) and everything in the other circle has another attribute (for example, red) and buttons with both attributes (large and red) are placed in the intersection of the two circles. Buttons that do not belong in either circle should be left off to the side (for example, small non-red circles or large blue circles). Once sorting by two intersecting sets is understood, the students can go back to taking turns having one pair sort and the other pair identify how the buttons have been sorted (what each circle represents).

References

Balka, D. *Attribute Logic Block Activities.* Oak Lawn, Ill.: Ideal School Supply Co., 1985.

Baratta-Lorton, M. *Mathematics Their Way.* Menlo Park, Calif.: Addison-Wesley, 1995.

Lobel, A. *Frog and Toad are Friends.* New York: Harper Collins Publishers, 1970.

Introduction

Teachers play many different roles in the classroom. Think about how the work of a teacher may be compared to the work done by a gardener, policeman, parent, sculptor, architect, friend, counselor, or cheerleader. Can you think of other metaphors to describe some of the roles that teachers play?

You may find yourself playing a number of these different roles as a teacher. The roles you play depend upon your personality, your school, and many other factors including the students in your class. This chapter focuses on the more traditional roles that all teachers must assume in the classroom: choosing tasks; planning lessons; asking questions; listening to, observing, and helping students; assessing understanding; and assigning grades. This chapter serves as a organizer for much of what you will learn throughout the rest of this text because each of these teacher roles will be elaborated upon and more fully described in subsequent chapters when you read about how to help children learn specific mathematics concepts and skills.

In Chapter 2, you read about the research on how children learn mathematics. Growing accep-tance that children actively construct their own un-derstandings as they build new ideas upon what they already know has significantly influenced how mathematics is being taught in many contemporary schools. NCTM's Teaching Principle affirms the im-portance of designing instruction to build upon stu-dents' prior knowledge:

> Effective mathematics teaching requires under-standing what students know and need to learn and then challenging and supporting them to learn it well. (NCTM 2000, p. 16)

In this chapter we briefly discuss general recom-mendations for mathematics teaching in today's technological and global society and provide con-crete suggestions for how you, as a teacher, may ap-proach the challenges of teaching mathematics.

RECOMMENDATIONS FOR TEACHING FROM WHAT WE KNOW ABOUT LEARNING MATHEMATICS

Let's begin by considering some general recommen-dations for teaching. The recommendations that follow are based on what we know about how children learn, and they involve expectations, tasks, discourse, tools, and the learning environment.

Expectations

- Establish a mathematics class motto: Do only what makes sense to you. This motto will encourage students to question, reflect, and seek explanations that make sense to them. It will pave the way for constructing knowledge that is meaningful and understood by them.

- Another class motto might be: Maybe one answer—for sure, many paths. Focusing on answers places the priority on the end result. As teachers, we must help students realize that processes are valued, too. We must probe behind the scenes to learn the paths—that is, where the answers come from. This focus on process requires communication, which may be oral explanations or notes in journals.

- Maintain high expectations for every child regardless of gender or cultural background. Make it clear that you expect all children to be successful in mathematics, and be careful to involve both boys and girls in all aspects of mathematics learning.

- Encourage children to reflect on their learning. Metacognition is an important part of the learning process. Individual reflection or interaction with others (both teachers and peers) encourages students to communicate and explain their thinking.

Tasks

- Provide rich learning situations to involve students. Interesting problems are more stimulating and effective in promoting mathematics. Often, these situations are driven by real-world applications that involve, connect, integrate, and use many different mathematical concepts and skills. Select a balance of problem situations to appeal to different groups and involve your students in choosing the contexts.

- Make reading and writing an integral part of mathematics. As the Snapshot of a Lesson that opens this chapter shows, many children's books offer starting points for mathematical thinking and rich mathematics lessons. Such books help make interdisciplinary connections that stimulate student interest and provide reminders of the power and usefulness of mathematics. These books also provide a context for a variety of rich mathematical experiences. Writing is a natural extension of reading and of talking. Writing provides valuable insight into, as well as develop-

ment of, students' thinking and communication skills.

Discourse

- Encourage children to talk about their mathematical thinking as well as to listen and respond to other students' ideas. Interaction among children provides them opportunities to talk about their ideas, obtain feedback, and learn other points of view. Students can learn from one another as well as from the teacher.

Tools

- Use models, manipulatives, and technology to explore problems and provide experiences that will help children build their mathematical thinking. Provide a variety of different models (through multi-embodiments). Allow children ample time to become familiar with the materials, and help them construct knowledge as they make connections between the models and materials.

Learning Environment

- Provide a safe and intellectually stimulating environment for learning mathematics. Incorrect answers and conceptual errors are natural as children construct their mathematical knowledge. Children uninhibited with concerns about intuitive responses and faulty answers are more likely to observe patterns, make conjectures, engage in discussions, and take risks when doing mathematics.

- Accept the fact that confusion, partial understanding, and some frustration are a natural part of the process of learning mathematics. Not all students will learn the same things at the same time, nor will they all demonstrate the same level of proficiency. Learning mathematics is a long-term process. Sometimes progress is slow; at other times, it is reflected in moments of insight such as "I've got it!" or "Now I understand."

- Project a positive attitude toward mathematics. Children are influenced by their teachers. If a teacher has mathematics anxiety, this feeling is likely to influence students' feelings. Make it clear that you value mathematics, and help children become aware of the importance of mathematics.

- Use classroom organizations that facilitate learning. Whole-class instruction and cooperative small-group work have both been demonstrated to be effective ways to promote mathematics learning. The challenge for teachers is to know when and how to use them effectively.

THE PROFESSIONAL STANDARDS FOR TEACHING MATHEMATICS

The Professional Standards for Teaching Mathematics (NCTM 1991) provide a vision of teaching mathematics that aligns with the constructivist view of how children learn. The introduction to the *Professional Standards* suggests five important shifts in classroom environment that help children develop mathematical power (see Table 3–1).

The *Professional Standards* also make it clear that mathematical discourse ("the ways of representing, thinking, talking, and agreeing and disagreeing that teachers and students use to engage in [mathematical] tasks") plays an extremely important role in mathematics learning (p. 20). Thus the first section of the *Professional Standards,* which outlines six standards for teaching school mathematics, pays particular attention to the role of discourse in the classroom.

Standard 1, shown in Figure 3–1, focuses on *tasks*: "the projects, questions, problems, constructions, applications, and exercises in which students engage" (p. 20). These tasks must encourage students "to reason about mathematical ideas, to make connections, and to formulate, grapple with, and solve problems." (p. 32).

Lappan (1993) states: "No other decision that teachers make has a greater impact on students' opportunity to learn and on their perceptions about what mathematics is than the selection or creation of the tasks with which the teacher engages the students in studying mathematics. Here the teacher is the architect, the designer of the curriculum"

Table 3–1 • Five shifts in classroom environment

Mathematics Instruction Should Shift:	
Toward	*Away From*
Classrooms as mathematics communities	Classrooms as simply a collection of individuals
Logic and mathematical evidence as verification	The teacher as the sole authority for right answers
Mathematical reasoning	Mere memorizing procedures
Conjecturing, inventing, and problem solving	An emphasis on the mechanistic finding of answers
Connecting mathematics, its ideas, and its applications	Treating mathematics as a body of isolated concepts and procedures

Adapted from *Professional Standards for Teaching Mathematics* (NCTM 1991).

NCTM Standard 1: Worthwhile Mathematical Tasks

The teacher of mathematics should pose tasks that are based on

- Sound and significant mathematics
- Knowledge of students' understandings, interests, and experiences
- Knowledge of the range of ways that diverse students learn mathematics

and that

- Engage students' intellect
- Develop students' mathematical understandings and skills
- Stimulate students to make connections and develop a coherent framework for mathematical ideas
- Call for problem formulation, problem solving, and mathematical reasoning
- Promote communication about mathematics
- Represent mathematics as an ongoing human activity
- Display sensitivity to, and draw on, students' diverse background experiences and dispositions
- Promote the development of all students' dispositions to do mathematics

Figure 3–1 • Standard focusing on tasks (Reprinted with permission from "Professional Standards for School Mathematics," p. 25, copyright 1991 by the National Council of Teachers of Mathematics. All rights reserved.)

(p. 524). Expanding on this idea, Reys and Long (1995) suggest that good tasks

- Are often authentic in that they come from the students' environment
- Are challenging yet within students' reach
- Pique the students' curiosity
- Encourage students to make sense of mathematical ideas
- Encourage multiple perspectives and interrelated mathematical ideas
- Nest skill development in the context of problem solving

Standards 2, 3, and 4, which are shown in Figure 3–2, concern, respectively, the role of the teacher, the students, and mathematical tools in the classroom (with special attention to their roles in mathematical discourse).

NCTM Standard 2: The Teacher's Role in Discourse

The teacher of mathematics should orchestrate discourse by

- Posing questions and tasks that elicit, engage, and challenge each student's thinking
- Listening carefully to students' ideas
- Asking students to clarify and justify their ideas orally and in writing
- Deciding what to pursue in depth from among the ideas that students bring up during a discussion
- Deciding when and how to attach mathematical notation and language to students' ideas
- Deciding when to provide information, when to clarify an issue, when to model, when to lead, and when to let a student struggle with a difficulty
- Monitoring students' participation in discussions and deciding when and how to encourage each student to participate

NCTM Standard 3: Students' Role in Discourse

The teacher of mathematics should promote classroom discourse in which students

- Listen to, respond to, and question the teacher and one another
- Use a variety of tools to reason, make connections, solve problems, and communicate
- Initiate problems and questions
- Make conjectures and present solutions
- Explore examples and counterexamples to investigate a conjecture
- Try to convince themselves and one another of the validity of particular representations, solutions, conjectures, and answers
- Rely on mathematical evidence and argument to determine validity

NCTM Standard 4: Tools for Enhancing Discourse

The teacher of mathematics, in order to enhance discourse, should encourage and accept the use of

- Computers, calculators, and other technology
- Concrete materials used as models
- Pictures, diagrams, tables, and graphs
- Invented and conventional terms and symbols
- Metaphors, analogies, and stories
- Written hypotheses, explanations, and arguments
- Oral presentations and dramatizations

The role of the teacher obviously involves orchestrating mathematical discourse and much, much more. The teacher is responsible for choosing appropriate tasks and for establishing a classroom environment in which all children have opportunities to engage in "doing" mathematics. The teacher is the organizer, cheerleader, and orchestrator of the entire process, making appropriate tools available and finding ways to help the children assume major responsibility for their own learning (as described in the standards on the role of the student and the role of tools). A flow of ideas, with interactions not only from teacher to student but from student to teacher and student to student, using a variety of modes, is expected in order to help every child learn more mathematics.

The *environment* is the focus of Standard 5, which is shown in Figure 3–3. This standard is concerned

NCTM Standard 5: Learning Environment

The teacher of mathematics should create a learning environment that fosters the development of each student's mathematical power by

- Providing and structuring the time necessary to explore sound mathematics and grapple with significant ideas and problems
- Using the physical space and materials in ways that facilitate students' learning of mathematics
- Providing a context that encourages the development of mathematical skill and proficiency
- Respecting and valuing students' ideas, ways of thinking, and mathematical dispositions

and by consistently expecting and encouraging students to

- Work independently or collaboratively to make sense of mathematics
- Take intellectual risks by raising questions and formulating conjectures
- Display a sense of mathematical competence by validating and supporting ideas with mathematical argument

with the physical setting and more: "If we want students to learn to make conjectures, experiment with alternative approaches to solving problems, and construct and respond to others' mathematical arguments, then creating an environment that fosters these kinds of activities is essential" (p. 56). Clearly, the teacher is responsible, in large part, for ensuring that an appropriate environment is established.

Finally, Standard 6 (Figure 3–4) considers *analysis*: "the systematic reflection in which teachers engage . . . [to consider] how well the tasks, discourse, and environment foster the development of every student's mathematical literacy and power" (p. 20). Such analyses are a primary source of information for planning and improving instruction during the course of a lesson and as lessons build during the year.

We have focused on the first six standards—tasks, teacher's role, students' roles, tools, learning environment, and teacher's analysis of teaching and learning—because they so clearly affect your work as a mathematics teacher. These standards deal with six key elements in teaching that we will return to repeatedly throughout this chapter and throughout this entire book.

NCTM Standard 6:
Analysis of Teaching and Learning

The teacher of mathematics should engage in ongoing analysis of teaching and learning by

- Observing, listening to, and gathering other information about students to assess what they are learning
- Examining effects of the tasks, discourse, and learning environment on students' mathematical knowledge, skills, and dispositions

in order to

- Ensure that every student is learning sound and significant mathematics and is developing a positive disposition toward mathematics
- Challenge and extend students' ideas
- Adapt or change activities while teaching
- Make plans, both short- and long-range
- Describe and comment on each students' learning to parents and administrators, as well as to the students themselves

---

Figure 3–4 • **Standard focusing on analysis**
(Reprinted with permission from "Professional Standards for School Mathematics," p. 63, copyright 1991 by the National Council of Teachers of Mathematics. All rights reserved.)

THE IMPORTANCE OF PLANNING

At the heart of good teaching lies planning. Children learn best from lessons that are interesting and carefully organized, directed by thoughtful questions, and enriched by activities and materials that give them the opportunity to develop ideas about mathematics. Careful development of ideas, with clear explanations, careful questioning, and manipulative materials, is particularly important in teaching mathematical content.

Teachers plan mathematics lessons in a variety of ways. Some teachers just list the objectives they want children to attain or at least take a step toward attaining. Some jot down key questions they want to ask. Some teachers lay out the materials for children to use or run off a worksheet for the children to use. Others read the comments in the teacher's guide to the textbook. All of these approaches require teachers to think through what they plan to do.

Few teachers have the time to write out a complete, detailed plan for every mathematics lesson they teach. Some do it occasionally, when they know the idea they want to teach must be developed especially carefully. Experienced teachers often have detailed mental plans, although they may not write more than a page of sketchy notes. They may have taught a very similar lesson many times before and therefore have a good sense of appropriate sequencing, timing, questioning, and potential pitfalls. For beginning teachers, however, writing detailed lesson plans is particularly important because they are not likely to have rich mental memories from teaching the lesson before. Careful planning helps to make initial teaching experiences good ones, for both the children and the teacher.

Lesson plans give you the security of knowing what you will do and say, of having interesting activities and materials ready for the children's use, and of anticipating what the children might do. A detailed lesson plan also gives you a way to judge how well the lesson went. Even though you might not have been able to follow your plan precisely, it helps you evaluate your behavior and assess the actions and responses of the children. A written lesson plan also makes your plans and ideas accessible for sharing with other teachers, who can provide helpful comments and suggestions. Moreover, through writing detailed plans you learn how to plan "in your head."

Planning for mathematics instruction is important for a number of reasons:

1. Planning establishes definite goals and helps to ensure that all essential content will be included,

whether you are considering the year's work, a unit's work, or a day's work. The purposes of each lesson will be delineated clearly to help you to avoid omissions and mistakes.

2. Planning permits scheduling work in feasible units of time and in a sensible sequence. The amount of time allotted to teaching a particular topic is determined on the basis of relative importance and relative difficulty. The sequence of topics is determined on the basis of the specific mathematics content and the developmental level of the children. Mathematics appears to be more highly sequenced than some other bodies of knowledge. For example, it is difficult to teach how to multiply with fractions before children know how to multiply with whole numbers.

On the other hand, sometimes a particular sequencing is not as mandatory as it seems. For instance, for many years, it was considered mandatory to delay instruction on decimals until after instruction on whole numbers was well under way—that is, until the intermediate grades. As children use calculators, however, they encounter decimals much earlier, and we find that they can learn decimal ideas before the intermediate grades.

Developmental level must also be considered, however. For example, a child who is at the concrete operations level, where ideas must be rooted in concrete illustrations and it is difficult to manipulate abstract relationships, would find it difficult (if not impossible) to learn with understanding how to find the volume of a cube from a two-dimensional drawing or picture.

3. Planning helps to ensure that a lesson begins interestingly and involves each child, throughout the lesson. Time is relatively flexible in most elementary schools, with no ringing of bells to signify that students are to move on to the next class. Nevertheless, there are constraints such as lunch time or another subject that must be taught. Often, however, you will be able to allow more time than you'd originally planned for a lesson in which the children are totally involved or in which they need more help in grasping an idea. Sometimes you will be able to end a lesson sooner than you'd thought because they have learned the content quickly or have had difficulty so that you need to reconsider how to teach them.

4. Planning aids in holding the children's interest and attention, whether they are working as a total class, in small groups, or individually. We know from research that "time on task" is associated with achievement gains. That is, the more time a student spends actively engaged in tasks related to the topic, the more he or she achieves on a test of that content. Thus the teacher's goal is to have the children spend as much as possible of the time available for mathematics instruction actually working on content. Moreover, children who are actively involved are less likely to create discipline problems.

5. Planning helps to avoid unnecessary repetition while ensuring necessary repetition for review and practice. In most schools, with most textbooks, you will be using a spiral approach, in which mathematical ideas and skills are taught at several points in a year or over a several-year period, as discussed in Chapter 2. At each encounter, a topic should be approached in more depth. As you plan, you will need to consider the extent to which your pupils are ready for another look at a topic they have previously encountered. Sometimes you will want to delay instruction on a particular topic. But be wary of scheduling all the instruction on a given topic for a single period of time. Children may need the "time between" to assimilate it.

Some schools take a "mastery learning" approach, in which children are to master each topic or skill before they go on to the next. This approach has decided advantages, not the least of which may be achievement. But mastery learning also has some disadvantages, in that children who have not yet learned a skill may be "stuck" at that point in the curriculum, unable to go on to new mathematical ideas with which they might be more successful. Frequently, a later topic will provide practice related to the earlier idea, and then the child learns it. Also, some educators argue against the mastery approach by observing that the level of achievement a student demonstrates one day—right after practicing a skill—may be quite different from what he or she can do a couple of days later. Thus, even if students seem to have mastered an idea or skill, it is important for them to continue to work with it in subsequent lessons. The advantage of requiring all children to master prerequisite topics before they go on to new material must be carefully weighed against the disadvantages—and efforts must be made to compensate for those disadvantages.

6. Planning creates a feeling of confidence for you. You know what you want to do, and your class will recognize that you are prepared. If you think about the "good teachers" you have had, you

will probably recognize that they were well prepared for teaching.

As Rathmell (1994) indicates:

> Planning for instruction that promotes the development of children's thinking and reasoning about mathematics not only helps them make sense of the content they are studying but also helps them learn ways of thinking that later will enable them to make sense of *new* content. (p. 290)

Levels of Planning

You must plan more than each day's mathematics lesson. At the beginning of the school year, you will need to consider what you want to have the children in your class accomplish during the year. These goals are not something you must develop on your own. Most schools prepare scope-and-sequence charts or guides, or they rely on the ones provided with the textbook series they use. Your district or state may provide a curriculum framework for your grade level, and NCTM's *Principles and Standards for School Mathematics* (NCTM 2000) indicates, in broad terms, the mathematical content and processes appropriate for students at each of the grade bands Pre-K–2, 3–5, 6–8, and 9–12).

You should be familiar with the NCTM Standards and with your school's scope-and-sequence guide or chart before you do any planning. Such materials are designed to ensure that children will be taught the desired range of content across grade levels. It would also be wise to check with your principal and other teachers to determine whether any changes have been made to meet the needs of children in your school and to learn how much flexibility you will have in making changes for your class.

After ascertaining the goals of mathematics instruction and the order in which topics will be taught, you will need to consider the approximate amounts of time you want to spend on each phase of the curriculum in terms of its relative importance. This allotment helps you to fit in all the mathematics content you want to include.

The goals for the year need to be considered by textbook units or chapters and the specific objectives to be taught about each topic. The NCTM Standards and your school's curriculum guide or the textbook's planning chart will help you here and with the decision about how much time to assign to teaching each topic, which is also important. Most mathematics textbooks contain 130 to 150 lessons. Given the typical 180-day school year, you may have some opportunity to spend extra time on some topics or to teach others that are not included in the textbook.

In planning for a unit or chapter, you begin by outlining, in sequence, what topics are to be taught and how much time you will spend on each. Next, outline what you want to accomplish each week, and then you are ready to develop daily lesson plans. Some schools require teachers to maintain a lesson plan book in which they note the objectives (and sometimes other details as well) for each day's lessons for a week. Even if this practice is not required, it is a good idea. It keeps you aware of progress toward the goals for the year, and it gives you a guide to follow each day. You cannot expect to follow it exactly, but it will serve as a guide, and as you plan each week, you can review the progress of the children in your class and then vary or pace the content to be taught to meet their individual needs. Or you can plan to teach different content to small groups or individuals.

Components of a Lesson Plan

The most important consideration in planning a lesson is deciding what sort of tasks the students will be doing. Students learn best when tasks are motivating and challenging but not out of reach and when tasks involve them in actually *thinking* about the mathematics at hand. The *Professional Standards for Teaching Mathematics* (NCTM 1991, p. 25) suggests:

> Teachers should choose and develop tasks that are likely to promote the development of students' understanding of concepts and procedures in a way that also fosters their ability to solve problems and to reason and communicate mathematically. Good tasks are ones that do not separate mathematical thinking from mathematical concepts or skills, that capture students' curiosity, and that invite them to speculate and to pursue their hunches.

Remember to keep the importance of appropriate tasks in mind. If you do, then the following guidelines may be useful as you develop lesson plans for a particular mathematical topic:

- State clearly the objective or objectives. What mathematical skill or idea are you trying to teach? What do you want the children to learn? Is the purpose to introduce a new topic, develop understanding, or provide review? What do the children already know? Do they have the necessary prerequisites?

- Decide how the class is to be organized. Should the lesson involve the total class, small groups, individual work, or some combination of these?

- Determine the procedures to be followed. What teaching strategy will be most effective? What type of motivation will capture the children's interest and attention? What must be reviewed to relate this lesson to previous work? What will you do and what will the children do? What questions will you ask? How will you and the children interact? What varied activities will be incorporated? What materials will you and the children use? How will the materials and activities be tailored to meet individual needs? Should practice be assigned—and if so, will it be from the textbook, from worksheets, or from a follow-up activity? Will there also be homework? What and how much? (The assignment of homework depends on school policy. You will need to find out what role homework has in your school.)

- Decide how much time to spend on each part of the lesson. What is the lesson's relative importance in terms of the time available, as well as the difficulty it might present to the children?

- Decide how you will assess or evaluate—both as the lesson proceeds and after it is completed. What should you look for during the lesson? How will you and the children know what they have learned? Will writing be involved? Will each child meet with some success during the lesson?

- Write the plan for the lesson. Putting your plan into writing will help you clarify many of your ideas and also give you a record that can be used in evaluating the lesson and in planning subsequent lessons. Moreover, if you diverge from the plan, you will be able to pinpoint the point of divergence and return later to pick up where you left off.

Planning Different Types of Lessons

This section describes three different structures for lessons: investigative, direct instruction, and review/practice. You will probably choose to use different types of lessons on different days depending upon your goals and your students' previous experiences with the content at hand. It is important to keep in mind that within each of these lesson structures the overarching goals of ensuring student understanding and maintaining active student involvement should be maintained. It is quite likely that you will design many lessons that incorporate aspects of more than one of these lesson formats at the same time. A direct instruction lesson might also involve some review and practice, or an investigative lesson might also include some direct instruction. In other words, the three lesson structures should not be seen as entirely distinct. Nevertheless, it seems useful to outline the general characteristics of each form.

Investigative Lessons Investigative lessons are most appropriate for developing problem-solving skills, learning new concepts, or applying and deepening understanding of previously learned ideas. An investigative lesson involves students in pursuing a problem or exploration on their own. The task at hand may have been identified by the teacher or by some of the students, but the lesson itself revolves around ideas that the students generate through their own investigations of the task. Obviously, the teacher is responsible for guiding the lesson, but the students are expected to identify their own approaches, strategies, and solutions. An investigative lesson generally involves three phases: launch, explore or investigate, and summarize (Lappan et al. 1996). The lesson plan outline in Figure 3–5 gives more information about how the lesson is organized.

In the launch phase, motivation is provided for the lesson and the problem at hand is explained. The launch might come from a student presenting a problem that he or she has been struggling with and asking classmates to work on it, too. Or the teacher might provide motivation for a task, situation, or problem by reading a children's story, sharing a newspaper clipping, playing a game, presenting a puzzle, or using any of many other motivators.

Once all the students understand the challenge, the investigate phase of the lesson involves students in working on it, either independently or with others. This phase of the lesson might involve learning stations, individual work, paired problem solving, or cooperative groups. Students might be using models, manipulatives, computers, calculators, or other tools. Note that in an investigative lesson, the challenge should be a true problem for the students, so it is important that you do not explain how to address the challenge up front. The students should not be simply mimicking strategies or skills that you have just shown them. Instead, they themselves should be deciding how to get started and what to try. Your role as teacher is to let them go. You should circulate around the room, listening in on conversations, observing what individuals or groups are doing, and occasionally interjecting questions or comments to help students recognize where they may be going wrong or to suggest a different approach. (More advice about questioning is provided in a later section in this chapter and also in Chapter 5.)

During the summarize phase of the lesson, the class comes back together to talk about their findings. Using information you gathered from observing while the children were working independently, you orchestrate a discussion where various groups

Investigative Lesson Plan Outline

Grade Level _____

Title and topic of lesson _____

Purpose   What is it, exactly, that you want students to get from this lesson?

Rationale   Why are these ideas important?

Prerequisites   What background do the students need prior to participating in this lesson?

Materials   List all materials needed:
  a. math manipulatives (and how many of each)
  b. books, including page numbers (and how many of each)
  c. other supplies (scissors, markers, posters, etc., and how many of each)
  d. handouts—attach a copy of each

Lesson Outline (include approximate times for each segment of your lesson)

I. LAUNCH: Setting the Stage for the Lesson
Describe briefly how you will launch the lesson. Your aim is to motivate students to get involved in the activities to follow and to ensure that everyone understands what they are to do.

II. INVESTIGATE: Lesson Development
This part of the lesson may involve one continuous activity (whole class, small group, or individual), or it may be divided into several lesson segments that involve different activities. For each segment, give a step by step description of what you (the teacher) will be doing and what the students will be doing. In particular, provide examples of the types of questions you may ask and of any products that the students will produce. If your lesson is segmented, include approximate times for each segment and describe your plans for transitions from one segment to the next.

III. SUMMARIZE: Closure
Describe how you will bring the lesson development to a close. Include questions you may ask yourself and/or your students to help you know if the lesson was a success.

Gearing Down   What will you do if your lesson, as planned, turns out to be too advanced for some or all students? How can the lesson be modified (on the spot) for slower students?

Gearing Up   What will you do if your lesson, as planned, turns out to be too easy for some or all students? How can the lesson be modified (on the spot) for faster students?

Assessment   Identify what types of data you will collect to help determine how well individual children understood the goals of your lesson and where they had trouble. Assessment data may come from a variety of sources: for example, classroom observations, written classwork (either individual or group), homework, etc. Your dual goals in planning for assessment are to be able to make appropriate follow-up instructional decisions and to be able to report on the progress of students (e.g., assign grades or write a narrative report).

References   Include titles and pages of books or other references consulted in planning the lesson.

Figure 3–5 • Investigative lesson plan format

or individuals report what they tried and what they discovered. It is important to be neither too judgmental nor too affirming about student ideas and responses. Encourage the students themselves to challenge each other's ideas. They need practice in learning how to judge when mathematical ideas are valid and when they are not. It is also important to avoid finalizing the solution to the problem prematurely. Students learn a lot from listening to each other and from hearing about alternative approaches. Your job is to encourage the students to share their ideas while maintaining control of the discussion and trying to guide it in ways that advance your curricular agenda. During the final portion of the summarize phase, it may be important to help students be explicit in stating what they have learned from the investigation. This is the appropriate point for identifying generalities or stating rules that have been formulated.

Direct Instruction Lessons   The main difference between investigative lessons and direct instruction lessons is the central role of the teacher in directing the latter. For example, direct instruction lessons are appropriate when the teacher wants to communicate specific knowledge, to introduce new vocabulary, or to teach certain procedures. In a direct instruction lesson, the teacher exercises more control than in an investigative lesson and the lesson generally has a tighter focus.

A lesson plan for a direct instruction lesson usually consists of three major parts—launch, instruct, and summarize—each of which may be subdivided into smaller segments of various types, depending on the content of the lesson. In the first part of the lesson, the teacher introduces the students to a problem or task and the class talks together, led by the teacher, about how they might approach the problem and what previously learned concepts and skills may be brought to bear. In the second part, the teacher should not merely *show* the students how to proceed but should elicit ideas from the students while helping them to move toward the concepts or skills that are the goal of the lesson. The students then have a chance to work with the ideas presented earlier in the lesson and to make them their own. The task during this phase should be closely related to the original task but not so similar that the students are simply copying what the teacher has just shown them. Finally, the teacher summarizes. Figure 3–6 provides an template for a direct instruction lesson plan.

Review-Teach-Practice Lessons The most familiar form of mathematics lesson, review-teach-practice, may also be one of the least effective. Most Americans are very familiar with this lesson format, where the teacher begins by reviewing homework or problems worked during a previous lesson, moves to explaining a new concept or showing how to perform a new skill and demonstrating on sample problems, and then assigns exercises (of the very same type just demonstrated) for student practice. The remainder of the lesson usually involves students practicing solving similar problems on their own while the teacher assists individual students.

The Third International Mathematics and Science Study (TIMSS) indicated that this sort of mathematics

---

Direct Instruction Lesson Plan Format

Topic:

Grade:

Objective What are the major concepts or skills that students will work with in this lesson? What do you expect them to be able to do as a result of the lesson?

Theme Can the mathematics of the lesson be connected to some non-mathematical context that can serve as a theme for the lesson? If so, how will that context be motivated?

Materials List all materials needed:
  a. math manipulatives (and how many of each)
  b. books, including page numbers and how many of each
  c. other supplies (scissors, markers, posters, etc., and how many of each)
  d. handouts or worksheets—attach a copy of each

LAUNCH

Describe how you will begin the lesson.

How is this lesson connected to previous lessons?

INSTRUCT

Whole-Class Teacher Instruction What concepts, definitions, formulas, algorithms, etc. will you use in your instruction?

List all examples that you will use, and order them appropriately.

Provide a list of directions for the class/individual activities to follow.

Class/Individual Activities This part of the lesson may be individual or small group. Students work on problems or exercises that follow rather closely from what they learned during your whole-class instruction.

You circulate, assisting students, answering questions, and providing extension tasks to students who finish early.

Include a copy of the task, assignment, or worksheet that students will work on.

Make a list of the questions you will be asking as you circulate.

Include several simpler problems that you may use in helping students who have trouble.

Include several more challenging problems that you may pose to early finishers.

SUMMARIZE

How will you decide whether students have learned what you wanted them to?

What sort of grades, if any, will you be able to record as a result of this lesson?

Provide an answer key for any worksheets or problem sets.

Provide a plan for documenting student progress on the objectives of the lesson.

References Include titles and pages of books or other references consulted in planning the lesson.

Figure 3–6 • Direct instruction lesson plan format

lesson is very common in the United States and Germany (*Pursuing Excellence* 1996). Unfortunately, neither Germany nor the United States performed particularly well on tests of student achievement. Many educators attribute much of this poor performance to the ineffective nature of the review-teach-practice lesson format.

By contrast, typical lessons in Japan (whose students were top TIMSS scorers) have a structure that is much more similar to the investigative lesson: the teacher poses a thought-provoking problem, and then students struggle with the problem and present ideas or solutions to the class, which discusses these solution methods. Then the teacher uses the discussion to highlight the key mathematical concepts before students practice similar problems.

Review-teach-practice lessons in the United States and Germany concentrate on skill acquisition, or teaching students to do something, while in Japan the typical lesson focus is on understanding mathematical concepts. More than twice as much time in U.S. and German classrooms includes practice on routine procedures (although many Japanese students practice skills in paid tutoring sessions after school). Japanese students spend most of their class time inventing new solutions and being engaged in conceptual thinking about mathematics.

Analysis of TIMSS data suggests that what occurs in lessons is critical to students' learning. The specific topics taught and how these topics are presented and developed shapes what students learn and are able to do. Rather than the focused coherence seen in other countries, U.S. lessons often consist of "episodic encounters" between students and curricular content. Topics and concepts are presented in a fragmented and disjointed manner in which underlying themes or principles are either not identified or merely stated but not developed.

Using the Strategic Moment

Despite careful lesson planning, teachers must make many minute-to-minute decisions. It would be very sad if you did not take advantage of a situation because you had not planned for it (see Figure 3–7). Making use of teachable or strategic moments and events is imperative.

To some extent, you can encourage strategic moments by the way you arrange the environment—by bringing in something new and therefore exciting, for instance. You must know what concepts you want to teach and how these develop for the children in your class—and then recognize the strategic moment when it arises.

Experience will also help you as you make the many on-the-spot decisions that are a part of teach-

Several first-grade children come into the room all excited by the parade they saw yesterday, with "hundreds" and "thousands" of marchers. You've planned a lesson on measurement for that day. What do you do?

All the traffic lights in town are off. Why? The computer has failed. You've planned a lesson on multiplication with two-digit numbers. Do you discuss the computer's role in society instead?

You are teaching a lesson on estimation. You have the class use calculators to find 3762.5×795.6 quickly. A child asks, "Why is there no zero after the decimal point in the answer?" How do you continue the lesson on estimation?

Figure 3–7 • **Some examples of strategic moments**

ing. You will learn what works and what doesn't. Try to define for yourself the goals you want to attain and how to attain them, and then try to work within that framework. Consider how children develop and learn. Observe the children in your class as individuals, and watch for their errors and their successes. These observations will help you diagnose their needs and plan their instruction. The better you know your children, the more ready you will be to see and grasp strategic moments and make valid decisions.

Adapting Textbook-Based Lessons

Beginning teachers often wonder how much to depend upon a textbook for lesson planning. To what extent can textbook lessons be used "as is"? How and why should they be adapted for individual use? Obviously, answers to these questions depend upon the textbook and how closely its goals and methods align with your own. Schmalz (1990, 1994) offers suggestions for planning with a textbook yet maintaining the spirit of the teaching suggestions made in the Standards. She suggests, for instance, that the first topic to be taught need not be Chapter One of the text but instead one of which most of the students are unsure. Avoiding the obvious review, which seems boring to many students, is only one of her reasons. It certainly does not make sense to try to develop your own original lesson plans if you have a textbook that provides a general outline for each lesson. If you determine that the lessons are developmentally appropriate for your students and that they engage the students in genuine problem solving and conceptual development, then there is no reason not to use them or adapt them as seems necessary. Teacher's guides to textbooks provide a variety of ideas for teaching a lesson incorporating the textbook page. Suggestions are often given for follow-up activities, such as seatwork and games. Many guides also provide suggestions for remediation, enrichment, and variation for children with learning disabilities and other special needs.

In some cases, textbook lessons can be considerably enhanced by embedding them in a motivating theme or context. The context provides an organizing framework for teaching and learning the lesson and helps tie the lesson (or several lessons) together. Contexts for lessons may be taken from real-life situations found in current events or on the calendar or developed from integrative themes tied to other subjects such as science, social studies, or children's literature. Table 3–2 shows some examples of how contexts or themes can enhance mathematics lessons.

Using Children's Literature to Motivate Mathematics Lessons

Teachers often use children's trade books to enhance lessons in language arts, social studies, science, music, art, dance, and drama, but it is also easy, effective, and appropriate to use children's literature in mathematics lessons. Notice how the Snapshot of a Lesson that opens this chapter uses *Frog and Toad are Friends,* a Caldecott award–winning "I can read" book, as a springboard for a lesson on sorting and classifying. Fiction and nonfiction books can provide "rich, authentic explorations of time and place and human experiences that make the concepts children are exploring vivid, relevant, and involving" (Whitin and Wilde 1992, p. xi). Stories provide children with a common starting point from which to share and discuss mathematical ideas. Mathematics and language skills develop hand-in-hand as children talk about problems and read and write about mathematical ideas. Use of children's literature in mathematics lessons can enhance learning in many ways. Children's literature:

- Integrates mathematics into other curriculum areas
- Provides a meaningful context for mathematics
- Supports the art of problem posing
- Demonstrates that mathematics develops out of human experience
- Fosters the development of number sense
- Addresses humanistic, affective elements of mathematics
- Celebrates mathematics as a language
- Restores an aesthetic dimension to mathematical learning (Whitin and Wilde 1992).

Table 3–2 • Using contexts or themes for planning lessons

This Is a Context or Theme	*This Is Not a Context or Theme*
Sorting M&Ms for party favors gives a reason for using this manipulative.	M&Ms (alone) are a manipulative, not a context.
Planning a schedule for a class field trip involves telling time.	Time is a math topic, not a context.
Ordering carpet for classrooms in the school is a context. We need to know the area of the room to find out how much to order.	Area of rectangles is a math concept, not a context.
Measuring classroom objects to decide how to fit them into storage containers gives purpose to a lesson.	Measuring length of classroom objects doesn't give a reason for doing so.

If you want to integrate use of children's literature with a lesson on a particular mathematics topic, many teacher reference books are available to help you identify stories that work well. These books include *Math and Literature* (Grades 4–6) (Bresser 1995), *Math and Literature* (K–3) (Burns 1992), *Story Stretchers for the Primary Grades: Activities to Expand Children's Favorite Books* (Raines and Canady 1992), *The Wonderful World of Mathematics: A Critically Annotated List of Children's Books in Mathematics* (Thiessen and Matthias 1998), *How to Use Children's Literature to Teach Mathematics* (Welchman-Tischler 1992), *Read Any Good Math Lately?* (Whitin and Wilde 1992), and *It's the Story That Counts* (Whitin and Wilde 1995).

POINTS TO CONSIDER IN PLANNING AND TEACHING

Maintaining a Focus on the Mathematics

It's extremely important when planning mathematics lessons to maintain a focus on the mathematics. Lessons can certainly be considerably enhanced by using children's literature as a springboard, by involving students in hands-on explorations, or by setting problems in real-world contexts, but the primary question when planning a lesson should be "What mathematics will the children learn from this?" rather than just "Will they have fun?" It is not appropriate to use manipulative materials just as toys, to engage students in talking and writing only about their feelings (and never about the mathematics itself), or to do lessons that are just fun for fun's sake. Mathematics lessons should involve students in tasks that are mathematically problematic. When children are genuinely engaged in solving mathematical problems, the learning that they take away from that experience is likely to be deep and lasting.

Meeting the Needs of All Students

Equity of educational opportunity is one of NCTM's fundamental principles. NCTM's Equity Principle states that "excellence in mathematics education requires equity—high expectations and strong support for all students" (NCTM 2000, p. 12). Similarly, the *Professional Standards* call for every child to have equal opportunities to learn mathematics, and state (NCTM 1991, p. 4):

By "every child" we mean specifically

- Students who have been denied access in any way to educational opportunities as well as those who have not

- Students who are African American, Hispanic, Native American, and other minorities as well as those who are considered to be a part of the majority

- Students who are female as well as those who are male

- Students who have not been successful in school and in mathematics as well as those who have been successful.

Throughout this book we will discuss strategies that promote this goal of equity, and you will find a number of references to help you (for example, see Cuevas and Driscoll 1993 and Koontz 1997).

It is important to note that providing equal opportunities to learn does not necessarily mean providing exactly the same instruction. The key to equity is fairness and justice, adapting instruction appropriately for the needs of students. In an equitable mathematics classroom, the teacher does the following (Koontz 1997):

- Fosters a climate of openness
- Encourages student interaction and cooperation
- Demonstrates an attitude of acceptance
- Encourages students to gather and organize information

- Provides visual cues to develop cognitive strategies
- Makes connections to past concepts and applications
- Elicits the verbalization of students' reasoning
- Promotes silent reflection
- Encourages equity

As our country becomes more culturally diverse, teachers face increased challenges and opportunities in making mathematics relevant for all students. It is important to plan lessons and activities that take into account the realities of students' daily lives, as well as to ensure that students' cultural backgrounds are reflected in the mathematics curriculum. Some useful resources for planning mathematics lessons that celebrate cultural diversity include *The Multicultural Math Classroom: Bringing in the World* (Zaslavsky 1996) and *Multicultural Mathematics Materials* (Krause 1983). Some interesting articles by teachers telling how they addressed issues of cultural diversity or gender equity in their classrooms include De La Cruz (1999), Karp et al. (1998), Smith et al. (1999), Tevebaugh (1998), and Zanger (1998).

If students in your classroom are at different academic levels or if they have identified learning problems or disabilities, providing equitable treatment may mean adapting instruction to meet their particular needs. To meet the needs of individual children learning mathematics, you must first determine what their strengths and weaknesses are, using one or more of the procedures mentioned here or using a specific diagnostic test. The results of such evaluations are used to select instructional materials, to group students for instruction, to adapt materials, or to decide what needs to be taught or retaught to individuals and to the class. Guidelines for diagnosis in mathematics include the following (Driscoll 1981):

1. Make sure that a child's apparent mathematical deficiency is really a deficiency.

2. Remember that each child progresses through several stages of development before reaching an adult conceptual level.

3. Strengthen your diagnosis with the liberal use of manipulative materials.

4. Don't lose sight of the emotional side of students in your diagnosis.

5. Be flexible and patient in piecing together an accurate picture of a child's thinking.

6. Maintain a climate of acceptance.

7. Distinguish between errors that are random and those that occur more systematically.

Both observations and interviews are highly effective in revealing behaviors that are not noticeable from paper-and-pencil tests, but tests are also useful tools in diagnosis, especially when you analyze how children reached their answers, not merely their final scores.

Effective remediation begins with effective diagnosis. Once you have a clear picture of a child's needs, you can plan activities to provide the missing prerequisites that are at the source of a difficulty, develop the understanding that has been missed, provide the practice that is needed, and give the encouragement that is so vital in effective remediation.

At times you will be able to group pupils who need help on a particular point; sometimes you will decide to adapt regular classroom instruction for the special needs of individuals; at other times you will need to work with individuals in small groups or one-on-one.

Ebling et al. (1994) identify nine ways (see Figure 3–8) that curriculum and instruction can be adapted for students who have special needs. These students may include, for example, those who are gifted, those who have a learning disability, or those who need accommodation because of a physical handicap. Deciding which type(s) of adaptation are appropriate for a given student is a matter of the teacher's familiarity with three things: (1) the individual student and his or her special needs, (2) the activity and its subject-content demands (what is required to successfully complete the assignment), and (3) options available for adaptations, modifications, or accommodations.

Nine Types of Adaptation

Size

Adapt the number of items that the learner is expected to learn or complete.

For example:
Reduce the number of social studies terms a learner must learn at any one time.

Time

Adapt the time allotted and allowed for learning, task completion, or testing.

For example:
Individualize a timeline for completing a task; pace learning differently (increase or decrease) for some learners.

Level of Support

Increase the amount of personal assistance with a specific learner.

For example:
Assign peer buddies, teaching assistants, peer tutors, or cross-age tutors.

Input

Adapt the way instruction is delivered to the learner.

For example:
Use different visual aids; plan more concrete examples; provide hands-on activities; place students in cooperative groups.

Difficulty

Adapt the skill level, problem type, or the rules on how the learner may approach the work.

For example:
Allow the use of a calculator to figure math problems; simplify task directions; change rules to accommodate learner needs.

Output

Adapt how the learner can respond to instruction.

For example:
Instead of answering questions in writing, allow a verbal response; use a communication book for some students; allow students to show knowledge with hands-on materials.

Participation

Adapt the extent to which a learner is actively involved in the task.

For example:
In geography, have a student hold the globe, while others point out locations.

Alternate Goals

Adapt the goals or outcome expectations while using the same materials.

For example:
In social studies, expect one student to be able to locate just the states while others learn to locate capitals as well.

Substitute Curriculum

Provide different instruction and materials to meet a learner's individual goals.

For example:
During a language test one student is learning computer skills in the computer lab.

Figure 3–8 • Nine types of curriculum and instruction adaptations (Reproduced, with permission, from Ebeling, D. G.; Deschenes, C.; and Sprague, J. (1994). Adapting curriculum and instruction in inclusive classrooms: Staff development kit. Bloomington, Ind.: Institute for the Study of Developmental Disabilities.)

Grouping for Instruction

There are three basic patterns of grouping for mathematical instruction:

- Whole class, with teacher guidance
- Small group, either with teacher guidance or with pupil leaders
- Individuals working independently

Whole-class instruction is used extensively by many teachers, yet small-group work can mean that children work on content that is focused on their particular needs and at the same time learn to work together to solve problems. Most effective teachers use some combination of whole-class, direct instruction with small group cooperative learning, and other student-centered modes of instruction.

Here are some guidelines to aid you in determining which grouping pattern to use.

1. Use large-group instruction:
   - If the topic is one that can be presented to all pupils at approximately the same point in time (that is, if all pupils have the prerequisites for understanding the initial presentation)
   - If pupils need continuous guidance from the teacher to attain the knowledge, skill, or understanding
2. Use small-group instruction:
   - If pupils can profit from pupil-to-pupil interaction with less teacher guidance
   - If exploration and communication about mathematics are being encouraged
   - If cooperative learning skills and effects are being fostered
3. Use individual instruction:
   - If pupils can follow a sequence or conduct an activity on their own
   - If individual practice for mastery is the focus

The kind of teaching envisioned by the NCTM Standards (NCTM 1991, 2000) is probably very different from the kind of teaching you experienced. The emphasis is shifting from a teacher-directed classroom to one in which students are actively involved in learning. The teacher is, of course, still in control, but involves the students through discussions and activities, usually by incorporating much small-group work. Presentations and discussions with the whole class have not disappeared, but we have learned that children learn much more effectively when they work with materials to solve problems and talk about their results with each other.

Farivar and Webb (1994) point out that, "Simply putting students in small groups will not guarantee that they will interact in ways that are beneficial to learning" (p. 521). They draw on extensive research to outline how students learn how to "use one another" as resources for doing mathematics by developing skills in communication, team building, small-group socialization, and helping.

At times, instruction should be teacher directed. This approach has been found to be particularly effective in teaching basic skills to young students and those who are slow-learning or otherwise "educationally at risk" (Thornton and Wilson 1993). These learners succeed better with structured activities, close supervision, and active, teacher-led instruction. Even so, most effective teachers use a combination of grouping patterns. For example, a teacher might develop new material with the whole class and allow children to break up for individual or small-group work during part of the period for one or more activities. The class is then brought together for a teacher-mediated discussion so that children can hear ideas from students in other groups. The teacher ends the discussion by providing closure on the lesson for the day. This method of integrating whole- and small-group work has proved more effective than direct instruction alone for developing higher-level thinking skills (Thornton and Wilson 1993, p. 275).

Guidelines from research that can help teachers to merge active student learning with active mathematics teaching include the following:

- Be proactive by constructing detailed long- and short-range plans and by checking prerequisite concepts or skills.
- Make students aware of the major objective(s) of the lesson.
- Spend at least half of the period developing material in a way that *actively* engages all students and emphasizes understanding.
- Involve students in important problem solving, estimation, mental math, and mathematical extensions related to the lesson.
- Communicate the expectation that, if students attend, they will be able to master the material.
- Be clear. Provide relevant examples and non-examples.
- Ask many "why," "how," and other high-level questions.

- Be organized; maintain a brisk pace to foster time-on-task.
- Allow time for guided seatwork before independent seatwork.
- Regularly assign a small amount of homework (or seatwork) to develop fluency with knowledge or skills previously mastered, to stimulate thinking about the next day's lesson, or to provide open-ended challenges. (Thornton and Wilson 1993, p. 274)

Research has indicated the effectiveness of such student-centered learning modes as cooperative learning and peer teaching or tutoring (Thornton and Wilson 1993). Cooperative learning involves setting a group goal and having students collaborate in groups to help each other. Those who have experienced it find that it brings a sense of relief that the burden for coming up with an answer is not solely on the individual. A student can learn *from* the group as well as contributing *to* the group, and both actions result in more positive attitudes.

The lesson might begin with the teacher meeting with the whole class to provide an overall perspective, present new material, pose problems or questions for investigation, and clarify directions for the group activity. The class then divides into small groups, usually with four members each. Students work together cooperatively in each group, discussing the problem or question, making and testing conjectures, verifying that each student is satisfied that the group answer is reasonable. This communication of ideas with one another is especially valuable in the learning process because the students help each other learn mathematical ideas. The teacher moves from group to group, providing assistance by asking thought-provoking questions as needed (Davidson 1990).

Despite the additional planning and class time needed for cooperative learning, it seems easy to justify the time spent when one considers the positive factors: increase in mathematical communication, the social support for learning mathematics, an opportunity for all students to experience success in mathematics, the possibility that several approaches to solving a problem might arise, and the opportunity to deal with mathematics through and discussion of meaningful problems. (Fitzgerald and Bouck 1993, pp. 251–252)

Cooperative learning may evolve to two children working together to teach each other in a peer-teaching situation. The process of teaching—of deciding how to help someone else learn—promotes the learning of both children.

Whatever the structure of lesson—whether it is more teacher-directed or more student-centered—the teacher orchestrates the classroom discourse by "deciding when to provide information, when to clarify an issue, when to model, when to lead, and when to let students struggle with a difficulty" (NCTM 1991, p. 35). You learn to make these decisions through planning and through experience. Research indicates that no one mode of instruction can be considered best. Teachers should learn many instructional modes and use them when appropriate. The NCTM Standards urge teachers to consider the goal, the task, and the students—that is, to ask what will best help them learn.

The Importance of Questioning

Questions can be aimed at checking children's knowledge of a fact or their ability to perform a skill. These are relatively low-level questions. At a higher level are questions that require the analysis or synthesis of information—as when we ask a child to explain why a procedure works. In mathematics lessons, teachers often use questions of the first type and only infrequently those of the latter type (Evertson et al. 1980). Although the ability to answer fact-checking, lower-level questions may be correlated with the ability of children to score high on some achievement tests, such questions give the child an erroneous picture of mathematics as involving only short answers, with one correct answer per question. We need to encourage children to do more talking about mathematics—why a procedure works, what would happen if something were changed in the problem, how the mathematics could be applied in a real-life situation.

As you plan a lesson, give thought to the types of questions you want to ask. Try to include a range of them, with more requiring children to think rather than merely to supply a fact from memory or to perform a learned procedure. Encourage them to make conjectures, to examine the validity of their thoughts, and to consider how they would convince someone else that they are right (Burns 1985). Ask such questions as:

Who has a different solution?

Can you find another way to explain that?

Why do you think that's true?

Why doesn't Becca's answer make sense to you?

Vacc (1993) proposes three types of questions: factual, reasoning, and open questions with a wide range of acceptable answers. Her aim is in accord with the NCTM *Professional Standards* (NCTM 1991, pp. 3–4), which look at five categories of questions that teachers should ask.

- In the first category are questions that help students work together to make sense of mathematics: "What do others think about what Janine said?" and "Can you convince the rest of us that that makes sense?"

- The second category contains questions that help students rely more on themselves to determine whether something is mathematically correct: "Why is that true?" and "How did you reach that conclusion?"

- The third category of questions seeks to help students learn to reason mathematically: "How could you prove that?" and "What assumptions are you making?"

- The fourth category focuses on helping students learn to conjecture, invent, and solve problems: "What would happen if . . . ?" and "Do you see a pattern?"

- The questions in the fifth category relate to helping students connect mathematics, its ideas, and its applications: "How does this relate to . . . ?" and "Have we ever solved a problem like this one before?"

The Use of Manipulative Materials and Models

All through this book, we stress the importance of having children use manipulative materials to model mathematical ideas. Commonly used materials in the elementary school include chips or tiles, interlocking cubes, pattern blocks, attribute blocks, tangrams, base ten blocks, fraction models, geoboards, measuring instruments, spinners and dice, and play money. Research indicates that lessons using manipulative materials have a higher probability of producing greater mathematical achievement than do lessons without such materials (Sowell 1989). Handling the materials appears to help children construct mathematical ideas and retain them. Thompson (1994) points out that some discrepant findings in research stem from the fact that "concrete materials do not automatically carry meaning for students" (p. 557). Like many others, he suggests that the focus must continually be on *understanding*. Clements and McMillen (1996) are also concerned with what *concrete* means, and report evidence on the value of computer manipulatives as concrete. Furthermore, research indicates that student learning is enhanced when the children connect real-world situations, manipulatives, pictures, and spoken and written

symbols. Clearly, it is helpful when students are able to "see" concepts as the result of experiencing them through the use of models.

When planning a lesson involving manipulatives, Ross and Kurtz (1993, p. 256) suggest the teacher should be certain that:

1. Manipulatives have been chosen to support the lesson's objectives.

2. Significant plans have been made to orient students to the manipulatives and corresponding classroom procedures.

3. The lesson involves the active participation of each student.

4. The lesson plan includes procedures for evaluation that reflect an emphasis on the development of reasoning skills.

One of the challenges a teacher faces is how to store materials so that they can be found and used easily (Suydam 1990). Shelves and small plastic boxes (or dishpans) help to make them manageable. Children should be able to reach and remove things easily themselves without assistance from the teacher. It is also helpful to:

- Color code or label the materials and put a matching code or label on the appropriate storage space.

- Prepackage manipulatives into sets for one student, two students, or a small group.

- Put extra pieces into a "spare parts" container.

- Package sets of materials in durable individual containers, such as heavy plastic bags or transparent containers.

- Store individual sets of materials in "trays," such as box lids, shallow plastic pans, or stackable vegetable bins.

To help children who are disorganized, you might use materials with built-in organization (such as bead frames or an abacus) or materials that fit together (such as Unifix cubes) rather than separate objects such as lima beans or blocks. Or you can use containers that keep counters separated, such as egg cartons, muffin tins, or mats with clearly delineated spaces. There is one more thing to consider: have the children pass out and collect the materials as much as possible. You don't have to do it all!

The Role of Drill and Practice

It should be obvious that students need drill and practice in order to be able to perform a desired behavior or procedure at will. Just as we practice learning to walk or drive a car, we practice basic addition facts or how to multiply fractions. The choice is not if but when. Research has long indicated that drill and practice should follow, not precede, the development of meaning (Brownell and Chazal 1935). Research also indicates that drill-and-practice activities should not consume as much time as developmental work that helps children to understand an idea or procedure (Suydam and Weaver 1981).

Workbooks published to accompany textbook series provide practice on the content presented in the textbook, lesson by lesson. Whether to assign this practice material (in addition to all the practice that students get incidentally in the course of problem solving, or in addition to practice already presented in the textbook itself) is a decision you must make in terms of children's needs. Keep in mind that they must understand an idea or procedure before they are asked to practice it. On the other hand, practicing a skill that has already been mastered is boring and thus can be harmful. Therefore, it is advisable to include practice on previously learned topics as a small but regular component of each practice session.

Many teachers use worksheets in place of workbooks. When these are purchased, they are little different from workbooks. But when the teacher prepares them with the needs of particular children in mind, they can become a valuable tool. They can be used to aid slower learners by providing practice on subskills, to challenge faster learners with extension activities, and to provide personalized practice for the whole class.

Many games can also be used to provide practice. They offer a motivating format and a competitive aspect that many children love. An example of such a game is Bingo. By changing the rules slightly and perhaps producing specialized "math bingo" cards you can make it into a game that provides practice on place value ("the number has 3 tens and 2 ones"), one of the operations ("the number is the sum of 50 and 24"), or geometric ideas ("the number of sides in a hexagon").

Incorporating Technology

Recent increases in the availability of technology in today's homes and classrooms is having a profound effect on teaching and learning. In the fall of 1998, 89 percent of public schools were connected to the Internet (as compared with only 35 percent just four years before; National Center for Education Statistics—NCES). Computers have become an essential tool in our society. Between 1984 and 1996, the percentage of students reporting using computers in school increased substantially, with 72 percent of the fourth graders reporting using a computer at school at least once a week (The Condition of Education 1998, NCES). The NCTM has affirmed the importance of this trend with its Technology Principle: "Technology is essential in teaching and learning mathematics; it influences the mathematics that is taught and enhances students' learning" (NCTM 2000, p. 24).

A wide variety of electronic technology can be useful in various ways in the classroom. Students use each type of computer software in a slightly different way, and the different types of software also offer different benefits to children.

Drill-and-practice software provides practice for a skill that has been previously taught. The computer presents a problem to the student, waits for an answer, and indicates whether the student is right or wrong. Some drill-and-practice programs keep records or provide a score, or they may even be sophisticated enough to adjust the difficulty level of problems presented as a result of the types of responses (and errors) that the student makes.

Tutorial software actually provides instruction on new skills. It may introduce information, present examples, and provide practice. If the student either grasps the concept easily or has difficulty, the program may branch to a more difficult lesson or provide additional instruction.

Simulation software allows students to experience events or to explore environments that might otherwise be too expensive, messy, dangerous, or time-consuming to experience in the classroom. For example, through computer simulation, students may run a business, go on an expedition, or conduct a probability experiment (such as flipping coins or drawing randomly from a collection) with many more trials than would be feasible to conduct by hand.

Educational games engage students in fun activities that address specific educational objectives or aid in the development of logical thinking or problem-solving skills. Games usually include randomized events, offer an opportunity to "win," and present some obstacles to winning that the child must overcome.

Problem-solving programs are designed to aid in the development of higher-order problem-solving strategies. Although similar to a simulation, where students are placed in a situation where they can manipulate variables and receive feedback, problem-solving programs do not necessarily model real-life situations. One type of problem-solving software involves programming. Students may write programs in computer languages such as Logo or Pascal to instruct the computer to operate in a particular way; in the process the students may develop logical thinking and problem-solving skills.

Finally, technology may be used as a *tool* to enhance both teaching and learning. Technology efficiently and effortlessly provides assistance with graphing, visualizing, and computing. Useful classroom technological tools include word processors, databases, spreadsheets, hypermedia, dynamic geometry software, computer microworlds, and graphing calculators. And the *World Wide Web* offers teachers and students access to data and resources that were never before so accessible.

Integrating Assessment and Instruction

Assessment should be an integral aspect of mathematics instruction. Teachers need to ascertain whether they have taught what they think they have taught and whether each child has learned what they think he or she has learned. As you will read in Chapter 4—which is devoted entirely to the topic of assessment—teachers assess for several purposes (NCTM 1995):

1. To monitor student progress
2. To make instructional decisions
3. To evaluate students' achievement
4. To evaluate their mathematics program

In the process, teachers may well ask such questions as

- Is the content appropriate for the students?
- How well are they progressing toward the goals and objectives?
- Are they able to apply their knowledge and skills in new situations?
- Do they enjoy doing and using mathematics?

Among the procedures teachers use are observations, interviews, inventories and checklists, tests, reports from parents, samples of students' work collected in portfolios, and attitude scales. Increasingly, writing is being incorporated into mathematics as a means of helping children reflect on what they have learned, as well as providing another means of enabling teachers to gauge both student learning and their own effectiveness. Chapter 4 provides a detailed discussion of all these methods of assessment.

In the final analysis, all the assessment information teachers collect is useful as they plan lessons. They know more about the achievement and progress of each child, as well as what his or her individual needs are.

In addition, many teachers have found it helpful to keep an evaluative record of the effectiveness of their lessons. They jot down notes in their planbooks or their teacher's guides about the things that went well and the things that didn't during each lesson (see Figure 3–9). They keep records of activities tried, articles read, ideas they want to try, and other anecdotal records. These notes help them to plan the following year. You may think you will remember what happened, but you will probably forget without such notes.

▶ A Glance at Where We've Been

Among the many roles that teachers play, some of the most important involve choosing tasks; planning lessons; asking questions; listening to, observing, and helping students; assessing understanding; and assigning grades. From research on learning come recommendations that teachers must work at the following: identifying expectations and choosing appropriate tasks, managing classroom discourse, using learning tools effectively, and ensuring an appropriate learning environment. Planning lies at the heart of good teaching. Planning helps to ensure that all essential content will be included, permits scheduling the work in feasible periods of time and in a sensible sequence, helps to control the pace of a lesson, aids in holding children's attention, helps to avoid unnecessary repetition while ensuring necessary review and practice, and creates a feeling of confidence for you. Planning must be done for the year, the unit, and the day. Lesson plans should include clearly stated objectives, procedures, and evaluation. There are certain guidelines to aid in determining when and how to use various types of lessons (investigative, direct instruction, review-teach-practice) and which grouping pattern to use (large-group, small-group, or individual instruction). Knowing how to take advantage of strategic moments is also important.

Observations in classrooms have indicated the importance of meeting the needs of all students. Children's attention, initiative, and understanding, are crucial to their successful achievement. Also critical are the teacher's skill in questioning, the use of appropriate use of manipulative materials and tech-

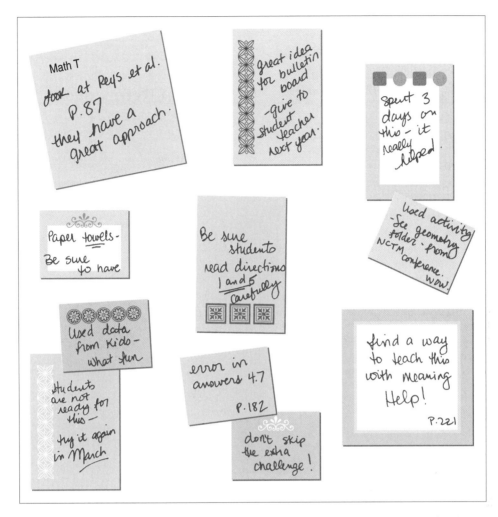

Figure 3–9 • A sampling of stick-on notes from a fifth-grade teacher's textbook

nology, and the role of drill and practice. Finally, assessment is another integral part of mathematics instruction.

Things to Do: From What You've Read

1. According to the NCTM's *Professional Teaching Standards,* there are five ways that mathematics instruction and classroom environments have been changing in recent years. Consider the classroom snapshot that opens this chapter, and point out instances where each of these shifts in classroom environment is evident or where they could be made more prominent.

2. General recommendations for teaching can be drawn from what we know about how children learn mathematics. The recommendations provided in this chapter involve five major areas of concern. Describe each of these areas briefly.

3. Why is lesson planning important?

4. What must be considered as you plan a lesson?

5. What should be included in a daily lesson plan?

6. Briefly describe the most important differences among the three different types of lessons described in this chapter. When and why would you choose to use each type?

7. How can lessons be adapted for students with specific sorts of special needs?

8. Describe the five varieties of questions that teachers should be prepared to incorporate into their daily teaching activities.

9. Write a lesson plan for the Snapshot of a Lesson at the beginning of Chapter 10.

10. Plan a follow-up activity to assess learning resulting from the lesson snapshot at the beginning of this chapter.

Things to Do: Going Beyond This Book

field Additional activities, suggestions, and questions are provided in *Teaching Elementary Mathematics: A Resource for Field Experiences.*

1. Compare two different scope-and-sequence charts from textbooks for a particular grade level. How does the scope of the content included differ? What proportion is the same? How does the sequence differ?

2. Select a content topic. Compare the way it is taught in two different textbooks.

3. Select a content topic. Follow its development through three grade levels in a textbook series. Trace what is review and what is new development of mathematical content.

4. Examine a textbook and the supplemental materials that accompany it to see what assistance is provided for adapting instruction for various levels of students. Are suggestions for modifying lessons included? Are there extra challenge worksheets or review sheets for students who need extra practice? How would you use these materials if your class included students with widely varying levels of understanding and skill?

5. Read one of the following articles: De La Cruz (1999), Karp et al. (1998), Smith et al. (1999), Tevebaugh (1998), or Zanger (1998). Prepare to describe to others what you learned about specific classroom-tested ways of addressing issues of diversity in the classroom.

6. Select a topic and plan a week's work for it for a particular grade level.

7. Design a lesson in which children will work in cooperative learning groups.

8. *field* Analyzing Classroom Discourse. Observe in a classroom, recording the way teacher and pupils interact. What proportion of time does the teacher talk? What types of questions are asked? What evidence is there that children have learned some mathematics? How many of the children have an opportunity to talk? Make a list of what they say (either to the class or to each other). In your opinion, is the classroom discourse about significant mathematics? Why?

9. *field* Grouping in the Classroom. Consider the suggestions for planning and grouping offered by Larson (1983). Talk over these suggestions with a classroom teacher, and write a summary of the ideas you want to try in your classroom.

10. *field* The Learning Environment. Read the NCTM standard on the learning environment in the *Professional Standards* (NCTM 1991, pp. 57–61). Compare the kind of teaching portrayed there with what you recall from your elementary school experiences or what you have observed in a school recently.

Selected References

Artzt, Alice F., and Newman, Claire M. *How to Use Cooperative Learning in the Mathematics Class.* Reston, Va.: NCTM, 1990.

Balka, D. *Attribute Logic Block Activities.* Oak Lawn, Ill.: Ideal School Supply Co. 1985.

Baratta-Lorton, M. *Mathematics Their Way.* Menlo Park, Calif.: Addison-Wesley, 1995.

Bresser, Rusty. *Math and Literature (Grades 4–6).* White Plains, N.Y.: Cuisenaire, 1995.

Bright, George W. "Understanding Children's Reasoning." *Teaching Children Mathematics,* 3 (September 1996), pp. 18–22.

Brownell, William A., and Chazal, Charlotte B. "The Effects of Premature Drill in Third-Grade Arithmetic." *Journal of Educational Research,* 29 (September 1935), pp. 17–28.

Burns, Marilyn. "The Role of Questioning." *Arithmetic Teacher,* 32 (February 1985), pp. 14–16.

Burns, Marilyn. *Math and Literature (K–3).* White Plains, N.Y.: Cuisenaire, 1992.

Burns, Marilyn. "What I Learned from Teaching Second Grade." *Teaching Children Mathematics,* 3 (November 1996), pp. 127–134.

Bush, William S., and Kincer, Lisa A. "The Teacher's Influence on the Classroom Learning Environment." In *Research Ideas for the Classroom: Early Childhood Mathematics* (ed. Robert J. Jensen). Reston, Va.: NCTM, and New York: Macmillan, 1993, pp. 311–328.

Clements, Douglas H., and McMillen, Sue. "Rethinking 'Concrete' Manipulatives." *Teaching Children Mathematics,* 2 (January 1996), pp. 270–279.

Cuevas, Gilbert, and Driscoll, Mark (eds.). *Reaching All Students with Mathematics.* Reston, Va.: NCTM, 1993.

Davidson, Neil. *Cooperative Learning in Mathematics: A Handbook for Teachers.* Reading, Mass.: Addison-Wesley, 1990.

De La Cruz, Yolanda. "Reversing the Trend: Latino Families in Real Partnerships with Schools." *Teaching Children Mathematics,* 5(5) (January 1999), pp. 296–300.

Driscoll, Mark J. "Diagnosis: Taking the Mathematical Pulse." In *Research within Research: Elementary School Mathematics.* Reston, Va.: NCTM, 1981.

Ebeling, David G.; Deschenes, Cathy; and Sprague, Jeffrey. *Adapting Curriculum and Instruction in Inclusive Classrooms: Staff Development Kit.* Bloomington, Ind.: Institute for the Study of Developmental Disabilities, 1994.

Farivar, Sydney, and Webb, Noreen M. "Helping and Getting Help—Essential Skills for Effective Group Problem Solving." *Arithmetic Teacher,* 41 (May 1994), pp. 521–525.

Fitzgerald, William M., and Bouck, Mary Kay. "Models of Instruction." In *Research Ideas for the Classroom: Middle Grades Mathematics* (ed. Douglas T. Owens). Reston, Va.: NCTM, and New York: Macmillan, 1993, pp. 244–258.

Good, Thomas L.; Grouws, Douglas A.; and Ebmeier, Howard. *Active Mathematics Teaching.* New York: Longman, 1983.

Karp, Karen; Allen, Candy; Allen, Linda G.; and Brown, Elizabeth Todd. "Feisty Females: Using Children's Literature with Strong Female Characters." *Teaching Children Mathematics,* 5(2) (October 1998), pp. 88–94.

Kelly, Margaret. "A Script for a Mathematics Lesson." *Arithmetic Teacher*, 38 (December 1990), pp. 36–39.

Koehler, Mary Schatz, and Prior, Millie. "Classroom Interactions: The Heartbeat of the Teaching/Learning Process." In *Research Ideas for the Classroom: Middle Grades Mathematics* (ed. Douglas T. Owens). Reston, Va.: NCTM, and New York: Macmillan, 1993, pp. 280–298.

Koontz, T. *Multicultural and Gender Equity in the Mathematics Classroom: The Gift of Diversity.* Reston, Va.: NCTM, 1997.

Krause, Marina C. *Multicultural Mathematics Materials.* Reston, Va.: NCTM, 1983.

Lappan, Glenda. "What Do We Have and Where Do We Go from Here?" *Arithmetic Teacher*, 40 (May 1993), pp. 524–526.

Lappan, Glenda; Fey, James; Fitzgerald, William; Friel, Susan; and Phillips, Elizabeth. *Getting to Know Connected Mathematics: A Guide to the Connected Mathematics Curriculum.* White Plains, N.Y.: Dale Seymour Publications.

Larson, Carol Novillis. "Organizing for Mathematics Instruction. *Arithmetic Teacher*, 31 (September 1983), pp. 16–20.

Lindquist, Mary Montgomery. "Assessing through Questioning." *Arithmetic Teacher*, 35 (January 1988), pp. 16–18.

Lobel, A. *Frog and Toad are Friends.* New York: Harper Collins Publishers, 1970.

Long, Madeleine J., and Ben-Hur, Meir. "Informing Learning through the Clinical Interview." *Arithmetic Teacher*, 38 (February 1991), pp. 44–46.

Madsen, Anne L., and Baker, Kendella. "Planning and Organizing the Middle Grades Mathematics Curriculum." In *Research Ideas for the Classroom: Middle Grades Mathematics* (ed. Douglas T. Owens). New York: Macmillan, 1993, pp. 259–279.

Meyers, Marcee J., and Burton, Grace M. "Yes You Can . . . Plan Appropriate Instruction for Learning Disabled Students." *Arithmetic Teacher*, 36 (March 1989), pp. 46–50.

National Council of Teachers of Mathematics. *Professional Standards for Teaching Mathematics.* Reston, Va.: NCTM, 1991.

National Council of Teachers of Mathematics. *Assessment Standards for School Mathematics.* Reston, Va.: NCTM, 1995.

National Council of Teachers of Mathematics. *Principles and Standards for School Mathematics.* Reston, Va.: NCTM, 2000.

Pursuing Excellence: A Study of U.S. Eighth-Grade Mathematics and Science Teaching, Learning, Curriculum, and Achievement in International Context. Washington, D.C.: National Center for Education Statistics, 1996.

Raines, Shirley C., and Canady, Robert J. *Story Stretchers for the Primary Grades: Activities to Expand Children's Favorite Books.* Mt. Rainier, Md.: Gryphon House, 1992.

Rathmell, Edward C. "Planning for Instruction Involves Focusing on Children's Thinking." *Arithmetic Teacher*, 41 (February 1994), pp. 290–291.

Reys, Barbara J., and Long, Vena M. "Teacher as Architect of Mathematical Tasks." *Teaching Children Mathematics*, 1 (January 1995), pp. 296–299.

Ross, Rita, and Kurtz, Ray. "Making Manipulatives Work: A Strategy for Success." *Arithmetic Teacher*, 40 (January 1993), pp. 254–257.

Scheibelhut, Carolyn. "I Do and I Understand, I Reflect and I Improve." *Teaching Children Mathematics*, 1 (December 1994), pp. 242–246.

Schmalz, Rosemary. "The Mathematics Textbook: How Can It Serve the Standards?" *Arithmetic Teacher*, 38 (September 1990), pp. 14–16. Reprinted in *Arithmetic Teacher*, 41 (February 1994), pp. 330–332.

Smith, Nancy L.; Babione, Carolyn; and Vick, Beverly Johns. "Dumpling Soup: Exploring Kitchens, Cultures, and Mathematics." *Teaching Children Mathematics*, 6(3) (November 1999): 148–152.

Sowell, Evelyn J. "Effects of Manipulative Materials in Mathematics Instruction." *Journal for Research in Mathematics Education*, 20 (November 1989), pp. 498–505.

Suydam, Marilyn. "Planning for Mathematics Instruction." In *Mathematics for the Young Child* (ed. Joseph N. Payne). Reston, Va.: NCTM, 1990.

Suydam, Marilyn N., and Weaver, J. Fred. *Using Research: A Key to Elementary School Mathematics.* Columbus, Ohio: ERIC Clearinghouse for Science, Mathematics and Environmental Education, 1981.

Tevebaugh, Tara N. "Mathematics is *Not* a Universal Language." *Teaching Children Mathematics*, 5(4) (December 1998), pp. 214–216.

Third International Mathematics and Science Study (TIMSS). *U.S. National Research Center Report No. 7*, East Lansing, Mich.: TIMSS U.S. National Research Center, Michigan State University, December 1996. http://ustimss.msu.edu/

Thompson, Patrick W. "Research into Practice: Concrete Materials and Teaching for Mathematical Understanding." *Arithmetic Teacher*, 41 (May 1994), pp. 556–558.

Thornton, Carol A., and Wilson, Sandra J. "Classroom Organization and Models of Instruction." In *Research Ideas for the Classroom: Early Childhood Mathematics* (ed. Robert J. Jensen). Reston, Va.: NCTM, and New York: Macmillan, 1993, pp. 269–293.

Thiessen, Diane, and Matthais, Margaret. *The Wonderful World of Mathematics: A Critically Annotated List of Children's Books in Mathematics.* Reston, Va.: NCTM, 1998.

Vacc, Nancy Nesbitt. "Questioning in the Mathematics Classroom." *Arithmetic Teacher*, 41 (October 1993), pp. 88–91.

Vacc, Nancy Nesbitt. "Planning for Instruction: Barriers to Mathematics Discussion." *Arithmetic Teacher*, 41 (February 1994), pp. 339–341.

Welchman-Tischler, Rosamond. *How to Use Children's Literature to Teach Mathematics.* Reston, Va.: NCTM, 1992.

Whitin, David, and Wilde, Sandra. *Read Any Good Math Lately?* Portsmouth, N.H.: Heinemann, 1992.

Whitin, David, and Wilde, Sandra. *It's the Story That Counts.* Portsmouth, N.H.: Heinemann, 1995.

Zanger, Virginia Vogel. "Math Storybooks." *Teaching Children Mathematics*, 5(2) (October 1998), pp. 98–102.

Zaslavsky, Claudia. *The Multicultural Math Classroom: Bringing in the World.* Portsmouth, N.H.: Heinemann, 1996.

Assessment: Enhanced Learning and Teaching

Snapshot of a Teacher's Thoughts on Assessment

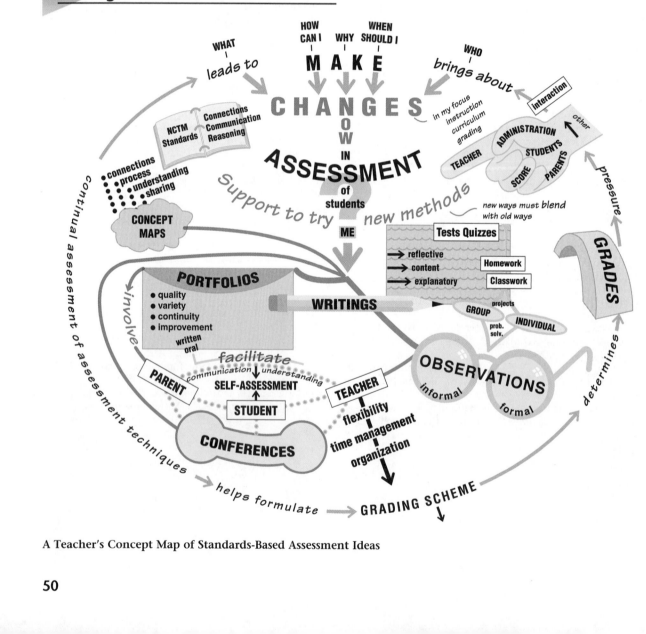

A Teacher's Concept Map of Standards-Based Assessment Ideas

Introduction

In previous chapters you were introduced to a new vision of teaching mathematics. That vision includes the mathematics we expect children to know and be able to use and the ways that they learn it, as well as how their progress is assessed. This chapter begins with a concept map drawn by a sixth grade teacher who was thinking deeply about how her methods of assessing students needed to change as a result of all the other changes in her instruction. Her concept map illustrates the many different methods of assessment that she used with her students, and shows how those methods interact with one another and with her classroom goals. Most of the ideas and connections shown in the concept map are elaborated upon in this chapter.

Many people tend to equate assessment with testing, but it is important to think much more broadly. NCTM's Assessment Principle asserts that "assessment should support the learning of important mathematics and provide useful information to teachers and students" (NCTM 2000, p. 22) According to NCTM's *Assessment Standards for School Mathematics* (NCTM 1995) assessment is "the process of gathering evidence about a student's knowledge of, ability to use, and disposition toward, mathematics and of making inferences from that evidence for a variety of purposes" (p. 3). As a teacher, you will need to plan assessments, gather evidence in many ways such as those discussed in this chapter, interpret the evidence you collect, and use the results for a variety of purposes. Many books have been written on the subject of assessment, so what we present here represents only a brief overview of the information available. For more in-depth coverage on any of the topics surveyed here, refer to some of the references we've provided. Two very useful edited books on assessment are Webb (1993) and Lambdin et al. (1996).

NCTM's six Assessment Standards are short but powerful statements against which your assessment practices can be judged.

The first standard focuses on the *mathematics*. You should always ask yourself if you are assessing mathematics that is important for students to learn. Although this may sound like a rhetorical question, it is not. Often the easiest aspects of mathematics to assess are the most trivial. It makes no sense to assess a mathematical skill or concept just because it is easy to assess. You need to plan assessments that tap important mathematics in ways that are meaningful to children.

The second standard asks if your assessments enhance students' opportunities for *learning* mathematics. Have you thought of tests as a way to help in the learning or as a hurdle to jump? Assessing

should be integral to learning, not something separate. Children will infer what we value in mathematics by what we consider important enough to assess. For example, if we think that problem solving is important and yet never or rarely assess problem solving, students will soon conclude that it is not an important part of their learning. Result: they will not become problem solvers.

There are many questions that you could ask yourself about the third standard, the *equity* standard. As you strive to help all children learn mathematics, look carefully at your assessment procedures and ask questions such as these:

- What opportunities has each student had to learn the mathematics being assessed?
- How does the assessment help students demonstrate their best work?
- How have the effects of bias been minimized throughout the assessment? (NCTM 1995, p. 16)

These three standards and the other three (openness, inferences, and coherence) can be used to judge the appropriateness of a wide variety of forms of educational assessment.

More specifically, NCTM's *Assessment Standards* identifies four purposes of assessment: making instructional decisions, monitoring student's progress, evaluating students' achievement, and evaluating programs (see Figure 4–1).

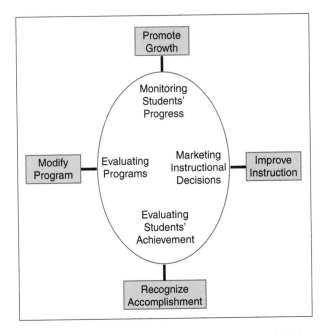

Figure 4–1 • Four purposes of assessment and their results (Reprinted with permission from "Assessment Standards for School Mathematics," p. 25, copyright 1995 by the National Council of Teachers of Mathematics. All rights reserved.)

In this chapter, however, we will focus on the first three purposes of assessment because they are the aspects you are most likely to be involved with in the classroom.

Making Instructional Decisions

As a teacher, you will be making many instructional decisions. As with any decision, the better informed that we are, the wiser the choices we usually make. The *Assessment Standards* suggest ways that you may use assessment information differently in making instructional decisions than teachers did years ago (see Table 4–1).

One shift in assessment practices is a move toward gathering assessment data continuously rather than periodically. Another is toward using a wide variety of sources of information (rather than tests primarily). And the third is related to keeping the needs and progress of students in mind when making long-range teaching plans (rather than following a set plan of study regardless of how well students are doing).

Monitoring Student Progress

As teachers monitor student progress, there are also several shifts in assessment practice being called for by the *Assessment Standards* (Table 4–1). These include assessing a wide range of student abilities rather than focusing on testing students' factual knowledge and skills, providing more extensive and elaborated feedback to students on their progress, using a wider variety of methods for gathering information (rather than relying primarily on tests and quizzes), and involving students themselves more in the assessment process.

Evaluating Student Achievement

There are also a number of things teachers today are doing differently in terms of grading and certifying students' achievement. One change is a move toward judging students' performance against stated criteria rather than by comparing students with each other. The second and third shifts were mentioned earlier: assessing a broad range of components of mathemat-

Table 4–1 • Major shifts in assessment practices

Toward	*Away From*
Shifts in Assessing to Make Instructional Decisions	
Integrating assessment with instruction	Depending on scheduled testing
Using evidence from a variety of assessment formats and contexts	Relying on any one source of information
Using evidence of every students' progress toward long-range planning goals	Planning primarily for content coverage
Shifts in Assessing to Monitor Students' Progress	
Assessing progress toward mathematical power	Assessing knowledge of specific facts and isolated skills
Communicating with students about performance in a continuous, comprehensive manner	Simply indicating right or wrong answers
Using multiple and complex assessment tools	Primary reliance on answers to brief questions on quizzes and tests
Students learning to assess their own progress	Teachers and external agencies as the sole judges of progress
Shifts in Assessing to Evaluate Students' Achievement	
Comparing students' performance with performance criteria	Comparing student with student
Assessing progress toward mathematical power	Assessing knowledge of specific facts and isolated skills
Certification based on balanced, multiple sources of information	Relying on only a few, narrowly conceived sources of evidence
Profiles of achievement based on public criteria	Single letter grades based on variable or nonpublic criteria

ical power rather than isolated skills and knowledge and using a variety of sources for gathering assessment information. And finally, there are trends toward making achievement criteria more open and public.

The number of shifts listed in this opening section is an indication of the need for change in many of our assessment practices. This will come through time and open minds; this chapter is an opportunity for you to begin asking yourself questions about how you will assess students in order to make decisions, monitor progress, and evaluate achievement.

Phases of Assessment

The assessment process has four phases: (1) deciding what to assess and what kind of assessment tool to use, (2) gathering evidence, (3) interpreting the evidence, and (4) using the results. In the boxes around the edge of Figure 4–1 you see how the results of an assessment may be used differently depending upon the reason for undertaking the assessment. If the purpose of your assessment is to make an instructional decision (for example, whether to continue working on a particular concept with your students or whether to move on to a new topic), you are using the results of your assessment to improve instruction. By contrast, assessments undertaken to monitor students' progress generally result in actions to promote individual student growth (for example, you might determine that a particular student could benefit from more hands-on work with fractions).

When you are planning an assessment, it is important to think about the purpose of the assessment, the methods you will use to collect data, how you will interpret the evidence you collect (for example, how you will award points for students' written problem-solving work), and how you will summarize and use your findings. Will the outcome of your assessment be to change your lesson plans for the next week? Or will you use the information when explaining to parents what their child's strengths and weaknesses are? How you answer these questions may have an impact on the sorts of data you decide to collect.

When you are gathering evidence, think about the variety of tasks or activities you might use and try to choose appropriately. For example, if you want to find out what your students understand about decimals, you could have them complete some worksheets on addition and subtraction of decimals. But that might not provide you with as much information as having them show you how they could use base ten blocks to represent an addition or subtraction problem with decimals or hav-

ing them write about using base ten blocks and draw pictures to accompany their writing.

When you are interpreting evidence, it is important to think ahead of time about the criteria you will use to judge the adequacy of responses. You should think about how you *hope* your students will respond to a task or question, and what sorts of difficulties or misconceptions they *might* have. What sorts of responses will you consider exemplary, adequate, or flawed? What will you consider adequate evidence of understanding?

Finally, when using results from assessments, think about how you will communicate your judgments and how they will affect future instructional decisions. For example, how well will a numeric or letter grade help your students understand where they went wrong and what they need to do differently in the future? Can you supplement the grade with written comments? Can you find time for brief individual conferences with some of your students? How will you use what you've learned about your class, as a whole, in planning for future instruction?

WAYS TO GATHER AND MAKE JUDGMENTS ABOUT EVIDENCE

There are many different ways to gather information about the abilities, dispositions, and interests of students. What type of information to collect and how to obtain it depend on the purpose for which it will be used. You first need to ask yourself what mathematics learning you want to assess.

For example, if you want to assess the principle discussed in Chapter 2—that mathematics learning should be meaningful—then you will want to find out whether students have attached meaning to what they are doing by observing them and by asking questions that elicit their level of understanding. If you want your students to be persistent and willing to approach problems in a variety of ways, then you will assess these characteristics through problems of a challenging nature. If you want your students to be able to communicate well and to work well with others, as discussed in Chapter 2, then you will make those characteristics part of your assessment.

Once you have engaged your students in activities likely to elicit the behaviors that you want to judge, you need some sort of guidelines or framework to use in looking at the data you collect. (For example, if you want to see how well your students can communicate about the notions of area and perimeter, you might ask them to write a letter to a younger child comparing and contrasting these two ideas and providing an example of a real-world problem using each measure.) But how will you judge which student letters are better than others? You may choose to use a rubric.

A *rubric* is a rating scale that can be designed or adapted for use with a certain class of students or a particular task. Generally, a rubric is used to assign anywhere from 0 to 10 points to student work to provide a generalized rating of performance. Unlike awarding points when grading a quiz or test, you generally do not count the number of items correct to arrive at rubric score. Instead, you look at overall performance on the task and rate that performance along a continuum. The very simplest type of rubric simply has three or four points and very general descriptors of the achievement necessary to attain them. For example, you might award points for a student's problem-solving work as shown in the rubric in Figure 4–2.

Another way of thinking about constructing a rubric is to think about sorting students' work into three piles: (1) students who do not understand the outcome (the concept or process), (2) students are developing the outcome (but not quite there), (3) students who have attained the outcome and can apply it and communicate it. For any specific task, you can develop *performance indicators* to help you judge which student work to put in which categories. For example, you might design a task for students to show what they know about the meaning of decimals by using base-10 blocks to build specified decimal numbers (for example, 3 tenths or 1 and 5 hundredths) and to demonstrate decimal relationships (for example, build 2 tenths and build 22 hundredths and explain which one is larger). Each flat block could represent a whole number, each rod a tenth, and each little cube a hundredth.

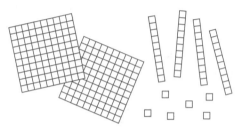

Figure 4–3 shows a three-category rubric of performance indicators for this task.

In the rest of this section, we consider a broad range of different techniques for obtaining information to assess students' learning and their dispositions according to the NCTM's vision. Scoring rubrics such as those described earlier can be adapted for use with many of these data collection techniques. We also look at some combinations of assessment methods—for example, giving a written test and then asking individual children to explain how they arrived at the solution.

Observation

Observing students as they work and making judgments about their performance from observation is probably one of the most commonly used assessment methods in the classroom. Yet many teachers never go one important step further: to make notes about their observations or to think carefully about what they want to look for and why. Watching and listening may seem easy and commonplace, but it takes practice and planning to hone your observation skills. For example, it is helpful to plan what you will observe on a given day. Suppose you are teaching first grade and your students are solving problems involving addition facts. You may want to observe and record which students are using physical materials, which are doing most of the problems mentally, which are using thinking strategies to determine basic facts (which will be discussed in

4	Exemplary work	Goes well beyond expectations of the task (for example, problem solved in more than one way, or student has extended the problem and completed a more difficult version)
3	Excellent work	Task as stated is completed with no errors, work is clear and complete
2	Good work	Task is completed with only a few minor errors. Work shows understanding of the problem and uses anticipated approaches.
1	Needs more instruction	Student work may include evidence that the problem was not understood completely; may use inappropriate methods or faulty reasoning; may make significant errors.

Figure 4–2 • General holistic rubric for math problem solving

Sample performance indicators for a student who:		
Does not understand	**Is developing understanding**	**Understands**
• When told to use one flat to represent a whole, cannot use blocks to show how many tenths would be equivalent to that one whole • When told to use one flat to represent a whole, cannot use blocks to show how many hundredths would be equivalent to that one whole • Has difficulty understanding that the same blocks can be used to represent different powers of ten in different problems (may think a flat must represent 100 if earlier experiences assigned a value of 1 to each small cube)	• When told to use one flat to represent a whole, can state which block would represent one tenth (rod) and which block would represent one hundredth (little cube) • Can use blocks to show why ten tenths and one hundred hundredths are each equivalent to one whole • May interchange value of blocks when building decimals • May have difficulty building decimals with blocks, especially when the decimal includes zeros (for example, 3.04). • May have difficulty stating what number is represented by a given collection of blocks (for example, 5 flats, 2 rods, and 3 little cubes)	• Understands that the same blocks can be used to represent different powers of ten in different problems • When told which block represents one, can state what number is represented by any collection of blocks • Can build, order, and compare decimals using blocks to illustrate • Can build alternative models for the same decimal (for example, can represent 3.45 either with 3 flats, 4 rods, and 5 little cubes or with 3 flats and 45 little cubes)

Figure 4–3 • **Rubric of performance indicators for base-10 block task on decimals**

Chapter 8), and which are relying on memorized facts. At times, you may plan to observe only one student in a cooperative group setting:

> Does José jump right in or wait for others to begin?
>
> Is he willing to listen?
>
> Does he know his doubles facts? Does he know the facts that make ten?
>
> Is he able to use known facts to figure out unknown facts? If so, what strategies does he use?
>
> Does he accept or challenge the ideas of others?
>
> Is he willing to play different roles within the group?
>
> Is he persistent? Does the problem interest him?

From such observations, you can gain insight into a student's attitude and disposition toward mathematics. This knowledge, in turn, can help you plan ways to encourage strengths and work on weaknesses.

Sometimes, you may want to scan all your students while they are engaged in tasks:

> What does the frown on Rhonda's face mean?
>
> Why is the cluster of students at the back table off the task?

> How is Roger attempting to arrive at an answer?
>
> Which students in the class do not appear to be grasping the new concept?

Your notes about what you have observed will certainly be useful for anecdotal records that you can use for individual assessment and for future planning. However, your observations can also help you decide what to do immediately in the classroom, while you are leading a discussion or presenting a new concept.

Some practical tips are helpful in organizing yourself for classroom observations (Beyer 1993). Some teachers find it helpful to set aside a page in a notebook for each student or to use individual notecards in a file. But it can be clumsy to have to page through the notebook or fumble through the cards when you are walking around the room. To make observation notes easier to handle, some teachers like to tape an index card for each student in the class on a single page of heavy cardboard, with the cards overlapping as shown in Figure 4–4. When you want to write notes about a particular individual, you just flip to his or her card. When a card is full, you can file it away in that student's file and replace it with a fresh card. Another handy idea is to carry a page of computer labels on your clipboard as you circulate around the class. Make notes about individual students on the labels

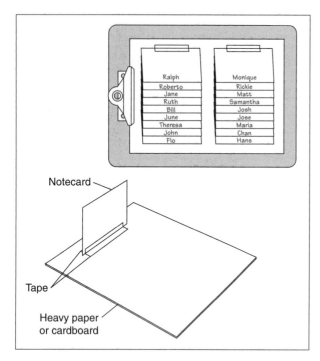

Figure 4–4 • **Flip cards for recording classroom observations**

(putting name and date on each). Later you can paste the labels into the individual students' folders or pages in your observation notebook. If you want to remember to collect data on certain students on a given day, you can write their names on labels in advance as a reminder.

Some interesting articles about classroom observation include Beyer (1993), Chambers (1995), Cross and Hynes (1994), Ross and Kurtz (1993), and Sgroi et al. (1995).

Questioning

Observation is complemented and enlightened by asking questions. For example, suppose Rhonda was frowning during a sixth-grade class in which students were investigating the decimal representations of fractions using calculators. The calculator has shown these results:

$$\frac{1}{9} = 0.1111111$$

$$\frac{2}{9} = 0.2222222$$

$$\frac{3}{9} = 0.3333333$$

You know that Rhonda is a confident and capable mathematics student, so what might be the cause of

the frown? In this case, a direct question to Rhonda about what is puzzling her may be appropriate. (Maybe Rhonda recognizes that the calculator is limited in how many decimal places it can represent. She may already understand that the ones and twos will repeat indefinitely in the decimal expansions for $\frac{1}{9}$ and $\frac{2}{9}$, respectively. In fact, she may already be thinking about the implications of the pattern she has observed and be bothered by extrapolating to $\frac{9}{9} = 0.9999999 \ldots$, since she knows that $\frac{9}{9} = 1$ and finds it hard to believe that 1 and .9 repeating indefinitely are equal.) In other cases, asking a direct question such as "What don't you understand?" may not help because a less-confident or less-capable student may not know how to talk about what's confusing. You may need to ask a series of questions to probe for the cause.

For example, suppose Raymond, thinks that $\frac{1}{9}$ is exactly equal to 0.1111111 because the calculator shows it. To help Raymond understand that this result is only an approximation, you may need to ask Raymond:

> What does $\frac{1}{9}$ mean? Can you show what it means by drawing a picture or performing a computation?
>
> If Raymond responds that it means one of nine equal parts of a whole, you could proceed in this manner:
>
> Can you draw a sketch and label the parts with both notations (fractional and decimal)?
>
> If each part is equal to $\frac{1}{9}$, what is the total of all nine parts? Can you explain why so that your little brother could understand?
>
> If each part is equal to 0.1111111, so what is the total of all nine parts? Can you explain why?
>
> Is this total exactly equal to one?
>
> Is it near to one?
>
> What do you think now about $\frac{1}{9}$ and 0.1111111? Do they represent exactly the same amount?

Alternatively, instead of responding that $\frac{1}{9}$ means one of nine parts, Raymond might respond that $\frac{1}{9}$ means one divided by nine. In that case, your questions to him should be a bit different. You might ask him to divide 1 by 9 using paper and pencil to see what happens. After working on this computation he is likely to observe that there is always a remainder no matter how many places you carry out the division. So $\frac{1}{9}$ must be represented by a decimal with ones repeating indefinitely after the decimal point.

Asking good questions is an art that needs to be developed and practiced. When you teach through questioning, you actively involve students and know more about what they are thinking. In planning your lessons, you should think of questions that will help you gauge whether students are understanding the mathematics, whether they are approaching a problem in different ways, whether they can generalize, or whether they can explain their thinking. Limit the number of questions that can be answered yes or no or with one-word responses. For example, instead of asking "Should we add, subtract, multiply, or divide to solve this problem?" ask "What could we do to understand this problem better?" or "What sort of picture can we draw to help decide what operation to use?" As a teacher, you should also work to develop more high-level and open-response questioning, asking students to explain or defend their answers or to describe another way to solve the problem. For example, look at the lesson that opens Chapter 12, and examine the questions that Mr. Flores asked. The questions about which students took the most and the least shots are low-level questions that do not give you much information. The questions about who is the best shot, however, elicit a great deal of information about students' thinking and their understanding of the mathematics. Remember that students need time to think about their answers to such questions. Practice waiting silently.

Finally, recognize that you can involve many more of your students in thinking deeply about mathematics if you think of ways to get everyone involved in question asking and answering. For example, you can pose a question to the class and ask everyone to "think-pair-share." The students should first think about their own answers, then pair up with a partner to talk about their ideas, and finally be ready to offer suggestions to the entire class. (For even more opportunities for small group discussion, you can have the pairs join up for discussion in groups of four or six before you bring the whole class together to talk about the question.) With this questioning model, everyone is encouraged to think and talk about the question. The conversation in the classroom is no longer "ping-pong" from teacher to individual student and back.

Some useful references on questioning include Burns (1985), Mumme and Shepherd (1990), Spangler (1992), Sullivan and Clarke (1991), and Vaac (1993).

Interviewing

Interviewing is a combination of questioning and observing, usually done with one student in a quiet place. It is a powerful way to learn about a student's thinking and to give her or him some special attention. Key factors in a successful interview are establishing rapport with the child, accepting responses without judging, and encouraging the child to talk and explain.

Although you will certainly not have time to interview all of your students each day or even every week, choose a few to interview each week until you have had a chance to talk with each one individually. Teachers are often surprised at how students value private time with them and how much they learn in a short time about the individual student. You may be able to squeeze in an interview or two each day during whole-class silent reading time or during work-station time (when other students are circulating from station to station) or during seat-work time.

Before interviewing a student, you need a basic plan of what you want to investigate, what materials you will need, what questions you will ask, and when and how you will record the information. You may want to have alternative paths to take if the interview proceeds in different ways.

The interview itself generally has three parts: initiation, questioning/hypothesis formulation, and questioning/hypothesis testing (Long and Ben-Hur 1991). During the initiation phase, the interviewer puts the student at ease by chatting informally, asking nonthreatening personal interest questions, showing the child the materials that will be used and ensuring that he or she is familiar with them, and explaining the purpose of the interview. Next, the interviewer begins posing tasks, always making certain, when necessary, to rephrase questions in the student's own language and to encourage the student to explain, elaborate, and show what he or she knows. Students often understand more than it appears at first glance.

It is the interviewer's responsibility to ask questions in a variety of ways in order to formulate hypotheses about how the child is thinking about the task and what the child does and does not understand. It is critical that the interviewer remain nonjudgmental about student responses, even though students often will look for subtle clues about the correctness of their answers. Some noncommittal phrases that are helpful in prompting children to explain their thinking further (without indicating whether previous responses have been right or wrong) include:

- I am interested in knowing more about your thinking. Talk to me about it.
- Pretend you are the teacher and I am your student. Please help me understand.
- Can you explain that a different way?

- I like it when you take the time to explain your thinking.
- I think I understand now, but what if . . . ?

As the second phase of the interview is proceeding, the interviewer begins to formulate hypotheses about what the child knows and where the child has trouble.

The third phase of the interview is the time to ask questions specifically designed to test those hypotheses, to see if the difficulties really are what they seemed to be. A big temptation for many teachers is to slide into teaching during a interview, rather than maintaining a more distant stance that focuses just on learning what the student knows and can do. If there is lots of time, teaching may be appropriate. But reteaching or tutoring is often better reserved for another time or another day. The focus of a classroom interview should be to figure out what a student knows, not to help him or her on the spot.

In the Classroom 4–1 is a plan for interviewing third-grade students about their understanding of place value.

A very useful chapter about classroom interviews is "Listening to Children: The Interview Method" (Labinowicz 1985). Cross and Hynes (1994), Kamii and Lewis (1991), Labinowicz (1987), Long and Ben-Hur (1991), Peck et al. (1989), and Weaver (1955) are additional sources of information on interviews.

Performance Tasks

In a class that is alive with problem solving and investigations, many valuable opportunities will arise to observe students working on performance tasks. In fact, the only way we can assess some skills will be through performance tasks. For example, if one objective is for children to know how to measure with a ruler, then they need to be assessed doing such measuring. Questions on written tests that line up a picture of a ruler with the object do not reveal much about the actual skill of measuring.

Performance tasks often mirror the real world, are open-ended, and require time for grappling with a problem. It often is helpful to pair children when observing performance of such tasks so that you can hear their conversation as they work. In planning, you will want to list some of the areas you want to observe as the pairs work on appropriate tasks.

As an example of a performance task, look back at In the Classroom 2–1 (Chapter 2). In that activity, children are provided with some blocks and asked to build different boxes (right prisms). As they build boxes of various dimensions and various volumes, the formula for the volume of a box evolves natu-

---

In The Classroom 4–1

Primary Interview on Place Value

Objective: To determine students' understanding of place value.

Materials: Unifix cubes, paper and pencil, base-ten blocks

Tasks:

1. Can you show me twenty-four Unifix cubes? Observe if child counts accurately (says numbers in proper order, uses one-to-one correspondence, has a method for keeping track of which cubes have been counted)
2. Now let's suppose we want thirty-four cubes. Can you show me that? Does child count out ten more or count over from beginning?
3. Can you write the number thirty-four here?
4. Let's put the thirty-four cubes into groups of ten. How many tens do you think we can make? Do you think you'll have any cubes left over? Shall we count out the thirty-four cubes into piles to make sure?
5. Let's look at thirty-four, the number you wrote. Can you show me with the cubes what the 3 means? Can you show me what the 4 means?
6. Now let's make four piles of ten cubes each. And let's have five leftover. Do you know how many cubes we have here altogether? How can you tell? (Does student know to count the piles by ten and add the leftovers? Or does he or she count all?)
7. a. If the child has trouble with the questions above, check further by asking again to count out several different numbers of cubes—for example, 17, 26, or 30—and to predict how many tens and how many left over. Ask the reverse question. For example, if we have 2 tens and 7 left over, how many cubes would that be?
   b. If the child has no trouble with the questions above, probe for understanding of place value of larger numbers such as 123 or 347 using base-ten blocks and asking how many piles of one hundred could be made and how many piles of ten and how many ones. Also ask the reverse question: if we have three flats and six sticks and two units, how many cubes would that be altogether? Extension: Check to see how many different ways the child can show 136.

Interview Reminders:

Listen and watch carefully! Let them do it! Don't teach!

Be flexible. Ask for more examples, if needed.

Ask: How would you show a friend? How would you explain it to a little kid?

rally. The children are involved in using models, making decisions, and thinking mathematically, rather than just applying a formula. Figure 4–5 lists three areas you might plan to observe and examples of the notes you might make while observing the performance task from In the Classroom 2–1.

As indicated in Chapter 3, emphasis on worthwhile mathematical tasks is a core dimension of the *Professional Standards for Teaching Mathematics* (NCTM 1991). Figure 3–1 gives the standard describing the type of tasks and the goals of this focus on task performance. You may want to begin with simple tasks and then build up to longer, more complicated ones. Often you will be surprised at the tenacity of very young children on a task that is engaging them; you should not rule out richer tasks for this age. Badger (1992), Moon (1993), and Sanford (1993) provide additional interesting reading about performance assessment in the elementary math classroom.

	Jason	Amy	Lawanda	Tyler	Zaria	Kristin	Becca	Drew
Strategy								
Used trial and error								
Organized by length (or height or width)								
Found and used patterns								
Made other comparisons								
Used a combination of strategies								
Result								
Found few or all combinations								
Found the connection to factors of the number								
Found/did not find the formula								
Able/unable to describe the procedure								
Attitude								
Worked well with others								
Curious, explored other shapes, other numbers								
Enthusiastic								
Remained engaged								

Figure 4–5 • Observation guide for block building activity

Self-Assessment and Peer Assessment

Self-assessment is an activity that many people engage in. For example, actors, athletes, and musicians often study videotapes of their performances in order to figure out how to improve. In a similar way, when math students engage in activities that promote self-awareness and self-evaluation, they can eliminate weaknesses and become better problem solvers. Students are often the best assessors of their own work and feelings. When students evaluate their own work, the responsibility for their learning is theirs. You can begin the self-assessment process by having students validate their own thinking or their answers to selected exercises. For example, in a nonthreatening way, you could ask Dwayne to show you how he arrived at the answer in the following case:

$$
\begin{array}{r}
28 \\
\times 46 \\
\hline
168 \\
122 \\
\hline
290
\end{array}
$$

You will also want to ask him to explain how he obtained the answer to this problem:

$$
\begin{array}{r}
24 \\
\times 39 \\
\hline
216 \\
72 \\
\hline
936
\end{array}
$$

It is important to ask about correct answers as well as incorrect ones, and standard approaches as well as nonstandard, so that children do not think that they are questioned only when something is wrong. Asking only about incorrect answers will not help build their self-esteem or establish the feeling that they have control of the mathematics.

It is helpful for students to learn to ask themselves a variety of mental self-assessment questions while they are engaged in problem solving. You can help students develop the habit of self-assessing by prompting them with questions such as "What are you doing now?" "Why are you doing that?" "How will it help you find the solution?" (Kenney and Silver 1993). Eventually, these questions will become second nature to the students, and you will no longer need to prompt them. Being able to think about one's own thinking and to monitor one's own problem-solving efforts (metacognition) is one of the goals of problem-solving instruction.

Engaging students in self-assessment of their problem-solving efforts after they have finished solving problems is another useful way to improve their monitoring abilities. For example, you might ask students to write a sentence or two in response to prompts like those in Figure 4–6 after they have finished a problem-solving activity.

Students can also analyze each others' strategies for solving problems. As they listen to and discuss how another student or group of students solved a problem, they will begin to see different ways to

---

Think about the problem you just worked on. Then answer these questions by circling what you think:

1. How sure are you that your answer is right?

| ABSOLUTELY SURE | PRETTY SURE | SORT OF SURE | NOT SO SURE | I KNOW I GOT IT WRONG |

Why are you sure (or not sure) about your answer?

2. How hard was this problem for you?

| VERY, VERY HARD | PRETTY HARD | SORT OF HARD | NOT SO HARD | REALLY EASY |

Why was this problem at this difficulty level for you?

3. Have you ever solved a problem like this one before?

| YES MANY TIMES | YES, ONCE OR TWICE | NOT SURE | DON'T THINK SO | NO, DEFINITELY NOT |

If so, describe the other problems and tell why they were like this one. If not, what was different about this problem from the others you've seen?

Figure 4–6 • **Self-assessment questions for problem solving**

proceed and to make judgments about which way makes the most sense to them, which seems easier or different, and which leads to stumbling blocks. Not only will they learn from such discussions and self-assessments, but you will also learn a lot about the students.

Sometimes knowing about students' attitudes, beliefs, and feelings about mathematics and mathematical tasks helps you, as a teacher, know how to design lessons more effectively. No one is better at assessing how a student feels about a given task than the student who is doing it. You may want to give a simple attitude inventory (see Figure 4–7).

Or you might assign students to write math journals or letters to themselves or to others. One teacher had her students write letters to themselves about their strengths and weaknesses at the beginning of each grading period. Months later, they would read back over their letters to see if they had made progress in any of the areas they had previously self-identified as weaknesses (see Figure 4–8).

You may learn more from young children by asking them to answer questions or complete tasks such as the following:

What are you really good at in math? What things do you need to improve on?

Draw a picture of what mathematics looks (feels) like to you.

If you were telling a friend about the favorite thing you do in mathematics class, what would you tell him or her? What other things about math class might you tell your friend? Why?

You can learn much about older children's view of mathematics through discussions. Several questions suggested by Spangler (1992) included the following:

If you and a friend got different answers to the same problem, what would you do?

If you were playing "Password" (one-word clues) and you wanted a friend to guess the word mathematics, what clues would you give?

How do you know when you have solved a problem correctly?

Attitude Inventory Items

Pretend your class has been given some math story problems to solve. Mark true or false depending on how the statement describes you. There are no right or wrong answers for this part.

_____ 1. I will put down any answer just to finish a problem.
_____ 2. It is no fun to try to solve problems.
_____ 3. I will try almost any problem.
_____ 4. When I do not get the right answer right away I give up.
_____ 5. I like to try hard problems.
_____ 6. My ideas about how to solve problems are not as good as other students' ideas.
_____ 7. I can only do problems everyone else can do.
_____ 8. I will not stop working on a problem until I get an answer.
_____ 9. I am sure I can solve most problems.
_____ 10. I will work a long time on a problem.
_____ 11. I am better than many students at solving problems.
_____ 12. I need someone to help me work on problems.
_____ 13. I can solve most hard problems.
_____ 14. There are some problems I will just not try.
_____ 15. I do not like to try problems that are hard to understand.
_____ 16. I will keep working on a problem until I get it right.
_____ 17. I like to try to solve problems.
_____ 18. I give up on problems right away.
_____ 19. Most problems are too hard for me to solve.
_____ 20. I am a good problem solver.

Figure 4–7 • A problem-solving attitude survey for elementary students (Reprinted with permission from "How to Evaluate Progress in Problem Solving," copyright 1987 by the National Council of Teachers of Mathematics. All rights reserved.)

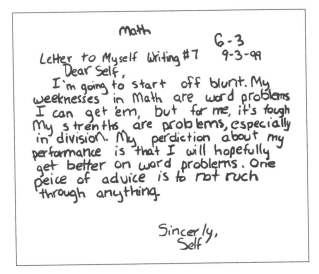

Figure 4–8 • Example of student self-assessment "letter to myself"

Student self assessment instruments for mathematics can be found in a variety of sources (for example, Charles et al. 1987; Stenmark 1991). Other useful resources on self- and peer-assessment include Clarke (1992), Collinson (1992), Garafalo and Bryant (1992), and Kenney and Silver (1993).

Work Samples

Work samples can include written assignments, projects, and other student products that you collect and evaluate. Figure 4–9 reproduces the work of four children on the following problem:

> A carpenter makes only three-legged and four-legged tables. At the end of one day, he had used thirty-one legs. How many stools and tables did he make?

Figure 4–10 provides a typical analytic scoring scale for assessing children's work in problem solving on three measures (understanding the problem, planning a solution, and getting an answer).

Figure 4–9 • Samples of children's problem-solving work

Analytic Scoring Scale

Understanding the Problem

0: Complete misunderstanding of the problem

1: Part of the problem misunderstood or misinterpreted

2: Complete understanding of the problem

Planning a Solution

0: No attempt or totally inappropriate plan

1: Partially correct plan based on part of the problem being interpreted correctly

2: Plan could have led to a correct solution if implemented properly

Getting an Answer

0: No answer, or wrong answer based on an inappropriate plan

1: Copying error, computational error, partial answer for a problem with multiple answers

2: Correct answer and correct label for the answer

Figure 4–10 • **A scale for scoring problem solving** (Reprinted with permission from "How to Evaluate Progress in Problem Solving," copyright 1987 by the National Council of Teachers of Mathematics. All rights reserved.)

Table 4–2 shows one teacher's scores for each of the four children on the three measures in Figure 4–10. There are, in fact, many different schemes for scoring problem solving, and each involves judgment. For example, try scoring the papers in Figure 4–9 using the same analytic scoring scale to see whether you agree with the scorer in Table 4–2. (You may well disagree, but you should be able to justify your position.)

Perhaps more important than scoring children's work is analyzing it to see what you can learn about the students. Looking again at the work of the four students in Figure 4–9, for example, we could conclude that only Suzy searched for more than one answer to the problem.

Portfolios

Portfolios have been used for evaluation of works of art for a long time, but only recently has there been an emphasis on using this technique in mathematics. A portfolio is a "purposeful collection of student work that exhibits the student's efforts, progress, and achievement in one or more areas. The collection must include student participation in selecting the contents, the criteria for selection, and criteria for judging merit, and evidence of student self-reflection" (Paulson et al. 1991, p. 60). A student's mathematics portfolio might include such things as special problem-solving tasks, writings, investigations, projects, and reports. These could be presented through a variety of media, including paper and pencil, audio or videotapes, and computer disks.

If you have your students keep portfolios, you will need to make many decisions:

What is the purpose of the portfolio? Who will be the audience? (The students themselves? You as teacher? parents?)

What will be included and who selects? (Problem-solving work? Tests and quizzes? Writing about math? Only "best efforts" or a collection of "representative work"?) See Figure 4–11 for a list of the items one teacher chose to require.

Table 4–2 • **Scoring for children's work in Figure 4–9 using the scale in Figure 4–10**

	Understanding the Problem	Planning a Solution	Getting an Answer	Total
Suzy	2	2	1	5
Toby	1	1	0	2
Katie	2	2	1	5
Ralph	2	2	1	5

Minimum requirements for inclusion in your portfolio at the end of each grading period:

1. 3 homework assignments
2. 3 writing samples
3. 2 quizzes
4. 2 examples of class notes
5. 1 example of special project work
6. 1 example of cooperative group work

Your portfolio is not limited to the above. At the end of each grading period, you will choose five pieces of work to remain in your portfolio to represent the grading period's work.

Figure 4–11 ● **One teacher's specifications for portfolio contents**

Where will the portfolios be kept? (In notebooks? In folders? In the classroom? In student desks or lockers or at home?)

Will you grade the portfolios? (If so, on what basis? Will the portfolio include already graded items, and if so, is a student graded twice on the same material? Is the portfolio graded on the basis of completeness, comprehensiveness, insight, etc.? Can a well-compiled portfolio that contains many poor papers receive a high grade? Can a messy, incomplete portfolio belonging to an excellent math student—and containing all A papers—receive a low grade?)

How often will you give feedback? (Monthly, quarterly, at the end of each grading period?)

These are only representative questions. There are many more to be considered. Once you have decided these things for yourself, portfolios can be a rich source of information for you and your students.

A particular benefit of portfolios is their value as a self-assessment tool for students. It is important for students to date the entries so that they (and others) can see their growth over time. It is also helpful if they describe each task and reflect on it.

Figure 4–12 provides some advice for getting started with math learning portfolios.

Some useful references on the subject include: Clarke (1992), Kuhs (1997), Lambdin and Walker (1994), and Mumme (1990).

Writings

The NCTM Standards call for more emphasis on communication in mathematics. As shown in the follow-

ing illustration, numeracy and literacy go hand in hand. Student writings as a form of communication can provide another source for assessment. You may want students to keep a journal or to add writing to other assignments.

Words and numbers are of equal value,
for, in the cloak of knowledge,
one is warp and the other woof.
It is no more important to count the sands
than it is to name the stars.

(From THE PHANTOM TOLLBOOTH by Norton Juster. Text copyright © 1961 by Norton Juster. Text copyright renewed 1989 by Norton Juster. Reprinted by permission of Random House Children's Books, a division of Random House, Inc.)

A simple way to begin is to ask students to write about what they understood and did not understand for one assignment, how they felt about an activity, what they learned today in class, or what they like about math. Your creativity in providing suggestions will help spark theirs. For example, you might ask them to write a letter to a friend about math class or to write a poem about triangles. As writing becomes a part of math class, you can use it to assess children's knowledge of and attitudes toward mathematics. Figure 4–13 provides some sample ideas for writing prompts.

Teacher-Designed Written Tests

Tests can inform and guide your instruction, rather than simply determine grades. Students learn from tests, but too often the lessons they learn may not be those intended. When too much emphasis is placed on written tests, students can learn that they do not have to know why some procedure works, to explain how they solved a problem, or to be able to

Getting Started with Portfolios

Start small and simple
• Especially if you have many students, portfolios are a lot of work

Developing a rationale is important
• Why do you want your students to keep portfolios?
• What will you say to students and parents about your goals?

Portfolios need to be accessible
• Establish a central place in your classroom for keeping portfolios

Class time allocated for portfolio work is time well spent
• Students need guidance in labeling and choosing
• Sharing samples of student work in class is important
• Students need guidance in being reflective

A table of contents is essential

The criteria you identify for judging students' portfolios reflect your goals and values
• What categories of mathematical tasks will you require be included?
• Will you require examples of both draft and revised work?
• Will you require written reflections?
• Will you put grades on the portfolios? If so, how?

Figure 4–12 • Tips for getting started with portfolios

solve word problems, since a passing grade may be obtained without ever doing these things.

Carefully constructed and correctly analyzed tests can tell us a lot about students. For example, the children's papers in Figure 4–14 are for a simple test on subtraction of two-digit numbers, but they reveal a lot about the students. Notice how many of them missed the problems with zeros. If the first or seventh item had not been on the test, the teacher might not have realized that Jim regroups—and then ignores—even when regrouping is not necessary. (Try analyzing the kinds of errors the other students made and what characterizes each student.)

Most paper-and-pencil tests will not give you the opportunity to learn how a student arrived at an answer. One way to gain more insight is to ask the students to explain in writing what they did. If children are accustomed to explaining orally in class, then this task will be easier for them, and you will receive more meaningful explanations. Ask for explanations on a few items, and accept them in the children's

Describe an activity our class might do to help us understand how big one million really is.

Let's play teacher! You want to teach some first graders how to subtract two-digit numbers. Give examples of the problems and materials you will use. Tell what you will say and what you will have the children do.

Audrey claims that her teacher could improve the average test score in the class by 10 points if she just added 10 points to everyone's score. Kelly doesn't believe that would work. What do you think? Explain your thinking.

Which decimal is closer to one-half, 0.307 or 0.32? How do you know? Explain how you could show or prove it.

What connections are there between fractions and decimals? Explain and use examples in your explanation.

Figure 4–13 • Sample writing prompts

language. Otherwise, they will soon learn to parrot explanations that are meaningless to them.

There is no reason why paper-and-pencil tests cannot include estimation items and require manipulatives and calculators. These tests can also permit the use of textbooks or notebooks, ask thought-provoking questions, and require students to connect new learnings to previous ones. They need not be races against time in which the students regurgitate all they remember from the week or about the procedure last taught.

Thoughtful, well-constructed tests are one way—often a very efficient way—to gather information. Alone, they will not give a complete assessment of students' knowledge, but they can add one more piece to the puzzle.

Achievement Tests

At some point you will undoubtedly be asked to administer standardized or state-wide tests. The results of these tests may often be reported back too late to be applied to instruction that year, but they can be used to take a look at your students' achievement in general. For example, if you see that your students did poorly in measurement, then you need to rethink what you are doing in that area. If student test results come back very late in the year at your school, you might ask to see the results from the previous year for students in your class. Sometimes this information can provide valuable insight into what areas of study need extra work this year.

Edie

27	94	60	41	52
− 14	− 37	− 48	− 26	− 39
13	57	12	15	13

80	76	57	66	92
− 25	− 53	− 49	− 8	− 16
55	23	8	58	76

Steve

27	94	60	41	52
− 14	− 37	− 48	− 26	− 39
13	63	28	25	23

80	76	57	66	92
− 25	− 53	− 49	− 8	− 16
65	23	12	2	84

Mary Beth

27	94	60	41	52
− 14	− 37	− 48	− 26	− 39
13	57	28	25	23

80	76	57	66	92
− 25	− 53	− 49	− 8	− 16
65	23	18	58	86

Jim

27	94	60	41	52
− 14	− 37	− 48	− 26	− 39
13	67	22	25	23

80	76	87	66	92
− 25	− 53	− 49	− 8	− 16
65	23	18	518	76

Becky

27	94	60	41	52
− 14	− 37	− 48	− 26	− 39
13	58	12	15	14

7 8 9 10 11 12 13 14   9 10 11 12

80	76	57	66	92
− 25	− 53	− 49	− 8	− 16
65	23	8	60	77

59   58

30 40 50 60 70 80   58

HSM

27	94	60	41	52
− 14	− 37	− 48	− 26	− 39
13	57	28	15	13

80	76	57	66	92
− 25	− 53	− 49	− 8	− 16
65	23	8	58	76

Herbie

27	94	60	41	52
− 14	− 37	− 48	− 26	− 39
13	57	12	15	21 / 13

80	76	57	66	92
− 25	− 53	− 49	− 8	− 16
		8	68	76

Brad

27	94	60	41	52
− 14	− 37	− 48	− 26	− 39
12 / 13	56	18	14	12

80	76	57	66	92
− 25	− 53	− 49	− 8	− 16
65	23	7	57	75

Fran

27	94	60	41	52
− 14	− 37	− 48	− 26	− 39
13	57	12	67	91

80	76	57	66	92
− 25	− 53	− 49	− 8	− 16
55	29	106	8	76

Figure 4–14 • Samples of children's papers for a written test of subtraction

Remember that norm-referenced tests are designed to spread children across the whole normal distribution. There will always be 50 percent of the students below average and 50 percent above average. Thus some items on such tests are not intended for everyone at a grade level to do correctly. The fact that an item on multiplying fractions appears on a fourth-grade test does not mean that this is a recommended skill for all students at this level. Refer to your school, district, or state curriculum framework for expectations for your grade level.

Achievement tests are changing. Some allow the use of calculators, some ask questions in an open format rather than multiple choice format, some ask for explanations, and some include problem-solving situations.

If you help your students learn in a way that is meaningful to them and help build their confidence and attitude that they can do mathematics, then you will not have to worry about the results of achievement tests.

KEEPING RECORDS AND COMMUNICATING ABOUT ASSESSMENTS

It is important to keep both informal and formal records of students' learning and their disposition toward mathematics. Certain types of record-keeping may be required by your school system, but you can always keep additional records of your own.

A word of caution: do not become burdened with a multitude of records but do keep enough that you can reflect on your students' progress and can justify any major decisions about them or what to teach. The type of records you keep also will depend on the ways you report information to students, parents, and the school administration.

Recording the Information

Teachers are aware of many things about their students and keep many informal records about them.

For example, you may know from daily interactions that Treena is always willing to answer in math class, that Joshua does not work well with Katrina, that Yong knows how to compute but seems to lack understanding about when and why certain operations are used, and that Cary is often absent on math test days. But maybe you need to jar your memory about Rachel before her parents come for the next parent conference. Or maybe you are thinking about changing the composition of cooperative groups and wondering if Jerry and Richard worked well together in the past.

Because of the volume of information about students that may be useful, it is often helpful as well as necessary to record some of it. Several techniques for recording information are described here. You may find others or modify these to suit your needs.

Checklists Checklists may be used in a variety of ways to record individualized information about students' understandings, attitudes, or content achievement. They may be simply lists that are marked in different ways, rating scales, or annotated checklists (see Figures 4–15, 4–16, 4–17, and 4–18, 4–19, 4–20). The beauty of checklists is that they can

Figure 4–15
This checklist of student participation in math class activities is useful for tracking which children need to be encouraged to participate and which need to be supported in their involvement. For example, as Brenda's teacher, you would see that she has worked at the math centers and has been responsible for materials, and you could use this information as a reminder to support her interest by making her a group leader.

MATH CLASS PARTICIPATION

NAME — DATE: March	Center A	Center B	Center C	Group Leader	Group Recorder	Group Reporter	Bulletin Board	Materials	Other
Atkins, Willie	2	4	6	5	13	10	✓	✓	MCounts
Bero, Chuck	9	10	11	10	5			March	
Connel, Brenda	2	3	5			10		✓	
Cosby, Kim			2		5		✓	✓	
Coroi, Troy	11	10	9	5		13	✓	March	MCounts
Foster, Greg	12		2		10	5		✓	
Hale, Carol	2	4	6	13	5		✓	✓	
Jones, Tempie		12	13				March		
Jones, Zelda	10	9	6			5		March	
McGee, Leslie	6	4		5	13		march	✓	
Mory, Kelly	11		12	13	10		✓		
Navarro, Sarita		10	4	10			✓	march	
Nelson, Clara	5	6	2			5	March	✓	
Odom, Ruby			2	5		13		✓	
Pak, Yong	12	11	10	13				march	
Porter, Jessie		5		10	5		March		
Roy, Lulu	10		12			10			
Stewart, Scott		2				5	✓		
Tucker, Enoka	11		3	5	13		March		MCounts
Watt, Mary Lee	10	2	3		5	10		March	
Weaver, J. T.	12	2	5	10				✓	
White, Emma	3		5	13	10			✓	MCounts
Wortaszek, Sam	4	10	3		10	5	March		
Yi, Sik			11	10					
Zuber, Albert		11				10			

Figure 4–16
This annotated checklist is useful for recording classroom observations as well as actions the teacher took when necessary. Such checklists are also useful for providing reminders of points to discuss when communicating with parents and students.

CLASS OBSERVATION Class _5th period_		ACTION	
NAMES	COMMENTS	NEEDED	TAKEN
Atkins, Willie			
Bero, Chuck	Needs a challenge	✳	Yes
Connel, Brenda			
Cosby, Kim	No homework for 3 days	✳	Called
Coroi, Troy			
Foster, Greg			
Hale, Carol	Doing much better with fractions – fraction bars helped		
Jones, Tempie			
Jones, Zelda	What a difference in geometry – good spatial sense		
McGee, Leslie			
Mory, Kelly			
Navarro, Sarita			
Nelson, Clara	Wants to be on math team next year – mother says yes ✳		Called mother
Odom, Ruby			
Pak, Yong			
Porter, Jessie	Spend some time with Jessie – he can do this		
Roy, Lulu			
Stewart, Scott	Is beginning to work well in a group		
Tucker, Enoka			
Watt, Mary Lee			
Weaver, J. T.			
White, Emma			
Wortaszek, Sam			
Yi, Sik	Loves group work – helps with language		
Zuber, Albert			

Week _Feb. 6-10/13-17_

Figure 4–17
This annotated checklist is used to record the teacher's observations of group work. Notes such as these can help the teacher in assessing group interactions and to make decisions on how to group students for future work.

GROUP OBSERVATION	DATE	TASK	COMMENTS	DATE	TASK	COMMENTS
GROUP A	1/18	Problem:	Group worked well			
John		Quarter	together – would not			
Caryl		Change	stop until they had all			
Luther			the possibilities			
Jara						
GROUP B						
Todd						Need to observe!
Kate						
David						
Cathy						
GROUP C	1/18	Problem:		1/22	Data	
Tamia		Quarter	Need to watch, that			Brandi made a real effort
Larry		Change	Brandi doesn't take			to obtain the ideas from
Maude			over – talk with her –			others – they arrived at
Brandi			give some questions to ask			a neat different question
GROUP D		Data:				
Otis		What's	Chose TV programs –			
Sandra		My	finally focused on			
Gloria		Favorite?	G-4 – were on task			
Chon ho						
GROUP E	1/22	Data:		1/24	Same	
Renea		Favorite	Could not agree on			
Lisa			topic – all wanted			
Tamio			their own			
Gary						

Figure 4–18
This checklist of student dispositions is helpful in determining which students might need special activities or encouragement to help boost their confidence or perseverance in problem solving, for example. It can also be used for support in parent conferences or in discussions with students.

STUDENT DISPOSITIONS	Helen	Art	Whit	Beverly	Anita	Jim
CLASS: 3rd Grade Math MONTH: October						

Confidence
  Is sure of answer
  Knows how to proceed
	✓
	✓
				✓
				✓		

Flexibility
  Will change direction
  Tries several ways
	If prodded ✓		✓
			✓
					✓	

Perseverance
  Stays with task
  Enjoys involved problems
	✓	✓		✓		

Curiosity
  Wants to find out why
  Challenges
		✓	✓	✓		✓

Sharing
  Works well with others
  Shows leadership
		✓		✓		✓

Student Profile in Mathematics K–4

Date Feb.

Student Jeremy Gelder   Teacher Matt Bell   Grade 2

Content Areas
Number Sense & Numeration   Still sees numbers as ones – needs to develop place value
Estimation   Good feel for numbers – size of quantities
Concepts of Operations   Good problem solver
Computation
Geometry & Spatial Sense   Geometry he loves
Measurement
Statistics & Probability
Fractions & Decimals
Patterns & Relationships   Better at spatial patterns

Math Power
Problem Solving   Likes to think in creative ways
Reasoning
Communication   Explains well
Connections
Concepts   Developing
Procedures   Doesn't like to follow procedures – invents his own

Dispositions
Confidence   Growing
Flexibility
Perseverance   On many tasks
Curiosity   Great
Reflection

Other Comments

Figure 4–19 • Student profile

I can draw these shapes ☐ yes ☐ not yet	I recognize patterns ☐ yes ☐ not yet	I can sort ☐ yes ☐ not yet	I can count ___ objects ☐ yes ☐ not yet
I can count by 1's (to 127) ☐ yes ☐ not yet	I can count by 2's (to 106) ☐ yes ☐ not yet	I can count by 5's (to 125) ☐ yes ☐ not yet	I can count by 10's (to 120) ☐ yes ☐ not yet
I can read a graph ☐ yes ☐ not yet	I can match sets ☐ yes ☐ not yet	I can make a pattern ☐ yes ☐ not yet	I can make a graph ☐ yes ☐ not yet
I can do addition to 10 ☐ yes ☐ not yet	I can do subtraction from 10 ☐ yes ☐ not yet	I can give number sentences ☐ yes ☐ not yet	I can recognize and count money ☐ yes ☐ not yet
I can read and use the calendar ☐ yes ☐ not yet	I can tell time ☐ yes ☐ not yet	I can write number sentences ☐ yes ☐ not yet	I can recognize numbers 0-20 ☐ yes ☐ not yet
I can build a double digit number ☐ yes ☐ not yet	I can build a triple digit number ☐ yes ☐ not yet	I know and use > and < signs ☐ yes ☐ not yet	I can recognize random 2 digit numbers ☐ yes ☐ not yet

Figure 4–20 • **Primary development checklist** (Reprinted with permission of the McGraw-Hill Companies from "The Whole Language Catalog: Forms for Authentic Assessment," p. 3, by Lois Bridges Bird, Kenneth S. Goodman, and Yetta M. Goodman, copyright 1994 by SRA. All rights reserved.)

be adapted to your situation and, in fact, may help you think about your goals and the needs of each child you are teaching.

You cannot spend all your time keeping records, so select a few significant aspects of students' learning and attitudes and target a few children each day. For example, you may want to observe and keep records about children working in cooperative groups one week and focus on individual children's understanding of a new topic the next week.

If you use a checklist, you will want to keep it handy so that you can make quick entries as children are engaged in tasks. If you wait until the end of the day, you may forget some of the day's gems or be too preoccupied with other tasks to jot them down.

If you are recording information that is meant only for you, keep the checklist away from the eyes of your students. Be especially sensitive to children's feelings. A public checklist that shows the progress of each class member's skill attainment may be a great boost for those at the top but quite detrimental to those at the bottom, who often need the most encouragement.

Student Files Many teachers keep a record of students' learning in the form of a file of work samples from each. If children are keeping their own portfolios, those may suffice and you will not need to keep additional samples of their work in your own student files. In either case, you may want to keep a summary profile for each child, like the one shown in Figure 4–19. Sometimes the school's format for reporting to parents will require that you keep such a record.

Class Records Often the only class record is the grade book. Although it may be necessary to keep such a record, you must realize the limitations of a grade book. Alternatively, you could modify it with shorthand entries of your choosing to tell you more than attendance; grades on assignments, quizzes, and tests; and cumulative grades.

You could also supplement the grade book with a cumulative checklist made from your daily or weekly checklists. You can determine which items to include by reviewing the usefulness and frequency of your entries in these earlier checklists. The cumulative checklist will then give you a picture of the class as a whole and help you plan.

Communicating the Information

Most teachers have three main audiences to whom the information they have gathered will be communicated. Each group—students, parents, and administration—will receive different amounts of information in different ways.

To Students Much of your communicating of information to students will be done orally or through actions, but also you will be writing comments on work samples, portfolios, tests, journals, or other forms of assessment materials. And, perhaps, you will give a letter or number grade. All these communications influence children's feelings about the value of different aspects of mathematics, their expectations of what they can accomplish, and their sense of their own worth.

Be positive and fair. Use information from your checklists or from student portfolios when letting each student know whether he or she is meeting expectations, and look for ways to demonstrate to each that he or she can do what is expected. Finally, remember that it is important that children grow in their ability to self-assess. One of your goals should be to help children become independent learners. If they always have to rely on you to validate their work and their thinking, they will not reach this goal.

To Parents You will be reporting to parents both in written form and orally. The format of these reports is often determined by the school system, but you are responsible for the quality. You will grow in your ability to communicate with parents, but it is important from the beginning that you keep records and use them to illustrate or justify your oral and written comments. Phone calls can be useful for immediate feedback to parents not only when there is a problem, but also to applaud good behavior or outstanding achievement. Parents and children are often surprised and gratified when a teacher calls home to report something good. Some teachers try to make "good" calls home to all students early in the year. This practice can set up good relationships with parents and establish the expectation that a teacher phone call need not necessarily mean bad news. Some teachers use regular newsletters to keep parents informed about classroom activities and goals or letters to parents to tell them about special events or request their help. (Figure 4–21 shows a letter one teacher sent to parents to enlist their assistance in developing and maintaining their children's math portfolios.)

At parent conferences, you have an opportunity to explain goals for your instruction and to enlist parents' aid in helping their child meet those goals. It is helpful if you have collected a wide variety of samples of student work to share with the parents as you talk about their child's progress. Parent conferences are also times for gathering information. Parents often provide insights about their children that may not be evident to you in the classroom. The information you glean from them should be included in notes in your student files.

To the School Administration When you begin teaching, you will need to find out what type of

Dear Parents,

Your child will be developing a "portfolio" in math class this year. One of the primary purposes of this project is to allow students the opportunity to reflect on their work, including exemplary work, work that is considered a "personal best," or work that they feel is in some way memorable. Through this project, students can begin to develop critical self-evaluative tools that will be extremely valuable in the years ahead.

A second purpose of the portfolio project is to allow students to share some of their work with you. Please take some time this week to discuss your child's portfolio with him or her. Your child has been given written guidelines for the portfolio project. Please review the guidelines together.

Please help your child this week as he or she finalizes selections for the portfolio. There is no set number of pieces required, but a selection of 5 or 6 pieces is suggested. Help your child select pieces that *best* meet the guidelines and that are *most* representative of the major math content areas that we have covered during this grading period. The attached "news bulletin" from this grading period may provide you with a better idea of the topics your child has studied and the activities he or she has participated in. Students have been asked to provide written accounts about *why* they chose particular pieces for their portfolios, so be sure to talk with your child about why he or she is choosing each piece for inclusion in the portfolio. (If you wish, you too may include some written comments about the pieces selected or the selection process.)

After you have read the news bulletin and have helped your child with his or her portfolio selections, please sign and detach the form below. Your child is to return the signed form, along with his or her portfolio by Friday, November 15.

Thank you for helping to make your child's mathematical experience a memorable one!

Sincerely,

_____

I have read and discussed the "News Bulletin" with my child and have helped him or her select choice pieces for his or her portfolio. _____

Figure 4–21 • Letter to parents about math portfolios

records and grades are required in your school and how they are used.

- What sort of report card format is used (A/B/C letter grades? S/I/N (satisfactory, improving, needs improvement) progress indicators? Numeric grades? Narrative reports?)
- Does the administration expect written reports on each child?
- Is there an official checklist?
- Is the class grade record sufficient?
- Is information on students passed to the next teacher, kept in a permanent file, or used to make tracking decisions?
- Is the information used in teacher evaluations?

The type and use of records vary from school to school, so it is necessary to find out about your own situation. When you know how the records are to be used, you will be better able to provide information that is suitable for particular uses.

A Glance at Where We've Been

Assessment is an integral part of teaching. This chapter looks at student assessment to help you make informed decisions about instruction, monitoring student progress, and evaluating student achievement. There are many ways to gather, analyze, and present the information from assessments.

The different ways to gather information range from informal observations to formal achievement tests. Collecting information about students' learning is only one goal. The other is to collect information regarding their dispositions toward mathematics. Information needs to be recorded in some way so you can analyze it. There are numerous techniques for recording and communicating information. Portfolios, in particular, can provide a broad and useful picture of student progress.

Assessment can make a difference in how you help your students learn mathematics. You can use it in a positive way to encourage the children to become independent learners, to modify your instruction, and to communicate with parents.

Things to Do: From What You've Read

1. Make a list of as many assessment-related concepts and terms as you can think of (for example, achievement, portfolio, observation, conference, test). Draw a concept map to show how these ideas are related to one another in your mind. (The concept map on assessment that opens this chapter was drawn by a sixth grade teacher who had been giving a lot of thought to changing assessment practices in her classroom.)

2. Describe the four different purposes of assessment and their results.

3. What recommendations for shifts in assessment (Table 4–1) are most closely connected to the classroom? How are they connected?

4. A narrow view is that assessment in mathematics focuses on how well students can carry out procedures in a limited amount of time. Describe a broader view of mathematics assessment.

5. Identify an error pattern in the work of at least four of the students in Figure 4–9.

6. Write a "letter to self" similar to that shown in Figure 4–8. In your letter you should reflect upon your current strengths and weaknesses, as well as your future goals, as a teacher of elementary school mathematics.

7. What records could you keep to assist with a parent-teacher conference? What other ways can you communicate with parents about their child's progress?

8. List three ideas for keeping records of your observations of students as they work during class.

Things to Do: Going Beyond This Book

field Additional activities, suggestions, and questions are provided in *Teaching Elementary Mathematics: A Resource for Field Experiences.*

1. Watch the videotape *A Look at Children's Thinking* (Richardson 1990) or a similar video on interviewing students. Describe what you learned from the students and the interviewer.

2. Read one of the articles on interviewing listed in the Selected References. Design an interview and use it with three students. Describe what you learned about each student.

3. *field* *Scoring Problem Solving.* Collect a set of problem-solving papers from students. Analyze and score them using the analytic scale in Figure 4–10.

4. Develop a test that involves the use of manipulatives.

5. Analyze a test in an elementary mathematics textbook. Would it make a difference if the students used calculators? What items would you need to change?

6. Analyze a test in an elementary mathematics textbook to determine whether it requires writing about mathematics. If not, what changes could you make so that it would do so?

7. *field* *Observing Students in Class.* Observe one or two students during a mathematics class. Describe what you observed. If you were to work with these students in mathematics, what course of action would you take?

8. *field* *Trying a Performance Task.* Try a performance task with a couple of students. Make a list of observations and use it as the basis for your description of the children's performance. You may find samples in *Measuring Up: Prototypes for Mathematics Assessment* (Mathematical Sciences Education Board 1993).

9. Examine a standardized test. Does it allow use of calculators? Identify examples of good and poor questions, and explain your opinions.

10. Many teachers use cooperative learning methods during instruction but face the problem of aligning assessment techniques with that instruction. Read the article by Kroll et al. (1992), which describes methods to include cooperative problem solving in assessment and offers suggestions for choosing appropriate problems and incorporating aspects of both individual and group grading. Identify a math problem that you think would be useful as a group problem-solving assessment and design a rubric for scoring student work on it, adapting Kroll et al.'s suggestions.

11. **field** *How Teachers Grade.* Talk to one or more classroom teachers about how they grade their students in math. Ask what sorts of tasks are figured into the grade and how they are weighted. Ask to see the teacher's gradebook so you can understand what sorts of records it includes. Find out what other records the teacher keeps (folders, portfolios, notes, etc.).

Selected References

Ann Arbor Public Schools. *Alternative Assessment: Evaluating Student Performance in Elementary Mathematics.* Palo Alto, Calif.: Dale Seymour Publications, 1993.

Badger, Elizabeth. "More than Testing." *Arithmetic Teacher,* 39 (May 1992), pp. 7–11.

Beyer, Ann. "Assessing Students' Performance: Using Observations, Reflections, and Other Methods." In *Assessment in the Mathematics Classroom,* 1993 Yearbook (ed. Norman Webb). Reston, Va.: NCTM, 1993.

Bird, Lois Bridges; Goodman, Kenneth S.; and Goodman, Yetta M. *The Whole Language Catalog: Forms for Authentic Assessment.* New York: SRA, 1994.

Burns, Marilyn. "The Role of Questioning." *Arithmetic Teacher,* 32 (February 1985), pp. 14–16.

California Mathematics Council. *Assessment Alternatives in Mathematics: An Overview of Assessment Techniques That Promote Learning.* Berkeley, Calif.: EQUALS, 1989.

Chambers, Donald L. "Improving Instruction by Listening to Children." *Teaching Children Mathematics,* 1 (February 1995), pp. 378–380.

Charles, Randall; Lester, Frank; and O'Daffer, Phares. *How to Evaluate Progress in Problem Solving.* Reston, Va.: NCTM, 1987.

Clark, H. Clifford, and Nelson, Marvin N. "Evaluation: Be More Than a Scorekeeper." *Arithmetic Teacher,* 38 (May 1991), pp. 15–17.

Clarke, David J. "Activating Assessment Alternatives in Mathematics." *Arithmetic Teacher,* 39 (February 1992), pp. 24–29.

Clarke, David J.; Clarke, Doug M.; and Lovitt, Charles J. "Changes in Mathematics Teaching Call for Assessment Alternatives." In *Teaching and Learning Mathematics in the 1990s,* 1990 Yearbook (ed. Thomas J. Cooney). Reston, Va.: NCTM, 1990.

Collinson, Judith. "Using Performance Assessment to Determine Mathematical Dispositions." *Arithmetic Teacher,* 39 (February 1992), pp. 40–47.

Cross, Lee, and Hynes, Michael C. "Assessing Mathematics Learning for Students with Learning Differences." *Arithmetic Teacher,* 41 (March 1994), pp. 371–377.

Garafalo, Joe, and Bryant, Jerry. "Assessing Reasonableness: Some Observations and Suggestions." *Arithmetic Teacher,* 40 (December 1992), pp. 210–212.

Garnett, Cynthia M. "Testing—Do Not Disturb? A Parent's View of Testing." *Arithmetic Teacher,* 39 (February 1992), pp. 8–10.

Harvey, John G. "Using Calculators in Mathematics Changes Testing." *Arithmetic Teacher,* 38 (March 1991), pp. 52–54.

Juster, Norton. *The Phantom Tollbooth.* New York: Random House, 1993.

Kamii, Constance, and Lewis, Barbara Ann. "Achievement Tests in Primary Mathematics: Perpetuating Lower-Order Thinking." *Arithmetic Teacher,* 38 (May 1991), pp. 4–9.

Kenney, Patricia Ann, and Silver, Edward A. "Student Self-Assessment in Mathematics." In *Assessment in the Mathe-matics Classroom,* 1993 Yearbook (ed. Norman Webb). Reston, Va.: NCTM, 1993.

Kroll, Diana L.; Masingila, Joanna O.; and Mau, Sue Tinsley. "Cooperative Problem Solving: But What about Grading?" *Arithmetic Teacher,* 39 (February 1992), pp. 17–23.

Kuhs, Therese M. *Measure for Measure: Using Portfolios in K-8 Mathematics.* Portsmouth, N.H.: Heinemann, 1997.

Labinowicz, Ed. *Learning from Children: New Beginnings for Teaching Numerical Thinking.* Menlo Park, Calif.: Addison-Wesley, 1985.

Labinowicz, Ed. "Assessing for Learning: The Interview Method." *Arithmetic Teacher,* 35 (November 1987), pp. 22–25.

Lambdin, Diana V., and Walker, Vicki L. "Planning for Classroom Portfolio Assessment." *Arithmetic Teacher,* 41 (February 1994), pp. 318–324.

Lambdin, Diana V.; Kehle, Paul E.; and Preston, Ronald V. *Emphasis on Assessment: Readings from NCTM's School-Based Journals.* Reston, Va.: NCTM, 1996.

Lester, Frank, and Kroll, Diana L. "Assessing Student Growth in Mathematical Problem Solving." In *Assessing Higher Order Thinking in Mathematics* (ed. Gerald Kulm). Washington, D.C.: American Association for the Advancement of Science, 1990.

Lindquist, Mary M. "Assessing through Questioning." *Arithmetic Teacher,* 35 (January 1988), pp. 16–18.

Long, Madeleine J., and Ben-Hur, Meir. "Informing Learning through the Clinical Interview." *Arithmetic Teacher,* 38 (February, 991), pp. 44–46.

Mathematical Sciences Education Board. *Measuring Up: Prototypes for Mathematics Assessment.* Washington, D.C.: National Academy Press, 1993.

Mathematical Sciences Education Board. *Measuring What Counts: A Conceptual Guide for Mathematics Assessment.* Washington, D.C.: National Academy Press, 1993.

Moon, C. Jean. "Connecting Learning and Teaching through Assessment." *Arithmetic Teacher,* 41 (September 1993), pp. 13–15.

Mumme, Judy. *Portfolio Assessment in Mathematics.* Santa Barbara, Calif.: Regents of the University of California, 1990.

Mumme, Judith, and Shepherd, Nancy. "Implementing the *Standards:* Communication in Mathematics." *Arithmetic Teacher,* 38 (September 1990), pp. 18–22.

National Council of Teachers of Mathematics. *Curriculum and Evaluation Standards for School Mathematics.* Reston, Va.: NCTM, 1989.

National Council of Teachers of Mathematics. *Professional Standards for Teachers of Mathematics.* Reston, Va.: NCTM, 1991.

National Council of Teachers of Mathematics. *Assessment Standards for School Mathematics.* Reston, Va.: NCTM, 1995.

National Council of Teachers of Mathematics. *Principles and Standards for School Mathematics.* Reston, Va.: NCTM, 2000.

Paulson, F. Leon; Paulson, Pearl R.; and Meyer, Carol A. "What Makes a Portfolio a Portfolio?" *Educational Leadership,* 48 (February 1991), pp. 60–63.

Peck, Donald M.; Jencks, Stanley M.; and Connell, Michael L. "Improving Instruction through Brief Interviews." *Arithmetic Teacher,* 37 (November 1989), pp. 15–17.

Richardson, Kathy. "Assessing Understanding." *Arithmetic Teacher,* 35 (February 1988), pp. 39–41.

Richardson, Kathy. *A Look at Children's Thinking. Assessment Videos for K-2 Mathematics.* Norman, Okla.: Educational Enrichment, 1990.

Robinson, G. Edith. "Assessing for Learning: The Purposes of Testing." *Arithmetic Teacher,* 35 (September 1987), p. 33.

Ross, Rita, and Kurtz, Ray. "Making Manipulatives Work: A Strategy for Success." *Arithmetic Teacher,* 40 (January 1993).

Sanford, Susan. "Assessing Measurement in the Primary Classroom." In *Assessment in the Mathematics Classroom,* 1993 Yearbook (ed. Norman Webb). Reston, Va.: NCTM, 1993.

Sgroi, Laura A.; Gropper, Nancy; Kilker, Mary Tom; Rambusch, Nancy M.; and Semonite, Barbara. "Assessing Young Children's Mathematical Understandings." *Teaching Children Mathematics,* 1 (January 1995), pp. 275–277.

Smith, Jacque. "Assessing Children's Reasoning: It's an Age-Old Problem." *Teaching Children Mathematics,* 1 (May 1996), pp. 524–528.

Spangler, Denise A. "Assessing Students' Beliefs about Mathematics." *Arithmetic Teacher,* 40 (November 1992), pp. 148–152.

Stenmark, Jean K. (ed.). *Mathematics Assessment: Myths, Models, Good Questions, and Practical Suggestions.* Reston, Va.: NCTM, 1991.

Sullivan, Peter, and Clarke, David. "Catering to All Abilities through 'Good Questions.'" *Arithmetic Teacher,* 39 (October 1991), pp. 14–18.

Trafton, Paul. "Assessing for Learning: Tests—A Tool for Improving Instruction." *Arithmetic Teacher,* 35 (December 1987), pp. 17–18.

Vaac, Nancy Nesbitt. "Implement the *Professional Standards for Teaching Mathematics:* Questioning in the Mathematics Classroom." *Arithmetic Teacher,* 41 (October 1993), pp. 88–91.

Weaver, J. Fred. "Big Dividends from Small Interviews." *Arithmetic Teacher,* 2 (April 1955), pp. 40–47.

Webb, Norman (ed.). *Assessment in the Mathematics Classroom,* 1993 Yearbook. Reston, Va.: NCTM, 1993.

Zawojewski, Judith. "Polishing a Data Task: Seeking Better Assessment." *Teaching Children Mathematics,* 1 (February 1996), pp. 372–378.

Zawojewski, Judith, and Lesh, Richard. "Scores and Grades: What Are the Problems? What Are the Alternatives." *Teaching Children Mathematics,* 1 (May 1996), pp. 776–779.

5 ▶ *Five Mathematical Processes*

▶ Snapshot of a Classroom Investigation

Rebecca is a second grader in a colorful, lively, multi-age classroom. The desks are arranged in groups of four, although the children typically spend a good portion of each day working at various learning centers around the perimeter of the classroom—an art center, a pet center, and a reading corner with a cozy rug and comfy pillows. Similarly, a significant amount of time is spent on mathematical problem solving. Rebecca and her classmates are often actively engaged in hands-on, investigative activities, many of which grow out of questions that they themselves bring up.

One day Rebecca was proudly showing her new size 2 sports shoes to everyone. When she was chatting with Marisa, she noticed that they were approximately the same height. "You're just about the same size as me," she observed, "What size shoe do you wear?" "Two," Marisa responded. "So do I!" said Rebecca, "I wonder if people who are the same size have the same shoe size?"

Rebecca and Marisa ran to share this thought with their teacher. They were very familiar with posing questions and figuring out how to investigate them. They were eager to poll their classmates to see whether their idea about shoes and heights was right. Rebecca designed a recording sheet by borrowing a class list from the teacher and copying everyone's name onto the page. She drew two boxes next to each name, one for height and the other for shoe size.

Marisa and Rebecca recruited Tyler to help them go around the classroom asking people about their shoe sizes and their heights. Rebecca was the recorder. It wasn't hard to figure out shoe sizes because if a person didn't know, they just took off their

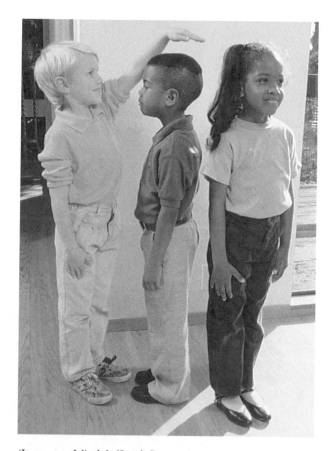

(Lawrence Migdale/Stock Boston.)

shoe and looked inside. But very few of the children knew how tall they were, so most of the boxes for height had to be left blank.

Rebecca, Marisa, and Tyler sat on the floor by the reading corner and looked at their data. "Hey, you know what? I just thought of something." said Tyler. "I was thinking about who is big and who is small in our class, even if we don't really know exactly how big they are. Some of the biggest kids in the class have shoe sizes that are smaller than some of the smaller kids. Something doesn't make sense here!"

"Who do you mean?" asked Marisa.

"Well, Sammy is one of the biggest kids, but he only wears size 3. Jenna wears size 12, but she's smaller than Sammy," said Tyler.

"Maybe boys' and girls' shoes come in different sizes," Rebecca mused.

Even Mrs. Lester didn't know for sure if that was true, but this idea led Rebecca, Marisa, and Tyler to try comparing the heights and shoe sizes of girls and boys separately.

Marisa made a new recording sheet. She wrote boys' names on the left and girls' names on the right and put shoe sizes next to the names. She and Rebecca looked on the list for two girls or two boys with the same shoe sizes. She planned to asked them to stand back to back to see whether they were the same height. The students had decided that they didn't have to bother with finding a way to measure heights because they could just compare people directly. (Note that they were now investigating a new statement—if you have the same shoe size, then you are the same height—rather than the converse—if

you're the same height, you have the same shoe size—which they had started out with.)

Chip and Frank had the same shoe size on the chart, so Rebecca drew a line to connect those two names. But when Chip and Frank stood back to back, they were not the same size. Rebecca decided to note this by scribbling over the arrow connecting their names. Rebecca also connected Gavin's and Jake's names with a scribbly line because they were different heights, even though they wore the same size shoes. She used smooth lines to mark pairs of students who matched both in shoe size and in height.

Rebecca, Marisa, and Tyler were *doing mathematics*. They were involved in observing apparent patterns and regularities, formulating conjectures, gathering data, talking with their peers and with their teacher about their ideas, and inventing ways to represent their findings. Their work involved the fundamental mathematical processes that this chapter is all about: problem solving, reasoning and proof, communication, connections, and representations.

(This Shapshot of a Lesson is adapted from a true story in *Mathematics in the Making* by Heidi Mills, Timothy O'Keefe, and David Whitin, 1996).

Introduction

As we have seen in earlier chapters, school mathematics is moving in new directions. In many mathematics classrooms today it is rare for a lesson to consist primarily of rows of children studiously bent over worksheets, practicing computations, rules, and formulas. Instead, it is more common to observe children first working in small groups while talking and using tiles or blocks to model a problem, then moving to their desks to write individually about what they have discovered, and finally engaging in a whole class discussion about what has been learned. The students are encouraged to share their ideas, observations, and problem-solving processes. They listen carefully to each other and they challenge and question each other. "Doing mathematics" means being actively involved in a wide variety of physical and mental actions—actions that can be described by verbs such as *exploring, investigating, patterning, experimenting, modeling, conjecturing,* and *verifying*.

Principles and Standards for School Mathematics (NCTM 2000) highlight this active vision of learning and doing mathematics by identifying the five "process" standards listed in Table 5–1 (problem

solving, reasoning and proof, communication, connections, and representations).

These process standards share equal billing with the five "content" standards (number, algebra, geometry, measurement, and data). The NCTM Standards make it very clear that "doing mathematics" means engaging in these fundamental processes. This chapter provides a brief introduction to these five important processes for doing mathematics, with special attention to problem solving as a foundation on which the entire mathematics curriculum can be organized.

THE FIVE MATHEMATICAL PROCESSES

Problem Solving

What comes to mind when you think of problem solving? Some people think of challenging situations they may have encountered in real life, such as when their car got stuck in a snow bank, but they were able to get it out by putting floor mats under the wheels to provide greater traction. When you think of problem solving in the mathematics

Table 5–1 • **Process standards for school mathematics**

Problem Solving	Instructional programs from prekindergarten through grade 12 should enable students to: • build new mathematical knowledge through problem solving • solve problems that arise in mathematics and in other contexts • apply and adapt a variety of appropriate strategies to solve problems • monitor and reflect on the process of mathematical problem solving
Reasoning and Proof	Instructional programs from prekindergarten through grade 12 should enable students to: • recognize reasoning and proof as fundamental aspects of mathematics • make and investigate mathematical conjectures • develop and evaluate mathematical arguments and proofs • select and use various types of reasoning and methods of proof
Communication	Instructional programs from prekindergarten through grade 12 should enable students to: • organize and consolidate their mathematical thinking through communication • communicate their mathematical thinking coherently and clearly to peers, teachers, and others • analyze and evaluate the mathematical thinking and strategies of others • use the language of mathematics to express mathematical ideas precisely
Connections	Instructional programs from prekindergarten through grade 12 should enable students to: • recognize and use connections among mathematical ideas • understand how mathematical ideas interconnect and build on one another to produce a coherent whole • recognize and apply mathematics in contexts outside of mathematics
Representations	Instructional programs from prekindergarten through grade 12 should enable students to: • create and use representations to organize, record, and communicate mathematical ideas • select, apply, and translate among mathematical representations to solve problems • use representations to model and interpret physical, social, and mathematical phenomena

Reprinted with permission from "Principles and Standards for School Mathematics," p. 52, 56, 60, 64, 67, copyright 2000 by the National Council of Teachers of Mathematics. All rights reserved.

classroom, you may think of similarly challenging situations involving numbers or shapes or patterns. For example, a state may need to figure out how many distinct license plates can be produced if each must be printed with a unique identifier consisting of exactly six characters. Maybe the characters may be chosen only from among the ten numeric digits (0–9) and twenty-five of the twenty-six letters of the alphabet (with the letter *o* excluded because it can be confused with the numeral zero). How many different license plates are possible? That's a problem!

Alternatively, when you think of mathematical problem solving you may conjure up images of the "story problems" that often came at the end of each chapter of the mathematics text when you were in elementary school. After you had learned to perform certain computations (say, multiplication of fractions), your text may have provided problems in context that used those very same skills. In many cases, these may not have been genuine "problems" because the techniques to use had been clearly outlined in the preceding pages. Problem solving, as envisioned by the NCTM Standards, is much more than just finding answers to lists of exercises. By general agreement, a problem is a situation in which a person wants something and does not know immediately what to do to get it. Problem solving is the foundation of all mathematical activity. As such, problem solving should play a prominent role in the elementary school mathematics curriculum.

Let's consider another problem, actually a game that you can play with one or more opponents. You'll need two dice, twelve small chips or tiles or markers each, and a piece of paper on which to make a game board for each person (see In the Classroom 5–1).

Place your chips on the game board, putting as many or as few as you like on each of the twelve numbered spaces. (For example, you might choose to put all your chips on your favorite number, 4, or one chip on each space, or two chips on each of the even spaces and leave all the odd spaces empty. It's your decision.) Roll the dice. Say you get 3 and 5. Find the sum (3 + 5 = 8). If you have any chips on the 8 space, you may remove one of them. When anyone rolls, everyone plays, so your opponents also should be removing a chip from the 8 space on their boards, if they can. Roll the dice again and sum the results. The goal of the game is to be the first person to remove all your chips from your board. Try the game a couple of times before reading on.

Here's the problem: find a good strategy for placing your chips at the start of this game, so that you are likely to be able to clear your board as quickly as possible. Which squares are good to avoid? Are there certain sums that rarely (or never) came up when you rolled the pair of dice? Why? Which squares are good to put chips on? Are there certain sums that came up rather often? Why? Can you explain why some sums are more likely than others? A fourth-grade class played this game several times, worked on the problem of finding a useful game strategy, talked about what they discovered, and then wrote about their findings. See Figure 5–1 for what some of the children wrote.

In a classroom where mathematics is taught through problem solving, students given the challenge of the dice game might already have had previous experiences with making organized lists or making tables. Nevertheless, their teacher would *not* have provided them with advice about exactly how

In The Classroom 5–1

Rolling the Dice

Objective: Using a dice game to investigate experimental and theoretical probabilities and to develop logical reasoning skills.

Materials: Twelve counters or chips for each player, one pair of dice for each four players.

Rules of the Game

Up to four players can play together with one pair of dice. Each player has his/her own game board. You begin by placing all twelve of your counters on your game board. The game board has twelve spaces numbered 1–12. You may place as many counters as you choose (from 0 to 12) on each space. You may leave spaces blank, and you may put one or more than one counter on any space.

Players take turns rolling the dice. The first player rolls the two dice and finds their sum. (For example, if 2 and 3 are rolled, the sum is 5.) Each player may remove one counter from his or her 5 space. Even if there is more than one counter on that space, only one may be removed. If there are no counters on that space, no counters may be removed from any space. The next player rolls the two dice and finds their sum (for example, 4 + 4 = 8). Each player now removes one counter from his/her 8 space, and so on. The goal of the game is to empty your board. The first player with no counters left on his/her board is the winner.

Analyzing the Game

When you have played several times, talk with each other about these questions:

- Which sums were rolled most often?
- Which sums were never rolled, or not rolled very often?
- Why do you think some sums came up more often than others?
- Can you prove which sums are most likely to occur?
- What do you think is a good strategy for placing your counters on the game board? Why?

Writing about the Game

Write advice to a friend who is new to the game. Tell him or her your favorite strategy for placing counters on the game board, and explain why you believe this strategy is a good one.

Rolling the Dice Game Board

What I learned was that when playing with two dice your best odds are with seven. And when you see a pattern, go with it sometimes, not all the time.

If you bett on something you allways bett on a seven. Never on a one, tow, three, four, five, six, eight, nine, ten, elven, or trelv.

That number seven is the best number to beat on not to [two] or twelve if you go to a cuceno [casino] you should no [know] that.

Figure 5–1 • Fourth-grade students' writing about playing the dice game

to solve the problem if he or she wanted this to be a true problem-solving challenge. A reasonable approach is to begin experimenting by playing a few games. It is helpful to keep a list of the sums obtained when the dice are rolled. If you don't keep a list, it may be hard to be sure which sums came up more often than others. Haphazard experimentation is not likely to produce a good, well-justified solution. Solving this problem requires students to think logically and to make some important decisions, particularly about how to keep track in a systematic way of the sums that come up. (Perhaps even better is keeping track of the pairs of dice that lead to those sums; writing down $5 + 2 = 7$ is more informative than just writing 7, since 7 could be obtained in a number of different ways.)

When you roll two dice, you are much more likely to roll a sum of 7 than a sum of 3, since there are only two ways to get 3 ($1 + 2$ and $2 + 1$), but there

are many more ways to get 7. A skill such as making an organized list or a table can be useful in a wide variety of problem situations. As this problem helps develop general problem-solving expertise, it also deepens students' understanding of probability (helping them to recognize that we can compare the likelihood of rolling various sums by seeing how many ways those sums can be formed). The probability of rolling a 7 is actually $\frac{6}{36}$, whereas the probability of rolling a 3 is only $\frac{2}{36}$ (refer to Figure 5–2 to see two ways of representing the 36 different possible sums: $1 + 1$, $1 + 2$, . . . all the way up to $6 + 6$). Students who work on this problem are learning about probability *through* problem solving.

What kinds of problems are appropriate for elementary school students? In the early grades, most school mathematics problems are related in some way to the children's own experiences because their world is relatively circumscribed and children relate best to concrete situations. By upper elementary, however, the universe of problem contexts should diversify. Increasingly, problems can grow out of situations in the world at large or from the investigation of mathematical ideas. Mathematics instruction in the upper grades can take advantage of the increasing sophistication of students and their growing knowledge of such topics as probability, statistics, and geometry. Upper elementary students can deal with messier and more complex problems than primary children can, not only because they are more capable and confident in working with mathematical ideas than younger children but also because they can use technology to alleviate much of the drudgery that—until very recently—often constrained school mathematics to considering problems with "nice numbers." Computers, calculators, and electronic data gathering devices such as calculator-based laboratories (CBLs) and calculator-based rangers (CBRs) provide simple methods for gathering and analyzing data that in years past might have been considered too much trouble to deal with. Similarly, classroom Internet connections make it possible for students to look up facts and figures quickly and easily for use in posing and solving a wide variety of real-world problems. Graphing calculators and easy-to-use computer software enable students to move effortlessly between different representations of problem data and to compute with large quantities of data and with messy numbers, both large and small, with relative ease. As a result, problems in the elementary school can and should be responsive to student questions and interests. (Note: Later sections in this chapter deal with issues of how to use problems in teaching mathematics and how to assess students' problem-solving work.)

							6+1				
						5+1	5+2	6+2			
					4+1	4+2	4+3	5+3	6+3		
				3+1	3+2	3+3	3+4	4+4	5+4	6+4	
			2+1	2+2	2+3	2+4	2+5	3+5	4+5	5+5	6+5
		1+1	1+2	1+3	1+4	1+5	1+6	2+6	3+6	4+6	5+6	6+6
Sums		2	3	4	5	6	7	8	9	10	11	12

+	**1**	**2**	**3**	**4**	**5**	**6**
1	2	3	4	5	6	7
2	3	4	5	6	7	8
3	4	5	6	7	8	9
4	5	6	7	8	9	10
5	6	7	8	9	10	11
6	7	8	9	10	11	12

Figure 5–2 • Two tables showing possible outcomes for rolling two dice

Reasoning and Proof

From their very earliest experiences with mathematical challenges and problems, children should understand that they are expected to supply reasons for their arguments. The question "Why do you think so?" should be commonplace in the classroom. Teachers should not be the only ones asking, "Why?" Asking why comes naturally to small children. They should be encouraged to sustain their natural curiosity for justification as they share their mathematical ideas with each other. When children observe a pattern (for example, whenever you add two odd numbers, the answer is even), they should be encouraged to ask why. One second grader drew some pictures (see Figure 5–3) and then explained his reasoning as follows: "All the even numbers are just rectangles. But all the odd numbers are rectangles with 'chimneys.' If you put two with chimneys together, the new one doesn't have a chimney. So two odds makes an even." If students are consistently expected to explore, question, conjecture, and justify their ideas, they learn that mathematics should make sense, rather than believing that mathematics is a set of arbitrary rules and formulas.

Russell (1999) identifies four important points about active mathematics reasoning in elementary school classrooms: (1) reasoning is about making generalizations, (2) reasoning leads to a web of generalizations, (3) reasoning leads to mathematical memory built on relationships, (4) learning through reasoning requires making mistakes and learning from them.

Reasoning Is about Making Generalizations
Mathematics is about much more than just finding answers to specific problems or computations. Indeed, in today's world we have machines that can do much of the computational drudgery for us. Reasoning mathematically involves observing patterns, thinking about the patterns, and justifying why they should be true in more than just individual instances. A very simple example of mathematical reasoning was illustrated when a kindergartner, proud of his new-found ability to think about big numbers, eagerly challenged his mother by asking, "Do you know how much 2 trillion plus 3 trillion is? It's 5 trillion!" There was no doubt that this boy had never seen a trillion of anything, nor was he able to write numbers in the trillions. But he was familiar with the pattern in smaller cases (2 apples + 3 apples = 5 apples, 2 hundred + 3 hundred = 5 hundred), so he was able to generalize to adding trillions.

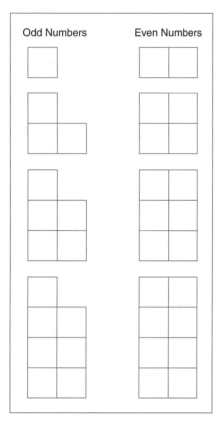

Figure 5–3 • **Pictures of odds and evens**

Another example of making generalizations is offered by Russell (1999). She reports the story of a third grader named Katie who was working with a partner to find factor pairs for 120. The students believed at first that 3 × 42 might be such a factor pair (a result obtained by incorrectly counting squares on a rectangular array on graph paper). However, Katie reasoned that answer must be incorrect because she remembered that 6 × 20 was a valid factor pair for 120, and from previous experience in finding factor pairs, she had figured out that if you halved one factor, you should double the other factor to keep the product the same. This is a very powerful and useful generalization. Using this line of reasoning, Katie reported that the correct factor pair must be 3 × 40, not 3 × 42. When children go beyond specific instances of mathematical ideas to consider general cases, they are reasoning mathematically.

Reasoning Leads to a Web of Generalizations
A second point about mathematical reasoning is that it "leads to an interconnected web of mathematical knowledge within a mathematical domain" (Russell 1999, p. 1). Students should expect newly encountered mathematical ideas to fit with ideas they have already learned. A student has much

more mathematical power if he or she has many ways to think about a number or fact or assertion. A student might understand as early as the first grade that "three quarters" is between "one half dollar" and "one dollar," but he has a much more extensive understanding of the fact that three quarters is between one half and one when he also understands this relationship in terms of fractions ($\frac{1}{2}$, $\frac{3}{4}$, 1), in terms of equivalent fractions ($\frac{2}{4}$, $\frac{3}{4}$, $\frac{4}{4}$), in terms of decimals (.5, .75, and 1.00), and by visualizing pieces of a pie or portions of a collection of trading cards. When students incorrectly claim that .25 must be larger than .5 because 25 is more than 5, they probably have not developed a robust web of connections for such ideas. They are unable to reason about the other meanings they may know for these two numbers, and they are thereby unable to recognize the contradiction in their thinking.

Reasoning Leads to Mathematical Memory Built on Relationships A third point about mathematical reasoning is that the development of a web of mathematical understandings is the foundation of what Russell calls *mathematical memory* (or mathematical sense), a capability that provides the basis for insight into mathematical problems. For example, consider the problem of finding the sum of the first 100 counting numbers: 1 + 2 + 3 + · · · + 100. Sometime in your years of studying mathematics, you probably encountered a formula that would allow you to calculate the sum of any arithmetic series (a list of numbers where the difference between consecutive numbers is always the same—here, the difference is always just one). If you are like most people, you have long since forgotten that formula because it is not something that you use every day. On the other hand, if you have ever seen a geometric illustration of that formula, your web of mathematical understanding may be strong enough to help you reconstruct the formula with very little trouble.

Picture the sum from 1 to 100 as a set of stairs. Picture another identical set of stairs. Turn the second set of stairs upside down on the first, and you will have a rectangle (100 wide, 101 high). (See Figure 5–4 for a picture of a related, simpler problem: a 10 by 11 rectangle built from two staircases from 1 to 10.) It's easy to find the area of the 100 by 101 rectangle (100 × 101 = 10100). The sum you want is half of this (100 × 101 divided by 2, or 5050) because the rectangle is made of two staircases instead of just the one original staircase.

Using the same idea, you can figure out how to find the sum, S, from 1 to any number, n. It's just $S = n(n + 1)/2$. A similar line of reasoning can be used to find the sums for various other arithmetic series

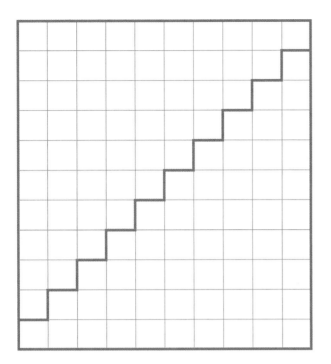

Figure 5–4 • A 10 × 11 rectangle built from two staircases from 1 to 10

(such as 1 + 3 + 5 + · · · 175 or 12 + 15 + 18 + · · · 639). In other words, if you can connect the idea of summing numbers in a series with the geometric illustration of the dual staircases, you'll never need to worry about forgetting the formula for the sum of an arithmetic series again.

Learning through Reasoning Requires Making Mistakes and Learning from Them A final, very important point about mathematical reasoning is that one of the best ways to develop deeper reasoning ability is to study flawed or incorrect reasoning. There will be many times that your students think they've figured something out, but their reasoning just isn't quite right. That's just human nature. For example, a student might observe that you can make the problem 29 + 95 easier to do mentally by adding 29 and 100, then subtracting 5 (obtaining the correct sum, 124). Can this same shortcut be used to make the problem 29 × 95 easier to do mentally (that is, can you multiply 29 times 100, and then subtract 5)? It turns out that just isn't correct! Why? Rather than just tell your students that this doesn't work, it would be much better to help them investigate why the shortcut works for addition and why it does not work for multiplication. Some possible approaches would be to try adding and multiplying a wide variety of examples to try to figure out

what is going on. Or it might help to represent the problems geometrically (using a 29 by 95 array to represent the multiplication and comparing it with a 29 by 100 array may offer some insights—see Figure 5–5).

Your role as a teacher will be to encourage students to constantly examine their own thinking and the thinking of others, and to help them uncover and understand flawed reasoning when it occurs.

Communication

Because language is a powerful tool for organizing thinking about mathematical ideas, it is extremely important for students to have many experiences with talking and writing about mathematics, describing and explaining their ideas. Conversely, it is also important that students are often on the receiving end of communications: hearing about, reading about, and listening to the descriptions and explanations of others. Two-way communication about mathematical ideas helps students identify, clarify, organize, articulate, and extend their thinking. Have you ever noticed how struggling to explain an idea helped you figure out what you really were thinking? Reflection and communication are intertwined. To share ideas with others through talking or writing, we are forced to think more deeply about those ideas. And in thinking about our ideas we often deepen our understanding and, consequently, are able to communicate even more clearly. Communication is obviously a process rather than an end in itself.

Students should be encouraged to communicate their mathematical thinking in a variety of modes: for example, through pictures, gestures, graphs, charts, and symbols, as well as through words (both spoken and written). Figures 5–3, 5–4, and 5–5 clearly illustrate the power of visuals in communicating about mathematics. Such nonverbal communication is often very useful in promoting learning.

Especially at first, students' efforts at verbal communication about mathematical ideas may be idiosyncratic (they may use symbols and expressions that they have made up on their own). Over time, with more experience and practice, students learn to use conventional and more precise language to express their ideas. Indeed, mathematics as a language has a vocabulary, syntax, and symbolism all its own. Sometimes words or phrases used in everyday conversation may be used in mathematics with different, more precise, meanings. The symbolism of mathematics (particularly equations and graphs) often helps clarify concepts and promote understanding. Throughout their elementary school years, students should have daily opportunities for

Figure 5–5 • **Visualizing 29 × 95 and 29 × 100**

communicating about mathematical ideas. Gradually, they should be expected to incorporate more precise mathematical terms in their explanations.

Making writing a regular part of the mathematics curriculum provides students with opportunities to review, reiterate, and consolidate their thinking about mathematical ideas. One of simplest yet most effective modes of writing about mathematics is open-ended writing as follow-up to a lesson. In response to the prompt "What did you learn today?", even young children can describe their activities and their understanding in a variety of ways. Wilde (1991) shares writing about a fraction lesson by Vilavanh, a fifth grader who needed extra help in math:

> When you do fractions you have to think what number is higher or lower than can equal a whole pizza. When you are splitting a pizza you have to think how many pieces will each person get. When you have a number like this—$\frac{1}{2}$, $\frac{1}{8}$—the number that is higher has to give eight pieces to a person. You'll only have a little piece. The person who gets $\frac{1}{2}$ gets a bigger piece, gets a lot, because $\frac{1}{2}$ is bigger than $\frac{1}{8}$.

Vilavanh apparently is beginning to understand that a fraction with a larger denominator represents division into more pieces, and thus the pieces will be smaller. Teachers can use students' writing diagnostically. When the writing, of many students in a group or class reveal similar confusions or misconceptions, the teacher can more appropriately plan future lessons.

Mathematics journals can be used to prompt students to write about mathematics. The regularity of writing in a journal can help students monitor their own understanding of mathematical concepts. Students can be encouraged to write about such questions as "What am I puzzled about?" and "what mistakes do I make and why?" When teachers take time to respond to student journals on a regular basis, however briefly, the journals can become a regular chain of communication between student and teacher.

Other forms of writing in math class include having students write their own word problems, having them describe their solutions to problem-solving activities, having them describe a procedure or process, and writing about connections between and among ideas. Young children can be encouraged to use their own invented spelling, and all students can benefit by accompanying words with pictures and symbols so they can express themselves as fully and completely as possible.

Some useful references on writing and communication in mathematics classes include Azzolino (1990), Ciochine and Polivka (1997), Countryman (1992), Ford (1990), Van Zoerts and Enyart (1998), and Wilde (1991).

Connections

Although mathematics is often represented—particularly in textbooks—as a list of topics or a collection of skills, this is a very shallow view. Mathematics is actually a very well-integrated domain of study. The ideas of school mathematics are richly connected. It is important for the elementary school curriculum to provide children with ongoing opportunities to experience and appreciate the connectedness of the subject.

At least three types of connections are important in learning mathematics. First, ideas within mathematics itself are richly connected with one another. Students who learn about fractions, decimals, and percentages in isolation from one another miss an important opportunity to see the connections among these ideas. For example, in Figure 5–6, we can see why $\frac{1}{4}$, .25, and 2 tenths + 5 hundredths are actually all names for the same quantity.

A second important type of connection is between the symbols and procedures of mathematics and the conceptual ideas that the symbolism represents. For example, why do we refer to 3^2 as "3 squared"? 3^2 is 3×3, or 9. A drawing of 9 dots, arranged in a 3-by-3 array forms a square. Similarly, any array of x-by-x dots would form a square; thus we have come to read x^2 as "x squared."

When we find the area of any geometric figure, we generally report it in square units (square feet, square centimeters, square miles, etc.). Why? Because measuring area is actually just measuring how many "squares" it would take to cover a surface. If the squares are one inch on each side, then we are measuring in square inches. In fact, we can write "in.^{2}" instead of "square inches" for the same reason. So here we see connections between number theory (the "square numbers": 4, 9, 16, etc., as shown in Figure 5–7), algebraic language (x squared), and measurement (square inches).

A third type of connection is between mathematics and the real world (or mathematics and other school subjects). Classroom instruction should pro-

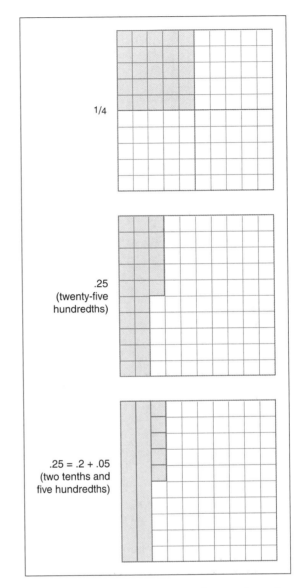

Figure 5–6 • Representations for $\frac{1}{4}$, .25, 2 tenths and 5 hundredths

vide many opportunities for children to experience how mathematics is used in domains such as science, business, home economics, social studies, and art. Applications of mathematics can be highlighted through integrated or thematic curricula, through mathematics lessons motivated by problem situations or by situations in children's literature, and through consistently engaging students in real-world problems as they occur in the classroom. (For example, our class has 24 students. Today 4 desks are empty. Everyone who is here today wants to buy the school lunch. How many orders for lunch should be sent to the office?) As they encounter problems from real-world contexts where mathematics is a

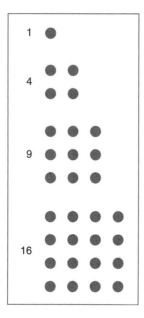

Figure 5–7 • Square numbers

significant part of the solution, students come to recognize and value the utility and relevance of the subject.

Representations

When most people think of mathematics, they may think of numbers such as 2, 29, or 5280. Or they may think of numeric or symbolic expressions such as 5×2, $(a + b)(a - b)$, or $5798 \div 13$ or equations such as $x^2 + y^2 = r^2$ or $2x + 7 = 13$. Alternatively, they may think of tables of numbers or graphs or geometric figures. All are commonly used representations for mathematical ideas. Interestingly, it often is possible to use a variety of these very different representations to illustrate the very same mathematical ideas. Different representations for an idea can lead us to different ways of understanding and using that idea. This is the power of representation.

The school mathematics curriculum has traditionally involved children in learning about a wide variety of representations for mathematical ideas. However, different representations were often learned in isolation, one from the other (for example, students might have learned about fractions in one chapter and decimals in another but not have been provided with enough opportunities to connect these two very different representations for the same numbers). It is important to challenge and encourage students to connect and to compare and contrast the utility and power of different representations.

Principles and Standards (NCTM 2000) discusses three major goals for representation as a process in

school mathematics: (1) creating and using representations to organize, record, and communicate mathematical ideas, (2) selecting, applying, and translating among representations to solve problems, and (3) using representations to model and interpret physical, social, and mathematical phenomena.

Creating and Using Representations In the snapshot that opened this chapter we see children developing their own idiosyncratic representations for organizing, recording, and communicating data about the heights and shoe sizes of their classmates. When they discovered that their initial recording sheet wasn't very helpful in showing how heights and shoe sizes were related (or not related) and didn't help with sorting out boy–girl differences, they devised a new representation. It is important for young children to have repeated opportunities both to invent their own ways of recording and communicating mathematical ideas and to work with conventional representations. The mathematical symbols and representations that we use every day (base ten notation, equations, coordinate graphs, etc.) have been polished and refined over many centuries. When students come to understand them in deep ways, they are provided with a set of tools that expands their capacity to think mathematically.

Selecting, Applying, and Translating Among Representations As mentioned earlier, mathematical ideas can often be represented in very different ways, and each of those representations may be appropriate for very different purposes. For example, a student who can think flexibly about numbers is probably able to think about the number 24 in many different ways: 2 tens and 4 ones, 1 ten and 14 ones, a little less than 25, double 12, the perimeter of a square with side 6, the area of rectangles with sides 2×12 or 4×6, etc. Depending on the problem at hand, some of these representations may be more useful than others. Technology now offers students many opportunities for experiences with translating among representations. For example, data analysis software can help students easily compare and contrast a bar graph, a histogram, a circle graph, a box-and-whisker plot, or a line plot for the set of data. It is important that students consider the kinds of data and questions for which each of these representations is appropriate.

Using Representations to Model and Interpret Phenomena Much of what we do in mathematics is to simplify problems, stripping away context and excess information to reduce them to symbols or representations that we can work with more easily. This is mathematical modeling. For example, to solve the following word problem, we might reduce it to a picture or to a table of numbers:

> Alice is stacking soup cans for display on a shelf at the end of a supermarket aisle. She wants the display to look like a pyramid. On the top row she wants to put just one can, on the next-to-top row, 3 cans, on the next row down 5 cans, and so on. Alice decides the display can be 6 rows high. How many cans should she put on the bottom row?

Once you've made a picture or a table of numbers, the fact that the problem is about stacking soup cans is no longer really important. You've modeled the problem and used the power of mathematics to solve it. Similarly, when students ask, when solving word problems, "Do I add or do I subtract?" they are asking for advice about modeling the situation at hand. It is important to encourage students not to move too quickly and unthinkingly from real-world situations to abstract models. The best answer to the question about adding or subtracting is to ask, "What's going on in the problem?" "Can you draw a picture or can you act it out to help you decide which operation to use?" It is also important to check back at the end of solving a problem to ensure that the solution obtained from the mathematical model actually fits the contextualized situation. A classic example is a problem where students are asked to determine how many buses will be necessary to transport a school on a field trip. The problem tells how many students need to be transported and how many can fit in each bus. Many students correctly pick out the numbers in the problem and divide, but then offer nonsensical answers such as $3\frac{1}{4}$ or 3.25. They have forgotten to check back with the context of the problem, to see that a more sensible answer would be 4 buses or perhaps 3 buses and a minivan.

In sum, representations are ways of thinking about ideas. Individuals develop their own idiosyncratic ways of thinking, but mathematics itself offers a broad repertoire of conventional representations that are helpful in problem solving and in communicating about mathematical ideas. One of the most important goals of mathematics instruction should be to help students build bridges from their own ways of thinking to the conventional, so that they come to understand, value, and use these powerful mathematical tools.

TEACHING MATHEMATICS VIA PROBLEM SOLVING

In our earlier discussion about problem solving as one of the five fundamental processes for school mathematics, we discussed the general nature of problem solving and briefly considered the types of problems that may be appropriate for elementary school students. In the remainder of this chapter, we provide more specific advice about how problem solving can serve as a foundation for all your mathematics teaching because it involves students in work with all the fundamental processes of doing mathematics (reasoning, communicating, connecting, and representing).

Problem solving is a way of teaching. This means it involves more than the presentation of word problems; it involves the way we encourage children to approach mathematical learning. A situation is posed, as in a word problem, and then there is a search for a resolution, very often using some of the same processes or procedures as are used in solving a word problem. But the situation that is posed often has a mathematical basis beyond the application of some procedures. The problem may be posed by students, or it may be initiated by the teacher. In either case, using problems as a jumping-off point for mathematics instruction involves the teacher in posing questions that provoke student thought and also in encouraging students to pose their own questions. Using problem-solving as a foundation for mathematics instruction requires students to engage in a search for a reasonable solution or solutions.

One group of researchers proposes that

> students should be allowed to make the subject problematic . . . allowing students to wonder why things are, to inquire, to search for solutions, and to resolve incongruities. It means that both curriculum and instruction should begin with problems, dilemmas, and questions for students. (Hiebert et al. 1996)

Franke and Carey (1997) are among those who have begun the process of documenting the changes in children's perceptions about mathematics when they are taught in an environment reflecting the spirit of the NCTM Standards. They write about students who have been involved in the Cognitively Guided Instruction (CGI) program. In the CGI model of instruction, the teacher poses a rich mathematical task. Students take time to work individually or in small groups to solve the problem, and then share their approaches with each other. Students are encouraged to listen carefully to each other and to question each other about processes and strategies. The teacher's role is to choose appropriate tasks and to orchestrate the classroom discourse, using what he or she knows about the students' developmental level. A key aspect of CGI is the teacher's ability to analyze the children's thinking and to guide classroom problem solving accordingly. The CGI first graders studied by Franke and Carey (1997) "perceived of mathematics as a problem-solving endeavor in which many different strategies are considered viable and communicating mathematical thinking is an integral part of the task" (p. 8). In a study of another problem-centered mathematics program, after two years in the program third graders scored significantly higher on standardized measures of computational proficiency and conceptual understanding and held stronger beliefs about the importance of finding their own or different ways to solve problems than those in "textbook classes" (Wood and Sellers 1996).

It seems to be generally accepted that Japanese students do quite well on conceptual mathematics questions and problem-solving items in international assessments. Therefore, it is interesting to learn what sorts of problem solving are typical in Japanese elementary classrooms. Sawada (1999) describes a typical grade 5 Japanese lesson in which the teacher poses a single contextualized problem that the students spend more than 35 minutes working. Although the teacher functions as a guide with a definite agenda, student contributions to the follow-up class discussion are used to structure both the content of the lesson and its flow. Similarly, in the United States today, problem solving as a way of teaching is merging with problem solving as only a curriculum component. Problem solving has been the focus of numerous books, collections of materials, and research studies, but many questions continue to be raised about the nature and scope of problem solving:

● What is a problem and what does problem solving mean?
● How can problem solving be taught effectively?
● What problem-solving strategies should be taught?
● How can problem solving be evaluated?

The remainder of this chapter addresses these questions.

WHAT IS A PROBLEM AND WHAT IS PROBLEM SOLVING?

A *problem* involves a situation in which a person wants something and does not know immediately what to do to get it. If a problem is so easy that chil-

dren know how to obtain the answer or know the answer immediately, there is really no problem at all.

To gain skill in solving problems, one must have many experiences in doing so. Research indicates that children who are given many problems to solve score higher on problem-solving tests than children who are given few. This finding has led many textbooks and teachers to offer a problem-solving program that simply presents problems—and nothing more.

Unfortunately, children have often been expected to learn how to solve word problems merely by solving them, with virtually no guidance or discussion of how to do it. Thus, a typical page in a children's textbook (after students have been taught how to add large numbers) might begin with exercises such as the following:

3194	5479	6754
5346	3477	8968
+ 8877	+ 6399	+ 7629

Next would appear "story problems" such as the following:

(A) 7809 people watched television on Monday.

9060 people watched on Tuesday.

9924 people watched on Wednesday.

How many people watched in the three days?

Whether story problems such as these really are problems for most children is debatable.

In effect, these "problems" are exercises with words around them. The biggest difficulty lies in doing the computation. The choice of what computation to perform is obvious. Do what you have been doing most recently. If the past week's work has been on addition, solve the problems by adding; if the topic has been division, then find two numbers in the word problem and divide. The problems generally provide practice on content just taught, with the mathematics placed in a more-or-less real-world setting. It is little wonder that children taught in this way flounder on tests, where problems are not conveniently grouped by operation.

Consider, as an alternative, the following problem—and try it yourself:

(B) Begin with the digits:

1 2 3 4 5 6 7 8 9

Use each of them at least once, and form three four-digit numbers with the sum of 9636.

To obtain a solution (or solutions), the children will have the desired practice in addition—but they will have to try many possibilities. They will be aided in reaching a solution if they apply some mathematical ideas. For instance, knowing that the sum of three odd numbers is odd will lead them to avoid placing 1, 3, and 5 all in the ones place. The children have the prerequisites for solving the problem, but the solution is not immediately apparent. They may have to guess and check a number of possibilities.

The decision to add the three numbers in problem (A) presents little if any challenge to most children in terms of determining what to do. The problem is merely a computational exercise that provides practice with addition. The children know what to do because the pattern has been set by the examples before it. With problem (B), however, they will probably have to try several alternatives. Interest in obtaining a solution or solutions and acceptance of the challenge of trying to do something you have not done before (but believe you can do) are key aspects of problem solving.

Whether a problem is truly a problem or merely an exercise depends on the person faced with it. For example, tying a shoelace is no longer a problem for you, but it is for a three-year-old. What is a problem for Ann now may not be a problem for her in three weeks, or it may not be a problem now for Armando. Problems that you select for children must truly be seen as problems.

Many teachers are prone to select only problems that can be solved immediately, which often means the problems are too easy for children. Children form the idea that problems should be solved readily, so a problem where the route to solution is not immediately apparent is viewed as "impossible." Finding the right level of challenge for students is not easy, but you can do it by trying out a range of problems, providing time, and then encouraging students to explore many ways around the obstacles initially posed. Don't underestimate their abilities. Weinberg (1996) comments on her fear that a problem was too difficult for her second-grade class and how amazed she was by their strategies for solving the problem.

A distinction is sometimes made between routine and nonroutine problems. *Routine problems* can be solved by application of a mathematical procedure in much the same way as it was learned. Many textbook word problems are routine problems. *Nonroutine problems* often require more thought because the choice of mathematical procedures to solve them is not as obvious.

Results from national assessments have shown that the majority of students have difficulty with problems that require some analysis or thinking.

Students are generally successful in solving routine one-step problems like those found in most textbooks. They have great difficulty, however, in solving multistep or nonroutine problems, particularly those that involve application of more than one single arithmetic operation. The 1992 National Assessment of Educational Progress included some non-multiple-choice items where students had to construct their own answers and provide rationale for their responses. Students at all grades tended to have difficulties with these problem-solving items (Kouba et al. 1997).

Results from the sixth assessment indicate that students at all three grade levels (4, 8, and 12) performed well on addition and subtraction word problems set in familiar contexts and involving only one step or calculation (Kenney and Silver 1997). Eighth- (and twelfth-) grade students did well on multiplication and division problems involving one step as long as one of the factors was a whole number. Difficulties arose when fourth-grade students applied an incorrect strategy of "when in doubt, add," and when some students at all three grade levels but especially grade four attempted to solve multistep problems as though they involved a single step.

Unfortunately, in many mathematical programs, problem solving has been limited to finding the answers to word problems in textbooks. Mathematical problem solving involves more. Whenever children are faced with providing a solution to a task they have not mastered, they are solving a problem.

HOW CAN PROBLEM SOLVING BE TAUGHT EFFECTIVELY?

Because problem solving is difficult to teach and to learn, researchers have devoted much attention to it over the years. Their work has focused on characteristics of those children who are successful or unsuccessful at solving problems, on characteristics of problems, and on teaching strategies and classroom conditions that may help children to be more successful at problem solving. On the basis of this research, some broad generalizations can be made (Hembree and Marsh 1993; Kroll and Miller 1993; Suydam 1982).

- Young children enter school able to solve many problems. Instruction should build on what children already know.

- Students can begin solving problems in the earliest grades. Engaging students in problem solving should *not* be postponed until after they have "mastered" computational skills.

- Problem-solving strategies can be specifically taught, and when they are, not only are they used more but students also achieve correct solutions more frequently.

- No *one* strategy is optimal for solving all problems. Some strategies are used more frequently than others, with various strategies being used at different stages of the problem-solving process.

- Teaching a variety of strategies (in addition to providing an overall plan for how to go about problem solving) provides children with a repertoire from which they can draw as they meet a wide variety of problems. They should be encouraged to solve different problems with the same strategy and to discuss why some strategies are appropriate for certain problems.

- Students need to be faced with problems in which the way to solve them is not apparent, and they need to be encouraged to test many alternative approaches.

- Children's problem-solving achievements are related to their developmental level. Thus, they need problems at appropriate levels of difficulty.

Major factors that contribute to students' difficulties with problem solving in the middle grades are knowledge, beliefs and affects, control, and sociocultural factors (Kroll and Miller 1993). At all levels, teachers should be aware of the importance of each of these areas in problem-solving instruction.

Knowledge Students need experiences throughout their school years that encourage them to connect their thinking about problems at hand to problems they have solved in the past. Students need to learn to recognize problems that are structurally similar (schema knowledge) and to choose appropriately among approaches for solving them, rather than to rely on surface problem features in deciding how to attack problems. For example, the use of key words in problem-solving instruction (for example, *in all* means to add, *how many left* means to subtract) is counterproductive because it relies on a problem's surface features only. Students should choose a solution approach based on a clear understanding of a problem.

Beliefs and Affects Students' success in solving problems is often strongly linked to their attitudes, confidence, and beliefs about self as a problem solver. It is important for teachers to show students that they believe *all* students can be good problem solvers, and it is also important for them to encourage students to develop their own strategies for and approaches to problem solving. Teachers who believe there is only one way to solve a problem prevent students from truly experiencing what it means to be a problem solver and to do mathematics.

Control It is extremely important for students to learn to monitor their own thinking about problem solving. Research indicates that good problem solvers often spend a considerable amount of time up front, making sure they understand a problem, and at the end, looking back to see what they did, how their solution might be modified or improved, and thinking about how this problem is similar and different from other problems they have seen. By contrast, weaker problem solvers tend to be impulsive, jumping right into trying to solve (often crunching numbers with little regard for what they mean), without stopping to think about what approach might be most productive. Teachers can help students monitor their thinking and develop better control mechanisms by structuring opportunities where students are encouraged to engage in reflection on their own thinking processes.

Sociocultural Factors The atmosphere of the classroom should encourage students to use and further develop problem-solving strategies developed naturally through experiences outside the classroom. Furthermore, the classroom climate itself (with its opportunities for discussion, collaboration, sharing, and encouragement among students) plays an important role in helping students develop as problem solvers.

In other words, a strong problem-solving program builds on the natural, informal methods that the child has when entering school. Many of the best problem-solving situations come from everyday happenings. "How many more chairs will we need if we're having five visitors and two children are absent?" or "How many cookies will we need if everyone is to have two?" may be of concern to a group of first graders. "Who has the higher batting average, Benny or Marianne?" or "What's the probability of our class winning the race?" may be urgent questions for a group of fifth graders.

A problem-solving approach should pervade the mathematics curriculum. Teachers need to use problem situations to introduce new topics, as a continuing thread throughout instruction, and as a culmination to ascertain whether children can apply what they have learned. To teach problem solving effectively, teachers need to consider the time involved, planning aids, needed resources, the role of technology, and how to manage the class.

Time

Effective teaching of problem solving demands time. Attention must be focused on the relationships in the problem and on the thinking processes involved in reaching a solution. Thus, students must have time to digest, or mull over, a problem thoroughly—time to understand the task, time to explore avenues of solution, time to think about the solution. Moreover, teachers need to encourage students to extend the amount of time they are willing to work on a problem before giving up. It takes more time to tackle a problem that you do not know how to solve than to complete an exercise where you know how to proceed. (Consider problems (A) and (B) on page 88. How long did it take you to solve each?)

Some time for problem solving is already included as part of the mathematics program. Additional time can be gained by organizing instructional activities so that some of the time allotted for practicing computational and other skills is directed toward problem solving. This approach is logical, since students use such skills and thus practice them as they solve many problems.

Planning

Instructional activities and time must be planned and coordinated so that students have the chance to tackle numerous problems, to learn a variety of problem-solving strategies, and to analyze, write about, and discuss their methods of attack. You will probably use a textbook when you teach mathematics; you need to consider how to use it most effectively to help you teach problem solving. For instance, you might identify your objectives for using problem-solving materials in the textbook, examine the entire book for problems to use, regroup textbook materials to suit your objectives, use the textbook to develop questions to ask about problem solving, extend textbook problems with materials you develop yourself, and make use of "challenge problems" (found in many textbooks) with all children.

As you plan, consider including problems with the following characteristics:

- Problems that contain superfluous or insufficient information:

  (C) A bag contains 2 dozen cookies for 99¢. Becca bought 3 bags. How many cookies did she get?

  (D) Andy would like to be as tall as his uncle, who is 6 feet 4 inches. How much more must Andy grow?

- Problems that involve estimation:

  (E) Anita has 75¢. Does she have enough money to buy a candy bar costing 35¢ and a notebook costing 49¢?

- Problems that require students to make choices about the degree of accuracy required:

  (F) Kurt is helping his father build a pen for his rabbit. He finds three pieces of lumber in the garage that they can use for the frame. One piece is 8 feet long; the other two are each 7 feet long. What is the largest size rectangular pen that they can build?

- Problems that involve practical applications of mathematics to consumer or business situations.

  (G) Which is the better buy, a 6-ounce jar of jelly for $1.79 or a 9-ounce jar for $2.79?

- Problems that require students to conceptualize very large or very small numbers:

  (H) Have you lived one million hours?

- Problems that are based on students' interests or events in their environment or can be personalized by adding their names:

  (I) Some of you play soccer every Tuesday. If today were Wednesday, January 21st, on what date would you play next?

- Problems that involve logic, reasoning, testing of conjectures, and reasonableness of information:

  (J) Three children guessed how many jelly beans were in a jar. Their guesses were 80, 75, and 76. One child missed by 1. Another missed by 4. The other child guessed right. How many jelly beans were in the jar?

- Problems that are multistep or require the use of more than one strategy to attain a solution:

  (K) Ellie had $10.00 in her pocket. A ticket to the movie is $5.50. The theater offers a popcorn and drink special for $3.79. If Ellie buys the popcorn and drink, does she have enough money for a $1.45 candy bar too?

- Problems that require decision making as a result of the outcome (perhaps there are many answers—or no answers):

  (L) Is a traffic light needed in front of the school?

In addition, you should choose sometimes to pose problems that are open ended. Such problems have no one "correct" answer, but rather an answer that depends on the approach taken. Each solution is, however, expected to be reasonable. Such problems are especially appropriate for cooperative group work and should be followed with a class discussion in which the mathematical ideas and planning skills are explored and students get a chance to clarify their thinking and validate their decisions. Consider the following open-ended problems:

(M) You have just been given $50, and you have decided to plan a special outing for your family. Where will you go? Plan a schedule for the day. What time will you get to your destination? What time will you leave? How long will you stay? What will you do? Will $50 be enough money to cover all activities? If not, how much more money will you need?

(N) Your group has decided to plan a track-and-field competition. What events would be fun? What equipment will you need? Where and when should different events be held so that they will not interfere with each other? Develop a map and time schedule for the competition. How will you collect and display data from the events to determine winners?

It is important to recognize that open-ended problems such as (M) and (N) are much more effective when reasonable constraints are specified to ensure that the level of mathematics in the problems remains high. For example, you could improve problem (M) considerably by specifying that students must state the size of their family (three, four, or five people) and by requiring them to list lunch costs for that family from their choice of restaurant menus that you provide. You might also offer a choice of transportation options (for example, car or bus). For the car, you could provide (or students could research) information about gas costs per gallon, the car's gas efficiency, and the distance to various attractions. For the bus option, you might provide information about individual and group costs of tickets to the same destinations. If you do not include constraints such as these in an open-ended problem such as (M), students are likely to spend most of their time simply debating where to go and what to do, with very little time spent estimating or computing how to spend their $50. The unfortunate result can be a fun activity with very little mathematics involved. By contrast, providing reasonable and interesting constraints can turn an open-ended problem into a much more realistic challenge.

Problems (O) and (P) are a different sort of open-ended problem from (M) and (N). The numeric answer is not at all difficult to determine in these problems (and everyone should get the same answer). The challenge is to see how many different and interesting ways there are to find that answer.

(O) Squares are made by using matchsticks as shown in the picture. When the number of squares is eight, how many match sticks are used?

(P) How many marbles are in the picture? Find the answer in as many different ways as you can.*

Resources

Although many textbooks include a range of problems, if your textbook does not provide sufficient challenges you may find it helpful to acquire additional problems to stimulate and challenge your students. Fortunately, there are many sources of problems. The list of references at the end of this chapter includes several such sources. In addition, you can do the following:

- Collect problems from newspapers, magazines, Web sites, and so on.

- Write problems yourself (possibly using ideas from newspapers or from events in your community). (For example, see Silbey (1999) for a description of a broad assortment of problems drawn from a single newspaper circular describing activities related to Washington, D.C.'s annual cherry-blossom festival.)

- Use situations that arise spontaneously, particularly questions children raise ("If a bank robber stole a million dollars, how heavy and bulky would it be? Could he run down the street with it in his pocket? In a shopping bag?").

- Attend problem-solving sessions at professional meetings.

- Share problems with other teachers.

*Problems (M) and (N) are adapted from Chancellor and Porter (1994, pp. 304–305); problems (O) and (P) are from Becker (1992).

- Have children write problems to share with each other (Kliman and Richard 1992; Silverman et al. 1992).
- Make videotapes to bring real-life problem situations into the classroom (Kelly and Wiebe 1993, Cognition and Technology Group 1993).

It is never too soon to start a problem file, with problems grouped or categorized so you can locate them readily. File them by mathematical content, by strategies, by how you are going to use the file. Laminating the cards permits them to be used over and over by students for individual or small-group problem solving.

Technology

Ever since calculators dropped in price and it became feasible to use them throughout the school program, their potential for increasing problem-solving proficiency has been recognized. Many problems can now deal with more realistic numbers rather than merely with numbers that come out even. Calculators also help us to shift attention from computation to problem solving. However, research has indicated that use of calculators will not necessarily improve problem-solving achievement (Suydam 1982). The student must still be able to determine *how* to solve a problem before he or she can use a calculator to attain the solution.

Research also indicates that children tend to use more and different strategies when they use calculators (Wheatley 1980). The main reason is that the time once spent on performing calculations can be spent on extending the use of problem-solving strategies. More problems also can be considered when calculations are no longer as burdensome. Consider using calculators whenever they:

- Extend a child's ability to solve problems
- Eliminate tedious computations and decrease anxiety about inability to do computations correctly
- Allow time to devote extended attention to a problem or to consider more problems
- Allow consideration of more complex problems or of problems with realistic data
- Provide motivation and confidence that a problem can be solved

Computers also can be an important problem-solving tool. As with calculators, computers allow for the processing of problems with realistic data. But computers also can be used to present problems of different types—for instance, problems involving graphics and graphing.

Many fine software programs provide a variety of problem-solving experiences. Some, such as What Do You Do with a Broken Calculator? involve computation. Others, such as The Factory and The Super Factory, address spatial visualization. Still others, such as Math Shop, provide direct experiences with problem solving. The Cruncher teaches spreadsheet skills for solving such real-life problems as how many weeks of allowance equal a new CD player.

Logo and BASIC, still available to students in some schools, also can provide rich problem-solving experiences. These languages encourage students to think about what will happen, try it and see what happens, and then try something else. Other tools, such as the Geometer's Sketchpad provide opportunities to create geometric figures, make conjectures, and explore relationships. In recent years, the World Wide Web has become an extremely rich resource for mathematics education. On the Web, teachers and students can find a wealth of challenging and interesting mathematics problems, search for data for real-world problem-solving investigations, and seek answers to mathematical queries and conundrums.

Class Management

When you teach problem solving, you will find it useful at times to teach the whole class, to divide the class into small groups, or to have children work individually or with one other child. Large-group activities are effective for presenting and developing a new problem-solving strategy and for examining a variety of strategies for solving the same problem. You can focus children's attention on a problem's components, pose questions to help them use one strategy or find one solution, lead them to use other strategies or find other solutions, and encourage them to generalize from the problem to other problems. Individuals may suffer, however, because the faster students will tend to come up with answers before others have had a chance to consider the problem carefully. Moreover, what may be a problem to some students may appear trivial or impossibly difficult to others. Discussions about problem solving are feasible with large groups, but the process of solving problems should be practiced in small groups as well as individually.

Small-group instruction makes it possible to group students by problem-solving ability and interests. They have the opportunity to work cooperatively at an appropriate level of difficulty in this type of group.

Their anxiety level is lowered as they all work together, discussing problems, sharing ideas, debating alternatives, and verifying solutions. In small groups, students can generally solve more problems than when working alone, although the groups may take longer on each problem. Research indicates that when groups discuss problem meanings and solution paths, they achieve better results than when they are told how to solve the problem (Suydam and Weaver 1981). Groups are clearly a means of promoting communication about mathematics.

When pairing children to work together, you may want to pair children of comparable abilities or of slightly different abilities so that one child can help the other. Both children can end up learning from a peer-teaching situation.

Some problem solving should be done individually so that children can progress at their own pace and use the strategies with which they are comfortable. You will also want to have in the classroom sources of problems to which individual children can turn in their free time: a bulletin board, a problem corner, or a file of problems.

Problem Posing

Another way to help students with problem solving is to encourage them to write, share, and solve their own problems. Through problem-posing experiences, students become better aware of the structure of problems, develop critical thinking and reasoning abilities, and learn to express their ideas clearly.

It is often helpful to begin problem posing by having students modify familiar problems. For example, third-grade students may have read the story *The Doorbell Rang* (Hutchins 1986) and considered problems such as "If Mama baked 12 cookies, how many cookies can each child have if there are 2 children (or 4 or 6 or 12 children)?"

The problem can be rewritten in various ways. One very simple modification is to change the numbers. Some changes in number leave the difficulty level of the problem essentially unchanged (18 cookies, 6 children). Other changes may make an important difference in the problem solution (12 cookies shared by 8 children or 12 cookies shared by 5 children). Another interesting way to reformulate a problem is to exchange the known and unknown information. For example, "Mama baked a lot of cookies, and each child got 3. How many cookies did Mama bake, if there were two children (or 4 or 6 or 12 children)?" Alternatively, we might consider a more open-ended problem: "If we want to be able to share 18 cookies fairly with different groups of children, without breaking any cookies, what different sizes can the groups be?"

Moses et al. (1990) suggest four principles for helping students as they learn to pose problems:

1. Focus students' attention on the various kinds of information in problems: the kinds of information a problem may give us (the *known*), the kind of information we are supposed to find (the *unknown*), and the kinds of *restrictions* that are placed on the answer. Encourage students to ask "what if" questions. For example, what if we make the known information different? What if we switch what is known in the problem and what is unknown? What if we change the restrictions?

2. Begin with mathematical topics or concepts that are familiar.

3. Encourage students to use ambiguity (what they are not sure about or what they want to know) as they work toward composing new questions and problems.

4. Teach students about the idea of domain (the numbers we are allowed to use in a particular problem). Extending or restricting the domain of a problem is an interesting way to change it. For example, the problem "name three numbers whose product is 24" is very different depending upon whether we consider a domain of all whole numbers, only even whole numbers, all integers (both positive and negative), or perhaps even fractions and decimals.

The teacher plays a key role in establishing a classroom environment where thinking deeply about problems and how the problems can be changed or rewritten is encouraged. The teacher can model an inquiring mind by frequently asking "What if?" when problems are discussed and by encouraging conjecturing and problem reformulation.

Another very useful problem-posing activity is having students write their own problems (rather than modify problems already at hand). This is generally best done after students have had considerable experience with posing problems that are modifications of familiar problems. When asking students to compose problems on their own, it is often important for the teacher to specify certain goals or constraints for the task. Otherwise, the assignment may become nothing more than an exercise in creativity (students may write fantastic stories with no discernible mathematics content or pose problems that are so convoluted or complicated that no solution is possible). For example, students might be assigned to write a word problem that matches a given mathematical number sentence or figure:

- Write a word problem for $250 \div 5 = 50$.
- Write a comparison word problem for $12 - 8 = 4$.

- Write a multiplication word problem for the tree diagram (for example, two kinds of ice cream and three possible toppings for each gives six different types of sundaes).

Other effective problem-posing prompts can be provided by situations or data offered in magazine advertisements, newspaper articles, world records, sales flyers, and so on. A sixth-grade teacher challenged her students to write and illustrate problems that involved multiplication or division and that included extraneous information. Here is a problem written by one of her students (from Kroll and Miller 1993, p. 67).

At midnight, the wind over Jamaica started to increase as Hurricane Lucas came closer. Every 10 minutes from then on, the wind doubled, and five trees were pulled from the ground. At 12:30, the wind speed was 120 miles per hour. At what speed was the wind blowing at 12:00 midnight?

Students need help with learning to write problems. Lessons of this sort can easily be integrated with language arts instruction. A writing workshop approach may be used, consisting of stages such as: brainstorming and prewriting, writing, several rounds of peer critique followed by rewriting, and, finally, editing and publication. Student problems may be "published" on bulletin boards, on cards (to be made available for other students to solve), or in a class "book" of problems. The sixth-grade teacher mentioned earlier obtained a small classroom grant to produce enough copies of her class's illustrated book of problems to distribute one to each sixth-grade class in the school district. Her students proudly went on a field trip, which took them from school to school delivering their books to sixth-grade classrooms, where they shared problem-solving experiences with other students their own age. A third-grade teacher in another state engaged her students in taking "the mathematician's chair" as they challenged their peers with mathematics problem-solving situations they had authored themselves (Hildebrand

et al. 1999). She assessed their written work using a 4-point rubric that considered three aspects of each problem they authored: problem attributes, problem structure, and use of language conventions.

WHAT PROBLEM-SOLVING STRATEGIES SHOULD BE TAUGHT?

You cannot consider problem solving in mathematics education without finding numerous references to the contribution of George Polya (1973). He proposed a four-stage model of problem solving:

1. *Understand* the problem.
2. *Devise* a plan for solving it.
3. *Carry out* your plan.
4. *Look back* to examine the solution obtained.

This model forms the basis for the problem-solving approach used in most elementary school mathematics textbooks. Such an approach, which focuses on teaching students to see, plan, do, and check, can help them see problem solving as a process consisting of several interrelated actions. Students have a guide to help them attack a problem because actions are suggested that will lead them to the goal.

However, Polya's model can also be misleading if taken at face value. Except for simple problems, it is rarely possible to take the steps in sequence. Students who believe they can proceed one step at a time may find themselves as confused as if they had no model. Moreover, the steps are not discrete; nor is it always necessary to take each step. As students try to understand a problem, they may move unnoticed into the planning stage. Or, once they understand the problem, they may see a route to a solution without any planning. Moreover, the stages do not always aid in finding a solution. Many children become trapped in an endless process of read, think, reread—and reread—and reread—until they give up.

Specific strategies are needed to help children move through the model. Polya himself delineates many of these. Many textbooks provide lists of the strategies presented at various grade levels. These strategies are tools for solving problems, whereas the four-stage model provides a guideline for how a problem solver may move through the process of solving a problem.

In this section, we will describe and give examples of a number of problem-solving strategies (see Table 5–2).

The discussion here is not exhaustive, but it provides a useful set of strategies that can be applied in a wide variety of problem settings.

Table 5–2 • **A list of useful problem-solving strategies**

Act it out
Make a drawing or diagram
Look for a pattern
Construct a table
Identify all possibilities
Guess and check
Work backward
Write an open sentence
Solve a simpler or similar problem
Change your point of view

A teacher needs a plan for introducing the strategies; it is not feasible to focus on them all in a given year. Children need time to gain confidence in applying each. A plan also will ensure that students are exposed to the range of strategies you want them to learn, and that they have the opportunity to practice them at an appropriate level. Thus you may decide to introduce "act it out" and "make a drawing" in grade 1, "look for a pattern" and "solve a simpler or similar problem" in grade 2, and so on. No one sequence is best. In successive grade levels, children will practice and use the strategies they have already learned. Of course, students should not be limited to using the strategies that you have already discussed with the class. They should always be encouraged to use their own ideas in approaching novel situations. If you see a student successfully using a strategy that you haven't yet talked about in class, you might encourage her to share her ideas with the rest of the class, and you might help the children identify a label for that new strategy so it can be referred again in future class discussions. For example, Jessica might discover that solving a simpler, parallel problem is a good way to get started on problems that involve large numbers or numbers that seem hard to think about. In a follow-up whole-class discussion, you might suggest naming this "Jessica's simpler strategy" and you might begin future problem-solving discussions by asking whether Jessica's simpler strategy might be useful in attacking the problem at hand.

Textbooks also outline the scope and sequence for any strategies included in the series. Use this outline to compare the scope of your textbook's program with what you want to implement. Then you can devise a plan, if necessary, for extending children's learning beyond what the textbook covers.

The discussion that follows includes a number of illustrative problems, covering a range of mathematical topics and grade levels, that could be used to develop each problem-solving strategy. Usually a problem also can be solved with another strategy; it is rare that a problem can be solved only with one strategy. For this reason, a repertoire of strategies is useful. (On the other hand, not all strategies can be used effectively to solve a given problem.) Often more than one strategy must be used to solve a problem. For example, students may begin to use the identify-all-possibilities strategy but find there are so many possibilities that they also need to use the make-a-table strategy to keep track of them. By becoming familiar with possible strategies, a student acquires a repertoire that can be drawn on to attack a problem, and making a start is often the most difficult point. Moreover, when one strategy fails, the child has others to turn to, thus enhancing his or her confidence that a path to a solution can be found.

As you read, do stop and try to solve the problems!

Act It Out

This strategy helps children visualize what is involved in the problem. They actually go through the actions, either themselves or by manipulating objects. This physical action makes the relationships among problem components clearer in their minds.

When teaching children how to use the act-it-out strategy, it is important to stress that other objects may be used in place of the real thing. Obviously, real money is not needed when a problem involves coins—only something labeled "25¢" or whatever. Because children are adept at pretending, they probably will suggest substitute objects themselves. Make sure they focus their attention on the actions rather than on the objects per se.

Many simple real-life problems can be posed as you develop the act-it-out strategy in the early grades:

(1) Six children are standing at the teacher's desk. Five children join them. How many children are at the teacher's desk then?

The value of acting it out becomes clearer, however, when the problems are more challenging:

(2) Twelve people met at a public park for a nature walk. Before they set off to look for birds, they all introduced themselves and each person shook hands with each of the other people. How many handshakes were exchanged?

(3) A man buys a horse for $60, sells it for $70, buys it back for $80, and sells it for $90. How much does the man make or lose in the horse-trading business?

(4) Gum balls cost 5¢ each. There are gum balls of 5 different colors in the machine. You can't see them because it's dark. What would be the least

number of nickels you'd have to spend to be sure of getting at least 3 gum balls of the same color?

(5) I counted 7 cycle riders and 19 cycle wheels go past my house this morning. How many bicycles and how many tricycles passed?

Make a Drawing or Diagram

Probably within the past week or so you have used the drawing strategy to help solve a real-life problem. Perhaps you had to find someone's house from a complicated set of directions, so you drew a sketch of the route. Or maybe you were rearranging a room and drew a diagram of how the furniture was to be placed. This strategy provides a way of depicting the information in a problem to make the relationships apparent (Kelly 1999).

When teaching this strategy, stress to the children that there is no need to draw detailed pictures. Encourage them to draw only what is essential to tell about the problem. For example, the appearance of the bus, the pattern of the upholstery, the presence of racks above the seats, and similar details are irrelevant in drawing a picture that will help to solve the bus problem:

(6) A bus has 10 rows of seats. There are 4 seats in each row. How many seats are there on the bus?

(7) You enter an elevator on the main floor. You go up 6 floors, down 3 floors, up 9 floors, down 7 floors, up 8 floors, down 2 floors, down 5 more floors. Then you get off the elevator. On what floor are you?

(8) How much carpet would we need to cover our classroom floor?

(9) A snail is at the bottom of a jar that is 15 cm high. Each day the snail can crawl up 5 cm, but each night he slides back down 3 cm. How many days will it take the snail to reach the top of the jar?

(10) It takes 3 minutes to saw through a log. How long will it take to saw the log into 4 pieces?

(11) A patch of lily pads doubles its size each day after it starts growing in a pond. If a pond was completely covered just today, what part of it was covered in lily pads five days ago?

At times you can reverse this strategy by presenting a picture for which the children have to make up a problem:

(12)

Look for a Pattern

In many early learning activities, children are asked to identify a pattern in pictures or numbers. When pattern recognition is used to solve problems, it involves a more active search. Often students will construct a table, then use it to look for a pattern.

(13) Triangle dot numbers are so named because that number of dots can be used to form a triangle with an equal number of dots on each side:

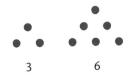

What triangle dot number has 7 dots on a side? Ten dots on a side? What about 195 dots on a side? Is 57 a triangle dot number?

(14) How long would it take to spread a rumor in a town of 90000 people if each person who heard the rumor told it to 3 new people every 15 minutes?

(15) Little Island has a population of 1000 people. The population doubles every 30 years. What will the population be in 30 years? 60 years? 300 years? When will the population be over a million? Over a billion?

(16) An explorer found some strange markings on a cave wall. Can you find and complete the pattern between the numbers in the first row and the numbers in the second row?

5	6	1	3	0	8	16
11			7		17	

Construct a Table

Organizing data into a table helps children to discover a pattern and to identify information that is missing. It is an efficient way to classify and order large amounts of information or data, and it provides a record so that children need not retrace nonproductive paths nor do computations repeatedly to answer new questions.

(17) Can you make change for a quarter using only 9 coins? Only 17? Only 8? How many ways can you make change for a quarter?

(18) About how many direct ancestors have you had in the last 400 years?

(19) A carpenter makes only 3-legged stools and 4-legged tables. At the end of one day he had used 31 legs. How many stools and how many tables did he make?

(20) Ann, Jan, and Nan all like pizza. One likes her pizza plain. One likes pizza with mushrooms. One likes pizza with anchovies. Which kind of pizza does each girl like? Here are three clues:

1. Ann doesn't know the girl who likes her pizza plain.
2. Jan's favorite kind of pizza is cheaper than pizza with mushrooms.
3. The one who likes mushrooms is Ann's cousin.

(21) Your teacher agrees to let you have 1 minute of recess on the first day of school, 2 minutes on the second day, 4 minutes on the third day, and so on. How long will your recess be at the end of 2 weeks?

Notice that the mathematical idea involved in problem (21) can be stated in terms of other situations. Such reformulation can alter the difficulty level of the problem. It can also give children practice in recognizing similarities in problem structure—an ability that appears to be closely allied to good problem-solving skills. Here is one alternative to that problem:

(22) Suppose someone offers you a job for 15 days. They offer you your choice of how you will be paid. You can start for 1¢ a day and double the new amount every day. Or you can start for $1 and add $1 to the new amount every day. Which would you choose? Why?

Textbooks frequently teach part of the table-constructing strategy. They have students read a table or complete a table that is already structured. It is important for students to learn to read a table, and thus problems such as this one are presented:

(23) Here is a bus schedule. What time does the bus from New York arrive? (Ask other questions about arrival, departure, and traveling times.)

It is also vital that children learn how to construct a table. They need to determine for themselves what its form should be (for example, how many columns are needed), what the columns or rows should be labeled, and so on. For this purpose, you can present problems that require children to collect information and then organize it into a table in order to report it. A spreadsheet can be quite helpful with this task.

(24) Make a table that shows how many cars pass through the traffic lights at each intersection by the school.

Identify All Possibilities

This strategy is sometimes used with "look for a pattern" and "construct a table." Children don't always have to actually examine all possibilities—rather, they have to account for all in some systematic way. They may be able to organize the possibilities into categories and then dismiss some classes of possibilities before beginning a systematic search of the remaining ones. Sometimes, however, they do need to actually check all possibilities.

(25) In how many different ways can a bus driver get from Albany to Bakersville? The driver always moves toward Bakersville.

(26) In how many ways can you add 8 odd numbers to get a sum of 20? (You may use a number more than once.)

(27) Ask a friend to think of a number between 1 and 10. Find out what number it is by asking him or her no more than five questions that can be answered only by yes or no. How many questions would you need to ask to find any number between 1 and 20? Between 1 and 100?

(28) If each letter is a code for a digit, what is the following addition problem? Use 1, 2, 3, 6, 7, 9, and 0.

$$\begin{array}{r} \text{SUN} \\ + \text{FUN} \\ \hline \text{SWIM} \end{array}$$

(29) You need 17 lb. of fertilizer. How many bags of each size do you buy to obtain at least 17 lb. at the lowest cost?

Guess and Check

For years, children have been discouraged from guessing. They have been told, "You're only guessing," in a derisive tone. But guessing is a viable strategy when they are encouraged to incorporate what they know into their guesses, rather than making "blind" or "wild" guesses.

An educated guess is based on careful attention to pertinent aspects of the problem, plus knowledge from previous related experiences. There is some reason to expect to be "in the ballpark." Then the child must check to be sure. It is also very important to recognize that the guess-and-check strategy involves making repeated guesses, and *using what has been learned from earlier guesses to make each subsequent guess better and better*. Too often, children just check a guess and, upon finding that it is wrong, make another guess that may be even more off the mark. It is essential to help children learn how to refine their guesses efficiently. Consider the following problem:

> **(30)** Suppose it costs 20¢ to mail a postcard and 33¢ for a letter. Bill wrote to 12 friends and spent $3.57 for postage. How many letters and how many postcards did he send?

We might begin by making a guess of 6 letters and 6 postcards. On checking, we find that results in postage of $3.18. It is important not to just make another guess randomly. $3.18 is not enough postage (because Bill spent $3.57), so we need to *guess more letters*. Maybe we guess 8 letters and 4 postcards. That produces postage of $3.44—almost enough. When we try 9 letters and 3 postcards, we discover the solution.

> **(31)** If two whole numbers have a sum of 18 and a product of 45, what are the numbers?

> **(32)** Place the numbers 1 through 9 in the cells so that the sum in each direction is 15.

(33) Margie hit the dartboard with 4 darts. Each dart hit a different number. Her total score was 25. Which numbers might she have hit to make that score?

(34) Use the numbers 1 through 6 to fill the 6 circles. You may use each number only once. Each side of the triangle must add up to 9.

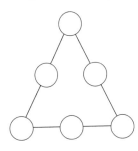

Work Backward

Some problems are posed in such a way that children are given the final conditions of an action and are asked about something that occurred earlier. In other problems, children may be able to determine the endpoint and work backward (many mazes are like that).

(35) Complete the following addition table:

+			3		
	12		11	15	
6		6			7
2			5	9	
					13
5					14

(36) Sue baked some cookies. She put half of them away for the next day. Then she divided the remaining cookies evenly among her three sisters so each got 4. How many cookies did she bake?

Write an Open Sentence

The open-sentence (or equation) strategy is often taught in textbooks; in some, in fact, it is the only strategy taught. Research indicates that it is useful (Suydam and Weaver 1981) but not so useful that it should be taught exclusively. True, once you can write an open sentence, you probably can solve the problem, but writing the sentence in the first place may be difficult. Thus some problems cannot be solved easily with this strategy, and sometimes other problem-solving strategies may be needed first to clarify the problem. In particular, children must be able to perceive a relationship between given and sought information in order to write the sentence. Also, children need to learn that more than one sentence may be formed to solve some problems.

(37) An ant travels 33 cm in walking completely around the edge of a rectangle. If the rectangle is twice as long as it is wide, how long is each side?

(38) Two thirds of a number is 24 and one half of the number is 18. What is the number?

Solve a Simpler or Similar Problem

Some problems are made difficult by large numbers or complicated patterns, so the way to solve them is unclear. For such a problem, making an analogous but simpler problem may aid in ascertaining how to solve it. Thus, for the following problem, you might have second or third graders first consider what they would do if Cassie had 3¢ and Kai had 5¢:

(39) Cassie saved $3.56. Kai saved $5.27. How much more money has Kai saved?

(40) We get 32.7 miles per gallon of gas in our van. If our van's tank holds 14 gallons and we fill it up, how far can we go without filling up again?

(41) Tickets to the college football game cost $15.95 for bleacher seats in the end zone and $25.95 for seats on the home sidelines. Last week 2340 people sat in the endzone bleachers and 6020 people sat on the home sidelines. How much money was collected from the sale of endzone bleacher seat tickets?

You may need to encourage students to break some problems down into manageable parts. When problems require a series of actions, children often fail to recognize the need to answer one question before another can be answered. They need help in identifying the questions that must be answered.

Many kinds of problems are interrelated. Knowing how to solve one problem usually means that children can solve another problem that is somewhat similar. The insight and understanding that permit them to solve more complicated problems are built through solving easier problems, where relationships are easier to see and possibilities for solving can be readily considered. Momentarily, children can set aside the original problem to work on a simpler one; if that problem can be solved, then the procedure used can be applied to the more complicated problem.

(42) Place the numbers 1 to 19 into the 19 circles so that any three numbers in a row will give the same sum.

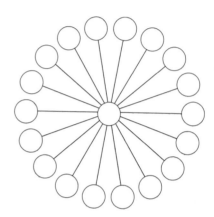

Students might tackle this problem by first trying simpler problems such as placing the numbers 1 to 5 or 1 to 7 or 1 to 9 in a similar pattern of circles.

Often, children need to restate a problem, expressing it in their own words. Sometimes this repetition will indicate points at which they do not understand the problem, and you can then help them to clarify it. At other times, the rephrasing will help them to ascertain what the problem means or requires, so that they see a possible path of solution. Rephrasing can be a way of getting rid of unimportant words or of changing to words that are more easily understood. Try rewording each of the following problems so that children will understand the terms.

(43) Find 3 different integers such that the sum of their reciprocals is an integer.

(44) I bought some items at the store. All were the same price. I bought as many items as the number of cents in the cost of each item. My bill was $2.25. How many items did I buy?

Change Your Point of View

Often, this strategy is used after several others have been tried without success. When children begin to work on most problems, they tend to adopt a particular point of view or make certain assumptions. Often they quickly form a plan of attack and implement it to determine whether it produces a plausible solution. If the plan is unsuccessful, they tend to return to the problem with the same point of view to ascertain a new plan of attack. But there may be some faulty logic that led them to adopt that point of view. They need to try to redefine the problem in a completely different way. Encourage them to ask themselves such questions as, "What precisely does the problem say and not say? What am I assuming that may or may not be implied?"

Problem (20), the pizza problem, is one version of a set of logic problems that are useful in presenting this strategy. Following are some other problems that most students will rather quickly attack in a particular way. Only when it is apparent that an incorrect answer has been obtained (or no answer) will they see the value of looking at the problem from another point of view.

(45) How many squares are there on a checkerboard? (Note: The answer is more than 64.)

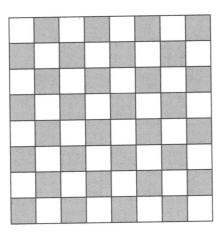

(46) Without lifting your pencil from the paper, draw four straight line segments through the 9 dots.

(The key to solving this problem is recognizing that the lines you draw are allowed to extend beyond the edges of the rectangle formed by the dots.)

(47) A state with 750 schools is about to begin a "single elimination" basketball tournament—one loss and you're out. How many games must be played to determine a champion? (Note: Here it may be helpful to think about how many games each individual team plays in the tournament, rather than to focus on counting games played by pairs of teams.)

THE IMPORTANCE OF LOOKING BACK

Some of the best learning about problem solving may occur after the solution has been attained. It is important to think about how a problem was solved. In fact, research indicates that time spent discussing and reconsidering their thinking may be more important than any other strategy in helping children become better problem solvers (Kroll and Miller 1993; Suydam and Weaver 1981). Thus, this step, which should be included regularly in instructional planning, may focus on one or more helpful strategies.

Generalize

The generalization strategy is used to extend the solution to broader and more far-reaching situations. Analyzing the structural features of a problem rather than focusing only on details often results in insights more significant than the answer to the specific situation posed in the problem. This sort of thinking about generalizations is very important in developing students' mathematical reasoning abilities.

According to research (Suydam 1987), being able to see similarities across problems is one of the characteristics of good problem solvers.

(48) First solve: A boy selling fruit has only three weights and a double-pan balance. But with them he can weigh any whole number of pounds from 1 to 13 pounds. What weights does he have? Then consider: Should he buy a fourth weight? How many additional weighings could be made with the four weights?

(49) When five consecutive numbers are added together their sum is 155. Find the numbers. How can this problem be symbolized so that other totals could be considered?

Getting children to focus on the relationships involved in a problem and then generalizing can sometimes be accomplished by giving children problems without numbers:

(50) A store sells Ping-Pong balls by the box. For the amount of money Maria has, she can buy a certain number of boxes. What price does she pay per ball?

Check the Solution

Checking has long been advocated as a way to help children pinpoint their errors—provided they do not simply make the solution and the check agree. One way of checking is going through the procedures again. Another is verifying the reasonableness of the answer. Is it a plausible answer to the question posed in the problem? Estimating the answer before obtaining the solution will aid in this verification process.

Find Another Way to Solve It

Most problems can be solved with many different strategies. Use of each strategy adds to an understanding of the problem. You have probably felt uncomfortable with the classification of some of the problems in this chapter under one or another strategy. But even for the problems where you felt the classification was satisfactory, there is probably another way each could be solved. (Try it and see!)

Find Another Solution

Too often, children are given problems for which there seems to be one and only one correct solution. Many textbook problems are like that. In real-life situations, however, two or more answers may be acceptable (depending, sometimes, on the circumstances or the assumptions) or only one answer may be obtained via very different approaches. You probably noticed that some of the problems given here have several solutions. For many others, such as the following, each person tackling the problem will have a different answer:

(51) Find out how many days (or minutes) old you are.

Study the Solution Process

This strategy aims to help the child put the problem into perspective: the thinking used at each stage, the facts that were uncovered, the strategies that were employed, and the actions that were productive and nonproductive. Again, giving a problem without numbers helps children to focus on the process they follow, as well as the relationships in the problem, as they describe how they would go about finding the answer. Different students can also be asked to share with the group the varying ways in which they proceeded to reach the same solution. Having children write about how they solved a problem also adds to their understanding of the problem-solving process.

USING PROBLEM-SOLVING OPPORTUNITIES

This chapter has presented a variety of problems. Many of the problems have involved students in mathematical reasoning and communication. We have noted the possible use of nonverbal problems, embodied in different representations such as pictures or materials. Real-world problems arise in a variety of modes, offering many opportunities for making connections. Make use of problems posed spontaneously by children or by situations in which you find yourself. Bring in games that present good problem-solving situations, games that will present children with the opportunity to use many different strategies. Have children work cooperatively in small groups. And be aware that personalizing problems—for instance, by substituting the names of children in your class—can help many children to accept problems that otherwise would seem remote or uninteresting.

Throughout your instruction, you need to encourage enjoyment in solving problems. You have helped children achieve this sense of enjoyment in part when they begin to believe that they *can* solve a problem. They need an atmosphere in which they feel both free and secure. Your positive attitude toward problem solving will stimulate a similar attitude on the part of the children.

HOW CAN PROBLEM SOLVING BE ASSESSED?

It is more difficult to assess children's problem-solving skills than many other skills in the mathematics curriculum. We are interested in knowing whether students can:

- Formulate problems
- Apply a variety of strategies to solve problems
- Solve problems
- Verify and interpret results
- Generalize solutions

To assess problem solving, we need to go beyond the open-ended or multiple-choice format of a paper-and-pencil test. Chapter 4 describes the assessment process, and many of the points to follow are also discussed in Chapter 4. We present them briefly here as well, because it is so important that assessment be considered a vital component of teaching children to be problem solvers.

It takes a long time to develop problem-solving skills. Therefore, assessment is a long-term process that can not be accomplished solely with short-term measures. It needs to be continuous over the entire school mathematics program (Charles et al. 1987).

Assessment of problem solving should be based on your goals, using techniques consistent with those goals. If the mathematics program encompasses the ability to solve both routine and nonroutine problems, then assessment measures must include both types of problems. If the program includes emphasis on the process of problem solving, then assessment measures must incorporate ways of evaluating children's use of the process.

As you plan each lesson, consider how you will determine whether or not its objectives have been attained. Paper-and-pencil measures have a place in this type of evaluation. But consider, also, such procedures as these:

- Presenting students with a problem-solving situation and observing how they meet it
- Interviewing students
- Having students describe to a group how they solved a problem
- Having one student teach another how to solve a problem

You will need to assess as you go along because you will want to ascertain children's understanding and difficulties with understanding, for guidance in developing the next lesson. Remember that problem solving cannot be learned in any one lesson. The process must develop and thus be assessed over time.

Observations

As children work individually or in small groups, you can move about the room, observing them as they work, listening as they talk among themselves, making notes, questioning, offering suggestions. Focus on how each goes about the task of solving a problem. You might want to consider the following points:

- Is there evidence of careful reading of the problem?
- Do individual children seem to have some means of beginning to attack a problem?

- Do they apply an appropriate strategy, or do they simply try to use the last procedure you taught?
- Do they have another strategy to try if the first one fails?
- How consistent and persistent are they in applying a strategy?
- Are careless errors being made, and if so, when and why?
- How long are they willing to keep trying to solve a problem?
- How well are they concentrating on the task?
- How quickly do they ask for help?
- What strategies does each child use most frequently?
- Do they use manipulative materials? How?
- What do their behaviors and the expressions on their faces indicate about their interest and involvement?

Then make a brief note—an anecdotal record—that describes the situation and the behaviors you have observed.

Interviews

An interview is an attempt to remove the limitations of writing—your own limitations in developing a written test item and the child's in developing a written answer. An interview lets you delve further into how a student goes about solving a problem. You can follow the child's thought patterns as he or she describes what is done and why.

Basically, you need to present the student with a problem; let the student find a solution and describe what he or she is doing; and question the student, eliciting specific details on what he or she is doing and why. Make notes as the student works and talks. Sometimes it is helpful to have an exact record of the replies.

You may want to have a student use a tape recorder when working alone. Or have a group of students discuss various ways of solving a problem. You can play the tape back later and analyze students' thinking more carefully and from a different perspective than if you are involved in the interview.

Inventories and Checklists

An inventory can be used to check on what a student knows about problem-solving strategies. You might give students one or several problems and ask them to solve each with a specified strategy or to solve each using two or three specified strategies. Your aim is to find out whether or not the student can apply each strategy—not what the answer to the problem is. You can also record your observations on a checklist, which then serves as an inventory.

Paper-and-Pencil Tests

You will also want to use written tests to assess children's ability to solve problems. Make sure that those you develop follow the guidelines of your problem-solving program—that is, select good problems that are interesting and challenging, allow sufficient time for the process, and so on. Of particular interest are paper-and-pencil tests that assess the stages of problem solving (see Schoen and Oehmke 1980; Charles et al. 1987).

Evaluation should be an ongoing component of the problem-solving program. You use it not just to assess where students are, but also to help you plan what to do next. If children do not use a strategy you have taught, you need to consider why, and then try again. If they try to use a strategy, you have evidence on how well they use it and whether they need more practice. Do not let evaluation become just a recording process. It is a way of helping you solve the problem of how to teach problem solving more effectively!

A Glance at Where We've Been

Learning and doing mathematics involves engaging in five key processes: problem solving, reasoning and proof, communication, connections, and representations. These processes are inextricably linked to the mathematics content that students learn (number, algebra, geometry, data, and measurement). Through the key mathematical processes, students engage actively in making sense of the mathematics they are learning.

Problem solving should pervade the mathematics curriculum. Children need many experiences with problems that they do not immediately know how to solve. Moreover, they should be taught to use a variety of problem-solving strategies, providing them with a repertoire from which they can draw. You will need to provide not only a large resource of good problems but also enough time for problem solving. Your instruction must coordinate textbook materials with the use of calculators and other technology, as well as large-group, small-group, and individual work.

An overall strategy for approaching problems is desirable (understand, plan, carry out, look back), plus specific strategies that give children ways to begin to attack a problem. This chapter has described

such strategies, provided sample problems, and discussed the assessment of problem solving by means of observations, interviews, inventories, and tests.

Things to Do: From What You've Read

1. What are the five key mathematical processes described in this chapter? For each process, briefly describe how the classroom snapshot story that opens this chapter shows children engaging in that process.

2. Make a list of as many different representations for the number 75 as you can think of. Compare your list with the lists of others. You might use equivalent expressions, models, words, pictures, and so on. It is a sign of flexibility in thinking to be able to represent numbers and other mathematical ideas in many different ways.

3. What are the three distinct types of connections that are important in school mathematics? Give two examples of each type of connection.

4. Describe why Polya's four-step plan is inadequate for helping students become good problem solvers. Why is it useful?

5. Discuss: We don't teach textbook word problems any more because no one has to solve that kind of problem.

6. Identify levels (such as primary or intermediate) for problems presented in the chapter.

7. Identify problems in the chapter for which calculators would be useful. Are there problems for which having a calculator available would take away all of the challenge? (These are important considerations when you are choosing problems for your class and deciding when students may and may not use calculators in their problem-solving efforts.)

8. Answer true or false, then defend your answer: Before solving a problem, pupils should be required to draw a picture of it.

9. Solve problems (5), (11), and (38) using two different strategies for each.

10. Why isn't finding the answer the final step in solving a problem?

Things to Do: Going Beyond This Book

field Additional activities, suggestions, and questions are provided in *Teaching Elementary Mathematics: A Resource for Field Experiences.*

1. Read *Counting on Frank* (Clement 1991). Write a lesson plan where this book would be read aloud to Grade 4–6 students as a motivator for some sort of problem-solving lesson.

2. *field* *Assessing Problem-Solving Strategies.* Choose a problem from this chapter and pose it to two children. Identify the strategies each child uses, use the analytic scoring scale in Figure 4–10 to score their work, and write an evaluation of their efforts.

3. Start a file with problems from this chapter and add other problems, especially nonroutine ones. Many math education Web sites offer long lists of interesting problems. Categorize the problems in the way you find most useful.

4. Make up problems using newspaper or magazine articles or data from reference books (for example, *Guiness Book of Records*) or Web sites. Add the problems to your file.

5. *field* *Mathematical Processes in the Classroom.* Observe an elementary school classroom while children are engaged in a math lesson or investigation. Make a list of instances in which the children show evidence of using one or more of the five mathematical processes. Tell what the children were doing or saying and what tasks were involved. What role did the teacher play?

6. Search textbooks for a particular grade level. Find at least one problem that could be solved by using the following strategies: Make a drawing or diagram, act it out, and solve a simpler or similar problem.

7. Choose a content topic for a particular grade level (for example, number, geometry, data). Make up at least one interesting problem for that topic that can be solved by each of these strategies: Look for a pattern, make a drawing or diagram, and construct a table.

8. Plan a bulletin board focused on problem solving.

9. Obtain catalogs from software companies; select promising software to promote problem solving.

10. Check a textbook for a list of the problem-solving strategies taught. Write an evaluation of it.

11. *field* *What Is "Doing Math"?* Talk to one or more elementary teachers about their vision of what it means to "do mathematics." Ask whether they connect math to other areas of their curriculum and, if so, how. Write a reflection about how teachers' views of mathematics fit (or do not fit) with a view involving the five mathematical processes discussed in this chapter.

12. Read O'Brien and Moss (1999). Choose your own context and problems similar to those used by these authors with fifth graders (problems with consistent data and with inconsistent data). If possible, try these problems with students of a similar age and analyze how they approach them.

BOOK NOOK FOR CHILDREN

Clement, Rod. *Counting on Frank.* Milwaukee: Gareth Stevens Publishing, 1991.

Hamm, Diane Johnston. *How Many Feet in the Bed?* New York: Simon and Schuster, 1991.

Hutchins, Pat. *The Doorbell Rang.* New York: Green Willow Books, 1986.

Sciedzka, Jon. *Math Curse.* New York: Viking, 1995.

Selected References

Azzolino, Aggie. "Writing as a Tool for Teaching Mathematics: The Silent Revolution." In *Teaching and Learning Mathematics in the 1990s* (1990 Yearbook) (ed. Thomas J. Cooney and Christian R. Hirsch). Reston, Va.: NCTM, pp. 92–100.

Becker, Jerry P. (ed.). *Report of U.S.–Japan Cross-National Research on Students: Problem Solving Behaviors.* Carbondale, Ill.: Southern Illinois University, 1992.

Bird, Elliott. "What's in the Box? A Problem-Solving Lesson and a Discussion about Teaching." *Teaching Children Mathematics,* 5 (May 1999), pp. 504–507.

Brown, Sue. "Integrating Manipulatives and Computers in Problem-Solving Experiences." *Arithmetic Teacher,* 38 (October 1990), pp. 8–10.

Carpenter, Thomas P.; Corbitt, Mary Kay; Kepner, Henry S., Jr.; Lindquist, Mary Montgomery; and Reys, Robert E. *Results from the Second Mathematics Assessment of the National Assessment of Educational Progress.* Reston, Va.: NCTM, 1981.

Chancellor, Dinah, and Porter, Jeanna. "Calendar Mathematics." *Arithmetic Teacher,* 41 (February 1994), pp. 304–305.

Charles, Randall, and Lester, Frank. *Teaching Problem Solving: What, Why & How.* Palo Alto, Calif.: Dale Seymour Publications, 1982.

Charles, Randall; Lester, Frank; and O'Daffer, Phares. *How to Evaluate Progress in Problem Solving.* Reston, Va.: NCTM, 1987.

Ciochine, John G., and Polivka, Grace. "The Missing Link? Writing in Mathematics Class!" *Mathematics Teaching in the Middle School,* 2 (March-April 1997), pp. 316–320.

Cognition and Technology Group at Vanderbilt University. "The Jasper Experiment: Using Video to Furnish Real-World Problem-Solving Contexts." *Arithmetic Teacher,* 40 (April 1993), pp. 474–478.

Countryman, Joan. *Writing to Learn Mathematics: Strategies that Work.* Portsmouth, N.H.: Heinemann, 1992.

Ford, Margaret I. "The Writing Process: A Strategy for Problem Solvers." *Arithmetic Teacher,* 38 (November 1990), pp. 35–38.

Franke, Megan Loef, and Carey, Deborah A. "Young Children's Perceptions of Mathematics in Problem-Solving Environments." *Journal for Research in Mathematics Education,* 28 (January 1997), pp. 8–25.

Gilbert-Macmillan, Kathleen, and Leitz, Steven J. "Cooperative Small Groups: A Method for Teaching Problem Solving." *Arithmetic Teacher,* 33 (March l986), pp. 9–11.

Hembree, Ray, and Marsh, Harold. "Problem Solving in Early Childhood: Building Foundations." In *Research Ideas for the Classroom: Early Childhood Mathematics* (ed. Robert J.

Jensen). Reston, Va.: NCTM, and New York: Macmillan, 1993, pp. 151–170.

Hiebert, James; Carpenter, Thomas P.; Fennema, Elizabeth; Fuson, Karen; Human, Piet; Murray, Hanlie; Olivier, Alwyn; and Wearne, Diana. "Problem Solving as a Basis for Reform in Curriculum and Instruction: The Case of Mathematics." *Educational Researcher* 25 (May 1996), pp. 12–21.

Hildebrand, Charlene; Ludeman, Clinton. J.; and Mullin, Joan. "Integrating Mathematics with Problem Solving Using the Mathematician's Chair." *Teaching Children Mathematics*, 5 (March 1999), pp. 434–441.

Hutchins, Pat. *The Doorbell Rang.* New York: Green Willow Books, 1986.

Kelly, Janet. "Improving Problem Solving Through Drawings." *Teaching Children Mathematics,* 6 (September 1999), pp. 48–51.

Kelly, M. G., and Wiebe, James H. "Using the Video Camera in Mathematical Problem Solving." *Arithmetic Teacher,* 41 (September 1993), pp. 41–43.

Kenney, Patricia Ann, and Silver, Edward A. (eds.). *Results from the Sixth Mathematics Assessment of the National Assessment of Educational Progress.* Reston, Va.: NCTM, 1997.

Kliman, Marlene, and Richards, Judith. "Writing, Sharing, and Discussing Mathematics Stories." *Arithmetic Teacher,* 40 (November 1992), pp. 138–141.

Kouba, Vicky L.; Zawojewski, Judith S.; and Strutchens, Marilyn E. "What Do Students Know about Numbers and Operations?" In *Results from the Sixth Mathematics Assessment of the National Assessment of Educational Progress,* (eds. Patricia Ann Kenney and Edward A. Silver). Reston, Va.: NCTM, 1997.

Kroll, Diana Lambdin, and Miller, Tammy. "Insights from Research on Mathematical Problem Solving in the Middle Grades." In *Research Ideas for the Classroom: Middle Grades Mathematics* (ed. Douglas T. Owens). Reston, Va.: NCTM, and New York: Macmillan, 1993, pp. 58–77.

Kroll, Diana Lambdin; Masingila, Joanna O.; and Mau, Sue Tinsley. "Cooperative Problem Solving: But What about Grading?" *Arithmetic Teacher,* 39 (February 1992), pp. 17–23.

Krulik, Stephen, and Rudnick, Jesse A. *The New Sourcebook for Teaching Reasoning and Problem Solving in Elementary School.* Boston: Allyn and Bacon, 1995.

Krulik, Stephen, and Reys, Robert E. (eds.). *Problem Solving in School Mathematics.* 1980 Yearbook. Reston, Va.: NCTM, 1980.

Leitze, Annette Ricks. "Connecting Process Problem Solving to Children's Literature." *Teaching Children Mathematics,* 3 (March 1997), pp. 398–406.

Lindquist, Mary Montgomery. "Problem Solving with Five Easy Pieces." *Arithmetic Teacher,* 25 (November 1977), pp. 7–10.

Lubinski, Cheryl Ann. "The Influence of Teachers' Beliefs and Knowledge on Learning Environments." *Arithmetic Teacher,* 41 (April 1994), pp. 476–479.

Middleton, James A. and Goepfert, Polly. *Inventive Strategies for Teaching Mathematics: Implementing Standards for Reform.* Washington, D.C.: American Psychological Association, 1996.

Mills, Heidi; O'Keefe, Timothy; and Whitin, David. *Mathematics in the Making: Authoring Ideas in Primary Classrooms.* Portsmouth, N.H.: Heinemann, 1996.

Morris, Janet. *How to Develop Problem Solving with a Calculator.* Reston, Va.: NCTM, 1981.

Moses, Barbara; Bjork, Elizabeth; and Goldenberg, E. Paul. "Beyond Problem Solving: Problem Posing. In Thomas J. Cooney (ed.), *Teaching and Learning Mathematics in the 1990s* (1990 Yearbook). Reston, VA: NCTM, 1990, pp. 82–91.

National Council of Teachers of Mathematics. *Principles and Standards for School Mathematics.* Reston, Va.: NCTM, 2000.

National Council of Teachers of Mathematics. *Reaching Higher: A Problem-Solving Approach to Elementary School Mathematics.* Reston, Va.: NCTM, 1990.

O'Brien, Thomas C., and Ann C. Moss. "On the Keeping of Several Things in Mind." *Teaching Children Mathematics,* 6 (October 1999), pp. 118–122.

Polya, George. *How to Solve It.* Princeton, N.J.: Princeton University Press, 1973 (1945, 1957). Worth, Ill.: Creative Publications.

Russell, Susan Jo. "Mathematical Reasoning in the Elementary Grades." In *Developing Mathematical Reasoning in Grades K–12* (ed. Lee V. Stiff). Reston, Va.: NCTM, 1999, p. 1–12.

Sanfiorenzo, Norberto R. "Evaluating Expressions: A Problem-Solving Approach." *Arithmetic Teacher,* 38 (March 1991), pp. 34–35.

Sawada, Daiyo. "Mathematics as Problem Solving: A Japanese Way." *Teaching Children Mathematics,* 6 (September 1999), pp. 54–58.

Schoen, Harold L., and Oehmke, Theresa. "A New Approach to the Measurement of Problem-Solving Skills." In *Problem Solving in School Mathematics, 1980* (eds. Stephen Krulik and Robert E. Reys). Reston, Va.: NCTM, 1980, pp. 216–227.

Silbey, Robyn. "What Is in the Daily News? Problem-Solving Opportunities." *Teaching Children Mathematics,* 5 (March 1999), pp. 390–394.

Silverman, Fredrick L.; Winograd, Ken; and Strohauer, Donna. "Student-Generated Story Problems." *Arithmetic Teacher,* 39 (April 1992), pp. 6–12.

Suydam, Marilyn N. "Update on Research on Problem Solving: Implications for Classroom Teaching." *Arithmetic Teacher,* 29 (February 1982), pp. 56–60.

Suydam, Marilyn N. "Indications from Research on Problem Solving." In *Teaching and Learning: A Problem-Solving Focus* (ed. Frances R. Curcio). Reston, Va.: NCTM, 1987, pp. 99–114.

Suydam, Marilyn N., and Weaver, J. Fred. *Using Research: A Key to Elementary School Mathematics.* Columbus, Ohio: ERIC Clearinghouse for Science, Mathematics and Environmental Education, 1981.

Thornton, Carol A., and Bley, Nancy S. "Problem Solving: Help in the Right Direction for LD Students." *Arithmetic Teacher,* 29 (February 1982), pp. 26–27, 38–41.

Van Zoerts, Laura E. and Enyart Ann. "Discourse of Course: Encouraging Genuine Mathematical Conversations." *Mathematics Teaching in the Middle School* 4(3), 1998, pp. 150–157.

Weinberg, Susan. "Going Beyond Ten Black Dots." *Teaching Children Mathematics,* 2 (March 1996), pp. 432–435.

Wheatley, Charlotte L. "Calculator Use and Problem-Solving Performance." *Journal for Research in Mathematics Education,* 11 (November 1980), pp. 323–334.

Wilde, Sandra. "Learning to Write About Mathematics." *Arithmetic Teacher,* 38 (February 1991), pp. 38–43.

Wood, Terry, and Sellers, Patricia. "Assessment of a Problem-Centered Mathematics Program: Third Grade." *Journal for Research in Mathematics Education,* 27 (May 1996), pp. 337–353.

6 Beginning Number Sense: Counting and Early Benchmarks

Snapshot of a Lesson

Key Ideas for an Early Lesson on Numbers

1. Maintain and/or improve skill in recognizing the number of objects in small groups.
2. Increase awareness of number patterns.
3. Develop counting skills.

Necessary Materials

Overhead projector and about twenty counters or beans.

Orientation

The children are learning to recognize by sight the number of objects in small groups. The teacher, Miss Chen, spends a few minutes each day on this activity. She has just placed four beans on the face of the overhead. She turns on the overhead for two seconds, then turns it off.

Miss Chen

MISS CHEN: How many beans did you see?

Less than half the children raise their hands, so Miss Chen decides to do it again. This time nearly all the children raise their hands.

MISS CHEN: How many beans? Barry?

BARRY: Four.

One child, Susan, is in obvious disagreement, so Miss Chen calls on her.

SUSAN: Five.

MISS CHEN: Okay, let's check. I will turn on the overhead and Susan can count the beans for us.

Susan counts the images.

SUSAN: There are only four. When I saw the pattern, I thought there was one in the middle.

MISS CHEN: I am glad Susan is looking for patterns. That is the key to recognizing groups of things. Let's try another one, and be sure to look for patterns.

Miss Chen places five beans on the overhead, turns it on for two seconds, and then turns it off.

MISS CHEN: How many beans?

All the children have a hand up; Miss Chen points to one of them, who says five. The others agree.

MISS CHEN: We will try one more.

Miss Chen places five beans on the overhead in a different arrangement. She then turns it on for two seconds.

MISS CHEN: How many beans did you see? Bonny?

BONNY: Five, but it looks different than the other five.

SUSAN: It is different because there are six. It fits the pattern for six.

MISS CHEN: Let's check it.

Miss Chen turns the projector on, and Bonny confirms there are five. Susan and many other children are looking for patterns, but their recognition skills need sharpening. They see part of a pattern but are not sensitive to small differences. That's why this activity is used for a couple of minutes each day.

MISS CHEN: Thanks, Bonny, there are only five. We really have to watch those patterns carefully. That's enough for today.

Many children groan and plead for more. They really enjoy this activity, but Miss Chen realizes the value of not overdoing a good thing. Therefore, she is careful not to "burn them out" with too much at one time. Even though the children don't realize it, this activity reviews counting and increases their readiness for addition and subtraction.

Introduction

Number sense, like common sense, is difficult to define or express simply. It refers to an intuitive feel for numbers and their various uses and interpretations, many of which are shown in the Number and Operation Standard of the *Principles and Standards for School Mathematics* (NCTM 2000) in Appendix A. Number sense also includes the ability to compute accurately and efficiently, to detect errors, and to recognize results as reasonable. People with number sense are able to understand numbers and use them effectively in everyday living (McIntosh et al. 1997). Good number sense also includes recognizing the relative magnitude of numbers and establishing referents, or benchmarks, for measures of common objects and situations in their environments.

These ideas regarding number sense are reminiscent of Brownell's ideas about meaningful learning (see Chapter 2). Students need to develop concepts meaningfully so that numbers are used effectively both in and out of school. Helping students to develop such number sense requires appropriate modeling, posing process questions, encouraging thinking about numbers, and in general creating a classroom environment that nurtures number sense.

Let's explore several examples of number sense in action. What does the number 5 mean to young children? It can mean many things. It might be their current age or their age next year. It might be how old they were when they started kindergarten.

Figure 6–1 illustrates a few uses and interpretations of the number 5 suggested by young children. Other children would provide different examples. In fact, the examples in Figure 6–1 might be different for the same children tomorrow because children's concept of numbers continuously grows and changes. A few examples illustrating the multidimensional nature of number sense for older children are shown in Figure 6–2.

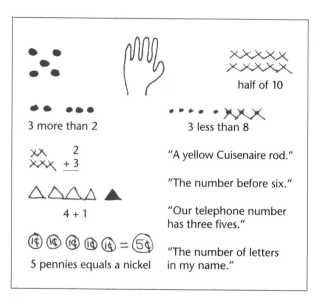

Figure 6–1 • The meanings of the number five suggested by young children

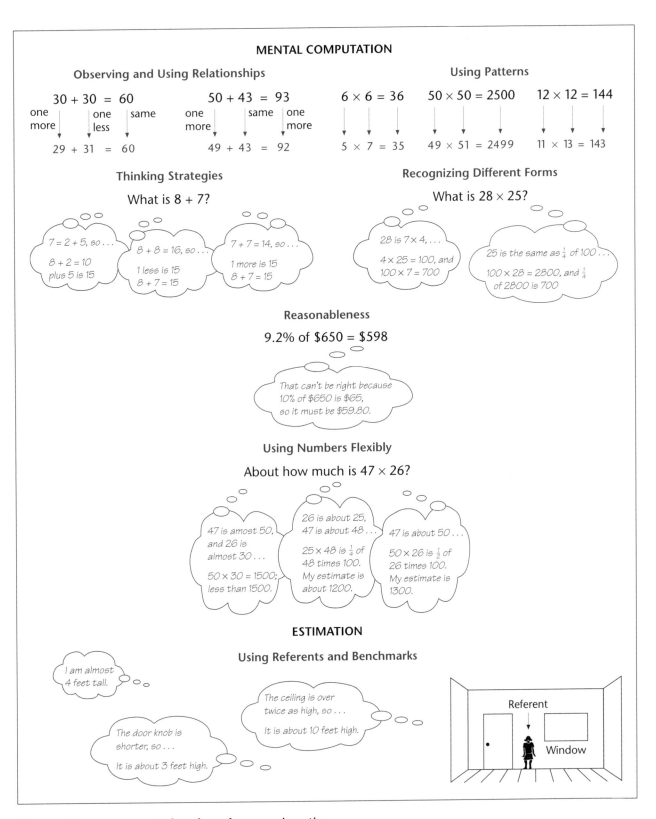

Figure 6–2 • Some examples of number sense in action

It should be understood that number sense is not a finite entity that a student either has or does not have. Its development is a lifelong process. In an effort to facilitate the development of number sense in elementary school, the NCTM has published several books on number sense (Burton et al. 1993; Reys et al. 1991).

Children begin to develop some sense about numbers long before they begin to count. For example, young children can answer these kinds of questions:

How old are you? [two]

What channel should we watch? [thirteen]

On what floor is your doctor's office? [four]

How many sisters do you have? [one]

Such early experiences introduce the number names as well as their symbols—13 on the channel indicator or 4 on the elevator. These names and symbols are memorized through sound and sight recognition and provide an important beginning, but a child's knowledge of these alone does not indicate the child's grasp of number.

For one thing, these experiences underscore a very important characteristic of number. It is an abstraction. It can't be adequately illustrated in just one situation. The multiple meanings of 5 illustrated in Figure 6–1 demonstrate how quickly the concept of *five* becomes associated with different situations. Research into how children develop number sense makes it clear that the more varied and different their experiences, the more likely it is that they will abstract number concepts from their experiences (Payne and Huinker 1993). Helping children further their development of number and number sense has a high instructional priority. The goal of this chapter is to stimulate your thinking about number sense and its development during the early stages of prenumber experiences and counting.

PRENUMBER CONCEPTS

Numbers are everywhere, and thus even young children have a vast amount of early number experience, as was shown in Figure 6–1. Many of these experiences do not rely on numbers per se but provide the basis for building early number concepts and the foundation for later skills. Such experiences are called *prenumber experiences* and, as teachers, we often need to help children take advantage of them. Different steps are involved in developing prenumber concepts that will lead eventually to meaningful counting skills and number sense. Although the learning paths that children take are bound to differ greatly, they all begin with classifying whatever is to be counted.

Classification

Classification is fundamental to learning about the real world, and it can be done with or without numbers. For example, children can be separated into groups of boys and girls (which is classification) without considering number. Yet classification skills are prerequisite to any meaningful number work. If we want to know how many girls are in the class, we must be able to recognize (that is, classify) the girls. Thus, before children can count, they must know what to count, and classification helps identify what is to be counted.

Young children learn to distinguish between dogs and cats, reptiles and mammals, toys they enjoy and those they never use. These distinctions are examples of classification in action. Classification not only helps children make some sense of things around them but also helps them become flexible thinkers. Classifying objects in different ways fosters the development of thinking skills.

As children classify, or sort, materials, such as buttons (see Snapshot of a Lesson Plan in Chapter 3), they must decide whether or not each object has the given characteristic. If children disagree on how an object should be classified, it forces them to defend their answers and clarify how the classification process was done. This type of argumentation is the beginning of helping children see the need for explaining their thoughts in mathematics, one of the goals of the *Principles and Standards*. At this point, there may be no counting as materials are classified, although words such as *more, few, many, most,* and *none* will likely be used in describing the resulting collections.

Classification allows us to reach general agreement on what is to be counted. For example, consider a pile of buttons and the following question: How many plastic buttons have two holes? The answer is a number that tells *how many*. When a number is used in this way, it is called a *cardinal number*. However, before finding the specific cardinal number, we must first decide which buttons are plastic and how many of them have exactly two holes. Once this classification is done, the members to be counted are well defined, and the results should be the same.

Stories provide opportunities for classification. Books such as *Where's Waldo?* by Martin Handford challenge students to find objects in a vast and often complex picture containing many different things. Such search-and-find challenges provide practice in visual discrimination as well as in classification.

Attribute blocks, sometimes called *logic blocks,* provide an excellent model for classification activities and help develop logical thinking. These blocks can be made from cardboard (see Appendix B for an attribute block master), but they are also commercially available in wood or plastic. They differ in several attributes, including color, shape, and size. Consider, for example, the twenty-four pieces shown in Appendix B and In the Classroom 6–1. These pieces illustrate three attributes:

Size: Large, Small (L, S)

Color: Black, White, Gray (B, W, G)

Shape: Square, Triangle, Pentagon, Circle (S, T, P, C)

In The Classroom 6–1

Who Am I?

Objective: Using attribute pieces to develop classification and reasoning.

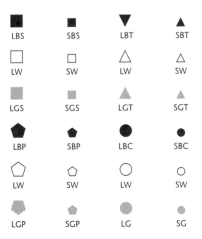

LBS	SBS	LBT	SBT
LW	SW	LW	SW
LGS	SGS	LGT	SGT
LBP	SBP	LBC	SBC
LW	SW	LW	SW
LGP	SGP	LG	SG

▼ Match me with the attribute blocks shown here:

A. I have three sides.
I am black.
I am large.

Who am I? _____

B. I am black or white.
I have three sides.
I am not large.

Who am I? _____

C. I am not black.
I am not white.
I have five sides.
I am small.

Who am I? _____

D. I am not large.
I have more than four sides.
I am gray.

Who am I? _____

• Which clues describe more than one piece? _____

• Which clues describe only one piece? _____

▼ Your turn:

Play "Who Am I?" with a partner.

The first block can be described in words as the "Large Black Square." Later in primary and elementary school, symbols, such as LBS, can be meaningfully attached to the attribute pieces, but at this stage a clear verbal description of the pieces by young children is the goal. As children manipulate the blocks and describe them, they begin to make natural connections between the concrete model and different ways of representation. Many of the twenty-four pieces are alike in some attributes, but no two pieces are alike in all attributes, which provides opportunities for "Who am I?" games, as presented in In the Classroom 6–1. Such activities encourage children to think logically and develop communication skills. In the process, children informally explore fundamental notions, including matching, comparison, shape, sets, subsets, and disjoint sets as well as set operations.

Communication and language can be further developed as the set operations of union and intersection are encountered. The combining, or union, of *disjoint sets* (sets with no members in common) is a natural model for addition. The logical connection *or* can be used to develop the union of two or more sets. For example, as Figure 6–3 shows, the union of triangles and squares produces a set that contains all attribute blocks that are either triangles *or* squares.

The intersection of sets can be used to explore the logical connective *and*. Using the attribute blocks, we could examine the pieces that are pentagons *and* blue. Children might place these in yarn loops as shown in Figure 6–4. This arrangement also allows children to identify other subsets, such as pieces that

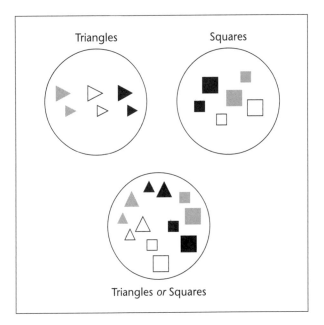

Figure 6–3 • The union of two sets

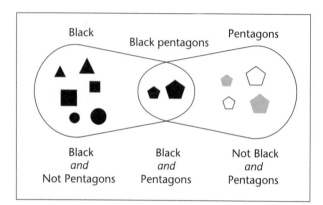

Figure 6–4 • The intersection of two sets

are blue and not pentagons. Using *not* to describe a relationship is an important step in development.

The logical connectives *and, or,* and *not* can be used to help children classify pieces according to their attributes. For example, the "alike and difference trains" shown in In the Classroom 6–2 provide opportunities for students to use attribute blocks to classify and to search for patterns and use logical thinking as well. Children at all grade levels can benefit from structured activities with these materials.

Attribute blocks almost guarantee student involvement, but they also require teachers to assume an active role. When children are engaged in activities with attribute blocks, directed questions and probes can provide clues about their thinking processes. Observing children's actions reveals much about their maturity. For example, when asked to choose a piece that is black and a triangle, one child might choose a black piece but not a triangle. Another might select a triangle that is not black. These responses may only reflect poor listening skills. However, additional questioning may show the two children don't understand what the word "and" means or are unable to keep two different attributes in mind simultaneously. Carefully observing and questioning children as they are using these materials will help you better understand what they are thinking, which in turn will help you design more appropriate learning activities.

Many different experiences are needed to sharpen children's observation skills and provide them with the basis on which the notion of numbers is built. Consider another example, in which children are asked to count money:

| 1¢ | 1¢ | 5¢ |

In The Classroom 6–2

Alike-and-Difference Trains

Objective: Using attribute pieces to recognize patterns and identify relationships.

Each car in a train is like the car it follows in two ways, *or* it is different from the car it follows in two ways.

▼ Find the alike-and-difference pattern in each train, and describe the missing car:

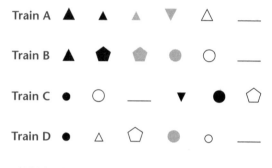

Train A
Train B
Train C
Train D

• Which of these are one-difference trains? ____

• Which of these are two-difference trains? ____

▼ Your turn:

• Begin with ■. Make a train (with at least six cars) in which each car has exactly one attribute different from the car it follows. Compare your train with someone's train. Are they the same?

• Begin with ■. Make a train (with at least six cars) in which each car has exactly one attribute the same as the car it follows. Compare your train with a classmate's train. Tell how they are alike.

How much money is this?

Three, if coins are counted

Seven, if cents are counted

This example provides a reminder that a number name alone, such as three or seven, is rarely reported. In this case, "three coins" tells us both *cardinality* (that is, how many) and what was actually counted. This example also provides another reminder that what is to be counted must be well defined or clearly understood. If there is any confusion about what is being counted, then counting discrepancies are certain to happen.

Such discrepancies occur in many different forms but are particularly troublesome with a number line. Two children standing on a number line that has been made from a roll of adding machine tape and fastened to the floor provide an example:

We can ask,

How far is it from Barb to Scott?

Is it 4? or 3? or 5?

The solution depends on what is to be counted:

Should the intervals between the dots be counted?

Should the dots be counted?

All of the dots?

Research confirms that confusion between dots and intervals often contributes to later misunderstanding with a number line (Sowder 1992). Confusion over what should be counted is a classification problem that must be solved before counting can be meaningful. Thus, classification is a very important step in developing number sense and early counting skills (Payne and Huinker 1993).

Patterns

Mathematics is the study of patterns. Creating, constructing, and describing patterns require problem-solving skills and constitute an important part of mathematics learning. Patterns can be based on geometric attributes (shape, symmetry), relational attributes (sequence, function), physical attributes (color, length, number), or affective attributes (like, happiness). Sometimes patterns combine several attributes. For example, a child's list of favorite colors provides a pattern involving physical attributes (color) and affective attributes (like).

Paper, cubes, attribute blocks, pattern blocks, and other manipulatives (objects) provide opportunities for children to stack, arrange, and order objects in various ways. Number sense and mathematical exploration grow from such patterning. In the early grades, patterns help children develop number sense, ordering, counting, and sequencing (Coburn et al. 1992). Later, patterns are helpful in developing thinking strategies for basic facts, as will be discussed in Chapter 8. As children grow older, their experiences with patterns accelerate as they explore graph-

ing, number theory, and geometry. Patterns, as with puzzles, are usually intellectually inviting and stimulating for people of all ages.

Exploring patterns requires active mental involvement and often physical involvement. The opportunities to do patterning are limitless, but there are several different types of pattern activities that children should encounter regularly. Let's consider four different ways that patterns might be used in developing mathematical ideas.

Copying a Pattern Children are shown a pattern and then asked to make one "just like it." The original pattern might take many different forms. For example, children might be given a string with beads and asked to make the same pattern:

Or pattern blocks could be laid out for children to copy:

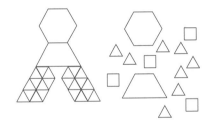

This experience requires students to choose the same pieces and arrange them in the same order. Or one could model a figure on a geoboard (see Appendix B for a geoboard master)

and ask children to copy the figure on an empty geoboard.

Finding the Next One The trains in In the Classroom 6–2 illustrate problems where children "find the next one." In that case, "the next one" was the next car in the train. Consider a somewhat easier pattern suggested by "stairs" of Cuisenaire rods:

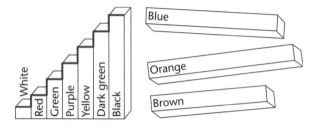

Children might be asked to find the next rod for the staircase. This find-the-next activity naturally leads to continuing or extending the pattern.

Extending a Pattern Children are shown a pattern and asked to continue it. For example, an initial pattern can be made with blocks, and children can be asked to continue the pattern:

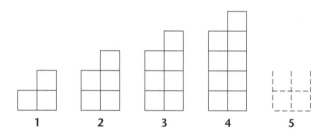

Notice how this visual pattern might serve as the foundation for exploring several important mathematical ideas. It could lead to classifying odd numbers. It could be used to observe something common about the representations—that they are all a rectangle plus one. This latter observation might lead to the algebraic generalization $2N + 1$ to describe odd numbers.

Making Their Own Patterns Children need opportunities to create their own patterns and are eager to do so. Sometimes the patterns they make are highly creative and reveal insight into their mathematical thinking.

Language and communication are important elements of patterning activities. Children should be encouraged to "think out loud" as they search for patterns. Ask them to explain why they selected a certain piece or why they did what they did. Sometimes children "see" different patterns than we anticipate. As teachers, we must try to learn and understand children's patterns and encourage them to share their thinking.

Comparisons

Comparison of quantities is another important part of learning to count and is also essential in developing number awareness. Comparisons are plentiful in classrooms as children use materials. Teacher-led activities frequently provide opportunities for comparisons, with questions such as

> Does everyone have a piece of paper?
>
> Are there more pencils or desks?

These questions either directly or indirectly involve comparisons, which may lead to the very important and powerful mathematical notion of one-to-one correspondence.

Look at Figure 6–5A and consider this question: are there more hearts or gingerbread cookies? Counting would provide a solution, particularly with the cookies scattered on a plate. However, if the cookies are arranged in an orderly fashion (Figure 6–5B), we can make direct comparisons and answer the question without counting. Sometimes placing connectors (laying string or yarn; drawing lines or arrows) provides a visual reminder of the one-to-one correspondence that underlies many comparisons, as in Figure 6–5C.

When making comparisons, students must be able to discriminate between important and irrelevant attributes. In Figure 6–6A, for example, who has more leaves—Bonnie or Sammy? The leaves are very different; their sizes, shapes, and colors vary. Still, the procedure for setting up a correspondence is the same.

To ensure that members of two sets are arranged in an orderly fashion for comparison, a method that is sometimes helpful involves using pieces of square paper or index cards. In this case placing each leaf on a card and then stacking the cards on a common base as in Figure 6–6B provides a helpful framework. This method provides a graphical representation of the information, allowing quick and accurate visual comparisons.

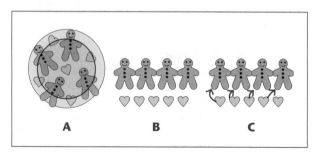

Figure 6–5 • Models for counting (A) versus comparison (B) with one-to-one correspondence (C)

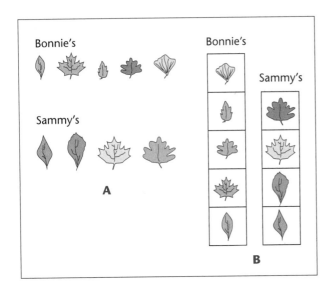

Figure 6–6 • A framework for comparison that eliminates irrelevant attributes

Several different but equally valid verbal descriptions may be used for the example given in Figure 6–6:

> Bonnie has more leaves than Sammy.
>
> Sammy has fewer leaves than Bonnie.

Children need to become familiar with descriptions of relationships such as *more than, less (fewer) than,* and *as many as.* A grasp of these terms is followed by more explicit characterization:

> Bonnie has one more leaf than Sammy.
>
> Sammy has one less leaf than Bonnie.

In these cases, the notion of order and succession are being developed. Children must come to realize that 4 is the number between 5 and 3 as well as one more than 3 and 1 less than 5. Understanding of such relationships can evolve naturally as comparisons are made and discussed.

When comparisons are made among several different things, ordering is involved. For example, children can print their first names on some grid paper:

Then they can physically compare their names with others' names to answer questions such as these:

> Who has the longest name?
>
> Who has the shortest name?

Can you find someone with a name the same length as yours?

Can you find someone whose name has one more (less) letter than your name?

Ordering often requires several comparisons, and a graph might help organize the information. The graph in Figure 6–7 was constructed by classifying children's names according to length. It summarizes much information and presents it in an organized form. The graph could be used to answer the previous questions and additional questions such as these:

> Which length name is most popular?
>
> Greg wasn't here today. Where should his name go on our graph?
>
> Can you think of anyone you know who has a shorter name than Tim?

As more things are ordered, the ordering process becomes more complicated, and most children need some guidance to be able to order things efficiently. That's why organizational techniques, such as graphing (see Chapter 16), are particularly helpful and will contribute to the early development of numbers.

Conservation

The phenomenon of *conservation of number*—that a given number does not vary—reflects how children think. We need to be aware of the symptoms of the

Figure 6–7 • Classification of children's names on a graph for comparison

lack of conservation of number in children and its implications for early number development and counting. This phenomenon occurs in different forms, but we'll look at an example involving counting and numbers.

Two rows of blocks are arranged side by side, and a teacher and a five- or six-year-old child look at them together:

The teacher, asking the child to make a comparison to decide whether there are more white blocks or purple blocks, initiates the following dialogue.

T: How many purple blocks?

S: (Counting them) Six.

T: How many white blocks?

S: (Counting again) Six.

T: Are there more purple blocks or white blocks?

S: They are the same.

Now the teacher spreads out the white blocks as follows:

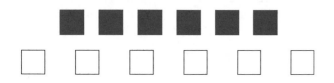

T: How many purple blocks now?

S: Six.

T: How many white blocks now?

S: Six.

T: Are there more purple blocks or white blocks?

S: More white blocks.

T: I thought you said there were six purple and six white.

S: I did, but this six (pointing to row of white blocks) is bigger.

This example illustrates a typical case where a young child thinks a number varies and depends on arrangement or configuration. Here the child believes that stretching out the row makes it longer; the fact that the number remains the same creates no conflict. Look at the following grouping of marbles.

Some children count six in each of these groups but report one group has more. For adults it seems inconceivable that "this six" could be more than "that six," but as this and other examples in this book show, children's logic and adults' logic are very different.

The phenomenon of conservation was described by Jean Piaget and has been the subject of much research. Rarely do children conserve number before five or six years of age. Children up to this age don't realize that moving the objects in a set has no effect on the number of the objects. Thus, many children in kindergarten and some in first and second grade are nonconservers. A child can be very adept at counting and remain naive about conservation. Whenever this happens, instructional activities (such as the different configurations of five objects on the overhead in the opening Snapshot Lesson) should be used to increase the child's awareness of the invariance of number.

Group Recognition

The patterns encountered in classifying and making comparisons provide many number-sense experiences. In fact, prior to actually counting, children are aware of small numbers of things: one nose, two hands, three wheels on a tricycle. Research shows that most children entering school can identify quantities of three things or less by inspection alone without the use of counting techniques (Clements 1999; Payne and Huinker 1993).

The skill to "instantly see how many" in a group is called *subitizing*, from a Latin word meaning "suddenly." It is an important skill to develop. In fact, one instructional goal for first-grade students is to develop immediate recognition of groups of up to five or six. Sight recognition of quantities up to five or six is important for several reasons:

1. It saves time. Recognizing the number in a small group is much faster than counting each individual member of that group.

2. It is the forerunner of some powerful number ideas. Children who can name small groups give ev-

idence of knowing early order relations, such as 3 is more than 2 and 1 is less than 4. Some may also realize that 3 contains a group of 2 and a group of 1.

3. It helps develop more sophisticated counting skills. Children who recognize the number in a small group will more quickly begin counting from that point.

4. It accelerates the development of addition and subtraction. Early work with these operations involves manipulation with objects. Being able to recognize the quantity in a small group will free children of the burden of counting small quantities to be joined or removed and allow them to concentrate on the action of the operation.

The teacher in the opening Snapshot Lesson used beans and the overhead projector to develop sight recognition. The overhead projector allowed careful control of time so that the children could not count individual beans. The teacher placed the beans in different arrangements to encourage children to identify different patterns—and to do so quickly. Several different approaches were demonstrated as the children counted. Sight recognition is also evidenced by children's skills in reading the number of dots on the face of a die or on a domino. In fact, both of these materials provide natural as well as interesting models for developing and practicing this skill.

As children grow older, their ability to recognize quantities continues to improve, but it is still very limited. Certain arrangements are more easily recognized or subitized. For example, look at these arrangements:

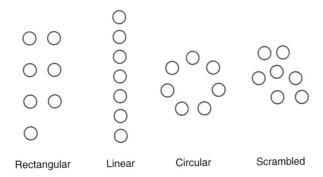

| Rectangular | Linear | Circular | Scrambled |

Children usually find rectangular arrangements easiest, followed by linear, and circular, whereas scrambled arrangements are usually the most difficult. If the arrangement does not lend itself to some grouping, people of any age have more difficulty with larger quantities. Few adults can recognize by inspection groups of more than 6 or 8, and even these

groups must be in common patterns such as those found on playing cards or dominoes. For example, look at these birds:

How many birds do you see? Each picture shows 12 birds, but you probably used different processes to count them. The picture at the left provides no clear groups, so you could either count every bird or perhaps immediately identify the numbers in some subset of the birds and then count the rest. In the other two pictures, some natural groupings are suggested: four groups of 3 and two groups of 6. It is even more difficult to recognize larger groupings without counting or forming some subsets of numbers. Nevertheless, small-group recognition is a powerful ally in counting larger groups.

COUNTING

Patterns facilitate the counting process. However, there are no sound patterns within the first twelve number names. Children learn these number names by imitating adults and older children. As young children practice counting, they often say nonconventional sequences of number names. It is not unusual to hear a young child count "one, two, five, eight, fifteen, twenty, six, hundred." This counting may sound strange, but it is perfectly natural. It reflects the child's struggle to remember both the number names and their order, both of which are necessary to count.

Eventually children may count apples, blocks, cards, rocks, stones, twigs, even petals on a flower. Try counting the petals on the flowers shown in Figure 6–8. They provide a very interesting setting for practicing counting and remind us that numbers are everywhere in nature.

Items such as blocks or petals are *discrete objects*—that is, materials that lend themselves well to handling and counting. *Continuous quantities,* such as the amount of water in a glass or the weight of a person, are measured rather than counted.

What is counting? It is a surprisingly intricate process by which children call number values by name. A close look at the counting process shows that finding how many objects are present involves two distinct actions. A child must say the number-name series, beginning with one, and point to a

Figure 6–8 • Models from nature for counting practice

different object as each number name is spoken. Children exhibit several different but distinct stages of counting, which we will soon discuss.

Counting Principles

How do children count? Let's look at an actual counting situation. Suppose seven shells are to be counted. A child who is what we will call a "rational counter" says each number name as the shells are counted, as indicated in Figure 6–9. The last number named, "seven," reports the total.

As adults, we probably cannot recall our own struggle with counting. Yet observing young children can remind us how counting strategies vary and are developed sequentially over a period of

years (Fuson 1988). Here are four important principles on which the counting process rests:

1. Each object to be counted must be assigned one and only one number name. As shown in Figure 6–9, a one-to-one correspondence between each block and the number name was established.

2. The number-name list must be used in a fixed order every time a group of objects is counted. The child in the figure started with "one" and counted "two, three, . . . , seven," in a specific order. This is known as the *stable order rule*.

3. The order in which the objects are counted doesn't matter (this is known as the *order irrelevance rule*). Thus the child can start with any object and count them in any order.

4. The last number name used gives the number of objects. This principle is a statement of the *cardinality rule,* which connects counting with *how many.* Regardless of which block is counted first or the order in which they are counted, the last block named always tells the number.

These principles help us recognize the levels of children's counting skills. Careful observation of children, coupled with a good understanding of these principles, will pinpoint counting errors. Once the trouble is diagnosed, instruction can focus on the specific problem.

Counting Stages

There are several identifiable counting stages, and each reflects one or more of the counting principles. For example, some children may count the objects correctly and still not know how many objects have been counted. In response to the question "How many shells are on the table?" a child might correctly count "one, two, three, four, five, six, seven," as shown in Figure 6–9, and yet be unable to answer the question. This child does not realize that the last number named tells how many.

Rote Counting A child using rote counting knows some number names, but not necessarily the proper sequence, as shown in Figure 6–10A. In this case, the child provides number names, but these names are not in correct counting sequence. Research shows that such children may "count" the same objects several times and use a different counting sequence each time (Fuson 1988).

Rote counters may know the proper counting sequence, but they may not always be able to maintain a correct correspondence between the objects being

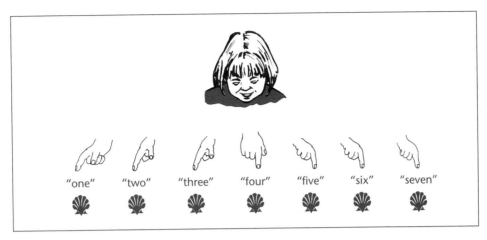

Figure 6–9 • Rational counting: Correct sequence, with correct correspondence

counted and the number names. Figure 6–10B shows an example in which the rote counter is saying the number names faster than pointing, so that number names are not coordinated with the shells being counted. Rote counters may say the number names until they perceive all the objects as being counted. It is also possible that the rote counter points faster than saying the words, as illustrated in Figure 6–10C. This rote counter is pointing to the objects but is not providing a name for each of them.

Thus, rote counters may not have their number names in the proper sequence, or they may not consistently provide a number name for each object being counted. A one-to-one correspondence may

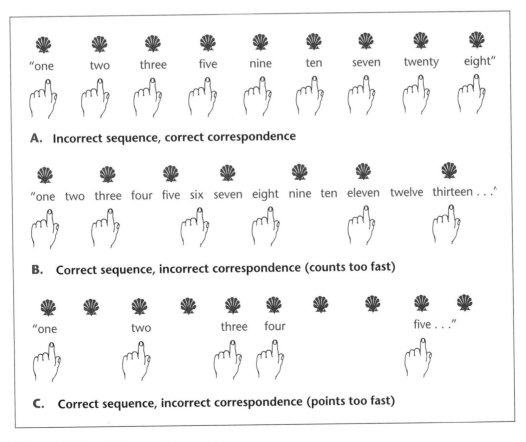

A. Incorrect sequence, correct correspondence

B. Correct sequence, incorrect correspondence (counts too fast)

C. Correct sequence, incorrect correspondence (points too fast)

Figure 6–10 • Rote counting errors

not be shown, which is a critical distinction between rote and rational counting. Using a one-to-one correspondence in counting represents significant progress and establishes one of the prerequisites to rational counting.

Rational Counting In rational counting, the child gives a correct number name as objects are counted in succession. However, in rational counting the child not only uses one-to-one correspondence in counting but also is able to answer the question about the number of objects being counted. In fact, rational counters exhibit all four counting principles.

Rational counting is an important skill for every primary-grade child. Children notice their own progress in developing this skill and become proud of their accomplishments. Early in first grade, some children will count to 10, others to 20, some to 50, and a few to over 100 (Fuson 1988). No upper limit should be imposed, although a goal of 100 is clearly reasonable for most children by the end of first grade. Instruction should provide regular practice and encourage each child to count as far as he or she can.

Counting Strategies

Once mastery of rational counting to 10 or 20 has been reached, more efficient and sophisticated counting strategies should be encouraged.

Counting On In counting on, the child gives correct number names as counting proceeds and can start at any number and begin counting. For example, the child can begin with 8 pennies and count "nine, ten, eleven"; or begin with 78 pennies and count "seventy-nine, eighty, eighty-one"; or begin with 98 pennies and count "ninety-nine, one hundred, one hundred one." Counting-on practice leads children to the discovery of many valuable patterns. Counting on is also an essential strategy for developing addition.

Counting Back When children count back, they give correct number names as they count backward from a particular point. For example, to count back to solve the problem, "Bobbie had 22 rabbits and 3 were lost," a child might count "twenty-one, twenty, nineteen" and conclude there were 19 left. At an early stage, counting back can be related to rockets blasting off (counting down—five, four, three, two, one, blast off); later, it becomes helpful in developing subtraction.

Many children find it very difficult to count backward, just as many adults find it difficult to recite the alphabet backward. The calculator provides a valuable instructional tool to help children improve their ability to count backward. Many children are surprised to learn that it is as easy to count backward on a calculator as it is to count forward.

Instruction in counting should include practice counting backward as well as forward. Counting backward, "Five, four, three, two, one," helps children establish sequences and relate each number to another in a different way. In the Classroom 6–3 provides an activity that integrates such practice with pattern recognition.

In The Classroom 6–3

Hunting for Numbers

Objective: Using a hundred chart to identify patterns and develop number sense.

▼ Look at this chart:

1	2	3	4	5	6	7	8	9	10
11	12	13	14	15	16	17	18	19	20
21	22	23	24	25	26	27	28	29	30
31	32	33	34	35	36	37	38	39	40
41	42	■	44	45	46	47	48	49	50
51	52	53	54	55	56	57	58	59	60
61	62	63	64	65	66	67	68	69	70
71	72	73	74	75	76	77	78	79	80
81	82	83	84	85	86	87	88	89	90
91	92	93	94	95	96	97	98	99	100

- What is hidden by the ■ ?
- What number is after ■ ?
- What number is before the ■ ?

▼ Put a ● on any number.

- Begin at ● : Count forward five.
- Begin at ● again: Count backward five.

▼ Put a ▲ on a different number.

- Begin at ▲ : Count forward five.
- Begin at ▲ again: Count backward five.

▼ Tell about any patterns you see.

Skip Counting In skip counting, the child gives correct names, but instead of counting by ones, counts by twos, fives, tens, or other values. The starting point and direction are optional. In addition to providing many patterns, skip counting provides readiness for multiplication and division.

Skip counting, coupled with counting on and counting back, provides excellent preparation for counting change. Thus, given the coins shown, children would be encouraged to choose the largest-valued coin and then begin counting on—"twenty-five, thirty, thirty-five, forty."

25¢

5¢   5¢   5¢

Counting change is a very important skill whose usefulness children recognize. It holds great appeal for them. It should be introduced and extended as far as possible in the primary grades. Interestingly enough, most of the difficulties associated with counting change can be traced to weaknesses in counting. This finding suggests that teachers should take advantage of every opportunity to encourage accurate and rapid counting.

Counting Practice

Counting practice should include counting on and counting back by ones. Situations that encourage thoughtful counting often present problems embedded in real-world models. These situations may provide practice in counting either forward or backward. For example:

If the six numbers on the cube must be consecutive (that is, whole numbers in order for the cube)

Name some possible numbers that could be on the six faces of this cube.

What is the smallest possible number on the cube?

What is the largest possible number on the cube?

This problem requires counting, but it also encourages higher-level thinking and logical reasoning. For example, questions such as, "Is there more than one correct answer?" should be raised and discussed. The problem also illustrates that unique answers don't always exist. These experiences may even encourage children to formulate similar problems.

Books such as *Anno's Counting Book* and *Anno's Counting House* by Mitsumasa Anno, *Bears on Wheels* (Berenstain and Berenstain 1969), and *I Can Count the Petals of a Flower* by John and Stacy Wahl provide a variety of rich and stimulating contexts for counting. These books engage children in counting and provide insight into how children count. Other books, such as *How Many Snails? A Counting Book* by Paul Giganti and *Count On Your Fingers African Style* by Claudia Zaslavsky, focus on numerical relationships. These and many other books are included in *The Wonderful World of Mathematics: A Critically Annotated List of Children's Books in Mathematics* (Thiessen & Matthias 1998). Such books are very useful for counting-based discussions between children and adults. For example, *Anno's Counting Book* provides a sequence of pictures of different scenes of the house where little people move from one house to another. Initially the teacher or parent can ask questions such as:

How many children are in the house?

How many are boys?

How many are girls?

How many are wearing hats?

How many are on the second floor?

Starter questions are provided to encourage active participation and maintain a high level of interest. After students start counting, not only are many new things to count identified but important aspects of early number sense also are experienced.

Practice in skip counting from 1 and other start numbers, including 0, contributes to developing good counting skills and greater number sense. The hundred chart is an ideal model for practicing skip counting, as in In the Classroom 6–4. Here, finding

Bumps in the road for successful counters

Not only is the calculator a valuable instructional tool that helps children improve their ability to count, but it also is a powerful counting tool that they love to explore. Early counting with the calculator should emphasize the physical link between pressing the keys and watching the display. Because the display changes constantly, the students begin to recognize patterns. Calculator counting involves a physical activity (pressing a key each time a number is counted), through which students relate the size of a number to the amount of time needed to count.

Children are usually surprised to find that it is as easy to count by any number on the calculator as to count by ones. A calculator can start at zero and count by ones (In the Classroom 6–5) or begin at any starting point and skip count by any number (In the Classroom 6–6). Calculators can also easily count backward (In the Classroom 6–7).

Estimation is a natural part of counting, and In the Classroom 6–5 encourages students to estimate the time it takes to count by ones to 100 and 1000 with the calculator. By expanding this activity, students will come to realize that it takes about the same amount of time to count to 1000 by ones as to count to 1000000 by 1000 or to 100 by 0.1. Such counting experiences develop important place-value concepts and contribute to number sense.

Counting from a particular number or by a certain number leads students to see many patterns. For example, using the hundred chart in In the Classroom 6–4 helps students recognize that adding 49 to a number is the same as adding 50 and subtracting 1, which is a powerful pattern often used in mental computation. Calculator counting opens exciting mathematical explorations and promotes both critical thinking and problem solving.

EARLY NUMBER DEVELOPMENT

Comparing and counting experiences help children develop early foundations for number sense. Today's children also have had many experiences, primarily while watching television (*Sesame Street,* for example), that develop counting skills. Classroom instruction for early number development should be designed to build on these experiences.

patterns and problem solving are integrated with the counting practice.

Research has shown some predictable trouble spots for children when counting. For example, children often slow down, hesitate, or stop when they reach certain numbers, such as twenty-nine. However, as soon as they establish the next number as thirty, their counting pace quickens, until they are ready to enter the next decade (set of ten). Bridging the next century (set of one hundred) poses a similar challenge. As children count ". . . one hundred ninety-eight, one hundred ninety-nine," they may pause and be uncertain how to name the next number. Bridging to the next ten or hundred are among the common transitional points of counting difficulty identified by Labinowicz (1985):

In The Classroom 6–5

Counting
On . . . and On . . . and On . . .

Objective: Using calculators to count and develop number sense.

- How long did it take
  to count from 1 to 100?_____

- Guess how long it will
  take to count from 1 to 1000. _____

- Count from 1 to 1000.
  How long did it take?_____

Developing Number Benchmarks

Number benchmarks are perceptual anchors that become internalized from many concrete experiences, often accumulated over many years.

The numbers 5 and 10 (the number of fingers on one and two hands) provide two early number benchmarks. Children recognize four fingers as being

In The Classroom 6–6

Skipping Around

Objective: Using calculators to practice skip counting.

▼ Start at 5 every time:

Count by:

9	*14*	__	__	__	__	__	__
10	*15*	__	__	__	__	__	__
49	__	__	__	__	__	__	__
50	__	__	__	__	__	__	__

one less than five and eight as being three more than five or two less than ten:

"one less than five"   "three more than five"
                        "two less than ten"

The five-frame (5 × 1 array) and the ten-frame (5 × 2 array) (Appendix B) use these early benchmarks:

In The Classroom 6–7

Counting Backward

Objective: Using calculators to skip count backward.

10, 9, 8, 7, 6, . . .

▼ Try these:

15 – 1 = _14_ , _13_ , ___ , ___ , ___ , ___

20 – 2 = _18_ , ___ , ___ , ___ , ___ , ___

35 – 3 = ___ , ___ , ___ , ___ , ___ , ___

In The Classroom 6–8

Decide If It's 👍 Up or 👎 Down

Objective: Comparing quantities with specific benchmarks.

- Circle the 👍 if the number of dots is *more than* the number symbol.
- Circle the 👎 if the number of dots is *less than* the number symbol.

In Japan, the early benchmarks of 5 and 10 are later used with the ten-frame and the Japanese *soroban* (which is similar to an abacus) to promote counting, quick recognition of quantities, and mental computation (Shigematsu et al. 1994).

In the Classroom 6–8 illustrates an activity that encourages the development of benchmark numbers. Because the goal is to develop an intuitive sense of the anchor number (not laborious counting), these early activities show numbers of dots that are significantly different from the anchor.

Of course, many different anchors can be drawn from children's experiences. You might show a bowl of peanuts and ask, "About how many can you hold in one hand?" Change the contents of the bowl to other things, such as erasers, centimeter cubes, marbles, or balls. As children grow older, they should be comfortable and skilled with more and more benchmark numbers.

Making Connections

The development of the numbers 1 through 5 will be principally done through sight recognition of pat-

terns, coupled with immediate association with the oral name and then the written symbolization. For example, as Figure 6–11 illustrates, a picture of a tricycle and the question, "How many wheels?" can be used to develop the number 3. It is important that the number of wheels be linked to both oral name and written symbol. It is also important to provide different configurations of dots, blocks, and other

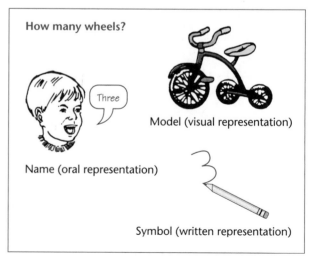

Figure 6–11 • A number development model linking visual, oral, and written representations

objects, as well as different forms of the numerals, such as *3* and 3, to broaden their experiences.

Many valuable relationships are established as the numbers 1 through 5 are developed, but none are more useful than the notions of *one more* and *one less*. These connections are fundamental in early counting and also in learning place value with larger numbers. The notions *one more* and *one less* evolve from many different real-world experiences, such as these:

> David has one less cookie than Jean-Paul.
>
> Mira has one more apple than Beth.
>
> They have one less player on their team.
>
> Their group has one more girl than our group.

The concepts of *one more* and *one less* can be modeled in different ways. Figure 6–12 shows three such models. These arrangements provide a basis for developing the concept of 5 as well as discussing *one more* or *one less*. Using these models for discussion will help children establish important connections that link numbers such as 4 and 5. For example, children might say,

> The yellow rod is one step longer than the purple rod.
>
> The five card is just like the four card except it has an extra dot in the middle.

Having many experiences with such models and patterns helps children abstract numbers and establish useful connections between them.

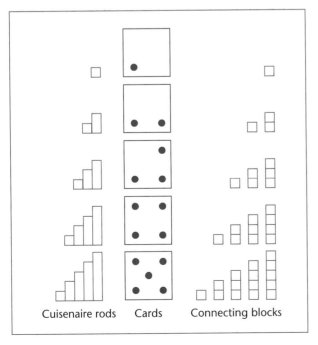

Figure 6–12 • Three models for *one more* or *one less*

The dots on the cards and the trains of blocks in Figure 6–12 provide clear reminders of the numbers represented and the notion of *one more* or *one less*. Both the staircase of rods and the trains of blocks vividly illustrate not only these concepts but also an important, yet subtle, difference between the models. The staircase of rods illustrates the concept of *more*, but it is not absolutely clear how much more until the length of the rods has been made clear. If we used a single rod without identifying a unit rod, it would not be possible to associate the rod with a unique number. Thus, the rods are a very different model for developing numbers than the dot cards or trains of blocks.

Some models illustrate zero more clearly than others. For example, a rod of length zero is more difficult to grasp than a card with zero dots. Care should be taken to introduce zero as soon as it becomes natural to do so, using models appropriate for the purpose. Help children distinguish between zero and nothing by encouraging the use of zero to report the absence of something. For example, when reporting the score of a game, it is better to say "Cardinals three, Bears zero" than to say "three to nothing."

As the numbers through 10 are developed, it is important that various patterns among them be discovered, recognized, used, and discussed. Many patterns suggesting many different relationships are shown in this number chart:

For example, the number 7 is shown by 5 dots and 2 more dots. The number 10 is composed of two groups of 5 dots. It is also useful to explore other patterns.

On the number chart, 6 is shown as 5 dots and 1 dot, but other representations are possible, as shown in Figure 6–13, and they should be explored and discussed with students. Part (B) of Figure 6–13, for example, shows that 6 can be represented as one group of 3, one group of 2, and one group of 1. It can also be shown as two groups of 3, as in parts (A) and (D), or three groups of 2, as in part (C). No mention is made of addition or multiplication in this context, but such observations provide helpful connections when these operations are developed.

Similar illustrations and applications of the numbers 7 through 10 should be presented. For example, 7 days in a week may suggest a natural grouping; 8 vertices (corners) of a cube suggest two groups of 4;

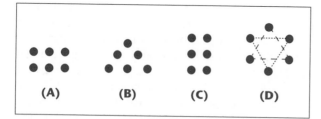

Figure 6–13 • Some representations of 6

Figure 6–14 • Representations of 8 on a ten-frame

and the number of boxes in a tic-tac-toe grid suggest three groups of 3.

Most children realize very early that 10 is a very special number. At the early stage of number development, the most unusual thing about 10 is that it is the first number represented by two digits, 1 and 0. In addition to having 10 fingers and toes, children encounter the number 10 in many situations such as in playing games and changing money.

These experiences can be extended to include discussion about different representations of 10:

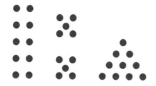

Can you find two groups of 5?

Can you find five groups of 2?

Does the group of 4, 3, 2, and 1 remind you of bowling?

The number 10 provides the cornerstone for our number system, and its significance is developed further in Chapter 7.

A ten-frame is certainly one of the most effective models for facilitating patterns, developing group recognition of numbers, and building an understanding of place value. The ten-frame can be made from an egg carton shortened to contain ten boxes, or it may simply be outlined on paper or tagboard (see ten-frame in Appendix B). This frame is a powerful organizer and helps provide the base for many thinking strategies and mental computation. Initially, children might use counters to make different representations of the same number in the ten-frame, as illustrated in Figure 6–14. Encountering a variety of groupings on the ten-frame should stimulate discussion about different patterns.

Figure 6–15 shows some of the connections that might be constructed as children examine different representations on the ten-frame. These relationships encourage children to think flexibly about

numbers, thereby promoting greater number sense. Experiences with the ten-frame also facilitate the development of addition, subtraction, multiplication, and division, as well as place value.

CARDINAL, ORDINAL, AND NOMINAL NUMBERS

We have discussed some important considerations in number development. The emphasis has been on finding a correct number name for a given group. This aspect of number provides a *cardinal number*, which answers the question "How many?" Another important aspect of number emphasizes arranging things in an order and is known as *ordinal number;* it answers the question "Which one?"

An emphasis on ordering, seriating, or arranging things in a given sequence leads to ordinal numbers. The order may be based on any criterion such as size, time of day, age, or position in a race. Once an order is established, however, the counting process not only produces a set of number names but also names each object according to its position. Thus, in counting the rungs on the ladder in Figure 6–16, number 1 is first, 2 is second, 3 is third, and so on.

Research shows that many children know some ordinal numbers such as first, second, and third before they begin school (Payne and Huinker 1993). Encounters with statements such as the following provide early and valuable experience with ordinal numbers:

The first letter of the alphabet is A.

Bob is second in line.

Cary was third in the race.

It is important that the development of early number concepts provides children with opportunities to learn both ordinal and cardinal numbers.

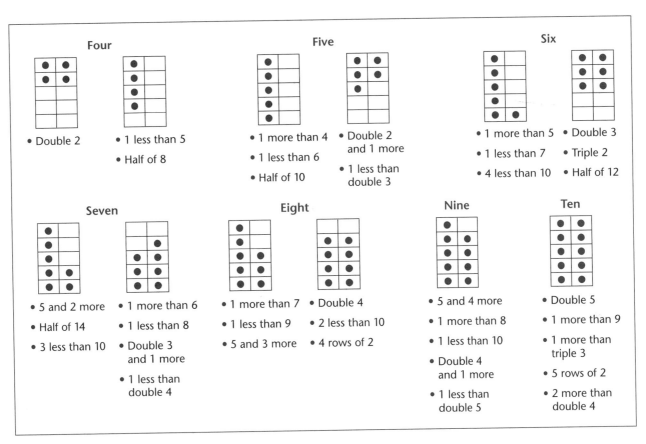

Figure 6–15 • Connections from representations on the ten-frame

Don't worry about which to teach first; just be sure both are given attention.

It is possible for a child to recognize a pattern of 4 beans but not be able to count to 4 correctly. Such a child could give the cardinal number 4 to answer the question "How many beans do you see?"

For this child, the notion of cardinal number is very limited but has preceded the use of ordinal number in counting. Such instances are rare, and, when they do occur, they are limited to small numbers.

A knowledge of ordinal relationships, along with logical thinking, leads to more challenging experiences, such as those suggested in Figure 6–17. These questions are guaranteed to generate much discussion as they help children further clarify notions of ordinal numbers.

Another aspect of number provides a label or classification and is known as *nominal*. Examples are the number on a player's uniform, the license plate of a car, a postal zip code, and a telephone number. The nominal numbers provide essential information for identification but do not necessarily use the ordinal or cardinal aspects of the number.

When using cardinal, ordinal, and nominal numbers, children do not need to distinguish between the terms. Distinctions can be made informally by asking questions within problem situations such as

How many pieces are on the chess board?

Which pawn is third?

Where is the queen?

These questions not only help children think about numbers but also illustrate that numbers have different uses.

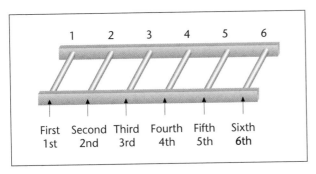

Figure 6–16 • A counting model for ordinal numbers

Race Day Riddles

Tell how many people were in the race, and explain your reasoning.

How could I be last but second in a race?

The number on my shirt is 9. How could I be first and last in a race?

How could I be seventh in a race but finish last?

How could I be third from winning and also third from last?

Figure 6–17 • Thinking about ordinal relationships

WRITING NUMERALS

Young children should focus their attention on number development and relationships among numbers and spend less time writing numerals. This recommendation is based on research studies that document that young children typically have difficulty writing numerals as well as letters (Payne and Huinker 1993). The lack of development of the small muscles needed to write presents one problem, and the limited eye-hand coordination of many young children constitutes another difficulty. Both of these make it difficult or impossible for young children to write numerals. If children are pressured into premature symbolization, it can create unnecessary frustrations and anxieties.

First graders can usually recognize a number symbol and say it correctly long before they write it. Many young children initiate early writing of numerals on their own, and they get a feeling of great accomplishment from it. However, research shows that children learn these writing skills much more quickly as second graders than as kindergarteners! They should begin by tracing the digits:

0 1 2 3 4 5 6 7 8 9

Textbooks provide guidance to children in different forms. Usually a starting point is indicated as well as the direction:

2 2 2 2 ʾ

Encourage children to draw the appropriate number of objects beside the numeral being written to help them connect the number concept with its symbolic representation. We recommend that when children are learning to write numerals, the writing skill be developed aside from "mathematics." Thus, children should master this skill and use it freely before applying it in written computational situations; otherwise, the writing task consumes all their concentration, and they forget about the mathematics being done.

Many children develop the necessary writing skills on their own. Even then, these youngsters need monitoring and maybe some occasional guidance. Others, however, need systematic step-by-step procedures to help them. Although there is no one best way to form a numeral, there are some patterns that may help. Guiding a child's hand until the child takes the initiative in writing helps him or her get started. Later, outlines of numerals for children to trace is helpful. Here are some additional suggestions; these will not be necessary in all cases, but some children will profit from them.

1. Cut out shapes of numerals. Use the overhead projector to project a numeral on the chalkboard or wall and have a child trace the numeral's silhouette.

2. As one child is tracing the projected numeral, have class members trace it in the air. As the tracing is being done, describe it verbally such as "go to the right and then down." This activity can be extended to using only dots to form the outline or pattern for the children to follow.

3. Have a child who can make numerals stand behind someone who cannot. Ask the skilled child to use a finger and gently "write" a numeral on the other child's back. The child in front should identify the numeral and write it on the chalkboard, trace it on the wall, or write it in the air. This approach calls

on the tactile sense and helps some children better develop their writing skills.

4. Use numerals that have been cut from sandpaper and pasted to cards, or take some cord and glue it in the shape of numerals. Place a mark on each numeral to show the child where to begin tracing it with his or her finger. This approach is particularly helpful with children who persist in reversing numerals.

5. Cover numerals to be traced with a transparency. Then give the child a water-soluble pen and have him or her practice tracing the numerals.

6. For children having difficulty writing numerals, a calculator is helpful. The calculator display provides a visual reminder of a number's symbolization and removes the burden of writing complicated numerals.

The fact that numerals take different forms also should be mentioned but not belabored.

$$4 \quad 4 \quad 4 \quad 4$$

Some familiarity with these forms will help avoid confusion when a 4 appears as a printed number or as a digital display on a clock or calculator. The wide use of digital numbers in everyday living demands planned instruction to make children familiar with them.

A Glance at Where We've Been

Good number sense is a prerequisite for all later computational development. Young children need to recognize small groups of objects (up to 5 or 6) by sight and name them properly. Activities involving sight recognition of the numbers of objects in small groups provide many opportunities to introduce and use key terms such as *more, less, after, before, one more*, and *one less*. To foster a better number sense, instruction on the numbers through 5 should focus on patterns and develop recognition skills. Models such as the ten-frame provide a powerful tool for helping children explore and construct relationships for numbers to 10 and beyond.

Counting skills are started before children begin school but must be developed by careful and systematic instruction before written work is appropriate. Counting processes reflect various levels of sophistication, beginning with rote counting and eventually leading to rapid skip counting forward and backward. Although the four counting principles are established in the primary grades, counting skills are extended in the intermediate grades and often are further refined throughout our lives.

Competence with and understanding of the numbers 0 through 10 are essential for meaningful later development of larger numbers. The relation of the sets of objects, the number names, the written symbols, and the order between numbers must be well understood. This knowledge is the basis for the successful study of elementary mathematics, and it prepares children for the necessary understanding of large numbers and place value.

Things to Do: From What You've Read

1. Why is number sense difficult to define?

2. Check the Numbers and Operations Standard in Appendix A. Identify three expectations related to number sense.

3. Suppose you send a note home to parents encouraging them to help their child improve sight-recognition skills. One parent responds, "Why should my child learn to recognize a group of 5? After all, you can just count them." How would you respond?

4. Four fundamental principles of counting were identified in this chapter. Describe in your own words what each means and why it is necessary.

5. Distinguish between rote and rational counting.

6. What is meant by conservation of number? Why is its development an important part of number sense?

7. Describe how the following activity could help older children sharpen their understanding of ordinal and cardinal numbers.

   a. How many ordinal numbers are in this sentence? "The 500 residents of Centerville celebrated the 100th anniversary of the town's founding by setting off a $200 fireworks display at the corner of Fifth and Broadway on January 1st."

8. Describe how counting could be used to answer these questions:
   a. How many floors are between the seventh and fifteenth floors?
   b. If Alfinio has read to the bottom of page 16, how many pages must he read to reach the top of page 21?

9. Describe how the ten-frame serves as a useful model for early number development.

10. What is subitizing? Tell why it is an important skill to help children develop.

Things to Do: Going Beyond This Book

field Additional activities, suggestions, and questions are provided in *Teaching Elementary Mathematics: A Resource for Field Experiences.*

1. Examine *Number Sense and Operations* (Burton et al. 1993), *Developing Number Sense in Middle Grades* (Reys et al. 1991), or the *SENSE* series (McIntosh et al. 1997). How do these books characterize number sense? Report on several instructional activities designed to foster number sense.

2. Select a patterning activity from *Patterns* (Coburn et al. 1992) that would be appropriate for primary grades. Describe how you would prepare for, use, and extend this activity.

3. Examine the chapter "Concepts of Number" by Van de Walle (1990) in *Mathematics for the Young Child*. Describe three different instructional activities for promoting early number sense.

4. Read "Bring on the Buttons" (Whitin 1989) and describe some ways in which buttons could be used to develop classification skills.

5. *field* Counting. Observe a young child counting. Identify any counting errors and where they took place, such as bridging to the next decade. Also identify any counting principles that were exhibited

6. *field* Counting Resources. Find the instructor's guidebook or teacher's edition being used in mathematics in K–2. Examine it to learn how resources, such as calculators and children's books, are used to support counting.

7. Compare two current textbook series.
   a. Find how far each series expects children to be able to count when they begin first grade and when they complete first grade.
   b. Find examples of activities designed to develop number sense. Describe the activities and identify the grade level. Do you think these activities would be effective? Tell why.
   c. Find an example of a visual pattern that connects numbers to geometry.

8. Review *The Wonderful World of Mathematics: A Critically Annotated List of Children's Books in Mathematics* (Thiessen and Matthias 1998). Find three multicultural books related to counting that are highly recommended.

9. Read one of the vignettes in the *Professional Standards for Teaching Mathematics* (NCTM 1991) that involves early development of number. Describe the role of the teacher.

10. Read the book *How Many Snails: A Counting Book* (Giganti 1988). Then read the article by Whitin, Mills, and O'Keefe (1994) to see how this book was used to explore mathematical problem solving. Discuss how the project was done and how the examples of children's work provides insight into their development of number sense.

11. View a segment from the videotape series *Number Sense Now!* (Fennell 1992). Discuss ways in which this tape might help students become more sensitive to the importance and power of number sense.

12. *field* In the Classroom 6–1 and 6–2 provide several patterning and logical reasoning activities using attribute pieces with children. Explore these trains with several children. How many different correct solutions did children find for Train A? Did your children find one-difference trains to be the same difficulty as two-difference trains? Did students feel comfortable knowing that more than one correct answer exists?

13. *field* In the Classroom 6–5, 6–6, and 6–7 provide structured calculator counting activities. Try one or more of them with some children in a classroom that has calculators available. Were the children experienced at using the calculators or were they viewed as a novelty? Were the childen comfortable making estimates for the counts? Describe some patterns that emerged.

BOOK NOOK FOR CHILDREN

Anno, Mitsumasa. *Anno's Counting Book*. New York: Thomas Y. Crowell, 1977.

Anno, Mitsumasa. *Anno's Counting House*. New York: Philomel Books, 1982.

Berenstain, Stanley, and Berenstain, Janice. *Bears on Wheels*. New York: Random House, 1969.

Carle, Eric. *The Very Hungry Caterpillar*. New York: Putnam, 1990.

Carter, David A. *How Many Bugs in A Box?* New York: Simon & Schuster, 1988.

Clement, Rod. *Counting on Frank*. Milwaukee, Wis.: Gareth Stevens, 1991.

Dee, Rudy. *Two Ways to Count to Ten*. New York: Henry Holt, 1988.

Feelings, Muriel. *Maja Means One: A Swahili Counting Book*. New York: Dial Books for Young Readers, 1971.

Giganti, Paul. *How Many Snails? A Counting Book*. New York: Greenwillow Books, 1988.

Handford, Martin. *Where's Waldo?* Boston: Little, Brown, 1987.

Hawkins, Colin, and Hawkins, Jacqui. *How Many Are in This Old Car? A Counting Book*. New York: G. P. Putnam's Sons, 1988.

Hoban, Russell, and Selig, Sylvie. *Ten What? A Mystery Counting Book*. New York: Scribner's, 1975.

Kingsley, Emily Perl; Moss, Jeffrey; Stiles, Norman; and Wilcox, Daniel. *Sesame Street One, Two, Three Story Book*. New York: Random House, 1973.

Nozaki, Akihiro, and Anno, Mitsumasa. *Anno's Hat Tricks*. New York: Philomel Books, 1985.

Pinczes, Elinor. *One Hundred Hungry Ants*. Boston: Houghton Mifflin, 1993.

Pluckrose, Henry. *Numbers*. New York: Franklin Watts, 1988.

Robinson, Shari. *A First Number Book*. New York: Grossett & Dunlap, 1981.

Thomson, Ruth. *All about 1, 2, 3*. Milwaukee, Wis.: Stevens Publishing, 1986.

Wahl, John, and Wahl, Stacy. *I Can Count the Petals of a Flower*. Reston, Va.: NCTM, 1976.

Yeoman, John. *Sixes and Sevens*. New York: Macmillan, 1974.

Zaslavsky, Claudia. *Count on Your Fingers African Style*. New York: Crowell Publishers, 1980.

Selected References

Baratta-Lorton, Mary. *Mathematics Their Way*. Palo Alto, Calif.: Addison-Wesley, 1976.

Burton, Grace; Mills, Ann; Lennon, Carolyn; and Parker, Cynthia. *Number Sense and Operations*. Reston, Va.: NCTM, 1993.

Clements, Douglas G. "Subitizing: What is it? Why teach it?" *Teaching Children Mathematics* (March 1999), pp. 400–405.

Coburn, Terrence G.; Bushey, Barbara J.; Holton, Liana C.; Latozas, Debra; Mortimer, Debbie; and Shotwell, Deborah. *Patterns*. Reston, Va.: NCTM, 1992.

Economopoulos, Karen. "What come next? The mathematics of pattern in kindergarten." *Teaching Children Mathematics,* 5 (December 1998), pp. 203–233.

Fennell, Francis. *Number Sense Now!* (video tape and guidebook). Reston, Va.: NCTM, 1992.

Fuson, Karen C. "Adding by Counting on with One Handed Finger Patterns." *Arithmetic Teacher,* 35 (September 1987), pp. 38–41.

Fuson, Karen C. *Children's Counting and Concepts of Number*. New York: Springer-Verlag, 1988.

Howden, Hilde. "Teaching Number Sense." *Arithmetic Teacher,* 36 (February 1989), pp. 6–11.

Labinowicz, Ed. *Learning from Children: New Beginnings for Teaching Numerical Thinking*. Menlo Park, Calif.: Addison-Wesley, 1985.

McIntosh, Alistair; Reys, Barbara J.; and Reys, Robert E. "A Proposed Framework for Examining Basic Number Sense." *For the Learning of Mathematics,* 12 (November 1992), pp. 2–8.

McIntosh, Alistair; Reys, Barbara; and Reys, Robert. *Number SENSE, Simple Effective Number Sense Experiences: Grades 1–2 & 3–4*, Palo Alto, Calif.: Dale Seymour Publications, 1997.

National Council of Teachers of Mathematics. *Professional Standards for Teaching Mathematics*. Reston, Va.: NCTM, 1991.

Payne, Joseph N., and Huinker, DeAnn M. "Early Number and Numeration." In *Research Ideas for the Classroom: Early Childhood Mathematics* (ed. Robert J. Jensen). Reston, Va.: NCTM, and New York: Macmillan 1993, pp. 43–70.

Reys, Barbara J.; Barger, Rita; Bruckheimer, Maxim; Dougherty, Barbara; Hope, Jack; Lembke, Linda; Markovitz, Zvia; Parnas, Andy; Reehm, Sue; Sturdevant, Ruthi; and Weber, Marianne. *Developing Number Sense in the Middle Grades*. Reston, Va.: NCTM, 1991.

Shigematsu, K.; Iwasaki, H.; and Koyama, M. "Mental Computation: Evaluation, Curriculum and Instructional Issues from the Japanese Perspective." In *Computational Alternatives for the 21st Century: Cross Cultural Perspectives from Japan and the United States* (eds. Robert E. Reys and Nobubiko Nohda). Reston, Va.: NCTM, 1994.

Sowder, Judith, and Schappelle, Bonnie. Number Sense-Making, *Arithmetic Teacher,* 41(6) (February 1994), pp. 342–345.

Sowder, Judith T. Estimation and number sense. In *Handbook of Research on Mathematics Teaching and Learning* (ed. D. A. Grouws). New York: Macmillan, 1992, pp. 371–389.

Thiessen, Diane, and Matthias, Margaret (eds.). *The Wonderful World of Mathematics: A Critically Annotated List of Children's Books in Mathematics*. Reston, Va.: NCTM, 1998.

Thompson, Charles S. "Number Sense and Numeration in Grades K–8." *Arithmetic Teacher,* 37 (September 1989), pp. 22–24.

Thornton, Carol A.; Jones, Graham A.; and Neal, Judy L. "The 100s Chart: A Stepping Stone to Mental Mathematics." *Teaching Children Mathematics,* 1(8) (April 1995), pp. 480–483.

Van de Walle, John. "Concepts of Number." In *Mathematics for the Young Child* (ed. Joseph N. Payne). Reston, Va.: NCTM, 1990, pp. 62–87.

Whitin, David J. "Bring on the Buttons." *Arithmetic Teacher,* 36 (January 1989), pp. 4–6.

Whitin, David J.; Mills, Heidi; and O'Keefe, Timothy. "Exploring Subject Areas with a Counting Book." *Teaching Children Mathematics,* 1(3) (November 1994), pp. 170–177.

7 Extending Number Sense: Place Value

Key Ideas for a Primary-Grade Lesson on Place Value

1. Develop number sense by using tens (bean sticks) for a quick benchmark estimate.

2. Illustrate the place-value concept with two different models.

3. Provide concrete representation of two-digit numbers and their corresponding symbolization.

Necessary Materials

- *Bean Sticks:* Each child should have a set of 10 bean sticks and a small pile of loose beans. (A bean stick is a tongue depressor or popsicle stick on which ten lima or butter beans are glued. Children should each make their own bean sticks, thereby convincing themselves that there are indeed ten beans on a stick. Gluing on the beans will also instill a pride in ownership of the sticks.) The teacher also needs some loose beans and a set of bean sticks.

- *Place-Value Mat:* Each child should have a place-value mat and a water-soluble pen. (A place-value mat is a piece of heavy construction paper that has been laminated so children can write on it. It has two columns—for tens and ones.) The teacher needs a transparency of a place-value mat for use on the overhead projector.

Tens	Ones

Orientation

In previous lessons, these second graders have been counting by ones and tens, as well as counting on (by ones). This lesson continues to develop number sense and place value, as the children count the sticks and beans in several different ways. (For example, they count the sticks first and then the separate beans or count the beans first and then the sticks—which is more difficult for the children but an important skill to develop.) To encourage students to decide about how many beans there are without counting, Mrs. Golden places the bean sticks and four beans on the overhead, turns it on for only a couple of seconds, and then turns it off.

MRS. GOLDEN: Did you see more than 30?

Tranh raises his hand immediately.

TRANH: Yes.

MRS. GOLDEN: Tell us how you knew that so quickly. Did you count them?

TRANH: No, I didn't need to count. There are 3 sticks—that makes 30. There are also some other beans, so I know there are more than 30.

MRS. GOLDEN: Are there more than 40?

SANDRA: No. You have 30, but there are not 10 more beans to make 40, so I know there are not more than 40.

MRS. GOLDEN: Good. Now let's count them together.

Ten, twenty, thirty, thirty-one, thirty-two, thirty-three, thirty-four

Mrs. Golden points to appropriate pieces as the children count.

MRS. GOLDEN: Now, let's start with the beans instead of the sticks and count them a different way.

One, two, three, four, fourteen, twenty-four, thirty-four

Mrs. Golden again points to appropriate pieces as the children count.

MRS. GOLDEN: Does it matter how you count the beans?

DERREK: No, you get the same answer. But it's easier for me to start with the sticks first.

MRS. GOLDEN: That's fine, Derrek. We will learn to count in different ways, but you should use what is easiest for you. Now everyone try modeling the number with beans and then writing this number on our number mats.

Tens	Ones
3	4

Before continuing, Mrs. Golden checks for any difficulties in modeling the number or writing the correct numerals. Writing the numerals on the place-value mat helps children naturally associate the symbol with the model, and understand the significance of place value in a concrete way.

MRS. GOLDEN: Here are some practice numbers for you to pair and share:

25   52   forty-one   89

I want you to take turns and show each of them on your mat to your partner one at a time. Be sure to model the number with your beans and sticks first and then write the number on your mat. When you finish, ask your partner to check the number before you clear the mat. Then your partner does the next one and you check it.

Introduction

Children must make sense of numbers and the ways in which numbers are used in and out of school. This sense making of numbers is a hallmark of the *Principles and Standards for School Mathematics* (NCTM 2000). It is elegantly stated in the Grade 3–5 Number and Operations Standard that all children should "understand numbers, ways of representing numbers, and relationships among numbers" (p. 32).

Place value is critical to this understanding or sense making and one of the cornerstones of our number system. We say "our" number system, but it is multicultural, and it is "ours" only to the extent that it is a part of our cultural heritage. History tells us that "our numeration system" is really the result of continuous development and refinement over many centuries.

Called the Hindu-Arabic system, the number system we use was probably invented in India by the

Hindus and transmitted to Europe by the Arabs, but many different countries and cultures contributed to its development.

OUR NUMERATION SYSTEM

Our numeration system has four very important characteristics:

1. *Place value:* The position of a digit represents its value; for example, the 2 in $23 names "twenty" and has a different mathematical meaning from the 2 in $32, which names "two."

2. *Base of ten:* The term *base* simply means a collection. Thus, in our system, 10 is the value that determines a new collection, and the system has ten digits, 0 through 9.

3. *Use of zero:* A symbol for zero exists and allows us to represent symbolically the absence of something; for example, 309 shows the absence of tens in a number containing hundreds and ones.

4. *Additive property:* Numbers can be summed with respect to place value; for example, 123 names the number that is the sum of 100 + 20 + 3.

These properties make the system efficient and contribute to the development of number sense. That is, once these characteristics are understood, the formation and interpretation of numbers—either large or small—is a natural development.

Thinking Place Value

Place value is an essential feature of our number system. In fact, place value, together with base ten, allows us to manipulate, read, and symbolize both large and small numbers. The power of place value can and should be developed early. For example, each of the piles shown has the same number of buttons. Decide how many buttons are in each pile.

Which pile would you use to decide how many? Explaining which pile and telling why that pile was chosen leads to a discussion of how grouping by tens facilitates counting and organizing larger quantities.

The ten-frame (Appendix B) provides a convenient model for counting, grouping, and eventually representing two-digit numbers. It is a natural model for place value and often provides valuable mental imagery for children in naming and distinguishing between two numbers. For example, Mrs. Golden asked the children to illustrate 25 and 52:

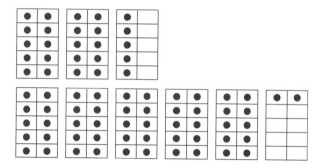

This exercise alerts students to the physical differences between these values, which are formed with the same digits but are different because of place value.

Grouping or Trading

Children in the first three grades need experience in counting piles of objects; trading for grouped tens, hundreds, and thousands; and talking about the results. The fourth national mathematics assessment reported that fourth-grade students had not mastered grouping and place value (Kouba et al. 1989). The Snapshot of a Lesson at the beginning of this chapter demonstrated how students might count and model different numbers. The bean sticks and ten-frame thus provide two early models for counting and grouping. As children work with these models, they need piles of materials (beans, buttons, cubes, or other counters) to practice counting and grouping.

Lesson Idea 7–1 provides some early guided practice in grouping by tens. These models (beans and interlocking cubes) are different, but each shows how grouping by ten helps determine the number in the group more quickly. The interlocking cubes in the train stay together and provide a natural step toward the base ten blocks shown later in Figures 7–2 and 7–4.

Trading and grouping by tens provide problem-solving activities that contribute to number sense and provide opportunities for developing mental computation. Lesson Idea 7–2 illustrates another grouping experience that further facilitates counting and trading. Although it may be easy to decide which group has more or less when the values differ greatly (as between B and the others), it may be very difficult when the values differ only slightly (as between A and C). Furthermore, as the number in the

Lesson Idea 7–1

Getting Started

▼ Provide a pile of beans or counters.

▼ Provide a pile of interlocking cubes.

▼ Ask children to group by ten.

▼ Ask children to build trains with ten cubes in a train.

▼ Some questions to ask:

- How many beans in each group?
- How many groups of ten?
- How many beans left over?
- Which pile is easier to count?

- How many cubes in each train?
- How many trains of ten?
- How many cubes left over?
- Which group is easier to count?

Developing Representation

▼ Some questions to ask:

- How many groups (trains) do you have?_____
- How many beans (cubes) are left over?_____

These questions help connect the concrete to symbolic representation.

---

groups increase, it often becomes more difficult (and sometimes impossible) to decide without counting and grouping. The activities highlighted in Lesson Ideas 1 and 2 provide opportunities for students to tell what they are doing and establish a firm foundation for the later development of written computation.

Asking children to group by tens as they count the larger piles serves several valuable purposes. First, if a child loses count, correction is often easier if these smaller groups have been formed. It is also easier to check for errors by inspecting groups of 10 than to recount the entire pile. However, the most important purpose of this practice is that it shows children how an unknown quantity can be organized into a form that can be interpreted by inspection. This process of grouping by tens is the framework for place value.

Nature of Place Value

A thorough understanding of place value is necessary if computational algorithms for addition, subtraction, multiplication, and division are to be learned

Lesson Idea 7–2

▼ Provide several piles of beans or other counters

A   B   C

▼ Some questions to ask:

• Which group has the most? Least?

• Can you decide without counting?

• Do you know the exact number without counting?

▼ Now have the children arrange in groups of ten.

• Does trading help you decide which group has the most? Tell why.

• Do you know the exact number in each group? Tell why.

and used in a meaningful way. However, place value develops from many various experiences, such as counting and mental computation (for example, $1 plus $0.25 to get $1.25). Development of place value promotes number sense, which facilitates estimation and sharpens a sense of reasonableness about computational results. Place value rests on two key ideas.

1. Explicit grouping or trading rules are defined and consistently followed. These ideas are implicit in the bulletin board display shown in Figure 7–1. Such a display provides a constant reminder of the importance of grouping by tens to place value. Our base-ten system is characterized by trading 10 ones for 1 ten (or 1 ten for 10 ones), 10 tens for 1 hundred, 10 hundreds for 1 thousand, and so on. The two-way direction of these trades (for example, 10 tens for 1 hundred or 1 hundred for 10 tens) should be stressed because there are times when each type of trade must be used. It also should be noted that similar trades are followed with numbers less than one—decimals. Thus, 1 can be traded for 10

tenths (or 10 tenths for 1), 10 hundredths for 1 tenth (or 1 tenth for 10 hundredths), and so on.

2. The position of a digit determines the number being represented. For example, the 2 in 3042 and the 2 in 2403 represent completely different quantities: 2 ones in 3042 and 2 thousands in 2403. Furthermore, the zero plays a similar yet different role in each of these numbers. It has positional value in each case, but it reports the lack of a quantity for that place. Although the notion of zero will continue to be expanded and developed throughout elementary school mathematics, children should experience the role of zero in place value early and often.

In our number system, place value means that any number can be represented using only 10 digits (0–9). Think about the problems of representing numbers without place value! Each number would require a separate and unique symbol. Our memory storage would quickly be exceeded, and we would probably have to use only the few numbers with symbols we could remember. Nevertheless, place

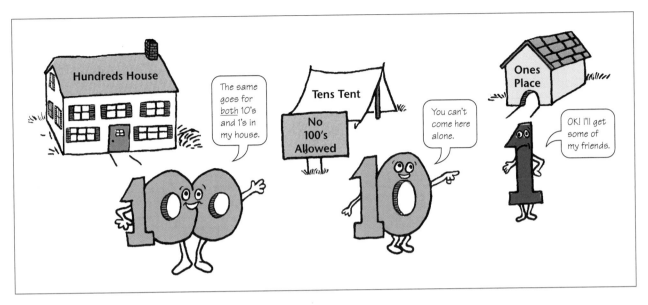

Figure 7–1 • **A bulletin board display for place value**

value is difficult for some children to grasp. Oral counting or rote recitation of numbers by young children is often interpreted as understanding of place value. Yet many children who can count correctly have absolutely no concept of place value. In most cases, the confusion or misunderstanding can be traced to a lack of counting and trading experiences with appropriate materials and the subsequent recording of these results. Early and frequent hands-on counting activities, similar to those described in Chapter 6, are essential in establishing this concept.

Place-value concepts are encountered before starting school. For example, many children distinguish between the one- and two-digit numbers on a channel indicator of a television, a timer for a microwave oven, and house or apartment numbers. Children learn early that apartments 201 and 102 are different.

Modeling

Hands-on experience with manipulatives is essential in establishing and developing the concept of place value. Research suggests that instruction should focus on concrete models that are connected to oral descriptions and symbolic representations of the models (Thompson 1990; Wearne and Hiebert 1994). Bean sticks and the ten-frame provide two effective models for developing place value.

Figure 7–2 illustrates some additional physical models that are effective in helping students understand not only place value but larger numbers as well. All of the models shown in Figure 7–2 represent the same three-digit number, 123. The value of using different embodiments is that a child will be less likely to associate place value with a particular model. In fact, a key instructional goal is to develop concepts to a level that does not depend on any one physical model, instead providing for abstraction of the commonalty among all models.

Models may be either proportional or nonproportional, but all are based on groups of 10. In proportional models for base ten, such as popsicle sticks, the material for 10 is ten times the size of the material for 1; 100 is ten times the size of 10, and so on. Measurement provides another proportional model. For example, a meter stick, decimeter rods, and centimeter cubes can be used to model any three-digit number.

Nonproportional models, such as money, do not maintain any size relationships. Ten pennies are bigger than a dime, but are fair trade in our monetary system. Ten dimes are the same as a dollar, but they are not proportional. These ideas introduce children to a level of abstraction based entirely on trading rules. Young students often focus on proportionality, which is why they are often willing to trade a dime for one or two pennies, or why they prefer to have a few dimes rather than a dollar bill.

Although both types of embodiments are important and should be represented, proportional models are more concrete, and we recommend that children use and clearly understand them before moving on to nonproportional models.

Of the nonproportional models shown in Figure 7–2, the abacus and the counters are very similar. In

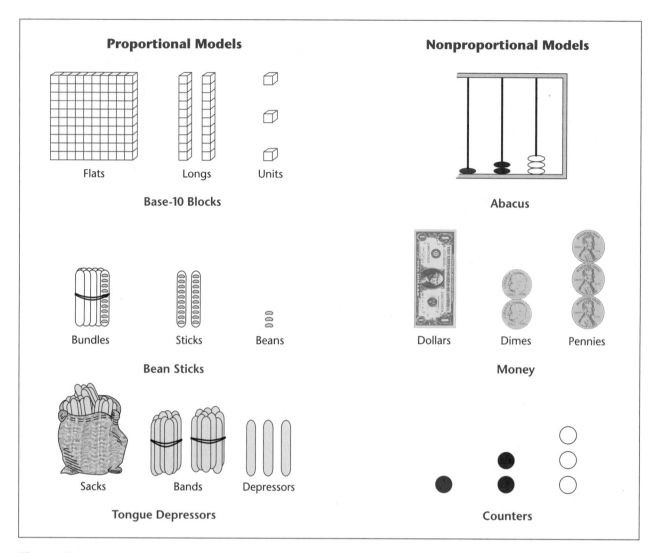

Figure 7–2 • **Place-value models**

each model, different-colored beads or counters provide the basis for trading. For example, 10 white beads (or counters) might be traded for 1 black, 10 black for 1 purple, and so on. Use of a trading mat can help keep the counters in order. The beads on an abacus are arranged in a fixed order. The color distinction is important for the early establishment of proper trades, but it should be dropped as soon as possible so that attention will shift from color of the beads or counters to their position. It is only the position of the bead counter that has long-range significance.

DEVELOPING PLACE VALUE

A Place to Start

In developing place value and establishing number names, it is far better to skip beyond the teens and start with the larger numbers. The names for the numbers 11–19 are not consistent with the names for other numbers, even though the symbolization or visual pattern is wholly consistent. The numbers 11–19 do not exhibit the place-value characteristic in their names that other numbers do. To do so, they would have to be renamed onety-one (1 ten and 1 one), onety-two, . . . , onety-nine, which would make them consistent with larger numbers, such as forty-one, forty-two, . . . , forty-nine. In many other countries, such as Japan, the naming pattern for the numbers 11–19 is consistent with the naming of larger numbers. This feature reinforces place value early and helps Japanese children name the teen numbers (Yoshikawa 1994).

What does a number such as 25 mean? It is important that children have the capability of thinking of numbers in various ways. With such number sense, 25 might be thought of several different ways. When multiplying, a square array of 5 × 5 may come to mind. When thinking of money, several combinations of coins, such as 25 pennies, 2 dimes and 5 pennies, 5 nickels, and 1 quarter may be envisioned. With certain items, such as eggs, 1 more than 2 dozen and 4 six-packs plus 1 are two different representations of the quantity 25. With metric measures, 25 centimeters might be thought of as 2 decimeters and 5 centimeters. However, it could also be thought of as 0.25 or ¼ meter. Children with good number sense know when a particular form is useful.

Of course, if place value is to be called upon, the tens and ones model is needed. It might use money (2 dimes and 5 pennies) or another model, such as bean sticks. With the bean sticks, 25 could be represented several different ways:

Which way is better? It depends on what is to be done with the 25 beans because there are times when each form may be useful. The grouping at the top, for example, would be easier to divide among several people. Either of the groupings on the bottom would be easier to count.

The notion of representing a quantity with the least number of pieces for a particular model is critical in place value. Establishing its importance at an early stage will eliminate some later errors such as:

Because 10 or more of something (namely, ones) exist on the place-value mat, a trade must be made. Making the ten-for-one trade results in the least number of pieces and thus 25 becomes the only representation that is meaningful:

Figure 7–3 highlights the advancement from a concrete model to symbolic representation. The bridges from the physical models to the symbolic representation must be crossed back and forth many times if meaningful learning is to occur.

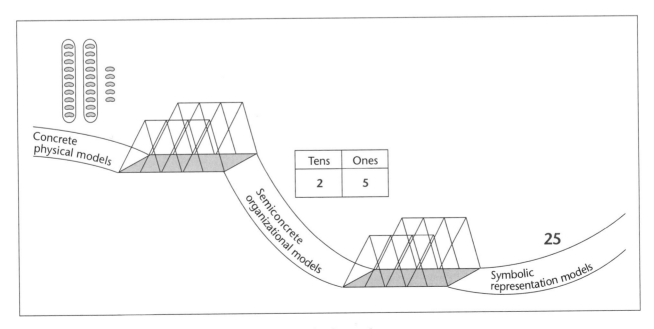

Figure 7–3 • From the concrete to the symbolic with place value

Careful attention must be given to linking modeling with the language. As children become fluent in talking about their models, it will become natural to them to describe 25 in different ways.

Many children reverse the digits of numbers. Although this error is generally caused by carelessness, it may be symptomatic of a disability known as *dyslexia*. In either case, it is very important that children understand the consequences of such reversals. That's why Mrs. Golden included the first two practice numbers at the end of the Snapshot of a Lesson at the beginning of this chapter.

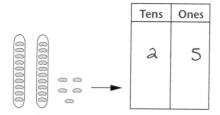

How many tens? [2]

How many ones? [5]

Name this number. [25]

Although the same digits are used, the resulting numbers—25 and 52—are very different. Children should compare the modeled numbers and talk about them in an effort to better appreciate the magnitude of the differences.

The base-10 blocks, together with the place-value mat, as shown in Figure 7–4, can be used to model the additive property and illustrate expanded notation. A variety of strips, such as those in Figure 7–4, which connect the base-10 blocks to number symbols in an expanded form, can be used effectively to review key ideas.

Lesson Idea 7–3 shows two slightly different hundred charts. One chart goes from 1 to 100, the other from 0 to 99. One advantage of the latter chart is that the tens digit in each row is constant, whereas in the 1-to-100 chart the tens digit always changes in the last column. Either hundred chart can be used to ex-

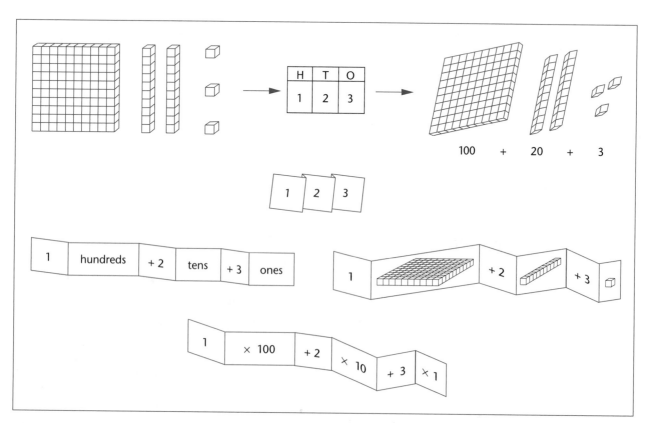

Figure 7–4 • Connecting models and symbols that reinforce place value

Lesson Idea 7–3

▼ Provide a hundred chart for each student to use.

1	2	3	4	5	6	7	8	9	10
11	12	13	14	15	16	17	18	19	20
21	22	23	24	25	26	27	28	29	30
31	32	33	34	35	36	37	38	39	40
41	42	43	44	45	46	47	48	49	50
51	52	53	54	55	56	57	58	59	60
61	62	63	64	65	66	67	68	69	70
71	72	73	74	75	76	77	78	79	80
81	82	83	84	85	86	87	88	89	90
91	92	93	94	95	96	97	98	99	100

↑ Fifth column

0	1	2	3	4	5	6	7	8	9
10	11	12	13	14	15	16	17	18	19
20	21	22	23	24	25	26	27	28	29
30	31	32	33	34	35	36	37	38	39
40	41	42	43	44	45	46	47	48	49
50	51	52	53	54	55	56	57	58	59
60	61	62	63	64	65	66	67	68	69
70	71	72	73	74	75	76	77	78	79
80	81	82	83	84	85	86	87	88	89
90	91	92	93	94	95	96	97	98	99

▼ Some questions to ask:

- What is alike for all the numbers in the fifth column?
- How are the numbers in the fourth and sixth columns alike? Different?
- Tell where you stop, if you start on any square in the first three rows and count forward ten more squares.
- Start on a different square in the first three rows and count forward ten more squares. Where did you stop?
- After you have done this several times, tell about a pattern that you found.

▼ Cut out a piece like this ⌐ and lay it on the chart.

- What numbers are covered? Tell how you found them.
- Move the piece to a different place, and tell what numbers are covered.
- Do it again with different shapes like ▭ and ▢

▼ Here is only a part of a hundred chart:

		A
		46
	B	
		C	D

- Use what you know about a hundred chart to
- Find A_____ B_____ C_____ D_____
- Tell two different ways to find C.
- Suppose 46 is replaced by N.
- Find A_____ B_____ C_____ D_____

plore place value, patterns, mental computation, and algebraic thinking. For example, 43 + 30 can be determined by counting mentally 43, 53, 63, 73 and is a natural by-product of counting by tens on the hundred chart. Furthermore, 43 + 29 can be found by counting 43, 53, 63, 73 and then dropping back one to 72. Counting by tens and then dropping back or bumping up illustrate how to adjust numbers and be flexible when using and thinking about numbers.

Consider the diagram and how patterns and generalizations lead to algebraic thinking:

Patterns from the hundred chart suggest these solutions

$$A = 46 - 10$$
$$B = 46 + 10 - 1$$
$$C = 46 + 20$$
$$D = 46 + 30 - 1$$

directly from the hundred chart. If the diagram is shifted on the hundred chart then 46 changes to some number N. Although the starting number N has changed, the solutions are similar, as

$$A = N - 10$$
$$B = N + 10 - 1$$
$$C = N + 20$$
$$D = N + 30 - 1$$

Such activities illustrate a variable, and the power of patterns in promoting algebraic thinking.

Lesson Idea 7–4 highlights an activity that extends the modeling to three-digit numbers and provides some opportunities to order numbers according to place value. Modeling three-digit numbers establishes the importance of position for each digit more clearly. It provides an early reward for looking at the "front-end" (lead) digits of a number. For example, when students are asked to show the number closest to 400 in Lesson Idea 7–4, they can concentrate on the values with 4 hundreds. Furthermore, when asked to show a number that is at least 100 more than 314, students can focus on hundreds and ignore the other digits. This ability to focus on certain digits in numbers is an important part of number sense.

In the Classroom 7–1 reinforces place value and also provides practice in important mental computational skills. Scores are found by counting the darts in each circle, which provides practice counting by ones, tens, and hundreds, and then computing the totals.

A calculator provides many opportunities to practice and develop important place-value concepts. Wipe Out is a place-value game that involves either addition or subtraction using a calculator. The goal is to change (wipe out) a predetermined digit by subtracting or adding a number. This activity can be made into a competitive game for two people. The players take turns entering a number and naming a specific digit the other player must change to 0.

For example, Kelly enters 431, naming the 3 to be wiped out:

Tanya wipes out the 3 by subtracting 30, which also leaves the other digits unchanged:

A player scores a point for changing the digit to 0 on the first try. A record of the game in table form reinforces the identification of the correct place value:

WIPE OUT RECORD   Name: Tanya

Entered	Wiped Out	Keys Pressed	Display	Score
431	3	−30	401	1
24	4	+6	30	1
849	8	−800	49	1
206	2	−200	6	1

Lesson Idea 7–4

Make That Number

Materials: A deck of 40 index cards with the numerals 0–9 or discard face cards from a regular deck and let an ace be 1 and a ten be 0.

Activity: Shuffle the cards and select two, three, or or four cards at random. Pose questions for children to model all possible resulting numbers with base-10 blocks.

For example, suppose these three cards were selected:

▼ Show the smallest number with the cards. Model it.

▼ Now show the largest number and model it.

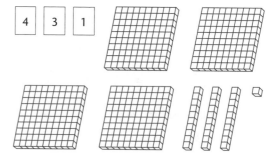

▼ Show a number between the largest and smallest number.

▼ Show the number closest to 400.

▼ Show as many different numbers as you can make with these three cards.

▼ Show a number at least 100 more than 314.

▼ Show a number almost 30 more than 314.

A variation of Wipe Out that has been developed focuses more attention on the place value of the digits (Hopkins 1992). In this variation, which can be played with or without a calculator, the teacher chooses a multidigit number with no two digits the same, such as 5849. The teacher identifies a digit (for example, the 5 in 5849) to be "wiped out," and students must try to change only that digit to 0 by using one operation. Students are called upon until the correct answer is given, and points are awarded according to their responses.

Response	Scoring
Student names operation and number: "Subtract five."	Teacher scores 2 points.
Student names operation and number: "Subtract five, zero, zero, zero")	Teacher scores 1 point.
Student names operation and number: "Subtract five thousand."	Class scores 2 points.

Although Wipe Out or a variation of it can be played without a calculator, it is much more exciting with one. Children don't get bogged down with computation. The focus remains on place value. Furthermore, they are often surprised by what happens when they make a place-value error, which increases their place-value understanding.

The challenge of wipe-out type activities is illustrated by a question included on a recent national assessment, shown in Figure 7–5. The figure shows this open-ended question along with examples of satisfactory responses. Although calculators were available, the decision as to whether or not to use a calculator was made by each student. However, more than 60 percent of the fourth graders made no response or provided an incorrect response. This performance level indicates the value of the "wipe-out" type of activities and reminds us that connections

Question: Laura wanted to enter the number 8375 into her calculator. By mistake, she entered the number 8275. Without clearing the calculator, how could she correct her mistake?

Satisfactory Responses:

1. 8275 + 100 = 8375

2. She could add 100 more.

3. If she subtracted 100 she could add 200.

Figure 7–5 • An example from a national assessment test that reinforces the connection between wipe-out-type calculator game and mental computation skills

need to be established between such activities and mental computations.

Research reports that many children lack an understanding of the relative sizes of numbers greater than 100 (Payne and Huinker 1993). This results from many factors, one of which may be the lack of opportunities to model which help children develop a visual awareness of the relative size of numbers. Large numbers can be modeled using variations of the models shown in Figure 7–2. For the base-10 blocks, lay another place-value mat to the left of the mat holding hundreds, tens, and ones. This thousands mat holds thousands, ten-thousands, and hundred-thousands. Figure 7–6 provides another demonstration of how two numbers can have the same digits but be very different. How are 2130 and 1032 alike and different? As children engage in discussion to answer this question, their knowledge of place value and their sense of numbers will grow. Using the same digits to represent different numbers helps children appreciate the importance of representing the place values accurately. Although the numbers 2130 and 1032 use the same digits, the models that represent these numbers are dramatically different (see Appendix B). This type of experience helps develop number sense and alerts children to the importance of the front-end, or lead, digits, which in this case denote thousands.

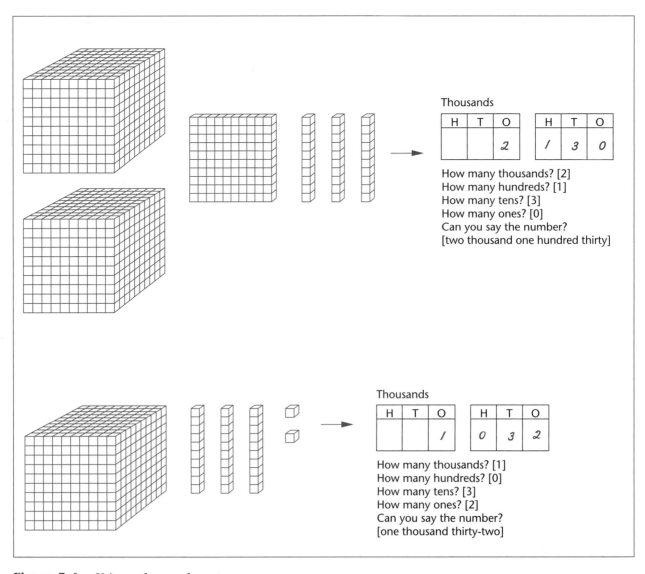

Figure 7–6 • Using a thousands mat

As the number of digits increases, children should be encouraged to focus on the front-end digits. The front-end digits are used when comparing and ordering numbers, as well as when computing mentally and estimating:

3000 + 4000   5286

Mental computation   Estimating

The front-end approach can be naturally extended and applied to larger numbers. For example, students could be asked to decide which number is larger when the front-digits are the same:

| 5 | 4 | 1 | 2 |

| 5 | 4 | 8 | 9 |

And then asked the same question when the end digits are the same:

| 2 | 4 | 5 | 6 |

| 1 | 4 | 5 | 6 |

This task helps students compare and order larger numbers.

Try this problem:

Norway has an area of 125181 square miles.

New Mexico has an area of 121400 square miles.

Greece has an area of 50944 square miles.

Why is it easy to tell which has the least area?

Can you tell which is the greatest area by comparing the first front-end digit? The first two front-end digits? The first three front-end digits?

Which has the greatest area?

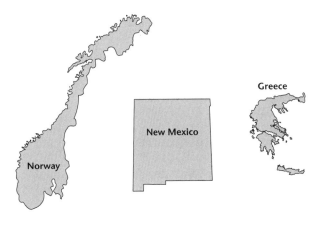

This problem reminds students of the importance of place value when comparing numbers. For example, the front-end approach is used only when the numbers have the same number of digits. It is not needed to compare 125181 square miles with 50944 square miles because the numbers of digits are different.

Counting and Patterns

As noted in Chapter 6, calculators are useful in counting and pattern recognition. Seeing each value displayed on the calculator helps students develop important insight into what digits are changing and when. For example, as Figure 7–7 shows, when counting on the calculator by ones, children observe that the digit on the right (ones place) changes every time they "count," while the next digit (tens place) changes less frequently, and it takes much counting to change the third digit (hundreds place).

Calculator counting provides many opportunities to discuss patterns related to place value. Such counting can also contribute to a better grasp of large numbers, thereby helping to develop students' number sense. For example, in Chapter 6, In the Classroom 6–5 asked pupils to record how long it took to count from 1 to 1000 by ones. Students might also be asked to find how long it takes to count from 1 to 1000000 by thousands.

Many pupils are surprised to learn that it takes about the same time. One fourth grader said, "That

Figure 7–7 • Calculator counting to illustrate place-value patterns

means there are as many thousands in one million as ones in one thousand." This is a profound observation—of the type that leads to a better understanding of both place value and large numbers, and it also reflects a growing sense of numbers.

As Figure 7–7 shows, counting on by tens or by hundreds never changes the ones place. However, when counting by tens, the tens place changes on each count and the next digit (hundreds) changes every ten counts. Observing these patterns in counting larger and larger numbers helps students recognize place-value properties. In the Classroom 7–2 uses calculators and patterns to help students add multiples of 100. Similar exercises should be provided with other powers of ten.

As we have seen, the hundred chart provides useful model for counting and pattern recognition related to place value. Activities involving counting with multiples of 10 were illustrated in Lesson Idea 7–3. In the Classroom 7–3, shows how similar ideas can be extended to a thousand chart. For example, consider this diagram and the thousand chart In the Classroom 7–3:

A solution for this diagram:

$$A = 430 - 100 - 10$$
$$B = 430 - 100$$
$$C = 430 + 100 + 10$$
$$D = 430 + 200$$

requires the use of patterns and leads to algebraic thinking when 430 is replaced by any number N. Then

$$A = N - 100 - 10$$
$$B = N - 100$$
$$C = N + 100 + 10$$
$$D = N + 200$$

This activity further develop students' number sense and provide practice in important mental computation skills. (See Appendix B for copies of several master charts.)

Regrouping and Renaming

Counting suggests many patterns, but one of the most important for young children is observing what happens when the number after 9 (or 19, 29, etc.) is modeled. Trading occurs in every case. The pattern involved in bridging from one decade to another should be recognized and clearly understood by children.

Regrouping and place value are intertwined in later development of computation. Regrouping happens whenever bridging occurs, as from 1 ten to another (such as 29 to 30) or from 1 hundred to another (such as 799 to 800). Regrouping also happens when 6 tens 7 ones are considered as 5 tens 17 ones, or 245 is thought of as 24 tens 5 ones, or 40 pennies are traded for 4 dimes. The importance of clearly understanding the regrouping process cannot be overstressed. Understanding is most likely to develop when children experience this bridging with physical models and practice trading and regrouping.

Whenever trading occurs, there are accompanying changes in how the number is recorded. An understanding of this symbolization requires many experiences with problems involving trading and the related recording process. Figure 7–8 shows how regrouping affects digits and place value.

Figure 7–9 further illustrates the regrouping process with two different models. Similar models with larger numbers should be used as soon as children have grasped the trading principles involving ones, tens, and hundreds. In fact, it is this extension process that demonstrates the power of mathematical abstraction. Extending to thousands should be done with proportional models to illustrate the dramatic size increase that continues to occur as new places are

---

In The Classroom 7–3

The Power of 10 on the Thousand Chart

Objective: Using a thousand chart to identify patterns and skip count by tens and hundreds.

10	20	30	40	50	60	70	80	90	100
110	120	130	140	150	160	170	180	190	200
210	220	230	240	250	260	270	280	290	300
310	320	330	340	350	360	370	380	390	400
410	420	430	440	450	460	470	480	490	500
510	520	530	540	550	560	570	580	590	600
610	620	630	640	650	660	670	680	690	700
710	720	730	740	750	760	770	780	790	800
810	820	830	840	850	860	870	880	890	900
910	920	930	940	950	960	970	980	990	1000

▼ Count by 10:

- Start on any square in the first three rows.
- Count forward 10 squares, and tell where you stopped.
- Start at a different square, and count forward 10 squares.
- After you have done this several times, tell about a pattern that you found.
- Describe a quick way to count "a hundred more" on this thousand chart.

▼ Count by 100:

- Tell how you could use the thousand chart to add 300 to 240.
- Tell how you could use the thousand chart to add 290 to 240.

▼ Connect the charts:

- Tell how using the hundred chart helps you use the thousand chart.

---

used. Children will soon recognize that it becomes very cumbersome to model large numbers with proportional models (see Powers of Ten in Appendix B).

The calculator can be used with very large numbers. Minor variations of In the Classroom 6–5 (such

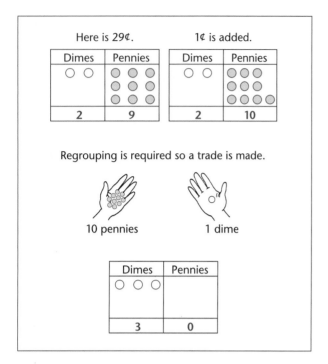

Figure 7–8 • Nonproportional model illustrating relation between regrouping and place value

as finding how long a calculator takes to count to one million or one billion) can help students develop a better grasp of large numbers.

READING AND WRITING NUMBERS

Reading and writing numbers are symbolic activities and should follow much modeling and talking about numbers. The key word is *symbolic*. This recommendation is based on research with young children and alerts us to the danger of a premature focus on symbols (Payne and Huinker 1993). A sustained development of number sense should precede the reading and writing of numbers. This approach ensures that the symbols the students are writing and reading are meaningful to them.

Now let's consider some ways in which understanding place value helps develop the reading and writing of numbers. Let us again take the example of the number 123. We can identify the places (hundreds, tens, ones) as well as the value of each (1, 2, 3). We know that the 1 means one hundred. We also know that 23 is both 2 tens 3 ones and 23 ones, and that 123 is 1 hundred 2 tens 3 ones; 12 tens 3 ones; and 123 ones.

These representations may be shown on the place-value mat:

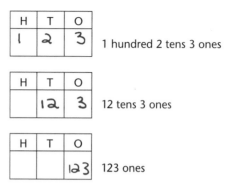

The skill of reading numbers in different ways (and the understanding of the grouping that allows this to be done) can be useful in many operations with whole numbers. For example, rereading provides a nice stepping stone to mental computation; more specifically, it leads to multiplying a number by 10:

H	T	O
3	8	O

Reads: 3 hundreds 8 tens 0 ones.
Realizes there are no ones.
Rereads: 38 tens, which is 380.

Although it seems logical to write number words as they sound, this procedure can lead to difficulty. If this were done, sixty-one would be incorrectly written as 601 and one hundred twenty-three as 100203. The exercise in the Snapshot of a Lesson where children were asked to show forty-one was aimed at detecting this error. If a child made this mistake, the teacher could use the place-value mat as a model to demonstrate:

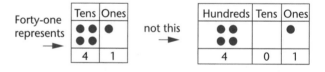

Modeling several numbers on the mat will help clarify this notion.

Similar problems exist in naming and representing larger numbers. Consider the following questions from a national assessment:

The census showed that three hundred fifty-six thousand, ninety-seven people lived in Middletown. Written as a number, the population is

350697

356097

356907

356970

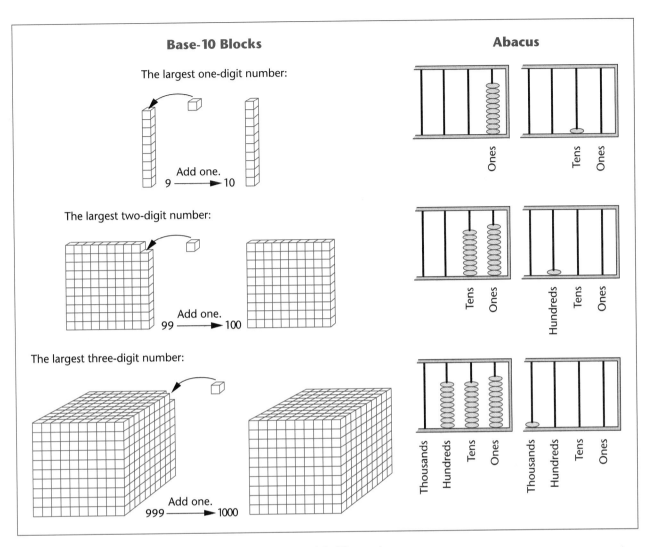

Figure 7–9 • Proportional and nonproportional models illustrating some relationships between regrouping and place value

What number is four hundred five and three tenths?

45.3

405.3

453

4005.3

About 70 percent of fourth graders and 90 percent of eighth graders correctly connected the place-value language and symbolic representation. Yet research shows that number sense development lags behind language (McIntosh et al. 1997). Children need to make sense of large numbers in order to read and write them and calculator counting (In the Classroom 6–5) provides an effective way of contributing to their number sense. Open-ended questions such as those shown in Figure 7–10 encourage

How Big Is BIG?

A million . . .

- dollars is _____ $100 bills.

- days is about _____ years.

- miles is about _____ times around the equator of the earth.

A billion . . .

- dollars would buy about _____ trail bikes.

- seconds is about _____ years.

- people live in _____ .

Figure 7–10 • A poster to promote thinking about numbers and benchmarks

Figure 7–11 • **Children constructing a cubic meter box**   (Photo by Gene Sutphen.)

children to estimate and think about numbers. As they share their answers and talk about different ways of understanding millions and billions, their number sense grows. Reading books listed in the Book Nook for Children such as *If You Made a Million* (Schwartz 1989) and *In One Day* (Parker 1984), found in *The Wonderful World of Mathematics: A Critically*

Annotated List of Children's Books in Mathematics (Thiessen and Matthias 1998) gives children additional insight and appreciation of larger numbers.

It is helpful for students to link some of the models to larger numbers. For example, the students might begin with a one-cubic-centimeter block. If they then make a cubic-meter box, that box will hold one million cubic-centimeter cubes, as illustrated in Figure 7–11.

Base-10 blocks also can be used to help students make the connection between the concrete model and the symbolic representation, as in Figure 7–12. This model helps mentally "see" that ten thousand is a long piece made up of ten cubes, where each cube is one thousand. Although this model can be constructed with physical models, children quickly appreciate the power of constructing mental images to represent larger numbers.

When students begin to develop an intuitive grasp of larger numbers and begin to use millions and billions intelligently, they are ready to write and read these larger numbers. Place-value mats can be naturally expanded to represent larger numbers:

Billions				Millions				Thousands				Ones		
H	T	O		H	T	O		H	T	O		H	T	O

Figure 7–12 • **Connecting the symbolic representation of one million with a concrete model**   (Adapted from Labinowicz 1989.)

To develop facility in reading large numbers, children need careful instruction and practice in actually naming them aloud. For example, would you read 12345678 as "one ten-million two million three hundred-thousand four ten-thousand" and so on? Certainly not! You would use the period names and read it as "twelve million, three hundred forty-five thousand, six hundred seventy-eight." This example is a clear application of an organizing strategy: the digits within each period are read as hundreds, tens, and ones, as with "three hundred forty-five thousand." For this reason, children need to think of larger numbers (those of more than three digits) in blocks of three digits.

Recognition and understanding of the hundreds, tens, and ones pattern provide a powerful organizational strategy that can be called upon in naming numbers.

Only the key terms—ones, tens, and hundreds—along with the recognition of the periods for thousands, millions, and billions are needed to name very large numbers.

Did you know that in many countries, commas are not used to separate blocks of three digits? Instead, for example, the number 2346457 is written as 2 346 457. The blocks of digits remain visible but are separated by spaces rather than commas. Some newspapers, journals, and textbooks in the United States now print numbers this way. This change has instructional implications for both reading and writing numbers. In particular, children must become even more sensitive to the importance of writing numbers clearly and distinctly.

Speaking of reading and writing, newspapers provide a rich context to explore numbers of all sizes. Examine a newspaper and highlight all of the numbers reported in headlines and related stories. We were surprised at the high frequency in which numbers occurred. It reminds us of the importance of developing notions of place value and number sense. Figure 7–13 illustrates how newspapers provide a powerful source way to help students to become more sensitive to the frequent use of numbers in newspapers and some related activities to engage students in writing about them.

Naming numbers is clearly an important skill. Yet with the widespread use of calculators, a more efficient way to read multidigit numbers is being used. For example, 32764 is read as "three two seven six four" and 4.3425 as "four point three four two five." Each of these readings is correct and much easier to say than the respective periods. There is the danger that children will say the digits without any realization of the value of the numbers involved, but such interpretations are not necessary at every

Making More Sense of Numbers by Reading and Writing

Use a front page of a daily newspaper:

1. Find a headline or sentence that contains a number.

2. Is the number exact or an estimate? How can you tell?

3. Rewrite the headline or sentence without the number.
   - Does this change the meaning?
   - Do you like the headline with or without the number best? Tell why.

4. Does a newspaper article always have at least one number in it?

5. How many articles on your front page can you find that do not include a number?

Figure 7–13 • Newspapers report many numbers

stage of the problem-solving process. If it is only desired to copy a number displayed on a calculator, then a direct translation of digits is without a doubt the best way to read the number. Rather than requiring children to read numbers in a specific way, it is far better to recognize the value of each technique and encourage children to choose wisely—namely, to select the technique that is most appropriate for a given situation.

ESTIMATION AND ROUNDING

An important aspect of developing number sense is recognizing that some numbers are approximate (such as our national debt) and some are exact (such as the number of people killed in a fatal airplane crash). Approximate values are associated with estimation, often involving rounding, and are encountered regularly in our daily lives.

Estimation

Estimation provides a natural way to develop number sense and place-value concepts. Children love to estimate, and they enjoy many types of estimating situations that challenge their skills:

About how many balloons could fill this room?

About how many pennies tall are you?

About how many dollar bills can you lift?

These types of questions stimulate thinking and invite involvement.

In this section, our focus is on estimating quantities. This experience provides an important foundation for number sense and place value, but practice situations must be well chosen. If the number of objects is small, it is natural to count and unnecessary to estimate. However, when the number becomes large and tedious or too time-consuming to count, then estimates are useful.

Research has demonstrated that children use several different techniques for estimating, and there is a wide range of performance at each grade level.

Providing opportunities for children to share strategies is an effective way to help children develop competence and confidence in estimating (Sowder 1992).

Figure 7–14 illustrates three different thinking processes students use in making an estimate. Students also should be encouraged to share their thinking strategies. Sharing may offer insight into not only the thinking processes used but also any misconceptions held by the students.

Experience in making comparisons of different quantities is important at every grade level.

Benchmarks are a very important and useful tool in estimating (see Figure 6–2). If you know your own height, for example, that information can help you estimate someone else's height. You can decide if the other person is taller or shorter than you are, and this decision helps you make an estimate. In this case, you have used your height as a benchmark for comparison.

Good estimation skills require the development of number sense; thus, they evolve slowly over time. The foundation for estimation includes counting, models, and meaningful interpretations of real-life encounters with numbers of all sizes. For example, the bulletin board display shown in Figure 7–15 provides some benchmarks that can help children better grasp the relationships between small and large numbers when estimating length. Frequent practice with the lower portion of the display provides an enjoyable activity that helps develop both estimation skills and number sense.

The benchmark principle is used in many different ways. Figure 7–16 demonstrates how providing

Figure 7–14 • **Examples of children's thinking when making an estimate**

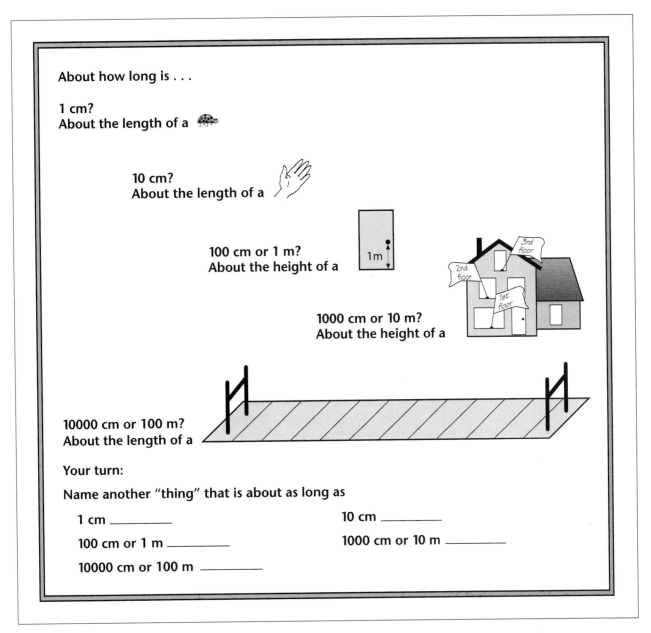

About how long is . . .

1 cm?
About the length of a

10 cm?
About the length of a

100 cm or 1 m?
About the height of a

1m

3rd floor

2nd floor

1st floor

1000 cm or 10 m?
About the height of a

10000 cm or 100 m?
About the length of a

Your turn:

Name another "thing" that is about as long as

1 cm _____   10 cm _____

100 cm or 1 m _____   1000 cm or 10 m _____

10000 cm or 100 m _____

Figure 7–15 • A bulletin board display to develop benchmarks of length

additional information (new benchmarks) can be helpful in producing closer estimates. It is important that students make initial estimates and then refine or adjust these in light of new information. For example, Figure 7–16 produces a "trail" of estimates, with each estimate reflecting changes resulting from new benchmarks. This trail encourages students to continue to think about numbers and provides teachers with insight into their thinking.

Rounding

As students estimate, they become more comfortable with numbers that are not exact. Thus, early es-

timation of quantity and use of benchmarks provide some useful preparation for rounding numbers.

Rounding is an important skill that integrates understanding of approximate values with place value and naming numbers. Numbers are usually rounded to make them easier to use or because exact values are unknown. How numbers are rounded depends on the uses that will be made of the rounded numbers. For example, attendance at a major league baseball game may be 54321. Although the attendance could be rounded to the nearest ten (54320) or the nearest hundred (54300), it is more likely to be reported as "about 54000" or "over 50000" or "less

Figure 7–16 • Using benchmarks to estimate

than 60000" because these values are convenient and a little easier to comprehend and remember.

As they develop rounding skills, children should come to realize that rounding rules may vary and are not universal. For example, here are two different rules from current textbooks for rounding a number ending in 5:

(a) Increase the previous digit by 1.

(b) If the digit preceding the 5 is even, leave the 5 alone; if it is odd, increase the 5 to the next even digit.

In either case, 75 would round to 80. However, 85 would round to 90 using rule (a) and 80 using rule (b). Neither rule is "right" or "best," but this variability across textbooks can confuse children. Checking to make sure students understand the specific rules of rounding that are to be used avoids some of the confusion.

Regardless of the rounding rule used, the precision of the rounded numbers reflects the problem context. For example, a meter stick could serve as a number line. Consider this train of Cuisenaire rods, with 7 decimeter rods and 4 centimeter rods:

Is the train closer to 7 or 8 decimeters?

Is it closer to 0 or 1 meter?

If we round to the nearest decimeter, then the length is 7 decimeters. If we round to the nearest meter, the length is 1 meter. How numbers are rounded depends on how the values will be used. For example, if we were to cut a strip of cloth to cover this train, it would be foolish to round to the nearest decimeter and cut a length of 7 decimeters, but a meter of cloth would provide plenty of material to cover the train. Children must think about numbers before rounding them and not just indiscriminately apply rounding rules.

Even in a context, interpretation of rounded numbers is challenging, as illustrated by this national assessment question:

> The length of a dinosaur was reported to have been 80 feet (rounded to the nearest 10 feet). What length other than 80 feet could have been the actual length of the dinosaur?

Several different answers, such as 76 or 84 feet, were acceptable. Only 20 percent of the fourth graders and less than half of the eighth graders reported an acceptable answer. This performance shows that interpreting a rounded result needs to be addressed in elementary and middle grades.

The base-10 blocks provide a natural method for developing rounding skills with larger numbers. Questions such as these focus attention on the quantity and the idea of *closer to,* which is essential in rounding:

Is this more than three hundred? [yes]

Is this more than four hundred? [no]

Is this closer to three or four hundred? [closer to three hundred]

This model can also be extended to help children become more aware that 350 is halfway between 300 and 400.

A roller coaster model could be used to develop rounding skills. If children understand the number line, the roller coaster provides an effective tool for rounding.

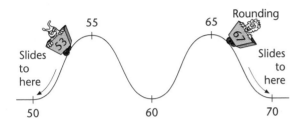

Children know what happens when the coaster stops at certain points. The model also suggests that something special happens at the top: The coaster could roll either way. This observation provides an opportunity to discuss a rule of rounding, such as "if the number ends in 5, you go over the hump to the next valley." In rounding, attention is given to the back-end digit or digits. Children should view rounding as something that not only makes numbers easier to handle but, more important, makes sense.

Perhaps the biggest difficulty related to rounding is knowing whether to round to the nearest ten, hundred, thousand, or whatever. Normally this decision depends on the purpose of rounding and the context of the problem. Consider for example, the following situation:

> Carl Furillo (former baseball player for the Brooklyn Dodgers) had a lifetime batting average of .2994 in the major leagues, yet he is not considered a .300 hitter.

This suggests that Major League baseball has a particular procedure for rounding batting averages.

Encourage students to explore different ways to round. For example, consider these prices:

> How would you 'round' these prices if you wanted to round them to the same number?

> What would you 'round' these prices to, in deciding how much money is needed to make each purchase?

Such real-world situations encourages students to think about both the advantages and consequences of rounding numbers. Meaningful rounding (knowing how much precision is necessary and what to round to) will improve through practice in many different problem contexts.

A Glance at Where We've Been

Children must have a clear understanding of our number system if they are going to be mathematically literate. They must be able to distinguish characteristics of our number system, the role of zero, the additive property of numbers, a base of ten, and place value. Many counting and trading experiences (particularly grouping by tens) are necessary.

As children develop their skills with the aid of various models (such as bean sticks, base-10 blocks, and an abacus), they need to learn how to organize the results in some systematic fashion and record them. Place-value mats serve as a visual reminder of the quantities involved and provide a bridge toward the symbolic representation of larger numbers. Establishing these bridges from the concrete to the abstract is the heart of good teaching. It is particularly critical in developing place value, whose importance is second to none in all later development of number concepts.

Place-value concepts are developed over many years. The trading rules help plant the seeds early, but recognition of the power and importance of place value is developed, refined, extended, and expanded throughout the study of mathematics. Estimation provides a natural setting for students to experience larger numbers and develop place-value concepts via rounding.

Systematic study of place value over a long period is essential. For example, review of important place-value concepts must be provided as computation is being established. This type of study also provides an opportunity not only to maintain but to extend many place-value concepts learned earlier. The point is that place value is not just taught for a couple of days in one or two grades; rather, systematic instruction on place value must be planned and integrated throughout the elementary school mathematics program.

Things to Do: From What You've Read

1. Identify four characteristics of our number system. Select one characteristic and make a visual representation of it.

2. Show how 201 and 120 would be represented with three different place-value models.

3. Distinguish between proportional and nonproportional models. Name an example of each.

4. Tell why trading activities are so important with respect to place value. Describe several materials that could be used for trading.

5. Estimation provides many opportunities to explore place value. Describe an estimation activity that would encourage students to think about 10, 100, 1000, and 10000 and distinguish among these values.

6. Describe some ways that benchmarks are used in estimating length and quantity.

7. Describe ways in which modeling, reading, and writing numbers can be used to get children actively involved in talking about mathematics and linking concrete materials with their symbolic representations.

8. It has been suggested that centuries decades, and millenniums can be used to demonstrate some notions of place value. Describe how this could be done.

9. Examine Lesson Idea 7–3. Show the six different numbers that could be made with the three cards. Which is closest to 400? Which number less than 400 is next closest to 400?

10. Use your calculator. Enter the largest number possible in the display and name this number. How many digits does it have? Add one to this number and describe what your calculator does.

Things to Do: Going Beyond This Book

field Additional activities, suggestions, and questions are provided in *Teaching Elementary Mathematics: A Resource for Field Experiences.*

1. *field* *Early Number Sense.* Ask a child some questions (such as, What number comes before seventeen? Thirty? Two hundred? What number comes after thirty-nine? Two-hundred nine? How many tens are in forty? Forty-seven? Try to capture the words students use to describe how they did it. Explain how their answers help you better understand their thinking and their level of number sense.

2. *field* In the Classroom 7–2 provides a structured counting activity that can be facilitated with a calculator. Use this activity as a guide and ask primary grade students to count by hundreds and predict which of the results will occur. Ask them to count with the calculator and compare results. Describe any difficulties or discoveries that you observed.

3. Different models exist for helping children develop a concept of large numbers. Each of the articles

(Bickerton-Ross 1988; Harrison 1985; Joslyn 1990; Parker and Widmer 1991; Thompson 1989) shows and describes useful physical models. Examine one or more of the articles and describe the approach taken to help children better understand large numbers.

4. Select either *Number Sense and Operations* (Burton et al. 1993), *Developing Number Sense in the Middle Grades* (Reys et al. 1991), or SENSE (McIntosh et al. 1997). Choose an activity that you think would be useful to help students develop a better understanding of large numbers and demonstrate how you would implement the activity.

5. *field* *Checking Place-Value Concepts.* Give a second or third grader some of the following tasks: Write three hundred forty eight. Write a large number. Name that number. How many tens are in 250? How many hundreds are in one thousand? Tell how the answers to these questions helped you better understand the child's development of place value.

6. Make bean sticks for base five. Describe how to demonstrate any number up to 24 with your bean sticks and loose beans. Alternatively, use pennies and nickels for base five, and describe how you would show all numbers up to 24.

7. View a segment from the videotape series *Number Sense Now!* (Fennell 1992). Discuss ways in which this tape might help students become more sensitive to the importance and power of number sense.

8. Check the Number and Operation Standard for Pre-K–2 (www.standards-e.nctm.org/) for additional explorations of groups of ten and place value. Discuss how the samples of student work influence your thinking of place value.

9. *field* In the Classroom 7–3 provides an extension of the hundred chart. (See Appendix B for other variations.) Show the chart to at least three children (grades 3–5) and say, "Please tell me about some patterns that you see." After each description, say, "Tell me about any other patterns you see." Be sure to allow them time to think and reflect—pattern recognition takes time. Make a list of the patterns for each child and compare their observations.

BOOK NOOK FOR CHILDREN

Berry, David. *The Rajah's Rice: A Mathematical Folktale from India.* New York: W. W. Freeman & Company, 1994.

Demi. *Demi's Count the Animals 1-2-3.* New York: Gossett Dunlap, 1986.

Diagram Group. *Comparisons.* New York: St. Martin's Press, 1980.

Howard, Katherine. *I Can Count to One Hundred . . . Can You?* New York: Random House, 1979.

Parker, Tom. *In One Day.* Boston: Houghton Mifflin, 1984.

Paulos, John Allen. *Innumeracy.* New York: Hill and Wang, 1988.

Schwartz, David M. *How Much Is a Million?* New York: Lothrop, Lee and Shepard Books, a division of William Morrow, 1985.

Schwartz, David M. *If You Made a Million.* New York: Lothrop, Lee and Shepard Books, a division of William Morrow, 1989.

Selected References

Auriemma, Susan. "How Huge Is a Hundred?" *Teaching Children Mathematics,* 6(3) (November 1999), pp. 154–159.

Bickerton-Ross, Linda. "A Practical Experience in Problem Solving: A '10,000' Display." *Arithmetic Teacher,* 35 (December 1988), pp. 14–15.

Bobis, Janette F. "Using a Calculator to Develop Number Sense." *Arithmetic Teacher,* 38 (January 1991), pp. 42–45.

Bove, Sandra. "Place Value: A Vertical Perspective." *Teaching Children Mathematics,* 1(9) (May 1995), pp. 542–546.

Burton, Grace et al. *Number Sense and Operations.* Reston, Va.: NCTM, 1993.

Curcio, Frances R., and Zarnowski, Myra. "Revisiting the Powers of 2." *Teaching Children Mathematics,* 2(5) (January 1996), pp. 300–304.

Fennell, Francis. *Number Sense Now!* (videotape and guidebook). Reston, Va.: NCTM, 1992.

Gluck, Doris. "Helping Students Understand Place Value." *Arithmetic Teacher,* 38 (March 1991), pp. 10–13.

Harrison, Marilyn, and Harrison, Bruce. "Developing Numeration Concepts and Skills." *Arithmetic Teacher,* 33 (February 1986), pp. 18–21.

Harrison, William B. "How to Make a Million." *Arithmetic Teacher,* 32 (September 1985), pp. 46–47.

Hopkins, Martha H. "Wipe Out Refined." In *Calculators in Mathematics Education,* 1992 Yearbook (eds. James T. Fey and Christian R. Hirsch). Reston, Va.: NCTM, 1992.

Joslyn, Ruth E. "Using Concrete Models to Teach Large Number Concepts." *Arithmetic Teacher,* 38 (November 1990), pp. 6–9.

Kouba, Vicky L.; Carpenter, Thomas P.; and Swafford, Jane O. "Number and Operations." In *Results from the Fourth Mathematics Assessment of the National Assessment of Educational Progress* (ed. M. Lindquist). Reston, Va.: NCTM, 1989.

Labinowicz, Ed. *Learning from Children: New Beginnings for Teaching Numerical Thinking.* Menlo Park, Calif.: Addison-Wesley, 1985.

Lara-Alecio, Rafael; Irby, Beverly J.; and Morales-Aldana, Leonel. "A Mathematics Lesson from the Mayan Civilization." *Teaching Children Mathematics,* 5(3) (November 1998), pp. 154–158.

McIntosh, Alistair; Reys, Barbara; and Reys, Robert. *Number SENSE: Simple Effective Number Sense Experiences: Grades 3–4 & 4–6.* Palo Alto, Calif.: Dale Seymour Publications, 1997.

Nagel, Nancy G., and Swingen, Cynthia C. "Students' Explanations of Place Value in Addition and Subtraction." *Teaching Children Mathematics,* 5(3) (November 1998), pp. 164–170.

National Council of Teachers of Mathematics. *Principles and Standards for School Mathematics.* Reston, Va.: NCTM, 2000.

Parker, Janet, and Widmer, Connie. "How Big Is a Million?" *Arithmetic Teacher,* 39 (September 1991), pp. 38–41.

Payne, Joseph N., and Huinker, DeAnn M. "Early Number and Numeration." In *Research Ideas for the Classroom: Early Childhood Mathematics* (ed. Robert J. Jensen). Reston, Va.: NCTM, and New York: Macmillan, 1993, pp. 43–70.

Rathmell, Edward C., and Leutzinger, Larry P. "Number Representations and Relationships." *Arithmetic Teacher,* 38 (March 1991), pp. 20–23.

Reed, Kristine. "How many spots does a Cheetah have?" *Teaching Children Mathematics,* 6(6), (February 2000), pp. 346–349.

Reys, Barbara J.; Barger, Rita; Bruckheimer, Maxim; Dougherty, Barbara; Hope, Jack; Lembke, Linda; Markovitz, Zvia; Parnas, Andy; Reehm, Sue; Sturdevant, Ruthi; and Weber, Marianne. *Developing Number Sense in the Middle Grades.* Reston, Va.: NCTM, 1991.

Ritchhart, Ron. *Making Numbers Make Sense: A Sourcebook for Developing Numeracy.* Menlo Park, Calif.: Addison-Wesley, 1994.

Rinker, Ethel. "Eight-Ring Circus: A Variation in the Teaching of Counting and Place Value." *Arithmetic Teacher,* 19 (March 1972), pp. 209–216.

Sowder, Judith. "Estimation and Number Sense." In *Handbook of Research on Mathematics Teaching and Learning* (ed. Douglas Grouws). New York: Macmillan, 1992, pp. 371–389.

Thiessen, Diane, and Matthias, Margaret (eds.). *The Wonderful World of Mathematics: A Critically Annotated List of Children's Books in Mathematics.* Reston, Va.: NCTM, 1998.

Thomas, Cynthia S. "100 Activities for the 100th day." *Teaching Children Mathematics,* 6(5) (January 2000), pp. 276–280.

Thompson, Charles S. "Place Value and Larger Numbers." In *Mathematics for the Young Child* (ed. Joseph N. Payne). Reston, Va.: NCTM, 1990, pp. 89–108.

Thornton, Carol A.; Jones, Graham A.; and Neal, Judy L. "The 100s Chart: A Stepping Stone to Mental Mathematics," *Teaching Children Mathematics,* 1(8) (April 1995), pp. 480–483.

Wearne, Diane, and Hiebert, James. "Place Value and Addition and Subtraction," *Arithmetic Teacher,* 41(5) (January 1994), pp. 271–275.

Yoshikawa, Shigeo. "Computational Estimation: Curriculum and Instructional Issues from the Japanese Perspective." In *Computational Alternatives for the 21st Century: Cross Cultural Perspectives from Japan and the United States* (eds. Robert E. Reys and Nobubiko Nohda). Reston, Va.: NCTM, 1994.

Operations: Meanings and Basic Facts

Snapshot of a Lesson

Purpose

To provide initial experiences with multiplication (as repeated addition) and division (as repeated subtraction).

Needed Materials

Flannelboard or magnetic board; flannel or magnetic "candies": 20 small yellow, 15 medium orange, and 12 large red; disks for each child: 25 yellow, 20 orange, and 15 red.

Procedures

Read this story to children, stopping to ask questions and model each situation on the board:

Once upon a time there was a little old lady who lived in a little old house in the middle of a little old town. She was such a nice little old lady that all the children who lived in the town liked to come to visit her. For a special treat, she would often give them candy. She had three kinds, each wrapped in a different color:

- small yellow ones
- medium orange ones
- large red ones

Put a sample of each on the board.

She let the children choose the kind they wanted, but she realized there could be a problem—everyone might want the largest. So she made a rule: each child could have

- 4 yellow, or
- 3 orange, or
- 2 red

Put each grouping on the board.

1. One day 3 children came to visit. They all took red candies. How many red candies could each child take? Who can show how many pieces the children took altogether?

Expected response: 2 + 2 + 2 = 6; possibly 3 groups of 2, 3 twos are 6, or 3 × 2 = 6. Have child show and count.

2. Another day, 2 children took red.
   (a) How many pieces altogether?
   (b) How do you know?
   (c) Is there any other way to know?

Ask questions (a), (b), and (c) for the next examples. After several with whole group watching the board, have each child use disks.

3. 3 children—orange
4. 2 children—yellow
5. 4 children—orange
6. 3 children—yellow.
7. If needed:
   2 children—orange
   4 children—yellow

8. 6 children—3 took yellow, 3 red

9. 4 children—2 took red, 2 orange

10. 5 children—2 took orange, 3 yellow

11. If needed:

5 children—all took yellow

6 children—all took red

Suppose the old lady had 8 pieces of yellow candy. How many children could choose yellow? How do you know?

After several examples with board, have each child solve with disks.

1. 15 orange (how many children?)

2. 10 red

3. 12 red

4. 12 yellow

5. 12 orange

6. 9 orange

7. 8 red

Practice

Worksheet paralleling lesson (use to evaluate):

> 3 children.
> All took red.
> Make a drawing.

Extension

1. If the old lady gave away 2 candies, how many children came? What color candies did she give? What if she gave 9 candies? 15?

2. If she gave away 6 candies, how many children might have come, and what color candies did they get? Can you find more than one answer to this question? Find some other numbers of candies that have more than one answer.

3. Pretend you see boots all lined up outside a classroom. How many children are in the room if there are 18 boots and each child left boots?

4. Ask children to make up similar problems.

Introduction

The Snapshot of a Lesson incorporates several essential components of a well-planned classroom activity involving computation. First and foremost, it involves the student in an active way in manipulating objects to answer questions. It provides problem-solving experiences that promote reasoning and discussion. "How do you know?" is an important question because it encourages students to think about "why" and not just "what." Also, computational ideas are posed in a potentially real situation.

These components are important in elementary school mathematics lessons, particularly as understanding of the relevance and meaning of computational ideas is being developed. An understanding of addition, subtraction, multiplication, and division and knowledge of the basic facts for each of these operations provide a foundation for all later work with computation. To be effective in this later work, children must develop broad concepts for the operations. This development is more likely to happen if each operation is presented through a multi-embodiment approach using various physical models. Such experiences help children recognize that an operation can be used in several different types of situations. Children also must understand the properties that apply to each operation and the relationships between operations.

Learning the basic facts is one of the first steps children take as they refine their ideas about each operation. By using the facts, plus an understanding of place value and mathematical properties, a child can perform any addition, subtraction, multiplication, or division with whole numbers. Understanding the operations and having immediate recall of number facts are essential in doing estimation, mental computation, and pencil-and-paper algorithms; but these skills are just as essential when calculators and computers are used. Without such devices, the basic facts form the building blocks for performing more difficult, multidigit calculations; when calculators are readily available, the basic facts (along with operation sense and understanding of place value) provide a means of quickly checking the reasonableness of answers.

Moreover, knowing the basic facts lets children perform calculations or estimate answers in many everyday situations where it would be slower to use a calculator. So no matter what type of computation a child is using—mental computation, estimation, paper-and-pencil, or a calculator—quick recall of the basic facts for each operation is essential.

HELPING CHILDREN DEVELOP NUMBER SENSE AND COMPUTATIONAL FLUENCY

Ultimately, the instructional goal is that children not only know how to add, subtract, multiply, and divide, but, more important, know *when* to apply each in a problem-solving situation. Children also should be able to recall the basic facts quickly when needed.

How do we help them to attain these skills and understandings? We begin by finding out what each child knows. Then we capitalize on this knowledge as we help them to continue to build on the number concepts they have already constructed (Kouba and Franklin 1993). Most children entering school will be ready in some ways and not ready in others for formal work on the operations. Of the prerequisites for such work, four seem particularly important: facility with counting, experience with a variety of concrete situations, familiarity with many problem-solving contexts, and experience in using language to communicate mathematical ideas.

Facility with Counting

Children use counting to solve problems involving addition, subtraction, multiplication, and division long before they come to school, as research has indicated (Baroody and Standifer 1993; Suydam and Weaver 1981). Any problem with whole numbers can be solved by counting, provided there is sufficient time. Because there is not always the time to solve problems by counting, children need to be able to use more efficient operations and procedures that help them cope with more difficult computation. Figure 8–1 illustrates this idea by comparing the counting method with the multiplication operation.

Counting nevertheless remains an integral aspect of children's beginning work with the operations. They need to know how to count forward, backward, and by twos, threes, and other groups (see Chapter 6). They need to count as they compare and analyze sets and arrays as they affirm their initial computational results. But they need more than counting to become proficient in computing.

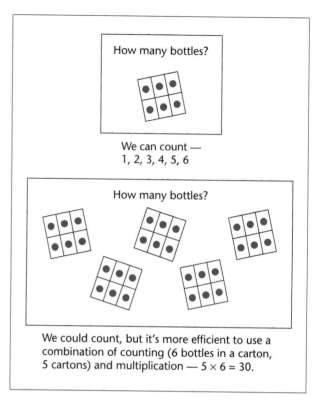

Figure 8–1 • An example showing the efficiency of using operations

Experience with a Variety of Concrete Situations

Children need to have many experiences in real-life situations and in working with physical objects to develop understanding about the operations. Research has indicated that work with actual physical objects promotes achievement for most children (Sowell 1989). Understanding improves if they can relate mathematical symbols to some experience they have had or can visualize. A basic fact cannot be learned with meaning unless it has been experienced in a situation that gives it meaning.

Manipulative materials serve as a referent for later work with the operations, as well as for constructing the basic facts. They also provide a link to connect each operation to real-world problem-solving situations—and whenever a child wants to be sure that an answer is correct, materials can be used for confirmation.

Familiarity with Many Problem-Solving Contexts

As with other mathematical content, a variety of problem-solving contexts or situations should be used to familiarize students with the four basic operations and all along the way until practice for computational mastery is the goal. We want children to think of mathematics as problem solving—as a means by which they can resolve problems through applying what they know, constructing possible routes to reach solutions, and then verifying that the solutions are plausible. We want them to realize that mathematics is a tool that has real-life applications. Most children already know that computation is used in everyday life. We want to connect the mathematics lesson to those experiences, but we also want them to realize that $6 \times 8 = \square$ or $9 + 2 = \square$ also may be problems—ones that they can resolve. We want them to have the attitude, "I don't know the answer, but I can work it out."

Experience in Using Language to Communicate Mathematical Ideas

Children need to talk and write about mathematics; experiences to develop meanings need to be put into words. Manipulative materials and problems can be vehicles for communicating about mathematics. Such discussion of mathematics is a critical part of meaningful learning. All early phases of instruction on the operations and basic facts should reflect the important role language plays in their acquisition. The *Principles and Standards for School Mathematics* (NCTM 2000) discusses the roles of language in great depth in presenting the recommendations on communication and thus provides a valuable source of additional information.

Frequently, the move to symbols is made too quickly, and the use of materials dropped too soon. Instead, the use of materials should both precede and then parallel the use of symbols. Recording of symbols should be done as materials are manipulated. As illustrated in the lesson that opened this chapter, language should be used to describe what is happening in a given situation. Then and only then will children see the relation of the symbols to the manipulation of materials and to the problem setting (Carey 1992).

The language that is learned as children communicate about what they are doing and what they see happening as they use materials helps them to understand the symbolism related to the operations. Thus, the referent for each symbol is being strengthened. Children should begin their work with operations after talking among themselves and with their teacher about a variety of experiences. They need to be encouraged to continue talking about the mathematical ideas they meet as they work with the operations. And, as soon as feasible, they need to put their ideas on paper—by drawings alone at first. As soon as they are able to write, children should also be encouraged to write number sentences and narrative explanations of their thinking.

DEVELOPING MEANINGS FOR THE OPERATIONS

As explained earlier, children encounter the four basic operations in very natural ways when they work with many diverse problem situations. By representing these problem situations (acting them out, using physical models, or drawing pictures), children develop meanings for the addition, subtraction, multiplication, and division. Mastery of basic facts and later computational work with multidigit examples must be based on a clear understanding of the operations. The following general sequence of activities is appropriate for helping children develop meaning for the four basic operations:

1. Concrete—modeling with materials: Use a variety of verbal problem settings and manipulative materials to act out and model the operation.

2. Semiconcrete—representing with pictures: Provide representations of objects in pictures, diagrams, and drawings to move a step away from the concrete toward symbolization.

3. Abstract—representing with symbols: Use symbols (especially numeric expressions and number sentences) to illustrate the operation.

In this way, children move through experiences from the concrete to the semiconcrete to the abstract, linking each to the others.

The four operations are clearly different, but there are important relationships among them that children will come to understand through modeling, pictorial, and symbolic experiences:

- Addition and subtraction are inverse operations; that is, one undoes the other:

$$5 + 8 = 13 \longleftrightarrow 13 - 5 = 8$$

- Multiplication and division are inverse operations:

$$4 \times 6 = 24 \longleftrightarrow 24 \div 4 = 6$$

- Multiplication can be viewed as repeated addition:

$$4 \times 6 \longleftrightarrow 6 + 6 + 6 + 6$$

- Division can be viewed as repeated subtraction:

$$24 \div 6 \longleftrightarrow 24 - 6 - 6 - 6 - 6$$

These relationships can be developed through careful instruction with a variety of different experiences.

Addition and Subtraction

Figure 8–2 illustrates a variety of models (including counters, linking cubes, balance scale, and number line) that can be used to represent addition. In each, the idea that addition means "finding how many in all" is depicted.

The models for addition also can be used for subtraction. Each can be applied in the three different situations that lead to subtraction.

1. Separation, or take away, involves having one quantity, removing a specified quantity from it, and noting what is left. Research indicates that this subtraction situation is the easiest for children to learn. However, persistent use of the words *take away* results in many children assuming that this is the *only* subtraction situation and leads to misunderstanding of the other two situations. This is why it is important to read a subtraction sentence such as 8–3 = 5 as "8 minus 3 equals 5" rather than "8 take-away 3 equals 5." Take-away is just one of the three types of subtraction situations.

Peggy had 7 balloons. She gave 4 to other children. How many did she have left?

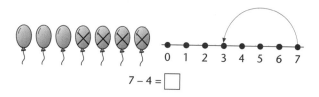

2. Comparison, or finding the difference, involves having two quantities, matching them one-to-one, and noting the quantity that is the difference between them. Problems of this type are also solved by subtraction, even though nothing is being "taken-away."

Peggy had 7 balloons. Richard had 4 balloons. How many more balloons did Peggy have than Richard did?

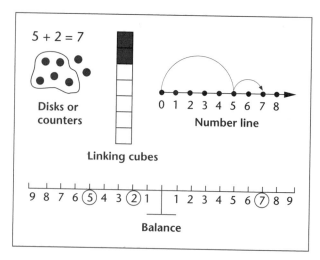

Figure 8–2 • **Some models for addition**

3. The final type of subtraction situation is known as part-whole. In this type of problem, we have a set of objects that can logically be separated into two parts. We know how many are in the entire set and we know how many are in one of the parts. We want to find out how many must be in the remaining part.

Peggy had 7 balloons. Four of them were red and the rest were blue. How many were blue?

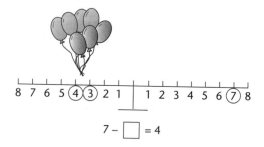

Some educators refer to this sort of subtraction situation as a "missing-addend" problem because it may be helpful to "think addition" to find the answer. For example, in the preceding problem, we could ask ourselves: 4 plus what equals 7?

The importance of providing many varied experiences in which children use physical objects to model or act out examples of each operation cannot be overemphasized. The lesson at the beginning of this chapter provided one such experience. It illustrates a way to involve each child in forming equal-sized groups as a lead-in to learning about multiplication. Writing symbols for each action is not essential at this early stage. Moving, counting, and questioning are the important components.

Lesson Idea 8–1 illustrates a slightly more symbolic activity. The children solve problems in a variety of ways using the dot sticks, followed by

Lesson Idea 8–1

Dot Sticks

Materials: Each child needs a set of dot sticks (6 popsicle sticks labeled 1–6, each with the appropriate number of dots).

Activity: Pose questions for children to model, solve, and discuss.

▼ Ask children to pick up 4 dots. (Most children will pick up the 4 stick.)

  • Is there another way to pick up 4 dots?

▼ Now ask them to pick up 6 dots.

  • How many ways can you do it?

  • Can you pick up 6 dots using 3 sticks?

▼ Ask for 11 dots.

  • Can you do it with 2 sticks?

  • 3 sticks?

  • 4 sticks?

▼ Ask for 8 dots using only 3 sticks.

▼ Ask how many different ways you can pick up 10 dots: List them on the chalkboard.

▼ Follow up with individual worksheets.

---

individual practice. Similar activities can be done with counters, linking cubes, or other objects.

Initially, symbols are used as a complement to the physical manipulation of objects. They are a way of showing the action with the materials and should always be introduced in conjunction with a concrete material or model. As the work progresses, the amount of symbolization you offer and encourage will increase.

The number line is used in some textbooks as a model for addition and subtraction, but it must be used with caution. Over the years, research has shown that children often find number lines difficult to use and interpret. Sometimes they are not sure whether they should count spaces between tic-marks or the tic-marks themselves when attempting to model a problem, or they may not be sure where on the number line to begin counting. (For example, to find 5 + 7 on a number line, they may put their finger on 5 as they begin counting from 1 up to seven—whereas they actually should begin counting when pointing at 6.) In other cases, children

seem unsure how to relate the number line to a problem situation. For example, consider this number line:

In the second national mathematics assessment, about twice as many nine-year-olds responded that "5 + 7" was pictured as did those responding with the correct answer, "5 + 2 = 7." The same error was made by 39 percent of the thirteen-year-olds. Carpenter et al. (1981, p. 19) suggested:

> Since the model does not seem to clearly suggest the operation, the meaning must be developed or misunderstandings may occur. The mathematics curriculum should be constructed to ensure that students have a meaningful development of the basic operations. Certainly, many types of models can help this development, but they must be carefully selected and meaningfully taught.

Multiplication and Division

The same sequence of experiences used for developing understanding of addition and subtraction—moving from concrete, to pictorial, to symbolic—should also be followed for multiplication and division. However, one important way that multiplication and division problems differ from addition and subtraction problems is that the numbers in the problems represent different sorts of things. For example, consider a problem such as "Andrew has two boxes of trading cards. Each box holds 24 cards. How many cards does he have altogether?" This problem may be written 2 × 24 = 48, where the *first factor* (2) tells us how many groups or sets of equal size we are considering, while the *second factor* (24) tells the size of each set. The third number (48), known as the *product,* indicates the total of all the parts (here, the total number of cards). By contrast, the old saying "you can't add apples and oranges" points out the fact that in addition and subtraction problems we must always be able to attach a common label to *all* the numbers involved. We can add apples and oranges only if we agree to relabel all the numbers in the problem with a common label (such as "fruits"). In the trading card problem, the labels for the numbers would be, respectively, boxes (2), cards per box (24), and cards (48).

Figure 8–3 illustrates some of the most commonly used models for illustrating multiplication situations: sets of objects, arrays, and the number line. Research indicates that children do best when

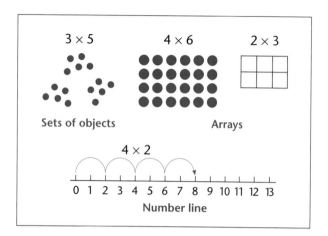

Figure 8–3 • **Commonly used models for multiplication**

they can use various representations for multiplication and division situations and can explain the relationships among those representations (Kouba and Franklin 1995).

Researchers have identified four distinct sorts of multiplicative structures: equal groups, multiplicative comparisons, combinations, and areas/arrays (Greer 1992). Problems involving the first two of these structures are most common in the elementary school, though students should eventually become familiar with all four. The four multiplicative structures are described here to help you, as the teacher, understand and recognize the variety of multiplicative situations. You are not expected to teach these labels to children, but you should try to ensure that they encounter a broad range of problem situations involving multiplication and division.

Equal-groups problems involve the most common type of multiplicative structure. When both the number and size of the groups are known (but the total is unknown) the problem can be solved by multiplication. The problem given earlier, about Andrew and his trading card collection, is an example of an equal-groups problem. When the total in an equal-groups problem is known, but either the number of groups or the size of the group is unknown, the problem can be solved by division. The two distinct types of division situations that can arise (depending on which part is unknown) are measurement or partition division (described later).

Comparison problems involve another common multiplicative structure. When we considered comparison problems for subtraction, we observed that we had two different sets which needed to be matched one-to-one to decide how much larger one was than the other. In similar fashion, comparison problems with multiplicative structures involve two

different sets, but the relationship is not one-to-one. Rather, in multiplicative situations, one set involves multiple copies of the other. An example of a multiplicative comparison situation might be: "Hilary spent $35 on Christmas gifts for her family. Geoff spent 3 times as much. How much did Geoff spend?" In this case, we are comparing Hilary's expenditures with Geoff's, and the problem is solved by multiplication. The question does not involve "How much more?" (as it would if the problem involved additive/ subtractive comparison). Instead, the structure of the problem involves "How many times as much?" If the problem is changed slightly to include information about how much Geoff spent but to make either Hilary's expenditures unknown or the comparison multiplier unknown, then the problem could be solved by division. Examples of these problem structures are: (a) Hilary spent a certain amount on Christmas gifts for her family, and Geoff spent 5 times as much. If Geoff spent $105, how much did Hilary spend? (b) Hilary spent $35 on Christmas gifts for her family, and Geoff spent $105. How many times as much money as Hilary did Geoff spend?

Combinations problems involve still another sort of multiplicative structure. Here the two factors represent the sizes of two different sets and the product indicates how many different pairs of things can be formed, with one member of each pair taken from each of the two sets. Combination problems are also sometimes known as Cartesian product problems (Quintero 1985). For example, consider the number of different sundaes possible with four different ice cream flavors and two toppings, if each sundae can have exactly one ice cream flavor and one topping:

	Vanilla	Cherry	Mint	Chocolate
Pineapple				
Butterscotch				

Other examples of combination problems are the number of choices for outfits given 5 T-shirts and 4 shorts or the number of different sandwiches possible with 3 choices of meat and 2 choices of cheese.

Finally, *area and array* problems also are typical examples of multiplicative structure. The area of any rectangle (in square units) can be found either by covering the rectangle with unit squares and counting them all individually, or by multiplying the width of the rectangle (number of rows of unit squares) by the length (number of unit squares in each row). Similarly, in a rectangular array—an arrangement of discrete, countable objects (such as chairs in an auditorium)—the total number of objects can be found by multiplying the number of rows by the number of objects in each row. The array model for multiplication can be especially effective in helping children visualize multiplication. It may serve as a natural extension of children's prior work in making and naming rectangles using tiles, geoboards, or graph paper:

| Tiles | Geoboard | Graph paper |

These illustrations show a 2-by-3 or 3-by-2 rectangle. Thus, each contains six small squares. Asking children to build and name numerous rectangles with various numbers is a good readiness experience for the concept of multiplication. In the Classroom 8–1 through 8–3 illustrate several experiences designed for this purpose.

Just as sets of objects, the number line, and arrays are useful in presenting multiplication, they can also be useful in presenting division, with the relationship to repeated subtraction frequently shown. However, for division, two different types of situations must be considered: *measurement* and *partition*.

1. In *measurement* (or repeated subtraction) situations, we know how many in each group and must determine the number of groups.

> Jenny had 12 candies. She gave 3 to each person. How many persons got candies?

Here, we can imagine Jenny beginning with 12 candies and making piles of 3 repeatedly until the candies are all gone. She is "measuring" how many groups of 3 she can make from the original pile of 12.

| Person 1 | Person 2 | Person 3 | Person 4 |

Another example might be measuring how many 2-foot hair ribbons can be made from a 10-foot roll of

---

In The Classroom 8–1

Construct a Rectangle!

Objective: Building rectangles with tiles to develop visual representations for multiplication facts.

▼ Use 12 tiles.

▼ Make a rectangle using all 12 tiles.

Draw the rectangle you made here.

▼ Write a multiplication number sentence to describe your rectangle:

_____ × _____ = 12.

▼ Use 12 tiles over and over again to make different rectangles. Draw a picture and write a number sentence for each.

_____ × _____ = 12

_____ × _____ = 12

How many different ways can you do it?

Have you tried a 6-by-2 rectangle? How about a 12-by-1?

In The Classroom 8–2

Rectangles and More Rectangles!

Objective: Building rectangles with tiles to develop visual representations for multiplication facts.

▼ How many ways can you make a rectangle with this many tiles? Draw pictures. The first one is done for you.

▼ List the ways:

6 tiles

1×6 or 6×1

2×3 or 3×2

4 tiles

_____ or _____

3 tiles

_____ or _____

8 tiles

_____ or _____

_____ or _____

9 tiles

_____ or _____

_____

2 tiles

_____ or _____

10 tiles

_____ or _____

_____ or _____

ribbon. We can imagine repeatedly stretching out 2 feet and cutting it off, thus "measuring" how many hair ribbons can be made.

2. *Partition,* or sharing, situations are those in which a group is separated into a given number of equivalent groups and we seek the number in each group. By contrast with measurement situations, here we already know how many groups we want to make, but we don't know how many must be put in each group.

Gil had 15 shells. If he wanted to share them equally among 5 friends, how many should he give to each?

Here we can imagine Gil passing out the shells to his five friends (one for you, one for you, one for you, then a second to each person, and so on) until they

are all distributed, and then checking to see how many each person got.

Friend 1   Friend 2   Friend 3   Friend 4   Friend 5

Partitioning (or sharing) is very difficult to show in a diagram, but it is relatively easy to have children act out. Dealing cards for a game is another instance of a partition situation.

In The Classroom 8–3

How Many Squares in a Rectangle?

Objective: Drawing rectangles on grid paper to develop visual representations for multiplication facts.

▼ Draw a 3×4 rectangle:

 That's 3×4 or 4×3. It's a rectangle with 12 squares.

▼ Your turn:

Draw each rectangle, color it in, then tell how many squares.

$5 \times 3 =$ _____ $4 \times 4 =$ _____

$4 \times 1 =$ _____ $2 \times 3 =$ _____

It is certainly not necessary for children to learn these terms or to name problems as measurement or partition situations. But it is important for you as a teacher to know about the two types of division situations so you can ensure that your students have opportunities to work with examples of each. It is vital that students be able to identify when a problem situation requires division, and that means being able to recognize both types of situations as involving division. Lesson Idea 8–2 illustrates an activity that can be used to introduce the idea of division to children in a meaningful way.

Lesson Idea 8–2

Lots of Links

Materials: 20 links (or other counters) for each child; an overhead projector

Activity: Discuss with children different ways to separate the links into equal-sized groups.

▼ Scatter 12 links on an overhead projector.

- How can we place these links into equal-sized groups? (6 groups of 2, 4 groups of 3, 1 group of 12, etc.)

- How many different ways can we do it?

▼ Scatter 15 links on the projector.

- How many different ways can these links be split into equal-sized groups?

- What happens if we try dividing 13 links into groups of 5?

CCCCC CCCCC CCC   2 groups and 3 leftovers

▼ Focus on numbers that can be divided into equal-sized groups without "leftovers":

- Which of these numbers can be divided into groups of 3 without having leftovers?

  8   4   7   3   18

  Try each one.

- Name a number that will have no leftovers if we divide it into groups of 5. How many numbers like this can you name?

- Name a number that will have 1 leftover if we divide it into groups of 5. Can you name 3 numbers like this?

MATHEMATICAL PROPERTIES

An understanding of the mathematical properties that pertain to each operation (Table 8–1) is vital to the child's understanding of the operation and how to use it. This understanding is not a prerequisite to work with operations, but it must be developed as a part of the understanding of the operations.

In elementary school, children are not expected to state these properties precisely or identify them by name. Rather, the instructional goal is to help children understand the commutative, associative, distributive, and identity properties and to use them when it is efficient. Table 8–1 gives the meaning of each property, states what children should understand, and provides examples to illustrate how the property can make learning and using the basic facts easier.

Understanding these properties implies knowing when they apply. For example, both addition and multiplication are commutative, but neither subtraction nor division is:

$$7 - 3 \text{ is } not \text{ equal to } 3 - 7$$

$$28 \div 7 \text{ is } not \text{ equal to } 7 \div 28$$

Many children have difficulty with the idea of commutativity. They tend to "subtract the smaller number from the larger" or to "divide the larger number by the smaller" regardless of their order. Care needs to be taken to ensure that they construct correct notions.

OVERVIEW OF BASIC FACT INSTRUCTION

As children develop concepts of the meanings of the operations, instruction begins to focus on certain number combinations. These are generally referred to as the *basic facts*:

- *Basic addition facts* each involve two one-digit addends and their sum. There are 100 basic addition facts (from 0 + 0 up to 9 + 9; see Figure 8–4 on page 173). To read off a fact (say, 4 + 9 = 13), find the first addend (4) along the left side and the second addend (9) along the top. By reading horizontally across the 4-row from the left and vertically down the 9-column from the top, you find the sum (13).

- *Basic subtraction facts* rely on the inverse relationship of addition and subtraction for their definition. The 100 basic subtraction facts result from the difference between one addend and the

Table 8–1 • Mathematical properties for elementary-school children

Property	Mathematical Language	Child's Language	How It Helps
Commutative	For all numbers *a* and *b*: $a + b = b + a$ and $a \times b = b \times a$	If 4 + 7 = 11, then 7 + 4 must equal 11, too. If I know 4 × 7, I also know 7 × 4.	The number of addition or multiplication facts to be memorized is reduced from 100 to 55.
Associative	For all numbers *a, b,* and *c*: $(a + b) + c = a + (b + c)$ and $(ab)c = a(bc)$	When I'm adding (or multiplying) three or more numbers, it doesn't matter where I start.	When more than two numbers are being added (or multiplied), combinations that make the task easier can be chosen. For example, $37 \times 5 \times 2$ can be done as $37 \times (5 \times 2)$ or 37×10 rather than $(37 \times 5) \times 2$.
Distributive	For all numbers *a, b,* and *c*: $a(b + c) = ab + ac$	8 × (5 + 2) is the same as (8 × 5) + (8 × 2). 24 ÷ 3 is the same as (12 ÷ 3) + (12 ÷ 3).	Some of the more difficult basic facts can be split into smaller, easier-to-remember parts. For example, 8 × 7 is the same as (8 × 5) + (8 × 2) or 40 + 16.
Identity	For any whole number *a*: $a + 0 = a$ and $a \times 1 = a$	0 added to any number is easy; it's just that number. 1 times any number is just that number.	The 19 addition facts involving 0 and the 19 multiplication facts involving 1 can be easily remembered once this property is understood and established.

sum for all one-digit addends. Thus, the one hundred subtraction facts are also pictured in Figure 8–4, the same table that pictures the 100 basic addition facts. You read off a basic subtraction fact (say, 13 – 4 = 9) by finding the box in the 4-row that contains the sum 13, then reading up that column to find the difference (9) at the top of the table. Note that a sentence such as 13 – 2 = 11 is neither represented in Figure 8–4 nor considered a basic subtraction fact sentence because 2 + 11 = 13 is not a basic addition fact (since 11 is not a one-digit addend).

- *Basic multiplication facts* each involve two one-digit factors and their product. There are 100 basic multiplication facts (from 0 × 0 up to 9 × 9).
- *Basic division facts* rely on the inverse relationship of multiplication and division, but there are only 90 basic division facts. Because division by zero is not possible, there are no facts with zero as the divisor.

Development and mastery of the addition and subtraction facts begins in kindergarten or first grade and continues as multiplication and division facts are developed and practiced in third and fourth grade.

Some children, however, have not mastered the facts several years later. Sometimes the problem may be a learning disability that makes it virtually impossible for a child to memorize the facts. Use of a calculator may allow such a child to proceed with learning mathematics. (Or, as research by Clark and Kamii (1996) indicates for multiplication, a child may have trouble with multiplication facts because he or she has not developed the ability to think multiplicatively.) More commonly, however, children's difficulties in mastering basic facts may stem from one (or both) of the following two causes, and in these cases teachers can definitely provide help. First, the underlying numerical understandings may not have been developed. Thus, the process of remembering the facts quickly and accurately becomes no more than rote memorization or meaningless manipulation of symbols. As a result, the child has trouble remembering the facts. Second, the skill of fact retrieval itself may not be taught by teachers or understood by children, resulting in inefficient strategies. Teachers can do something about both of these lacks by using a three-phase process for helping children learn basic facts:

- *Get ready:* Start from where the children are.
- *Get set:* Build understandings
- *Go:* Focus on how to remember facts.

Get Ready: Starting Where Children Are

Many children come to school knowing some basic facts. For instance, the chances are great that they can say "one and one are two," "two and two are four," and maybe even "five and five are ten." They may know that 2 and 1 more is 3, and that 6 and "nothing more" is still 6. But they probably don't know that 6 + 7 = 13, nor do they have a clear concept of the meanings of symbols such as + and =.

Similarly, they may know that if you have 3 and take away 2, you have only 1 left. But they probably won't know 3 − 2 = 1 (or "three minus two equals one"). They may know that buying three pieces of gum at 5¢ each will cost 15¢, but they won't know that 3 × 5 = 15. They may know that eight cookies shared among four children means that each child will get two cookies, but they won't know that 8 ÷ 4 = 2.

In other words, they can solve simple problems involving facts, but they are not likely to be able to either recognize or write the facts. Nor do many children understand *why* 5 + 5 = 10 or realize that 4 + 2 = ☐ asks the same question as:

$$\begin{array}{r} 4 \\ +2 \\ \hline \end{array}$$

It is our task to help children organize what they know, construct more learning to fill in the gaps, and, in the process, develop meaning.

We need to begin by determining what each child knows, using responses from group discussions, observations of how each child works with materials and with paper-and-pencil activities, and individual interviews. Many teachers use an inventory at the beginning of the year, administered individually to younger children and in a questionnaire format in later grades. The purpose of such an inventory is to discover:

- Whether the children have the concept of an operation: "What does it mean to add?" "Why did you subtract?" "When can you multiply?"

- What basic facts they understand (demonstrated by drawing a picture to illustrate a written fact or, conversely, by writing the fact for a given illustration)

- What strategies they use to find the solution to combinations: "How did you know 7 + 9 = 16?"

- What basic facts they know fluently (can answer within about 3 seconds, without stopping to figure them out).

We use such information to plan instruction. Do some children need more work with manipulative materials to understand what multiplication means? Do some children need help in seeing the relationship of 17 − 8 and 8 + 9? Do some children need to be taught that counting on from a number is quicker than counting each number? Which children need regular practice in order to master the facts? We can group them to meet individual needs (as suggested in Chapter 3) and provide activities and direct instruction to fill in the missing links and strengthen understanding and competency. The calculator can be one of the tools. Research has indicated that the development of basic facts is enhanced through calculator use.

Get Set: Building Understanding of the Basic Facts

The emphasis in helping children to learn the basic facts is on aiding them in organizing their thinking and seeing relationships among the facts. Children should learn to use strategies for remembering the facts prior to drill to develop fluency.

Generally, the facts with both addends or factors greater than 5 are more difficult for most children, but relative difficulty is not a simple matter to determine with accuracy. What is difficult for an individual child is really the important point. Although many textbooks, workbooks, and computer programs emphasize practice on the generally difficult facts, many also encourage the child to keep a record of those facts that are difficult for him or her and suggest extra practice on those. The teacher should suggest or reinforce this idea.

How can the basic facts for an operation be organized meaningfully? Many textbooks present facts in small groups (for example, facts with sums to 6: 0 + 6 = 6, 1 + 5 = 6, 2 + 4 = 6, and so forth). Other textbooks organize the facts in "families" (for example, facts in the "2 – 3 – 5 family" are 3 + 2 = 5, 2 + 3 = 5, 5 − 3 = 2, and 5 − 2 = 3). Still other textbooks organize the facts by "thinking strategies" (for example, all facts where 1 is added, or containing "doubles" such as 7 + 7). No one order for teaching the basic facts has been shown to be superior to any other order. Thus, the teacher can use professional judgment about what each group of children needs and choose whether to use the sequence in a given textbook.

A variety of thinking strategies can be used to recall the answer to any given fact. Thinking strategies are efficient methods for determining answers on the basic facts. The more efficient the strategy, the more quickly the student will be able to construct the correct answer for the sum, difference, product, or quotient of two numbers and, eventually, develop fluency with the facts so he or she can quickly recall them.

Research has shown that certain thinking strategies help children learn the basic facts (Rathmell 1978; Thornton and Smith 1988). Understanding of the facts develops in a series of stages characterized by the thinking children use. Some of these thinking strategies involve using concrete materials or counting. Others are more mature in the sense that a known fact is used to figure out an unknown fact. We want to help children develop these mature, efficient strategies to help them recall facts.

Many children rely heavily on counting—in particular, finger counting—and fail to develop more efficient ways of recalling basic facts. For example, a child might count 4 fingers and then 5 more to solve 4 + 5. This strategy is perfectly acceptable at first. However, this counting process should not be repeated every time 4 + 5 is encountered. We want the child to move beyond counting on from 4 (which is relatively slow and inefficient), to thinking "4 + 4 = 8, so 4 + 5 is 9" or using some other more efficient strategy. Eventually, we want the child to be able to recall "4 + 5 = 9" quickly and effortlessly. Some children discover efficient fact strategies on their own, but many need explicit instruction. When the teacher is satisfied that the children are familiar with a particular strategy (able to model it with materials and beginning to use it mentally), it is time to practice the strategy.

Go: Mastering the Basic Facts

Consider this scene: Pairs of children are keying numbers on a calculator and passing it back and forth. Other pairs are seated at a table, some playing a card game and others playing board games. Several are busily typing numbers on computer keyboards. Still others are working individually with flashcards. What are they all doing? Probably they are practicing basic facts.

If children are to become skillful with the algorithms for addition, subtraction, multiplication, and division and proficient at estimation and mental computation, they must learn the basic facts to the level of immediate, or automatic, recall. When should this mastery level be attempted? As soon as children have a good understanding of the meanings of the operations and the symbols, the process of developing fluency with basic facts can begin. That is, as Ashlock and Washbon (1978) suggest, children should be able to:

- State or write related facts, given one basic fact
- Explain how they got an answer, or prove that it is correct
- Solve a fact in two or more ways

Research has shown that drill increases speed and accuracy on tests of basic facts (Wilson 1930). In the Classroom 8–4 contains several interesting individual activities that provide drill practice for basic facts. However, drill alone will not change a child's thinking strategies so that they become efficient. Drill will, therefore, be most effective when the child's thinking is already efficient.

In The Classroom 8–4

Test Your Facts!

Objective: Using a variety of activities and puzzles to practice multiplication and division facts.

▼ Fill in the empty box:

▼ Complete these five-facts and match them with the clock minutes.

$7 \times 5 = \mathbf{35}$

$2 \times 5 = \_$

$6 \times 5 = \_$

$4 \times 5 = \_$

$5 \times 5 = \_$

▼ Fill in each empty box to make the next number correct:

▼ Multiply each number in the middle ring by the number in the center:

Some principles for drill have been proposed, based on research with primary-grade children (Davis 1978):

- Children should attempt to memorize facts only after understanding is attained.

- Children should participate in drill with the intent to develop fluency. Remembering should be emphasized. This is not the time for explanations.

- Drill lessons should be short (five to ten minutes) and should be given almost every day. Children should work on only a few facts in a given lesson and should constantly review previously learned facts.

- Children should develop confidence in their ability to remember facts fluently and should be praised for good efforts. Records of their progress should be kept.

- Drill activities should be varied, interesting, challenging, and presented with enthusiasm.

Computer software provides a natural complement to more traditional materials and activities, such as flashcards, games, and audiotaped practice, for establishing the quick recall of basic facts. For example, in Alien Intruder children encounter invading spaceships, each containing an addition problem. Children must provide the correct answer to "equalize" the spaceship before the aliens invade.

Most programs keep track of the number of exercises attempted and the number answered correctly. Some display the time taken to give correct answers, thus encouraging students to compete against their own records for speed as well as mastery. Requiring short response time (within three or four seconds) is very important, because it promotes efficient strategies and encourages children to develop fluent recall.

Many children enjoy computer software that displays a cumulative record of their individual progress. This feature allows children to diagnose for themselves the basic facts they know and don't know. It also provides a source of motivation because each student can compete against himself or herself, with the goal of complete mastery always in mind.

When using flashcards, the child should go through the entire set and separate the cards into a pack of those known and a pack of those unknown. Each time the child works with the cards, he or she should review those in each pack, moving newly learned facts to the known pack. This approach makes progress evident.

Another point from research also must be taken into account: the frequency with which basic addition and multiplication facts occur in elementary school textbooks is probably a source of the difficulty. Facts with numbers larger than 5 occurred up to half as frequently as those in the range of 2 to 5; 0 and 1 occurred relatively infrequently. Thus, teachers need to assure that more practice is provided with facts involving 0, 1, and especially 6 through 9.

Several types of drill-and-practice procedures in the form of games are noted in In the Classroom 8–5 through 8–8 (see pages 172–173). Children in all age groups find such games an enjoyable way to practice what they know. These activities supplement the many other drill-and-practice procedures that you will find in textbooks, journals, computer software, and other sources.

In The Classroom 8–5

Multig

Objective: Using a game to practice basic multiplication facts.

▼ Use the playing board here or make a larger one on heavy construction paper. Each player needs some buttons, macaroni, or chips for markers.

Don't forget the spinner. You can't play this game without it!

1. Take turns. Spin twice. Multiply the 2 numbers. Find the answer on the board. Put a marker on it.

56 25 40
36 49 20 81
30 64 35 48 32
56 42 63 28 54 45
32 48 54 72 24 16 35
16 24 28 36 40 30 25 20
63 45 81 56 49 42 64
20 25 72 45 24 36
40 49 32 28 54
30 16 72 48
42 35 63

2. Score 1 point for each covered ◊ that touches a side or corner of the ◊ you cover.

3. If you can't find an uncovered ◊ to cover, you lose your turn.

4. Opponents may challenge any time before the next player spins.

5. The winner is the player with the most points at the end of 10 rounds.

In The Classroom 8–6

Addition Bingo!

Objective: Using a bingo game to practice basic addition facts.

▼ Each player needs a different Bingo card and some buttons or macaroni for markers.

9	6	17	11	5
5	8	10	3	7
15	11	Free	13	14
7	9	2	1	12
2	13	11	18	17

The leader needs a pack of cards like these with all possible combinations (basic facts).

▼ It's easy to play:

• The leader draws a card and reads the addends on it.

• Each player covers the sum on his or her Bingo card.

Not all sums are given on each card.

Some sums are given more than once on a Bingo card, but a player may cover only one answer for each pair of addends.

The winner is the first person with 5 markers in a row!

THINKING STRATEGIES FOR BASIC FACTS

In the four following sections, thinking strategies for basic facts for addition, subtraction, multiplication, and division are discussed, and ways to teach them are illustrated.

Thinking Strategies for Addition Facts

The one hundred basic facts for addition are shown in Figure 8–4. They are not presented to children in this completed form; rather, the children gradually and systematically learn the facts and may fill in or check them off on the chart.

Lesson Idea 8–3 presents questions that a teacher might use to help children see the orderliness of the basic addition facts. This overview will help children see their goal as they begin to work on fluency with facts.

The thinking strategies that can be used when teaching basic addition facts include commutativity; adding 0, 1, and doubles; counting on; and adding to

In The Classroom 8–7

Zero Wins!

Objective: Using a game to develop number sense and practice addition and subtraction facts.

▼ Make two identical sets of 19 cards with a number from 0 to 18 on each!

▼ Follow these rules:

• After shuffling, the leader deals 4 cards to each player and puts the remaining cards face down in the center of the table.

• Players must add or subtract the numbers on their 4 cards so they equal 0. For example, suppose you had these cards:

• With these cards you could write

$$10 - 6 + 2 - 6 = 0$$

or

$$6 + 6 - 10 - 2 = 0$$

or various other number sentences.

• On each round of play, the players may exchange one card if they wish, and each player takes a turn being first to exchange a card on a round. To make an exchange, the first player draws a card and discards a card, face up. Other players can draw from either the face-down pile or the face-up discard pile.

The first player to get 0 on a round wins the round!

10 and beyond. For many facts, more than one strategy is appropriate.

1. *Commutativity* The task of learning the basic addition facts is simplified because of the commutative property. Changing the order of the addends does not affect the sum. Children encounter this idea when they note that putting 2 purple objects and 3 white objects together gives the same quantity as putting 3 purple objects and 2 white objects together:

In The Classroom 8–8

21 or Bust!

Objective: Using a game to develop logical reasoning and to practice addition.

▼ Play this game with a partner:

• Enter 1, 2, 3, 4, or 5 in your [calculator]

• Give the [calculator] to your opponent, who adds 1, 2, 3, 4, or 5 to the displayed number.

• Take turns adding 1, 2, 3, 4, or 5 to the total.

The first player to reach 21 wins!
If you go over 21, you "bust," or lose!

What next?

+	0	1	2	3	4	5	6	7	8	9
0	0	1	2	3	4	5	6	7	8	9
1	1	2	3	4	5	6	7	8	9	10
2	2	3	4	5	6	7	8	9	10	11
3	3	4	5	6	7	8	9	10	11	12
4	4	5	6	7	8	9	10	11	12	13
5	5	6	7	8	9	10	11	12	13	14
6	6	7	8	9	10	11	12	13	14	15
7	7	8	9	10	11	12	13	14	15	16
8	8	9	10	11	12	13	14	15	16	17
9	9	10	11	12	13	14	15	16	17	18

Figure 8–4 • **The 100 basic facts for addition**

We encourage the use of commutativity by using materials such as a chain of loops:

Have the children note that 5 is followed by 2 and 2 is followed by 5 all around the chain. The chain can be turned as they read and add:

$$5 + 2 = 7, 2 + 5 = 7, 5 + 2 = 7, \ldots$$

The calculator also can help children verify that the order of the addends is irrelevant. Have them key into their calculators:

$$5 + 8 = \quad \text{and} \quad 8 + 5 =$$

Use a variety of combinations, so the idea that the order does not affect the outcome becomes evident. In the Classroom 8–9 presents another way of helping them develop and use the idea of commutativity.

The blank boxes in Figure 8–5 help us see that the commutative property reduces the number of facts to be learned by 45. Each blank box below the diagonal of the table can be matched with a box above the diagonal with the same addends and sum. (If there are 100 facts altogether, why are there 55 distinct facts to learn, rather than just 50?)

In work with the basic addition facts, children will see or write, for example:

$$\begin{array}{c} 2 \\ +5 \\ \hline \end{array} \quad \text{and} \quad \begin{array}{c} 5 \\ +2 \\ \hline \end{array}$$

or

$$2 + 5 = \boxed{} \quad \text{and} \quad 5 + 2 = \boxed{}$$

We want them to realize that the same two numbers will have the same sum, no matter which comes first. We want them to be able to put this idea into their own words; they do not need to know the term *commutative property*. We want them to use the idea as they work with basic facts, not merely parrot a term.

Lesson Idea 8–3

The Big Picture

Materials: Activity sheet for each child; a transparency of it for use on the overhead projector.

Objective: To discover the orderliness of the basic addition facts to be memorized.

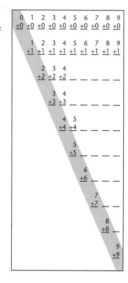

▼ Ask each child to study carefully examples on the activity sheet.

- What is alike about the examples?

- What patterns are apparent?

▼ Discuss the top row of examples—those involving 0. Have the children fill in each of the sums.

▼ Discuss the second row of examples.

- Why isn't $\overset{0}{\underline{+1}}$ included? (This fact is in the top row.)

- How can each sum be found quickly? (By counting on one.)

▼ Look at the diagonal containing these facts:

0	1	2	3	4	5	6	7	8	9
+1	+1	+2	+3	+4	+5	+6	+7	+8	+9

- Find the sums.

▼ On the overhead projector, quickly fill in the remaining sums. Then focus attention on the entire table.

- What patterns are apparent?

- What is the largest sum? What are its addends?

- What is the smallest sum? What are its addends?

- Ask children to circle all examples whose sum is 8.

- Where are they?

- What patterns do you see in the addends?

- Why isn't $\overset{5}{\underline{+7}}$ in the chart?

▼ Continue discussing patterns as long as you feel your children are benefitting from the experience. Encourage the children to understand that all the basic facts to be memorized are included on this sheet.

In The Classroom 8–9

Arranging and Rearranging

Objective: Developing number sense by using counters to illustrate different sums to 10.

▼ Use 10 counters and string for the rings to make this arrangement:

A   B

- How many counters are in Ring A? _____

- How many counters are in Ring B? _____

▼ Rearrange your counters and rings to show the same numbers, and then move 1 counter from Ring A to Ring B.

- How many counters are now in Ring A? _____

- How many counters are in Ring B? _____

▼ See how many different ways you can put 10 counters in the two rings.

- Use your counters and rings, and list the ways here:

  4 + 6   _____   _____

  _____   _____   _____

  _____   _____

+	0	1	2	3	4	5	6	7	8	9
0	0	1	2	3	4	5	6	7	8	9
1		2	3	4	5	6	7	8	9	10
2			4	5	6	7	8	9	10	11
3				6	7	8	9	10	11	12
4					8	9	10	11	12	13
5						10	11	12	13	14
6							12	13	14	15
7								14	15	16
8									16	17
9										18

Figure 8–5 ● **Addition facts derived by the commutative thinking strategy**

2. *Strategies for Adding One and Adding Zero. Adding one* to a number is easy for most children. In fact, most learn this idea before they come to school, and they only have to practice the recognition and writing of it rather than develop initial understanding. To reinforce their initial concept, experiences with objects come first, followed by such paper-and-pencil activities as these:

5 + 1 = ☐

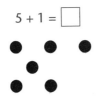

Recognition of the pattern is then encouraged:

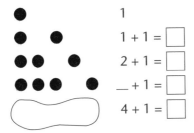

The strategy for *adding zero* applies to facts that have zero as one addend. These facts should be learned, through experience, as a generalization: *Zero added to any number does not change the number.* This idea follows from many concrete examples in which children see that any time they add "no more" (zero) they have the same amount. Activities then focus on this pattern:

○   1 + 0 = ☐   0 + 1 = ☐
○○   2 + 0 = ☐   etc.
○○○   3 + 0 = ☐
○○○○   4 + 0 = ☐

Although adding zero may seem very easy to adults, this is actually one of the hardest strategies for children to learn. Concrete modeling of the situation is tricky because it is difficult to picture adding nothing. Therefore, explicit work on facts involving zero should be postponed until children have mastered some of the other fact strategies.

3. *Strategies for Adding Doubles and Near Doubles. Doubles* are basic facts in which both addends are the same number, such as 4 + 4 or 9 + 9. Most chil-

dren learn these facts quickly, often parroting them before they come to school. Connecting doubles facts to familiar situations often helps students remember them (for example, two hands shows 5 + 5 = 10, an egg carton shows 6 + 6 = 12, two weeks on a calendar shows 7 + 7 = 14, etc.) Students can profit from work with objects followed by drawings:

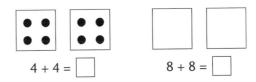

Another strategy, "near doubles," can be used for the facts that are one more or one less than the doubles:

Think

7 + 8 = ☐   7 + 7 = 14
              So 7 + 8 is one more.
              7 + 8 = 15

Think

7 + 6 = ☐   7 + 7 = 14
              So 7 + 6 is one less.
              7 + 6 = 13

Lesson Idea 8–4 shows one way of presenting this strategy.

The four thinking strategies in the preceding two sections can be used with the addition facts shown in Figure 8–6, parts A and B.

3. *Counting On* The strategy of *counting on* can be used for any addition facts but is most easily used when one of the addends is 1, 2, or 3. To be efficient, it is important to count on from the larger addend. For example,

Think

2 + 6 = ☐   6 . . . 7 . . . 8
              2 + 6 = 8

Initially, children will probably count all objects in a group, as noted in Chapter 6.

They need to learn to start from the larger addend, 6, and count on, 7, 8. (Notice that understanding of the commutative property is assumed.)

Lesson Idea 8–4

Nearly Double

Materials: Flannel board or magnetic board and disks for demonstration, 1 die, a pile of chips or tiles, and paper for each pair of children for seat work.

▼ Put a group of 6 disks on the board and have children do the same at their seats.

▼ Have them add a second group of 6 (and do so for demonstration too).

• Ask: How many in each group? How many in all?

▼ Write 6 + 6 = 12 on the board.

▼ Have children add one more disk to the second group:

• Ask: How many in the first group? How many in the second group? How many in all?

▼ Write 6 + 7 = 13 on the board.

▼ Demonstrate how children can use their dice and chips to build more examples like this and to write the corresponding sentences on their papers. Each pair of children should repeatedly roll their die. After each roll they should model, say, and write a near doubles fact. For example, if they roll 5, they use chips to model, say, and write 5 + 6 = 11.

A Addition facts derived by the adding one and adding zero strategies.

+	0	1	2	3	4	5	6	7	8	9
0	0	1	2	3	4	5	6	7	8	9
1	1	2	3	4	5	6	7	8	9	10
2	2	3								
3	3	4								
4	4	5								
5	5	6								
6	6	7								
7	7	8								
8	8	9								
9	9	10								

B Addition facts derived by the adding doubles and near-doubles strategies.

+	0	1	2	3	4	5	6	7	8	9
0	0	1								
1	1	2	3							
2		3	4	5						
3			5	6	7					
4				7	8	9				
5					9	10	11			
6						11	12	13		
7							13	14	15	
8								15	16	17
9									17	18

Figure 8–6 • Addition facts derived by four strategies

Research indicates that young children will count on but not necessarily from the larger addend (Ginsberg 1977). Thus, the strategy must be taught to many children using activities such as this one:

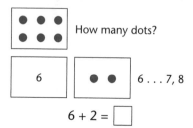

The counting-on strategy can be rather efficiently used with the addition facts noted in Figure 8–7 (where at least one addend is 1, 2, or 3). However, it is *not* efficient to use counting on when both addends are larger than 3 (for example, for 6 + 8 = 14 or 5 + 8 = 13 or 9 + 8 = 17). Counting on for facts such as these is both slow and also prone to error. Unfortunately, some children develop the habit of using counting on all the time and thereby fail to develop more efficient strategies, sometimes still relying on counting on even after they have graduated to middle school or high school. It is important to help students move beyond counting on because fluency (efficiency and accuracy) is extremely im-

+	0	1	2	3	4	5	6	7	8	9
0										
1		2	3	4	5	6	7	8	9	10
2		3	4	5	6	7	8	9	10	11
3		4	5	6	7	8	9	10	11	12
4		5	6	7						
5		6	7	8						
6		7	8	9						
7		8	9	10						
8		9	10	11						
9		10	11	12						

Figure 8–7 • Addition facts derived by the counting-on strategy

portant for work with basic facts. When students are slowed down by inefficient strategies for basic fact retrieval, they are often hampered in doing more advanced work in mathematics.

4. *Adding to 10 and Beyond* With the strategy of *adding to 10 and beyond,* one addend is increased and the other decreased, to make one of the addends 10. This strategy is used most easily when one of the addends is 8 or 9, although some children also find it useful when adding 6 or 7. Here is an example.

$$8 + 5 = \boxed{}$$

Think

8 + 2 = 10, and 5 = 2 + 3
So 10 + 3 = 13, so
8 + 5 = 13

The child recognizes that 8 is close to 10, and then mentally breaks 5 apart into 2 + 3. The 2 is used with the 8 to "add to ten," and the 3 is used to go "beyond." A ten-frame can be very helpful in teaching this strategy because it provides a visual image of adding to ten and going beyond:

$$10 + 3 = \boxed{}$$

The research of Funkhouser (1995) indicates that working with five-frames as a base and then moving

to ten-frames may be particularly helpful for children with learning disabilities.

Children must know the sums to 10 well in order to use the "adding-to-ten-and-beyond" strategy. Practice with regrouping to 10 is needed to help them become proficient. They also need to realize how easy it is to add any single digit to ten to get a number in the teens, without having to think about counting on. Which is easier?

$$10 + 5 \quad \text{or} \quad 9 + 6$$
$$7 + 8 \quad \text{or} \quad 5 + 10$$

As another example, change this problem to an easier one:

$$9 + 6 = \boxed{}$$

In all cases, talk the strategy through with drawings as well as objects:

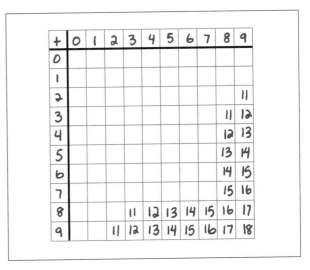

The adding-to-10-and-beyond strategy can be used with the addition facts shown in Figure 8–8.

In many cases, more than one strategy can be used to aid in recalling a fact. This point should be

+	0	1	2	3	4	5	6	7	8	9
0										
1										
2										11
3									11	12
4									12	13
5									13	14
6									14	15
7									15	16
8				11	12	13	14	15	16	17
9			11	12	13	14	15	16	17	18

Figure 8–8 • Addition facts derived by the adding-to-10 strategy

made with the children. It encourages them to try different ways of recalling a fact, and it may strengthen their understanding of the relationships involved. Notice from Figure 8–9 that, when the strategies for adding one, adding zero, adding doubles and near doubles, counting on, and adding-to-10-and-beyond have been learned, only six basic facts remain. These missing facts can be derived using one of the strategies (and commutativity) or simply taught separately. Children should be encouraged to look for patterns and relationships because almost all of the 100 basic addition facts can be developed from a variety of relationships with other facts.

It also should be noted that children may invent strategies of their own, such as:

$$6 + 7 = \square \quad \begin{array}{l} \textit{Think} \\ 6 \text{ is } 5 + 1 \\ 7 \text{ is } 5 + 2 \\ \text{So } 10 + 3 \\ 13 \end{array}$$

$$6 + 8 = \square \quad \begin{array}{l} \textit{Think} \\ 3 + 3 + 8 \\ 3 + 11 \\ 14 \end{array}$$

Encourage their ideas!

Thinking Strategies for Subtraction Facts

For each basic addition fact, there is a related subtraction fact. In some mathematics programs, the two operations are taught simultaneously. The relationship between them is then readily emphasized, and learning of the basic facts for both operations proceeds as if they were in the same family. Even when they are not taught simultaneously, however, the idea of a fact family is frequently used (see Figure 8–10).

"Think addition" is the major thinking strategy for learning and recalling the subtraction facts. Encourage children to recognize, think about, and use the relationships between addition and subtraction facts. They can find the answers to subtraction facts by thinking about missing addends. For example,

$$15 - 7 = \square \quad \begin{array}{l} \textit{Think} \\ 7 + 8 = 15 \\ \text{So } 15 - 7 = 8 \end{array}$$

Other strategies for finding subtraction facts also can be taught: using 0 and 1, doubles, counting back, and counting on.

1. *Using 0 and 1* Once they have learned strategies for adding 0 and adding 1, most children find it rather easy to learn the related subtraction facts involving 0 and 1. They can profit from work with materials and from observing patterns similar to those used for addition facts.

2. *Doubles* The strategy for doubles may need to be taught more explicitly for subtraction facts than for addition facts. It rests on the assumption that children know the doubles for addition. Here is an example:

$$16 - 8 = \square \quad \begin{array}{l} \textit{Think} \\ 8 + 8 = 16 \\ 16 - 8 = 8 \end{array}$$

3. *Counting Back* The strategy of counting back is related to counting on in addition, and therefore it is

+	0	1	2	3	4	5	6	7	8	9
0	0	1	2	3	4	5	6	7	8	9
1	1	2	3	4	5	6	7	8	9	10
2	2	3	4	5	6	7	8	9	10	11
3	3	4	5	6	7	8	9	10	11	12
4	4	5	6	7	8	9			12	13
5	5	6	7	8	9	10	11		13	14
6	6	7	8	9		11	12	13	14	15
7	7	8	9	10			13	14	15	16
8	8	9	10	11	12	13	14	15	16	17
9	9	10	11	12	13	14	15	16	17	18

Figure 8–9 • Addition facts derived by all thinking strategies for addition

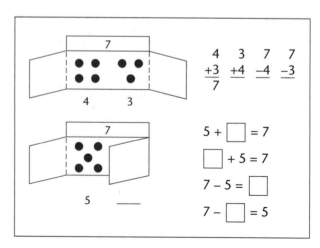

Figure 8–10 • Examples of fact families

most effectively used when the number to be subtracted is 1, 2, or 3:

Think

$$9 - 3 = \square \qquad 9 \ldots 8, 7, 6$$
$$9 - 3 = 6$$

As for other strategies, use problems and a variety of manipulative materials to help children gain facility in counting back from given numbers. Focus especially on the numbers involved in subtraction facts, as in the following examples.

Write the numbers in order backward:

Write the numbers you say when you count back. Write the answer.

$$6 - 2 = \square$$

$6, \_\_, \_\_$

4. *Counting On* The strategy of counting on is used most easily when the difference is 1, 2, or 3 (that is, when it is easy to see that the two numbers involved in the subtraction are close together). "Think addition" by counting on:

Think

$$8 - 6 = \square \qquad 6 \ldots 7, 8$$
$$8 - 6 = 2$$

Activities for developing this strategy include the following:

$$\begin{array}{r} 12 \\ \underline{-9} \end{array}$$ 9 ☐ ☐ ☐ ☐

Begin with 9. Count on until you reach 12. How many?

1 2 3   8
               −5

0 1 2 3 4 5 6 7 8 9

Begin with 5. Count on until you reach 8. How much?

The emphasis in using the counting-on strategy can also encompass adding on: "How much more would I need?" The child is encouraged to use

known addition facts to reach the solution. This is particularly valuable with missing-addend situations, such as $6 + \square = 9$.

Thinking Strategies for Multiplication Facts

Multiplication is frequently viewed as a special case of addition in which all the addends are of equal size. The solution to multiplication problems can be attained by adding or counting, but multiplication is used because it is so much quicker.

Instruction on multiplication ideas begins in kindergarten as ideas about groups, numbers, and addition are developed. In grades 1 and 2, counting by twos, threes, fours, fives, tens, and possibly other numbers should be taught. Such expressions provide a basis for understanding the patterns that will occur with the basic multiplication facts. Use of the calculator as described in Chapter 6 can aid teachers in developing ideas about these patterns of multiplication. Using the constant function on calculators, children realize that two sixes equal 12, three sixes equal 18, and so on.

The basic multiplication facts pair two one-digit factors with a product, as shown in Figure 8–11. The basic multiplication facts should not be given to children in the form of a table or chart of facts until they have been meaningfully introduced. Rather, the facts should be developed through problem situations, experiences with manipulative and other materials, and the use of various thinking strategies. The table becomes the end result of this process of developing understanding of the operations and of the facts.

The thinking strategies for multiplication facts provide an efficient way for a child to attain each fact. These strategies include commutativity, using 1

×	0	1	2	3	4	5	6	7	8	9
0	0	0	0	0	0	0	0	0	0	0
1	0	1	2	3	4	5	6	7	8	9
2	0	2	4	6	8	10	12	14	16	18
3	0	3	6	9	12	15	18	21	24	27
4	0	4	8	12	16	20	24	28	32	36
5	0	5	10	15	20	25	30	35	40	45
6	0	6	12	18	24	30	36	42	48	54
7	0	7	14	21	28	35	42	49	56	63
8	0	8	16	24	32	40	48	56	64	72
9	0	9	18	27	36	45	54	63	72	81

Figure 8–11 • **The 100 basic multiplication facts**

and 0, skip counting, repeated addition, splitting into known parts, and patterns.

1. *Commutativity* Commutativity applies to multiplication just as it does to addition. It is, therefore, a primary strategy for helping students learn the multiplication facts. In the Classroom 8–2 through 8–4 (presented earlier) emphasize this property. The calculator is also useful in reinforcing the idea. Children can multiply 4 × 6, then 6 × 4, for example, and realize that the answer to both is 24.

Here are some other examples:

$$3 \times 6 = 18 \longrightarrow 6 \times \square = 18$$

$$7 \times 5 = 35 \longrightarrow \square \times 7 = 35$$

After they have tried many combinations, students should be able to verbalize that the order of the factors is irrelevant. Figure 8–12 (where each box in the upper right can be matched with an unshaded box in the lower left) shows that, as for addition, there really are only 55 multiplication facts to be learned if we recognize the power of commutativity.

2. *Skip Counting* The strategy of skip counting works best for the multiples children know best, twos and fives, but it also may be applied to threes and fours (or other numbers) if children have learned to skip count by them.

Here is an example for 5:

Think

$$4 \times 5 = \square \qquad 5, 10, 15, 20$$
$$4 \times 5 = 20$$

Skip counting around the clock face (as we do when counting minutes after the hour) is a good way to re-

inforce multiples of 5 by skip counting. The facts that can be established with the skip-counting strategy for twos and fives are noted in Figure 8–13.

3. *Repeated Addition* The strategy of repeated addition can be used most efficiently when one of the factors is less than 5. The child changes the multiplication example to an addition example:

Think

$$3 \times 6 = \square \qquad 6 + 6 + 6 = 18$$
$$3 \times 6 = 18$$

Because this strategy is based on one interpretation of multiplication, children should have had many experiences with objects and materials. Drawings and the calculator can be used to provide additional experiences to help develop this strategy as well as the concept for the operation. Lesson Idea 8–5 illustrates these ideas. In Figure 8–14, note the facts that can be learned with this strategy.

4. *Splitting the Product into Known Parts* As children gain assurance with some basic facts, they can use their known facts to derive others. The strategy known as *splitting the product* is based on the distributive property of multiplication. It can be approached in terms of "one more set," "twice as much as a known fact," or "known facts of 5."

(a) The idea of *one more set* can be used for almost all multiplication facts. If one multiple of a number is known, the next multiple can be determined by adding a single-digit number. For example, to find 3 × 5 if doubles are already known, we can think of 2 × 5 (10) and add one more 5 (to get 15). The computation is slightly more difficult when

Figure 8–12 • Multiplication facts derived by the commutative thinking strategy

Figure 8–13 • Multiplication facts derived by the skip-counting strategy

Lesson Idea 8–5

How Many?

Materials: Counting chips, calculator.

▼ Look at these dots:

● ● ●   ● ● ●   ● ● ●   ● ● ●
● ●   ● ●   ● ●   ● ●

- How many groups of dots?
- How many dots in each group?
- How many dots in all?

Count them: __5__ , ___ , ___ , ___

Add them: 5 + 5 + 5 + 5 = ☐

Multiply them: 4 × 5 = ☐

▼ Now look at these dots:

● ● ● ● ● ● ●
● ● ● ● ● ● ●
● ● ● ● ● ● ●
● ● ● ● ● ● ●

- Ring sets of 7. How many sevens?
- How many dots in all?

Count them: __7__ , ___ , ___ , ___

Add them: 7 + 7 + 7 + 7 = ☐

Multiply them: 4 × 7 = ☐

▼ Do these using a calculator:

7 + 7 + 7 + 7 + 7 = ☐

5 + 5 + 5 + 5 + 5 = ☐

- Do you know a simpler way? Show it here:

_____

_____

the addition requires renaming (as, for example, below, where 8 × 7 is found by adding one more set of 7 to the known fact 7 × 7 = 49):

Think

8 × 7 = ☐   7 × 7 = 49
            8 × 7 = 49 + 7
            8 × 7 = 56

Each fact can be used to help learn the next multiple of either factor. Illustrating this strategy using an array model can be helpful:

Figure 8–14 • **Multiplication facts derived by the repeated addition strategy**

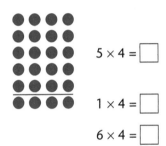

5 × 4 = ☐

1 × 4 = ☐

6 × 4 = ☐

Ask children to name each part of the array and write the multiplication fact for the whole array.

(b)   *Twice as much as a known fact* is a variation of the foregoing strategy. It can be applied to multiples of 4, 6, and 8, because an array with one of these numbers can be split in half. The product is twice as much as each half:

Think

6 × 8 = ☐   3 × 8 = 24
            6 × 8 is twice as much, or 24 + 24
            6 × 8 = 48

Note, however, that a difficulty may arise when renaming is needed to do the doubling by addition.

Again, using models helps provide a visual image of this strategy:

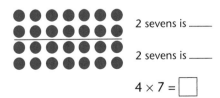

2 sevens is ____

2 sevens is ____

4 × 7 = ☐

In this case, children work with already-divided arrays.

As they progress, children can divide an array, such as the following; write about each part; and write the multiplication fact for the whole array.

Some options for the array above (6 × 8) might be:

(5 × 8) = 40 and 1 × 8 = 8, so 6 × 8 = 40 + 8 = 48

or 6 × 4 = 24 and 6 × 8 will be twice as much,

so 6 × 8 = 24 + 24 = 48.

(c)   Working from *known facts of 5* also will aid children. It can be helpful for any problem with large factors but is most useful for multiples of 6 and 8 because both five sixes and five eights are multiples of 10, so it is rather easy to add on the remaining part without renaming.

For example, to figure 7 × 6, recognize that 7 can be conveniently split into 5 + 2 because 5 × 6 (30) is easy to work with.

Think

7 × 6 = ☐   5 × 6 = 30
2 × 6 = 12
So 7 × 6 is 30 + 12, or 42.

To illustrate this strategy, the array is divided so that 5 sixes or eights (or some other number) are separated from the remaining portion:

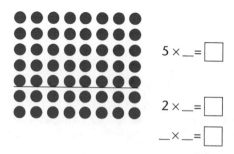

5 × __ = ☐

2 × __ = ☐

__ × __ = ☐

Call attention to how the array is divided. Have the children work with other arrays, determining when it seems reasonable to work with particular numbers. The facts that can be solved by splitting the product into known parts are shown in Figure 8–15.

5. *Using 0 and 1* The facts with zero and one are generally learned from experience working with multi-

plication. We want children to be able to generalize that "multiplying with 1 does not change the other number" and that "multiplying by 0 results in a product of 0." Figure 8–16 indicates the facts that can be learned with these strategies.

The preceding strategies account for all the multiplication facts. One more strategy is mentioned, however, because it can provide help with some difficult facts.

6. *Patterns* Finding patterns is helpful with a number of multiplication facts. One of the most useful and interesting patterns concerns nines. Look at the products of the facts involving nine. The digits of the products always sum to 9. Furthermore, the tens

X	0	1	2	3	4	5	6	7	8	9
0										
1										
2										
3										
4							24	28	32	36
5							30	35	40	45
6					24	30	36	42	48	54
7					28	35	42	49	56	63
8					32	40	48	56	64	72
9					36	45	54	63	72	81

Figure 8–15 • **Multiplication facts derived by the strategy of splitting the product into known parts**

X	0	1	2	3	4	5	6	7	8	9
0	0	0	0	0	0	0	0	0	0	0
1	0	1	2	3	4	5	6	7	8	9
2	0	2								
3	0	3								
4	0	4								
5	0	5								
6	0	6								
7	0	7								
8	0	8								
9	0	9								

Figure 8–16 • **Multiplication facts derived by strategies for 0 and 1**

digit of each product is always one less than whatever factor was being multiplied times 9.

$$1 \times 9 = \ 9 \qquad\qquad 0 + 9 = 9$$
$$2 \times 9 = 18 \qquad\qquad 1 + 8 = 9$$
$$3 \times 9 = 27 \qquad\qquad 2 + 7 = 9$$
$$4 \times 9 = 36 \qquad\qquad 3 + 6 = 9$$

The tens digit is 1 less than 4.

The *sum* of the digits of 36 is 9.

So for 5 × 9,

The tens digit is one less than 5 $\longrightarrow$ 4

The sum of the digits is 9, so 4 + $\square$ = 9 $\longrightarrow$ 5

Thus, 5 × 9 = 45

Now try 7 × 9 = $\square$

Challenge children to find this and other interesting patterns in a table or chart such as the one in Figure 8–11. They should note, for instance, that the columns (and rows) for 2, 4, 6, and 8 contain all even numbers, and the columns for 1, 3, 5, 7, and 9 alternate even and odd numbers.

You will probably find that children also enjoy various forms of "finger multiplication" (see Figure 8–17), seemingly magical tricks for using finger manipulations to determine basic facts. Actually, though, finger multiplication works because of the patterns that are inherent in the basic fact table.

Thinking Strategies for Division Facts

The teaching of division has traditionally consumed a large portion of time in the elementary school—so much that, with the increased use of calculators, many educators now advocate reducing the attention accorded to it. Nevertheless, children continue to need an understanding of the division process and the division facts. The facts help them to respond quickly to simple division situations and to understand better the nature of division and its relationship to multiplication.

Just as "think addition" is an important strategy for subtraction, "think multiplication" is the primary thinking strategy to aid children in understanding and recalling the division facts. Division is the inverse of multiplication; that is, in a division problem we are seeking an unknown factor when the product and some other factor are known. The multiplication table illustrates all the division facts; we simply read it differently. For the division fact 54 ÷ 9 = $\square$, we could look in the 9-row of the multiplication table for the number 54, then read up that

column to find the other factor, 6. Students generally do not learn division facts separately from multiplication facts. Instead, they learn division facts such as 48 ÷ 6 = 8 by remembering (and connecting with) multiplication facts such as 6 × 8 = 48.

However, it is important to realize that most division problems we encounter, in computations and in real-world problem situations, do not directly involve a multiplication fact that we have learned. For example, consider the computation 49 ÷ 6. There is no basic fact involving 49 and 6. So, what do you do? In this situation most people quickly and automatically mentally review the 6-facts that they know, looking for the facts that come closest to 49 (6 × 7 = 42—too small, 6 × 8 = 48—just a little too small, 6 × 9 = 54—too big). From this mental review, we can conclude that 49 ÷ 6 = 8, with 1 left over. Children need practice in thinking this way (mentally finding the answers to problems involving 1-digit divisors and 1-digit answers plus remainders).

Just as fact families can be developed for addition and subtraction, so can they be useful for multiplication and division:

$$8 \times 4 = 32$$
$$4 \times 8 = 32$$
$$32 \div 8 = 4$$
$$32 \div 4 = 8$$

Because of its relationship to multiplication, division can be stated in terms of multiplication:

$$42 \div 6 = \square \longrightarrow 6 \times \square = 42$$

Thus, children must search for the missing factor in the multiplication problem. Because multiplication facts are usually encountered and learned first, children can use what they know to learn the more difficult division facts. Moreover, division is related to subtraction, and division problems can be solved by repeated subtraction:

$$12 \div 3 = 12 - 3 - 3 - 3 - 3$$

Four threes

However, repeated subtraction and the related strategies of counting backward or skip counting are confusing for many children. You may discuss them as ideas children might like to try, particularly when these strategies occur spontaneously in the course of

Finger Multiplication for 9-Times Facts Only

1. Hold both hands in front of you with palms facing away.

2. To do 3×9, bend down the third finger from the left.

3. The fingers to the left of the bent finger represent tens. The fingers to the right of the bent finger represent ones. Read off the answer: 2 tens and 7 ones, or 27.

4. To do 5×9, bend down the fifth finger from the left, etc. Try this method for any 9-facts: 1×9 through 10×9.

Finger Multiplication for Facts with Factors 6 and Higher Only

1. Hold both hands in front of you with palms facing you.

2. Think of a multiplication in which both factors are 6 or more (up to 10). For example, you can do anything from 6×6 up to 10×10.

3. For each factor, find the difference from 10.
   - Let's try the example 8×9.
   - For the factor 8, think $10 - 8 = 2$, and bend down 2 fingers on the left hand.
   - For the factor 9, think $10 - 9 = 1$, and bend down 1 finger on the right hand.

4. Look at all fingers that are still up, and count by ten (10, 20, 30, 40, 50, 60, 70).

5. Look at the fingers that are bent down. Multiply the number of fingers bent down on the left hand by the number bent down on the right hand ($2 \times 1 = 2$).

6. So $8 \times 9 = 70 + 2$ or 72.

7. Try this method for any multiplication facts from 6×6 up through 10×10.

$3 \times 9 = 20 + 7 = 27$

$5 \times 9 = 40 + 5 = 45$

Multiply 8×9 · Difference between 8 and 10 is 2 (fold down 2 fingers) · Difference between 9 and 10 is 1 (fold down 1 finger)

$2 \times 1 = 2$
$70 + 2$
$8 \times 9 = 72$

Figure 8–17 • Two forms of finger multiplication

some students' work, but don't be surprised if only a few children actually use them.

$15 \div 3 = \boxed{}$

Think
15 . . . 12, 9, 6, 3, 0
That's 5 numbers.
$15 \div 3 = 5$

$28 \div 7 = \boxed{}$

Think
$\left.\begin{array}{l} 28 - 7 \\ 21 - 7 \\ 14 - 7 \\ 7 - 7 \end{array}\right\}$ 4 subtractions
0
$28 \div 7 = 4$

Splitting the product into known parts relies heavily on knowledge of multiplication facts, as well as on the ability to keep in mind the component parts.

Think

$35 \div 7 = \square$

$2 \times 7 = 14$
$3 \times 7 = 21$
$14 + 21 = 35$
$2 + 3 = 5$
So $35 \div 7 = 5$

As with multiplication, work with arrays helps children to relate the symbols to the action.

In general, children have little difficulty in dividing by one. They need to exercise caution when zero is involved, however. Division by zero and division of zero present two different situations. We can divide 0 by 6 ($0 \div 6$); the result is 0. We can check this by multiplying: $6 \times 0 = 0$. But division by zero is impossible.

For example, to solve $6 \div 0 = \square$ would require a solution so that $6 = \square \times 0$. However, there is no value for $\square$ that would make this sentence true. Therefore, $6 \div 0$ has no solution, and division by zero is undefined in mathematics. Just as you may have difficulty remembering which is possible, division *of* 0 or division *by* 0, so will children have difficulty in remembering and need to be given practice.

Thus, thinking strategies for division are far more difficult for children to learn than are the strategies for the other operations. The child must remember more, and regrouping is often necessary. When skip counting, for instance, the child must keep track of the number of times a number is named even as the struggle to count backward proceeds. Therefore, the primary burden falls on the child's facility with the multiplication facts. Being able to recall those facts quickly will facilitate recall of the division facts.

A Glance at Where We've Been

Skill in computation with whole numbers is developed through concrete experiences. In this chapter, the importance of experiences with counting, concrete experiences, problem-solving contexts, and language were considered, and meanings for each operation were described and modeled. Mathematical properties to be developed as part of the understanding of the operations were presented.

The remainder of the chapter focused on the basic facts for each operation. Starting from what children

know, the facts are developed using experiences that range from concrete to pictorial to symbolic. Thinking strategies for the basic facts for each operation help children move from counting to more mature, efficient ways of developing the facts. Finally, ways to help children master the basic facts for quick recall were discussed, with specific suggestions for drills and activities to provide practice and promote mastery.

Things to Do: From What You've Read

1. What prerequisites must children have before engaging in the lesson that opens this chapter?

2. Discuss each of these statements:
   (a) When you teach multiplication, you begin preparation for learning division.
   (b) Children should not be allowed to count on their fingers when they start addition.
   (c) With the wide use of calculators, there is little need for children to attain prompt recall of the basic facts.

3. What properties of addition and multiplication are especially helpful in teaching the basic facts?

4. Describe the thinking strategies a child might use with each of the following:

$8 + 0 = \square$
$18 \div 3 = \square$
$8 \times 5 = \square$
$16 - 7 = \square$
$7 + 8 = \square$

5. For each addition fact strategy (commutativity, adding one, doubles and near doubles, adding zero, counting on, adding to 10 and beyond), list three different facts that could use that strategy and explain what a child would think when using that strategy.

6. When is counting back an effective strategy for subtraction?

7. How can Cuisenaire rods be used to show the commutative property of addition? Sketch several examples and describe an activity using Cuisenaire rods that would involve students in investigating this property.

8. Explain, in your own words, why division by zero is considered "undefined" by mathematicians.

9. There are two types of division problems that arise in real-world problems: measurement (or repeated subtraction) division and fair sharing (or partitive) division. (a) Write a partitive (or fair sharing) division

word problem that would correspond to 24 ÷ 6. Draw a picture to illustrate the solution to your problem and in simple language explain why your numerical answer makes sense. (b) Write a measurement (or repeated subtraction) division word problem that would correspond to $4\frac{1}{2} \div \frac{3}{4}$. Draw a picture to illustrate the solution to your problem and in simple language, explain why your numerical answer makes sense.

Things to Do: Going Beyond This Book

field Additional activities, suggestions, and questions are provided in *Teaching Elementary Mathematics: A Resource for Field Experiences.*

1. Plan a bulletin board to help children learn about one or more thinking strategies for subtraction.

2. Find a vignette or game in *Professional Standards for Teaching Mathematics* (NCTM 1991) that focuses on basic facts. Share the ideas you find.

3. Consider the activity described in "Problem Solving with Combinations" (English 1992). How is it related to ideas presented in this chapter?

4. Examine a recently published textbook for grades 2, 3, or 4. Analyze how basic facts for the four basic operations are presented in that text. How are the facts grouped? Are thinking strategies presented? If so, how do they compare with the strategies described in this chapter? How would you use this text in teaching basic facts? If you think you would probably want to supplement the text, explain what sorts of supplementary materials and experiences you would use and why.

5. Look at the book *Mental Math in the Primary Grades* by Jack Hope et al. (1987). How do the strategies described in that book compare to those described in this chapter? The book includes black-line masters for instruction, activity sheets for individual seat work, and suggestions for using manipulatives to help children develop basic fact strategies. How might you integrate use of materials from that book with regular textbook instruction on basic facts?

6. *field* Building on Children's Literature. Find a popular trade book (perhaps from Book Nook for Children) that would be useful as a motivator for a problem-based lesson revolving around one of the four basic operations (addition, subtraction, multiplication, or division). Identify the operation that the story evokes and write a problem that you might challenge students to work on after hearing the story. If possible, read the story to some children, have them try solving your problem, and analyze their written work for evidence of understanding of the basic operation the story involves.

7. Read the "Number" Standards for Gradebands Pre-K–2 and 3–5 in NCTM's *Principles and Standards for School Mathematics.* What recommendations are made concerning teaching basic facts? Write a position paper in which you either agree with NCTM's recommendations or take an opposing position. In either case, clearly explain and defend your position.

8. Pick a concept or skill from this chapter and compile a brief bibliography of recent articles containing research or teaching ideas on this topic.

9. Find a computer program that claims to help children learn basic facts and play around with it. Many of these programs are on the market. Most focus on encouraging development of quick responses, but very few encourage use of thinking strategies. Write a half-page review of the computer program (similar to those published in teacher journals). In your review you should identify the name and publisher of the program, the cost, and the type of hardware required to run it. Explain how the program works. Include answers to the following questions: Does the program help children learn strategies for basic facts? Does the program keep track of student progress? Does it modify the facts presented to the student according to which ones he/she has gotten right or wrong in the past? Do you think the program would be effective in promoting quick recall of facts? Why? Do you think children would enjoy using this program? Why? How would you use such a program if your classroom had only one or two computers? Would you recommend this program to other teachers? Why?

10. *field* Timed Tests. Observe children as they take a timed test on basic facts. What behaviors and emotions can you document? How are the results of the test used by the teacher? Talk to at least five children or adults about their memories of timed tests on basic facts. What do they say about their experiences?

11. *field* Student Difficulties with Basic Facts. Talk to a fifth- or sixth-grade teacher about what he or she does with students who are not fluent in basic facts. Do the students receive special instruction in fact strategies? Do they use calculators routinely for classwork and homework? How many students in the class have problems with basic facts? Which facts cause the most difficulties?

BOOK NOOK FOR CHILDREN

Anno, Masaichiro, and Anno, Mitsumasa. *Anno's Mysterious Multiplying Jar.* New York: Philomel Books, 1983.

Burningham, John. *Pigs Plus.* New York: Viking Press, 1983.

Burningham, John. *Ride Off.* New York: Viking Press, 1983.

Butler, M. Christina. *Too Many Eggs.* Boston: David R. Godine Publisher, 1988.

Calmenson, Stephanie. *Ten Furry Monsters.* New York: Parents Magazine Press, 1984.

Charosh, Mannis. *Number Ideas Through Pictures.* New York: Crowell, 1974.

Dee, Ruby. *Ten Ways to Count to Ten.* New York: Henry Holt, 1988.

Enderle, Judith Ross, and Tessler, Stephanie Gordon. *Six Creepy Sheep.* Honesdale, Pa.: Boyds Mills Press, 1992.

Gerstein, Mordicai. *Roll Over!* New York: Crown Publishers, 1984.

Gretz, Susanna. *Teddy Bears 1 to 10.* New York: Four Winds Press, 1986.

Hamm, Diane Johnston. *How Many Feet in the Bed?* New York: Simon & Schuster Books for Young Readers, 1994.

Hawkins, Colin. *Adding Animals.* New York: G. P. Putnam's Sons, 1983.

Hawkins, Colin. *Take Away Monsters.* New York: G. P. Putnam's Sons, 1984.

Hawkins, Colin, and Hawkins, Jacqui. *How Many Are in This Old Car?* New York: G. P. Putnam's Sons, 1988.

Hulme, Joy N. *Counting by Kangaroos: A Multiplication Concept Book.* New York: Scientific American Books for Young Readers, 1995.

Hutchins, Pat. *The Doorbell Rang.* New York: Greenwillow Books, 1986.

Moerbeck, Kees, and Kijs, Carla. *Six Brave Explorers.* Los Angeles: Price Stern Sloan, 1988.

Owen, Annie. *Annie's One to Ten.* New York: Knopf, 1988.

Punnett, Dick. *Count the Possums.* Elgin, Ill.: Child's World, 1982.

Sendak, Maurice. *One Was Johnny.* New York: Harper & Row, 1962.

Srivastava, Jane Jonas. *Number Families.* New York: Crowell, 1979.

Selected References

Ashcraft, Mark H., and Christy, Kelly S. "The Frequency of Arithmetic Facts in Elementary Texts: Addition and Multiplication in Grades 1–6." *Journal for Research in Mathematics Education,* 26 (November 1995), pp. 396–421.

Ashlock, Robert B. *Error Patterns in Computation,* 7th ed. Upper Saddle River, N.J.: Simon & Schuster, 1998.

Ashlock, Robert B., and Washbon, Carolynn A. "Games: Practice Activities for the Basic Facts." In *Developing Computational Skills,* 1978 Yearbook (ed. Marilyn N. Suydam). Reston, Va.: NCTM, 1978, pp. 39–50.

Baratta-Lorton, Mary. *Mathematics Their Way.* Reading, Mass.: Addison-Wesley, 1976.

Baroody, Arthur J., and Standifer, Dorothy J. "Addition and Subtraction in the Primary Grades." In *Research Ideas for the Classroom: Early Childhood Mathematics* (ed. Robert J. Jensen). Reston, Va.: NCTM, and New York: Macmillan, 1993, pp. 72–102.

Bartek, Mary Marron. "Hands-on Addition and Subtraction with the Three Pigs." *Teaching Children Mathematics* 4 (October 1997), pp. 68–71.

Bruni, James V., and Silverman, Helene. "Let's Do It!: Making and Using Board Games." *Arithmetic Teacher,* 22 (March 1975), pp. 172–179.

Burns, Marilyn. "Timed Tests." *Teaching Children Mathematics* 1 (1995), pp. 408–409.

Burns, Marilyn. "What I Learned from Teaching Second Grade." *Teaching Children Mathematics* 3 (November 1996), pp. 124–127.

Campbell, Melvin D. "Basic Facts Drill—Card Games." *Arithmetic Teacher,* 36 (April 1989), pp. 41–43.

Carey, Deborah A. "Students' Use of Symbols." *Arithmetic Teacher,* 40 (February 1992), pp. 184–186.

Carpenter, Thomas P.; Carey, Deborah A.; and Kouba, Vicky L. "A Problem-Solving Approach to the Operations." In *Mathematics for the Young Child,* (ed. Joseph N. Payne). Reston, Va.: NCTM, 1990, pp. 111–131.

Carpenter, Thomas P.; Corbitt, Mary Kay; Kepner, Henry S., Jr.; Lindquist, Mary Montgomery; and Reys, Robert E. *Results from the Second Mathematics Assessment of the National Assessment of Educational Progress.* Reston, Va.: NCTM, 1981.

Carpenter, Thomas P.; Fennema, Elizabeth; and Franke, Megan L. "Cognitively Guided Instruction: A Knowledge Base for Reform in Primary Mathematics Instruction." *Elementary School Journal* 97 (1996), pp. 3–20.

Clark, Faye B., and Kamii, Constance. "Identification of Multiplicative Thinking in Children in Grades 1–5." *Journal for Research in Mathematics Education,* 27 (January 1996), pp. 41–51.

Davis, Edward J. "Suggestions for Teaching the Basic Facts of Arithmetic." In *Developing Computational Skills,* 1978 Yearbook (ed. Marilyn N. Suydam). Reston, Va.: NCTM, 1978, pp. 51–60.

English, Lyn. "Problem Solving with Combinations." *Arithmetic Teacher,* 40 (October 1992), pp. 72–77.

Feinberg, Miriam M. "Using Patterns to Practice Basic Facts." *Arithmetic Teacher,* 37 (April 1990), pp. 38–41.

Folsom, Mary. "Operations on Whole Numbers." In *Mathematics Learning in Early Childhood,* Thirty-seventh Yearbook (ed. Joseph N. Payne). Reston, Va.: NCTM, 1975, pp. 162–190.

Funkhouser, Charles. "Developing Number Sense and Basic Computational Skills in Students with Special Needs." *School Science and Mathematics,* 95 (May 1995), pp. 236–239.

Fuson, Karen C. "Research on Whole Number Addition and Subtraction" In *Handbook of Research on Mathematics Teaching and Learning* (ed. Douglas A. Grouws). New York: Macmillan, 1992, pp. 243–275.

Ginsberg, Herbert. *Children's Arithmetic: The Learning Process.* New York: Van Nostrand Reinhold, 1977.

Greer, Brian. Multiplication and Division as Models of Situations. In *Handbook of Research on Mathematics Teaching and*

Learning (ed. Douglas A. Grouws). New York: Macmillan, 1992, pp. 276–295.

Hope, Jack A; Leutzinger, Larry; Reys, Barbara J.; and Reys, Robert E. *Mental Math in the Primary Grades.* Palo Alto, Calif.: Dale Seymour, 1987.

Issacs, Andrew C., and Carroll, William M. "Strategies for Basic-facts Instruction." *Teaching Children Mathematics* 5 (May 1998), pp. 508–515.

Kamii, Constance; Lewis, Barbara A.; and Booker, Bobby M. "Instead of Teaching Missing Addends." *Teaching Children Mathematics* 4 (April 1998), pp. 458–461.

Kouba, Vicky L., and Franklin, Kathy. "Multiplication and Division: Sense Making and Meaning." In *Research Ideas for the Classroom: Early Childhood Mathematics* (ed. Robert J. Jensen). Reston, Va.: NCTM, and New York: Macmillan, 1993, pp. 103–126.

Kouba, Vicky L., and Franklin, Kathy. "Research into Practice: Multiplication and Division: Sense Making and Meaning." *Teaching Children Mathematics,* 1 (May 1995), pp. 574–577.

Leutzinger, Larry P. "Developing Thinking Strategies for Addition Facts." *Teaching Children Mathematics* 6 (September 1999), pp. 14–18.

Leutzinger, Larry P., and Nelson, Glenn. "Using Addition Facts to Learn Subtraction Facts." *Arithmetic Teacher,* 27 (December 1979), pp. 8–13.

Litwiller, Bonnie H., and Duncan, David R. *Activities for the Maintenance of Computational Skills and the Discovery of Patterns.* Reston, Va.: NCTM, 1980.

National Council of Teachers of Mathematics. *Principles and Standards for School Mathematics.* Reston, VA.: NCTM, 2000.

National Council of Teachers of Mathematics. *Professional Standards for Teaching Mathematics.* Reston, Va.: NCTM, 1991.

Page, Anita. "Helping Students Understand Subtraction." *Teaching Children Mathematics,* 1 (November 1994), pp. 140–143.

Quintero, Ana Helvia. "Conceptual Understanding of Multiplication: Problems Involving Combination." *Arithmetic Teacher,* 33 (November 1985), pp. 36–39.

Quintero, Ana Helvia. "Children's Conceptual Understanding of Situations Involving Multiplication." *Arithmetic Teacher,* 33 (January 1986), pp. 34–37.

Rathmell, Edward C. "Using Thinking Strategies to Teach the Basic Facts." In *Developing Computational Skills,* 1978 Yearbook (ed. Marilyn N. Suydam). Reston, Va.: NCTM, 1978, pp. 13–38.

Rightsel, Pamela S., and Thornton, Carol A. "72 Addition Facts Can Be Mastered by Mid-Grade 1." *Arithmetic Teacher,* 33 (November 1985), pp. 8–10.

Sowell, Evelyn J. "Effects of Manipulative Materials in Mathematics Instruction." *Journal for Research in Mathematics Education,* 20 (November 1989), pp. 498–505.

Sundar, Viji K. "Thou Shalt Not Divide by Zero." *Arithmetic Teacher,* 37 (March 1990), pp. 50–51.

Thiessen, Diane, and Matthais, Margaret. *The Wonderful World of Mathematics: A Critically Annotated List of Children's Books in Mathematics.* Reston, Va.: NCTM, 1998.

Thompson, Charles S., and Dunlop, William P. "Basic Facts: Do Your Children Understand or Do They Memorize?" *Arithmetic Teacher,* 25 (December 1977), pp. 14–16.

Thompson, Charles S., and Van de Walle, John. "Modeling Subtraction Situations." *Arithmetic Teacher,* 32 (October 1984), pp. 8–12.

Thompson, Charles S., and Van de Walle, John. "The Power of Ten." *Arithmetic Teacher,* 32 (November 1984), pp. 6–11.

Thornton, Carol. "Strategies for the Basic Facts." In *Mathematics for the Young Child* (ed. Joseph N. Payne). Reston, Va.: NCTM, 1990, pp. 133–151.

Thornton, Carol A. "'Look Ahead' Activities Spark Success in Addition and Subtraction Number Fact Learning." *Arithmetic Teacher,* 36 (April 1989), pp. 8–11.

Thornton, Carol A., and Smith, Paula J. "Action Research: Strategies for Learning Subtraction Facts." *Arithmetic Teacher,* 35 (April 1988), pp. 8–12.

Trafton, Paul R., and Zawojewski, Judith S. "Meanings of Operations." *Arithmetic Teacher,* 38 (November 1990), pp. 18–22.

Operation Sense: Calculators, Mental Computation, and Estimation

9

Snapshot of a Lesson

Third graders are working at tables in small groups. At each table paper, pencils, and calculators are available. Mr. Diggs has placed four items at the front of the room (prices are also shown on the board) for all the children to see. The focus of the lesson is to provide opportunities to use different computational tools.

MR. DIGGS: Here are some things you can buy. Please choose any two of them. Decide how much money the items you chose would cost.

He waits until children have decided. He also observes how children are doing their computations.

MR. DIGGS: Make a list of the money spent in your group, and then have a reporter from your group write the totals on the board.

After a few minutes, this list is compiled:

Amounts spent:	$0.50	$0.75	$1.00	$1.98
Number of Students:	8	6	9	4

MR. DIGGS: Many of you spent $1.00. Why do you think $1 was so popular?

WHITNEY: Because we like apples—I'm hungry and could eat two apples.

MR. DIGGS: I am hungry, too, and wish that I had a couple of apples. Is there another reason? Justin, what do you think?

JUSTIN: Because it is easy to add 50 cents plus 50 cents.

WILLIAM: I think it's easy to add 25 cents plus 25 cents. That is why I got 50 cents.

SARAH: It is also easy to add 50 cents and 25 cents.

JUSTIN: Easiest for me is 50 cents plus 50 cents because it makes a dollar.

This discussion provides insight into which computations are easy for the children and confirms Mr. Diggs' observation that the children did these computations mentally. He then moves the discussion to another sum that was reported.

MR. DIGGS: Four people spent $1.98. Would someone tell me what you bought and how you decided it was $1.98?

AARON: I bought two pens. Each cost $0.99, so that if it was one penny more, it would be a dollar. Two of them would make two dollars—minus 2 cents, that's $1.98.

KELLY: I did it a little differently. I knew that one more penny would make $0.99 a dollar. So I took one penny from the $0.99 and made it $0.98 and added one dollar to it to get $1.98.

ROBERT: I couldn't hold the numbers in my head, so I used paper and pencil.

MR. DIGGS: That sounds like another good way to get the answer.

BARBARA: I used a calculator. Is that okay?

MR. DIGGS: Barbara, you can use the calculator whenever you need it, but try to do it in your head first. If it is too hard to do in your head, then try doing it a different way, as Robert did.

189

Mr. Diggs wants to move this activity along to develop more number sense and include estimation. He asks, "Suppose I spent more than $3, what two items could I buy?"

WHITNEY: Four pens would be almost $4.

MR. DIGGS: That's right, Whitney, but I asked you to buy only two things.

LINDSEY: You could buy two toys.

MR. DIGGS: Lindsey, tell us more about how you decided two toys.

LINDSEY: Well—I thought $1.67 is more than one and a half dollars. I know that one plus one is two, and two halves make another dollar, so that makes three dollars. So it must be more than three dollars but less than four.

MR. DIGGS: Good thinking. It often helps to decide what is the most and least that could be possible when we compute. Why do you think no one chose to buy two toys?

Mr. Diggs anticipates an answer that the prices of the toys are hard to compute but asks this question to refocus the discussion on how we decide which computational tools to use. He plans to ask for other possibilities, such as a pen and a toy, and observe the strategies the children use. These activities give him insight into how his students are thinking and the level of confidence, as well as skill, his students have with various tools.

Introduction

Computation has evolved from using counting and calculating devices, such as piles of stones in ancient times or using a soroban in Japan, to using written computational algorithms. More recently, the calculator has become available, and no computational tool has the power for greater impact on school mathematics.

Competence with a variety of computational tools is not merely useful; it is essential. The importance of computational tools is reflected in the *Principles and Standards for School Mathematics*, which states that children should select appropriate computational methods from among "mental computation, estimation, calculators, and paper and pencil according to the context and nature of the computation and use the selected method or tool" (NCTM 2000, p. 148). Historically, elementary school mathematics has emphasized written computation far more than the other tools. This, together with the fact that learners are more likely to select tools with which they are familiar, means that students will often tend to use written computation even though other more efficient computational options exist.

A better balance of instructional attention to these tools needs to be established so children can learn to make appropriate computational tool choices. To make this happen, we must recognize and teach that different options are available for doing computation. One insightful view of computation is shown in Figure 9–1. It illustrates that all computation begins with a problem situation involving calculation and then highlights the series of decision-making stages that must be completed when doing computation. Notice that regardless of the type of computation done, estimation is always used to check on the reasonableness of the result.

In every computational situation, one must decide what type of result is needed and how that result will be produced. Thus, important goals of mathematics learning related to computation are to help people:

- Develop competence with each of the computational tools
- Make wise choices among the computational tools available
- Choose tools that are consistent with the computation desired and ability to use that tool
- Apply the tool chosen correctly
- Use estimation to determine the reasonableness of an answer (result) for the particular problem being solved

Helping students select and use these tools appropriately and effectively contributes to their number sense.

COMPUTATIONAL TOOLS

Developing competence with the four computational tools—mental computation, estimation, written computation, and calculators—is an important goal for elementary school mathematics. Three of these tools, mental computation, estimation, and calculators, are discussed here, and written computation is considered extensively in the next chapter.

As teachers we need to think about which computations are needed and important enough to learn in school, and how instructional time should be directed. Research reports that more than 80 percent of all mathematical computations in daily life involve mental computation and estimation of numerical quantities rather than written computation.

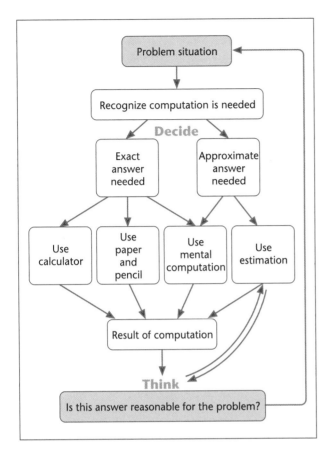

Figure 9–1 • **Computational decisions and tools to use**

Ironically, research in the United States also shows that 70 to 90 percent of the instructional time in elementary school mathematics directed toward computation has focused on written computation procedures (Sowder 1992).

Many proposals have been made regarding computation, ranging from prohibiting calculator use to eliminating the teaching of written algorithms. Thoughtful recommendations also have called for helping children learn to make appropriate computational tool choices. For example, a report by the National Research Council suggests:

> Children should use calculators throughout their school work, just as adults use calculators throughout their lives. More important, children must learn when to use them and when not to do so. They must learn from experience with calculators when to estimate and when to seek an exact answer; how to estimate answers to verify the plausibility of calculator results; and how to solve modest problems mentally when neither pencil nor calculator is convenient. (1989, p. 47)

Most people recognize the importance of each of the computational tools, and suggest that a redistri-

bution of instructional time is needed. We strongly support a better balance of instructional time for the computational alternatives than has historically occurred in elementary schools. What percentage of time to devote to each tool remains an unanswered question and will certainly depend on the developmental levels of the students.

Although we feel strongly that significant changes in the time devoted to computational alternatives are needed, we recognize that the specific percentages are open to debate. In the spirit of stimulating debate and discussion, please consider Figure 9–2; this depicts an approximation of what has happened in the past, the current situation, and our proposal for a better balance.

Any future prediction is subject to error. Thus the percentage of time devoted to these tools is subject

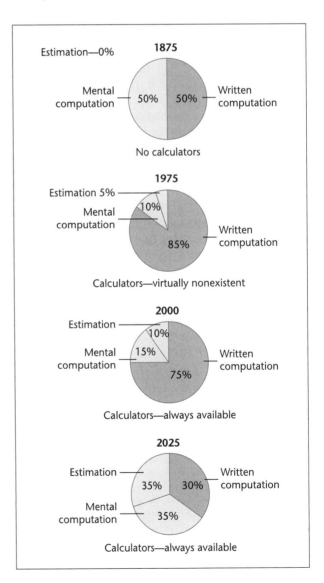

Figure 9–2 • **How time devoted to computation in elementary school is spent**

to question and challenge. Nevertheless, the decline in attention to standard written algorithms over the years and into the future is indisputable. Instructional time previously devoted to developing proficiency with written algorithms will become available for other uses. We anticipate that much of this time will be dedicated to developing increased number sense together with greater attention to the other computational tools, calculators, mental computation, and estimation. Reflecting on your experience and thinking about the future needs of your students will challenge you to develop ways of providing a proper balance in your computation instruction.

Calculators

The NCTM position statement on calculators has recommended that "appropriate calculators should be available to all students at all times." This statement suggests that, as the mathematical knowledge of students grows, their uses of calculators will change. Children outgrow calculators just as they outgrow shoes. The calculator needs of students in primary grades are different from those of students in the intermediate grades and middle school. The technology industry has anticipated these changing needs with the development of fraction calculators, scientific calculators, and graphing calculators.

Even though calculators have been in schools for more than twenty years, several myths continue to exist.

Myth 1. Calculator use does not require thinking.

As teachers, we must make it clear to parents that calculators don't think—they only follow instructions. Consider the following problem:

A bus holds 32 children. If 1,000 children are being bused to a concert, how many buses are needed?

Suppose a calculator is available. Does the calculator decide which keys to press and in what order to press them? Does the calculator interpret the result? The answer to both questions is no!

Research shows this problem is difficult to solve with or without a calculator. To use the calculator effectively, students must decide which buttons to use and the order in which to use them. Furthermore, a calculator result must be properly interpreted. For example, the calculator result of 31.25 requires students to decide if 31.25 makes sense for this problem situation or whether 31 or 32 buses are needed.

Children intent on producing an answer without reflecting on reasonableness are likely to get answers that don't make sense. Calculators don't discourage thinking! In fact, proper use of calculators will encourage thinking, as using a calculator frees students from tedious and laborious computation and allows them to dwell on the important problem-solving processes that generally precede, and often follow, the computation.

Myth 2. Use of calculators will harm students' mathematics achievement.

Research has addressed this issue and consistently reported that the use of "calculators in concert with traditional instruction . . . can improve the average student's basic skills with paper and pencil, both in basic operations and in problem solving" (Hembree and Dessart 1992). Moreover, "students using calculators possess a better attitude toward mathematics and an especially better self-concept in mathematics." Many parents and some teachers worry that students will become so dependent on calculators that they won't learn to compute. Research shows that is not the case. As teachers, we must not only make effective use of calculators in our teaching but also help any skeptics put their fears to rest.

Myth 3. Computations with calculators are always faster.

Calculators make tedious computations easy. For example, a calculator will compute 2345×67 or $34567 \div 89$ instantly, which shows the power of a calculator. However, it is much faster to do many simple calculations, such as 4×40, $99 + 99 + 99 + 99$, $\frac{1}{2} + \frac{1}{4}$ or 1000×23, mentally than to enter them into a calculator. In the Classroom 9–1 provides one way of helping children recognize the power of mental computations as well as the calculator.

Myth 4. Calculators are useful only for computation.

The most obvious use of calculators is to calculate, but in the process of calculating many powerful mathematical ideas emerge. For example, calculator counting forward and backward as was shown with In the Classroom 6–5, 6–6, and 6–7 provides patterns and practice in many important skills, such as basic multiplication and division facts. Using calculators to count by powers of ten (10, 100, 1000) and decimals (tenths, hundredths) suggests additional patterns for older children.

We recognize that computational skills must be learned, and view the calculator as a useful tool in this process (see In the Classroom 9–1). Our recommendation is that calculators be used whenever computation is needed and computational skills are not the main focus of instruction. Clearly, the estab-

In The Classroom 9–1

Grades 3–5

Calculators—To Use or Not to Use

Objective: Encourage recognition of the power of mental computation and wise use of calculator.

▼ Divide into two groups. One group must use calculators. The other group must NOT use calculators.

▼ Once groups are decided, the leader gives the following computations one at a time orally. Read the computation aloud, for example, "4 × 1000" → "four times one thousand."

▼ Decide who does the computation correctly the fastest. Then do the next computation.

	Must Use Calculators	Must NOT Use Calculators
1. 4 × 1000	_____	_____
2. 400 + 50 + 8	_____	_____
3. 99 + 99 + 99 + 99	_____	_____
4. 1000 − 200	_____	_____
5. 50 + 50 + 50 + 50 + 50 + 50	_____	_____
6. 1/2 + 3/4	_____	_____
7. 6300 ÷ 7	_____	_____
8. 10 × 10 × 10 × 10	_____	_____
9. 0.75 + 0.25 + .050	_____	_____
10. $1.00 − $0.25	_____	_____

▼ Which group got the most correct answers the fastest?

▼ Make a list of 5 computations that you think children *using calculators* will do the fastest.

▼ Make a list of 5 computations that you think children *NOT using calculators* will do the fastest.

lishment of basic facts must remain an important goal of primary grades. Basic facts are natural stepping stones to mental computation and estimation, and to the long-term development of number sense. It is essential that rapid recall of basic facts (for example, 4×7, $8 + 6$) be an instructional goal. However, as suggested previously, calculators can be used to facilitate basic fact learning in many meaningful ways that encourage students to think.

When is calculator use appropriate? Many teachers are unsure how to use calculators with their students. Some resort to unproductive uses of the calculator such as having students turn the calculator upside down to spell words or using the calculator to check written calculations. These activities may be somewhat motivational, but their educa-tional value is questionable. They may communicate the message that a calculator is only for playing games or, even worse, that using a calculator is cheating and should be used only after written computation. Research shows that the more teachers use calculators in their classroom, the more they develop creative and productive ways to use them (Fey 1992). We feel that a calculator should be used as a *computational tool* when it:

1. Facilitates problem solving

2. Relieves tedious computation

3. Focuses attention on meaning

4. Removes anxiety about computational failures

5. Provides motivation and confidence

In addition to making the calculator available as a computational tool, it also can be used productively as an instructional tool. Suggestions for how to do this may be found in the teacher's editions of most textbooks. Several resources are listed at the end of this chapter (CAMP-LA 1991). We believe that a calculator should be used as an *instructional tool* when it:

1. Facilitates a search for patterns
2. Creates problematic situations
3. Supports concept development
4. Promotes number sense
5. Encourages creativity and exploration

Calculators also provide a safety net for students having particular difficulties in learning computational procedures. If students are learning disabled, making it difficult or impossible for them to successfully use traditional computational procedures, the calculator provides equity and allows them to engage in other problem solving.

When using calculators with students we can provide experiences that will help them make appropriate use of this tool. As with any new tool, we should provide time for students to explore with the calculator on their own and discuss rules for handling and caring for them. We can help dispel the calculator myths discussed earlier by demonstrating:

1. Calculators do not think for themselves
2. Not all problems can be solved with a calculator
3. It is sometimes faster to compute mentally

Communicating with parents so that they understand what is happening and why calculator use is important. Often, a simple note to parents (see Figure 9–3) is effective. This note serves several useful purposes. It establishes communication between teacher and parents. It also lets parents know that calculators will be used in their child's classroom and tells why they are being used. Learning how and when to use calculators as well as other computational alternatives, such as estimation, mental computation, and written computation, is an important goal for every mathematics program.

Mental Computation

Mental computation is done without the aid of external tools. This sounds simple enough, and it certainly is a natural way to do many computations. The naturalness of "doing it in your head" is demonstrated in the Snapshot at the beginning of this chapter as well as by the fact that many young

Dear Parents:

We are using calculators in our second-grade class this year in many different ways. Sometimes we use them to develop skills in counting and recognizing patterns; other times to explore new topics, such as decimals; and often when solving problems that require tedious computations. Research suggests that a variety of early experiences with calculators will help young children make wise use of calculators both in and out of school.

If you have questions about how we are using calculators, please ask your child to share some things they have been doing with this tool. If you have further questions, please let me know.

Figure 9–3 • A sample note to parents about calculators in primary grades

children (before being able to write) have already developed ways of computing. In fact, research has documented a wide variety of creative mental computation techniques that children have constructed (Cobb and Merkel 1989; Kamii et al. 1993).

Doing mental computation builds onto and naturally extends thinking strategies used to develop basic facts that were discussed in Chapter 8. Extending basic facts is an early step in developing more powerful mental computation strategies and skills. For example, the basic fact 4×6 could serve as a foundation or stepping stone for many mental computations, such as:

4×600 is 4×6 hundreds, which is 24 hundreds, or 2400.

4×6000 is 4×6 thousand, which is 24 thousands, or 24000.

These extended facts build on basic facts, place-value concepts, and suggest different patterns and relationships in the process. Mental computation together with calculators can be used to explore a range of patterns that suggest different relationships and may stimulate conjectures and discoveries. As patterns emerge, students can explore relationships between

4×6 and 4×60 and 4×600 and 4×6000

Students can tell how these results are alike and how they are different. A slightly different exploration can be generated by challenging students to "Tell why these are the same."

$$4 \times 600 \qquad 40 \times 60 \qquad 400 \times 6 \qquad 4000 \times 0.6$$

Doing mental computation encourages flexible thinking and rewards thoughtful analysis that often uses very different techniques.

Notice the range of strategies used in Figure 9–4. Each strategy is meaningful to the student using it. However, that strategy may not be known by everyone and may even seem strange to others. Talking over ways different children compute mentally encourages freedom of thought and flexibility of strategies. Children often can learn new strategies by hearing their classmates' explanations. In fact, encouraging students to share and explain how they did it in their heads is an important part of instructional activities promoting mental computation (McIntosh et al. 1997).

As children develop their mental computation abilities, it is important that they encounter a range of activities that encourages and rewards the wide variety of skills used when doing mental computation. Rather than have everyone use the same strategy to solve a problem, the goal of mental computation instruction is to encourage individual students to use strategies that make sense to them. Here are some things children should be encouraged to do:

- Always try mental computation before written methods or calculator use.

- Use numbers that are easy to work with:

	One way to think
$397 \times 4 = ?$	$400 \times 4 = 1600$
	$3 \times 4 = 12$
	$1600 - 12 = 1588$
$\$6.98 + \$7.98 + \$9.98 = ?$	$7 + 8 + 10 = 25$
	$3 \times 2¢ = 6¢$
	$\$25 - 6¢ = \$24.94$

- Look for an easy way:

$2 \times 3 \times 7 \times 5 = ?$	$2 \times 3 = 6$
	$6 \times 5 = 30$
	$30 \times 7 = 210$
	or
	$2 \times 5 = 10$
	$3 \times 7 = 21$
	$10 \times 21 = 210$

$65 \times 8 \times 19 \times 0 = ?$	0 is a factor, which means the product is zero.

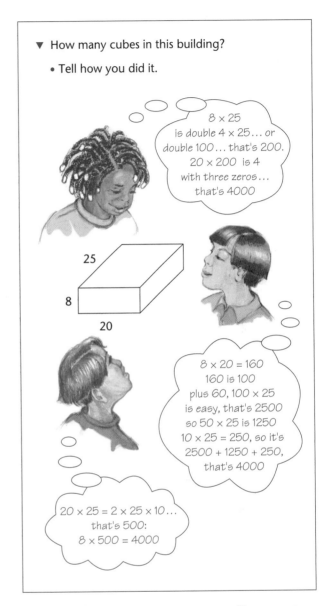

Figure 9–4 • Different ways to mentally compute

- Use logical reasoning

15×120	That's halfway between 10×120 and 20×120 . . . halfway between 1200 and 2400 . . . that's 1800
	or
	That's 10×120 plus half of 10×120 . . . 1200 + 600 that's 1800

● Use knowledge about the number system

56 – 24 =?   50 – 20 = 30
              6 – 4 = 2
              30 + 2 = 32
              or
              54 – 24 = 30
              so 56 – 24 = 32

Why emphasize mental computation? Here are several reasons for helping students develop mental computation:

● Mental computation is very useful. An overwhelming majority (more than three-fourths) of all calculations by adults are done mentally. Encouraging, developing, and rewarding mental computation early is an important step toward developing this practical and lifelong skill.

● Mental computation provides a direct and efficient way of doing many calculations. For example, research has shown that the computation 200 – 5 is easier to do mentally than in a written form. Students are more likely to make sensible judgments about the results and less likely to report 205 (a common error for the written form). Likewise, in the middle grades, computations such as $\frac{3}{4} - \frac{1}{2}$ are easier to compute mentally than in a written form (McIntosh et al. 1995).

● Mental computation is an excellent way to develop critical thinking and number sense and to reward creative problem solving. Students must choose (invent) a strategy and use it. In this process, they become aware that there is more than one way to perform most calculations mentally and are encouraged to seek simple and economical methods that make sense to them (Cobb and Merkel 1989).

● Proficiency in mental computation contributes to increased skill in estimation. Mental computation provides the cornerstone for all estimation processes, offering a variety of alternative algorithms and nonstandard techniques for finding answers.

Mental computation encourages flexible thinking, promotes number sense, and encourages creative work with numbers in an efficient manner. Thus, 165 + 99 might be solved in several different ways, such as:

"I subtracted 1 from 165 and added it to 99. Then I added 164 + 100 to get 264."

"I added 165 plus 100 and got 265, then I subtracted 1 and got 264."

Research has documented many insightful techniques. However, the dominant strategy among children above grade 2 was applying written algorithms mentally when doing the computation (McIntosh et al. 1997). Thus when asked to compute 165 + 99 mentally, the typical description was:

"I added 5 plus 9 and got 14. I carried the ten, and 5 + 9 plus 1 is 15. I carried that 1 and got 2. It's two-six-four or 264."

For many students, mental computation is thought of as applying written algorithms in their heads (Reys and Barger 1994). This notion of mental computation is far different than the mental computation we have in mind and is often very difficult and impractical.

Research suggests that practice with written computational algorithms increases the likelihood of students trying to apply written methods mentally. This phenomena is an international dilemma. Although the range of different mental computation strategies in Canada and the United States was far greater than in Japan, in each country a learned "paper/pencil" strategy was the dominant strategy reported by students. It appears that the application of written algorithms mentally most likely reflects the emphasis given to written algorithms in school and appears to inhibit the development of flexible and more efficient mental computation strategies (Shigematsu et al. 1994; Reys et al. 1995; Reys and Yang 1998). Increasing the acceptance of an emphasis on flexible, student-generated strategies will enable students to compute mentally without relying on written algorithms to do so.

Many useful mental computation strategies have been documented and identified. Just as teachers can help children develop a repertoire of problem-solving strategies, they also can help them develop a collection of mental computation strategies. In Figure 9–5, several common strategies for whole number addition are presented. As you examine these examples, see if you have ever used any of these strategies. Chances are, you have!

Among the guidelines you should follow when developing mental computation are these:

● Encourage students to do computations mentally. Make it clear that mental computation is not only acceptable but desired when possible. Students report that mental computation is not encouraged and often discouraged in school (Sowder 1992). It has been suggested that when teachers say, "Show your work," students interpret this to mean that mental computation is

Problem	Strategy	How I did it
43 + 48	Adding from the left	40 plus 40 is 80, 3 plus 8 is 11, 80 plus 11 is 91
43 + 48	Counting on	I'll count by tens. 48 . . . 58 . . . 68 . . . 78 . . . 88 Then I'll count by ones. 89 . . . 90 . . . 91
43 + 48	Making tens	48 plus 2 is 50, 50 plus 40 is 90, 90 plus 1 more is 91
43 + 48	Doubling	48 plus 48 is 96. Since 43 is 5 less than 48, 96 minus 5 is 91.
43 + 48	Making compatibles	43 and 7 are compatible because they make 50, 50 plus 40 is 90, 90 plus 1 more is 91
43 + 48	Bridging	I'll break up a number and add the parts. 43 plus 8 is 51, add 40 more is 91

Can you think of any other ways to solve this problem?

Figure 9–5 • Some examples of flexible mental computation strategies for whole number addition

unacceptable. Thus, instead of doing 1000×945 mentally, a student might write:

$$
\begin{array}{r}
945 \\
\times\ 1000 \\
\hline
000 \\
000 \\
000 \\
945 \\
\hline
945000
\end{array}
$$

Applying this written algorithm is both unnecessary and inefficient, yet it is often preferred by students, presumably because they think it is required.

- Check to learn which computations students prefer to do mentally. Research suggests that, when given the choice, students from grade 4 and up prefer to use written computations rather than calculators or mental computation. For example, a majority of fifth graders chose to do 1000×945 with either a calculator or paper/pencil. Although this is not a wise choice, research suggests that such choices typically reflect the student's lack of experience and confidence in doing computations mentally. In the Classroom 9–2 and 9–3 illustrate one way to explore the computational preferences of students with

whole numbers and with fractions. These In the Classroom activities include a range of computations. Some look easy, such as $1 - \frac{1}{3}$, yet only about 15 percent of fifth graders could produce a correct result (Reys et al. 1993).

- Check to learn if students are applying written algorithms mentally. Ask students to tell how they did a computation in their heads. When students tell how it was done, the strategies and thinking used become clear.

- Plan to include mental computation systematically and regularly as an integral part of your instruction. Systematic attention and practice will improve your students' mental computation performance. Experiences should focus on development of strategies and thinking patterns that make sense to students. These may be self-generated strategies as well as those learned from others.

- Keep practice sessions short—perhaps 10 minutes at a time. Many teachers use activities such as Follow Me while children are waiting in line: "3 + 7 + 10 – 4 + 20 . . ." or Today's Target, where the date serves as the target. For example, teachers post the date and ask students questions such as those shown in Figure 9–6A.

Figure 9–6A can be varied by changing target numbers to something beside dates. For example,

In The Classroom 9–2

How Would You Do It?

Objective: Encourage wise use of computational alternatives.

	In your head	With a calculator	With paper/pencil
60 × 60	☐	☐	☐
945 × 1000	☐	☐	☐
450 × 45	☐	☐	☐
24 × 5 × 2	☐	☐	☐
2000)‾16000	☐	☐	☐
45)‾450	☐	☐	☐
4 × 15	☐	☐	☐
50 × 17 × 2	☐	☐	☐

Follow Up

▼ Write a computation YOU would solve with a calculator _____

▼ Write a computation YOU would solve mentally _____

▼ Write a computation YOU would solve with paper/pencil _____

In The Classroom 9–3

How Would You Do It?

Objective: Encourage wise use of computational alternatives.

	In your head	With a calculator	With paper/pencil
½ + ¼	☐	☐	☐
1 − ⅓	☐	☐	☐
¾ + ¾	☐	☐	☐
⅕ + ⅙	☐	☐	☐
½ + ⅚	☐	☐	☐
1½ + 2¾	☐	☐	☐
2 − ¾	☐	☐	☐
½ − ⅓	☐	☐	☐

Follow Up

▼ Write a computation YOU would solve with a calculator _____

▼ Write a computation YOU would solve mentally _____

▼ Write a computation YOU would solve with paper/pencil _____

you might say, "Today's target is 100," and then ask students different ways to make 100. You might also change the questions and ask them to use "addition and subtraction."

- Develop children's confidence. Pick numbers that are easy to work with at first (such as 3 × 99 or $\frac{1}{2}$ of 84) then increase the difficulty (for example, try 5 × 75 or $\frac{2}{3}$ of 96).

   Experiences with compatible numbers (numbers easy to compute) such as those shown in In the Classroom 9–4 help develop confidence, number sense, and promote a valuable skill.

- Encourage inventiveness. There is no one right way to do any mental computation, but there may be certain ways that are more efficient and interesting. Asking students, "How did you do that?" can reveal highly ingenious mental computation strategies. For example, 60 × 15 was

given to students in an interview (Hope 1987). Among the strategies reported were:

"10 times 60 is 600. 5 times 60 is 300. 600 plus 300 is 900."

"60 times 10 is 600 and half of 600 is 300, so it is 600 plus 300 or 900."

"60 is 4 times 15, so that is 4 times 15 times 15. 15 squared is 225 times 4 is 900."

The latter strategy was reported by an eighth grader and is a reminder of the "interesting" techniques employed by students when doing mental computation. Many mental computational strategies are self-developed, and the power of self-learned out-of-school mental computation techniques has been documented (Sowder 1992).

- Make sure children are aware of the difference between estimation (in which answers are approximations) and mental computation (in which answers are exact).

Today's Target Date is May 24

Try to make today's target by:

Adding three numbers

Finding the difference between two numbers

Multiplying two numbers

Using a fraction

Figure 9–6A • Today's target and ways to hit the target

Some solutions to the 24 target

Adding three numbers

$8 + 8 + 8$

$20 + 12 + 2$

$10 + 10 + 4$

Finding the difference between two numbers

$30 - 6$

$25 - 1$

$100 - 76$

Multiplying two numbers

4×6

8×3

24×1

Using a fraction

$23 \, ^9/_{10} + \, ^1/_{10}$

$48 \times \, ^1/_2$

$24 \, ^1/_2 - \, ^1/_2$

Figure 9–6B • Some student solutions to target

Computational Estimation

Computational estimation is a process of producing answers that are close enough to allow for good decisions without making elaborate or exact computations. Real-world situations using estimation are diverse and plentiful. Computational estimation is typically done mentally, but there are circumstances that may require recording some results. Figure 9–7 illustrates how estimation serves as a monitoring

In The Classroom 9–4

Compatible Numbers

Objective: Finding sums of compatible whole numbers that total 100

▼ Find two numbers with a sum of 100.

17	46	15	39
83	61	54	43
92	85	8	75
25	57	80	20

A. Before computing

B. During computing

C. After computing

Figure 9–7 • Different times to estimate

function at three different places in the problem-solving process.

Estimation *prior to starting exact computation* helps build a general sense of what to expect. Estimation *while doing computation* provides an immediate or intermediate check to determine if the computation is moving in the right direction. *After the computation is completed* estimation provides an opportunity to reflect on an answer and helps determine if the result is reasonable. As children become aware of different uses of estimation, they develop a greater respect for its power and view it as an essential part of the total computational process.

Students proficient at written computations are not necessarily good estimators. In fact, research with Taiwanese students documented their considerable skill at tedious written computations, yet these same students performed much lower when asked to estimate the identical computations (Reys and Yang 1998). Several examples from that research are reported in Table 9–1. Notice that in each case, the numbers involved are tedious to compute, yet these same numbers lend themselves well to es-

timation. For example, 534.6×0.545 is rather complex with a written algorithm. Yet recognizing that 0.545 is about half, suggests that the only reasonable estimate is about 290 (that is, one-half times a number between 500 and 600 is between 250 and 300, so 290 is the only reasonable answer of the three choices). Nevertheless, nearly 90 percent of the Taiwanese students selected 29.1357. This is an unreasonable answer, yet one that might result by applying a "counting the digits to the right of the decimal point" rule. The low performance on estimating the sum of two fractions ($^{12}/_{13} + ^{7}/_{8}$) was similar to the results from second national assessment of 13-year-olds in the United States. Because both fractions were slightly less than one, the sum should be less than two. Yet more than half of these students (United States and Taiwanese) selected either 19 or 21. This research provides a vivid reminder that teachers must look beneath correct answers to check on students' understanding and their ability to produce reasonable answers.

Research has also confirmed that good mental computation skills and number sense provide the

Table 9–1 ● Percent Correct by Sixth Graders in Taiwan (Reys and Yang 1998)

Written Computation Items		Percent Correct by Sixth Graders
12/13 + 7/8		61
72 ÷ 0.025		54
534.6 × 0.545		61
Estimation Items		
Without calculating an exact answer, circle the best estimate for $\dfrac{12}{13} + \dfrac{7}{8}$.	A. 1	10
	*B. 2	25
	C. 19	36
	D. 21	16
	E. I don't know	13
Without calculating an exact answer, circle the best estimate for 72 ÷ 0.025.	A. A lot less than 72	31
	B. A little less than 72	18
	C. A little more than 72	18
	*D. A lot more than 72	33
This multiplication has been carried out correctly except for placing the decimal point: 534.6 × 0.545 = 291357 Place the decimal point using estimation.	A. 29.1357	87
	*B. 291.357	11
	C. Other Answer	2

foundation for the successful development of computational estimation techniques. Systematic attention to computational estimation can significantly improve performance. Students must be given the opportunity to estimate, and although some dramatic improvements can occur quickly, the development of good computational estimation skills is a lengthy process that will be accomplished only over a period of years (Sowder and Kelin 1992).

Estimation provides the first mathematical encounter that is not exact, yet it is nonetheless a natural part of mathematics. As young children talk about mathematics, their language and vocabulary include words such as *about, almost, just over,* and *nearly.* As children grow older, additional vocabulary is added to describe mathematical answers, including *approximate, reasonable,* and *unreasonable,* as well as phrases such as *in the ball park.* Developing comfort and confidence in using language to describe the inexactness found in the real world not only contributes to developing number sense but also prepares them for computational estimation.

Instruction should begin with making students aware of what estimation is about, so they develop a tolerance for error. Estimation involves a mind set different from that used to compute an exact answer. The "exact-answer mentality" must be changed before specific estimation strategies are developed. This change begins when students recognize that estimation is an essential and practical skill. That's why teachers must consistently emphasize computational estimation within different problem situations and along with computation procedures.

Immediate feedback to students on how well they have done in providing estimates is important. Be lenient in accepting responses initially. Ask students to explain how they obtained their estimates, because the discussion will help clarify procedures and may even suggest new approaches to estimating in a given problem. However, beware of letting them confuse estimation, which produces an answer that is close, with mental computation, which produces an exact answer.

One of the keys to developing good estimation strategies is to help children be flexible when thinking about numbers. Suppose you wanted students to evaluate 418 + 349. One child might think, "400 + 300 is 700, and 49 + 18 is less than 100, so the sum is between 700 and 800." This approach uses the leading digits. Another child might think, "418 is about 400 and 349 is almost 350, so the sum is about 750." This child rounded to numbers that are easy to compute, and used their number sense to make adjustments and produce an estimate.

As with mental computation, it is important that children develop different strategies, and it is critical that they think about the problem, the operations, and the numbers involved and not rely on a fixed set of rules to produce an estimate. When estimation is mentioned, many adults think of rounding. However, as in mental computation, several strategies can be developed with children so they possess a repertoire of strategies from which to choose. A few of these will now be discussed.

Front-End Estimation The front-end strategy for estimation is a very basic yet powerful approach that can be used in a variety of situations. Two important things must be checked: (1) the leading, or front-end, digit in a number, and (2) the place value of those digits. To help students understand this strategy, Figure 9–8 shows a three-digit number hidden behind a sheet of paper on the board. Give students the opportunity to see one digit of their choosing. Some students choose the ones digit, but others choose the hundreds digit and find that this gives the most useful information. A few exercises such as this help students begin to grasp the power of the leading, or front-end, digits.

Figure 9–9 shows how the front-end digits are used to obtain an initial estimate. The unique advantage of the front-end strategy is that all of the numbers to be operated on are visible in the original problem. Thus students can reach an estimate quickly and easily. The strategy also encourages students to use number sense as they think about the computations. In the Classroom 9–5 encourages students to use the front-end digits to make a quick estimate. A front-end estimate provides a lower bound, and this initial estimate can be adjusted as needed by using the remaining digits.

Adjusting or Compensating Number sense has many dimensions, one of which is recognizing when something is a little more or a little less. As students use any estimation strategy it becomes natural to begin refining their initial estimate by making adjustments or compensating. For example: About how much will 4 items at $0.78 each cost?

One person might think: 4 × $1 but less than $4. Another person might think: 4 × $0.75 is $3 but more than $3.

In each case, the amount "less than $4" or "more than $3" reflects an adjustment or compensation that is made to the initial estimate.

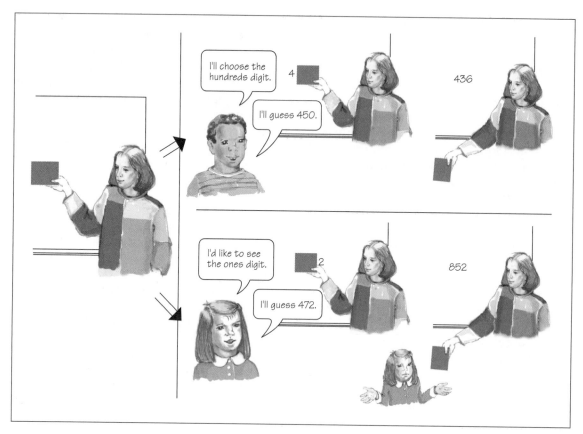

Figure 9–8 • **Illustrating the power of front-end estimation**

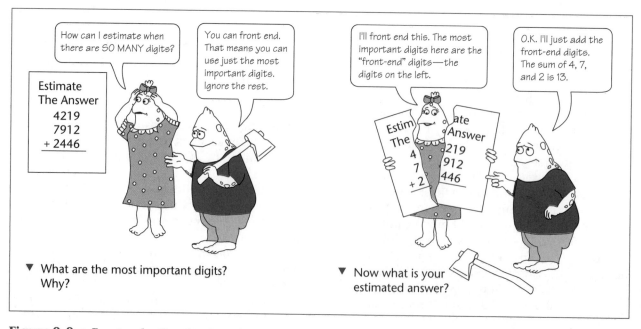

Figure 9–9 • **Front-end estimation in action**

Figure 9–10 • **Example of front-end estimation with adjustment**

Figure 9–10 illustrates how adjusting is accomplished. This process of adjustment or compensation cuts across all estimation strategies and all operations.

Compatible Numbers Compatible numbers, or friendly numbers, are easy to compute mentally and seem to go together naturally. Work with the ten-frame helps children recognize that 6 and 4 are compatible with 10. This experience extends naturally to help them recognize that 60 and 40 are compatible with 100. These compatibles aid the development of

other pairs, such as 65 and 35, that are also compatible with 100, and should be extended to other numbers. Figure 9–11 illustrates how compatible numbers can be used to make computations easier for a variety of different operations.

When the compatible numbers strategy is used, the numbers in the problem are rounded to numbers that are easier to work with. Figure 9–12 shows how the strategy works for division, with which it is particularly powerful. Given these problems, children

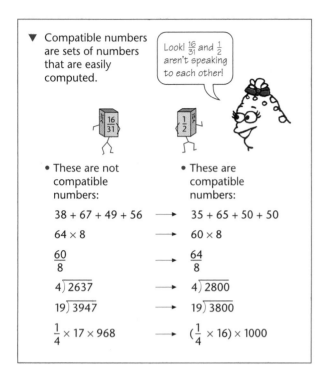

Figure 9–11 • **Examples of different compatible numbers**

need to be encouraged to think about why 7 and 2800 are compatible numbers for the problem. Asking students to pose possible "compatible numbers pairs" and asking them to tell why encourages thoughtful ideas and provides insight into their number sense. Consider some possible compatible pairs for

23)7029

23)6900   69 is divided evenly by 23, so 23 and 69 are compatible for division. Because both values are close to the original, the estimate of 300 is very close.

20)10000   10000 is divided evenly by 20. Although 20 and 10000 are compatible, 10000 is far removed from the original dividend—so the estimate of 500 will be very rough.

25)7500   75 is evenly divided by 25, so 75 and 25 are compatible. Both rounded values are close to the original values, so the estimate of 300 will be close.

Compatible numbers can be applied to all types of computations, and they are often used in addition. In the following example, the student first

used the front-end strategy and then compatible numbers to adjust the initial estimate:

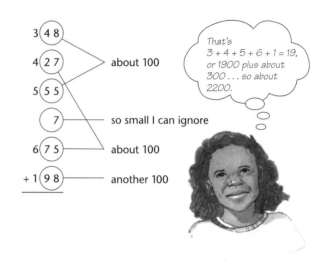

Flexible Rounding   Rounding to get easier numbers to work with was discussed in Chapter 7. Estimation also uses rounding to produce numbers that are easier to compute. Rounding in estimation is more sophisticated than front-end estimation because the numbers are changed or reformulated. However, rather than apply rigid rounding rules, the general premise for flexible rounding is to round to any numbers that are close but also easy to compute. Flexible rounding is appropriate for all operations with all types of numbers, but it is particularly well-suited to multiplication. Children should be adept at the process of rounding to compatible numbers. Figure 9–13 shows how students started with the same problem but rounded differently. Notice that each approach produced a different result, but each is a reasonable estimate. It is important for students to know they have the freedom to choose different estimation strategies, but they need to realize that different strategies will produce different estimates. Accepting a range of reasonable estimates, rather than a single best estimate, fosters number sense and encourages students to choose and use their own strategies.

Problems like the one shown in Figure 9–13 need to be accompanied by questions that go beyond those asking what the estimate is to those that encourage children to think about the process:

How have the numbers changed?

Why were these numbers changed?

The key to the effective use of rounding in estimation is to round to compatible numbers, which

Figure 9–12 • **Examples of the compatible numbers strategy for division**

involves substituting numbers that are close to the original numbers but are more manageable to compute mentally. Children should be encouraged to think of possible substitutions and to reason about

their choice from among them. The choices illustrated in the following example lead naturally to such questions as "Which pair would you choose to make the estimate?" and "Why?"

Figure 9–13 • **Example of flexible rounding and the different estimates that result**

Adjusting is often done to compensate for how the numbers were rounded, as in the following example in which an initial estimate is made by rounding:

Next, the student makes an adjustment to refine the initial estimate:

$$38 \times 47 = \left\{ \begin{array}{l} \text{a little} \\ \text{under} \\ 2000 \end{array} \right.$$

> It's gotta be less than 2000 because I rounded up on both numbers. 2000 is an overestimate.

Here are some other examples:

	Think	*Result*
42×61	$40 \times 60 = 2400$	A little more than 2400
39×78	$40 \times 80 = 3200$	A little less than 2400
27×32	$30 \times 30 = 900$	About 900

For the first two examples, the rounding procedure makes clear whether the result is an underestimate or an overestimate, but in the last example, it is not so obvious. Students must think about the numbers used to produce their estimate.

As students' mental computation skills progress, the rounding procedures they use to produce estimates reflect more flexibility. When estimating, people should always round to numbers that are easy for them to compute mentally. This means that traditional rounding rules (such as if the digit is more than 5, round the preceding digit up) are not necessarily followed, and common sense is the hallmark. It also means that different people may round the same numbers in a problem differently, depending on what is easiest to them, as was shown in Figure 9–13.

Clustering The *clustering,* or *averaging, strategy* uses a mean for an estimate. Whenever a group of numbers cluster around a common value, this two-step process is used:

1. Estimate the average value of the numbers.
2. Multiply by the number of values in the group.

Figure 9–14 gives a glimpse of this strategy in action. Questions such as the following can help give meaning to this strategy:

> What number do all the values cluster around?
>
> Why is the average estimated?
>
> Why is the estimated average multiplied by 6 (or by 5)?

Asking what the estimated total is for these and a range of similar problems helps children become adept at using this strategy.

Clustering is a limited strategy but a useful one. It is appropriate for estimating sums of groups of numbers quickly. A strength of this strategy is that it eliminates the mental tabulation of a long list of front-end digits or rounded numbers.

Choosing Estimation Strategies Estimation strategies take many different forms, often for the same problem. In fact, it is rare that a single strategy

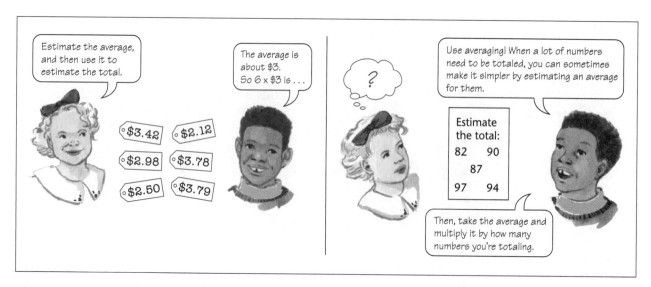

Figure 9–14 • **Examples of the clustering strategy for addition**

is used. Figure 9–15 illustrates how several different strategies might be applied to different situations. The choice of strategies depends on the situation, as well as on the numbers and operations involved. A challenge for us as teachers is to help our students become aware of the wide array of estimation strategies that exist and to help our students develop confidence in their ability to engage in estimation.

Among the guidelines we think are useful when developing computation estimation are these:

- Provide situations that encourage and reward computational estimation. For example, 78 + 83 should be computed mentally to produce an exact answer, but 78342 + 83289 is more likely to promote estimation. Thus, make sure the num-

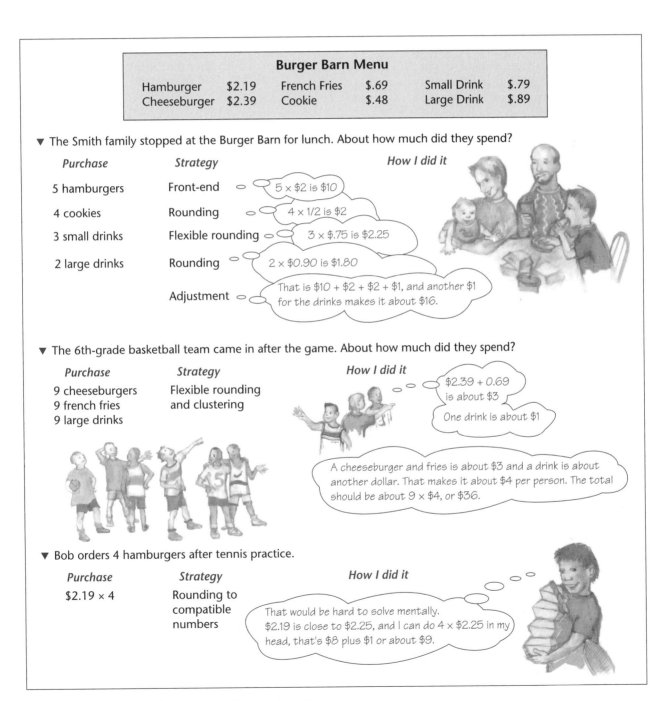

Figure 9–15 • Integrating computational estimation strategies

bers are messy enough so that students want to estimate, rather than use a different alternative.

- Check to learn if students are computing exact answers and then "rounding" to produce estimates. Research has documented the popularity of this technique (Sowder 1992), and unfortunately, these approaches often go undetected. Talking with students and observing their approaches to estimation provides checks to ensure that they are truly engaging in the process of estimating.

- Ask students to tell how their estimates were made. Research suggests that students often develop individual and unique approaches to computational estimation processes (Sowder 1992). By sharing them, students develop an appreciation of different estimation processes.

- Destroy the one-right-answer syndrome early. Help students realize that several different yet acceptable estimates might be made for the same problem. One way to do this is to invite students to identify acceptable intervals for good estimates. Their discussion will generally reveal different strategies and help everyone learn about other strategies. Such experiences help students become more comfortable with the notion that several different but correct estimates exist.

- Encourage students to think carefully about real-world applications where estimates are made. Critical thinking skills can be sharpened in deciding when to overestimate and underestimate. Figure 9–16 illustrates several situations to encourage such thinking.

A Glance at Where We've Been

As teachers we must help students develop confidence and skill in using computational alternatives. This should include ready access to and appropriate use of calculators. As basic facts are established, mental computation becomes an important tool for many computations. When the computations become too tedious to compute exact answers via mental computation, then estimation is a natural next step. Is the answer more than . . . Should it be less than . . . are questions encouraging estimation and number sense. When exact answers are too tedious to obtain mentally, calculators and written algorithms are the appropriate tools. However, in our judgment, care needs to be taken to develop confidence and proficiency with mental computation and estimation prior to introducing and practicing

---

Over or Under

1. Your car usually gets about 25 miles per gallon on the highway. Your gas tank is about one-quarter full and it is 100 miles to the next gas station. Is this a good time to over- or underestimate your gas mileage?

2. You are talking with a car dealer about buying a car, and you ask about the gas mileage. Do you think the car dealer will over- or underestimate the gas mileage of the car?

3. You have $20 to spend on groceries for a group picnic. As you place each item in the grocery cart, is this a good time to over- or underestimate the cost of each item?

4. You are forecasting the lava speed of an active volcano. As the lava is moving down the mountainside toward a town, a decision needs to be made when to evacuate the town. Should you over- or underestimate the speed of the lava?

5. Your plane is scheduled to leave at 4:00 and it usually takes about one hour to get to the airport. Should you over- or underestimate the time needed to get to the airport when deciding what time to leave?

Figure 9–16 • Examples of real-world situations in which under- or overestimations are needed

---

formal written algorithms. Such a plan will challenge each of us to reflect on the worth of different computational tools and strive to provide the balance of the instructional time that each deserves.

Things to Do: From What You've Read

1. What are some goals related to computation that involve computational tools?

2. How would you respond to the following statement by a parent? "Calculators should not be used in school, because if students use them, they will never have to think."

3. Do you think the proposal in Figure 9–2 regarding percent of instructional time devoted to developing computational alternatives applies to grades 2–6? If not, choose a grade level and decide how you think instructional time devoted to computation should be allocated. Be prepared to defend your proposal.

4. Distinguish between mental computation and estimation.

5. Several uses of the calculator as an instructional tool and a computational tool were discussed. Are these two approaches mutually exclusive? Explain and give an example to illustrate what you mean.

6. What do you think are the strongest reasons for encouraging and developing good mental computational skills?

7. A fifth-grader described this solution to 7 × 499 in her head: "I put the 499 on top and the 7 on bottom, then I get 3 and carry the 6 and 9 carry the 6 and 7 times 4 is 28 plus 6 is 34. . . ." Would you say this student was successfully doing mental computation? Explain why. Describe some other strategies that might be explored.

8. Discuss why it is important for students to develop a tolerance for an acceptable range of answers when doing computational estimation.

9. Tell why compensation and adjustment are an integral part of making estimates.

10. Why is the following not a good assignment? "I want you to estimate the answers to these problems, then compute the correct answers, and see how far off your estimate was from the correct answer."

11. Figure 9–3 shows a possible letter to parents about calculator use in second grade. Prepare a letter to sixth-grade parents telling them that calculators will be used in your class and can be used on homework. Briefly explain why you are allowing and encouraging calculator use.

12. Here is an actual quote from a fourth grader telling what she thinks her teacher wants:

I think she doesn't like us to use mental (computation) because she can't see the writing. And she doesn't like us to use the calculator a whole lot because then we'll get too used to it and we won't want to learn and stuff. . . . And she likes us to use written (computation) because she can see what we're doing, and if we're having problems she can see what we're doing wrong.

How would you respond to this student? Suppose you had an opportunity to talk with the student's teacher. What would you tell her teacher?

Things to Do: *Going Beyond This Book*

field Additional activities, suggestions, and questions are provided in *Teaching Elementary Mathematics: A Resource for Field Experiences.*

1. Keep a log of the computational tools (mental computation, estimation, calculator, written computation) that you use for one day. Estimate what percentage of your computations made use of each tool.

2. Read the article "Computation in the Elementary Curriculum: Shifting the Emphasis" by Reys and Reys. Do you agree or disagree with their proposal for change? Tell why.

3. Review one of the mental math books by Hope et al. (1987, 1988). Select a lesson and highlight the key ideas for your classmates.

4. Review one of the *Computation Estimation* books by Reys et al. (1987). Select a lesson and highlight the key ideas for your classmates.

5. Examine one of the Keystrokes books by Reys et al. (1980) or the CAMP-LA books. For the grade level of your choice, select an activity that illustrates a calculator activity you would like to use and tell why you chose the activity.

6. *field Do It Mentally.* Ask at least two students to compute 99+165 mentally. Ask them how they did it. Describe the strategies that were used.

7. *field About How Much?* Ask several people to estimate 29 × 24 and tell how they made their estimate. Describe their strategies and results. Did any of them use the strategies shown in Figure 9–13?

8. Examine the NCTM Yearbooks *Estimation and Mental Computation* (Schoen 1986) or *Calculators in Mathematics Education* (Fey 1992), for an article that you think will help you better develop computational alternatives with your students. Summarize this article and tell why you found it useful.

9. Select a standardized achievement test. Review the test and determine the attention given to assessing mental computation and computational estimation. Discuss the strengths and weakness of test items that you found addressing mental computation or estimation.

10. Check the article by Harries and Dobson (1996) or McIntosh et al. (1997) for a summary of different ways students do computations orally and on paper. Do you agree with the summary? Tell why.

11. *field* In the Classroom 9–1, 9–2, and 9–3 provide activities to check on student preferences for computing. Choose one of these activities to use with children in grades 2 to 5. Describe any surprises about how you thought students would do and how they actually did respond.

Selected References

CAMP-LA: *Activities Enhanced by Calculator Use.* Book 1, Grades K–2, Book 2, Grades 3–4; Book 3, Grades 5–6. Orange, Calif.: Cal State Fullerton Press, 1991.

Clayton, John C. "Encouraging Estimation." *Mathematics Teaching,* 157 (pp. 23–27), December 1996.

Cobb, P., and Merkel, G. "Thinking Strategies: Teaching Arithmetic Through Problem Solving." In *New Directions for Elementary School Mathematics* (eds. P. R. Trafton and A. P. Shulte). Reston, Va.: National Council of Teachers of Mathematics, 1989, pp. 70–81.

Fey, James. (ed.) *Calculators in Mathematics Education,* 1992 Yearbook of the National Council of Teachers of Mathematics. Reston, Va.: National Council of Teachers of Mathematics, 1992.

Harries, Tony, and Dobson, Alan. "Oral and Written Methods of Calculation." *Mathematics Teaching,* 154 (pp. 32–35), March 1996.

Hembree, Ray, and Dessart, Donald J. "Research on Calculators in Mathematics Education." In *Calculators in Mathematics Education,* 1992 Yearbook of the National Council of Teachers of Mathematics (ed. James Fey). Reston, Va.: National Council of Teachers of Mathematics, 1987, pp. 23–32.

Hope, Jack A.; Leutzinger, Larry; Reys, Barbara J.; and Reyes, Robert E. *Mental Math in the Primary Grades.* Palo Alto, Calif.: Dale Seymour Publications, 1988.

Hope, Jack A.; Reys, Barbara J.; and Reys, Robert E. *Mental Math in the Middle Grades.* Palo Alto, Calif.: Dale Seymour Publications, 1987.

Kamii, Constance; Lewis, Barbara A.; and Livingston, Sally Jones. "Primary Arithmetic: Children Inventing Their Own Procedures," *Arithmetic Teacher,* 41 (December 1993), 200–203.

McIntosh, Alistair; Nohda, Nobuhiko; Reys, Barbara J.; and Reys, Robert E. "Mental Computation Performance in Australia, Japan and the United States." *Educational Studies in Mathematics* 29 (1995), pp. 237–258.

McIntosh, Alistair; Reys, Robert E.; and Reys, Barbara J. "Mental Computation in the Middle Grades: The Importance of Thinking Strategies." *Teaching Mathematics in the Middle School,* 2(322–327), March-April, 1997.

National Council of Teachers of Mathematics. *Principles and Standards for School Mathematics.* Reston, Va.: NCTM, 2000.

National Research Council. *Everybody Counts: A Report to the Nation on the Future of Mathematics Education,* Washington, D.C.: National Academy Press, 1989.

Rathmell, Edward, and Trafton, Paul R. "Whole Number Computation." *Mathematics for the Young Child* (ed. Joseph N. Payne), Reston, Va.: NCTM, 1990, pp. 153–174.

Reys, R. E. "Computation versus Number Sense." *Mathematics Teaching in the Middle Grades,* 4(2), pp. 110–112, October 1998.

Reys, R. E.; Bestgen, B. J.; Coburn, T. G.; Schoen, H. L.; Shumway, R. J.; Wheatley, C. L.; Wheatley, G. H.; and White, A. L. *Keystrokes: Calculator Activities for Young Students* (Series). Palo Alto, Calif.: Creative Publications, 1980.

Reys, B. J., and Barger, R. "Mental Computation: Evaluation, Curriculum, and Instructional Issues from the United States Perspective." In *Computational Alternatives for the Twenty-First Century: Cross-Cultural Perspectives from Japan and the United States* (eds. R. E. Reys and N. Nohda). Reston, Va.: National Council of Teachers of Mathematics, 1994, pp. 31–47.

Reys, B., and Reys, R. "Computation in the Elementary Curriculum: Shifting the Emphasis." *Teaching Children Mathematics,* 5(4), pp. 236–241, December 1998.

Reys, R.; Reys, B.; McIntosh, A.; Emanuelsson, G.; Johansson, B.; and Yang, D. C. "Assessing Number Sense of Students in Australia, Sweden, Taiwan, and the United States." *School Science and Mathematics,* 99(2), pp. 61–70, (February), 1999.

Reys, R. E.; Reys, B. J.; Nohda, N.; and Emori, H. (1995). "Mental Computation Performance and Strategy Use of Japanese Students in Grades 2, 4, 6, and 8." *Journal for Research in Mathematics Education,* 26(4), pp. 304–326.

Reys, B. J.; Reys, R. E.; and Hope, J. A. "Mental Computation: A Snapshot of Second, Fifth, and Seventh Grade Student Performance." *School Science and Mathematics,* 93 (1993) pp. 306–315.

Reys, R. E., and Yang, D. C. "Relationship between Computational Performance and Number Sense among Sixth and Eighth Grade Students in Taiwan." *Journal for Research in Mathematics Education,* 29 (2) (March 1998), pp. 225–237.

Schoen, Harold (ed.) *Estimation and Mental Computation,* 1986 Yearbook of the National Council of Teachers of Mathematics. Reston, Va.: National Council of Teachers of Mathematics, 1986.

Shigematsu, K.; Iwasaki, H.; and Koyama, M. "Mental Computation: Evaluation, Curriculum, and Instructional Issues from the United States Perspective." In *Computational Alternatives for the Twenty-First Century: Cross Cultural Perspectives from Japan and the United States* (eds. R. E. Reys and J. Nohda). Reston, Va.: National Council of Teachers of Mathematics, 1994, pp. 19–30.

Sowder, J. T. "Estimation and Related Topics." In *Handbook for Research on Mathematics Teaching and Learning* (ed. D. Grouws). New York: Macmillan, 1992, pp. 371–389.

Sowder, J. T., and Kelin, J. "Number Sense and Related Topics." In *Research Ideas for the Classroom: Middle School Mathematics* (ed. D. T. Owns). New York: Macmillan, 1992, pp. 41–57.

Operations: Standard and Alternative Algorithms

10

Snapshot of a Lesson

On the chalkboard, the teacher has drawn a problem:

136 boxes in all · Put 8 boxes in each car · How many boxcars are needed?

TEACHER: As you can see, I've put a problem on the board. Can your group solve it using the materials in front of you? [Each group has a different type of material.] After you've had a chance to try, we'll share the ways we attacked it.

After seven or eight minutes, all the groups are ready to tell how they solved the problem:

> We first thought about using 10 boxcars, which would hold 80 boxes. That still leaves 56 boxes. But 7 X 8 = 56. So with 7 more cars, we can load all the boxes. We needed 17 boxcars altogether.

> We changed 136 to 13 tens and 6 ones, because we couldn't work well with 1 hundred. We took 8 from each one of the tens in our minds, but that got too mixed up. So we said, 10 boxcars would hold 80 boxes — that's 8 tens. 5 tens left. 5 more boxcars would hold 40 boxes. There's 1 ten and 6 ones left. That's 2 more eights. So you'd need 10 + 5 + 2 boxcars.

> We laid out 136 cubes, and then separated them into groups of 8.

H	T	O

> We keyed 8 on the calculator, then the division sign, then 136 — but the answer was less than 1! So we knew we'd used the wrong order. We had to key 136, then the division sign, then 8 — 136 divided by 8.

TEACHER: Good work! You all found reasonable ways to figure how many boxcars would be needed. Jenna's group recognized this as a division problem: 136 divided by 8. Now, how would you write that problem using math symbols?

Several children write each of these formats:

$$136 \div 8 \qquad \frac{136}{8} \qquad 8\overline{)136}$$

TEACHER: Yes, all show 136 divided by 8. We will use the third way when we work with paper and pencil. We know now that the answer is 17—will you put the answer in place, Karen?

Karen writes:

$$8\overline{)136}^{\,17}$$

Several other children say "No!" They are asked why.

CHILDREN: The answer has 1 ten and 7 ones, so it must be written in those places.

TEACHER: Good. Enrique, I noticed that you had a way of recording your thinking on your paper. Will you explain what you wrote?

We know there are at least 10 eights in 136, because 10 × 8 = 80. When I subtract, there are 56 left. 56 ÷ 8 is 7.

TEACHER: Great! Does what Enrique wrote make sense to you, Sarah? Tell us why. What about you, Jacob? Can you use your own words to explain what Enrique wrote? Okay. Now let's try: 259 ÷ 6. See if you can find an answer and also write down your thinking so others can understand it.

Introduction

For hundreds of years, computational skill with paper-and-pencil procedures, called *algorithms,* has been viewed as an essential component of children's mathematical achievement. The teaching of computation has become more exciting in the past few years. Instead of teachers merely presenting a stream of algorithms, showing children just what to do, step by step by step, we've begun to focus more attention on what children construct or develop for themselves. Computation has become a problem-solving process, one in which children are encouraged to reason their way to answers, rather than merely memorizing procedures that the teacher says are correct.

This change also means that children can explore alternative algorithms. The algorithms that teachers usually present have been refined over the centuries. They are highly efficient, but they do not necessarily reflect the way children think as they compute. We still want accuracy and efficiency, but the latter is of lesser importance. The focus is on reasoning and thinking.

Although calculators are readily available to relieve the burden of computation, the ability to use algorithms is still considered essential. The NCTM's *Principles and Standards for School Mathematics* (2000) stresses the need for children to be able to choose computational techniques that are appropriate for problems at hand and also to determine whether the answers they obtain are reasonable. To develop such an enhanced ability, revisions in the teaching of computation include the following:

- Fostering a solid understanding of and proficiency with simple calculations
- Abandoning the teaching of tedious calculations using paper-and-pencil algorithms in favor of exploring more mathematics
- Fostering the use of a wide variety of computation and estimation techniques—ranging from quick mental calculation to those using computers—suited to different mathematical settings
- Developing the skills necessary to use appropriate technology and then translating computed results to the problem setting
- Providing students with ways to check the reasonableness of computations (number and algorithmic sense, estimation skills).

Many parents and some teachers have worried that students will become so dependent on calculators that they will forget how to compute. This concern is not supported by research. Hembree and Dessart (1986) reported from an analysis of a large number of research studies that the use of "calculators in concert with traditional instruction . . . can improve the average student's basic skills with paper and pencil, both in basic operations and in problem solving" (p. 96).

Over the years, we have learned much about teaching computation. Key ideas that help to shape the role of computational skills in the curriculum, along with the belief that children are and must be actively involved in constructing their own mathematical learning, will guide our discussion. Of central importance is the need to teach children to choose an appropriate calculation procedure, depending primarily on whether an exact or approximate answer is needed.

Role of Materials in Learning Algorithms

The use of manipulative materials in developing understanding of the algorithms is essential. In the Snapshot Lesson that opened this chapter, the use of materials was the basis on which work with symbols was formed. Materials form a bridge between the real-life problem situation and the abstract algorithm, helping to forge the recognition that what is written down represents real objects and actions. Children must be given sufficient time to handle the materials and make the transition to pictures and symbols (Thompson 1991). Unifix cubes, base-ten blocks, rods, Popsicle sticks, beansticks and loose beans, buttons, and myriad other materials, either derived from the problem setting or representative of that setting, help children to construct understanding of when and how an algorithm works.

Importance of Place-Value Ideas

Each of the algorithms for whole-number computation is based on place-value ideas, many of which were discussed in Chapter 7. Children need to have a firm understanding of these ideas before they can work effectively with the algorithms. Linking place-value ideas directly with renaming ideas is a necessary step as the algorithms for each operation are explored and developed. Providing numerous trading activities is accompanied by renaming activities.

Regroup 138 ones into tens and ones:

138 is _____ tens _____ ones

Show 46 with bundles of tens and ones:

46 is _____ tens _____ ones

Rename: 7 tens 16 ones = 8 tens _____ ones
35 is 2 tens _____ ones

Rename 5 tens 3 ones to show more ones:

Tens	Ones
5	3

T	O
4 5̶	13 3̶

Write 6 tens 5 ones in five different ways.

Write 37 in all the different ways you can.

Don't be surprised at the many different ideas that arise in response to this last activity. Students frequently can handle challenges that you thought were "beyond them."

Developing the algorithms that work with multidigit numbers has to evolve from students' understanding of place value, which

> . . . involves building connections between key ideas of place value—such as quantifying sets of objects by grouping by ten and treating the groups as units—and using the structure of the written notation to capture this information about groupings. (Wearne and Hiebert 1994, p. 273)

ADDITION

You've just walked into a first-grade classroom. After a brief activity to review renaming (for example, renaming 52 as 5 tens 2 ones and also as 4 tens and 12 ones, and so on), a problem is posed to the children:

> Jill and Jeff both collected baseball cards. Jill had 27 cards and Jeff had 35. How many did they have together?

To focus attention on the reasonableness of the answers they will find, you might begin with such questions as

> Would they have more than 50 cards? Why do you think so?
>
> More than 100 cards? Why do you think so?

Then, actual cards or slips of paper to represent cards could be given to each group of four or five children, with the direction to figure out an answer, show it on paper, and be ready to tell why it is right. Instead of providing them with cards, the students might simply be encouraged to use whatever aids they are accustomed to using for math problem solving, such as tiles, base-ten blocks, abacus, or drawing pictures. At other times, instead of working in groups the children might be asked to solve the problem individually and to write an explanation of what they did. They need time and repeated opportunities to explore and invent strategies and to make connections between different ways of thinking about or doing the same process. After each group or individual has reached an answer, the whole class may meet to share the ways they solved the problem. The teacher may record on the board the essence of each explanation.

- Group 1 counted out 27 cards and counted out 35 cards, and then counted all the cards together, one by one:

$$27 + 35 = 62$$

- Group 2 made 2 piles of ten cards, with 7 extras and 3 piles of ten cards, with 5 extras:

$$\begin{array}{r} 2 \text{ tens} + 7 \\ + 3 \text{ tens} + 5 \\ \hline 5 \text{ tens} + 12, \end{array}$$ which is renamed as 6 tens + 2, or 62

- Group 3 recognized that 20 and 30 make 50, and 7 and 5 make 12:

$$\begin{array}{r} 20 + 7 \\ + 30 + 5 \\ \hline 50 + 12, \text{ or } 62 \end{array}$$

- Group 4 relied on what Kim's older brother had shown her, first adding 5 + 7, to get 12, writing the 2 ones and "carrying 1" ten, then adding it to 2 tens and 3 tens to get 6 tens, or 62 altogether. The teacher showed another way to record this way of thinking about the problem.

$$\begin{array}{r} \overset{1}{2}7 \\ + 35 \\ \hline 62 \end{array} \qquad \begin{array}{r} 27 \\ + 35 \\ \hline 12 \\ 50 \\ \hline 62 \end{array}$$

- Group 5 did almost the same thing, but because they thought about adding 20 + 30 before adding 7 and 5, the teacher proposed recording their work a little differently:

$$\begin{array}{r} 27 \\ + 35 \\ \hline 50 \\ 12 \\ \hline 62 \end{array}$$

- Group 6 decided to work with a multiple of ten that is easier to think about, and then compensated. They checked their answer by doing the problem a different way too!

$$\begin{array}{r} 27 + 3 = 30 \\ + 35 - 3 = 32 \\ \hline 62 \end{array} \qquad \begin{array}{r} 27 - 5 = 22 \\ + 35 + 5 = 40 \\ \hline 62 \end{array}$$

- Group 7 added 27 + 5 = 32, and then 32 + 30 = 62. Some of the students in the class pointed out that you could also think 27 + 30 = 57, and then 57 + 5 = 62.

Everyone was sure they were right and could tell why—and they were sure that the other groups were right, too! Is 62 correct just because it is the answer every group reached? No! retorted a number of children. It is a reasonable answer because 27 is almost 30, and 35 more would make it 65, but 27 is 3 less than 30, so 62 is right. Note that some of the students worked from left to right, as research has indicated children frequently do when constructing their own algorithms (Kamii et al. 1993). Not all used the manipulative materials, but those who did were able to describe or write an algorithm that modeled what they had done with the materials. Or they used procedures that they had "invented" outside of school.

Perhaps it has occurred to you that some of the procedures the children used were as plausible for mental computation as for paper-and-pencil computation. We want children to recognize this, too, as well as that much addition involving one- and two-digit numbers can and should be done mentally. Lots of activities with renaming have given these children a good base from which to tackle addition algorithms. Note that only the group that relied on what Kim's brother had told them came up with the "standard" algorithm:

$$\begin{array}{r} \overset{1}{2}7 \\ + 35 \\ \hline 62 \end{array}$$

Think
7 + 5 = 12
Write 2 in the ones column and 1 in the tens column.
2 + 3 + 1 = 6 tens

That most students did not use the standard algorithm should not surprise us. That algorithm is the result of centuries of refinement. It is commonly used because it is efficient (requires less writing than some other algorithms), but it is also less obvious. Someone probably needs to tell you about placing the one ten from 12 in the tens column. When students attempt to use the standard algorithm without understanding why it works, they may be more prone to errors than when they do addition in ways that intuitively make sense to them. As groups share their different ways of working, children learn from each other. At some point, the teacher will probably want to share his or her way (the standard algorithm)—noting that it is shorter than some of theirs and that this is probably the way that parents and other adults learned to add. The algorithm used by group 5 is very similar to the standard algorithm but less obscure because all the partial sums are shown separately, so there is less chance for errors with regrouping. As group 5 used it, they added from left to right (tens first, then ones), which is more natural than working right to left. But this same partial-sum algorithm works equally well starting with ones, then tens, and so on (as the teacher showed, for group 4). The partial-sum algorithm can be used as an alternative algorithm for addition (an end-goal for students) or it can be useful as a transitional algorithm (intermediate step on the way to learning the standard algorithm). Ideally, however, children should be encouraged to work with the procedure they find easiest to understand. There is no reason why all children should end up using the same algorithm.

The next problem the teacher posed to the children involved the addition of 13 and 54. Up until recently, teachers might have introduced this problem, which does not require regrouping (carrying), far earlier than the one involving 27 and 35, which does involve regrouping. We have come to realize, however, that this type of artificial control of problem situations leads students to misconceptions about the operation and the algorithm. It is more realistic and better pedagogically for them to work, from the outset, on addition computations stemming from problems that involve both regrouping and no regrouping.

The addition of

$$\begin{array}{c} 437 \\ +\ 25 \end{array} \quad \text{or} \quad \begin{array}{c} 437 \\ +521 \end{array} \quad \text{or} \quad \begin{array}{c} 254 \\ +283 \end{array} \quad \text{or} \quad \begin{array}{c} 672 \\ +188 \end{array}$$

is simply an extension of the regrouping procedure to the hundreds place. We want children to have enough experience with numbers with more than two digits so they realize that there are no hidden difficulties; if they had no calculators, they could do the computation. But most practice will focus on two-digit numbers, with which we do want them to become proficient.

Adding multiples of 10, 100, and so on is another simpler case, and it is an important skill for students to develop, for use both in mental computation and estimation and as a building block in performing written computations:

$$\begin{array}{c} 4 \\ +\ 2 \end{array} \qquad \begin{array}{c} 40 \\ +\ 20 \end{array} \qquad \begin{array}{c} 400 \\ +\ 200 \end{array}$$

As children work with addition (as well as the other operations), they should be encouraged to estimate in order to ascertain whether the answer they reach is approximately correct. Use of *compatible numbers*—numbers that are easy to compute mentally—is a powerful estimation strategy. Some problem-solving activities to practice mental computation and sharpen estimation skills, as well as deepen understanding of addition algorithms, are found on In the Classroom 10–1.

Column Addition

Column addition with three or more one-digit addends is often introduced after some of the basic addition facts are learned, so it may be used to provide varied practice. One new skill is required—adding an unseen addend. In this example, the 4 resulting from the addition of 3 + 1 must be added mentally to 2:

Think

$$\left.\begin{array}{r} 3 \\ 1 \end{array}\right\} \quad 3 + 1 = 4$$
$$\underline{+2} \quad\ \ 4 + 2 = 6$$

As with other topics, column addition is introduced through a problem situation:

Sasha bought a lollipop for 3¢, a jellybean for 1¢, and a gumdrop for 2¢. How much did he spend?

The children can model the situation using manipulative materials, flannelboard objects, or drawings:

3¢

1¢

+ 2¢

In The Classroom 10–1

Starters

Objective: Using compatible numbers to develop mental computation and estimation skills involving addition.

▼ Find each missing digit:

$$
\begin{array}{cccc}
52 & 29 & \square 8 & 452 \\
+\,16 & +\,36 & +\,21 & +\,\square 7 \\
\hline
6\square & \square 5 & 79 & 489
\end{array}
$$

▼ Use only the digits given in the cloud to make a problem with the sum shown:

$$
\begin{array}{c}
4\ \ 4 \\
+\,4\ \ 6 \\
\hline
9\ \ 0
\end{array}
\quad (4, 6)
\qquad
\begin{array}{c}
-\ \ - \\
+\,\_\ \ \_ \\
\hline
8\ \ 8
\end{array}
\quad (3, 5)
\qquad
\begin{array}{c}
-\ \ - \\
+\,\_\ \ \_ \\
\hline
7\ \ 0
\end{array}
\quad (7, 3)
$$

▼ Use 2, 4, 6, and 8 for these problems:

• Use each digit once to make the smallest sum possible.

$$
\begin{array}{c}
\square\,\square \\
+\,\square\,\square
\end{array}
$$

• Use each digit once to make the largest sum possible.

$$
\begin{array}{c}
\square\,\square \\
+\,\square\,\square
\end{array}
$$

• Use each digit once to make a sum as near 100 as possible.

$$
\begin{array}{c}
\square\,\square \\
+\,\square\,\square
\end{array}
$$

▼ Use only these numbers:

| 24 | 40 | 22 | 15 | 31 | 14 |

• Name two numbers whose sum is 64. _____

• Name two numbers whose sum is more than 70. _____

• Name two numbers whose sum ends in 8. _____

• Name three numbers whose sum is 93. _____

The materials or pictures help the children to bridge from the situation to the solution with symbols.

Is it better to teach children to add down, to add up, or to group numbers that add to 10 (using the associative property)?

Research has indicated that adding either up or down (and using the opposite to check) is better than grouping (Wheatley and Wheatley 1978). Fewer errors of omitting numbers or using a number more than once are likely to occur. "Be consistent" is the best rule.

Higher-Decade Addition

Combinations such as 17 + 4 or 47 + 8 or 3 + 28, called *higher-decade combinations,* are used in a strategy sometimes referred to as "adding by endings." Note that the two-digit number may come either before or after the one-digit number.

The need for higher-decade addition arises in many real-life problems; for instance, adding 6¢ tax to a purchase of 89¢. The skill is also necessary in column addition and in multiplication. The strategy of counting on will probably occur to some children, and it is clearly one way of solving this type of problem, but not necessarily the most efficient way. In the Classroom 10–2 focuses attention on the relationship of 9 + 5, 19 + 5, 29 + 5, and so on. As a result of this activity, we want children to realize the following:

• In each example, the sum has a 4 in the ones place because 9 + 5 = 14, and the tens place has 1 more ten.

• The sum of 9 + 5 is more than 10, so the sum of 19 + 5 is more than 20, and the sum of 29 + 5 is more than 30.

• For 59 + 5, there is a 4 in the ones place and 6 (5 + 1) in the tens place.

Children need to learn to perform such additions automatically, without adding ones and then

In The Classroom 10–2

Look for Patterns

Objective: Using observed patterns to develop mental computation skills with addition.

▼ Complete the sums in these addition problems:

$$3 + 6 = 9$$
$$13 + 6 = 19$$
$$23 + 6 = 29$$
$$53 + 6 = \boxed{}$$
$$83 + 6 = \boxed{}$$

Find a pattern in the answers!

▼ How does 4 + 8 help you to add 14 + 8?

4	14
+ 8	+ 8
12	22

▼ Your turn:

9	19	29	39	79	89
+ 5	+ 5	+ 5	+ 5	+ 5	+ 5

7	17	27	37	47	87
+ 3	+ 3	+ 3	+ 3	+ 3	+ 3

tens as they do with examples such as 27 + 32 and without always counting on. Children who have already developed good number sense and facility with basic-fact addition strategies (such as those described in Chapter 8) should have little difficulty thinking through higher-decade addition problems.

Looking for patterns such as those in In the Classroom 10–2, and explicitly discussing them with classmates and with the teacher not only encourages mental computation but also greatly increases the skill of higher-decade addition.

SUBTRACTION

Like addition, subtraction of multidigit numbers requires knowledge of basic facts and of place value.

The standard subtraction algorithm taught in the United States for the past 50 or 60 years is the *decomposition algorithm*. It involves a logical process of "decomposing" or renaming the sum (the number you are subtracting from). In the following example, 9 tens and 1 one is renamed as 8 tens and 11 ones:

Think

$$\begin{array}{r} \overset{8}{\cancel{9}}\overset{1}{1} \\ -24 \\ \hline 67 \end{array}$$

11 – 4 = 7 ones
8 tens – 2 tens = 6 tens

Before the decomposition algorithm gained prominence in this country, the *equal-additions algorithm* was taught. The equal-additions algorithm is still taught and used in many other countries around the world (Ron 1998). If you have children in your classroom whose parents were educated outside the United States—particularly in Europe or in South America—you may find that some confusion results when those parents attempt to help their children with computations. It helps if you, as the teacher, are well aware of the existence and validity of alternative algorithms. Asking students to explain their methods can help you uncover the reasons for errors that may arise if students confuse the steps from different algorithms.

In the equal-additions subtraction algorithm, both the sum and the known addend (the number you are subtracting) are renamed. In this example, ten is added to each number involved in the subtraction: here 10 ones have been added to the sum (91) and 1 ten has been added to the known addend (24):

Think

$$\begin{array}{r} 9\overset{1}{1} \\ -\overset{3}{2}4 \\ \hline 67 \end{array}$$

11 – 4 = 7 ones
9 tens – 3 tens = 6 tens

This algorithm works because the difference between the numbers (91 and 24) remains the same after both have been increased by the same amount [that is, 91 – 24 = (91 + 10) – (24 + 10)]. It may help to picture a number line. The distance between 91 and 24 on the number line is what we are finding when we subtract. If we move both numbers up the number line the same amount (10), the distance between them remains the same. The reason for adding 10 to each number (but adding it in different forms) is to make the subtraction possible without any "borrowing" or "regrouping." Although this algorithm may seem strange to many Americans, people who have learned to subtract this way generally find it easy and natural to use. What is important is that individuals understand *what* they are doing and *why* when they learn an algorithm. Research has confirmed that both the decomposition algorithm and the equal-additions algorithm are effective in terms of speed and accuracy when taught meaningfully (Brownell 1947), with a problem setting, manipulative materials, and clear rationale.

Children often quite naturally develop different algorithms for subtraction, just as they do for addition. They may try to work from left to right, and at this point some confusion may begin. But, if they think carefully about the numbers, they may construct alternatives such as the following:

$$
\begin{array}{r}
74 \\
-58 \\
\hline
20 \\
-4 \\
\hline
16
\end{array}
$$

or

$$
\begin{array}{r}
70 + 4 \\
-50 - 8 \\
\hline
20 - 4 = 16
\end{array}
$$

or

$$
\begin{array}{r}74\\-58\end{array} \rightarrow \begin{array}{r}58\\+\\\hline74\end{array} \rightarrow \begin{array}{r}\overset{1}{5}8\\+6\\\hline74\end{array} \rightarrow \begin{array}{r}\overset{1}{5}8\\+16\\\hline74\end{array} \rightarrow \begin{array}{r}74\\-58\\\hline16\end{array}
$$

To learn to use algorithms with understanding, children need to connect the steps that are used to solve a problem with manipulatives to the steps in the symbolic solution of the algorithm. Questions that encourage children to focus on the connections between manipulatives and symbols are very important. Consider the following example using a problem posed by Rathmell and Trafton (1990, p. 168):

There were 61 children who did not sign up for hot lunch. Of these, 22 went home for lunch. The rest brought a cold lunch. How many brought a cold lunch?

What are we trying to find? (How many brought cold lunch?)

Do you think it will be more or less than 60? (Less, because there are 61 children who didn't have hot lunch, but some of those went home for lunch.)

How many did not sign up for hot lunch? (61)

How many went home? (22)

How can we show this? (Use cubes to model 61, then separate out 22 cubes.)

Let's assume we want to subtract off the ones first.

Are there enough ones to subtract 2 ones? (No.)

How can we get more ones? (We can trade a stick of tens.)

If we trade in a 10 for ones, how many ones do we get? (10)

How many ones are there now? (11) And how many tens? (5)

How much is 5 tens and 11 ones? (61)

Now are there enough ones to subtract 2? (Yes, we have 11 ones. 11 is more than 2.)

What is 11 – 2? (9)

Now what do we subtract? (the tens)

What is 5 tens minus 2 tens? (3 tens)

So, if we have 9 ones and 3 tens, how many children are eating a cold lunch? (39)

Does this answer make sense? Why? (Yes, 39 makes sense because it is close to 40. There were about 60 kids who didn't have hot lunch. There were about 20 kids who went home. 60 – 20 = 40. So there should be about 40 kids who brought cold lunch. Because 39 is close to 40, it makes sense.)

Experiences with regrouping from tens to hundreds or in both places are also helpful. Lesson Idea 10–1 (Race-to-a-Flat and Give-Away-a-Flat) describes games played with base-ten blocks that can help de-

Lesson Idea 10–1

Race-to-a-Flat

Number of Players: 3–5

Materials: Base-10 blocks, place-value mat (full-sized paper divided into three columns) for each player, and one pair of dice

Place-Value Mat

Flats	Longs	Units

Before the Game Begins: Choose one player to be the base-10 "banker."

How to Play: Players take turns rolling the dice, adding the numbers on the tops of the two dice, and then asking the banker for that number of units. For example, if you roll a 4 and a 5 as shown on the dice, ask for 9 units.

Place the pieces on your place-value mat. You may never have ten or more pieces in any portion of your place-value mat. Whenever you can, you must trade units for a long (or longs for a flat). When all the trading is complete, it is the next player's turn to roll the dice, collect units, and trade pieces. The first player to trade up to a flat is the winner.

Give-Away-a-Flat

Number of Players: 3–5

Materials: Base-10 blocks, place-value mat for each player, and one pair of dice.

Before the Game Begins: Choose one player to be the base-10 "banker." Banker distributes one flat to each player who places it in the flats column on her or his place-value mat.

How to Play: Players take turns rolling the dice, finding the sum of the numbers on the tops of the two dice, and *giving away* that number of units to the banker. Clearly, trades will have to be made during each player's first turn and possibly again during subsequent turns. The first player to return all of her or his base-10 pieces to the banker is the winner.

Questions for Give-Away-a-Flat
1. Is it possible to give away one long with one roll of the dice?
2. Is it possible to give away two longs with one roll of the dice?
3. Can you win the game with one roll of the dice?
4. What is the fewest number of rolls required to give away all of the pieces?
5. What is the most number of rolls required to give away all of the pieces?

---

velop students' understanding of regrouping for addition or subtraction.

Zeros in the Sum

The presence of zeros in the sum demands special attention. In this example with zero in the ones place only, 50 is renamed as 4 tens and 10 ones:

$$\begin{array}{r} {\scriptstyle 4\ 10} \\ 8\cancel{5}\cancel{0} \\ -287 \\ \hline \end{array}$$

Zero in the tens place is slightly more difficult, especially when regrouping in the ones place is also necessary. Two ways to approach the regrouping (using either one step or two steps) are shown in Figure 10–1.

A larger difficulty lies with numbers having more than one zero. One alternative is multiple renaming, renaming from hundreds to tens, then renaming again from tens to ones:

$$\begin{array}{cccc} & & {\scriptstyle 4\ 10} & {\scriptstyle 9\ 10} \\ & & & {\scriptstyle 4\cancel{1}0} \\ 500 & \cancel{5}00 & \cancel{5}00 & \cancel{5}\cancel{0}0 \\ -257 & -257 & -257 & -257 \\ \hline & & & 243 \end{array}$$

If students learn a procedure like this rotely, without understanding, it is quite likely that they may make errors but be unable to notice or correct them. Place-value experiences are important in preparing children to cope with these problems. They must clearly understand that 500 can be renamed as 4 hundreds and 10 tens, or as 4 hundreds, 9 tens, and 10 ones. They will then find it easier to recognize the need for multiple regrouping when they see multiple zeros and will be able to do all the renaming at once:

$$
\begin{array}{r}
500 \\
-283
\end{array}
\qquad
\begin{array}{r}
\overset{4\ 9}{\cancel{500}} \\
-283
\end{array}
\qquad 500 = 4 \text{ hundreds, 9 tens, 10 ones}
$$

Alternatively, if they understand that 500 can be thought of as 50 tens, they can think of renaming it directly as 49 tens and 10 ones. In Figure 10–1, for

the problem 207 – 39, 207 can be renamed as 19 tens and 17 ones in one step. However, the need to do this is not readily recognizable to all children; those who need to do the double renaming should be allowed to do so.

MULTIPLICATION

Before children tackle the multiplication algorithms, they must have a firm grasp on place value, expanded notation, and the distributive property, as well as the basic facts of multiplication. As with the other operations, it is wise to review each of these prerequisites before beginning work with the multiplication algorithms. And it is also wise to develop situations or problems for which children compute mentally, without concern for the paper-and-pencil forms.

Multiplication with One-Digit Multipliers

Children should be encouraged to talk about their thinking, as the meaning of multiplication is reinforced with materials:

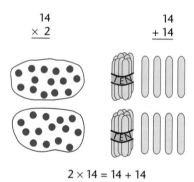

$$2 \times 14 = 14 + 14$$

When we look at the models above, we see not only that 14 can be represented by one bundle of tens and 4 ones, but also that 2×14 can be represented by *two* bundles of tens and *two* groups of 4 ones. Thus, use of the distributive property is pointed out:

$$2 \times 14 = 2 \times (10 + 4) = (2 \times 10) + (2 \times 4)$$
$$= 20 + 8 = 28$$

Arrays are also used to develop meaning and visual images of multiplication:

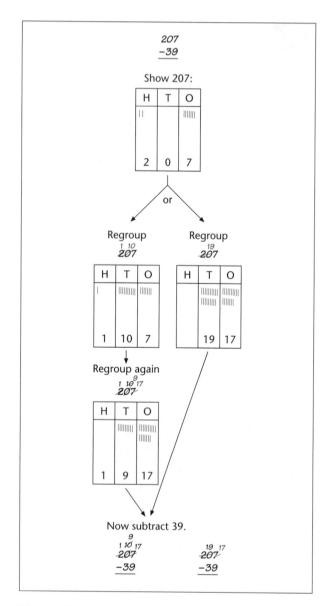

Figure 10–1 • Subtraction model

Place-value ideas are noted along with materials:

T	O
/ 1	4 ////
/ 1	4 ////
2	8

T	O
1	4
×	2
2	8

Expanded algorithms can be developed or constructed by the children easily:

$$\begin{array}{r} 14 \\ \times\ 2 \end{array}$$

$$\begin{array}{r} 1\ \text{ten}\quad 4\ \text{ones} \\ \times\qquad 2 \\ \hline 2\ \text{tens}\ 8\ \text{ones} \end{array}$$

$$\begin{array}{r} 14 \\ \times\ 2 \\ \hline 8 \\ +20 \\ \hline 28 \end{array}$$

$$\begin{array}{r} 2 \times 10 = 20 \\ 2 \times\ 4 =\ \ 8 \\ \hline 20 +\ 8 = 28 \end{array}$$

The partial-products algorithm for multiplication (Figure 10–2) is one form of expanded algorithm, where all the individual products produced by the multiplication are recorded on separate lines, then summed. Just as the partial-sums algorithm is a useful alternative or transitional algorithm for addition, the partial-products algorithm can be very useful for multiplication.

The traditional American multiplication algorithm is a streamlined version of the partial-products algorithm. In the traditional algorithm, some of the partial products are added mentally before we write down their sum. In some cases this traditional method is more efficient (because it requires less writing), but it is not as easy to understand step-by-step and it may be more susceptible to error (because steps are combined and done mentally).

The distributive property helps children understand the relationship between the partial-products algorithm and the traditional algorithm (see Figure 10–2). Lesson Idea 10–2 illustrates using the distributive property in mental computation, a skill that is quite useful for use in estimation as well. The calculator also promotes a focus on estimation, while decreasing the amount of time spent on written computations. Some activities with that focus are found on In the Classroom 10–3.

Multiplication with Two-Digit Multipliers

As children work with two-digit multipliers, the use of manipulative materials becomes cumbersome. Arrays or grids provide one means of bridging the gap from concrete materials to symbols and illustrating, once again, why the partial-products algorithm makes sense. As shown in Figure 10–3, a grid can also provide entirely new ways of viewing and writing about a multiplication example. Some other materials are used to tie the work to previously learned procedures, but increasingly the emphasis shifts to working with symbols, as shown in Figure 10–4. This approach is possible because of the earlier

$$\begin{array}{r} 57 \\ \times\ 3 \\ \hline 21 \\ +150 \\ \hline 171 \end{array}\quad \begin{array}{l} (3 \times 7) \\ (3 \times 50) \end{array}$$

$$3 \times 57 = (3 \times 50) + (3 \times 7)$$

$$\begin{array}{r} 452 \\ \times\ 7 \\ \hline 14 \\ 350 \\ +2800 \\ \hline 3164 \end{array}\quad \begin{array}{l} (7 \times 2) \\ (7 \times 50) \\ (7 \times 400) \end{array}$$

$$7 \times 452 = (7 \times 400) + (7 \times 50) + (7 \times 2)$$

Traditional

$$\begin{array}{r} 372 \\ \times\ 28 \\ \hline 2976 \\ 744 \\ \hline 10416 \end{array}$$

Partial Products

$$\begin{array}{r} 372 \\ \times\ 28 \\ \hline 16 \\ 560 \\ 2400 \\ 40 \\ 1400 \\ 6000 \\ \hline 10416 \end{array}\quad \begin{array}{l} (8 \times 2) \\ (8 \times 70) \\ (8 \times 300) \\ (20 \times 2) \\ (20 \times 70) \\ (20 \times 300) \end{array}$$

Figure 10–2 • The partial products algorithm

Lesson Idea 10–2

Use What You Know!

▼ Rename the larger factor and use the distributive property to make the multiplication easier to do in your head.

1. $7 \times 104 =$ __728__

   Think
   $7 \times (100 + 4)$
   $= (7 \times 100) + (7 \times 4)$
   $= 7$ hundreds and 7 fours
   $= 728$

2. $4 \times 59 =$ __236__

   Think
   $4 \times (60 - 1)$
   $= (4 \times 60) - (4 \times 1)$
   $= 240 - 4$
   $= 236$

3. $3 \times 99 =$ _____

4. $6 \times 51 =$ _____

5. $5 \times 95 =$ _____

6. $3 \times 76 =$ _____

7. $4 \times 24 =$ _____

8. $7 \times 205 =$ _____

9. $8 \times 36 =$ _____

10. $5 \times 47 =$ _____

base built on the use of materials and understanding of the distributive property.

It is always important for students to connect earlier understandings to new ideas, continually building upon a foundation of previous knowledge. Children should see that the process of multiplying by a two- or three-digit number is just an extension of the procedure for multiplying by a one-digit number. Similarly, illustrating this process by using an array is essentially the same no matter what the multiplier. Moreover, in the middle grades, when students begin to learn about symbol manipulation in algebra, they should be able to connect the new idea of multiplying binomials to their prior understanding of multidigit multiplication. In Figure 10–5, the illustration of the "foil" method for multiplying two binomials should look familiar because it is the same as the illustration for multiplying two two-digit numbers together; the very simple explanation is that the distributive property governs both of these parallel procedures.

An activity for using calculators with multidigit multipliers can be found in In the Classroom 10–4, which aids in strengthening the meaning of the algorithms and of multiplying by powers of ten.

In The Classroom 10–3

What's Missing?

Objective: Using number puzzles to develop estimation skills with multiplication.

▼ Guess the numbers that will go into the circles and boxes.

Write your number and then check it on a .
Score 2 points if correct on the first try and 1 point if correct on the second try.

$$\left(\; ④ \; ⑥ \; ⑦ \; ⑧ \qquad \boxed{32} \; \boxed{48} \; \boxed{68} \; \boxed{82} \; \right)$$

$\bigcirc \times \square = 408$ $\qquad \bigcirc \times \square = 272$

$\bigcirc \times \square = 476$ $\qquad \bigcirc \times \square = 336$

$\bigcirc \times \square = 384$ $\qquad \bigcirc \times \square = 492$

▼ Try these using only 2, 3, and 4:

$$
\begin{array}{r}
\square\,\square \\
\times \quad \square \\
\hline
4 \quad 6
\end{array}
\qquad
\begin{array}{r}
\square\,\square \\
\times \quad \square \\
\hline
6 \quad 6
\end{array}
$$

$$
\begin{array}{r}
\square\,\square \\
\times \quad \square \\
\hline
8 \quad 4
\end{array}
\qquad
\begin{array}{r}
\square\,\square \\
\times \quad \square \\
\hline
1 \quad 2 \quad 6
\end{array}
$$

▼ Now use only 4, 6, 8, and 9.

• Make the largest product.

$$
\begin{array}{r}
\square\,\square\,\square \\
\times \qquad \square \\
\hline
\end{array}
$$

• Make the smallest product:

$$
\begin{array}{r}
\square\,\square\,\square \\
\times \qquad \square \\
\hline
\end{array}
$$

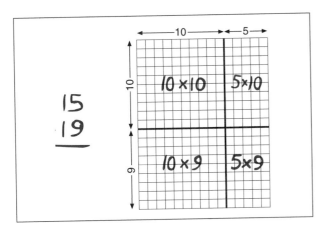

Figure 10–3 • Use of a grid to solve multiplication with two-digit multiplier

Figure 10–4 • Multiplication with two-digit multiplier

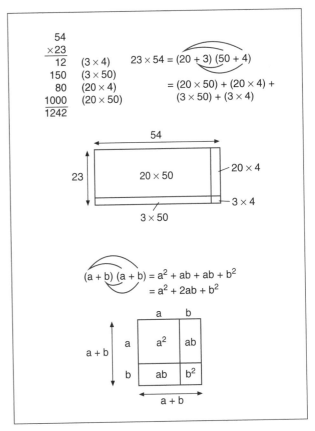

Figure 10–5 • Extending multiplication ideas to algebra

in the product. In the Classroom 10–5 shows how a calculator can help children develop ideas about the effect of multiplying by powers of ten.

Multiplying by 20, 30, 200, 300, and so on is an extension of multiplying by 10 and 100. The emphasis is placed on comparing what happens across examples and generalizing from the pattern. For example, have children consider 3×50:

$$3 \times 5 = 15$$
$$3 \times 5 \text{ tens} = 15 \text{ tens} = 150$$
$$3 \times 50 = 150$$

Then have them consider 4×50:

$$4 \times 5 = 20$$
$$4 \times 5 \text{ tens} = \underline{\quad} \text{ tens} = \underline{\quad}$$
$$4 \times 50 = \underline{\quad}$$

After several more examples, they are given other examples for which they are to find the pattern:

20	70	90		36	52
× 7	× 6	× 8	...	×20	×30

Multiplying by 10 and Multiples of 10

As we have seen, the ability to work flexibly with powers of ten is an important prerequisite to handling multiplication algorithms with understanding. Multiplying by 10 comes easily to most children, and it is readily extended to multiplying by 100 and 1000 as children gain understanding of larger numbers. The children can be shown a series of examples, after which they are asked to discuss and generalize, noting that, when there is a zero in the ones place, each digit moves one place to the left

In The Classroom 10–4

Analyzing Multiplication

Objective: Analyzing multiplication to develop number sense and mental computation skills.

▼ Use the partial product from the completed problems to help you find the missing numbers *mentally.*

```
  387
× 264
─────
 1548
23220
77400
──────
102168
```

387 × 60 = ____

2640 × 70 = ____

200 × 387 = ____

2640 × ____ = 79200

I know I can do these mentally!

```
  264
× 387
─────
 1848
21120
79200
──────
102168
```

264 × 80 = ____

264 × 300 = ____

▼ Check your mental answers with a calculator. Score one point for each correct answer.

A similar sequence is followed for examples with hundreds, such as 2 × 300:

$$2 \times 3 = 6$$
$$2 \times 3 \text{ hundreds} = \_\_\_ \text{ hundreds} = \_\_\_$$
$$2 \times 300 = \_\_\_$$

Finally, examples such as these might be given:

```
  273      418
×  50    ×  80
```

It is tremendously useful for children to be able to use multiplication by rounded numbers in making estimates. Consider one child's thinking when asked to make an estimate:

Think

```
  427
×  19
```
That's about 20 × 400.
2 × 4 = 8.
2 × 400 = 800.
So 20 × 400 would be 8000.

In The Classroom 10–5

Zeros Count

Objective: Using calculators to look for patterns and develop number sense involving multiplication by powers of ten.

▼ Use your calculator to find the product:

8 × 10 = _____

• How many 0's in 10? ____
• How many 0's in the product? ____

36 × 100 = _____

• How many 0's in 100? ____
• How many 0's in the product? ____

290 × 1000 = _____

• How many 0's in 1000? ____
• How many 0's in the product? ____   Why?

▼ Complete this multiplication table. Use your calculator to check your answers.

×	10	100	1000
7			
14		1400	
28			28000
240			
989			

Another child's thinking will differ:

Think

```
  427
×  19
```
That's about 20 × 425.
2 × 425 = 850.
20 × 425 = 8500.
So 19 × 427 is about 8500.

Both 8000 and 8500 are good estimates. When making estimates, students should round to numbers that are easy for them to compute. Consequently, different estimates are not only to be expected but also encouraged. In conjunction with estimation, students also need to answer questions such as these:

- How do I know how many zeros will be in the product?
- How is the number of zeros in the estimate related to the factors?
- How many digits will be in the estimated product?

Multiplying with Zeros

When zeros appear in the factor being multiplied, particular attention needs to be given to the effect on the product or partial product. Many children are prone to ignore the zero. Thus, for 9 × 306, their answer may be

$$\begin{array}{r} \overset{5}{306} \\ \times \quad 9 \\ \hline 324 \end{array}$$

When an estimate is made first, children have a way of determining whether their answer is "in the ballpark." Writing each partial product separately, rather than attempting to add them mentally, can also help avoid place value errors due to zeros. In the problem above, a student might actually write the partial products 54 and 0 and 2700. Use of a place-value chart may also help students to understand what the correct procedure must be, as will expanded notation:

Estimate

$$\begin{array}{r} 306 \\ \times \quad 9 \end{array} \qquad \begin{array}{l} 9 \times 3 = 27 \\ 9 \times 300 = 2700 \end{array}$$

T	H	T	O
3	0	6	
			9
2	7	5	4

$$\begin{aligned} 9 \times 306 &= 9 \times (300 + 6) \\ &= (9 \times 300) + (9 \times 6) \\ &= 2700 + 54 \\ &= 2754 \end{aligned}$$

Multiplication with Large Numbers

How can the calculator be used to solve computations involving numbers that appear too big for the calculator? As children experiment with using a calculator for multiplication, there will come a time when they overload the calculator. Sometimes the number to be entered will contain more digits than the display will show. At other times the product will be too big for the display. For instance, if this example is entered in a four-function calculator, an error message will result:

$$\begin{array}{r} 2345678 \\ \times \quad 4003 \end{array}$$

When this happens, children should be encouraged to estimate an answer and then use the distributive property plus mental computation along with the calculator.

Estimate:

$$4000 \times 2000000 = 8000000000$$
$$\begin{aligned} 4003 &= 4000 + 3 \\ &= (4 \times 1000) + 3 \end{aligned}$$

Calculate:

$$4 \times 2345678 = 9382712 \quad \text{(with the calculator)}$$
$$9382712 \times 1000 = 9382712000 \quad \text{(mentally)}$$
$$3 \times 2345678 = 7037034$$

Add:

$$\begin{array}{r} 7037034 \\ + 9382712000 \\ \hline \end{array}$$

Such examples show how an understanding of multiplication, plus problem-solving skills, can be used with calculators to reach a solution. Use of the calculator, mental computation, and paper-and-pencil recording may be integrated to solve a single problem. This sort of approach reminds us that calculator algorithms differ from the currently used paper-and-pencil algorithms.

DIVISION

The traditional division algorithm is without doubt the most difficult of the algorithms for children to master, for a number of reasons:

- Computation begins at the left, rather than at the right as for the other operations.
- The algorithm involves not only the basic division facts, but also subtraction and multiplication.
- There are a number of interactions in the algorithm, but their pattern moves from one spot to another.
- Trial quotients, involving estimation, must be used and may not always be successful at the first attempt—or even the second.

Teachers struggle to teach division, and children struggle to learn division; it is little wonder that the use of calculators is posed as a means of resolving the dilemma of the division algorithm. As *An Agenda for Action* (NCTM 1980, p. 6) indicates:

> For most students, much of a full year of instruction in mathematics is spent on the division of whole numbers—a massive investment with increasingly limited productive return.... For most complex problems, using the calculator for rapid and accurate computation makes a far greater contribution to functional competence in daily life.

On the national mathematics assessments, some exercises were given with and without the use of calculators. On the fourth assessment, third graders were given the problem $3\overline{)42}$. When calculators were not used, about 20 percent of the answers were correct; when calculators were used, about 50 percent were correct (Lindquist et al. 1988). On one item on the sixth assessment, students who reported using a calculator scored 82 percent correct, and those who reported they did not use a calculator scored only 35 percent (Kenney and Silver 1997). Even more dramatic were results from the second assessment (Carpenter et al. 1981). One exercise was given only to thirteen- and seventeen-year-olds when calculators were not used because nine-year-olds had not yet been taught division with a two-digit divisor. Thirteen-year-olds scored 46 percent and seventeen-year-olds scored 50 percent without calculators. With calculators, the scores rose dramatically, to 82 percent and 91 percent, respectively. And 50 percent of the nine-year-olds attained the correct answer when they used calculators. Considering that half of the seventeen-year-olds could not perform the division even after years of practice, is it not reasonable to let them use the tool with which they are successful—and which they will use anyway for the rest of their lives?

The NCTM *Standards* (2000) stress that in today's technological society we should rethink how computation is taught and how it is performed. Helping students to understand *when* division is appropriate and *how to estimate* answers to division problems is extremely important. In terms of actually performing computations, we strongly recommend that division with one-digit divisors should be the focus of instruction, followed by some work with two-digit divisors so that students understand how such division is done. Performing more complex division—perhaps any that takes more than 30 seconds to do—with paper and pencil is a thing of the past for adults. Thus, schools should not demand that children spend countless hours mastering an antiquated skill. Teachers can't afford the instructional time for this. Instead, estimation skills should be used to define the bounds of the quotient, so that the reasonableness of calculator answers can be determined—just as such estimates should be used with division with one-digit divisors and, in fact, with all addition, subtraction, and multiplication too.

Division with One-Digit Divisors

It is essential to begin division instruction with real-world problems. The most important thing is for students to develop an understanding of what division

is all about. Note that there is no reason for children not to encounter division problems with remainders from the very outset of their work with division. Children should be encouraged to use blocks or counters to model division situations and to explain their thinking. The teacher should help students see how their thinking can be clearly and efficiently recorded on paper. Thus, learning a paper-and-pencil algorithm will essentially turn into learning a way to record what is done concretely.

For example, Burns (1991) posed problems and had third-grade students explain their answers and the methods they used to reach them. One problem called for four children to divide 54 marbles equally. Group 1 counted out 54 cubes (to represent the marbles), divided them into four groups, and wrote:

> We think we get 13 each. We think this because we took the cubes and dealed out them one by one. We had two left. Bryce was sick so we gave the extra to him. (Burns 1991, p. 16)

Other groups wrote:

> Group 2: We had 54. We gave each person 10 because we thout if there was 40 there would be 4 tens and 14 would be left. Each person gets 3, witch leves 2. Each person gets 13.

> Group 3: We drew 54 marbles and then I numbered them 1, 2, 3, 4, and then we counted the ones and then we knew that each child gets 13 marbles and we lost the other two.

> Group 4: I wrote down 54. I took away 12. I got 42. I took anther 12 away. I got 30. I took another 12 away. I got 18. I took another 12 away. I got 6. Then I took away 4. I got 2. I chiped each of them into halves that made 4 halfs. Each person got 13 and a half. (Burns 1991, pp. 16–17)

Burns noted that, from listening to each others' methods, the children not only heard different approaches to solving division problems, but they also learned that division can be done in a variety of ways. Their teacher might have helped the class see how each of their different explanations could be recorded symbolically in a slightly different way, but always with the same final result. Refer to Figure 10–6 to see how each group's work might be recorded.

Obviously, there are many ways to figure and record the answer to a division computation and certain methods are much more efficient than others. Two algorithms have been used for division most frequently; both are effective. The *distributive algorithm* is most common and familiar and is considered the standard division algorithm by most

```
Group 1        Group 2          Group 3              Group 4

  54             54          ①②③④              4)54
 - 4 ①        - 40 ⑩        ①②③④①          - 12   3 × 4
 ----          ----          ②③④①②            ----
  50             14          ③④①②③             42
 - 4 ②         - 12 ③        ④①②③④           - 12   3 × 4
 ----          ----          ①②③④①            ----
  46              2          ②③④①②             30
 - 4 ③                       ③④①②③           - 12   3 × 4
 ----                         ④①②③④            ----
  42                          ①②③④①             18
 - 4 ④                        ②③④①②           - 12   3 × 4
 ----                         ③④①②③            ----
  38                          ④①②③④              6
                              ①②③④①            - 4    1 × 4
  10                          ②③④①②             ----
 - 4 ⑫                                               2
 ----                                          Our answer is
   6                                               13 ½
 - 4 ⑬
 ----
   2
```

Figure 10-6 • Solutions of groups 1–4—Marilyn Burns

```
A.
    2            23          238 r2
 4)954        4)954         4)954
   8            8             8
  ---          ---           ---
  15           15            15
               12            12
              ---           ---
               34            34
                             32
                            ---
                              2

B.                          C.
   238 r2                      238 r2
 4)954                       4)954
   200    50 × 4              120    30 × 4
  ----                       ----
   754                        834
   400    100 × 4             120    30 × 4
  ----                       ----
   354                        714
   200    50 × 4              120    30 × 4
  ----                       ----
   154                        594
   120    30 × 4              120    30 × 4
  ----                       ----
    34                        474
    32    8 × 4               120    30 × 4
   ---                       ----
     2    238                 354
                              120    30 × 4
D.                           ----
   238 r2                      234
 4)954                        120    30 × 4
   800    200 × 4            ----
  ----                        114
   154                         80    20 × 4
   120    30 × 4              ---
  ----                         34
    34                         32    8 × 4
    32    8 × 4               ---
   ---                          2
     2
```

Figure 10-7 • Some different division algorithms

Americans. Consider the problem of sharing $954 among 4 people (refer to Figure 10–7A):

When using the distributive algorithm for this problem, we first share as many of the 9 hundreds as possible (8 hundreds can be shared, 2 to each of the 4 people). We record how many were given to each person above (2 hundreds). We record the total number shared below (8 hundreds). We must be careful to preserve place value by writing these numbers in the proper columns. We "subtract and bring down" and note that we still have 1 hundred and 5 tens to be shared (or 15 tens). We begin the process again, sharing as many of the tens as possible, recording the number for each person above, recording the total shared below, and subtracting to see how much more still remains to be shared. We can share 12 of the 15 tens, 3 to each of the 4 people, so we write 3 above (in the tens place) and 12 below. Now we "subtract and bring down" again, noting now that we still have 3 tens and 4 ones to be shared (or 34 ones). Once again, we share as many as possible, this time writing 8 above and 32 below, and then subtracting. We now have just 2 ones left. Starting with $954, we were able to give $238 to each of 4 people, with $2 left over.

The *subtractive algorithm*, though not as familiar as the distributive algorithm, provides a very intuitive and straightforward method for helping children learn to divide. This algorithm is easier than the standard algorithm for most children to learn because it is flexible enough to be made to correspond to a wide variety of approaches to thinking about division. Refer to Figure 10–7B for an example of how the subtractive algorithm might be used to solve this same division problem. We have $954 to share among 4 people. Maybe we begin by giving each person $50. We subtract, and see that we still have $754 to share.

Obviously, we didn't need to start with such a small share. We might now choose to give each person $100. We still have $354 to share. Now we might give each person $50 again, leaving $154 still to share. We don't have enough to share $50 again, so maybe we'll give each person $30. That leaves $34. Now we can give each person $8, leaving $2 as remainder. The total each person received was $50 + $100 + $50 + $30 + $8, or $238, the same answer we obtained above with the standard algorithm. The choices made here in using the subtractive algorithm were arbitrary. We might instead have chosen to repeatedly distribute $30, over and over, and in that case the problem would take a long time to complete (see Figure 10–7C). On the other hand, if we were very efficient our solution would look very much like the standard algorithm solution (see Figure 10–7D).

The thinking process used in the subtractive algorithm is also clearly illustrated by the work of groups 2 and 4 in the problem involving marbles above. Both groups were computing 54 ÷ 4. Group 4 began by recognizing that 12 marbles could be shared fairly among 4 people (3 to each). So they first shared just 12 marbles (leaving 42 still to be shared). Then they repeatedly shared 12 more each time (leaving 30, then 18, then 6 still to be shared). Finally, they shared 4 of those final 6, leaving 2 marbles (which they, amusingly, cut in half to complete the sharing). Because each person was awarded 3 marbles 4 distinct times (for a total of 12 marbles), and also was awarded 1 more marble plus ½ marble, the solution can be written 54 / 4 = 13 ½. By contrast, Group 2 initially thought about sharing 40 of the 54 marbles among the 4 people (10 to each). That left 14 still to be shared. Those 14 could be distributed 3 per person. Thus, each person got 10 + 3 marbles (or 13), and 2 marbles were left over.

In using the subtractive algorithm, the child can choose to subtract off any multiple of the divisor at each step. Although the process may take more or less time, depending on how efficient the thinking is, the answer will be correct no matter how many steps are required. If children are extremely efficient, the subtractive algorithm can look almost exactly like the traditional division algorithm. Thus, the subtractive algorithm can serve as a transitional algorithm (a stage on the way to learning to divide using the traditional method), or children may learn it as an alternative algorithm.

Although we can help children to understand algorithms such as those described above, we also need to let them explore. As with the other operations, children develop their own algorithms. Some are closely allied with manipulative materials, as shown in Figure 10–8. Others make use of number sense, reasoning in terms of the numbers involved, as the following examples indicate:

52 ÷ 7   52 divided by 7 is close to 49 divided by 7, or 7. But there are 3 left over. So the answer is 7 remainder 3.

85 ÷ 5   20 divided by 5 is 4. There are four 20s in 80, so 4 × 4 = 16, and then there is one more 5. So the answer is 17.

69 ÷ 4   69 = 60 + 9. 60 divided by 4 is 15, and 9 divided by 4 is 2, with a remainder of 1. So the answer is 17 remainder 1.

Have you begun to believe that the possibilities for constructing ways to find an answer are myriad? Just when you think you've seen all the possible algorithms, another student will probably come up with a new one. Enjoy this process. Be an explorer right along with the children. But you also have another role. Just because all the algorithms we've dis-

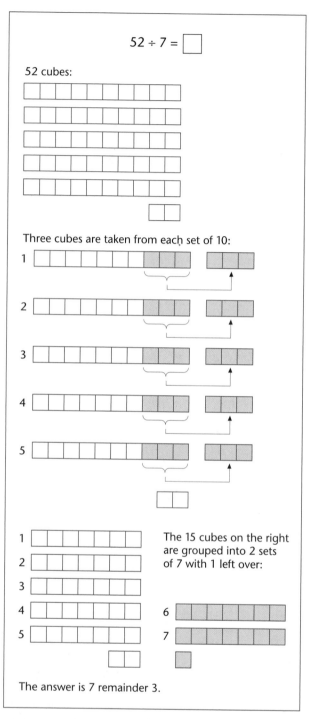

Figure 10–8 • **Alternative algorithm for division using manipulative materials** (Adapted from Harel and Behr 1991.)

played here are correct doesn't mean that children never come up with incorrect algorithms. They do.

You need to watch for this possibility—and you need to make children aware of the need to "prove" that a procedure really works across examples. You also need to be aware of consistent error patterns that crop up in children's work—error patterns that usually indicate some difficulty such as lack of knowledge about place value, or a lack of mastery of some basic facts, and some other misunderstanding. Fortunately, there are sources of information, such as Ashlock (1998), to which you can turn. This source not only helps you identify the patterns but provides specific suggestions for how to help the child get onto the right track. For additional help in working with children with learning problems, you could turn to such articles as Moyer and Moyer (1978) or Sears (1986).

As with the other operations, it is important that children work with manipulative materials as well as place-value charts. They need to keep in mind the problem situation, and not forget that it is the process of sharing that is of concern, not merely working their way through the algorithm. A variety of experiences, such as those in In the Classroom 10–6 and 10–7, may help children to gain facility with the division algorithm.

There is evidence from research that students also need to be encouraged to do more reasoning about their work. In particular, middle-school students were found to have a very difficult time providing written explanations of their reasoning about division problems with remainders (Silver et al. 1993). They did not associate "sense-making" with the solution of school mathematics problems. Some students assess their results by spurious criteria, such as whether a number "divides evenly" (Garofalo and Bryant 1992). We need to keep students aware of the real-world applications of the mathematics they are learning, but we also need to make them aware of how "reason-able" it is.

Determining a reasonable answer can be particularly difficult with the division algorithms, but questions can help students make sense of them. A necessary first step in determining a quotient is to estimate the number of places in the quotient:

$$6)\overline{839}$$

Are there as many as 10 sixes in 839? [Yes, 10 sixes are only 60.]

Are there as many as 100 sixes? [Yes, 100 sixes are 600.]

Are there as many as 200 sixes? [No, 200 sixes are 1200.]

So the quotient is between 100 and 200—and probably closer to 100.

An alternative to this is the following sequence:

$$3)\overline{187}$$

Are there enough hundreds to divide into three piles? [No.]

In The Classroom 10–6

The Missing Digits Game

Objective: Using a game to develop logical reasoning and number sense involving division.

▼ Try this game with several friends who have been divided into two teams.

- Teams take turns selecting the leader for a round of the game.

- The leader starts a round by working out a division problem and putting the pattern on the board.

- Players on each team take turns asking about the digits that go in the boxes. For example, a player on Team A might ask if there are any boxes containing 2's; then a player on Team B might ask if there are any containing 7's.

- If a digit appears in the problem, the leader writes it in the appropriate box(es).

- A team scores a point for each box that gets filled in during its turn. If there are no boxes for a digit, the team scores 0 for that turn.

- The winner for the round is the team with the highest score. (If a team guesses the problem before all the boxes are filled in, it wins the round and gets bonus points for the number of boxes that are still empty.)

▼ Play several rounds to determine which team wins the game!

Are there enough tens? [Yes—18 tens.]

So the quotient has two digits, and we decide that there are 6 tens.

So we know the answer is between 60 and 70.

Such procedures help to develop an early recognition of the range for a quotient. They help to provide meaning to the algorithm while developing valuable estimation skill.

Division with Two-Digit Divisors

Work with two-digit divisors should be aimed toward helping children understand what the procedure involves but not toward mastery of an

In The Classroom 10–7

Making Examples

Objective: Using number puzzles to develop number sense involving division.

▼ Make (and work out) a division example with

- A dividend of 47 and a divisor of 3
- A dividend of 81 and a divisor of 5

▼ Now make (and work out) a division example with

> I know I can do this . . .

- A quotient of 6 r2
- A quotient of 10 r4
- A quotient of 23 r5

▼ Try these:

- A divisor of 6 and a quotient of 15 r3
- A divisor of 3 and a quotient of 25 r2
- A dividend of 83 and a quotient of 11 r6

In The Classroom 10–8

Easy Does It!

Objective: Using calculators to develop number sense involving division.

▼ Use your calculator to find the missing numbers:

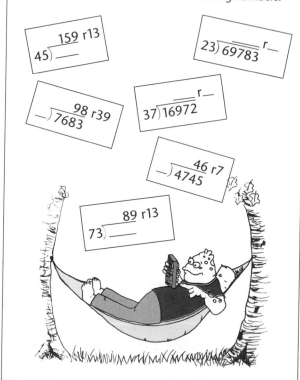

algorithm. The calculator does the job for most adults, and there is little reason to have children spend months or years mastering multidigit division. Other mathematics is of more importance for children to learn.

The development of division with two-digit divisors proceeds through stages from concrete to abstract, paralleling the work with one-digit divisors. Much practice may be needed with the symbolic form if proficiency is the goal. Use of the calculator is interwoven in the activities, as indicated in In the Classroom 10–8, where the calculator is used to strengthen understanding of the relationships between numbers.

Making Sense of Division with Remainders

Children should encounter division problems involving remainders from the time they begin to work with division ideas (just as they should encounter addition involving regrouping right from the outset). It is artificial and counterproductive to begin teaching division with problems that always come out even, saving problems involving remainders for later. As long as problems remain on a concrete level, the concept of remainder is rather easy. Here are some examples of varied situations:

- Pass out 17 candies to 3 children. (Each child receives 5 candies with 2 candies left over. Or, if

the candies can be cut into pieces, each child could have 5 candies plus ⅔ of a candy.)

- To make each Valentines card you need 3 pieces of lace. You have 17 pieces of lace. How many cards can you make? (You can make 5. You'll probably have to discard the two extra pieces of lace.)

- If 17 children are going on the class trip and 3 children can ride in each car, how many cars are needed? (You will need 6 cars. With 5 cars you could seat only 15 children, with 2 children still waiting for a ride. With 6 cars, you can seat all 17 children, with 1 seat left over.)

- Separate a class of 17 children into 3 teams. (There can be 5 children on each team and the 2 children left over can be the scorekeepers, or perhaps you could make two teams of 6 and 1 team of 5.)

Note that the "remainder" is handled differently in each of the real-world problems above. In the candy problem, both the whole number (5) and the remainder (⅔) are reported as parts of the answer. In the Valentine problem, the answer involves only the whole number part (the remainder must be discarded or ignored). In the class trip problem, the quotient is rounded up because the remainder cannot be ignored (no matter how small). In the team problem, we need to find some other use for the remainder (or we may abandon the attempt to form equal-sized groups if we want everyone to be able to play).

Thus it is important for children to think about and be able to deal with remainders as they appear in real-world problems. With calculators, the results of inexact division are expressed in decimal form, and children need to learn how to interpret the remainder when it is not an integer (see Chapter 12).

Initially, children are taught to write the remainder in one of the following ways:

$$\begin{array}{r} 2 \\ 6\overline{)13} \\ 12 \\ \hline 1 \end{array}$$ with 1 left over

$$\begin{array}{r} 5 \\ 5\overline{)27} \\ 25 \\ \hline 2 \end{array}$$ remainder 2 (later shortened to R2 or r2)

It is important to emphasize the real-life situations from which examples arise and to decide whether a "remainder of 2" makes sense in that situation. Activities such as the game in In the Classroom 10–9 provide practice in identifying the remainder.

Calculators can be used to solve problems with remainders, but the correct answer depends on the thinking a child does. Consider this problem:

A bus holds 36 children. If 460 children are being bused to a concert, how many buses are needed?

Does the calculator decide which keys to punch and in what order to punch them? Does the calculator interpret the result? Calculators don't solve problems—people do. Research shows the previous problem to be difficult for children to solve with or without a calculator. An answer of 12 remainder 28 is often reported without a calculator, and 12.777 buses is reported with a calculator. The children seem more intent on producing an answer than on deciding if their answer makes sense. A sensible answer would be 13 buses (12 buses will be full and the last bus will have some empty seats).

Some activities have been developed for calculators with "integer division" capabilities so that any remainder is displayed as a whole number. These activities were designed to help students develop conceptual understanding of division and the relationships among the dividend, divisor, and remainder. They involve estimation skills, so students have a bet-

In The Classroom 10–9

The Remainder Game
(A game for 2 to 4 players)

Objective: Using a game to practice mental computation involving division.

For this game, you will need

• A copy of this gameboard on heavy paper

• Four cards of each numeral 0 to 9

• A counter for each player

Game Rules

1. Place the cards face down in a pile.

2. The first player draws a card.

   • For a player's first turn, divide the first number or the board by the number drawn.

   • For a player's additional turns, the dividend is the number on the space where his or her counter landed on the previous turn.

3. Move the counter forward by the number of spaces indicated by the *remainder*. If the remainder is 0, no move is made.

4. Each of the other players go in turn.

5. To get "home," a player must be able to move the exact number of spaces left.

   The first person home wins!

ter chance of success if they are reasoning as they work. An example is given In the Classroom 10–10.*

CHECKING

Just as it is important to estimate before computing, it is important to check after computing. Ordinarily, addition and subtraction are used to check each other, as are multiplication and division. Unfortu-

*In the Classroom 10–10 is adapted from Usnick and Lamphere (1990).

In The Classroom 10–10

Number Net

Objective: Working with others to develop logical reasoning and number sense involving division.

▼ Work with a partner or in a small group to determine the missing values:

Dividend	Divisor	Quotient	Integral Remainder
632	73	——	——
345	——	——	45
——	34	——	27
——	——	——	18
——	746	89	——
7439	——	274	——
——	——	56	73

▼ If the solutions are not unique, explain why not. If no solution is possible, explain why.

• Which combinations result in unique solutions?

• Given any two numbers in a row, can a solution always be found? Why or why not?

• Given only one number in a row, can a solution always be found? Why or why not?

• Which combinations make finding a solution easy? Difficult? Why?

nately, checking does not always achieve its purpose of ascertaining correctness; research has indicated that children frequently "force the check"—that is, make the results agree without actually performing the computation (Grossnickle 1938). Obviously, children must come to understand the purpose of checking, as well as what they must do if the solution in the check does not agree with the original solution.

The calculator can serve many other functions, but its use in checking has not been overlooked by teachers. Nevertheless, we do not recommend that the calculator be used primarily to have children check paper-and-pencil computation. It insults students to ask them to spend large amounts of time on a computation and then use a machine that does the computation instantly. We do recommend that estimation be used extensively, both as a means of identifying the "ballpark" for the answer *and* as a means of ascertaining the correctness of the calculator answer. The words "use your calculator to check" should generally be used only when the calculator is to perform the computation following an estimate.

CHOOSING APPROPRIATE WAYS

As the NCTM *Standards* and the discussion in Chapter 9 make very clear, children must learn to choose an appropriate means of calculating. Sometimes paper and pencil is better; sometimes mental computation is more efficient. Other times use of a calculator is better than either, and sometimes only an estimate is needed. In the Classroom 10–11 illustrates one way of getting students to think about which method of calculation is most appropriate.

Encouraging students to defend their answers often yields valuable insight into their thinking. Children need to discuss when each method or tool is appropriate, and they need practice in making the choice, followed by more discussion, so that a rationale for their choice is clear. They need to realize that this is a personal decision. A problem that one child chooses to do with a calculator may be done with mental computation by another.

In The Classroom 10–11

Deciding How YOU Would Do It

Objective: Developing a sense for appropriate use of paper-and-pencil, mental, or calculator computation.

▼ Decide how you would do these computation exercises, and write your answers in the column that shows the method you decided to use. Explain your decisions.

	Mentally	Calculator
999 × 4 =	——	——
500 + 85 =	——	——
4200 ÷ 60 =	——	——
365 × 24 =	——	——
600 × 1000 =	——	——

▼ Follow up:

• Write a computation YOU would use a calculator with. ——————

• Write a computation YOU would do mentally. ——————

• Write a computation YOU would use a paper and pencil with. ——————

A Glance at Where We've Been

Although computational skill is viewed as an essential component of children's mathematical achievement, its role in the curriculum and the methods of teaching it are changing. The development of algorithms for each operation emphasizes the use of manipulative materials, place-value ideas, and estimation. Suggestions for developing the algorithms have been provided, and many transitional and alternative algorithms are presented. The use of calculators has been interwoven with many activities that use calculators as well as activities using other materials.

Things to Do: From What You've Read

1. What prerequisites must the child have in order to succeed in the chapter's opening lesson?

2. Consider each example. Describe what a child would think as he or she worked. What questions might you ask to develop or explain the procedure? How could manipulative materials be used?

   a.
   $$\begin{array}{r} \overset{1}{536} \\ 279 \\ +83 \\ \hline 8 \end{array}$$

   b.
   $$\begin{array}{r} \overset{2}{\cancel{3}}\overset{14}{\cancel{4}}9 \\ -184 \\ \hline 5 \end{array}$$

   c.
   $$\begin{array}{r} 73\overset{14}{\cancel{4}} \\ -2\overset{7}{\cancel{6}}9 \\ \hline 5 \end{array}$$

   d.
   $$\begin{array}{r} \overset{5}{79} \\ \times6 \\ \hline 4 \end{array}$$

   e.
   $$\begin{array}{r} 45 \\ \times3 \\ \hline 15 \\ 120 \end{array}$$

   f.
   $$38\overline{)291}\overset{9}{}$$

3. Explain why it is not recommended to spend long periods of time drilling students on the long-division algorithm. What level of facility with division would you be satisfied with? How would you justify this position when parents question your teaching of computational algorithms?

4. Analyze each of the following student-invented algorithms. Do they work all the time? If so, explain why they work. If not, explain why not.

   a. Subtraction—uses missing addend addition

   $$\begin{array}{r} 3452 \\ -1784 \\ \hline \end{array} \rightarrow \begin{array}{r} \overset{1}{1784} \\ +8 \\ \hline 3452 \end{array} \rightarrow \begin{array}{r} \overset{11}{1784} \\ +68 \\ \hline 3452 \end{array} \rightarrow \begin{array}{r} \overset{111}{1784} \\ +668 \\ \hline 3452 \end{array} \rightarrow \begin{array}{r} \overset{111}{1784} \\ +1668 \\ \hline 3452 \end{array}$$

   b. Subtraction—subtract from 10 when borrowing, then add on

   $$\begin{array}{r} \overset{4\ 10}{34\cancel{5}2} \\ -1784 \\ \hline 6 \\ +2 \end{array} \rightarrow \begin{array}{r} \overset{10}{\overset{3\ 4\ 10}{3\cancel{4}\cancel{5}2}} \\ -1784 \\ \hline 26 \\ +42 \end{array} \rightarrow \begin{array}{r} \overset{10\ 10}{\overset{2\ 3\ 4\ 10}{\cancel{3}\cancel{4}\cancel{5}2}} \\ -1784 \\ \hline 326 \\ +342 \end{array} \rightarrow \begin{array}{r} \overset{10\ 10}{\overset{2\ 3\ 4\ 10}{\cancel{3}\cancel{4}\cancel{5}2}} \\ -1784 \\ \hline 1326 \\ +342 \\ \hline 1668 \end{array}$$

   c. Subtraction—work left to right, crossing out when borrowing is needed

   $$\begin{array}{r} 3452 \\ -1784 \\ \hline 2 \end{array} \rightarrow \begin{array}{r} \overset{1}{3452} \\ -1784 \\ \hline \cancel{2}7 \\ 1 \end{array} \rightarrow \begin{array}{r} \overset{1\ 1}{3452} \\ -1784 \\ \hline 2\cancel{7}7 \\ 16 \end{array} \rightarrow \begin{array}{r} \overset{1\ 1\ 1}{3452} \\ -1784 \\ \hline 2\cancel{7}\cancel{7}8 \\ 166 \end{array}$$

   d. Division—uses distributive property to subtract twice for each multiplication by two-digit divisor

   $$\begin{array}{r} 2058\ \text{r}\ 20 \\ 23\overline{)47354} \\ \underline{40} \\ 7 \\ \underline{6} \\ 135 \\ \underline{100} \\ 35 \\ \underline{15} \\ 204 \\ \underline{160} \\ 44 \\ \underline{24} \\ 20 \end{array}$$

5. Some people wonder why it makes sense to encourage students to invent their own computational algorithms, because students are unlikely to discover the standard algorithms on their own. The standard algorithms—which are generally very quick and efficient—were refined through centuries of invention and modification. Why not just teach these standard algorithms directly to students?

6. Sketch a diagram to show how 12 × 17 can be modeled with an array on grid paper. Relate the model to the transitional algorithm for 12 × 17,

showing how each of the partial products in the array relates to the model.

7. Hands-on modeling of the traditional division algorithm: Consider a problem such as 798 ÷ 6. Model the dividend (798) with base-10 blocks. The divisor (6) tells how many equal-sized piles you want to make. Start by sharing the biggest blocks possible, and then make trades if necessary. Next, share the next biggest blocks. Again, make trades if necessary and continue the process until all blocks possible have been shared. Try several other problems such as 458 ÷ 3, 597 ÷ 2, 4782 ÷ 4, and 7365 ÷ 5. After doing several of these problems using just the materials, do them over again and record your findings step by step.

Questions to ask yourself (repeatedly), after sharing cubes or flats or longs or units:

- How many did you put in each pile? (Write this number up top in the appropriate place.)
- How many did you share altogether? (Write this number below.)
- How many do you still have left to be distributed? (Write this number after subtracting.)

8. Consider problems involving subtraction with regrouping, such as 52 – 25, 91 – 79, and 47 – 18. How would you approach these problems if you were teaching second grade? What do you think children need to understand or be able to do before they can start learning subtraction with regrouping?

9. Assume you are a sixth-grade teacher. You notice that several of your students are making the same mistake when multiplying multidigit numbers. When computing 15 × 23 or 173 × 234, they seem to forget to "move over the numbers" on each line. They are writing:

$$
\begin{array}{r} 23 \\ \times 15 \\ \hline 115 \\ 23 \\ \hline 138 \end{array}
\quad \text{instead of} \quad
\begin{array}{r} 23 \\ \times 15 \\ \hline 115 \\ 23 \\ \hline 345 \end{array}
\quad \text{and} \quad
\begin{array}{r} 234 \\ \times 173 \\ \hline 702 \\ 1638 \\ 234 \\ \hline 2574 \end{array}
\quad \text{instead of} \quad
\begin{array}{r} 234 \\ \times 173 \\ \hline 702 \\ 1638 \\ 234 \\ \hline 40482 \end{array}
$$

What will you do to help these students? How will you help them correct their mistake?

10. For the problem 4578 ÷ 7, find the quotient by using the transitional division algorithm known as the subtractive algorithm. Then do the problem again, using at least three more steps or three fewer steps than you used the first time to illustrate the flexible nature of this algorithm.

11. Write two story problems involving 35 ÷ 6 where the answers appropriate for the real world would actually not be the exact answer to the computation (5⅚). For your first story problem involving 35 ÷ 6, the appropriate answer should be 5. For your second story problem involving 35 ÷ 6, the appropriate answer should be 6.

12. Examine the games in Lesson Idea 10–1.

Answer the following questions about Race-to-a-Flat:

a. Can you win a long with one roll of the dice? Can you win two longs with one roll? Three longs?

b. Can you win a flat with one roll of the dice?

c. What is the fewest number of rolls you would need to win a flat? The most rolls to win a flat?

d. What is the fewest number of units a player will need to play this game?

e. How many units, longs, and flats should you give each student, so that he or she is sure to have enough pieces to play the game no matter what rolls he or she gets?

Answer the following questions about Give-Away-a-Flat:

a. Is it possible to give away a long with one roll of the dice? Two longs?

b. Can you win the game with one roll of the dice?

c. What is the fewest number of rolls required to give away all of the blocks?

d. What is the most number of rolls required to give away all of the blocks?

e. How many units, longs, and flats should you give each student, so he or she is sure to have enough pieces to play the game no matter what rolls he or she gets?

Things to Do: Going Beyond This Book

field Additional activities, suggestions, and questions are provided in *Teaching Elementary Mathematics: A Resource for Field Experiences.*

1. Choose a textbook for grade 3 or 4. Trace the development of multiplication algorithms. How are they introduced? What steps do children go through?

2. Choose a textbook series. Trace the development of division algorithms. What phases of development have been or should be modified because of the use of calculators?

3. **field** *Computation in Textbooks and Classrooms.* Choose a textbook for the grade level of a classroom you can visit and analyze a lesson plan on computation in the teacher's guide. What stages from concrete to abstract are involved in the lesson? Talk to the teacher about how he or she teaches computation. Is the textbook approach supplemented? How? What manipulatives, if any, are used? How?

4. **field** *Addition with Regrouping.* Develop three evaluation items that would assess students' understanding of adding two two-digit numbers with regrouping. Explain why you chose the examples

that you did. Try your items with several children and analyze their responses.

5. **field** *Transitional Algorithms.* Ask a classroom teacher if you can spend some time working with a student who is having trouble with paper-and-pencil computation (addition, subtraction, multiplication, or division, depending on age and grade level). See if you can figure out what the child's problem is. You might try helping him or her by suggesting the use of one of the transitional algorithms described in this chapter.

6. Becca investigating a multiplication problem is the focus of the article by Whitin (1993). After you have read about her investigation, write an evaluation of her work.

7. Read the "Number" Standards for Gradebands Pre-K–2 and 3–5 in *Principles and Standards for School Mathematics* (NCTM 2000). What recommendations are made concerning teaching computational algorithms? Write a position paper in which you either agree with NCTM's recommendations or take an opposing position. In either case, clearly explain and defend your point of view.

8. Pick a concept or skill from this chapter and compile a brief bibliography of recent articles containing research or teaching ideas on this topic.

9. You are a fourth-grade teacher. Following advice from NCTM's *Standards* (2000), you have decided this year to spend less time than in the past on multidigit multiplication and on long division. Instead, you will spend more time on mental computation, number sense, computations embedded in problem situations, and developing students' abilities to recognize and work with patterns and functions (early algebraic thinking). At the upcoming parent open house you want to explain to the parents how you have decided to modify your teaching approach and why. You decide that getting them involved with three or four problems as examples may be the best way to help them understand. Identify three problems to present at the open house. Write a brief narrative explaining why you chose each problem and how you would use it with the parents to convince them of the reasonableness of your new approach to teaching mathematics.

BOOK NOOK FOR CHILDREN

Anno, Mitsumasa. *Anno's Math Games.* New York: Philomel Books, 1987.

Anno, Mitsumasa. *Anno's Magic Seeds.* New York: Philomel Books, 1995.

Anno, Masaichiro, and Anno, Mitsumasa. *Anno's Mysterious Multiplying Jar.* New York: Philomel Books, 1983.

Froman, Robert. *The Greatest Guessing Game: A Book about Dividing.* New York: Crowell, 1978.

Pinczes, Elinor J. *One Hundred Hungry Ants.* Boston: Houghton Mifflin, 1993.

Trivett, John V. *Building Tables on Tables: A Book about Multiplication.* New York: Crowell, 1975.

Selected References

Ashlock, Robert B. *Error Patterns in Computation,* 7th ed. New York: Merrill, 1998.

Baek, Jae-Meen. "Children's Invented Algorithms for Multidigit Multiplication Problems." In *The Teaching and Learning of Algorithms in School Mathematics* (1998 Yearbook) (ed. Lorna J. Morrow and Margaret J. Kenney). Reston, Va: NCTM, 1998: pp. 151–160.

Baroody, Arthur J., and Standifer, Dorothy J. "Addition and Subtraction in the Primary Grades." In *Research Ideas for the Classroom: Early Childhood Mathematics* (ed. Robert J. Jensen). Reston, Va.: NCTM, and New York: Macmillan, 1993, pp. 72–102.

Brownell, William A. "An Experiment on 'Borrowing' in Third-Grade Arithmetic." *Journal of Educational Research,* 41 (November 1947), pp. 161–171.

Burns, Marilyn. "Introducing Division through Problem-Solving Experiences." *Arithmetic Teacher,* 38 (April 1991a), pp. 14–18.

Burns, Marilyn. *Math By All Means: Multiplication Grade 3.* Sausalito, Calif.: Math Solution Publications, 1991b.

Burns, Marilyn. *Math and Literature (K–3).* White Plains, N.Y.: Cuisenaire Company of America, 1992.

Campbell, Patricia F. "Connecting Instructional Practice to Student Thinking." *Teaching Children Mathematics* 4 (October 1997), pp. 106–110.

Campbell, Patricia F., and Johnson, Martin L. "How Primary Students Think and Learn." In *Prospects for School Mathematics* (ed. Iris M. Carl). Reston, Va.: NCTM, 1995, pp. 21–42.

Carpenter, Thomas P.; Corbitt, Mary Kay; Kepner, Henry S., Jr.; Lindquist, Mary Montgomery; and Reys, Robert E. *Results from the Second Mathematics Assessment of the National Assessment of Educational Progress.* Reston, Va.: NCTM, 1981.

Carpenter, Thomas P.; Franke, Megan L.; Jacobs, Victoria R.; Fennema, Elizabeth; and Empson, Susan B. "A Longitudinal Study of Invention and Understanding in Children's Multidigit Addition and Subtraction." *Journal for Research in Mathematics Education* 29(1) (1998), pp. 3–20.

Carroll, William M., and Porter, Denise. "Invented Strategies Can Develop Meaningful Mathematics Procedures." *Teaching Children Mathematics* 3 (March 1997), pp. 370–374.

Carroll, William M., and Porter, Denise. "Alternative Algorithms for Whole-Number Operations." In *The Teaching and Learning of Algorithms in School Mathematics* (1998 Yearbook) (ed. Lorna J. Morrow and Margaret J. Kenney). Reston, Va: NCTM, 1998: pp. 106–114.

Fennema, Elizabeth; Thomas P. Carpenter; Franke, Megan L.; Levi, Linda; Jacobs, Victoria R.; and Empson, Susan B. "A Longitudinal Study of Learning to Use Children's Thinking in Mathematics Instruction." *Journal for Research in Mathematics Education* 27(4) (1996), pp. 403–434.

Folsom, Mary. "Operations on Whole Numbers." In *Mathematics Learning in Early Childhood,* Thirty-seventh Yearbook (ed. Joseph N. Payne). Reston, Va.: NCTM, 1975, pp. 162–190.

Fuson, Karen. "Research on Whole Number Addition and Subtraction." In *Handbook of Research on Mathematics Teaching and Learning* (ed. Douglas Grouws). New York: Macmillan, 1992: pp. 243–275.

Garofalo, Joe, and Bryant, Jerry. "Assessing Reasonableness: Some Observations and Suggestions." *Arithmetic Teacher*, 40 (December 1992), pp. 210–212.

Graeber, Anna O., and Tanenhaus, Elaine. "Multiplication and Division: From Whole Numbers to Rational Numbers." In *Research Ideas for the Classroom: Middle Grades Mathematics* (ed. Douglas T. Owens). Reston, Va.: NCTM, and New York: Macmillan, 1993, pp. 99–117.

Grossnickle, Foster E. "The Effectiveness of Checking Subtraction by Addition." *Elementary School Journal,* 38 (February 1938), pp. 436–441.

Harel, Guershon, and Behr, Merlyn. "Ed's Strategy for Solving Division Problems." *Arithmetic Teacher,* 39 (November 1991), pp. 38–40.

Hembree, Ray, and Dessart, Donald J. "Effects of Hand-Held Calculators in Precollege Mathematics Education: A Meta-Analysis." *Journal for Research in Mathematics Education,* 17 (March 1986), pp. 83–99.

Huinker, DeAnn M. "Multiplication and Division Word Problems: Improving Students' Understanding." *Arithmetic Teacher,* 37 (October 1989), pp. 8–12.

Kamii, Constance. *Young Children Continue to Reinvent Arithmetic: 3rd Grade.* New York: Teachers College Press, 1994.

Kamii, Constance; Lewis, Barbara A.; and Livingston, Sally Jones. "Primary Arithmetic: Children Inventing Their Own Procedures." *Arithmetic Teacher,* 41 (December 1993), pp. 200–203.

Kamii, Constance; and Dominick, Ann. "The Harmful Effects of Algorithms in Grades 1–4" In *The Teaching and Learning of Algorithms in School Mathematics* (1998 Yearbook) (ed. Lorna J. Morrow and Margaret J. Kenney). Reston, Va.: NCTM, 1998: pp. 130–140.

Kenney, Patricia Ann, and Silver, Edward A. (eds.). *Results from the Sixth Mathematics Assessment of the National Assessment of Educational Progress.* Reston, Va.: NCTM, 1997.

Kouba, Vicky L., and Franklin, Kathy. "Multiplication and Division: Sense Making and Meaning." In *Research Ideas for the Classroom: Early Childhood Mathematics* (ed. Robert J. Jensen). Reston, Va.: NCTM, and New York: Macmillan, 1993, pp. 103–126.

Lindquist, Mary M.; Brown, Catherine A.; Carpenter, Thomas P.; Kouba, Vicky L.; Silver, Edward A.; and Swafford, Jane O. *Results from the Fourth Mathematics Assessment of the National Assessment of Educational Progress.* Reston, Va.: NCTM, 1988.

Merseth, Katherine Klippert. "Using Materials and Activities in Teaching Addition and Subtraction Algorithms." In *Developing Computational Skills,* 1978 Yearbook (ed. Marilyn N. Suydam). Reston, Va.: NCTM, 1978, pp. 61–77.

Morrow, Lorna J.; and Kenney, Margaret J. (eds.). *The Teaching and Learning of Algorithms in School Mathematics* (1998 Yearbook). Reston, Va.: NCTM, 1998.

Moyer, John C., and Moyer, Margaret Bannochie. "Computation: Implications for Learning Disabled Children." In *Developing Computational Skills,* 1978 Yearbook (ed. Marilyn N. Suydam). Reston, Va.: NCTM, 1978, pp. 78–95.

National Council of Teachers of Mathematics. *Agenda for Action.* Reston, Va.: NCTM, 1980.

National Council of Teachers of Mathematics. *Curriculum and Evaluation Standards for School Mathematics.* Reston, Va.: NCTM, 1989.

National Council of Teachers of Mathematics. *Professional Standards for Teaching Mathematics.* Reston, Va.: NCTM, 1991.

National Council of Teachers of Mathematics. *Principles and Standards for School Mathematics.* Reston, Va.: NCTM, 2000.

Ohanian, Susan, and Burns, Marilyn. *Math By All Means: Division Grades 3–4.* Sausalito, CA: Math Solutions Publications, 1995.

Phillipp, Randolph A. "Multicultural Mathematics and Alternative Algorithms." *Teaching Children Mathematics,* 3 (November 1996), pp. 128–133.

Rathmell, Edward, and Trafton, Paul. "Whole Number Computation." In *Mathematics for the Young Child* (ed. Joseph N. Payne). Reston, Va.: NCTM, 1990, pp. 153–172.

Reys, Robert E.; Bestgen, Barbara J.; Coburn, Terrence G.; Schoen, Harold L.; Shumway, Richard J.; Wheatley, Charlotte L.; Wheatley, Grayson H.; and White, Arthur L. *Keystrokes: Calculator Activities for Young Students: Addition and Subtraction, Multiplication and Division.* Palo Alto, Calif.: Creative Publications, 1980.

Ron, Pilar. "My Family Taught Me This Way." In *The Teaching and Learning of Algorithms in School Mathematics* (1998 Yearbook) (ed. Lorna J. Morrow and Margaret J. Kenney). Reston, Va: NCTM, 1998: pp. 115–119.

Sears, Carol J. "Mathematics for the Learning Disabled Child in the Regular Classroom." *Arithmetic Teacher,* 33 (January 1986), pp. 5–11.

Silver, Edward A.; Shapiro, Lora J.; and Deutsch, Adam. "Sense Making and the Solution of Division Problems Involving Remainders: An Examination of Middle School Students' Solution Processes and Their Interpretations of Solutions." *Journal for Research in Mathematics Education,* 24 (March 1993), pp. 117–135.

Smith, Jacque. "Assessing Children's Reasoning: It's an Age-old Problem." *Teaching Children Mathematics,* 2 (May, 1996), pp. 524–528.

Stanic, George M. A., and McKillip, William D. "Developmental Algorithms Have a Place in Elementary School Mathematics Instruction." *Arithmetic Teacher,* 36 (January 1989), pp. 14–16.

Sutton, John T., and Urbatsch, Tonya D. "Transition Boards: A Good Idea Made Better." *Arithmetic Teacher,* 38 (January 1991), pp. 4–8.

Suydam, Marilyn N., and Dessart, Donald J. *Classroom Ideas from Research on Computational Skills.* Reston, Va.: NCTM, 1976.

Thompson, Frances. "Two-Digit Addition and Subtraction: What Works?" *Arithmetic Teacher,* 38 (January 1991), pp. 10–13.

Trafton, Paul R., and Zawojewski, Judith S. "Implementing the Standards: Meanings of Operations." *Arithmetic Teacher,* 38 (November 1990), pp. 18–22.

Usnick, Virginia E., and Lamphere, Patricia M. "Calculators and Division." *Arithmetic Teacher,* 38 (December 1990), pp. 40–43.

Van de Walle, John A. "Implementing the Standards: Redefining Computation." *Arithmetic Teacher,* 38 (January 1991), pp. 44–51.

Van de Walle, John, and Thompson, Charles S. "Partitioning Sets for Number Concepts, Place Value, and Long Division." *Arithmetic Teacher,* 32 (January 1985), pp. 6–11.

Wearne, Diana, and Hiebert, James. "Place Value and Addition and Subtraction." *Arithmetic Teacher,* 41 (January 1994), pp. 272–274.

Wheatley, Grayson H., and Wheatley, Charlotte L. "How Shall We Teach Column Addition? Some Evidence." *Arithmetic Teacher,* 25 (January 1978), pp. 18–19.

Whitin, David J. "Becca's Investigation." *Arithmetic Teacher,* 41 (October 1993), pp. 78–81.

Fractions and Decimals: Meanings and Operations

Snapshot of a Lesson

Orientation

A fifth-grade class has reviewed ways to model fractions given a whole object or a set of objects. When we join the class, the teacher, Mrs. Benson, is introducing the lesson for today, in which a fractional part of a whole is given and the whole must be constructed.

MRS. BENSON: Good, you know a lot about fractions. Today, we are really going to test our brains. You found that it is fairly easy to show a fractional part of a whole. What if I give you a fractional part and you have to show me the whole?

JUSTIN: I'm not certain what you mean.

MRS. BENSON: Well, if I told you that this picture represents three-fifths of a cake, could you draw the whole cake?

$\frac{3}{5}$ of the cake

ROSA LEE: It sure would be a skinny cake.

CAMILLE: That depends on how the two-fifths was cut off.

MRS. BENSON: You are both right; you won't be able to tell exactly what the shape of the cake was before it was cut unless I tell you where it was cut. Let's pretend you can see that it was cut here (pointing to the right side). What do you know?

GILBERT: You have three of the five equal pieces. If we divide this into three equal parts, we know how large one-fifth is.

MRS. BENSON: Let's do that. Who can tell me how to finish the problem?

$\frac{3}{5}$ of the cake

OLAV: All you have to do now is add the missing two-fifths. Rosa Lee, you are right, it is a skinny cake. It would look like this. [Coming to the board, he draws two more parts.]

The whole cake

MRS. BENSON: How about another one? I have two-sevenths of a piece of licorice. How long was the licorice to begin with? Each of you draw a small line segment and label it two-sevenths.

JUSTIN: Does it matter how long it is?

MRS. BENSON: No, Justin, but we'll each be doing a slightly different problem. How long did you draw yours?

JUSTIN: About 5 centimeters.

MRS. BENSON: Do each one of you have a picture something like this?

$\frac{2}{7}$ of the licorice

What do you do next?

WINIFRED: That must be two of the seven parts, so one part would be about this long (holding up her fingers). Now, we need seven of those.

MRS. BENSON: Suppose I know that the twelve pieces of candy in a box are three-fifths of the original amount. How many pieces were in the box?

DENISE: I drew twelve pieces, but then I don't know what to do.

MRS. BENSON: Let's think, what does this picture tell you?

$\frac{3}{5}$ of the candy

DENISE: I think it means that three of five parts are in the box; this is three equal parts. Oh, there are twelve pieces so there must be four in each part.

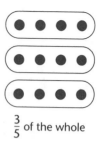

$\frac{3}{5}$ of the whole

- MRS. BENSON: Good, let's circle the three sets of four.

- DENISE: You need two more sets of four. So there must have been twenty pieces to begin with.

- MRS. BENSON: Does that make sense? Is twelve three-fifths of twenty?

After a few more examples using improper fractions and mixed numbers, the students continue to explore the problems that Mrs. Benson had ready for them. She ended the lesson by having the children make up problems and having a partner solve them.

Introduction

Fractions and decimals have long been a stumbling block for many students. One reason may be that curriculum materials—tend to rush to symbolization and operations without developing strong conceptual understandings for these numbers and operations with them. Thus, much of this chapter is devoted to concept development of fractions and decimals and the processes underlying the operations with these numbers using models and oral language.

As you will see in examining the concepts associated with fractions and decimals, they are complex. However, two rather simple but powerful ideas—*partitioning* and *equivalence*—can help tie many of the ideas together (Kieren 1980). In reference to fractions and decimals, partitioning is the process of sharing equally (a cake shared equally among five people or six candy bars shared equally among four people), and equivalence focuses on different representations of the same amount (three-fourths of a cake is the same amount as six-eighths of that cake, so three-fourths is equivalent to six-eighths).

One idea related to equivalence that you should keep in mind is that decimal fractions are another notation for common fractions. For example, 0.5 and $\frac{5}{10}$ are just two different ways to represent the same fractional part. Each of these fractions is equivalent to one-half.

Both common fractions and decimal fractions can represent fractional parts. However, decimal fractions represent only partitions of tenths, hundredths, and powers of tenths; common fractions can represent any partitioning.

Although we first concentrate on common fractions (simply called *fractions* from here on), we do not mean to imply that the entire study of fractions should be done before decimals. After a beginning foundation has been built with fractions, decimal notation can be introduced. In fact, many of the operations with decimals are easier than the corresponding operations with fractions and can be taught meaningfully before the entire study of operations with fractions is completed.

CONCEPTUAL DEVELOPMENT OF FRACTIONS

The *Principles and Standards for School Mathematics* (NCTM 2000) emphasize that students should be given the opportunity to develop concepts as well as number sense with fractions and decimals. A careful examination of the items on the seventh mathematics assessment of the National Assessment of Educational Progress (NAEP) reveals that concepts and models underlying fractions are not well developed by Grade 4 and although older students can relate fractions to pictorial models, they do not realize that these models can be helpful in solving problems (Wearne and Kouba 2000).

Many materials are available to help you help children develop concepts about fractions. However, some of the most effective materials, such as construction paper, white paper, and counters, are commonly found in the classroom.

Mathematics literature also can serve as an excellent basis for a conceptual development of fractions. For example, one book, *Ed Emberley's Picture Pie, A Circle Drawing Book* (Emberley 1984), allows students to see and make colorful pictures and patterns from fractional parts of a circle. Another book, *The Doorbell Rang* (Hutchins 1987), is an excellent source to use when introducing the concept of partitioning. Often books can help lay the groundwork for an understanding of mathematical concepts.

Three Meanings of Fractions

Three distinct meanings of fractions—part-whole, quotient, and ratio—are found in most elementary mathematics programs. Most fraction work is based on the part-whole meaning, often with little development of the other two meanings. Ignoring these other meanings may be one source of students' difficulty.

Part-Whole The part-whole interpretation of a fraction such as $\frac{3}{5}$ indicates that a whole has been partitioned into five equal parts and three of those parts are being considered. This fraction may be shown with a region model:

The whole

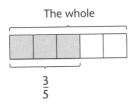

$$\frac{3}{5}$$

Quotient The fraction $\frac{3}{5}$ may also be considered as a quotient, $3 \div 5$. This interpretation also arises from a partitioning situation. Suppose you had some big cookies to give to five people. You could give each person one cookie, then another, and so on until you had distributed the same amount to each. If you had twenty cookies, you could represent this process mathematically by $20 \div 5$; each person would get four cookies.

Now consider this problem:

You have three big cookies and you want to give them to five people; that is, you want to divide the three cookies among five people, or $3 \div 5$.

How much would each person get?

Would anyone get a whole?

One way to solve the problem using pictures of the cookies is shown in Figure 11–1. This interpretation of fractions is used when a remainder in a division problem is expressed as a fraction. It is also the interpretation that is needed to change a fraction to decimal notation. For example, $\frac{5}{8}$ is $5 \div 8$ or 0.625.

Ratio The fraction $\frac{3}{5}$ may also represent a ratio, such as there are three boys for every five girls. Here is a model for this situation:

You can see that this interpretation is conceptually quite different from the other interpretations of fractions. In this chapter, we will consider only the other two interpretations; the ratio interpretation is discussed in Chapter 12.

Models of the Part-Whole Meaning

We will concentrate on four models for the part-whole meaning: region, length, set, and area. Any of

Begin with 3 cookies. Cut each into 5 parts.

Each person gets $\frac{1}{5}$ of each cookie.

Thus, each person gets

$$\frac{1}{5} + \frac{1}{5} + \frac{1}{5} \qquad \text{or} \qquad \frac{3}{5} \qquad \text{or} \qquad 3 \div 5 = \frac{3}{5}$$

Figure 11–1 • An example of the quotient interpretation of a fraction

these models may also be used for the quotient interpretation; however, the region model is most often used because it is the simplest. Other attributes, such as capacity, volume, or time, also can be used as models.

Region The region model is the most concrete form and is most easily handled by children. The *region* is the whole (the unit), and the parts are *congruent* (same size and shape). The region may be any shape, such as circle, rectangle, square, or triangle. A variety of shapes should be used when presenting the region model, so that the children do not think that a fraction is always a "part of a pie."

As Figure 11–2 indicates, the rectangle is the easiest region model for children to draw and to partition. (Try partitioning each of the shapes shown into three equal parts to see which is easiest.) The circle does have one advantage; it is easy to see as a whole. Because the region is the most common model, and the rectangle the easiest for children to draw, we will use it extensively throughout this chapter.

Length Any unit of length can be partitioned into fractional parts with each part being equal in length. Children can fold a long, thin strip of paper (*partition* it) into halves, fourths, and so on. Later this activity should lead to indicating fractions as points on a number line. That is, by partitioning a unit, or the distance between two points such as 4 and 5, into thirds, children can find one-third of the unit and will see that it is more than 4. If the children understand that each unit has been partitioned into thirds, they will realize that the point is $4 + \frac{1}{3}$, or $4\frac{1}{3}$, as shown in Figure 11–3.

Set The set model uses a set of objects as a whole (the unit). This model sometimes causes difficulty,

Figure 11–3 • **Length model of $4\frac{1}{3}$**

partly because students have not often considered a set of, say, twelve objects as a unit. About three-fourths of fourth-grade students could chose the region model for a given fraction, whereas only about half could choose the fraction that represented a set model (Wearne and Kouba 2000). The more likely reason for difficulty is that the students have not physically partitioned objects and considered this as sharing of a set. The set meaning is often presented only as a number out of the set such as five red pencils in a set of twelve pencils is $\frac{5}{12}$.

Without mentioning fractions, children should be given experiences partitioning sets, which provides a background for both division and fractions. For example, a child may be asked to give twelve toys to four children. Later, attention should be focused on whether or not a given number of objects can be partitioned equally among a given number of people:

Can 15 toys be partitioned (shared) equally among 5 people? [yes]

4 people? [no]

3 people? [yes]

2 people? [no]

With this understanding, the set model can be related to fractions; for example, finding fifths by partitioning the set into five equal parts. Figure 11–4 shows a set of fifteen marbles that have been partitioned into five equal parts. Each part is one-fifth of the whole set. From this modeling, children develop the set meaning of fractions and can answer questions such as these:

What is one-fifth of 15? [3]

Two-fifths of 15? [6]

Three-fifths of 15? [9]

Experience of this type allows children to solve many practical problems and gives background for multiplication of fractions.

Area The area model is a sophisticated one that is a special case of the region model. In the area model, the parts must be equal in area but not nec-

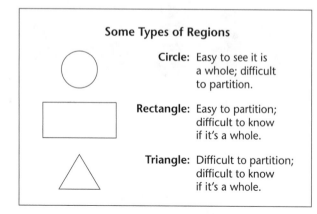

Some Types of Regions

Circle: Easy to see it is a whole; difficult to partition.

Rectangle: Easy to partition; difficult to know if it's a whole.

Triangle: Difficult to partition; difficult to know if it's a whole.

Figure 11–2 • **Types of regions for concrete models**

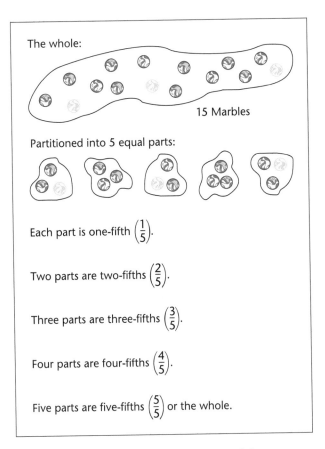

The whole:

15 Marbles

Partitioned into 5 equal parts:

Each part is one-fifth $\left(\frac{1}{5}\right)$.

Two parts are two-fifths $\left(\frac{2}{5}\right)$.

Three parts are three-fifths $\left(\frac{3}{5}\right)$.

Four parts are four-fifths $\left(\frac{4}{5}\right)$.

Five parts are five-fifths $\left(\frac{5}{5}\right)$ or the whole.

Figure 11–4 • An example of a set model

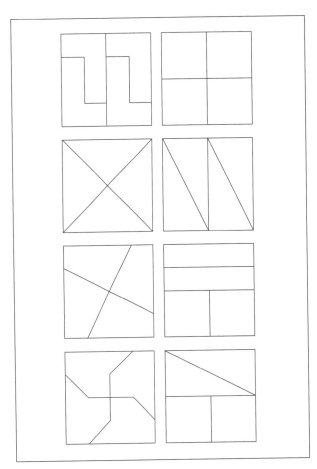

Figure 11–5 • Ways to partition an area model

essarily congruent (same size and shape). Before using this model, children must have some idea of when two different shapes have equal areas. Figure 11–5 shows eight squares partitioned into fourths in different ways. Can you see how the parts of each square are equal in area? This model is more appropriate for older children (about third and fourth grade) than for younger ones.

In the Classroom 11–1 gives examples and nonexamples of models of the fraction three-fourths. It is one way to assess children's understanding of the different models. Use it first as a self-assessment, and then try it with elementary students.

Making Fractions Meaningful

Explaining, in order, all the meanings and models, as done so far in this chapter, is not the way to teach fractions. If you are beginning to build children's conceptual understanding of fractions, start with the simplest meaning and model—something that can be made meaningful for children. The part-whole meaning and the region model provide a good starting place. After introducing this model and the language and symbols associated with fractions, begin using other part-whole models (length,

set, and area). Other meanings of fractions (quotient and ratio) can be introduced after children become more familiar with ordering and finding equivalent fractions and as they are introduced to improper fractions and mixed numbers.

Partitioning Underlying the idea of part-whole is the meaning of *part* and of *whole*. The whole is whatever is specified as the unit. At first, the whole should be obvious. Children must learn to partition the whole into equal parts, and then to describe those parts with fractional names.

Let the children do the partitioning. For example, each child could be given a "candy bar" (a piece of paper the size of a large candy bar) to share with a friend. Have them fold the "candy bar" to show how they would share. Talk about whether a fold like the one sketched here would be a "fair share" for two people.

In The Classroom 11–1

Three-Fourths

Objective: To assess children's understanding of three-fourths.

▼ In which of the following models does the shading show three-fourths of the whole? Why or why not?

A Whole: large rectangle

F Whole: large rectangle

B Whole: box of marbles

G Whole: box of candy

C Whole: large rectangle

H Whole: large rectangle

D Whole: large rectangle

I Whole: large triangle

E Whole: box of shapes

J Whole: large rectangle

Lesson Idea 11–1

Fraction Bars

Materials: 4 construction paper strips (3" × 9") of 4 different colors for each child

Preparation of Fraction Bars: Each child should fold a blue strip into halves, mark the fold with a dark line, and write halves on the back.

Make fraction bars for thirds, fourths, and sixths in other colors in the same way.

Activities:

▼ Ask each child to take the fourths bar, and count the parts:

1, 2, 3, 4 fourths

▼ Ask each to count the parts of other bars; for example, 1 sixth, 2 sixths, 3 sixths, . . .

▼ Ask a pair of children to count the fourths in two bars:

1, 2, 3, 4   5, 6, 7, 8 fourths

▼ See that 8 fourths is 2 wholes, 6 fourths is 1 whole and 2 fourths, and so on.

▼ Ask each to count all the sixths in the class.

▼ Challenge all children to tell how many strips it would take to show 11 sixths or 23 sixths. Let them experiment in groups of 4.

Through other examples, develop sharing equally among 4, 3, 6, and 5 people. For some of the more difficult sharing problems, such as with 5 people, you may want to use a strip of paper that has already been marked. See Lesson Idea 11–1 for an example of a way to start this sharing. Have the children make the models of the fractional parts using construction paper and keep for explorations about fractions. Doing a little work with fractions often will make them a natural part of the mathematics.

When children become familiar with the process of sharing regions and describing the parts with words and counting parts, move to the other models. Children especially like to share objects (set model) and tying it closely to sharing a "candy bar" will help extend their ideas about fractions. For example, share 12 marbles with 2 friends. Because you can share fairly, each friend gets half of the marbles. What about 4 friends?

Words As soon as you have developed the idea of equal parts, introduce the words *halves, thirds, fourths,* and so on. Be sure to ask such questions as, "How many equal parts in a whole would I have if each part was a fifth? An eighth? A twenty-fourth?" Only half of the fourth-grade students responded that 4 fourths made a whole in response to an item on the NAEP mathematics assessment (Wearne and Kouba 2000).

Counting Once children are familiar with the fractional part words, begin counting parts. This process should not be any more difficult than counting apples, but the children need to know what they are counting. A few ideas to practice counting fractional parts are given on Lesson Idea 11–1.

Symbols Both symbols and written words should be used together or alternately until students understand the meaning of the symbol.

> Using the written fraction symbol is appropriate only after children can name, count, and compare using oral language with facility. . . . Written symbols are developed in the same way as oral language. The same kind of questioning can be used, but now the model and the oral language are connected with the symbol. (Payne et al. 1990, p. 185)

We can depict these connections as follows:

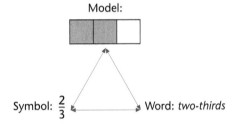

When children can match the words with the model, it is time to tell them that we write the symbol $\frac{2}{3}$ for the word *two-thirds*. Then, they need to have many opportunities to connect different representations:

1. Connect the model and the words.
2. Connect the model and the symbol.
3. Connect the words and the symbol.

Textbooks usually concentrate on tasks like 2, so you will find plenty of examples of these. Task 3 requires oral work, so you need to provide opportunities to have children solve problems and describe the solutions.

Drawing a Model In this developmental sequence, children have modeled fractions by folding paper or by choosing a picture. You also want them to be able to draw a picture. The rectangle is probably the easiest shape to use to show a "good approxima-

tion" to a fractional part. Encourage the children to be as accurate as possible, but do not worry if their drawings are not perfect. For example, which of these two drawings would you accept as a picture of two-thirds?

Bob's work is neater than Marilyn's, but he seems to have missed the point that the three parts must be equal. You might help Marilyn be a little neater, but she does seem to have the idea of two-thirds.

Extending the Model The results of a question on the second national mathematics assessment are in Table 11–1 (Carpenter et al. 1981). Little has changed in the almost twenty years since this item was given; the performance level on a similar question on the 1996 assessment was almost identical for fourth-grade students. There is no doubt that this model showing more parts than indicated by the denominator is more complicated than those described in the previous section, but it is useful for introducing equivalent fractions and for ordering fractions.

You also can use paper folding to introduce the model in Table 11–1 and to introduce equivalent

Table 11–1 • Results of national assessment question using the region model

What fractional part of the figure is shaded?

Responses	Percent Responding	
	Age 9	*Age 13*
Acceptable responses	20	82
$\frac{1}{3}$, $\frac{4}{12}$, .33		
Unacceptable responses		
$\frac{1}{4}$, .25	5	4
Top 4, top part, $\frac{4}{8}$	36	6
Other	15	6
I don't know	17	1
No response	7	1

fractions. For example, give each child a sheet of plain paper. Have each child fold the paper into thirds and shade two-thirds. Now fold the paper in half the other way. Ask how many parts and what kind of parts [6, sixths]. Then, ask what part is shaded. Encourage both $\frac{2}{3}$ and $\frac{4}{6}$. Tell the children that we call $\frac{2}{3}$ and $\frac{4}{6}$ *equivalent fractions* because they represent the same amount.

After more examples and practice with folding paper, children should be ready to understand what happens with the paper folding through drawings.

● Begin by drawing a picture of the paper folded in thirds and shade $\frac{2}{3}$:

Folded into thirds

$\frac{2}{3}$ shaded

● Now draw the fold made when partitioning it into halves, making certain the children can identify the way the paper was "folded" in both directions.

Folded into thirds

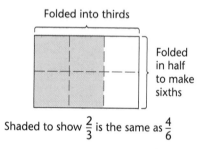

Folded in half to make sixths

Shaded to show $\frac{2}{3}$ is the same as $\frac{4}{6}$

● Ask children to show $\frac{1}{3}$, $\frac{2}{3}$, $\frac{4}{6}$, and so on and to name an equivalent fraction for each.

Next, move to pictures showing only the folded paper, such as the representation below:

Folded into fourths

Folded into thirds

Make certain the students can identify the way the paper was "folded" in both directions. Have them show

$$\frac{1}{3}, \quad \frac{2}{3}, \quad \frac{1}{4}, \quad \frac{3}{4},$$

and so on and give an equivalent fraction.

This sequence, which begins with partitioning and gradually introduces the words, symbols, and more complicated models and meanings, along with activities such as those in this chapter's Snapshot of a Lesson, provides a strong background for further development of fractions and operations with fractions. Before moving to operations with fractions, children need a firm understanding of equivalence. When children have worked with whole numbers, they most often have described the number of objects with only one number. That is, if they have counted eight objects, they will say eight and write 8. When we work with fractional parts, there are many ways to describe the amount depending on the sub-unit (denominator) that is chosen. For example, we can represent one-half of a pie with $\frac{1}{2}$, or $\frac{3}{6}$, or $\frac{4}{8}$. And, depending on the problem we are solving, one name may be more appropriate than another.

Ordering Fractions and Equivalent Fractions

Part of understanding fractions is realizing that they are numbers and can be ordered, added, subtracted, multiplied, and divided. The goal is to have children order fractions and find equivalent fractions symbolically, but you can help children build a bridge from the concrete to the symbolic. Not only will this bridge help children realize what they are doing when they are ordering and finding equivalent fractions, but it also will give another context in which to practice relating fractions and the models. Many problems involving ordering capture children's interest because they want to know which is more, which is shorter, which is larger, and so on. The problems about equivalent fractions are central to understanding fractions and being able to operate (add, subtract, multiply, and divide) with them.

Concrete Models If children have made concrete models, it is not difficult for them to order fractions and find equivalent fractions using various models.

For example, children can make fraction bars, as described in Lesson Idea 11–1, and then use them to find out which is larger, $\frac{2}{3}$ or $\frac{3}{4}$. Folding the thirds strip so that it is $\frac{2}{3}$ long and the fourths strip so that it is $\frac{3}{4}$ long provides a concrete model for the comparison.

This model can also be used to show equivalent fractions. Children can readily see that $\frac{2}{3}$ is the same amount as $\frac{4}{6}$. The extended model with paper folding, as described previously, also can be used to identify equivalent fractions.

For simplicity, we are emphasizing the rectangle and paper models. Children need to work with multi-embodiments representations as suggested by Principle 6 in Chapter 2. The pattern blocks (see Appendix B) are another model accessible to young children. See the Lesson Idea 11–2 for a mixture of ideas to begin your lesson planning using pattern blocks for ordering and finding equivalent fractions.

Pictorial Models   Children are able to order fractions if given pictures of the models, such as the fraction strips in Figure 11–6. (A more complete set of fraction strips is given in Appendix B.) The accurate scale of these models allows children to compare lengths to decide which is larger, $\frac{3}{4}$ or $\frac{2}{3}$. This set can also be used to identify equivalent fractions. It is clear that $\frac{1}{2}$, $\frac{2}{4}$, and $\frac{3}{6}$ all represent the same amount.

Children also can construct or draw their own pictorial models to represent fractions. Lesson Idea 11–3 illustrates one way that children can make a model of two fractions and easily compare the fractions. This model does not depend on the accuracy of the size of the parts, as the model in Figure 11–6 does. It also will lead to understanding a symbolic way of comparing fractions as well as to a way to add and subtract fractions.

Symbolic Representation   It is easier to compare two measurements given in the same unit (78 meters and 20 meters) than two measurements given in different units (83 meters and 4318 centimeters).

Similarly, it is easier to compare two fractions that are symbolically represented by the same subunit ($\frac{3}{5}$ and $\frac{2}{5}$) than two fractions that are represented by different subunits ($\frac{2}{3}$ and $\frac{5}{7}$). In mathematics, we often try to turn a more difficult situation into a simpler case—that is, representing the things to be compared in the same unit. With fractions, simpler means expressing each fraction as an equivalent fraction in the same subunit, or common denominator. The pictorial model shown in Lesson Idea 11–3 can be extended to develop this idea. Once the rectangle has been partitioned into both thirds and sevenths, it is partitioned into twenty-firsts so that $\frac{2}{3}$ is 14 of the 21 parts or $\frac{14}{21}$, and $\frac{5}{7}$ is 15 of the 21 parts or $\frac{15}{21}$.

Thus, 21 is the common denominator for comparing the fractions $\frac{2}{3}$ and $\frac{5}{7}$:

$$\frac{2}{3} = \frac{14}{21}$$

Lesson Idea 11–2

Comparing Models

Materials needed: Pattern blocks

The four basic shapes of the pattern blocks that you will use are the hexagon, triangle, rhombus, and trapezoid. Each child or pair of children will need multiple copies of each shape.

Let children have a chance to explore by making designs and seeing how they could make the hexagon with the other pieces.

Idea One: Use the hexagon as the whole. What is the size of each of the other pieces? Use the pieces to show that

$$\frac{2}{6} = \frac{1}{3} \qquad \frac{3}{3} = 1 \qquad \frac{3}{6} = \frac{1}{2} \qquad \frac{2}{3} > \frac{1}{2} \qquad 2\frac{2}{3} = \frac{8}{3}$$

Idea Two: Use the figure made from two hexagons as the whole.

Use ▱ to cover the yellow shape. How many does it take? What fractional part of the whole is the rhombus? What fractional part of the whole is the trapezoid?
Use the shape to show that $\frac{3}{4}$ is greater than $\frac{2}{3}$.

Idea Three: Give the shape of a fractional part and have children construct the whole as in the lesson snapshot.

If ▱ is $\frac{2}{3}$, what is the whole.

If ▽ is $\frac{3}{4}$, make the whole.

If △ is $\frac{1}{5}$, make the whole.

If △ is $\frac{2}{5}$, draw the whole.

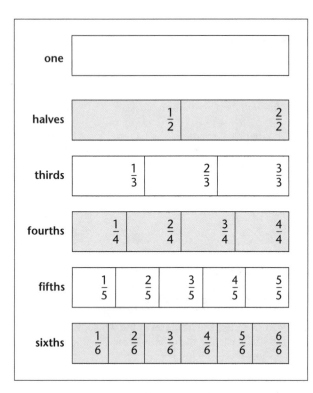

Figure 11–6 • Pictorial model of fraction strips

and

$$\frac{5}{7} = \frac{15}{21}$$

Therefore,

$$\frac{5}{7} > \frac{2}{3}$$

We have looked at models that represent fractional parts in more than one way, such as by $\frac{2}{3}$ and $\frac{3}{4}$.

Students with this background are familiar with the concept of equivalent fractions, but they may not have developed many of the skills associated with finding equivalent fractions symbolically. Finding an equivalent fraction rests on the generalization that both the numerator and denominator may be multiplied (or divided) by the same number.

To develop the generalization for finding an equivalent fraction symbolically, begin with the paper-folding model and symbolically describe what is happening.

- Make a model of $\frac{3}{4}$ by folding a piece of paper in fourths (A); then fold it in half the other way (B).

Lesson Idea 11–3

Comparing Fractions

Problem: Jacqui ate $\frac{1}{3}$ of the cake. Tom ate $\frac{2}{7}$ of the cake. Who ate more?

One way to model: Draw the cake twice. Show $\frac{1}{3}$ on one picture and $\frac{2}{7}$ on the other. Can you tell who ate the most?

It is difficult to compare these pictures, so show both partitions on each of the pictures.

Now you can see that Jacqui ate seven pieces and Tom ate six pieces. So Jacqui ate more cake.

What size are these pieces? That is, what part of the cake is each piece? Can you describe the $\frac{1}{3}$ as an equivalent fraction? Can you express $\frac{2}{7}$ as an equivalent fraction?

(A) Fold into fourths.

(B) Fold in half to make eighths.

- Ask what happened to the fourths when the paper was folded in half.

- Use shading to confirm that you created twice as many equal parts (or 2 ÷ 4) and twice as many shaded parts (or 2 ÷ 3).

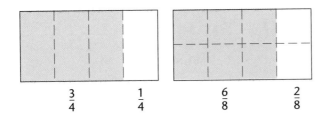

$$\frac{3}{4} \qquad \frac{1}{4} \qquad\qquad \frac{6}{8} \qquad \frac{2}{8}$$

• Express the model symbolically:

$$\frac{2 \times 3}{2 \times 4}$$

or

$$\frac{3 \times 2}{4 \times 2} = \frac{6}{8}$$

After more examples such as these, children should be able to make the generalization that both numerator and denominator may be multiplied by the same number and the resulting fraction is equivalent.

Conversely, you could begin with the model of eight parts and describe how to get to four parts. In this case, you begin with the eight parts and group them by two, or $8 \div 2$, which is 4. You also group the number of parts under consideration by two, or $6 \div 2$. Thus,

$$\frac{6}{8} = \frac{6 \div 2}{8 \div 2} = \frac{3}{4}$$

Again, examples of this type should lead to the generalization that the numerator and denominator may be divided by the same number.

After the students have made the generalization, which should not rest on the one example shown here, that both the numerator and denominator may be multiplied or divided by the same number, then they are ready to move to exercises such as these:

$$\frac{2}{3} = \frac{\square}{12}$$

$$\frac{4}{6} = \frac{\square}{3}$$

In this example, students need to think "What is 3 multiplied by to get 12?" Once they have established it is 4, they should think and write:

$$\frac{2 \times 4}{3 \times 4} = \frac{8}{12}$$

In the second example, they should realize that 6 was divided by 2 to obtain 3, so 4 would also have to be divided by 2:

$$\frac{4 \div 2}{6 \div 2} = \frac{2}{3}$$

The first example is the type of thinking needed in finding a common denominator; the second is the type needed in simplifying many problems. Both are ways to express fractions as equivalent fractions in order to solve some problem.

Children also should be helped to see that a common fraction cannot always be changed to an equivalent one with a certain specified denominator if the numerator must be a whole number. For example, $\frac{5}{12}$ cannot be changed to thirds even though you can divide 12 by 4 to get 3. When you divide 5 by 4, you do not get a whole number. Similarly, you cannot change $\frac{2}{3}$ to fifths:

$$\frac{2}{3} = \frac{\square}{5}$$

There is no whole number that you can multiply 3 by to get 5. Exercises such as those in Lesson Idea 11–4 focus on these skills.

In the past there has been much emphasis on finding the *least common denominator*. With a decreased emphasis on fractions, this skill is not as essential as it once was. However, to add or subtract fractions, one often finds a common denominator.

The product of the two denominators will always give a common denominator for the two fractions. We have already examined this as we ordered two fractions in Lesson Idea 11–3. We will return to this idea as we examine adding and subtracting fractions when a common denominator is needed.

At times, however, the product of the denominators is not the least common denominator. For example, a common denominator of $\frac{5}{6}$ and $\frac{3}{4}$ is 6×4, or 24, but the least common denominator is 12. The least common denominator is the smallest number that both 6 and 4 will divide. With small denominators, the least common denominator can often be found by inspection, which is probably a more beneficial approach than learning a routine.

When children can order fractions symbolically, they may enjoy the quick and easy game in In the Classroom 11–2. If they have difficulty playing, they may need to return to a concrete or pictorial representation. If the game is too easy, choose a game board with 48 squares and fractions less than $\frac{1}{3}$ that may be expressed as an equivalent fraction with denominator of 48 (for example, $\frac{1}{4}$ or $\frac{3}{16}$).

Benchmarks

Some fractions look intimidating, so children need to develop facility with some friendly fractions such as halves, thirds, and fourths, and be able to relate other fractions to these. By building what is referred to as benchmarks in *Principles and Standards for*

Lesson Idea 11–4

Can You Divide It?

Here is a few ideas to start your discussion. After children understand these, have them investigate other fractional parts.

▼ All of these regions have been divided into parts with vertical (up and down) lines. Use horizontal (across) lines to see if you can change the model to the fraction given. The first one has been done.

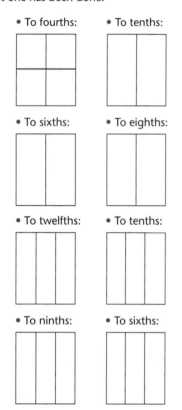

• To fourths: • To tenths:

• To sixths: • To eighths:

• To twelfths: • To tenths:

• To ninths: • To sixths:

▼ Choose the fractional part fifths. Draw the picture to decide whether you can change fifths to sixths, sevenths, eighths, ninths, tenths, and so forth. What is your conjecture? Write why you think this is true.

In The Classroom 11–2

Whole Hog

Objective: Practice in comparing fractions. Choose a partner, and each of you make your own gameboard by copying the H on the grid paper or drawing the 18 squares.

▼ Cut ten squares of paper. Write one of these fractions on each square:

$$\frac{1}{2} \quad \frac{1}{3} \quad \frac{1}{6} \quad \frac{2}{6} \quad \frac{1}{9} \quad \frac{2}{9} \quad \frac{3}{9} \quad \frac{1}{18} \quad \frac{2}{18} \quad \frac{3}{18}$$

▼ Be sure each of you has a crayon.

Now you are ready to go Whole Hog!

Game Rules

1. Put the fraction cards in a pile face down.

2. Each of you take a card from the top of the pile.

3. Turn your cards over and decide who has the larger fraction.

4. The player with the larger fraction must color that fractional part of her or his H.

5. Put both cards at the bottom of the pile.

6. Keep choosing a card and play as before.

7. If a player with the larger fraction cannot color the fractional part shown on the card, both players must put their cards back and take the next cards on top.

8. Continue playing until one person colors the whole H. That person is the first to go Whole Hog and loses the game.

▼ Make a new H and play again.

School Mathematics (NCTM 2000) children will be able to reason with these more complicated fractions. For example, what fractions are near one-half? Consider the following fractions:

$$\frac{6}{11} \quad \frac{11}{23} \quad \frac{18}{35} \quad \frac{44}{90} \quad \frac{354}{700} \quad \frac{800}{1605} \quad \frac{100001}{200000}$$

How do you know they each are near $\frac{1}{2}$? Which are more than $\frac{1}{2}$? Which are less than $\frac{1}{2}$? Beginning

with smaller numerators and denominators, children can build this same intuitive feel for fractions near the benchmark $\frac{1}{2}$.

Students should also be able to tell if a fraction is near 0 or near 1. Can you write a fraction that is near 0 (near 1)? How do you know? What would a model look like for any fraction near 0 (near 1)?

Let us look at the use of benchmarks to put in order a set of fractions: $^{13}/_{25}$, $^{2}/_{31}$, $^{5}/_{6}$, $^{4}/_{11}$, and $^{21}/_{20}$. This would be a time-consuming task if one tried to find a common denominator. If one uses benchmarks as shown in the number line below, the task becomes rather easy: $^{13}/_{25}$ is a little more $^{1}/_{2}$, and $^{4}/_{11}$ is a little less than $^{1}/_{2}$, $^{2}/_{31}$ is near zero, $^{5}/_{6}$ is a little less than one, and $^{21}/_{20}$ is a little more than one.

Children also can use the knowledge of benchmarks to check the reasonableness of computations with fractions or to estimate answers. For example, how do you know that $^{3}/_{5} + ^{6}/_{7}$ is not $^{9}/_{12}$? If one knows that $^{3}/_{5}$ is a little more than $^{1}/_{2}$ and $^{6}/_{7}$ is almost 1, then the sum must be more than 1.

Mixed Numbers and Improper Fractions

Through models, you can lead naturally into mixed numbers and improper fractions, even as children are learning the initial concepts of fractions. For example, a natural representation of the following model is the mixed number $2^{1}/_{4}$.

Adding partitions in the model to show all the fourths leads to the initial counting of 9 fourths and to the representation by the improper fraction $^{9}/_{4}$.

To help children gain experience with mixed numbers and improper fractions, use models as much as possible and ask them to write *both* types of numbers to represent the models. When children understand the process, they need practice in changing from one form to the other without the use of models. However, do not rush to a routine, but encourage students to think problems through, as in the example that follows. The thinking depends upon understanding the equivalence of a whole in terms of the fractional parts (for example, 5 fifths or 6 sixths make a whole).

Example: Change $8^{2}/_{3}$ to an improper fraction.

See if you can follow Cerise's thinking:

I know that 1 is 3 thirds.

So, I need to figure how many thirds in 8 wholes. That is 8 groups of 3 thirds, which is 24 thirds.

Now, I have to add on the 2 thirds, so it is 26 thirds.

It is also important that students can think through changing an improper fraction to a mixed number. For example, $^{17}/_{6}$ is 17 sixths; since 6 sixths make a whole, 17 would make 2 wholes, and there would be 5 sixths more. So $^{17}/_{6}$ is $2^{5}/_{6}$.

OPERATIONS WITH FRACTIONS

The key to a meaningful presentation of the operations with fractions is to establish a firm background in fractions, especially equivalent fractions. Problem situations that involve fractions and operations should be presented so that children will use what they know about the situation to make sense of the operations. Whenever possible, the meanings given to operations with whole numbers should be extended to fractions. There are, however, meanings of operations that do not extend directly. For example, for the multiplication of two fractions, multiplication is not repeated addition. Other differences also must be kept in mind, such as when multiplying two whole numbers, the product is always larger than either factor; but in multiplying two proper fractions, the product is always less than either factor.

Children gain a better understanding of operations with fractions if they learn to estimate answers by using whole numbers and benchmarks such as one-half. For example, before computing the answer to $3\frac{2}{3} + 4\frac{5}{6}$, they should be able to realize that the answer is more than 7. In fact, since $\frac{2}{3}$ and $\frac{5}{6}$ are each more than $\frac{1}{2}$, the answer is more than 8. Developing this type of number and operation sense will make it easier to establish what are reasonable answers to problems. Many calculators will perform operations with fractions. It is important that the conceptual understanding be firmly established so that answers can be checked for reasonableness.

Addition and Subtraction

Instead of beginning addition and subtraction with fractions with a symbolic sentence such as $\frac{2}{3} + \frac{1}{4}$, begin with joining and separating situations. Problems involving these situations, together with pictorial models, can:

- Help children see that adding and subtracting of fractions solve problems similar to those with whole numbers
- Give children an idea of what a reasonable answer will be
- Help children see why a common denominator is necessary when adding or subtracting

Use children's knowledge of solving whole number addition and subtraction word problems to begin examining how to add and subtract fractions. If children understand how to count fractional parts (for example, 3 sevenths and 2 more sevenths is 5 sevenths) and how to compare two fractions with a pictorial model, they may find their own ways to solve joining and separating problems with fractions.

Look at the set of word problems in Figure 11–7.

Children should have no problem solving the first two of these word problems. Have them show how they solved each one, encouraging them to tell how the two problems are alike (for example, by joining situations: in problem A, Cyrilla ate 2 apples, and in problem B she ate 2 fifths). Also, although quite simple, have children draw a picture to show the first two problems. Then let them try the next problem, discussing how problem C is like the other two and how it is different. Encourage children to draw a picture to show the cake.

Children may come up with many ways to approach the problem. If they have drawn pictures to

---

A

Cyrilla ate 2 apples, and Carey ate 1 apple. How many apples did they eat altogether?

B

Cyrilla ate $\frac{2}{5}$ of a pie, and Carey ate $\frac{1}{5}$ of a pie. How much pie did they eat altogether?

C

Cyrilla ate $\frac{2}{3}$ of a cake, and Carey ate ¼ of the cake. How much of the cake did they eat altogether?

Figure 11–7 • Three joining problems

---

compare fractions, they may draw a picture as shown here (like the model in Lesson Idea 11–3).

Math sentence: $\frac{2}{3} + \frac{1}{4} = ?$ Math computation

Cyrilla: $\frac{2}{3}$ Carey: $\frac{1}{4}$

$$\begin{array}{r} \frac{2}{3} \\ + \frac{1}{4} \\ \hline \end{array}$$

Show both partitions on each cake:

Cyrilla: $\frac{8}{12}$ Carey: $\frac{3}{12}$

$$\begin{array}{r} \frac{2}{3} \rightarrow \frac{8}{12} \\ + \frac{1}{4} \rightarrow \frac{3}{12} \\ \hline \frac{11}{12} \end{array}$$

Notice how the picture would change if Carey had eaten $\frac{3}{4}$ of the cake. Carey would have eaten $\frac{9}{12}$. Together, they would have eaten $\frac{17}{12}$. Do you see how the picture could then be used to see they ate one whole cake and $\frac{5}{12}$ of another?

Note that in adding fractions, we assume that the whole (the unit) is the same. If Cyrilla ate $\frac{2}{3}$ of a cake, and Carey ate $\frac{3}{4}$ of a cake, then there would have to be two cakes—and we assume the cakes are the same size. If Cyrilla eats $\frac{2}{3}$ of a very small cake and Carey eats $\frac{3}{4}$ of a very large cake, you would need more information about the size of each cake before telling how much they ate together.

Adding mixed numbers is no more difficult than the previous problem. Children who have made sense of adding proper fractions will put this together with their knowledge of adding whole numbers. You may want to watch to see how children handle a computation such as $5\frac{2}{3} + 3\frac{3}{4}$. Adding the whole numbers gives 8, and adding the fractions gives $\frac{17}{12}$ as shown previously, or $8\frac{17}{13}$. Children can then use their knowledge that $\frac{17}{12}$ is $1\frac{5}{12}$, so the total can be expressed as $9\frac{5}{12}$.

Often, children who have been taught a routine for this problem may say that the sum is $8\frac{7}{12}$. What error are they making?

You can approach subtracting two proper fractions in the same way that you did adding. If you begin with subtraction problems that involve comparison, such as how much more cake did Cyrilla eat than Carey in Problem C (Figure 11–7), then you can use the same model. Note that the background of knowing which fraction is larger is important in real-life situations. In Problem C, it would not make sense to ask how much more cake Carey ate than Cyrilla.

Subtracting fractions greater than one or mixed numbers is often more difficult, partly because children have not changed a mixed number to another mixed number or because they lack understanding of regrouping.

The subtraction example in Figure 11–8 requires regrouping $6\frac{3}{7}$ to $5\frac{10}{7}$. Help children understand that

$$1 \text{ is } \frac{7}{7} \quad \text{and} \quad 6 \text{ is } 5 + 1, \quad \text{or} \quad 5 + \frac{7}{7}$$

Thus,

$$6\frac{3}{7} \text{ is } 5 + \frac{7}{7} + \frac{3}{7}, \quad \text{or } 5\frac{10}{7}$$

If children are having difficulty with regrouping fractions, the following model can help them see, for example, that $6\frac{3}{7} = 5\frac{10}{7}$.

$6\frac{3}{7}$	Are the denominators the same?
$-2\frac{4}{7}$	Yes. (If not, change them to like fractions.)
	Can I take $\frac{4}{7}$ from $\frac{3}{7}$?
$5\frac{10}{7}$	No, I must regroup $6\frac{3}{7}$.
$-2\frac{4}{7}$	$(1 = \frac{7}{7}, \text{ so } \frac{3}{7} + \frac{7}{7} = \frac{10}{7}.)$
$3\frac{6}{7}$	Now subtract the fraction parts, then the whole parts.

Figure 11–8 • Subtracting mixed numbers

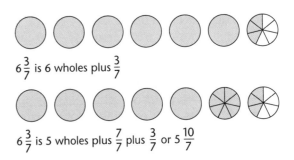

$6\frac{3}{7}$ is 6 wholes plus $\frac{3}{7}$

$6\frac{3}{7}$ is 5 wholes plus $\frac{7}{7}$ plus $\frac{3}{7}$ or $5\frac{10}{7}$

Multiplication

The algorithm for multiplication of fractions is one of the simplest. Multiply numerators to find the numerator, and multiply denominators to find the denominator.

This algorithm can be taught in minutes (and forgotten in seconds unless a great amount of practice is provided). However, simply teaching this algorithm does not provide insight into why it works or when to use it. We suggest a development that gives the underlying meanings of multiplication, an idea of the size of an answer, and the reason why the algorithm works before the algorithm itself is presented. Many children who have a good background with fractions will come up with their own methods (Warrington and Kamii 1999).

We will look at four different cases: a whole number times a fraction or mixed number, a fraction times a whole number, a fraction times a fraction, and a mixed number times a mixed number. In each case, we will tie the multiplication to a meaning of multiplication of whole numbers. We will use the knowledge that 3×4 means three groups of four and 3×4 is the area of a 3-by-4 rectangle.

Whole Number Times a Fraction Let's begin with a problem:

You have 3 pans each with $\frac{4}{5}$ of a pizza. How much pizza do you have?

How is this problem like having three bags each with four marbles? See if this sketch helps you to see the similarity between multiplying whole numbers and multiplying a whole number times a fraction:

3×4

3 groups of 4 is 12

$3 \times \frac{4}{5}$

3 groups of 4 fifths is 12 fifths

If we consider three groups of four to be 3 × 4, it makes sense to consider three groups of $\frac{4}{5}$ to mean $3 \times \frac{4}{5}$. How did we first find three groups of four? We could have put out three groups of four marbles and counted them. Similarly, if we want to find three groups of $\frac{4}{5}$, we can put out three pans of pizza, each having $\frac{4}{5}$ in it, and count the number of fifths. Or, to find 3 × 4, we can consider repeated addition:

$$4 + 4 + 4 = 12$$

Thus,

$$3 \times \frac{4}{5} \text{ is } \frac{4}{5} + \frac{4}{5} + \frac{4}{5} = \frac{12}{5}$$

After the students have solved problems like this one with pictures, see if they can solve them without pictures or repeated addition. Be sure to place strong emphasis on the words. Have them listen carefully as you read:

$5 \times \frac{2}{3}$ is 5 groups of two-thirds,
which is *5 groups of 2* or *10* (thirds),
or $\frac{10}{3}$

Fraction Times a Whole Number Again, let's begin with a problem:

> You have $\frac{3}{4}$ of a case of twenty-four bottles. How many bottles do you have?

If children have worked with the set model for fractions, they have the background to solve this problem with physical objects. Now, we want to move to solving it symbolically and tying it to multiplication.

First, let's look at why it makes sense to consider this problem as a multiplication problem. If we had 5 cases with 24 bottles in each, what would we do to find out how many? We would multiply 5 × 24.

Similarly, 20 cases would be 20 × 24, 53 cases would be 53 × 24, and, thus, $\frac{3}{4}$ case would be $\frac{3}{4}$ × 24.

Now let's review how we find $\frac{3}{4}$ of 24. We first partition (or divided) the set into 4 equal parts (each part would have 6), or, in other words, we first find $\frac{1}{4}$ of 24. Thus, $\frac{3}{4}$ would be 3 times as many, or 3 × 6 = 18.

Think

$\frac{3}{4} \times 24 = \boxed{}$ $\quad \frac{1}{4} \times 24 = 6$

$\frac{3}{4}$ is 3 times as many,

or 3 × 6 = 18

At first glance, this procedure looks slightly different from the algorithm for multiplying numerators and multiplying denominators. Physically, we first divided the number in the set by 4 and then multiplied that by 3. When we perform the standard algorithm, we multiply first and then divide:

$$\frac{3}{4} \times 24 = \frac{3}{4} \times \frac{24}{1} = \frac{3 \times 24}{4} = \frac{72}{4} = 18$$

One way to approach these problems is to use commutativity. Since 3 × 4 = 4 × 3, we want

$$\frac{3}{4} \times 24 = 24 \times \frac{3}{4}$$

We can then find $\frac{3}{4}$ × 24 by using the procedures discussed in multiplying a whole number by a fraction. Although this approach may be easier, the opportunity to present the "of" meaning of multiplication is lost. Children do not readily see that $\frac{3}{4}$ of a case of 24 is the same as having 24 groups of three-fourths.

Fraction Times a Fraction Consider another problem:

> If you own $\frac{3}{4}$ of an acre of land and $\frac{5}{6}$ of this is planted in trees, what part of the acre is planted in trees?

Why is this a multiplication problem? A picture may help you see how this is related to area of a rectangle and thus to multiplicaton. Consider first the acre partitioned into fourths and shade the amount you own, which is $\frac{3}{4}$:

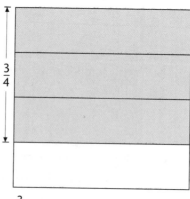

$\frac{3}{4}$ of an acre (the amount you own)

Since you know that 5 sixths of this is planted, partition your property into sixths. To find what part of the whole acre is planted in your trees, we need to identify the size of each of the small rectangles. Do you see that there would be 24 rectangles of this size? So each is one twenty-fourth of the acre, and you have planted 15 of them (or $^{15}/_{24}$ of the acre).

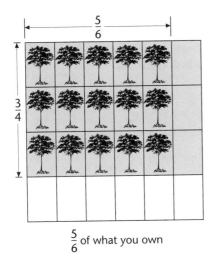

$\frac{5}{6}$ of what you own

What we have is a tree-planted rectangle that is $^3/_4$ by $^5/_6$, and its area is found by multiplying $^3/_4 \times ^5/_6$.

This model will need to be developed slowly and only after children have had experience with finding areas of rectangles. After children use a model for problems such as this, make a list of multiplication exercises and products (do not reduce the answers). See if the children notice a pattern for multiplying two fractions.

If children have had experience with finding area, this model can be used to see the procedure for multiplying fractions (multiply the numerators, multiply the denominators). You can refer to the diagrams to show why the procedure works. You have partitioned the acre into fourths one way and sixths the other way, thus creating 4 × 6, or 24, equal parts (the denominator). Trees were planted in three rows of five, or fifteen of these parts, so 3 × 5 is the numerator. Symbolically, we write

$$\frac{3}{4} \times \frac{5}{6} = \frac{3 \times 5}{4 \times 6} = \frac{15}{24}$$

At this point, return to earlier examples and let children know that this process holds for those cases also. A word of caution: do not rush to canceling. Be sure that children can do multiplication this way, reducing answers only if necessary and applying multiplication to problems, before introducing canceling.

Mixed Number Times a Mixed Number Problems that involve multiplication of mixed numbers also can be solved with models. Consider the following problem:

You have a piece of cloth that is $2^1/_4$ yards by $1^1/_2$ yards. How many square yards do you have?

Part A in Figure 11–9 presents a model that shows how to change both mixed numbers in this problem to improper fractions, and the model in part B shows how to multiply the mixed numbers without first changing them to improper fractions.

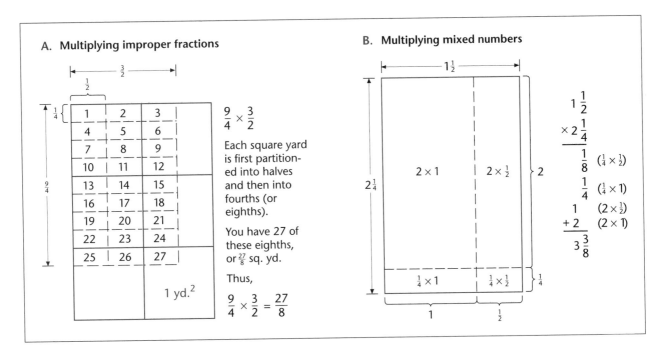

Figure 11–9 • Multiplication models

Division

The two meanings of division—partitioning and measurement—were explained in Chapter 8. In a partitioning situation with whole numbers, the whole is being shared equally among a given number of groups. In a measurement situation, a given number or amount is being put in each group. We will begin looking at the division of fractions by using the measurement situation and the same problem that was presented in Chapter 8:

> How many 2-foot hair ribbons can be made from a 10-foot roll of ribbon?

Here, you are finding how many 2-foot pieces (the size of the group) are in the whole, or how many twos in ten. If you were drawing a picture of how you could do this in real life, the picture might look like the following:

10-foot roll

2-foot ribbon

You can readily see that there would be five hair ribbons, each 2 feet long. We symbolized this by $10 \div 2 = \_\_$, or $10 \div 2 = 5$.

Following the same line of reasoning, draw a picture to show how to find the number of hair ribbons you could make from this roll if each were $\frac{1}{2}$ foot long? $\frac{1}{4}$ foot long? Although this is slightly tedious, do you see how the picture could be used? What is a symbolic shortcut for you?

See if your picture agrees with the one that Susie drew when she was finding the number of hair ribbons, each $\frac{1}{4}$ foot long, that she could make from a 3-foot long roll.

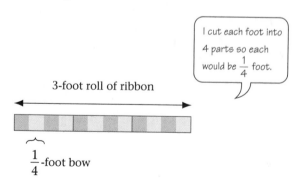

> I cut each foot into 4 parts so each would be $\frac{1}{4}$ foot.

3-foot roll of ribbon

$\frac{1}{4}$-foot bow

In this problem, we are finding how many one-fourths are in 3, or $3 \div \frac{1}{4} = \square$. We found that there

are 12, each $\frac{1}{4}$ foot long in a 3-foot roll of ribbon. Do you notice that the picture also shows that you have 3 groups of 4 (or 3×4 hair ribbons)?

How would you draw a picture to help you find how many $\frac{3}{4}$-foot long pieces there are in a 6-foot roll of ribbon? Again, we need to mark off lengths that are $\frac{3}{4}$-foot long. See the picture below.

$\frac{3}{4}$-foot

Note that we first marked off fourths and then grouped them by threes to see how many $\frac{3}{4}$-foot pieces are in a 6-foot roll. That is, we multiplied by 4 and divided by 3. You probably learned this as inverting the divisor and then proceeding by multiplying. Look at the symbolic algorithm:

$$6 \div \frac{3}{4} = \frac{6}{1} \times \frac{4}{3} = 6 \times \frac{4}{1} \times 3 = \frac{24}{3}, \text{ or } 8.$$

One difficulty that students, including adults, often have is with ribbon being left after cutting as many $\frac{3}{4}$-foot pieces as possible. For example, suppose that you only have 2 feet of ribbon on the roll and you want to cut as many $\frac{3}{4}$-foot long ribbons as you can. You know that you can cut at least two because you can get one from each foot of ribbon. Can you cut as many as three, each being $\frac{3}{4}$ foot long? Again, let's look at the picture.

We can cut two full ribbons as shown by the two shaded parts but do not have enough for another full hair ribbon. What part of another can we make? Do you see that the white parts are $\frac{2}{3}$ of a hair ribbon? If we use the algorithm, we would have

$$2 \div \frac{3}{4} = \frac{2}{1} \times \frac{4}{3} = 2 \times \frac{4}{1} \times 3 = \frac{8}{3} = 2\frac{2}{3}.$$

This last example also helps children to reason through problems in which the divisor is larger than the dividend. For example, how many bows, each $\frac{1}{2}$ foot long, could be cut from a strip of ribbon that is $\frac{1}{3}$ foot long, or $\frac{1}{3} \div \frac{1}{2}$? You know that since $\frac{1}{2}$ is larger than $\frac{1}{3}$ that you could not get a hair bow. What part of one do you have? Draw a picture to convince yourself that you would have enough ribbon to make $\frac{2}{3}$ of a hair bow.

DEVELOPMENT OF DECIMALS

In introducing decimals, you should link them to other knowledge—in particular, to common fractions and to place value. Although you will need to weave both of these ideas into your teaching, we have separated them for ease of discussion.

Relationship to Common Fractions

Decimal fractions are just another notation for tenths, hundredths, and other powers-of-ten parts of a unit. Thus, basic to decimals is understanding of these fractional parts. Hopefully, that understanding has been built in introducing common fractions. We will assume so.

Tenths Before introducing the decimal notation for tenths, let's review what students should know about tenths from their background with fractions. They should know that, to partition a unit into tenths, there must be ten equal parts. They also should be able to make the connection between the model, the oral name, and the fraction. And they should know that ten tenths make a whole, that seven tenths is less than a whole, and that twenty-seven tenths is more than a whole.

With this background, the children should be ready to learn that 0.3 is a new symbol for $\frac{3}{10}$. At this point, you should link the place-value ideas to the new notation (see the discussion on place value). You also need to stress that 0.3 is read just like $\frac{3}{10}$. Also look at $\frac{27}{10}$, or $2\frac{7}{10}$. This amount is written 2.7 and read as "two and seven-tenths." Note that the word *and* is said for the decimal point. Reading decimals in this way helps to connect decimal and fraction ideas. A quick game to play that provides practice in writing decimal and fraction notation is described in In the Classroom 11–3. Before introducing hundredths, you should make certain that the students have made all the connections in this triangle.

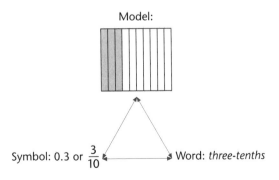

Model:

Symbol: 0.3 or $\frac{3}{10}$ ⟷ Word: *three-tenths*

Hundredths To begin extending decimals to hundredths, provide each child with copies of the model of hundredths, shown in Figure 11–10 (Ap-

pendix B contains a sheet with multiple copies). Make certain that the children know that the unit (entire square or grid) is one, and that each part (small square) is one hundredth. Using the model, ask them to shade in $\frac{3}{100}$, $\frac{7}{100}$, $\frac{10}{100}$, $\frac{21}{100}$....

Have the children color in the first and second columns on the hundredth model and three more small squares. Ask what part of the whole is covered. Elicit both responses, $\frac{2}{10} + \frac{3}{100}$ as well as $\frac{23}{100}$. Then write

$$\frac{23}{100} = \frac{2}{10} + \frac{3}{100}$$

Now connect the place-value interpretation and the decimal notation 0.23. You can also use the model to show that $0.2 = 0.20$. Continue having children make the connections shown in the triangle—that is, by connecting the model, the symbol, and the word.

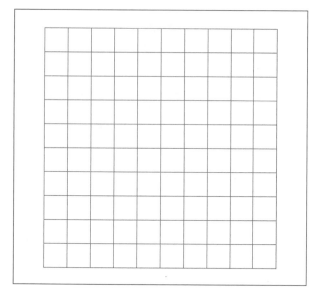

Figure 11–10 • **Model of hundredths**

Table 11–2 • **Results of national assessment items on equivalence of decimals and fractions**

Exercise	Percent Responding Age 13
A. Which decimal is equal to $\frac{1}{5}$?	
○ .15	12
● .2	38
○ .5	38
○ .51	3
○ I don't know.	6
B. Which decimal is equal to $\frac{5}{8}$?	
○ .6	7
● .625	27
○ .$\overline{714285}$	3
○ .85	30
○ I don't know.	30

Thousandths and Other Decimals One national assessment reported that

> . . . although thirteen- and seventeen-year-olds appeared to have facility with tenths and hundredths, their competency was less developed for thousandths and smaller decimal numbers. (Carpenter et al. 1981, p. 39)

This deficiency is partly because there is less emphasis on these decimals but also because teachers often expect children to generalize after hundredths to all the other places. Most of the work with smaller decimals should be done primarily through the place-value interpretation because the fractions become unwieldy. However, thousandths should be developed as one-tenth of a hundredth, and the understanding that ten thousandths is $\frac{1}{100}$ should be developed through a model.

Decimals and Other Common Fractions Students need to develop the ability to relate fractions with decimals. Hopefully, if decimals have been introduced carefully, students will be able to write the fraction notation for a decimal and the decimal notation for any fraction expressed in tenths, hundredths, and so on.

The ability to relate fractions to decimals when expressed in tenths, hundreds, and so on does not ensure that students can express other fractions as decimals. Table 11–2 shows two exercises from a national assessment as well as the responses of thirteen-year-olds. In each case, less than 30 percent responded correctly. Analyze the errors made in both examples and consider what they indicate about students' grasp of fractions and decimals. Would you not hope that more students would realize that $\frac{5}{8}$ is just a little more than one-half and thus could not equal 0.85, which is almost a whole?

When you have established that many fractions can be written as decimals, you can turn to the meaning of a fraction as division. Begin with an example that can be easily changed to a decimal, for example, $\frac{4}{5}$. Children should know that $\frac{4}{5} = \frac{8}{10} = 0.8$.

Then proceed to the idea that $\frac{4}{5}$ means $4 \div 5$. To divide 4 by 5, a child needs to be able to divide decimals and to realize that 4 is also 4.0:

$$\frac{4}{5} = 4 \div 5, \quad 5\overline{)4.0}^{\,0.8}$$

Therefore,

$$\frac{4}{5} = 0.8$$

Children can explore many interesting patterns that occur when converting fractions to decimals. Some can be investigated with a calculator. For example, look at the decimal equivalents for ninths:

$$\frac{1}{9} = .11111 \ldots$$

$$\frac{2}{9} = .22222 \ldots$$

$$\frac{3}{9} = .33333 \ldots$$

You should do a few of these calculations by hand to show that the pattern continues forever. If you use only the calculator, students may think that $\frac{1}{9} = 0.11111111$ (or the number of places on their calculator screen).

Students can also be helped to see that $\frac{1}{3}$ does not equal 0.33, 0.333, or 0.3333 by looking at the meaning of $\frac{1}{3}$. If $\frac{1}{3} = 0.33$, then each of three equal parts of a whole would be 0.33. Thus, the whole would be $0.33 + 0.33 + 0.33$, or 0.99, which is not one. Similarly, $\frac{1}{3} \neq 0.3333$, even though this is a better approximation.

Relationship to Place Value

The place-value interpretation of decimals is most useful in understanding computation with decimals. We look now at a way to develop this interpretation and how to use it in ordering and rounding decimals.

Interpretation Return to whole numbers and think about what children know about place value. Take, for example, the number 2463. Children can identify the places (ones, tens, hundreds, and thousands) as well as what number is in each (3, 6, 4, and 2). They know, for example, that the four means four hundreds. They also have learned how the places were formed: beginning with ones as a unit, grouping ten of these to form a new unit (tens), grouping ten of these to form a new unit (hundreds), and so forth.

In introducing place-value ideas with decimals, begin with ones as the unit. Instead of grouping by tens, take one-tenth of the one to form the new unit of tenths. To indicate this new unit in our place-value system, we use a decimal point after the ones place. Children also should be helped to realize that ten of the tenths make a one (just as ten of any unit make the next larger unit). They also should be able to identify the tenths place in a number. This interpretation should be integrated with the interpretation of decimals as fractions.

Again, when introducing hundredths, the place-value interpretation should be made. Given a number such as 51.63, a child should be able to tell what number is in the tenths place and the hundredths place as well as the relationships between the places (hundredths is $\frac{1}{10}$ of the tenths, or ten hundredths is one tenth). After introducing thousandths in a similar way, the children should be able to generalize to any decimal place.

Let us see how a place-value mat, or grid, can assist with decimals. When learning about decimals, it is most important that a decimal such as 24.09 be read as twenty-four *and* 9 hundredths—not "two, four, point, zero, nine." The words *tenths* and *hundredths* help students keep the tie between fractions and decimals. Consider 32.43, for example:

32 *and* 43 hundredths
or
32 *and* 4 tenths, 3 hundredths

Now let's use the grid for writing other decimals. (Remember to use models when first developing place value, as described in Chapter 7.)

Write 8 hundredths:

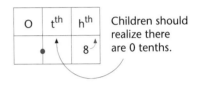

Children should realize there are 0 tenths.

What is 29 hundredths?

What is 29 tenths?

Now look at 4.3 on the grid:

How many tens? [0]

You could write a zero in the tens place, but this is not customary. However, sometimes it is helpful to write a zero in the hundredths place:

How many hundredths? [0]
What does that tell you?

4.3 is equivalent to 4.30.

Children who are well acquainted with the models and the grid for place value should be able to handle decimals with ease.

Ordering and Rounding Decimals

The ordering and rounding of decimals should follow directly from an understanding of decimals and the ability to order and round whole numbers. This understanding must include being able to interpret the decimals in terms of place value and being able to think of, for example, 0.2 as 0.20 or 0.200.

Here is an example of two children discussing which is larger—23.61 or 23.9?

CARTER: I think that 23.61 is larger because it has more places, just like 2361 is larger than 239.

BENNY: But we know that the 23 in each of them is the same, so all we have to do is compare the decimals.

CARTER: Okay, it's not like whole numbers.

BENNY: Well, sort of. We begin with the largest place—the tens are the same, the ones are the same, so we need to look at the tenths. The 9 is larger than the 6, so 23.9 is larger than 23.61.

CARTER: I follow you till that last. Now you have a 9 and a 61, and 61 is larger.

BENNY: But, the 9 is 9 tenths and the 61 is 61 hundredths. Want to look at a model?

CARTER: I get it, I remember the model. Nine tenths is 9 strips, or 90 little squares. It is 90 hundredths, so it is larger.

As you see from this conversation, if the children really understand the notation and the meaning of the decimals, they can figure out ways to compare decimals.

In rounding a decimal such as 24.78 to the nearest tenth, children need to ask themselves the same types of questions with whole numbers. Children must also understand that 24.7 = 24.70.

Questions	Expected Responses
What "tenths" is 24.78 between?	It's between 24.7 and 24.8 (or 24.70 and 24.80).
Is it nearer 24.7 or 24.8?	Looking at 24.70 and 24.80, it's nearer 24.80.
How will you round it?	To 24.8.

DECIMAL OPERATIONS

Certainly, one advantage of decimals over fractions is that computation is much easier and basically follows the same rules as for whole numbers. In teaching the algorithms for decimals, you should build on the place-value interpretations and the corresponding whole-number algorithms. Given the wide availability of calculators, it is important that you spend as much time seeing whether answers are

reasonable as on the algorithms. Thus, estimation skills (described in Chapter 9) become crucial.

In the Classroom 11–4 combines estimation skills and operations with decimals. To answer these questions, encourage students to use whole numbers that are compatible. They can be presented questions of this type before learning about decimal computation.

Addition and Subtraction

Children who have a good concept of decimals will have little trouble extending the whole number algorithms for addition and subtraction to decimals. They will realize that they need to:

- Add or subtract like units (tens with tens, hundredths with hundredths, and so forth)

- Regroup in the decimal places as they did with whole numbers.

In The Classroom 11–4

What's Your Answer?

Objective: Use estimations about decimal quantities to answer questions.

▼ Use the data in this table. These are data about the countries of the United Kingdom.

Country	Area (Thousands of km^2)	Population (Millions)
England	50.363	46.221
N. Ireland	5.452	1.543
Scotland	30.415	5.131
Wales	8.019	2.750

▼ Answer these questions:

- About how much larger is England than Scotland? _____

- About how large is the United Kingdom? _____

- About what is the population of the United Kingdom? _____

- Do twice as many people live in Wales as live in N. Ireland? _____

- Is England more than six times larger than Wales? _____

Difficulty with adding or subtracting decimals arises mainly when the values are given in horizontal format or in terms of a story problem and the decimals are expressed in different units; for example, 51.23 + 0.4 + 347. To deal with this difficulty, it is wise to have children first focus on an approximate answer. Will it be more than 300? More than 500? More than 1000? Some children may need help in lining up the like units and so may benefit from using a grid:

H	T	O	tth	hth
	5	1 • 2		3
		0 •	4	0
3	4	7 • 0		0

Multiplication and Division

Before we examine how to multiply or divide two decimals, let's consider multiplying and dividing a decimal by a whole number. These operations are conceptually easier to explain and allow for some development that will be helpful when multiplying or dividing two decimals. They also build the understandings needed for effective use of calculators.

Consider the following problem:

Six tables are lined up end-to-end. Each table is 2.3 meters long. How long is the line of tables?

Students should be able to solve this problem by adding decimals. From their previous work with multiplication, they also should realize it is a multiplication problem. Thus, they should see that:

$6 \times 2.3 = 2.3 + 2.3 + 2.3 + 2.3 + 2.3 + 2.3 = 13.8$

However, just as children moved away from repeated addition to find the product of two whole numbers, they need to do so with this type of problem. Here is another way to think about it: multiplication depends on a firm foundation of the place-value interpretation of decimals.

Think

2.3	23	tenths
× 6	× 6	
	138	tenths, which is 13.8
2.37	23	hundredths
× 6	× 6	
	1422	hundredths, which is 14.22

Working with the grid will help students remember that 138 tenths is 13.8. In using this method, you should first have the students decide on a reasonable answer. For example, is 6 × 2.37 more than 12? As much as 18? They can also check by repeated addition.

The distributive algorithm that was used for dividing whole numbers may be used for dividing a decimal by a whole number. Consider this problem:

A vinegar company distributed 123.2 million liters of vinegar equally to eight customers. How much vinegar did each customer receive?

First, ask for reasonable answers.

Did each customer get more than 10 million liters? [Yes, that would be only 80 million liters.]

Did each get more than 20 million liters? [No, that would be 160 million liters.]

What is the answer? [Between 10 and 20 million liters]

Talk through the division as follows:

How many hundreds? [1] Can 1 be distributed to 8 people? [No]

If we regroup so there are 12 tens, can 12 be distributed to 8 people? [Yes, each gets 1 ten.]

Thus, 8 × 1 ten or 8 tens have been distributed.

Subtracting leaves 43.2 to be distributed to 8 people. Can it? [Yes, each gets 5 ones.]

Subtracting again leaves 3.2, or 32 tenths, to be distributed. Can 32 tenths be distributed to 8 people? [Yes, each gets 4 tenths.]

Thus, 8 × 4 tenths, or 32 tenths, have been distributed.

After this method is introduced, do some problems with remainders and then develop division to a specified number of places:

```
      15.4
  8) 123.8
     80.0
     43.8
     40.0
      3.8
      3.2
       .6     Remainder is .6
```

Note that keeping the decimal in the algorithm helps one see that the remainder is 0.6, not 6.

Now try the same problem carrying out the division to two places (123.8 = 123.80):

$$
\begin{array}{r}
15.47 \\
8\overline{)123.80} \qquad 123.8 = 123.80 \\
\underline{80.0} \\
43.8 \\
\underline{40.0} \\
3.8 \\
\underline{3.2} \\
.60 \\
\underline{.56} \\
.04 \qquad \text{Remainder is .04}
\end{array}
$$

There are several ways to teach multiplication of a decimal by a decimal. If all teachers do is give students a rule for counting off decimal places, they will not help them develop a sense of decimals. Children can discover the rule by using calculators and examining patterns. Another way is to change the decimals to fractions and develop the rule through multiplication of fractions. Another method is to use place value and the knowledge that tenths times tenths is hundredths as shown here:

Think

$$
\begin{array}{rl}
3.2 & 32 \text{ tenths} \\
\times 1.6 & \times 16 \text{ tenths} \\
\hline
 & 512 \text{ hundredths or } 5.12
\end{array}
$$

No matter which method you choose to teach multiplication of decimals, it is important that children are able to check to see that their answers are reasonable.

To divide a decimal by a decimal, children can essentially turn the problem into one they already know how to do. That is, they can make the divisor a whole number by multiplying the divisor by a power of ten, such as 10, 100, or 1000. In order not to change the problem, the dividend must also be multiplied by the same number:

$$
.5\overline{)1.25} \qquad \text{Change to} \qquad 5\overline{)12.5}
$$

Multiply
by 10

There is a shortcut for this procedure: move the decimal point the number of places in the divisor needed to make it a whole number, and then do the same in the dividend.

Although this rule can be learned quickly, there is still the question of why it works. Students can easily be told why to turn the problem into one they can already do and convinced that it works (using the calculator or multiplying to check). However, what would you say to the inquisitive child who asks why it works? One way is to appeal to fractions. We know that:

$$
1.25 \div .5 = \frac{1.25}{.5}
$$

And we know that we can multiply the numerator and denominator by the same number. Thus,

$$
\frac{1.25}{.5} = \frac{1.25 \times 10}{.5 \times 10} = \frac{12.5}{5}
$$

or

$$
1.25 \div .5 = 12.5 \div 5
$$

Students need more practice with multiplication and division of decimals than with addition and subtraction. The reason is partly because multiplication and division of whole numbers is not as firmly fixed as addition and subtraction. It is also because new rules are needed. You will find a great variation in skill level among children in your class. You might want to begin collecting some challenging activities such as the one on In the Classroom 11–5 as well as games and other practice materials.

A Glance at Where We've Been

This chapter has examined how to approach fractions and decimals in a meaningful way. This goal can be reached through thoughtful teaching that first develops an understanding of the fractions and decimals through models and appropriate language. It involves careful sequencing and a pace that does not rush to the symbols alone. The operations with these numbers also can be developed in a meaningful way, instead of through rules learned by rote. A firm foundation of fractions and decimals and the operations will assist students in using these numbers to solve problems. Thus, throughout the development in this chapter, applications have been included to let students see how these numbers are used and to give meaning to the numbers and operations.

Ages or grade levels have not been given because we have found that older children often profit from some of the beginning concepts. It will be your job to realize which pieces of this topic your students are missing. This task will not be as difficult as it

In The Classroom 11–5

Plug-In Puzzles

Objective: Develop decimal number sense.

▼ Use these decimal fractions to fill in the blanks.

8.3   4.2   5.5   3.1   7.6   6.7

Do each multiplication or division. In the division problems, divide to the hundredths place. Sum the four answers.

____ × ____ = _____

____ ÷ 5 = _____

____ × ____ = _____

____ ÷ 3 = _____

Total _____

- What is the largest total you can get? _____

- Can you get a total greater than 50? _____

- Can you get one greater than 100? _____

▼ Arrange these four decimals in the boxes so that the sentence is true. (Remember to do the parts in the parentheses first.)

5.13   4.24   3.84   3.16

$$\left(\underline{\quad} \times 5\right) + \underline{\quad} = \left(4 \times \underline{\quad}\right) + \underline{\quad}$$

▼ Pick the two decimals from those listed that will make the sentence true.

21.21   42.42   36.36   63.63   27.27

$$\left(\underline{\quad} \div 7\right) \times 8 = \left(\underline{\quad} \div 9\right) \times 6$$

sounds if you are familiar with the background and how the concepts and skills interweave.

Things to Do: From What You've Read

1. The part-whole meaning of a fraction can be developed with different attributes such as length and numerosity (sets). Draw part-whole models for four different attributes to show $\frac{3}{4}$.

2. Illustrate three different meanings of $\frac{3}{4}$.

3. Explain how you would develop the idea of equivalent fractions.

4. What is partitioning? How is this process related to division and to fractions?

5. Explain why the areas are equal in each square in Figure 11–5.

6. Illustrate how two fractions may be ordered using the method shown in the Lesson Idea 11–3.

7. Show, with pictures, why $2\frac{3}{5}$ is equivalent to $\frac{13}{5}$; show why $2\frac{3}{5}$ is equivalent to $1\frac{8}{5}$.

8. What is a benchmark for fractions? How are benchmarks used?

9. How is multiplication of fractions different from multiplication of whole numbers?

10. Describe how decimal and common fractions are alike and different.

11. Describe how to explain, with meaning, that 2.8 × 3.7 is 10.36.

Things to Do: Going Beyond This Book

field Additional activities, suggestions, and questions are provided in *Teaching Elementary Mathematics: A Resource for Field Experiences.*

1. Create five story problems that ask children to order fractions.

2. Design a worksheet that would be a good follow-up to the Snapshot of a Lesson that opened this chapter. Include three models—region, length, and area—and a couple of challenging problems.

3. Develop a lesson plan to build on the ideas given in Lesson Idea 11–1, 11–2, or 11–3.

4. Read at least one article listed in the references from *Arithmetic Teacher, Teaching Children Mathematics,* or *Mathematics Teaching in the Middle School.* Describe how it complements or contradicts the suggestions in this chapter.

5. Examine an elementary mathematics textbook series to see how they introduce division of fractions, and contrast each to the methods in this book.

6. Experiment with a calculator that has a fraction key. What fraction skills and understanding would be important if such calculators were used?

7. *field* Fractions. Interview at least three children using the tasks found on In the Classroom 11–1.

8. *field* Fraction Bars. Use fraction bars to teach the concept of fractions as parts of a whole.

9. *field* Games. Play the game with children described in In the Classroom 11–2 (if you have only one child with whom you are working) or in In the Classroom 11–3 (if you have a small group).

BOOK NOOK FOR CHILDREN

Dennis, J. Richard. *Fractions Are Parts of Things.* New York: Crowell, 1971.

Emberly, Ed. *Ed Emberly's Picture Pie: A Circle Drawing Book.* Boston: Little, Brown, 1984.

Hutchins, Pat. *The Doorbell Rang.* New York: Greenwillow, 1987.

Matthews, Louise. *Gator Pie.* New York: Dodd, Mead, 1979.

McMillan, Bruce. *Eating Fractions.* New York: Scholastic, 1991.

Nelson, Joanne. *Half and Half.* Cleveland: Modern Curriculum Press, 1990.

Pomerantz, Charlotte. *The Half-Birthday Party.* New York: Clarion, 1984.

Silverstein, Shel. *A Giraffe and a Half.* New York: Harper and Row, 1964.

Selected References

Baker, Kay M., and Graeber, Anna O. "Little into Big Is the Way It Always Is." *Arithmetic Teacher,* 39 (April 1992), pp. 18–21.

Bezuk, Nadine, and Cramer, Kathleen. "Multiplication of Fractions: Teaching for Understanding." *Arithmetic Teacher,* 39 (November 1991), pp. 34–37.

Carpenter, Thomas P.; Corbitt, Mary Kay; Kepner, Henry S., Jr.; Lindquist, Mary Montgomery; and Reys, Robert E. *Results from the Second Mathematics Assessment of the National Assessment of Educational Progress.* Reston, Va.: NCTM, 1981.

Goldenberg, E. Paul. "A Mathematical Conversation with Fourth Graders." *Arithmetic Teacher,* 38 (April 1991), pp. 38–43.

Groff, Patrick. "It Is Time to Question Fraction Teaching." *Mathematics Teaching in the Middle School,* 1 (January-February 1996), pp. 604–607.

Hanselman, Cheryl A. "Stop Using Foul Language in the Mathematics Classroom." *Mathematics Teaching in the Middle School,* 3 (October 1997), pp. 154–160.

Kieren, Thomas E. "Knowing Rational Numbers: Ideas and Symbols." In *Selected Issues in Mathematics Education* (ed. Mary Montgomery Lindquist). Berkeley, Calif.: McCutchan Publishing, 1980, pp. 69–81.

Kouba, Vicky L.; Brown, Catherine A.; Carpenter, Thomas P.; Lindquist, Mary M.; Silver, Edward A.; and Swafford, Jane O. "Results of the Fourth NAEP Assessment of Mathematics: Number, Operations, and Word Problems." *Arithmetic Teacher,* 35 (April 1988), pp. 14–19.

Langford, Karen, and Sarullo, Angela. "Introductory Common and Decimal Fraction Concepts." In *Research Ideas for the Classroom: Early Childhood Mathematics* (ed. Robert J. Jensen). Reston, Va.: NCTM, 1992, pp. 223–247.

National Council of Teachers of Mathematics. *Principles and Standards for School Mathematics.* Reston, Va.: NCTM, 2000.

Ott, Jack M. "An Unified Approach to Multiplying Fractions." *Arithmetic Teacher,* 37 (March 1990), pp. 47–49.

Payne, Joseph N., and Towsley, Ann N. "Implications of NCTM's Standards on Teaching Fractions and Decimals." *Arithmetic Teacher,* 37 (April 1990), pp. 23–26.

Payne, Joseph N.; Towsley, Ann N.; and Huinker, DeAnn M. "Fractions and Decimals." In *Mathematics for the Young Child* (ed. Joseph N. Payne). Reston, Va.: NCTM, 1990, pp. 175–200.

Pothier, Yvonne, and Daiyo, Sawada. "Partitioning: An Approach to Fractions." *Arithmetic Teacher,* 38 (December 1990), pp. 12–16.

Romberg, Thomas A.; Harvey, John G.; Moser, James M.; and Montgomery, Mary E. *Developing Mathematical Processes* (DMP). Chicago: Rand McNally, 1974–1976.

Steffe, Leslie, and Olive, John. "The Problem of Fractions in the Elementary School." *Arithmetic Teacher,* 38 (May 1991), pp. 22–24.

Thompson, Charles S., and Walker, Vicki. "Connecting Decimals and Other Mathematical Content." *Teaching Children Mathematics,* 2 (April 1996), pp. 496–502.

Warrington, Mary Ann. "How Children Think about Division with Fractions." *Mathematics Teaching in the Middle School,* 2 (May 1997), pp. 390–394.

Warrington, Mary Ann, and Kamii, Constance. "Multiplication with Fractions: A Piagetian, Constructivist Approach." *Mathematics Teaching in the Middle School,* 3 (February 1998), pp. 339–343.

Wearne, Diana, and Kouba, Vicky L. "Rational Number Properties and Operations." In *Results from the Seventh Mathematics Assessment of the National Assessment of Educational Progress.* (eds. E. A. Silver & P. A. Kenney). Reston, Va.: NCTM, 2000.

Wentworth, Nancy M., and Monroe, Eula Ewing. "What Is the Whole?" *Mathematics Teaching in the Middle School,* 1 (April-May 1995), pp. 356–360.

Williams, Susan E., and Copley, Juanita. "Promoting Classroom Dialogue: Using Calculators to Discover Patterns in Dividing Decimals." *Mathematics Teaching in the Middle School,* 1 (April 1994), pp. 72–75.

12 Ratio, Proportion, and Percent: Meanings and Applications

Snapshot of a Lesson

Orientation

Mr. Flores and his students have been working on percents, a very important and often-misunderstood concept. He wants to help them appreciate the power of percents and recognize some of the difficulties in making interpretations and judgments based solely on percents. For today's lesson, Mr. Flores has collected the results from the first four basketball games for the sixth-grade team.

Mr. Flores has prepared the following data to be entered into a spreadsheet and projected the data from the computer screen to the overhead projector.

	A	B	C	D
1				
2	Player's	Shots	Shots	Percent
3	Name	Made	Taken	
4				
5	Billy	12	25	48%
6	Doug	8	17	47%
7	Harlan	1	8	13%
8	Bryan	3	5	60%
9	Rustin	15	43	35%
10	Eric	1	1	100%
11	Whitney	0	2	0%
12	Nick	0	0	#####

Mr. Flores begins by entering only the names and the middle column (shots taken) and asks:

Which students have taken the most shots?

Which students have taken the least shots?

Would this information help you decide who is the "best" shot? Tell why.

After some discussion, he also enters the first column of data (shots made) and asks:

If you wanted to find the best shooters, which students would you check? Why?

Is it easy to compare $^{15}/_{43}$ with $^{12}/_{25}$? Why? Why not?

Is it easy to compare $^{12}/_{25}$ with $^8/_{17}$? Why? Why not?

Before calculating Column D, the students share what they notice. Joe thinks Billy and Doug shot about the same because 12 is about half of 25 and 8 is about half of 17. He predicts both shooting percentages will be a little less than 50 percent. Susan notices that Rustin made about a third of his shots, so he wasn't as accurate as Billy and Doug. She predicts his shoooting percentage will be close to 33 percent. After more discussion, Mr. Flores has the spreadsheet calculate Column D and asks:

How does the percent column help us compare shooters? Do these results support what we noticed earlier?

How can Nick and Whitney have the same shooting percentage?

What if you looked only at the shooting percentages? Of all the players, who would be the best shot? Do you agree that that person is the best shot?

The class also noticed how the spreadsheet handled Nick's data by placing ##### in the percent column. This provided Mr. Flores with an opportunity to introduce how dividing column B12 by C12 results in division by zero, which is undefined. They also talked about how in the real world 0 percent would still be reported.

After discussing each of the next two questions, Mr. Flores reenters columns B and C, and the class examines the results.

What if each player took one more shot and missed it—which percents would change the most? The least? Tell why.

	A	B	C	D
1				
2	Player's	Shots	Shots	Percent
3	Name	Made	Taken	
4				
5	Billy	12	26	46%
6	Doug	8	18	44%
7	Harlan	1	9	11%
8	Bryan	3	6	50%
9	Rustin	15	44	34%
10	Eric	1	2	50%
11	Whitney	0	3	0%
12	Nick	0	1	0%

What if each player took one more shot and hit it—which percents would change the most? The least? Tell why.

	A	B	C	D
1				
2	Player's	Shots	Shots	Percent
3	Name	Made	Taken	
4				
5	Billy	13	26	50%
6	Doug	9	18	50%
7	Harlan	2	9	22%
8	Bryan	4	6	67%
9	Rustin	16	44	36%
10	Eric	2	2	100%
11	Whitney	1	3	33%
12	Nick	1	1	100%

The class continues to interpret the data, generate other "what if" questions, and use the spreadsheet to answer those questions. As the discussion continues, Mr. Flores also asks questions designed to help students gain a greater understanding of percents.

Introduction

"Family income this year increased by 10 percent."

"Ian did only half the work Angela did."

"Her salary is three times my salary."

"The cost of living tripled during the last eight years."

"Your chances of winning the lottery are less than one in a million."

Frequently heard statements like these reflect the fact that much of our quantitative thinking is relational. In such thinking, what is important is the equivalent relationship between numbers, rather than the actual numbers themselves. A greater emphasis on relational equivalence is a reflection of increased opportunities to use these relationships in real-world situations, which often require fluency in ratios, proportions, and percents as well as fractions and decimals.

Students in elementary and middle school grades must be able to show appropriate relationships by using fractions, ratios, proportions, and percents. This goal is expressed in the *Principles and Standards for School Mathematics*, where in grades 3–5 "all students should recognize and generate equivalent forms of commonly used fractions, decimals, and percents" and in grades 6–8 "all students should solve problems involving scale factors, using ratio and proportion" (NCTM 2000, Appendix A). For example, consider the prices of three carpets.

CARPET SALE

The difference in price between these carpets (A and B or B and C) is $1 per square yard. Yet B is twice as expensive as A, and C is 50 percent more expensive than B. In comparing relative cost, the ratio relationship of the prices rather than the prices themselves are important.

RATIOS

Ratios involve comparing things, and some of children's earliest experiences with comparisons involve rates. For example, if a child pays one dime for three stickers, the rate is three stickers for one dime.

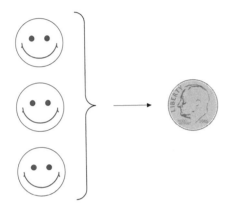

This ratio may be read as "three to one" and recorded as 3 to 1, 3:1, or $\frac{3}{1}$. Any of these forms is acceptable.

Ratios also can be formed to report the number of stickers to nickels as 3 to 2 or stickers to pennies as 3 to 10:

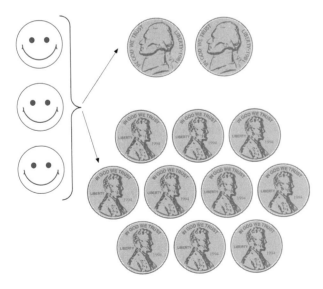

This ratio can also be expressed as ten pennies for every three stickers, which can be written as 10 to 3 or as the quotient 10 ÷ 3. The latter form provides a per-sticker cost of over three pennies and illustrates a powerful application of ratios.

Early experiences with ratios should stimulate children to think of two related numbers simultaneously. As children use manipulatives such as coins or draw pictures, they should be encouraged to think about ordered pairs of numbers, such as (3 stickers, 2 pennies). The models help link the operation of multiplication directly to ordered pairs and ratios.

Using facts about money (the number of pennies in a nickel, nickels in a quarter, and so on) provides natural and meaningful experiences with ratios. In the Classroom 12–1 shows how organizing such information not only visually displays many ratios but helps students realize that a ratio is a multiplicative comparison of two or more numbers in a given order. The activity also provides patterns that encourage students to explore relationships, generate formulas, and engage in algebraic thinking.

The money model also provides a natural extension of ratio to more than two numbers. For example, the ordered triple (2, 10, 50) relates 2 quarters, 10 nickels, and 50 pennies. Using a calculator to skip count by 5's or 25's or a spreadsheet to extend patterns are excellent uses of technology. The children's book *If You Made a Million* (Schwartz 1989) also provides photographs and explanations of ratios using coins.

Children encounter ratios in many different forms: "three video games for a dollar," "twice as long," "half as much," and so on. Real-world examples of ratios help develop a greater awareness and understanding. For example, the values (8–12–20) on a sack of lawn fertilizer use a ratio to report the percents of phosphorus, nitrogen, and potash the fertilizer contains. Prices such as two cans for 99¢, three pounds for $1.99, and 88¢ a dozen are frequently encountered and provide meaningful contexts for ratios.

This example is a reminder of the importance of the order of the entries and the need to understand what each entry represents. An ordered pair from In the Classroom 12–1, such as (5, 25), could represent 5 quarters and 25 nickels or 5 nickels and 25 pennies. Whether a ratio has two, three, or more entries, it has little meaning until the nature of the entries is known.

Although multiplication problems provide opportunities to discuss ratio informally, the concept of ratio is typically not studied until fifth grade. The concept of ratio is closely linked to multiplication, yet it is often difficult for students to make the necessary connections. Research shows that students often base their intuitive thinking about ratio on counting and adding, thereby reflecting a major misconception of ratio (Miller and Fey 2000).

In The Classroom 12–1

Grades 4–6

Know Your Coins

Objective: Using value of coins to develop patterns and proportions and to examine algebraic relationships.

▼ Use patterns to help complete this table:

Number of

Quarters	1	2		4	5	6	□
Nickels	5	10	15	20		30	△
Pennies	25	50	75		125	150	○

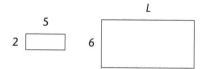

- Describe a pattern you found in each row.

- Write a ratio for the number of quarters to nickels. _____

- Write a ratio for the number of nickels to pennies. _____

- Write a ratio for the number of quarters to pennies. _____

▼ Try these:

- How many nickels will be needed for 8 quarters? ____
  Tell two different ways to decide.

- How many pennies will be needed for 10 quarters? ____
  Tell two different ways to decide.

- Give three numbers (not shown in the table) that could go

  in the △ row _____

  in the ○ row _____

- Give three numbers that could *not* go

  in the △ row _____

  in the ○ row _____

- How many quarters would you have

  when □+△+○ first exceeds $30? _____

For example, when asked to find the length of the side *L*, students frequently report 9 rather than 15:

$$\begin{array}{ccc} & 5 & L \\ 2\ \square & & 6\ \boxed{} \end{array}$$

Such students tend to add an amount rather than multiply by a scale factor. Research shows that this error reflects a students' misconception of ratio and is not simply the result of carelessness (Cramer et al. 1993).

Suppose you are ready to extend some ideas on multiplication to develop the concept of ratio. After the students use models and complete and discuss In the Classroom 12–1, you might consider how some of those tasks lead directly to writing ratios, as shown in Figure 12–1.

Students are sometimes confused by the different symbols used to record ratios. This confusion can be minimized by linking the symbols to appropriate models and promoting class discussion. Chips or cut-out wheels could be used to model these tasks before ratios are written. A table might be made to help organize the information. After the ratios are recorded, guided discussion centering on

Ratios, Ratios, Ratios, . . .

▼ Write a ratio to compare three bicycles with wheels.

- There are __3__ bicycles and __6__ wheels.

- We can write this ratio as __3 : 6__ or __3/6__ or __3 to 6__.

▼ Write a ratio to compare four bicycles with wheels.

- There are __4__ bicycles and __8__ wheels.

- We can write this ratio as __4 : 8__ or __4/8__ or __4 to 8__.

▼ Write a ratio to compare the number of wheels

- on a bicycle and a wagon __2 to 4__

- on a tricycle and a wagon __3 to 4__

Figure 12–1 • Writing record for ratios

the information and the situation helps children talk about the mathematics.

For example, questions such as the following will provide early practice in verbalizing and describing some of the mathematics surrounding the concept of ratio:

> If I have three bicycles and six wheels, is the ratio three to six or (3, 6)?
>
> If the ratio is four to eight, how many bicycles do I have?
>
> If the ratio is five to ten, how many wheels do I have?
>
> If I have six bicycles, how many wheels are there? What is the ratio?

Ratios provide one interpretation for fractions, namely, where one integer is compared to another. In elementary school, however, the emphasis is typically on smaller numbers such as 1-to-2, 2-to-3, and 3-to-4. These ratios are the most frequently used, and they are much easier to model and conceptualize than 7-to-9 or 11-to-14. Several real-life examples may be examined in the counting book, *Each Orange Had 8 Slices: A Counting Book* (Giganti 1992).

Far more important than how the ratio is expressed is the understanding of the relationship. Young children with a good understanding of numbers use "twice as much" just as often and as comfortably as "half as much." Instruction should take advantage of these different expressions to develop further reversible thinking.

PROPORTIONS

Proportions are two or more equal ratios and are frequently used in problem situations. Consider, for example, this problem:

SALE

Hot Cross Buns
3 for 49¢

About how much will a dozen cost?

In approaching such a problem, using words along with numerical symbols helps children not only organize the information but understand it more clearly. It is helpful, too, to get students to think and talk about reasonable answers before getting into specific computation. For example, children might think:

$\frac{1}{4}$ dozen is almost 50¢, so

$\frac{1}{2}$ dozen is almost \$1, so

1 dozen will be almost \$2

Such thinking is very productive. It should be both encouraged and rewarded. It uses estimation along with ratios to produce ballpark answers. Frequent experiences similar to this will improve students' judgment, making them less likely to fall victim to unreasonable answers resulting from indiscriminate number crunching.

Students also should realize that a single situation can be represented by several proportions. For example, here are some ways of writing proportions for the hot cross buns:

$$\frac{3}{49} = \frac{12}{\square} \qquad 3:49 = 12:\square$$

$$\frac{3}{12} = \frac{49}{\square} \qquad 3:12 = 49:\square$$

$$\frac{49}{3} = \frac{\square}{12} \qquad 49:3 = \square:12$$

$$\frac{12}{3} = \frac{\square}{49} \qquad 12:3 = \square:49$$

Although students should recognize the equivalence of these statements, they should feel free to use the form of their choice.

The pennies-nickels comparisons shown in In the Classroom 12–1 contain many equivalent ratios (1:5 = 2:10, 2:10 = 3:15, and so on). The concept of equivalent ratios is very important and can be anchored in different ways. For example, Figure 12–2 shows a table from a graphing calculator displaying

X	Y1
1	5
2	10
3	15
4	20
5	25
6	30
7	35

Figure 12–2 • Graphing calculator table display for $y = 5x$

the result of $y = 5x$. These tabular data provide opportunities to discover patterns, explore an algebraic relationship ($y = 5x$), and observe that the ratio of all of these proportions is constant.

After equivalent ratios are established, they can be used in a variety of ways. For example, comparative shopping relies heavily on determining which of two (or more) ratios is lower. Suppose the same product is packaged in two different sizes:

24 oz.   32 oz.

Do the two cans have the same unit price?

Although this problem can be solved in different ways, it involves ratios. More specifically, are these ratios equal?

$$\frac{\$1.90}{24} \stackrel{?}{=} \frac{\$2.65}{32}$$

This problem can be solved several ways, but one of the most natural is by finding equivalent ratios:

$$\frac{\$1.90 \times 4}{24 \times 4} = \frac{\$7.60}{96} \qquad \frac{\$2.65 \times 3}{32 \times 3} = \frac{\$7.95}{96}$$

Ratios are not equal

A calculator also could be used to demonstrate that $1.90 \div 24 \neq 2.65 \div 32$, so the ratios are unequal. Because the ratios are not equal, the prices are not equivalent.

Many problems involving proportions can be solved mentally without any paper-and-pencil computation. This approach should be encouraged whenever possible. However, when the computation becomes too messy, the proportion can be solved algorithmically. Figure 12–3 highlights two different mental strategies. Providing multiple ways to solve proportions mentally encourages students to analyze the problem before choosing an approach. Figure 12–4 illustrates how some students solved the same two proportion problems. Notice that although not all solutions are correct, the students tried to make sense of the problem and approached it in a way that was meaningful to them.

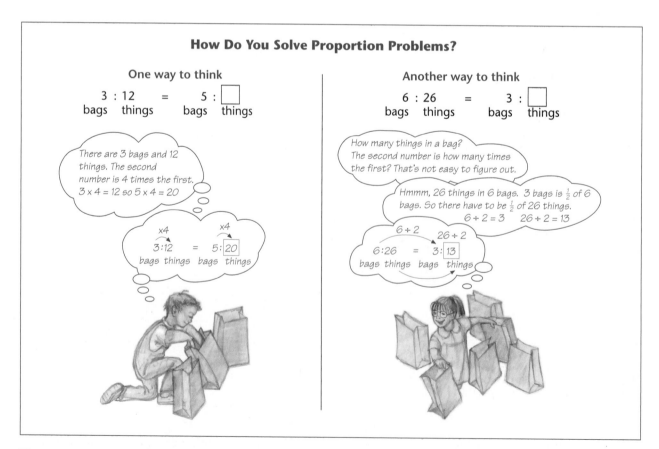

Figure 12–3 • Two different thinking strategies to solve proportions

Solve the following proportion. **Deanna**
Use whatever method is easiest for you.

A.   20 : 30 = 40 : 60
    doors walls doors walls

20×2=40
30×2=60 so 20:30=40:60

if there are 20 doors in 30 walls double that there'd be 40 doors in 60 walls. The numbers are equal.

Solve the following proportion. **Ned**
Use whatever method is easiest for you.

B.   9 : 81 = 15 : ___
    teams players teams players

If there are 9 & 81 then that means there are 9 players on every team. So when 135 players there are 15 teams. Then you have to take 15×9

Solve the following proportion. **Trevor**
Use whatever method is easiest for you.

A.   20 : 30 = 40 : 60
    doors walls doors walls

For every 20 doors there are 30 walls. The ratio is 2:3 or 2/3
40 is 2/3 of 60 so there are 60 walls for every 40 doors

Solve the following proportion. **Hal**
Use whatever method is easiest for you.

B.   9 : 81 = 15 : ___
    teams players teams players

9 : 81 = 15 : 135 I 9 into 81 one and I
teams players teams got that their was 9 players on each team So I add 6 more teams times total was 135.

Solve the following proportion. **Yang**
Use whatever method is easiest for you.

A.   20 : 30 = 40 : 50   20 40
    doors walls doors walls +10 +10
                                 30   50

Solve the following proportion. **Carmen**
Use whatever method is easiest for you.

B.   9 : 81 = 15 : 225
    teams players teams players

9 teams 81 players
9 players per team
ratio is 9:81 or 1/9 in simplest form
15 teams 15 players per team 15×15=225

Figure 12–4 • Samples of students' solutions to proportion problems

Consider using other real-life applications such as recipes, photographs and their negatives, maps, and scale drawings or models. Figure 12–5 highlights a project where students use scaling (ratios) and measurement skills to do some practical problem solving.

The concepts of ratio and proportionality can be naturally connected to geometry problems. One natural and powerful connection to geometry uses similarity. Two figures are similar if their respective sides are in the same ratio—that is, proportional. Thus, all squares are similar, but all rectangles are not.

Look for some patterns in the similar triangles in Figure 12–6. Triangle A is similar to triangle B because the extended ratios 1:2:4 and 2:4:8 are equal. Likewise, triangles B and C are similar. Now let's use triangles D and E for some additional problem solving. If triangle D is similar to A, describe how to find the length of the longest side of D. If triangle E is also similar to A, describe how the lengths of its

Draw Your Classroom

▼ First measure your classroom.

▼ Next decide on a scale to use.

▼ Now make a scale drawing of the room.

   • Show where doors, windows, tables, and desks are located.

   • Be sure to put your scale on your drawing, such as 1 in. : 5 ft   or   1 cm : 1 m

Our classroom

Figure 12–5 • A scaling project

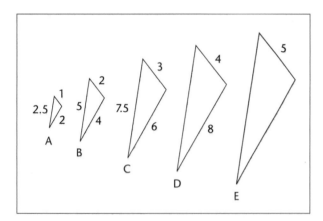

Figure 12–6 • Some similar triangles

other two sides can be found. Because the resulting ratios for E involve multiples of five, these values could be related to the ratios for coins on In the Classroom 12–1. This activity illustrates multi-embodiment and reminds students that the same numerical patterns can occur in very different settings.

An interesting application of ratio and proportion appears in many architectural designs. The ratio of the sides of the rectangle varies, but one ratio, known as the golden ratio, has occurred in many architectural structures and works of art.

Children's books such as *Anno's Math Games* (Anno 1987) provide different yet interesting contexts to explore ratios and proportions and connect them to percent. Other books such as *In One Day* (Parker 1984) encourage students to think about different ways of relating numbers.

PERCENTS

One need only read a newspaper or watch television to be reminded that percent is one of the most widely used mathematical concepts:

Save 23 to 55%

MONEY MARKET CERTIFICATES

14.70% YIELDS

16.07%

City Asks For 40% Budget Increase

Serious crimes drop 5 percent

Wholesale Price Index Up 0.6 Pct.

38 Percent Plunge In Profits

Understanding of percent is taken for granted, even though there is plenty of evidence to the contrary. Incorrect usage of percent is frequent among both secondary students and adults. Flagrant errors abound, suggesting that often the most basic ideas are unclear (Gay and Aichele 1997). For example, about one-third of the seventeen-year-olds and adults missed the following question on the first national assessment:

> If 5% of the students are absent today, then 5 out of how many are absent?

An error on such a fundamental idea suggests they did not know that 100 is the comparison base for percent. Low performance is found in other countries also, as only about half of the sixth graders tested in Japan correctly reported that 100% of 48 is 48 (Reys and Reys 1993).

Misconceptions, distortions, and confusion surrounding percent are surprisingly easy to find. Here are examples:

1. "Prices reduced 100%." If this advertisement were correct, the items would be free. Probably, the prices were reduced 50%. If an item that originally cost $400 was on sale for $200, then the ad based the 100% on the sale price, when it should have been based on the original price.

2. "Of all doctors interviewed, 75% recommended our product." This type of claim could be an effective advertisement for a company. If, however, the ad said "3 out of the 4 doctors we interviewed recommended our product," the consumer reaction might be different. Percents can often be used to disguise the number involved. Thus, they can be misused. Percents allow for easy comparisons because of the common base of one hundred, but they may appear to represent a larger sample than actually exists.

Discussing the following questions and providing real-life examples can help students develop a number sense for percents.

- Can you eat 50% of a cake?
- Can you eat 100% of a cake?
- Can you eat 150% of a cake?
- Can a price increase 50%?
- Can a price increase 100%?
- Can a price increase 150%?
- Can a price decrease 50%?
- Can a price decrease 100%?
- Can a price decrease 150%?

Ironically, the understanding of percent requires no new skills or concepts beyond those used in mastering fractions, decimals, and ratios. In fact, percent is not really a mathematical topic, but rather the application of a particular type of notational system. The justification for teaching percent in school mathematics programs rests solely on its social utility. Consequently, percent should be taught and learned in application situations similar to the one given in the Snapshot of a Lesson at the beginning of this chapter. Because the primary objective is to solve problems involving percent, the use of calculators would be appropriate and would allow students to focus on the concepts of percents rather than get bogged down in the written algorithm for multiplication. Special function keys such as the percent key and the memory keys also could be introduced.

As is true with decimals and fractions, percents express a relationship between two numbers. Percents are special ratios based on 100 and without a doubt are the most widely used of all ratios. Percent is derived from the Latin words *per centum,* which mean "out of a hundred" or "for every hundred." Thus, the origin of percent and its major uses are more closely associated with ratio than with either decimals or fractions.

When is percent understood? Students understand percent when they can use it many different ways. For instance, if a child understands 25%, he or she can do the following.

1. Find 25% in various contexts:

   Cover 25% of a floor with tiles.

   Determine 25% off the price of a given item.

   Survey 25% of the students in class.

In many such situations, estimates of 25% are not only appropriate but essential.

2. Identify characteristics of 25%:

   25% of the milk in a glass is less than half.

   If 25% of the milk in a glass is spilled, then 75% remains.

3. Compare and contrast 25% with a range of other percents and numbers such as 5%, 50%, 100%, one-fourth, one-half, and 0.25.

   25% is half as much as 50%, one-fourth as much as 100%, five times as much as 5%, less than one-half, and the same as one-fourth and twenty-five hundredths.

Understanding Percents

Percents should be introduced only after students thoroughly understand fractions and decimals and have had experience with ratios. Percent is not studied extensively in elementary school, although it is typically introduced in fifth or sixth grade.

Initially, students need a variety of experiences with the fundamental concepts of percent, and these experiences should be connected to various concrete models and real-world contexts. Computation applying percent in problem-solving situations is generally reserved for later. Students who understand that percent means parts out of one hundred and have a good pictorial representation of percent are more successful in solving percent problems than those who do not. Lembke found that students naturally use benchmarks to make initial judgments about percent situations (Lembke and Reys 1994). Helping students develop the concepts for common percent benchmarks and their fraction and decimal equivalents such as 10 percent, 25 percent, 33 percent, 50 percent, and 75 percent will help them apply their percent number sense to problem-solving situations.

Initial instruction should build on familiar models. A dollar is made up of one hundred cents; therefore, it provides a natural connection among percents, fractions, and decimals. For example, 25 cents is $0.25, one-fourth of a dollar, and also 25 percent of a dollar.

This model should be expanded to illustrate a wide range of percents, such as 50 percent, 90 percent, 5 percent, 100 percent, 99 percent, 1 percent, and 200 percent. These percents should be illustrated with a variety of different situations and models. For example, a meter stick provides an easily accessible and effective model. Cover part of the meter stick with blue paper and ask children to estimate the percent of the meter stick that is covered.

Students could be shown the meter stick face down (if the scale is on both sides, cover one side with masking tape) and then asked:

Estimate what percent of the meter stick is blue.

About what percent of the meter stick is not blue?

How can we check our estimate? [Turn the stick over.]

This model allows many different situations (25%, 50%, 1%, and so forth) to be presented and discussed quickly. Patterns may also emerge as students realize that the sum of the covered and uncovered portions will always total 100 percent. Shaded fraction circles (Appendix B) also can be used to pro-

vide multi-embodiment and help students see connections between fractions and percents.

A related activity involving area could have students using a stack of twenty cards with the B side down. On the A side, specific percents of the card are colored blue (0%, 10%, 20%, . . . , 100%), with the remainder (100%, . . . , 0%) white.

Side A

Side B

| | 30% |

Ask students to take turns trying to win cards by looking only at side A and trying to predict the percents shown on side B. Eleven-peg geoboards or four five-peg geoboards placed in a square (Appendix B) also may be used to model percents. Lesson Idea 12–1 provides some additional tasks that use models to develop important concepts about percent. Each of these tasks provides ideas that can be used to relate percents and fractions.

These early experiences with percent should be followed by activities that center around direct translation experiences involving 100. The national assessment data revealed that only 68 percent and 31 percent of seventh graders correctly wrote the decimals 0.42 and 0.9, respectively, as percents. These data remind us of the fragile nature of students' understanding and the importance of connecting percents with decimals and fractions. Having students use base-ten blocks or share decimal paper (Appendix B) provides another concrete model for percents and helps students see the connections between decimals and percents. Figure 12–7 illustrates how the same diagram can be represented symbolically by a fraction, a decimal, and a percent. It should be emphasized that each small square represents 1 percent and the large square represents 100 percent. Practice activities using this model to convert percents to fractions and decimals, and vice versa, should be plentiful. Calculators which convert fractions, decimals, and percents are useful when students are discovering patterns and relationships.

For example, Figure 12–7 provides a visual reminder that 17 percent can also be thought of as $17 \times \frac{1}{100}$, so the symbol % can be thought of as equivalent to the fraction $\frac{1}{100}$. Also, 17 percent can be thought of as $\frac{17}{100}$, so the concept of ratio is reinforced. This helps students feel comfortable with different interpretations of percent.

The importance of establishing 100 as the base for percent cannot be overemphasized, and 50 per-

Lesson Idea 12–1

Using Percent Models

Materials: Several different models, each of which displays clearly the 100 parts in a whole.

Activity: Pose additional questions to accompany the following teacher-led discussions.

1. Construct a model that has 100 parts but at the same time has the potential of displaying equivalent subsets of these 100 elements. Here are two models:

Rope with 100 discs arranged 10 black, 10 purple, 10 black, 10 purple, ...

Rectangle 5 × 20 with all small squares as shown.

2. Find representations of various percents on each model. For example, when representing 50 percent, help students realize that any 50 of the parts could be chosen — for example, in either of the two ways shown here:

3. Have students consider the model as a whole and ask for all the fractions that show the same amount as 50 percent. Write the results on the board:

Fifty percent — 50%

$$\frac{1}{2} \quad \frac{50}{100} \quad \frac{5}{10}$$

4. Repeat step 3 using 20 percent:

Twenty percent — 20%

$$\frac{2}{10} \quad \frac{1}{5} \quad \frac{20}{100}$$

5. Compare the representations for 50 percent and 20 percent on each model. Ask questions such as

• Which is greater, 50 or 20 percent?

• What fractional part is covered by 20 percent?

• What fractional part remains uncovered?

6. Any multiple of 10 can be illustrated easily with these models. Continue to model different percents and their corresponding fractions until generalizations of these relationships are established.

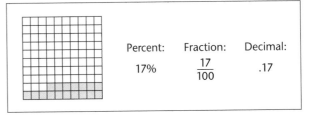

Percent: 17%   Fraction: $\frac{17}{100}$ Decimal: .17

Figure 12–7 • Models and symbolizations of 17%

cent should be recognized as the fraction $\frac{50}{100}$ or the product $50 \times \frac{1}{100}$. However, it is also important that students know that an infinite number of equivalent fractions ($\frac{1}{2}$, $\frac{2}{4}$, $\frac{3}{6}$, . . . , $\frac{50}{100}$, . . .) also represent 50%.

In the Classroom 12–2 provides a natural means of developing some important ideas in an informal and yet meaningfully structured way. Each of the four activities should further develop children's concept of percent. Activities B, C, and D require some collection and recording of data prior to reporting the percents. The use of three different base numbers (10 logs, 100 pennies, and 20 chips) will strengthen the link between ratio and percent. Even though answers on each activity depend on the data recorded, some patterns will emerge. A few questions from the teacher should trigger some stimulating discussion. For example, do the percents in each item total 100 percent? Why does this happen? Can you think of a time when it would not?

One particularly troublesome aspect of percents involves small percents between 0 percent and 1 percent. For example, $\frac{1}{2}$ percent, as in "$\frac{1}{2}$ percent milk fat," is not well understood. A visual representation, as in Figure 12–8, can help show that $\frac{1}{2}$ percent is indeed less than 1 percent. Understanding rests on the earlier agreement that each small square represents 1 percent, which cannot be mentioned too often. As is true with all percents, this percent also can be shown symbolically as a fraction or a decimal. However, it is more important in elementary school to establish the intuitive notion of relative size of small percents than to devote extensive time to the algebraic gymnastics of showing the fraction and decimal equivalents.

Development of percents greater than 100 percent also is challenging and should be illustrated with models. Once the idea is established that a given region represents 100 percent, more than one such region can be used to represent percents greater than 100 percent. For example, 234 percent could be represented by two completely shaded

In The Classroom 12–2

Using Percents

Objective: Using different models to relate quantities to percent.

A. Color this circle:

  • 25% red

  • 50% blue

What percent is uncolored? _____

B. Use 3 colors:

  • Blue

  • Green

  • Yellow

  Color each log with only one color. Color all logs.

	Number Colored	Percent Colored
Blue	_____	_____
Green	_____	_____
Yellow	_____	_____

C. Take 100 pennies, shake, and toss them in a box. Count the number of heads.

	Number	Percent
Heads	_____	_____
Tails	_____	_____

  Did you need to count the tails? _____

D. Here are 20 poker chips. Count the number of each color.

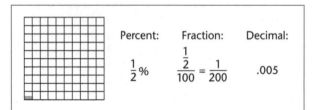

	Number	Percent
Purple	_____	_____
Black	_____	_____
White	_____	_____

	Percent:	Fraction:	Decimal:
	$\frac{1}{2}\%$	$\frac{\frac{1}{2}}{100} = \frac{1}{200}$	.005

Figure 12–8 • **Models and symbolizations of ½%**

large squares and a partially shaded one (see Figure 12–9). Using every opportunity to show equivalence of percents, fractions, and decimals helps establish and maintain these relationships.

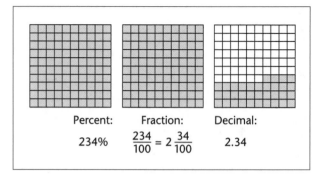

Percent:	Fraction:	Decimal:
234%	$\frac{234}{100} = 2\frac{34}{100}$	2.34

Figure 12–9 • **Model and symbolizations of 234%**

Applying Percents

In elementary school, students should solve percent problems meaningfully and avoid rushing toward symbolic methods. Whenever possible, students should be asked to discuss how to solve percent problems mentally using what they know about common percent benchmarks. Even when a formal method is required, using informal methods first to obtain an estimate will help students focus on the reasonableness of results obtained by formal methods.

Although percents are regularly encountered in many real-life problem-solving situations, only three basic types of problems involve percents. Several different formal methods can be used to solve percent problems, and we will illustrate two of them typically found in elementary and middle school textbooks—equation and ratio. The effective use of these methods requires a firm understanding of the concepts of percent and ratio as well as the ability to solve simple equations and proportions. Such skills are developed over a period of several years and need not be rushed.

In the equation method, the following equation is used:

$$\text{percent} \times \text{total} = \text{part}$$

The two known values are placed in the equation and one solves the equation for the third, unknown value.

In the ratio method, we know that a (part) is b (percent) of c (total). The variables are set up as equal ratios or a proportion:

$$\frac{b(\text{percent})}{100} = \frac{a(\text{part})}{c(\text{total})}$$

The three known values are placed into the proportion, and one solves for the fourth, unknown value.

Now let's take a brief look at each of the three types of percent problems and how they may be solved using both informal and formal methods:

1. **Finding the percent of a given number.**

    Lucas receives $60 a month for a paper route, and next month he will get a 10 percent raise. How much will his raise be?

The context of this problem suggests that the raise will be something considerably less than $60. The situation might be solved mentally or modeled as shown in Figure 12–10.

This problem could also be solved in these ways:

Ratio method: $\dfrac{10\%}{100\%} = \dfrac{R}{60}$ $R = \$6$

Equation method: $R = 10\%$ of $\$60$
$$R = .1 \times \$60$$
$$= \$6$$

The computation is simple and may disguise the level of difficulty this type of problem presents. Only about one-third of the seventh graders were successful at solving this type of problem on the fourth national assessment.

2. **Find what percent one number is of another number.**

    The Cardinals won 15 of their 20 games. What percent did they win?

Intuitively, it is clear that the Cardinals did not win all their games, so the answer must be less than 100 percent. Similarly, they won more than half their games, so it must be more than 50 percent. The situation could be solved mentally or modeled as shown in Figure 12–11.

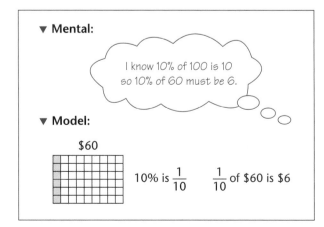

Figure 12–10 • Use of mental strategy or model for finding a percent of a number

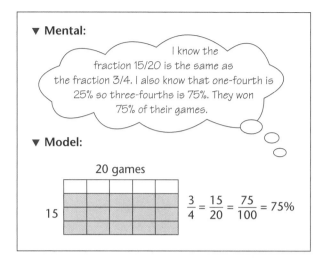

Figure 12–11 • Use of mental strategy or model for finding what percent one number is of another number

Here are two other ways to find the solution:

Ratio method: $\dfrac{P\%}{100\%} = \dfrac{15}{20}$ $P = 75\%$

Equation method: $P \times 20 = 15$
$$P = \dfrac{15}{20} \times 5$$
$$= \dfrac{75}{100} = 75\%$$

Once again the computation is easy, but the national assessment provides a reminder of the difficulty students have with percent. For example, 43 percent of seventh graders correctly answered "30 is what percent of 60?" but only 20 percent correctly answered "9 is what percent of 225?"

3. **Find the total (100%) when only a percent is known.**

    The sale price on a coat was $40, and it was marked down 50%. What was its original price?

Common sense suggests that the original price should be more than $40. Guess-and-test is often a very effective strategy in solving this type of problem. For example, if children guess an original price of $60, then the sale price of $30 is too low. Still, they are on the right track, and if this approach is continued, it will eventually lead to the correct price of $80. The problem could be solved mentally or modeled as shown in Figure 12–12. The model

▼ Mental:

> I know
> 50% is the same as one-half.
> If $40 is half of the original price and 40 is half of 80, the original price must be $80.

▼ Model:

$40 + $40 = $80

50% + 50% = 100%

Figure 12–12 ● **Use of mental strategy or model for finding the total when only a percent is known**

provides a base for either of these solutions, where *OP* is the original price:

Ratio method: $\dfrac{50\%}{100\%} = \dfrac{\$40}{OP} \qquad OP = \$80$

Equation method: 50% of $OP = \$40$

$$OP = \frac{\$40}{50} \times 2$$

$$= \frac{80}{100} = 80\%$$

This type of problem is typically more difficult to solve, as was confirmed by results from the fourth national mathematics assessment (Lindquist et al. 1988). Less than 22 percent of the seventh graders correctly answered a question of this type.

The consistently poor performance on percent problems means that instruction must become more meaningful. If emphasis is placed on a particular method before the problem is thought through and well understood, the result will probably be confusion and poor performance. Instructional emphasis in elementary school must be on thinking aloud and talking about what should be done and what a reasonable answer would be. These teacher-led discussions should occur before any serious efforts are made to solve the problem with pencil and paper. Early emphasis on writing a solution to a percent problem forces many students to operate mechanically (without any conscious thinking) on the numbers to produce an answer.

Students should be encouraged to think quantitatively in solving problems involving percent. Research does not support the teaching of a single method (such as ratio or equation) to solve such problems. Instruction, therefore, should be flexible and not locked into a single method. It is recommended that a variety of problems involving percent be presented and then student leads followed flexibly toward solutions. More specifically, some verbalization of the solution should accompany the actual problem-solving process. This helps clarify what was done (right or wrong) and provides some closure to the process. It also promotes consideration of the reasonableness of an answer.

This less formal, intuitive approach lacks the structure and security of emphasizing a particular method. Yet it has several important advantages. In particular, it encourages students to understand the problem in their own minds along with possible solutions, and it decreases the likelihood of their applying a method blindly.

A Glance at Where We've Been

Ratios compare two or more numbers. They take different forms and have many applications—money (pennies for nickels), measurements (12 inches in a foot), consumer purchases (3 for 29¢), scale drawings, and blueprints are but a few. Together with proportion, ratios provide an opportunity to practice many computational skills as well as strengthen problem-solving skills. Ratios also provide a natural means of studying percent, which has a comparison base of one hundred. Since few mathematical topics have more practical usage than percents, it is essential that meaningful and systematic development of percent be provided. Instruction should include the use of concrete models that support the development of number sense.

Things to Do: From What You've Read

1. Give a real-life example of a ratio and a proportion. How could you help children distinguish between them?

2. Describe how estimating the number of heartbeats in an hour or in a lifetime uses ratios. How could you use a calculator or a spreadsheet to solve the problem?

3. Describe how you could use a meter stick, graduated in millimeters, to illustrate each of the following percents:
   a. 35 percent
   b. 3.5 percent
   c. 0.35 percent

4. Make up a story for each of these sentences:

   a. $\dfrac{5}{12} = \dfrac{x}{\$1.80}$

   b. 40% of 95 =

5. Rose was making $26,000 a year. She received a 10 percent raise. Later in the year, the company started losing money and reduced all salaries 10 percent. Rose said, "I'm making less money than last year." Is her thinking correct? Tell why.

6. Here is a partially completed chart:

Decimal	Fraction	Percent
—	—	5%
.1	$\frac{1}{10}$	10%
—	$\frac{1}{4}$	—
.333 . . .	—	—
.5	—	—
—	$\frac{2}{3}$	—
—	—	75%

   Explain why it would be helpful to have students learn these popular percents and their related fraction and decimal forms.

7. Describe how you would think through a solution to this problem: the population of a city increased from 200000 to 220000. What is the percent increase?

8. Suppose you ask a student to enlarge the 1 × 2 rectangle shown here, and a 2 × 4 rectangle is correctly produced. Then you ask the student to enlarge it again so the base is 6. The student draws a 4 × 6 rectangle and says, "If I doubled it, the base would have been 8, so I added 2 on and the other side is 4." Would you say this student is an "adder" or a "multiplier"? Describe some additional questions you might ask to gain more insight into this student's understanding of ratio.

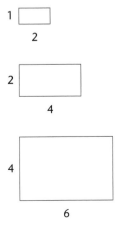

Things to Do: Going Beyond This Book

field Additional activities, suggestions, and questions are provided in *Teaching Elementary Mathematics: A Resource for Field Experiences.*

1. Read the article "Proportional Reasoning" by Miller and Fey (2000). Describe instructional suggestions they offer from research to help students better understand proportions.

2. *field* *Finding Out about Proportions.* Ask several fifth or sixth graders this questions: "A design is 2 cm wide and 2.4 cm long. If the picture is to be enlarged so that it is 5 cm wide, how long will it be?" Ask them to explain their reasoning and answer. Check to see if students tended to be "adders" (i.e., added 3 cm to the dimensions, thus getting 5 cm wide and 5.4 cm long). If they modeled the solution correctly and used multiplication, report the thinking they used.

3. Ratios may be used to determine the best buy. Use local newspaper advertisements to find information and set up ratios to compare prices for different sizes of the same product. Can you refute the claim "the larger the quantity, the lower the unit price"?

4. Read the article, "Our Diets May Be Killing Us" by Shannon (1995) or "Integrating Mathematics and Literature in the Elementary Classroom" by Kliman (1993). Describe how you could use ideas like those to make a ratio or percent lesson.

5. Describe how the white, red, purple, and brown Cuisenaire rods could be used to develop ratios. Describe several different equivalent ratios that could be made with these rods.

6. Review *The Wonderful World of Mathematics* (Thiessen and Matthias 1998). Several books focus on multiplication and division and use these concepts to develop ratio or proportion. Choose one of the books to read with some children and describe how they reacted.

7. *field* *Finding Out about Percent.* Ask a fifth or sixth grader some of these questions: What is 50% of $80? What is 100% of 50? What does the ½% on a milk carton mean? Is it possible to get a raise of 200%? In each question, ask the child to explain their thinking. Do you think this child has a good understanding of percent? Tell why.

8. Develop a spreadsheet similar to those in the article by Hoeffner et al. (1990) that will allow children to solve some real-life ratio and percent problems.

9. *field* In the Classroom 12–1 provides a structured activity for exploring patterns and connecting them to ratio. Use this activity as a guide to ask a fifth or sixth grader a series of questions. What patterns seemed to be the strongest? Explain how

experiencing this activity would help develop the notion of ratio.

10. Read the articles, "Toys 'R' Math" (Tracy and Hague 1997) or "Children's Literature: Impetus for a Mathematical Adventure" (Gibbons 1996). Discuss some ways these stories might be used to help students understand ratio and proportion.

BOOK NOOK FOR CHILDREN

Anno, Mitsumasa. *Anno's Math Games.* New York: Philomel Books, 1987.

Anno, Mitsumasa. *Anno's Math Games II.* New York: Philomel Books, 1989.

Banks, Lynne Reid. *The Indian in the Cupboard.* New York: Avon Books, 1980.

Burns, Marilyn. *The I Hate Mathematics! Book.* Boston: Little, Brown, 1975.

Clement, Ron. *Counting on Frank.* Milwaukee: Gareth Stevens Children's Books, 1991.

Diagram Group. *Comparisons.* New York: St. Martin's Press, 1980.

Giganti, Jr., Paul. *Each Orange Had 8 Slices: A Counting Book.* New York: Greenwillow Books, a division of William Morrow & Co., 1992.

Laithwaite, Eric. *Size: The Measure of Things.* New York: Franklin Watts, 1988.

Parker, Tom. *In One Day.* Boston: Houghton-Mifflin, 1984.

Schwartz, David M. *If You Made a Million.* New York: Lothrop, Lee and Shepard Books, Division of William Morrow, 1989.

Waverly, B. *How big? How fast? How hungry?* Milwaukee: Raintree, 1990.

Selected References

Allinger, Glenn D., and Payne, Joseph N. "Estimation and Mental Arithmetic with Percent." *Estimation and Mental Computation,* 1986 Yearbook (ed. Harold L. Schoen). Reston, Va.: NCTM, 1986, pp. 141–155.

Behr, Merlyn J.; Harel, Guershon; Post, Thomas; and Lesh, Richard. "Rational Number, Ratio, and Proportion." In *Handbook of Research on Mathematics Teaching and Learning* (ed. Douglas A. Grouws). New York: Macmillan, 1992, pp. 296–333.

Bennet, Albert B., and Nelson, Ted. "A Conceptual Model for Solving Percent Problems." *Mathematics Teaching in the Middle School,* 1 (April 1994), pp. 20–25.

Carpenter, Thomas P.; Corbitt, Mary Kay; Kepner, Henry S., Jr.; Lindquist, Mary Montgomery; and Reys, Robert E. *Results from the Second Mathematics Assessment of the National Assessment of Educational Progress.* Reston, Va.: NCTM, 1981.

Cramer, Kathleen; Post, Thomas; and Currier, Sarah. "Learning and Teaching Ratio and Proportion: Research Implications." In *Research Ideas for the Classroom: Middle Grades Mathematics* (ed. Douglas T. Owens). Reston, Va.: NCTM, and New York: Macmillan, 1993, pp. 159–178.

Gay, Susan, and Aichele, Douglas B. "Middle School Students' Understanding of Number Sense Related to Percent." *School Science and Mathematics,* 97 (January 1997), pp. 27–36.

Gibbons, Estelle. "Children's Literature: Impetus for a Mathematical Adventure." *Teaching Children Mathematics,* 3 (November 1996), pp. 142–147.

Glatzer, David J. "Teaching Percentage: Ideas and Suggestions." *Arithmetic Teacher,* 31 (February 1984), pp. 24–26.

Haubner, Mary Ann. "Percents: Developing Meaning Through Models." *Arithmetic Teacher,* 40 (December 1992), pp. 232–234.

Hoeffner, Karl; Kendall, Monica; Stellenwerf, Cheryl; Thames, Pixie; and Williams, Patricia. "Problem Solving with a Spreadsheet." *Arithmetic Teacher,* 38 (November 1990), pp. 52–56.

Hoffer, Alan R. "Ratio and Proportional Thinking." In *Teaching Mathematics in Grades K–8* (ed. Thomas R. Post, 2nd edition). Boston: Allyn and Bacon, 1992.

Kliman, Marlene. "Integrating Mathematics and Literature in the Elementary Classroom." *Arithmetic Teacher,* 40 (February 1993), pp. 318–321.

Lembke, Linda O., and Reys, Barbara J. "The Development of, and Interaction between, Intuitive and School-Taught Ideas about Percent." *Journal for Research in Mathematics Education,* 25 (May 1994), pp. 237–259.

Lindquist, Mary M.; Brown, Catherine A.; Carpenter, Thomas P.; Kouba, Vicky L.; Silver, Edward A.; and Swafford, Jane O. *Results from the Fourth Mathematics Assessment of the National Assessment of Educational Progress.* Reston, Va.: NCTM, 1988.

Miller, Jane L., and Fey, James T. "Proportional Reasoning." *Mathematics Teaching in the Middle School,* 5 (5) (January 2000), pp. 310–314.

Quintero, Ana Melvia. "Helping Children Understand Ratios." *Arithmetic Teacher,* 34 (May 1987), pp. 17–21.

Reys, Barbara J., and Reys, Robert E. *Mental Computation Performance and Strategy Use of Japanese Students in Grades 2, 4, 6, and 8.* Final Report NSF Int9000203. Columbia, Mo.: University of Missouri, 1993.

Romberg, Thomas A.; Harvey, John G.; Moser, James M.; and Montgomery, Mary E. *Developing Mathematical Processes.* Chicago: Rand McNally, 1974–1976.

Shannon, Brenda K. "Our Diets May Be Killing Us." *Mathematics Teaching in the Middle School,* 1 (April-May 1995), pp. 376–382.

Thiessen, Diane, and Matthias, Margaret. *The Wonderful World of Mathematics: A Critically Annotated List of Children's Books in Mathematics.* Reston, Va.: NCTM, 1998.

Tracy, Dyanne M., and Hague, Mary S. "Toys 'R' Math." *Mathematics Teaching in the Middle School,* 2 (January 1997), pp. 141–145.

Wiebe, James H. "Manipulating Percentages." *Mathematics Teacher,* 79 (January 1986), pp. 23–26.

13 Patterns, Relationships, and Algebra

Snapshot of a Lesson

Mr. Martinez and his second- and third-grade students have been thinking about the concept of equality and different expressions that represent equality. Recently, they have been exploring how you could change a quantity on one side of the balance to make it equal to the quantity on the other side. As we enter the scene, they are talking about what they have done in previous days.

JAIME: We did a lot of balancing. If there were 15 grams on one side and 8 grams on the other, we could balance the scales by taking away 7 grams from the 15 or adding 7 grams to the other side.

ANNA: You always do the same thing to both sides of the balance.

MR. MARTINEZ: I think I know what you mean, but say more.

ANNA: Well, add 7 to one side or subtract 7 from the other. Just like Jaime said. I guess you sort of do the opposite not the same.

JENNIFER: When we wrote the sentences (coming to the overhead), it's like this:

We are trying to balance 15 and 8, so we wrote:

$15 \neq 8$

$15 - 7 = 8$ You can take from the larger.

$15 = 8 + 7$ Or add to the smaller.

MR. MARTINEZ: What generalizations have we made? Can you think of a way to write them?

LEE: Well, it's like this. Say you started with 8 and 3. (Coming to the board). You can write (Lee writes these sentences on the board).

$8 \neq 3$

$8 - m = 3$

$8 = 3 + m$

The m is always the same like Anna said.

MR. MARTINEZ: Let's keep pushing. What if I start with A on one side of the balance and B on the other? (He points to the balance)

TAMI: Which is larger?

MR. MARTINEZ: Let's say A. How could we write that? (He pushes the A side down to show that it is heavier.)

CLASS: $A > B$

TAMI: So A take away something would equal B or B add that something equals A. (She is using her hands and writing $A -$ something $= B$ in the air, so Mr. Martinez knows Tami understands what she is saying,)

MR. MARTINEZ: How can we write what Tami is saying?

JAIME: $A - m = B$ $A = B + m$.

MR. MARTINEZ: That's a lot of letters. What do they mean?

YEON: The A and B are the things on the balance, and m is how you change the balance. You subtract m from the larger or you add m to the smaller.

MR. MARTINEZ: Jen said yesterday that you really could make the scales balance in other ways. Tell us what you were thinking.

JEN: Change both sides of the balance. Like you could take off some on one side and put it on the other. If that doesn't work, you can keep going.

MR. MARTINEZ: Let's explore that today.

Mr. Martinez sets up the class. He knows that some of his students are not yet ready to make generalizations, but others are. Even those that are not ready to generalize or to represent the generalization do grasp this meaning of equals and are practicing addition and subtraction facts.

Leon, who rarely contributes to these short discussions, was beaming at the end of the class.

> LEON: I got one! I got a generalization! If you take away everything from one side and everything from the other side, the scale will balance.

MR. MARTINEZ: Hold on to that, Leon. I'll write it on the generalization board. We will start with that tomorrow.

Introduction

In this chapter, we will examine ways to help children with algebraic thinking by focusing on patterns and relationships. We end the chapter by exploring special patterns and relationships as an illustration of how one topic, number theory, can be more closely related to algebraic thinking. Although we have chosen number theory, you will see ways to include algebraic thinking in other mathematical topics. Once children get into the habit of thinking and questioning this way, they will be less likely to approach algebra as a mysterious subject.

The *Principles and Standards for School Mathematics* (NCTM 2000) calls for us to include algebraic thinking in the mathematics we are teaching. Examine the algebraic expectations for elementary and middle school in Appendix A. Research is helping us focus on the thinking of children in this endeavor. For example, the article in *Teaching Children Mathematics* (Faulkner et al. 1999) reports research of elementary teachers' experiences in helping children with equality relationships. MacGregor and Stacy (1999, p. 79) state: "The language of arithmetic focuses on answers. The language of algebra focuses on relationships." This perspective allows us to include algebraic thinking in much of the mathematics we already do in elementary school.

We will concentrate on three aspects of algebraic thinking. This is not an exhaustive list, but it is a place to start thinking about elementary mathematics from an algebraic perspective rather than only as arithmetic. The first aspect is equality; we will look at understanding the relationship of equality and the language that lets us represent that relationship. The second aspect is change; we will examine patterns in terms of change and how children describe and symbolically represent change. The third aspect is generalizations; we will consider ways to help children make, describe, and represent generalizations.

PATTERNS

Before looking at repeating, growing, and number patterns, let's continue our examination of the three aspects of algebraic thinking.

Equality

What do you think that children would say about the truth of the following mathematical sentences?

$$\text{A. } 7 + 3 = 10$$
$$\text{B. } 9 = 5 + 4$$
$$\text{C. } 7 + 3 = 10 + 5$$

Children who say sentence A is true, often say that B is not true but C is true. At a very early age, they have tried to make sense of mathematics and have made the generalization that the equals sign means "get an answer." They will complete an open sentence such as $3 + \_\_ = 9$ with a 12. They are thinking, it says to add, 3 and 9 is 12. They are operating with the arithmetic language of getting answers. This reasoning makes A obviously true. What about the sentence B bothers children? Sometimes they say it is backwards or that the answer is 9. They are not focusing on the relationship between 9 and $5 + 4$, or that this expresses the equality between these two expressions. Why do you think they say C is true?

We know that children can develop an understanding of equality and how to represent it with mathematical sentences. Return to the Snapshot of a Lesson, and analyze the discussion in Mr. Martinez's class. These students understood that if you change one side of a balanced scale (one side of an equation) you must change the other to maintain equality. The concepts of equality, equivalent expressions, and equivalent fractions are central to all of mathematics.

Change

Think about how much mathematics involves dealing with change. From simple addition problems (You had three stuffed bears, Kiesha gave you four more bears. How many do you have now?) to exponential growth (How much money will you have in three years if you invest at 6 percent?) we are considering both the change as well as the final state. In the Snapshot of a Lesson, notice how the students were focusing on change. It took a change in the original state of the balance scale to make it balance. The students were able to describe that change.

As we are analyzing patterns, we often look for what is changing and what is not. Often we describe the next element of a pattern in terms of the previous term. For example, we may say that the next term is always 2 more than the last one. This is called a recursive description as opposed to one that relates the term to the number of that term (the *n*th term is always 5 times *n*).

Generalizations

You read how the children in the Snapshot of a Lesson were making conjectures and exploring generalizations and saw how Mr. Martinez was encouraging their thinking by having them explain what they were saying and having them represent their thoughts in a general way.

Look at what children do when given a generalization such as the conjecture $g + b - b = g$ (Carpenter and Levi 1999). See Figure 13–1. Young children in grades 1 and 2 often argue by example. They will choose a number for g and one for b as Margie did. She did realize that one example was not enough, but basically she was arguing from examples. Children may try to justify the conjecture by simply repeating the conjecture as Aaron did. Contrast Aaron's explanation with Jamal's. Maria is well on her way to deductive proof, using previous "proved" statements such as $b - b = 0$ and $g + 0 = g$. With ex-

perience, children in grades three and four are able to provide more general arguments like Jamal's and some that are more sophisticated, like Maria's.

Discussion of patterns opens many possibilities for algebraic thinking. You can build on the background children have in describing patterns with everyday language to help them represent those patterns with mathematical symbols. For example, if children have described a pattern as "each term is two more than the last one," they can describe the term after the *n*th term as $n + 2$. Here the children have focused on change and expressed a generalization. Later, they will learn to represent the relationship between two consecutive terms with an equation such as $N = L + 2$ (next term (N) is the last term (L) plus 2) or more sophisticated expressions such as $n_{i+1} = n_i + 2$. In the sections that follow, we will examine only a few of the different types of patterns and relationships. In each example, we will return to the three aspects of equality, change, and generalizations.

Repeating Patterns

Repeating patterns can be simple or puzzling; of course, you should begin young children with patterns that they can grasp. A pattern that has only two repeating elements in its core, known as an *ab* linear repeating pattern is the simplest.

Before doing patterns with pictures or even objects, you may want to start with oral patterns. Have the first few children do what you say (sit, stand, sit, stand) and ask "What should the next child do?"

Color is a very visual attribute for children. Ask them to describe the pattern shown below (use cubes or other blocks) and then to continue that pattern. You can use geometric shapes, sounds, numbers, and many other materials. When children become familiar with patterns such as these, they can extend other patterns that are begun or make their own patterns.

Purple   White   Purple   White   Purple   White

There are many variations of linear repeating patterns in which the core, the part that repeats, is not *ab*. For example, how would you describe the core in each of the following patterns?

Pattern A: ¿¿ □ ¿¿ □ ¿¿ □
Pattern B: # * # * * # * # * * # * # * *
Pattern C: □ $ □ $ $ □ $ □ $ $ □ $ □ $ $

Question: How would you prove this conjecture?

$$g + b - b = g$$

Margie: [writes $5 + 4 \rightarrow 9 - 4 \rightarrow 5$] That's the number you started with. I'll try $32 + 8 \rightarrow 40 - 8 \rightarrow 32$, so it's true.

Aaron: I plus b to g and I take it away, and I get g.

Jamal: [makes a stack of 8 stacking cubes, a stack of 6 stacking cubes, and puts them together] Then you take 6 right away, and you get these 8, just what you started with. It would work like that for any numbers. You're just taking away exactly what you added, so it's the same.

Maria: $g + b - b$ is the same as $g + 0$ since $b - b$ is 0, because I know that $b - b = 0$, and then $g + 0 = g$. So it's always true.

Figure 13–1 • Examples of children's justification strategies (From the Developing Conceptions of Algebraic Reasoning Project [Carpenter, pp. 57] reported in the 8th Semiannual Performance Report, National Center for Improving Student Learning and Achievement in Mathematics and Science, University of Wisconsin, November 1999.)

The core in Pattern A may be described as *aab* or something similar. Although the core in Pattern B may be described as *ababb,* some children may see that pattern as having two cores, *ab* followed by *aab* and then repeated, or as a pattern of single *a*s with one *b* then two *b*s in between. Ask children how Pattern B is like Pattern C.

Remember that children think about a pattern in a way that differs from you and that there is often more than one correct way to explain or extend a pattern.

Children's explanations of why they chose the next element of a pattern will help you understand their thinking and perhaps help you look at a pattern in a different way. Research from the Seventh Mathematics Assessment of NAEP indicates that fourth-grade students often have more difficulty inserting a missing element in a pattern than identifying the next element (Blume and Heckman 2000). Perhaps this is because they have been asked to continue patterns more often than filling in the missing parts. Your curriculum should include both types of experiences.

Begin to look for ways you can connect repeating patterns to number sequences. By simply numbering the elements, you can lead children to generalize. Consider the repeating pattern of geometric shapes in Figure 13–2.

Ask the following questions:

What shape is the ninth term? the twelfth term? (They are both squares.)

What is the sixteenth term? How do you know?

What can you say about the terms of all the squares?

In the upper elementary grades, children should begin to describe the terms of all the squares as multiples of 3. They also may see that the octagons are always one shape after the squares and represent this as $3s + 1$ or that the trapezoids are one shape before ($3s - 1$) the squares.

You could do a different linear repeating pattern each day because of the variety, but do not forget geometric patterns. Look for the use of geometric patterns in different cultures of the world. Quilts, fabrics, rugs, pottery, and other arts and crafts often use repetition as well as other intriguing patterns.

In the Classroom 13–1 is a variation in which the children must first find the change from one element to the next in terms of the geometric transformations: flips (reflections), turns (rotations), and slides (translations). The cores of the patterns vary from one to four squares. If children are having difficulty determining the transformation, have them color in the segmented pattern square, cut it out, and try the different motions.

The patterns we have considered thus far have repeated in a line. You can extend this to have patterns that extend in more than one direction. Beautiful patterns can be made by repeating geometric grids like the ones on In the Classroom 13–1 in a square grid, where the repetition occurs in each column as well as in each row. When the patterns are completed, have children focus on how each row (or each column) changes. Look for generalizations such as, if the core is two squares, then the even columns will be the same.

Growing Patterns

Another type of pattern, often called a growing pattern, may be linear as in patterns like these:

□○□○○□□○○○□□□○○○○□□□□○○○○
H H T H H H H T T H H H H H H T T T T T T
Y B B Y B B B B Y B B B B B B Y B B B B B B B B

Notice that only the Bs are growing in the last pattern.

Suppose we number the last pattern, as we numbered the repeated geometric pattern, as follows:

Y BB Y BBBB Y BBBBBB Y BBBBBBBB ?   ?   ?
1 2 3   4   5   6   7   8   9 10 11

Can you describe the change from term to term? How would you describe the odd-numbered terms? How would you describe the even-numbered terms? What is the 22nd term? What is 131st term? Can you describe the pattern in general? These are the types of questions that you could ask about this pattern. Do you see you are considering change, making generalizations, and perhaps even expressing the *n*th term as an equality?

Growing patterns may also be two-dimensional, such as the ones formed with squares in Figure 13–3. One way to help students see these growing patterns is to have them model a pattern with square tiles and then move the tiles as shown by the shaded squares in the pattern to see what shape is formed

Figure 13–2 • Repeated pattern with terms numbered

In The Classroom 13–1

Square Designs

Objective: Describe patterns in terms of transformations.

▼ Look at these designs made by sixth-grade students. The students began with the segmented square shown, colored part of it, and then flipped, turned, or slid it to the next square.

• For each pattern, tell which motion was used and the number of squares in the core (that is, the number of squares before the pattern repeats).

A. Motion: _____ Number of squares in core: _____

B. Motion: _____ Number of squares in core: _____

C. Motion: _____ Number of squares in core: _____

D. Motion: _____ Number of squares in core: _____

E. Motion: _____ Number of squares in core: _____

F. Motion: _____ Number of squares in core: _____

▼ Your turn:
  • Begin with this square:
  • Color part of it.
  • Flip, turn, or slide.

and how it relates to the term number. For each pattern, you can ask questions such as these:

> How many squares are in each of the terms: 1, 2, and 3?
>
> Do you see how the pattern is changing? Describe that change.
>
> Can you tell how many squares will be in the 4th term?
>
> How many squares will be in the 5th term?
>
> If you were to extend this pattern to the 100th term, how many squares would it take?
>
> How would you describe the nth term?
>
> How can you describe growing pattern A?

We can describe Pattern A with squared numbers. The 3rd term has 3^2 squares, the 100th term has 100^2 squares, and the nth term has n^2 squares.

See if you can see how Patterns B and C are changed from Pattern A. Do you see that each term in B has one more square than the corresponding term in A? The numbers of squares in the terms of B are 2, 5, 10 . . . . This sequence of numbers may not be easy for some children to represent. Yet, if you think about how A and B relate, you can see that the

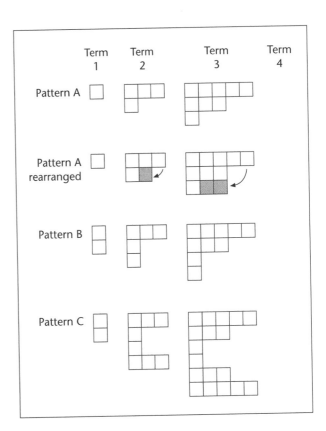

Figure 13–3 • Growing patterns

*n*th term of B has $n^2 + 1$ squares. See if you can describe the *n*th term of pattern C.

Number Patterns

Number patterns, like growing patterns, are about change. For example, consider a linear number pattern that begins 2, 4, 8. What would you say comes next? If you are focused on the fact that each term is twice the previous one, then you would say that 16 comes next. If the change that you observe is that there is a difference of 2 between the 2 and the 4, and a difference of 4 between the 4 and the 8, then you may say that next there should be a difference of 6. Thus, the next number may be 14.

This example points out two things about patterns that are especially true for number patterns. First, three terms are not sufficient to determine a pattern uniquely. Second, even with more terms given, there is usually more than one way to look at a pattern. The important thing is for children to see the change their own way, be able to extend that pattern, and explain their thinking. As they reach the upper grades, they should be able to give the next term for any given term (recursive form), and give the general term relating it to the number of that term.

Number patterns can also be two-dimensional. In every classroom there is an obvious two-dimensional pattern: the calendar. Figure 13–4 shows the calendar for April 2002 as an example. Have younger children look at the change. How does the calendar change as we look across a week? How does it change as we go down? Children may recognize that every other day has an even date or that the date of the next Friday after April 12th is 7 more, or the 19th. Have students find the sum of all the numbers in a square. After finding the sum of the numbers in this square and several other squares of the same size, students may observe that the sum is nine times the number in the center. Older students should be able to see why this result is true; often using letters to define the nine numbers in the square helps. If the middle number is represented by *m*, then the number a week later is *m* + 7. Note that the sum of all these expressions is 9*m*. This is not a difficult generalization for children in the upper elementary grades.

Many other number arrangements can be exciting to explore. The arrangement of numbers on In the Classroom 13–2 presents a variety of patterns. Challenge students in the upper elementary or middle school to find their own number pattern. You will be amazed at their creativity; there are many more than the ones suggested on the card. Again, focus the students on how each row is changing, how the sums of the numbers in successive "diamonds" are growing, or how the sums of the rows are changing. There are patterns that children can generalize such as describing the sum of the numbers in a row. Row *k* has a sum of *k* times the middle number. Although this relationship is not difficult, see if students can then find an expression for the middle number in terms of *k*.

RELATIONSHIPS

Relationships abound in mathematics; here we will touch on only a few. You can look at other chapters of this book for many other examples of relationships. We will focus on describing relationships with numbers and variables.

Young children can be asked how the number of boys in a group is related to the number of hands:

Figure 13–4 • Calendar patterns

APRIL 2002

	1	2–3–4	5	6
7	8	9 (10) 11	12	13
14	15	16–17–18	19	20
21	22	23 24 25	26	27
28	29	30		

```
2–3–4        2–3–4
9 (10) 11     9 (m) 11
16–17–18     16–17–18
```

Call the middle number *m*.

m – 8	*m* – 7	*m* – 6
m – 1	(*m*)	*m* + 1
m + 6	*m* + 7	*m* + 8

The day immediately above *m* is 7 days before *m* – 7.

In The Classroom 13–2

What Do You See in Me?

Objective: Exploring number patterns.

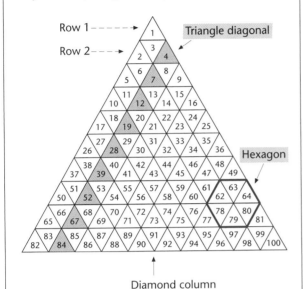

Row 1 → 1
Row 2 → Triangle diagonal

Diamond column

- Do you see the perfect squares?
- Where are the odd numbers?
- Find the sum of the numbers in each row. See if you can find a shortcut.
- Take any hexagon like the one outlined. What is its sum? Can you find a shortcut?
- Take any two adjacent numbers in a triangle diagonal (for example, 4 and 7). Find their product. Where is it?

Although this relationship may seem very similar to the one in the preceding example, it is a 3-to-1 relationship rather than a 1-to-2 relationship. Some children may have difficulty describing the general terms in this case because the relationship calls for division rather than multiplication. Again, begin slowly and write the results in a table:

Number of Girls	3	6	9	12			45		N
Number of Triangles	1	2	3	4			?		N ÷ 3

At times, you may want a relationship to be established by a "function machine," which outputs a number for every number input. The challenge for the students is to decide what the function machine did and how to describe it. These machines can be simple, such as one that always gives an output of one more than the number put in, twice as much as the number put in, or two less than the number put in. For a more complicated machine, inputs and outputs might be as follows:

In	3	5	12	25		53		N	
Out	7	11	25	51	29		163		S

You will need to help children focus on the change from the input to the output. Some children will focus on the change in the input, but this does

If multiplication symbols have been introduced, *B* boys and 2 × *B* hands describe this simple relationship. Begin by describing the number of hands of three boys as 2 × 3, of four boys as 2 × 4, and of ten boys as 2 × 10, writing the results for each in a table:

Number of Boys	1	2	3	4		10	B
Number of Hands	2	4	6	8		20	2 × B

Consider the relationship of girls to triangles if girls make triangles from string as shown in the following figure:

not help. So you need to ask questions about specific values that go in each direction:

Given the input _____, what is the output?

Given the output _____, what is the input?

Challenge your class to respond to an output of 64. Some students will say it is impossible because it is even and all the other outputs are odd. Others will give a fraction as an input. Discuss with the students why each could be a correct interpretation. If the machine will take only whole numbers, then 64 is not a possible output. But if the machine will take fractions, $31\frac{1}{2}$ is the input for 64.

Before talking about the general rule, describe many of the outputs in terms of the inputs or what the function machine is doing in words and numbers; then try the more abstract symbols. Students may generalize as follows: "you add the number twice and then add one more" or "double the number, and add one." When the students reach this stage, have them see that one way to write each of these is $N + N + 1$ and $(2 \times N) + 1$.

A fun way to slip into representing relationships is through number puzzles such as the one shown in Figure 13–5. As a first activity, have children do the puzzle with various numbers. After using many different numbers chosen by the children, let them use materials to model the steps. You can observe whether they have strongly developed concepts about the operations. If you discover, for example, that some children do not know how to model "multiply by two" or "divide by two," then you can reinforce the meanings. After the students are able to model, they will enjoy describing the steps with variables. Notice the concepts they can gain by doing this with simple algebraic representations. For example, it is easy to see that $2 \times (N + 4)$ is the same as $2N + 8$ because it is two ways of describing the same picture.

NUMBER THEORY

Number theory is the branch of mathematics concerned mainly with the natural numbers. Odd and even numbers, primes, prime factorization, number patterns, least common multiples, and greatest common divisors are some of the typical topics included in elementary and middle school curricula. We will consider some of the reasons that number theory should be included, illustrate some ways to include number theory, and tie number theory topics to algebraic thinking.

Figure 13–5 • A number puzzle

Number Theory

There are many reasons to include number theory in the elementary school curriculum. We have listed three of them here to begin your thinking.

1. Fascination with Numbers. From the time of ancient civilizations, people have been fascinated with numbers and number patterns. Ancients often thought numbers had mystical qualities, and the branch of mathematics called *numerology* was studied in great depth. Number theory topics often provide puzzle-like activities that intrigue some people.

Thus, one reason to study number theory is to awaken and encourage a fascination for numbers in settings that require looking for relationships and solving problems.

2. A Chance to Discover Mathematics. Many conjectures in number theory are easy to state, even though some may be difficult to prove. For example, the famous conjecture by Goldbach is easy enough for fourth and fifth graders to understand. In 1742, Goldbach conjectured that any even number greater than 2 could be written as the sum of two primes. For example, $8 = 3 + 5$, $18 = 11 + 7$, and $162 = 79 + 83$. After children have shown that this conjecture is reasonable for the first hundred even numbers, they can explore some conjectures of their own. (See In the Classroom 13–3). It is important that each child keep a record of conjectures that fail. It is just as important to know what will not work as it is to know what will work. Be sure to emphasize that students have not proved a conjecture by trying examples; they have only found out that it works for the examples chosen. In fact, no one has ever proved or disproved Goldbach's conjecture.

3. Extension and Practice. Teachers often need ways to help individualize within a topic. For example, suppose you need to review multiplication and division with some children in a fifth-grade class. Even though all of the children would probably benefit from some review, they all will not need the same amount. Consider the amount of computational practice suggested by the activities in this chapter. At the same time, we can extend children's experiences to include algebraic thinking.

Specific Number Theory Topics

In this section, we will examine some ways to develop some specific number theory concepts and skills and relate them to algebraic thinking. After developing any concepts or skills, they need to be used. To teach children what a prime number is in fourth grade and then never use primes again assures that primes will be forgotten. Beyond the skills to be developed, it is important to keep in mind the reasons for studying number theory. If all we do is have children learn definitions and rules, they have missed the real power of number theory.

Odds and Evens Classifying numbers as odd or even is one of the first number-theory topics that children encounter. As children count by twos—2, 4, 6, 8, 10—they learn that there is something different about these numbers; these are the even numbers, and the others are the odds. More precisely, an even number is a number that is a multiple of 2.

You can begin the study of odds and evens by having young children model the natural numbers with square tiles. Give each child a number (two through twenty) of square tiles. Young children may pretend they are making candy bars that are two squares wide. Have them tell what is the difference between the model of an even and an odd number. What changes as you go from an even number, say, 6, to the next number? What is the pattern, in counting, of the evens and odds? What is 0? Why?

In The Classroom 13–3

Do You Believe That?

Objective: Exploring conjectures about types of numbers.

▼ Try one of these conjectures about positive whole numbers. See if you can find examples that disprove each.

- *Tinbach's Conjecture:* Every number can be expressed as the difference of two primes.

  Examples: $14 = 17 - 3$ $5 = 7 - 2$ $28 = 31 - 3$

- *Zinbach's Conjecture:* Every number can be expressed as the sum of 3 squares (0 is permitted).

  Examples: $3 = 1^2 + 1^2 + 1^2$ $14 = 1^2 + 2^2 + 3^2$
  $9 = 3^2 + 0^2 + 0^2$

- *Aluminumbach's Conjecture:* Every odd number can be expressed as the sum of 3 primes.

  Examples: $15 = 5 + 5 + 5$ $11 = 3 + 3 + 5$

- *Brassbach's Conjecture:* Every square number has exactly 3 divisors.

  Example: $2^2 = 4$, 4 has 3 divisors 1, 2, and 4

- *Copperbach's Conjecture:* The product of any number of primes is odd.

  Examples: $5 \times 3 \times 7 = 105$ (3 primes)
  $7 \times 3 \times 3 \times 5 = 315$ (4 primes)

Later, have the children make a list of odd and even numbers. They should see the pattern that every other number is even and that even numbers end in 0, 2, 4, 6, or 8. Can they justify this conjecture? Do they use the pattern argument (every other number) or a definition of even (a multiple of 2).

There are many conjectures that children can make about even and odd numbers. For example, a child may claim that the sum of two odd numbers is even. How would you expect them to justify that statement? At first, many students will use specific numbers. If you have modeled evens and odds, they may explain through models like the ones in Figure 13–6. In middle school, they may use the following argument. Let one odd number be represented by $2m + 1$ and the other odd number by $2p + 1$. If we add these, we get $2m + 2p + 2$, which is a multiple of 2, or an even number.

Evens and odds arise on many occasions, and you should look for experiences in which the ideas of odds and evens are used. For example, students might find the sum of the first 50 odd numbers, find the probability of throwing an even number with two dice, or find the first odd number that is divisible by 11.

Factors, Primes, and Prime Factorization As children are learning about multiplication and division, they are also beginning to learn about multiples and factors.

Factors. Each of two numbers multiplied together to give a product is called a *factor* of that product. For example, 3 and 4 are factors of 12 because 3 times 4 is 12.

Children can begin exploring factors by using materials. For example, begin with 12 objects. See if they can group the 12 objects by ones, twos, threes, . . . , twelves. There are 12 groups of ones, 6 groups of twos, 4 groups of threes, 3 groups of fours, 2 groups of sixes, and 1 group of twelves, but 12 cannot be grouped by fives, sevens, eights, nines, tens, or elevens.

The 12 Story

$$12 = 12 \times 1$$
$$12 = 6 \times 2$$
$$12 = 4 \times 3$$
$$12 = 3 \times 4$$
$$12 = 2 \times 6$$
$$12 = 1 \times 12$$

Later, children should be able to find all the factors of a given number. For example, what are all the factors of 84? One place to begin is to see what numbers will divide 84. Have the children begin with the simplest divisor. You might lead them through a process such as this:

We know that 1 will divide 84, so 1 and 84 are factors. Write:

1   84

Now try 2 (in your head). [$2 \times 42 = 84$, so 2 and 42 are factors.] Write:

1, 2   42, 84

How about 3? (Do you really need your calculator?) [$3 \times 28 = 84$, so 3 and 28 are factors.] Write:

1, 2, 3   28, 42, 84

How about 4? [$4 \times 21 = 84$, so 4 and 21 are factors.] Write:

1, 2, 3, 4   21, 28, 42, 84

How about 5? No, so try 6. [$6 \times 14 = 84$, so 6 and 14 are factors.] Write:

1, 2, 3, 4, 6   14, 21, 28, 42, 84

How long do we continue? Do you see that we are closing in on it? Let's try 7. [$7 \times 12 = 84$, so 7 and 12 are factors.] Write:

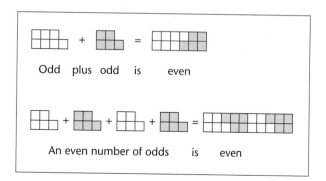

Figure 13–6 • Models for summing odd numbers

1, 2, 3, 4, 6, 7 ⤴ 12, 14, 21, 28, 42, 84

How about 8? 9? Do you need to try 10?

Children will need to try 10, 11, and perhaps some more numbers before they realize that, if they divide 84 by 10, 11, and so on, they always get a quotient smaller than 9, and they have checked each one of these.

In the Classroom 13–4 is a game that requires children to find the factors of the numbers 2 through 36 and to use some strategy. Although the objective indicates that it is practice in finding factors, you are

also developing a sense about which numbers have few and which numbers have many factors.

Multiples. A multiple of a number is the product of that number and any natural number. For example, 36 is a multiple of 4 because 36 is 4 times 9. In looking at multiples, we usually begin with the number and generate multiples of it. Here are the multiples of 4:

4, 8, 12, 16, 20, 24, 28, . . .

How did we generate this list? (We multiplied 4 by 1, 2, 3, 4, and so forth.)

Many different materials can be used to illustrate multiples such as the number line, Cuisenaire rods, and the hundred chart. Children should be familiar with the smaller multiples of the numbers 1 through 10 through learning the multiplication facts.

The concept of a multiple is not difficult—remember, it is a product. It is simply a new word, and children often confuse it with another new word, factor, or divisor. Confusion also arises when teachers ask, "What is 36 a multiple of?" They are actually asking children to find the factors of 36. Then when they ask, "What is 4 a factor of?" they are actually asking the children to find the multiples of 4. Children need to be able to think in both directions—for example, to list all the multiples of 7 and to find what 42 is a multiple of. But when you are first beginning the study of multiples and factors, keep the language consistent.

Primes and Composites. A whole number greater than one is prime if it has exactly two factors: one and itself. Otherwise, it is composite. There are several concrete models that you may use to introduce the idea of primes. The activity on In the Classroom 13–5 illustrates one model. After children have been introduced to primes, develop the definition with them. Then, have them identify which numbers are primes and which are composites.

There are other explorations that focus on primes, twin primes (pairs of primes that are two apart, such as 11 and 13), reversal primes (pairs of primes such as 79 and 97), or the infinitude of primes. Another investigation involves what is called a sieve (do you see why it is called that?). The most famous is the Sieve of Eratosthenes, in which the numbers are arranged in ten columns. The sieve, arranged in six columns, shown in In the Classroom 13–6, gives an easy method for generating the primes. At first, the process will seem long, but children will soon realize how quickly the primes can be generated. The beauty of the arrangement of the sieve in six columns is that

---

In The Classroom 13–4

Factor Me Out

Objective: Practice in finding factors.

▼ Choose a partner and make a chart to play this game:

●	2	3	4	5	6
7	8	9	10	11	12
13	14	15	16	17	18
19	20	21	22	23	24
25	26	27	28	29	30
31	32	33	34	35	36

▼ Rules:

- Player 1 chooses a number. He or she gets that many points. The opponent gets points equal to the sum of all the factors.

- Make a table to record scores:

Player 1	Player 2
10	7 (2 + 5)

- Mark out the number and the factors; these cannot be used again.

- Repeat with Player 2 choosing the number.

- Alternate turns until no numbers are left.

The player with the most points wins.

In The Classroom 13–5

Objective: Finding primes and composites.

Materials: A copy of the worksheet: The Hip-Hoppers Hop

Directions: Have the children do the worksheet after introducing the terms *prime* and *composite*. (The primes have two hopper stoppers; the composites have more than two hopper stoppers; and one is neither.)

When they have completed the chart, discuss the following questions with them:

- What numbers had two hopper stoppers? [2, 3, 5, 7, etc.]

- What numbers had more than two hopper stoppers? [4, 6, 8, 9, etc.]

- What number had only one hopper stopper? [1]

The Hip-Hoppers Hop

The hoppers are strange characters that can only hop a certain length. For example, the 5-hopper hops 5 spaces each time. They all begin at 0.

See where each hopper will land. The 1-hopper and the 2-hopper have been done for you.

Be a 3-hopper. You will land at 3 (write a 3 above the 3), you will land at 6 (write a 3 above the 6). Keep going. (You should have 3's above 9, 12, 15, 18, 21, 24).

Do the same for the 4-hopper, the 5-hopper, all the way to a 24-hopper. Then, answer the questions your teacher has.

---

after 2 and 3, all the primes occur in the first or the fifth column. Do you see why? This is a good time to encourage algebraic thinking as children make and justify conjectures about why this is true.

Prime Factorization. The fundamental theorem of arithmetic says that every composite number may be expressed as a product of primes in only one way. Many patterns and formulas in number theory, as well as some algorithms for finding the greatest common factor and the least common multiple, depend on expressing a number as a product of primes (prime factorization). In algebra, we often use prime factorization to find least common denominators of rational algebraic expressions.

How would you begin to find the prime factors of 3190?

In The Classroom 13–6

Sieve 6

Objective: To find all prime numbers (2–96).

▼ **Do it:**

- Circle 2, then mark out every multiple of 2 or every second number after.

- Circle 3, then mark out every third number (6, 9, 12, . . .) Some may already be marked out.

- Circle 5 (since 4 is marked out) and mark out every fifth number. Continue to 96.

②	3	X̶	5	X̶
7	X̶	9	10	11	12
13	14	15	16	17	18
19	20	21	22	23	24
25	26	27	28	29	30
31	32	33	34	35	36
37	38	39	40	41	42
43	44	45	46	47	48
49	50	51	52	53	54
55	56	57	58	59	60
61	62	63	64	65	66
67	68	69	70	71	72
73	74	75	76	77	78
79	80	81	82	83	84
85	86	87	88	89	90
91	92	93	94	95	96

▼ **Talk about it:**

- What numbers are circled? _____

- In what columns are they? _____

Two methods are commonly used to find the prime factorization of a number. One is the *factor tree method:*

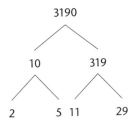

The other is the *division method,* in which the number is divided by primes:

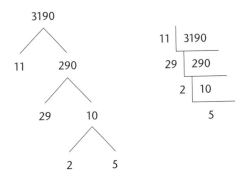

What is the difference between the two methods? In the factor tree method, the first step is to factor the number into any two factors. In the division method, you must divide by a prime. If, in the factor tree method, you made the rule that one factor must always be a prime, then the two methods would be the same except for notation.

No matter which method students use, make certain that they write the prime factorization. For example, they should express 3190 as 2 × 5 × 11 × 29.

Greatest Common Factor and Least Common Multiple We have looked at factors and multiples of individual numbers; now we will examine pairs of numbers to find the greatest common factor (GCF) and the least common multiple (LCM) by asking:

What is the largest number that is a factor of both numbers?

What is the smallest number that is a multiple of both numbers?

Understanding these concepts depends mainly on knowing how to find factors and multiples and keeping straight which is which. Algorithms for finding the GCF and the LCM are very similar. Often teachers develop GCF and LCM one right after the other and then do not use them. Or, if they develop the two ideas at separate times, they never bring them back together to compare and contrast them. If they are taught at all, these two concepts should be presented in a meaningful manner. Several algorithms are available for finding the GCF and LCM; the listing algorithm and the factorization algorithm are commonly used. Because the listing algorithm is the more concrete of the two, we will present it here. This would be a good time to let children develop their own algorithm. After seeing different ways that they found the GCF for two numbers, discuss the efficiency of some of the ways.

To find the GCF with the listing algorithm, you first list all the factors of the two (or more) numbers. For example, to find the GCF of 18 and 24, list the following:

Factors of 18: 1 2 3 6 9 18
Factors of 24: 1 2 3 4 6 8 12 24

Then we look for the common factors—1, 2, 3, 6—and choose the largest. Thus, 6 is the GCF.

Similarly, to find the LCM, list the multiples of each number until you find common multiples. For example, to find the LCM of 18 and 24, list the following:

Multiples of 18: 18 36 54 72 90 . . .
Multiples of 24: 24 48 72 96 . . .

By inspection, 72 is the smallest number common to both sets. Thus, the LCM is 72.

Children may use the LCM to find the least common denominator of two fractions, and they may use the GCF when they simplify fractions. Yet often we fail to teach them what they are using. For example, to simplify $^{18}/_{24}$, children may first simplify it to $^{9}/_{12}$ and then to $^{3}/_{4}$. If they see that the GCF of 18 and 24 is 6, then they can do the simplification in one step. However, the time saved by finding the GCF first is probably not worth the effort.

Similarly, at times it is important to find the least common denominator, but often it is sufficient to find a common denominator. Today, with the prevalence of calculators and decreased emphasis on complicated fractions, finding GCFs and LCMs is not as crucial as it once was. If you do teach these concepts, then you must develop them carefully and at a stage in the students' maturity when they can grasp what they are doing.

Divisibility Tests At one time, the divisibility rules were important. Today, they are an interesting sidelight in mathematics. It is the discovery of some of the rules, the making of conjectures and the justifying of those conjectures that is important to encouraging algebraic thinking.

Many children discover the rules for 2 and 5 through observing patterns in the multiplication

and division facts for those numbers. The rules for other numbers are not quite as evident. In the Classroom 13–7 provides a guided discovery activity for the divisibility rules for 3 and 9. It is important to discuss the results in the table with the class and to give more examples if the students don't answer the questions clearly. Here are some good questions to raise:

Does this divisibility test work for larger numbers?

Is this a test only for 3 and 9?

Why does this work?

This last question returns us to algebraic thinking. You can expect many children to explain by using a specific numerical example. Others may model the problem for numbers in the hundreds, such as 456 divided by 3 as shown in Figure 13–7. Still others in

---

In The Classroom 13–7

Divisibility Discovery

Objective: Discover divisibility rules for 3 and 9.

▼ Use your calculator. Fill in the chart and look for patterns.

Number	Divisible by 3?	Divisible by 9?	Sum of digits	Sum divisible by 3?	by 9?
456	yes	no	4 + 5 + 6 = 15	yes	no
891					
892					
514					
37					
78					
79					
1357					
1358					
1359					
1360					
1361					
1362					

▼ What do you think?

• A number is divisible by 3. Is it always divisible by 9?

• A number is divisible by 9. Is it always divisible by 3?

• What does the sum of the digits tell you?

• What did you notice about the sequence of numbers 1357, 1358, 1359, . . . 1362?

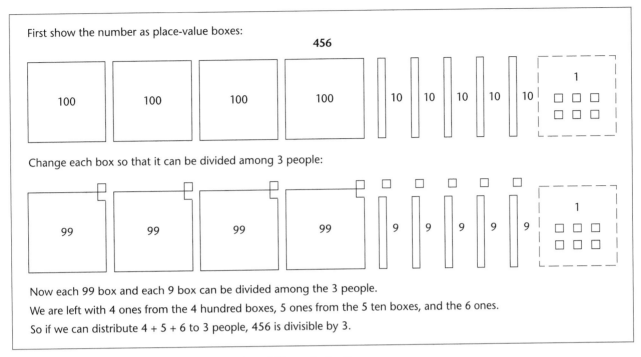

First show the number as place-value boxes:

456

Change each box so that it can be divided among 3 people:

Now each 99 box and each 9 box can be divided among the 3 people.

We are left with 4 ones from the 4 hundred boxes, 5 ones from the 5 ten boxes, and the 6 ones.

So if we can distribute 4 + 5 + 6 to 3 people, 456 is divisible by 3.

Figure 13–7 • **A model illustrating the divisibility rule for 3**

middle school may be ready to explain why the divisibility test for 3 works using symbolic representations.

You can look at other divisibility tests in a similar manner. For example, the divisibility test for 4 depends only on the tens boxes and the ones. The hundreds boxes, thousands boxes, and so on can always be divided or shared by 4, but a ten cannot be broken into four equal whole number parts. Thus, a number's divisibility by 4 depends on how many tens and ones it has. For example, 526 is not divisible by 4 because 26 is not, but 536 is divisible by 4 because 36 is divisible by 4.

A Glance at Where We've Been

This chapter has considered some reasons for including patterns and relationships in the elementary mathematics curriculum. From the very beginning of schooling, children can describe, extend, and create patterns in a variety of ways. As they progress through school, both the types of patterns and their descriptions can become more sophisticated. In describing patterns and relationships, variables can be used in a natural way. We approached patterns and relations by suggesting ways of extending children's thinking from arithmetic to algebra. In particular, we examined equality relations, change, and generalizations.

This chapter also has presented some reasons for studying number theory and ways to develop number theory concepts and skills. We used number theory as another site to develop algebraic thinking and ideas. Number theory is by no means the only, or even the primary, site; algebraic thinking can be developed throughout the mathematics curriculum.

Things to Do: From What You've Read

1. What is algebraic thinking to you? On what aspects of algebraic thinking does this chapter focus?

2. Why should children study patterns in mathematics?

3. What are three common types of patterns? How do they differ? How are they alike? In particular, how are they alike and different in developing the three aspects of algebraic thinking discussed in this chapter?

4. Use an example of a conjecture about number properties, such as the commutative property for addition or the zero property of multiplication, to illustrate how children give different levels of justifications.

5. Try the number puzzle in Figure 13–5 with friends. Can they explain why it worked? Can you show them with materials why it worked? Make up one of your own and try it.

6. List two reasons for teaching number theory. Discuss one number theory topic and how you could encourage algebraic thinking as students explore it.

7. Explain with a picture like that in Figure 13–7 why the divisibility test for eight works.

8. Use the picture method of Figure 13–7 to discover a divisibility test for 11.

9. Show how one can develop the concept of multiples with Cuisenaire rods, a number line, or any other concrete model.

Things to Do: Going Beyond This Book

field Additional activities, suggestions, and questions are provided in *Teaching Elementary Mathematics: A Resource for Field Experiences.*

1. Examine the treatment of patterns in an elementary mathematics textbook at a grade level of your choice. How does it differ from what is shown here? In particular, does it encourage algebraic thinking? How? If not, how could you extend their ideas to do so?

2. *field* Conjectures. Try one of the conjectures in In the Classroom 13–3 with a student. Record the student's procedure, comments, and hints that you provided.

3. *field* Strategies. Play the game in In the Classroom 13–4 with a group of students in upper elementary or middle school. What strategies did the students use?

4. Examine *Patterns* (Coburn et al. 1992). Try one of the activities with younger children; see how you can encourage algebraic thinking.

5. In a middle school textbook, locate the factoring algorithm for finding the GCF or the LCM. Compare that method with the listing algorithm presented here with respect to level of difficulty in developing meaning and ease of use.

6. *field* Divisibility. Talk with a couple of students as they are doing In the Classroom 13–7. Do they discover the rules for divisibility of 3 and 9? What generalizations do they make?

BOOK NOOK FOR CHILDREN

Anno, Misumasa. *Anno's Magic Seed.* New York: Philomel, 1995.

Clement, Rod. *Counting on Frank.* Milwaukee: Gareth Stevens, 1991.

Crews, Donald. *Ten Black Dots.* New York: Greenwillow, 1986.

Dee, Ruby. *Two Ways to Count to Ten.* New York: Henry Holt, 1988.

Kent, Jack. *The Twelve Days of Christmas.* New York: Scholastic, 1971.

Randell, Beverly. *At the Zoo.* New York: Nelson (Joining-in Books), 1986.

Selected References

Blume, Glendon W., and Heckman, David S. "Algebra and Functions." In *Results from the Seventh Mathematics Assessment of the National Assessment of Educational Progress* (eds. Edward A. Silver and Patricia Ann Kenney). Reston, Va.: NCTM, 2000.

Carpenter, Thomas P., and Levi, Linda. Developing conceptions of algebraic reasoning in primary grades. Paper presented at the annual meeting of the American Education Research Association, Montreal, Canada (April 1999).

Coburn, Terrence G.; Bushey, Barbara J.; Holtan, Liana C.; Latozas, Debra; Mortimer, Debbie; and Shotwell, Deborah. *Addenda Series, Grades K–6: Patterns.* Reston, Va.: NCTM, 1992.

Driscoll, Mark. *Fostering Algebraic Thinking: A Guide for Teachers Grades 6–10.* Portsmouth, N.H.: Heinemann, 1999.

Faulkner, Karen P.; Levi, Linda; and Carpenter, Thomas P. "Children's Understanding of Equality: A Foundation for Algebra." *Teaching Children Mathematics* 6 (December 1999), pp. 232–237.

Howden, Hilde. "Implementing the Standards: Patterns, Relations, and Functions." *Arithmetic Teacher,* 37 (November 1989), pp. 18–25.

National Council of Teachers of Mathematics. Principles and Standards for School Mathematics. Reston, Va.: NCTM, 2000.

Parker, Janet, and Widmer, Connie Carroll. "Patterns in Measurement." *Arithmetic Teacher,* 40 (January 1993), pp. 292–295.

14 ▶ *Geometry*

◢ Snapshot of a Lesson

Students are grouped in interest centers in a kindergarten. Several groups are building with blocks and decorating their structures with wooden geometric solids. Mrs. Pedro moves to a small group of children who are disagreeing about sharing the solids. She uses the opportunity to engage them in an activity to develop familiarity with simple properties of three-dimensional objects.

MRS. PEDRO: Jonathan, what seems to be the problem?

JONATHAN: We want these (pointing to some of the solids)—the ones we have won't stack.

MRS. PEDRO: Let's all solve a puzzle. Whoever can solve it, gets those solids. We need two of each solid and the mystery box.

MARIA: Oh, I remember this game. We have to find out what's in the box.

Turning around so the children cannot see her, Mrs. Pedro puts one solid in the box.

MRS. PEDRO: Right. I put one solid in the mystery box and two solids away so we can't see them. A solid that matches one of these three is in the box.

JONATHAN: Can we shut our eyes and feel?

MRS. PEDRO: No, this time we must only listen. Anthony, you may try listening to the box first. But all of you listen because you may be able to tell.

ANTHONY: It's not rolling like a ball.

JONATHAN: Let me hear. You're right, so it can't be the ball.

MRS. PEDRO: Does everyone agree? Joanne, could you hear?

JOANNE: No, let me try. Yeah, it sort of rolls, but not like a ball.

MRS. PEDRO: Let's put this one aside, since everyone agrees it isn't the ball. Now, it must be one of these two.

MARIA: This one (pointing to the cube) would just slide—slunk, slunk—and wouldn't roll at all.

EARL: This one (pointing to the cone) would roll if it was like this.

ANTHONY: Not if you shook the box. It might not roll.

JONATHAN: Right, so maybe it isn't this one.

MRS. PEDRO: So, which is it?

ALL: This one! Let us see.

Mrs. Pedro opens the box to let them see it was the cone.

JOANNE: Let's try again.

MRS. PEDRO: Yes, here's one that will really make all of you think.

They play several more rounds.

EARL: Let us try to stump you.

MRS. PEDRO: All right. I'll be back in a minute.

Mrs. Pedro hears talking and laughing. They hand her the box.

MRS. PEDRO: Oh, you rascals. You filled the box. You really stumped me.

Introduction

You may find yourself working with some teachers who respond to geometry in the following ways:

"Oh, I could never do proofs."

"The children don't understand it, so why do it?"

"We do it if we finish everything else."

There are many reasons for such responses. Some are based on past personal experiences such as an unsatisfactory geometry course in high school or having no geometry in elementary school. Some are based on inappropriate geometry curriculum materials that use, for example, an abstract, definitional approach. Some are based on a historical emphasis on computation—even though geometry has been recommended by various professional groups for over a hundred years.

You may find that you are working with some teachers who respond like this:

"It amazes me who is good in geometry; it's not always my best arithmetic students."

"What a joy it is to see a child's eyes light up as she discovers. . . ."

"Some of my students could work on a geometry problem for hours."

"Geometry gives me an opportunity to work on communication skills and to help children follow instructions."

"The change in the spatial ability of children after they work with geometric shapes always surprises me."

"I love to learn with my students; I never liked geometry before."

You will enjoy including geometry in your teaching if you adopt the philosophy of the teacher who said, "I love to learn with my students." As you read this chapter, begin the process of learning. You may encounter new ideas, but by trying the activities and brushing up on some things you may have once learned, you will begin to extend your knowledge of how to help children learn geometry.

Geometry in School Mathematics

The *Principles and Standards for School Mathematics* (NCTM 2000) calls for geometry to be an integral part of the mathematics programs of all elementary and middle school students. The standard for geometry states:

Instructional programs from prekindergarten through grade 12 should enable all students to—

- analyze characteristics and properties of two- and three-dimensional geometric objects and develop mathematical arguments about geometric relationships;
- specify locations and describe spatial relationships using coordinate geometry and other representational systems;
- apply transformations and use symmetry to analyze mathematical situations;
- use visualization, spatial reasoning, and geometric modeling to solve problems. (NCTM 2000, p. 41).

Before examining how we can help children learn and use these ideas, let's step back and examine what this standard means and look at some of the research on children's learning of these ideas.

Geometric Characteristics and Properties

All too often, elementary programs have concentrated on the names of geometric objects and have not helped children develop a deeper understanding of the properties of the objects or the relationships among different geometric objects.

The research of the Dutch couple Dina van Hiele-Geldof and Pierre Marie van Hiele gives us some guidelines on geometric thought. (Crowley 1987) They proposed and studied a model of five levels of understanding (see Table 14–1). When we examine the geometry provided many of our students in light of this model, it is not difficult to see why our students do not do well in geometry (U.S. Department of Education 1996). Geometry activities in many programs require little more than thought at the visualization level.

Our job as teachers is to provide activities that help children move from the level of thought at which they are operating. If we never ask children to tell about a property of a shape, why a rectangle is a rectangle or what all rectangles have in common, then we are not helping them deepen their understanding of solids and plane figures. Two major findings from the 1996 NAEP (Martin and Strutchens 2000) are relevant. First, in grades 4 and 8, students' performance on geometry items improved through the assessments given in the 1990s, and improved significantly on items that used geometric manipulatives. Second, many students can identify simple shapes unless the shapes are presented in unfamiliar contexts or positions, and they can identify simple but not complex properties of shapes.

This chapter will focus on questions that will help children build understanding of properties; it

Table 14.1. • Van Hiele levels of understanding

Level	Description	Sample Responses of Children
0 Visualization	Children view a geometric shape as a whole. They do not describe properties of the shape.	Shown a rectangle and asked to identify it, the child may say "It is a rectangle because it looks like a book cover."
1 Analysis	Children recognize the properties of figures. They do not see relations between properties.	A child may say that the rectangle has four sides and square corners.
2 Informal Deduction	Students see relations between properties of a class of shapes.	A student may say that since the angles of a rectangles are right angles, the opposite sides are parallel.
3 Deduction 4 Rigor	Both Level 3 (level at which students can use deduction in an axiomatic system to prove statements) and Level 4 (level at which students see geometry in the abstract) are beyond the scope of most students in middle school. Level 3 is the level at which a proof-oriented high school geometry course is taught.	

will also encourage you to have children give reasons or mathematical arguments to justify their thinking. The Snapshot of a Lesson that opened this chapter already began this process. The children were making the argument that since it must be one of the three solids, and it can't be two of them, it must be the remaining one.

As you read the chapter, see if you can classify the activities as to the level of geometric thought. As you design or select activities, make certain that they will help children move beyond Level 0.

Location and Spatial Relationships

Often, we think about geometry in elementary and middle school in terms of shapes. Another part of geometry deals with location and movement. Where are you? Are you above or below the floor? Are you in front of or behind your desk? Are you between the cabinet and the computer? Where would you be if you moved five steps forward? Starting at your desk, how far from your desk will you be if you move five steps forward and three steps backward? Examining locations and movements gives children a way to describe their world and to put order to their surroundings. It also provides an opportunity to build mathematical concepts such as that of positive and negative numbers (forward and backward) and skills connected to other subjects, such as map skills.

Later, we will regularize the space we live in by examining a coordinate system. The one most familiar to us is the rectangular coordinate system,

used in mapping and in mathematics. Again, we look at position and movement in the plane or in space and describe each abstractly: If I am at point (2,4) and move 5 spaces, where could I be?

Transformations

Geometry is often studied in terms of patterns. Think of wallpaper patterns, or look at the three patterns in Figure 14–1. What basic design is repeated? Is the basic design slid to a new position? Is it reflected so its mirror image appears? Or is it turned to the left? These are some of the transformations that young children can analyze and describe. Although these three motions (slide or translation, flip or reflection, and turn or rotation) can describe movements in three-dimensional space, we will only consider transformations in the plane because it is easier for children to check their conjectures.

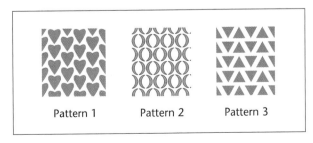

Figure 14–1 • **Wallpaper patterns**

Research (Jacobson and Lehrer 2000) with children who are investigating transformations points to the crucial role of the teacher. If students are asked to make conjectures and justify their thinking, they develop a deeper understanding of the transformations.

Visualization and Spatial Reasoning

Although you will help children learn geometric ideas by using physical materials, you also need to help them develop visual images of geometric shapes. And, as they mature, you will help them manipulate these images in their mind. For example, visualize a rectangle that is longer than it is wide. Now turn it (in your mind) to the right 90 degrees. What does it look like now? Draw a line from the top right corner to the middle of the bottom side. What two figures did you create?

In this chapter, we will look at visualizing the two-dimensional patterns that could be folded to make three-dimensional patterns. In so doing, you may visualize the folding, or you may use spatial reasoning to help you decide. For example, imagine trying to fold an open cube (no top face) from five connected squares. Which of the configurations in Figure 14–2 could be folded into an open cube? Which would be the bottom square?

Figure 14–2 • Open box

SOLID GEOMETRY

We live in a three-dimensional world that can be represented and described geometrically; this is the world of the young child, along with the flat, two-dimensional world of pictures. It is important that children explore their world in the geometric sense. In this section, we will consider some of the three-dimensional aspects of our surroundings.

Studying geometric properties of three-dimensional objects also provides an opportunity to emphasize the process goals of geometry. This section is built around some of these processes: describing and classifying, constructing, exploring and discovering, and relating three-dimensional shapes to two-dimensional shapes. We will often refer to a three-dimensional shape in this section as a *solid,* although the object may be hollow.

Models play an important role in solid geometry. If wooden or plastic solids are not available, you can make models as suggested later in this section. You and your students should also collect real objects that have particular geometric shapes, including spheres (balls), cylinders (cans), prisms (boxes), and cones, as well as shapes that may not have geometric names.

Describing and Classifying Objects

Children need to be able to describe properties of three-dimensional objects to see how two or more objects are alike or different according to geometric properties. Describing and classifying are processes that should be extended over time as new and more complex properties are added. These types of activities help children develop their thinking at Level 1 and begin to push them toward Level 2 thinking as described by the van Hiele model.

In the activities that follow, we suggest vocabulary and properties appropriate for beginning, intermediate, and more advanced students. Older children who have not been exposed to three-dimensional activities will benefit from activities such as the ones described in the beginning activities. Their responses, of course, will be more sophisticated.

Beginning Activities Often, children are taught the names of the geometric shapes, but they do not develop the discriminating power they need to use the names with meaning. In these beginning activities you should build on the children's own vocabulary, adding new words as appropriate. Although the names of the solids can be used, they need not be formally introduced until children have done activities like these.

1. *Who am I?* Put out three objects (such as a ball, a cone, and a box). Describe one of them (it is round all over, it is flat on the bottom, its sides are all flat), and have the children guess which one you are describing.

2. *Who stacks?* Provide a collection of solids for children to sort according to which will stack, which will roll, and which will slide. A more sophisticated sorting is one that requires three groups: solids that can be stacked no matter what face is down, solids that can be stacked if placed in some ways but not in other ways, and solids that cannot be stacked in any way.

3. *How are we alike or different?* Hold up two solids such as the following:

Ask children to tell how they are alike or different. For example, children may compare the two solids shown as follows:

"They are both flat all over."

"One is tall."

"One has bigger sides."

"They have some square faces."

"They have six faces."

4. *Who doesn't belong?* Put out three solids such as these:

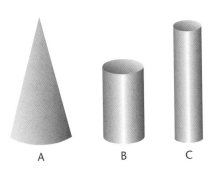

A   B   C

Ask children which does not belong with the other two. Since there are many ways to solve this problem, be ready to encourage lively discussion. For example, some children may say A doesn't belong because it has a point. Others may say B doesn't belong because it's short, or C doesn't belong because it's skinny or has a smaller bottom.

5. *How many faces have I?* A *face* is a flat side of a solid object. Have children count the number of faces on solids of various shapes. Then ask children to collect objects with six faces (boxes, books), with two faces (cans), and with zero faces (balls). You will be surprised at what they find.

6. *Can you find an object like me?* Put out a solid and see if children can find real objects that have the same shape. You may get disagreement about which are alike.

Intermediate Activities The following activities introduce the names of some solids and consider sizes (or measure properties) as well as edges, faces, and vertices.

1. *Using edges, vertices, and faces.* After introducing *edge* (a straight segment formed by two faces) and *vertex* (a point at which three or more edges come together), have children solve these riddles:

I am a solid with . . . :

- Eight edges—who am I?
- Six edges and four faces—who am I?
- Five corners—who am I?
- The same number of vertices as faces—who am I?
- No faces (no corners)—who am I?
- One face and no corners—who am I?

2. *Classifying solids.* Introduce each type of solid—cube, cone, pyramid, cylinder, and sphere—by putting out solids that are examples and nonexamples of each type of solid. For example, show two or three cylinders and two or three solids that are not cylinders. Ask the students to select other solids that would belong to the group of cylinders as well as those that do not. This is illustrated in Lesson Idea 14–1. Whether you do these types of activities with objects or on paper, the important part is the surrounding discussion. For example, many children think B is too "thin" to be a cylinder. They may be thinking at Level 0—it does not look like one. Discussion about the properties of a cylinder (a circular cylinder has two faces that are congruent circles joined by a curved surface), will help them move to a higher level of thought.

3. *Searching for solids.* Make up a set of activity cards that have children search out solids according to the size and shape of the faces and the length of the edges. The clues you give will depend on the solids you use, but here are some samples to get you started:

Search for a solid with . . . :

- exactly two faces that are the same size and shape (*congruent*)
- exactly three faces that are the same size and shape
- all edges the same length
- edges of three different lengths

Lesson Idea 14–1

Comparing Solids

▼ These are cylinders:

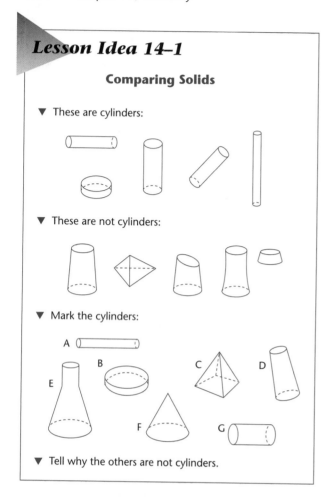

▼ These are not cylinders:

▼ Mark the cylinders:

▼ Tell why the others are not cylinders.

Advanced Activities These activities focus on the properties of parallel and perpendicular faces and edges as well as more careful definition and classification of the solids.

1. *Parallel faces*. This activity can be done after parallel faces have been introduced. It consists of questions about real objects and why faces are parallel. A few sample questions are given here to start you thinking:

> Why are the top and bottom of soup cans parallel?
>
> Why are shelves parallel to the floor?
>
> Why are roofs of houses in cold climates usually not parallel to the ground?
>
> Why is the front side of a milk carton parallel to the back side?

2. *Perpendicular edges*. In the Classroom 14–1 provides clues about particular solids focused on perpendicular edges and asks students to construct the solids from sticks and connectors. See the "stick" models section which follows for a variety of materials. Students enjoy making their own mysteries for

In The Classroom 14–1

Grades 4–8

Solid Mystery

Objective: To build three-dimensional objects with specified conditions about the perpendicularity of the edges.

▼ Solve each of these mysteries by constructing a "suspect" from sticks and connectors. If you think there is more than one suspect, look at Clue 2.

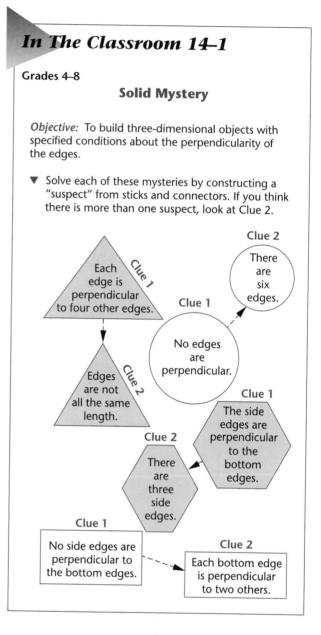

---

other students to solve. This provides excellent experience in writing descriptions that are clear, precise, and noncontradictory.

3. *Right prisms*. This activity introduces the definition of right prisms and how to name prisms. Show examples and nonexamples of right prisms (as in the second of the intermediate activities), and ask students to describe the bases and faces, ultimately encouraging them to come up with the definition of *prism*—a solid that has congruent and parallel bases (top and bottom) joined by rectangular faces. Then have students discuss how prisms are named. See if they can determine a way to distinguish between prisms. For example, if the base is a triangle it is a triangular prism.

Prisms

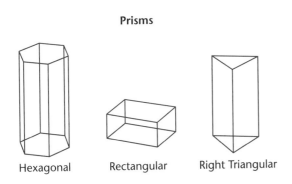

Hexagonal   Rectangular   Right Triangular

These activities are only suggestions to help children construct their knowledge of geometric ideas of three-dimensional objects. You will notice that many of the ideas are tied to the students' understanding of two-dimensional geometric objects. Although we have separated the discussion here, you should blend the study of solid and plane geometry. The activities in the rest of this section on solid geometry reinforce and extend the ideas discussed in this section.

Constructing to Explore and Discover

One of the difficulties that children have with three-dimensional geometry is visualizing the solids. It is essential to have models. If models are not available, there are many ways in which children can make three-dimensional models. In this section, we examine two ways to make "face models" and two ways to make "edge models." Face models (construction paper-tubes and polyhedra shapes) emphasize the faces, and edge models (newspaper-tape and gumdrops-toothpicks) focus on edges.

As children are making the models, they often discover many things about the solids. There are, however, other properties or relationships that they may not discover so we need other ways to explore the solids. The following activities provide examples of ways to structure students' investigations of various properties.

Paper Tubes Some of the easiest and most versatile models can be made from heavy construction paper. Figure 14–3 shows how open-ended tube models of prisms can be made. The top and bottom faces may be added to these models by tracing the top of the tube, cutting out the shape, and taping it to the tube. As Figure 14–3 suggests, many variations of prisms can be made, and these can be cut (truncated) to create many strange shapes.

The exploration in In the Classroom 14–2 is a variation of a famous formula, Euler's (pronounced "oil-ers") formula, which relates the number of edges (E), faces (F), and vertices (V) to each other: $V + F = E + 2$. This is a special case of the more gen-

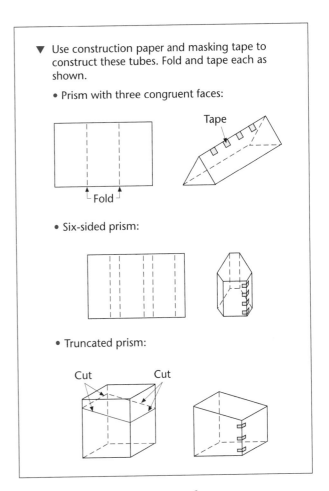

Figure 14–3 • Constructing tubes

eral formula because it uses only prisms. Since the prisms have no top or bottom face, we will call them tubes. The formula is $V + F = E$, which is more readily evident than Euler's more general formula, which holds for all polyhedra. Several other patterns can be found for these paper tubes; have your students look for them. For example, children may see that the number of edges is always three times the number of faces (not counting the top and bottom). This is a good place to have them describe the general case algebraically: $E = 3 \times F$ if E is the number of edges and F is the number of faces.

Polyhedron Models

Polyhedrons are the three-dimensional analogy to polygons in two dimensions. Prisms and pyramids are polyhedrons, but spheres, cones, and cylinders are not. Any solid whose faces are all polygons is a polyhedron. There are many examples that are neither prisms or pyramids. In the Classroom 14–3 explores making polyhedrons with regular polygons whose patterns are given on square or triangular grid paper. Commercial models are also available, either

In The Classroom 14–2

What Can You Discover?

Objective: To explore the relationship among the number of vertices, edges, and faces of prisms.

It's easy to complete this table if you've made the tubes in Figure 14–3!

	Tube 1	Tube 2	Tube 3
Faces	3		
Edges			
Vertices			

A. Count the number of faces of Tube 1. (Remember there is no top or bottom, so don't count them.)

B. Count the number of edges of Tube 1. (Don't forget the top and bottom edges.)

C. Repeat A and B for Tube 2.

- Do you see an easy way to tell how many edges if you know the number of faces?_____

- Write your conjecture: _____

  _____

D. Count the vertices of Tube 1 and Tube 2.

- Do you see an easy way to tell how many corners if you know the number of faces and edges?_____

- Write your conjecture: _____

  _____

Check your conjecture with Tube 3.

In The Classroom 14–3

Polyhedra Networks

Objective: To explore polyhedrons made from networks.

Materials: Triangular and square grid paper (see Appendix B for masters).

Directions: Color these shapes on your grid paper. Cut out the colored shape, and see if you can fold on the lines to make a polyhedron. Make your own design and try it.

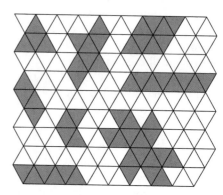

Now try square grid paper. Color six adjacent squares, then cut and fold into a cube. How many different ways can you color the adjacent squares? Which fold into a cube?

plastic shapes that clip together or card stock models that fit together with rubber bands. If you have these, then there are many different polyhedra to explore.

"Stick" Models Models can be made from straws, pipe cleaners, toothpicks, or other "sticks" that can be connected with clay, small marshmallows, gumdrops, or tape. There are also reasonably priced, commercial materials designed for this purpose.

Young children enjoy building stick models from toothpicks and gumdrops. In the Classroom 14–4 extends the exploration of building freely to building a stick model when the number of gumdrops (vertices) and the number of edges (toothpicks) are specified. If you need an even more sophisticated activity, return to In the Classroom 14–1.

Lesson Idea 14–2 (page 304) illustrates how to make a three-dimensional figure from newspaper sticks and tape. Rolling the paper tightly takes some practice for some children. However, as with many geometry activities, often you will be surprised at who can do this easily. When building three-dimensional objects with newspaper sticks, the children can investigate the rigidity of triangles, squares, or other polygons. They should find that the pyramid built with Lesson Idea 14–2 is a rigid structure, but the cube needs bracing to be sturdy.

Relating Three Dimensions to Two

Because three-dimensional objects often must be pictured in two dimensions, children must be able to relate the objects to pictures. They also need to be able to analyze a three-dimensional object in terms

In The Classroom 14–4

Gumdrops and Toothpicks

Objective: To construct three-dimensional figures with given number of edges and faces.

Materials: Gumdrops and toothpicks (about twenty of each for each child). Clay can be substituted for gumdrops.

Directions: Explore making three-dimensional shapes with the gumdrops and toothpicks. Here are a few examples. How many gumdrops and toothpicks did each take?

Now, try some with the given number of gumdrops and toothpicks.

Three rules to follow:

1. Two gumdrops can be used on each toothpick, one at each end.

2. Toothpicks should only be used to make the outline of a face (no extra ones stuck across the face).

3. The figure should be closed. Imagine it is a container with a hole in one face—you could fill it.

Some of these are not possible. See if you can figure out which ones and why. If you can make a shape, tell whether it is a prism, a pyramid, or another shape.

Letter	Gumdrops	Toothpicks	Can Make? (yes or no)	Name of shape
A	6	9		
B	5	8		
C	8	5		
D	6	10		
E	7	12		
F	8	12		
G	10	15		
H	12	18		
I	8	14		
J	10	3		
K	6	12		
L	5	9		

1. What is your conjecture about the ones that could not be made?

2. Which ones make pyramids? What is the relationship of the numbers? Using the models, explain why.

3. Which ones make prisms? What is the relationship of the numbers? Using the models, explain why.

Lesson Idea 14–2

Build Your Own Pyramid!

▼ Follow these easy steps to construct a "stick" pyramid from newspaper. Use masking tape for the connectors.

Step 1: Take three sheets from a newspaper and roll tightly from corner to corner.

Step 2: Tape to hold rod.

Step 3: Make several rods and tape together as shown.

Step 4: Put them together to make a pyramid.

▼ Your turn:

Use the same method to construct other three-dimensional shapes, such as a cube.

Lesson Idea 14–3

Which Solid Am I?

▼ I only have two different faces:

▼ Which solid could I be?

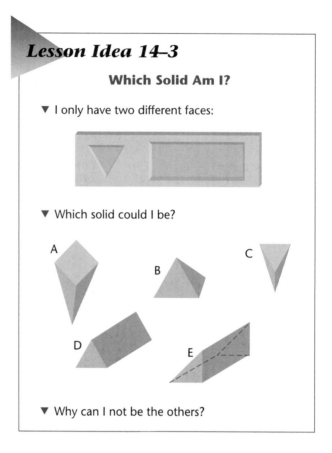

▼ Why can I not be the others?

Identifying Different Views of a Solid What happens if you view a solid from different perspectives? Pretend you are a fish, swimming below a pyramid that is sitting on top of the water. You can see the entire bottom of the pyramid. What do you see? Begin with putting the children in easy locations where they see only one face and then move to ones that show more than one face. Pretend you are a bird and you are looking down on the point of a (square) pyramid. Can you describe what it would look like? After children understand the task, put out solids and ask them to draw what they see from different views (down, under, directly in front, front when the solid is turned to see two faces).

Visualizing Cross Sections of Solids Cross sections of solids are often difficult for children to visualize. Cutting the paper tubes in the process of construction helps children to see the cross sections. If you have other objects that can be cut (oranges, carrots shaped in cones, or zucchini shaped in different solids), you can help the children see the cross sections.

The next time you eat cheese, cut some small cubes of cheese and then try slicing each cube so the slice shows different geometric shapes. Can you slice the cube to see a triangle? a different triangle? How can you slice the cube to make a rectangle that is not a square? Try a pentagon and hexagon.

of its two-dimensional parts. Constructing solids from networks and other materials assists in this skill, but you can help focus directly on the two-dimensional aspect by the activities you choose and the questions you ask.

Matching Imprints of Faces with the Solid Make imprints in play dough (homemade works great) of the faces of wooden geometric solids. Have children match each solid with a face. The faces can be traced instead of making imprints, but younger children can work easily with imprints. Lesson Idea 14–3, which provides a similar matching activity with pictorial models, also can be used.

Working with Drawings of Solids Many children need help in drawing three-dimensional objects. In the Classroom 14–5 shows how to use isometric paper to draw numerous views of prisms. (A master sheet of isometric paper can be found in Appendix B.) This activity also provides experience in interpreting two-dimensional drawings to construct the three-dimensional structures.

Experiences such as these will help children understand the concept of volume. As children build various shapes with a given number of cubes, they will be investigating the relationship of volume and shape. How many rectangular prisms can you build that have a volume of twenty-four cubes? Look at the pictures in Figure 14–4 (see page 307) these fifth-grade students drew of a prism made with twelve cubes. What concepts are being developed?

PLANE GEOMETRY

In this section, we consider properties of two-dimensional shapes, relationships among shapes, and classification schemes. The ideas mainly are presented through sample activities involving many types of physical materials, such as geoboards, pattern blocks (see Figure 14–5 on page 307), and paper strips. Many other engaging geometric activities can be done with paper and pencil, and computer programs also provide rich environments for geometric explorations.

In examining three-dimensional shapes, we often focus on the faces (two-dimensional); similarly, in examining two-dimensional shapes, we often focus on the sides or vertices (one-dimensional). We will build these one-dimensional concepts as they occur naturally within a two-dimensional context.

Properties of a Shape

Children first recognize shapes in a holistic manner (Van Hiele Level 0)—that is, a triangle is a triangle because it looks like a shape that someone has called a triangle. If an equilateral triangle with its base parallel to the bottom of the page is always used, then this shape will be children's image of a triangle. It is important to provide many examples and nonexamples of shapes so that children will have rich images of the different shapes.

Children have an intuitive feel for the differences among shapes, but they need ways to describe these differences. By considering the properties of shapes, you can help develop children's ability to describe and extend their knowledge of particular shapes. For example, think of how you would describe a rectangle to someone who had never seen one. Draw a strange shape that has no special name

---

In The Classroom 14–5

Grades 5–8

Views of Cubes

Objective: Connecting two- and three-dimensional drawings of cubes.

▼ Build this structure with seven cubes:

Front

• Use graph paper to draw your own front view:

Front view

• On the same paper draw and label the views from the back, bottom, top, right, and left sides.

▼ Use cubes to build this three-story structure:

• How many cubes did you use for all 3 stories?＿＿＿

• How many cubes did you use for the second floor?＿＿＿

• How many cubes did you use for the base?＿＿＿

• If you continue the pattern, how many cubes would be in the base if the structure were 4 stories high?＿＿＿ 5 stories high?＿＿＿ *n* stories high?＿＿＿

▼ Your turn:

• Build your own building with cubes and draw two views on isometric paper.

• See if a friend can build your building from the drawings. If the friend is having difficulty, draw all the views of the building.

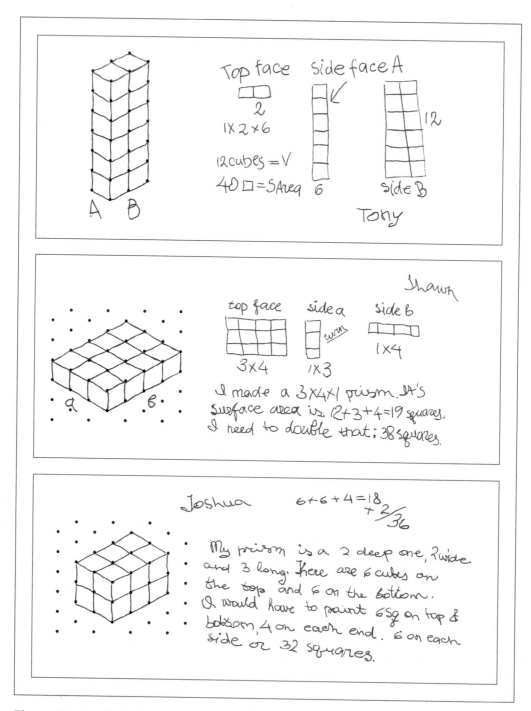

Figure 14–4 • Twelve cubes

to you, and try to describe it to someone. Consider the properties of the shape that you used.

There are many ways of describing geometric shapes, as illustrated in the activities that follow. The different properties are discussed separately but should be combined in activities similar to the ones given. Realize that keeping two or more properties in mind is more difficult than just focusing on one. For example, creating a figure with four sides on a geoboard is at a much simpler level than creating a figure with four sides that has two right angles and one side longer than the other.

Number of Sides One of the first properties children focus on is the number of sides. They readily count the number of sides (line segments) of a shape, unless a shape has many sides. Then they may need to mark the place where they begin counting. As you have children participate in activities such as the ones that follow, they will begin to make many conjectures about shapes and learn vocabulary.

1. *How many sides?* This simple activity uses pattern blocks (see Figure 14–5). If you do not have pattern blocks, you can use other shapes or cut shapes with different numbers of sides from construction paper. Each child needs only one shape for this activity.

- Call a number and ask children who have a shape with that number of sides to stand. Call numbers such as two and seven, for which no one will stand.

- Then have a search for all the different shapes that have three sides, four sides, five sides, six sides, and zero sides (the circle).

- Put a sample of each different shape somewhere within view of all children, and call on children to tell how the four-sided shapes differ (some are bigger than others, some are skinny, and some are slanty—accept their everyday words at this point). It is important for them to realize that the number of sides does not determine the shape.

2. *Can you make _____?* In this challenging activity, children make a figure of a given number of sides on a geoboard. (See Appendix B for a geoboard model.) Give each child a geoboard and one rubber band. Begin by asking them to make simple shapes, and gradually add other conditions. For example,

> Can you make a four-sided figure?
>
> Can you make a four-sided figure that touches only four pegs?
>
> Can you make a four-sided figure that touches six pegs?
>
> Can you make a four-sided figure that has two pegs inside (not touching) it?

3. *Less is best.* In the Classroom 14–6 provides a more advanced activity in which children put pattern blocks together to make new shapes with as few sides as possible. Two or more children choose three pattern blocks. Watch to see that they are counting the sides of the new shape, not the sides of the

In The Classroom 14–6

Grades 1–3

Less Is Best
(A game for two or more)

Objective: Make a shape with fewest sides.

▼ Choose a partner to play this game:

- Put an assortment of pattern blocks in a box.

- Without looking, each player chooses 3 blocks and puts them together to make a new shape.

- Count the number of sides on each of the new shapes. Whoever has the shape with the fewest sides wins—less is best!

▼ Make a table to record your scores, and play several rounds to determine the winner.

> I'm good at this game — only 4 sides!

> I've got 4 sides, too!

| Cos | 4 | | |
| Marrietta | 4 | | |

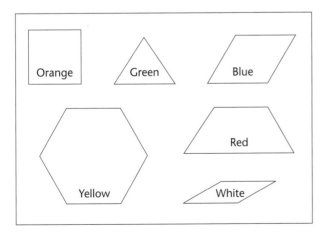

Figure 14–5 • Pattern blocks

pieces. For example, if Marietta said six, it is likely that she counted the sides of the pieces.

Number of Corners Closely related to counting the numbers of sides is counting the number of corners. Children will soon realize that any polygonal figure has the same number of sides as corners if they count both on each shape. The activities suggested for counting the number of sides can be modified for counting corners.

Symmetry Two types of symmetry—line or reflectional symmetry and rotational symmetry—may be used to describe geometric shapes as well as objects in the real world.

To introduce line symmetry, ask children to compare two snowmen:

When they say one looks lopsided, show them how they can fold the drawings in the center to see if the sides match. A child's first perception of symmetry is visual. Use this visual perception to help build the idea of "folding" to match the sides or edges. You may also want the children to explore with mirrors or miras to bring in the idea of reflection. A figure has line or reflectional symmetry if, when reflected over a line, the resulting image coincides with the original figure.

Have students find the line(s) of symmetry of geometric shapes. Be sure to let them try folding a square (four lines of symmetry), an equilateral triangle (three lines of symmetry), and a circle (an infinite number) to find lines of symmetry before moving to activities such as the one on In the Classroom 14–7. Older children can often see the lines of symmetry without folding, but some shapes are misleading. One of these is a parallelogram. Many children will say at first glance that a parallelogram has two lines of symmetry. (Try it yourself.)

It is important that children also see symmetry in things around them. You might have them make a bulletin board of pictures of things that are symmetric. They also enjoy making symmetric shapes. One way to make a symmetric shape is to fold a piece of paper and cut the folded piece, leaving the

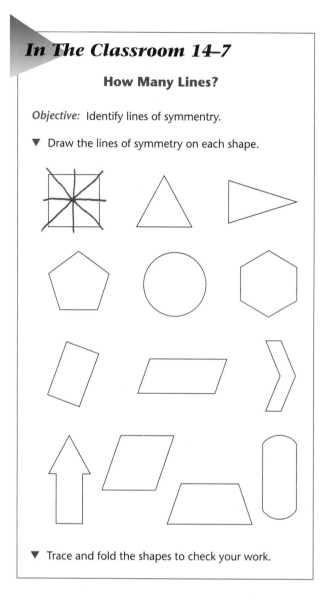

In The Classroom 14–7

How Many Lines?

Objective: Identify lines of symmetry.

▼ Draw the lines of symmetry on each shape.

▼ Trace and fold the shapes to check your work.

fold intact. (Can you figure out how to make a shape with two lines of symmetry?)

An unusual children's book to help establish the basic concepts of symmetry is *Reflections* (Jonas 1987). This book allows students to examine images in a variety of ways.

Length of Sides Many of the definitions of geometric shapes as well as classification schemes for them depend on the length of sides. Help children focus on the length by having them find the shape with the longest side, find the shortest side of a given shape, and measuring lengths of sides. In the Classroom 14–8 presents an example of a more advanced activity in which children make shapes on a geoboard according to certain specifications about the lengths of the sides. Try the items yourself, and classify each as to whether it is easy, medium, or challenging.

In The Classroom 14–8

Show My Sides

Objective: Make shapes with a specified number of congruent sides.

▼ Use a geoboard to show these figures:

1. Can you make a 4-sided figure with exactly two equal sides?

2. Can you make a 12-sided figure with all sides equal?

3. Can you make a 3-sided figure with three equal sides?

4. Can you make an 8-sided figure with four sides of one length and the other four of another length?

5. Can you make a 5-sided figure with exactly four equal sides?

6. Can you make a 4-sided figure with two pairs of equal sides that is not a parallelogram?

7. Can you make a 3-sided figure with two equal sides?

8. Can you make a 7-sided figure with no equal sides?

Size of Angles There are many ways to examine the angles of geometric figures. A more complete introduction to angles may be found in Chapter 15. Here are some of the properties related to angles that children may discover:

- The sum of the angles of a triangle is 180.

- The sum of the angles of a quadrilateral is 360.

- The base angles of an isosceles triangle are equal.

- Opposite angles of a parallelogram are equal.

- A polygon with more than three sides can have equal sides without having equal angles.

- The angle opposite the longest side of a triangle is the largest.

A guided activity such as the one in In the Classroom 14–9 will help students discover for themselves that the angles of a quadrilateral sum to 360°.

Logo programs and other software for computers offer a wide variety of activities for children to explore geometry. In Logo, an angle is considered as a turn, and a figure is a path that the turtle travels. With only a few simple commands, children can begin drawing pictures and hypothesizing about geometric figures. You can have children begin exploring Logo with In the Classroom 14–10 (see page 311).

Parallel and Perpendicular Sides In addition to examining parallel and perpendicular sides in geometric shapes, children need to be able to identify parallel lines and perpendicular lines in a plane and, later, in space. Two lines in a plane are parallel if they never intersect. (Remember, a line can be extended indefinitely in either direction.) Another useful definition states that two lines are parallel if they are always the same distance (perpendicular distance) apart. Two lines are perpendicular if they intersect at right angles.

It is important that children recognize perpendicular and parallel lines in the world around them. Have them search for perpendicular and parallel lines in the room. You might start a list together on the board, letting children add to it as they find other examples. Here is a start:

Parallel Lines
- Opposite sides of a book
- The horizontal lines in E
- The top and bottom of the chalkboard

Perpendicular Lines
- Adjacent edges of a book
- The vertical and horizontal lines in E
- The edge of the wall and the edge of the floor

You may also have the children identify parallel and perpendicular sides on the pattern blocks (Figure 14–5). Begin by asking them to find all the pieces that have one pair of perpendicular sides, next all the pieces with more than one pair of perpendicular sides, and then a piece with one pair of parallel sides. Use the puzzles in Lesson Idea 14–4 (see page 311), to challenge children to arrange pattern blocks to make shapes with a specified number of parallel sides.

Convexity and Concavity Often children are exposed only to convex shapes (any polygon with all angles less than 180°). Many of the activities

In The Classroom 14–9

How Many Degrees in a Quadrilateral?

Objective: To explore the sum of the degree of the angles in quadrilaterals and triangles.

▼ Try this method for finding the sum of the angles in a quadrilateral:

Trace and cut out.　　　　Tear off the　　　　　Arrange them
　　　　　　　　　　　　corners.　　　　　　around a point.

Name of shape *parallelogram*

Number of degrees of A + B + C + D　*360°*

▼ Use the same method for these quadrilaterals. (Reminder: there are 360°
　 around a point.)

Name of
shape _____

Number of
degrees _____

Name of
shape _____

Number of
degrees _____

Name of
shape _____

Number of
degrees _____

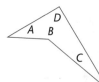
Name of
shape _____

Number of
degrees _____

▼ Now

　• Try some more 4-sided figures.　　• Try a 3-sided figure.

　• Try a 5-sided figure.　　　　　　 • What do you conclude?

---

suggested thus far have included concave shapes. When children are making shapes, concave examples will often give interesting variety.

Show children two shapes such as these and have them describe how they are alike and different:

They will probably express the idea that shape A "comes back" on itself or "caves in" (concave). Introduce the terms *concave* and *convex*. After children

classify shapes as convex or concave, you might have them investigate questions such as the following:

Can you draw a four-sided (five-sided, six-sided, seven-sided) figure that is concave?

Can you draw a five-sided (six-sided, seven-sided) figure that is concave in two places (or that has two angles greater than 180°)?

Can you draw a six-sided (seven-sided, eight-sided) figure that is concave in three places?

It is challenging to try these with Logo on the computer. Have the children keep a record of the steps it takes to make each figure.

Altitude The altitude (or height) of a geometric shape depends on what is specified as the base. Iden-

In The Classroom 14–10

Exploring with Logo

Objective: To draw shapes with a Logo program.

▼ Use a Logo program. You will need to know the following commands before trying this activity. If you do not, explore these first.

```
FORWARD (FD), RIGHT (RT), HOME,
SHOW TURTLE (ST), CLEARSCREEN (CS)
```

▼ Identify each of these figures. Write your guess and then draw the figure. Don't forget to CS after each figure is identified.

A _____   B _____   C _____   D _____

HOME	HOME	HOME	HOME
FD 40	FD 40	FD 40	RT 120
RT 90	RT 60	RT 120	FD 40
FD 20	FD 40	FD 40	RT 120
RT 90	RT 60	RT 120	FD 40
FD 40	FD 40	RT 40	RT 120
RT 90			FD 40
FD 20			

▼ Try the following:

  1. REPEAT 4 [FD 40 RT 90]

  • What did you draw? _____

  2. RT 45 REPEAT 4 [FD 40 RT 90]

  • What is the difference between 1 and 2? _____

  3. REPEAT 3 [FD 40 RT 120]

  • Have you drawn this one before? _____

▼ See if you can draw a hexagon.

  • What did you tell the turtle to do? _____

▼ For fun try these:

```
TO BOX
REPEAT 4 [FD 40 RT 90]
END
BOX
CS

TO BOXES
REPEAT 8 [BOX RT 45]
END
BOXES
```

Lesson Idea 14–4

Piezles

▼ Solve these *piezles* (puzzles) using pattern blocks. Draw a sketch of the shape you made.

  1. Use two different pieces; make a shape with

    • Exactly 2 pairs of parallel sides.

    • Exactly 1 pair of parallel sides.

    • No parallel sides.

  2. Use three different pieces; make a shape with

    • Exactly 3 pairs of parallel sides.

    • Exactly 2 pair of parallel sides.

    • Exactly 1 pair of parallel sides.

    • No parallel sides.

  3. What is the largest number of pairs of parallel sides of a shape you can make from

    • 2 pieces?

    • 3 pieces?

    • 4 pieces?

  4. Can you put all the pieces together to make a shape with no parallel sides?

tifying and measuring the altitude is essential in finding the area of geometric figures. Lesson Idea 14–5 is designed to help children realize that a geometric object has different heights or altitudes. After students do this with the triangular model, have them draw a triangle on paper and again measure each side and each altitude.

Names of Geometric Shapes

Often children are taught the geometric names without being given much opportunity to explore the properties or to solve problems. The sixth national assessment shows that students in the United States know the names of geometric shapes but have difficulty with complex geometric properties (Martin and Strutchens 2000).

Children should begin to recognize types of shapes through examples and nonexamples, not through definitions. By experiencing examples and discussing the properties, they can begin to realize what properties define a shape. In the Classroom 14–11 gives examples and nonexamples of triangles.

Lesson Idea 14–5

What's My Altitude?

▼ Make a triangle from a stiff piece of paper. Cut a strip 2 cm by 20 cm. Mark off segments of 9 cm, 4 cm, and 7 cm and label them A, B, and C, respectively. Fold and tape as shown:

1. Set the triangle on side A. This is the base.

   • How long is the base? ___9 cm___

   • What is the altitude? _____

   • How long is the altitude? _____

2. Set the triangle on side B. This is the base now.

   • How long is the base? _____

   • What is the altitude? _____

   • How long is the altitude? _____

3. Set the triangle on side C. This is the base now.

   • How long is the base? _____

   • What is the altitude? _____

   • How long is the altitude? _____

Do you see why the different shapes were included? If a child says that C, B, F, or G is a triangle, what property of triangles do you think is being ignored in each case? If a child fails to realize that D is a triangle, what do you think may be the reason?

Children also need to be able to recognize geometric shapes as models for real objects. For example, you might have young children write a "book" about circles. What is shaped like a circle? Let them find examples and draw pictures. Older children can be challenged to tell why certain objects are shaped in a certain way:

Why are most buttons shaped like a circle?

Why is paper rectangular?

Why are walls rectangular?

Why are support braces triangular?

Children should know the names of the most common shapes: triangle, square, rectangle, circle,

In The Classroom 14–11

Grades 2–6

Find Me

Objective: Identify examples and nonexamples of triangles.

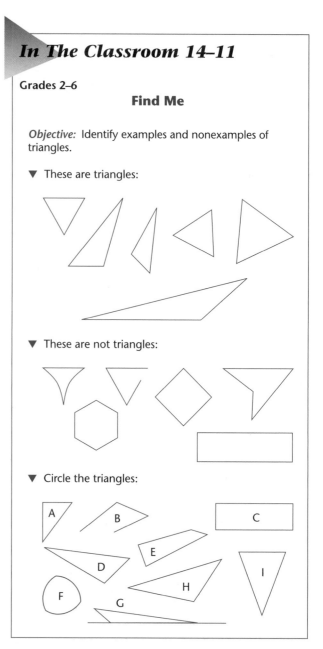

▼ These are triangles:

▼ These are not triangles:

▼ Circle the triangles:

and parallelogram. They also should be aware of other words that are used with shapes; for example, children should be able to identify the center, radius, diameter, and circumference of a circle. The most important thing with all vocabulary is that, after it is introduced, it is used.

Relationships between Shapes

In the preceding section we looked at properties of individual shapes. To emphasize those properties, it is often helpful to compare two or more shapes. When considering two or more shapes, you can examine two relationships, congruence and similarity, that are central to the study of geometry. After we look at these two relationships, we will consider how children at different levels might respond to comparing two shapes on all the properties we have mentioned so far.

Congruence Two shapes are said to be *congruent* if they have the same size and the same shape. Young children grasp this idea when they see that one shape can be made to fit exactly on the other. If the two shapes are line segments, they are congruent if they have the same length. If the two shapes are two-dimensional and they are congruent, then they have the same area. The converse is not true. Two shapes with the same area may not be congruent. Children have difficulty with this concept, and many middle-school students will respond that the parallelogram shown here is congruent to the rectangle:

This difficulty may be more a function of the word *congruence* than of the concept. Young children have little difficulty identifying figures with the same shape and size. Thus, the task becomes one of asking young children to match figures to see if they are the same size and shape and gradually introducing and using the word *congruence*.

You may have children begin to investigate the relationship of same area but different shape through activities such as those in Chapter 15.

Congruence is often investigated through motion geometry. If two shapes are congruent, they can be made to fit by one or more of the three motions illustrated in Figure 14–6. It sometimes takes more than one motion, as shown by the glide.

Similarity *Similarity* is a word that we use in everyday language to mean alike in some way. Although children may have an idea of similarity, they often have not developed the mathematical meaning. Intuitive notions about similarity have to be refined to a mathematical definition: Two figures are *similar* if corresponding angles are equal and corresponding sides are in the same ratio.

This definition is too formal for a beginning. Instead, you can begin by using a geoboard and geopaper. Children can make a design on the geoboard and transfer it to smaller geopaper, or they can copy designs from one size of graph paper to another.

After students have been introduced to ratio, they can investigate similarity in a more rigorous way. (The use of similar triangles is discussed in Chapter 13.)

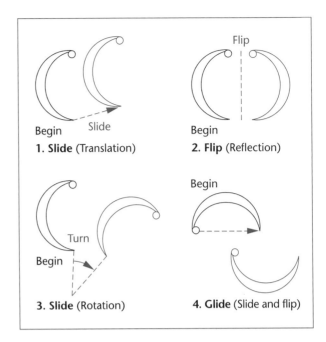

Figure 14–6 • **Motions for determining congruence**

Comparing Two Figures As children at all grade levels are learning about the properties of geometric figures, they should be given many opportunities to compare figures. As illustrated in Figure 14–7, children's understanding of geometric properties varies as they construct their knowledge through experiences.

Classification Schemes

We have examined many properties of and relationships among geometric figures. What makes a parallelogram a parallelogram? When is a rhombus a square? What is a regular polygon? When students understand the defining properties of two-dimensional shapes, they have moved into van Hiele Level 2.

Triangles Triangles are classified either by sides or by angles:

By Sides	By Angles

Equilateral
    three congruent sides
	Acute
	    all angles less than 90°

Isosceles
    at least two congruent sides
	Right
	    one angle equal to 90°

Scalene
    no sides congruent
	Obtuse
	    one angle greater than 90°

After children have learned to identify triangles by sides and by angles, the two classification schemes may be put together. For example, can you make an

Compare these shapes:

A

B

They have four sides.
A is a rectangle. B isn't.
A can be folded to match.
They each have corners.
B looks lopsided.

Primary Responses

They each have
4 sides and 4
corners.
A is a rectangle,
B is a parallelogram.
A has perpendicular
sides.
B has 2 pairs of
parallel sides: so
does A.
The angles of A are
equal: they are right
angles.
The length of
opposite sides
are equal.
They aren't congruent.

Intermediate Responses

All of the above and:
Both are parallelograms.
They have the same
height.
They have the same area,
but they aren't
congruent.
They are convex.
Opposite angles are
equal.
They are not similar.

Middle School Responses

Figure 14–7 • Examples of children's responses that reflect their understanding of relationships between figures at various stages

isosceles, right triangle? A scalene, obtuse triangle? An equilateral, right triangle?

Quadrilaterals There are many special names for quadrilaterals. The most common are parallelograms, rectangles, squares, rhombuses, trapezoids, and kites. These classes are not disjoint; one shape may fall into several categories. For example, a rectangle is also a parallelogram. This type of classifying process is more difficult for children than partitioning the whole set into disjoint classes, as is the case with triangles. It requires more than just recognizing examples of figures; it requires understanding the defining properties. For example, a parallelogram is a quadrilateral with two pairs of parallel sides. Assuming you know that a quadrilateral is a four-sided, closed, simple figure, can you identify which of the following are parallelograms? What other names do they have?

You are correct; they all are. Thus, a square, a rhombus, and a rectangle are all special types of parallelograms.

See if you can answer these questions, and discuss them with a colleague. What is a rhombus? A *rhombus* is a parallelogram with all sides congruent. Does that mean that a square is a rhombus? What is a rectangle? A *rectangle* is a parallelogram with right angles. Does that mean a square is a rectangle?

How do you begin to teach such relationships? Children must first begin to verbalize many properties of the figure. For example, they must be able to describe a square:

As a closed, four-sided figure (property 1)

With opposite sides parallel (property 2),

All right angles (property 3), and

All sides congruent (property 4).

Properties 1 and 2 make it a parallelogram; properties 1, 2, and 3 make it a rectangle; properties 1, 2, and 4 make it a rhombus; properties 1, 2, 3, and 4 make it a square. In the Classroom 14–12 helps students with this idea.

Polygons Polygons are named according to the number of sides:

3 sides: triangles

4 sides: quadrilaterals

5 sides: pentagons

6 sides: hexagons

In The Classroom 14–12

Classify Me

Objective: Classifying and naming quadrilaterals.

▼ Mark each of the figures with a
1. if it is a quadrilateral,
2. if it has two pairs of parallel sides,
3. if it has all right angles,
4. if it has all congruent sides.

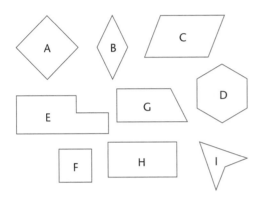

• Any figure marked 1 and 2 is a _____

• Any figure marked 1, 2, and 3 is a rectangle as well as a _____

• Any figure marked 1, 2, and 4 is a _____ as well as a _____

• Any figure marked 1, 2, 3, and 4 is a _____ and a _____ as well as a square.

In The Classroom 14–13

Can You Find It?

Objective: Shade polygons with given properties.

▼ See if you can find each of these in the design. Fill in the shape, and mark it with the matching letter.

A. triangle—isosceles
B. triangle—scalene
C. quadrilateral—not symmetric
D. quadrilateral—4 lines of symmetry
E. pentagon—concave
F. pentagon—convex
G. hexagon—exactly 2 pairs of parallel sides
H. hexagon—symmetric
I. heptagon (7 sides)—symmetric
J. heptagon—not symmetric
K. octagon

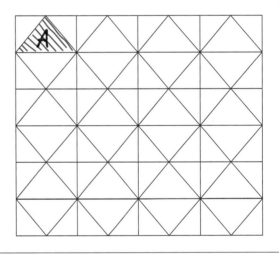

7 sides: heptagons
8 sides: octagons
9 sides: nonagons
10 sides: decagons

This classification scheme is not difficult, but often children are shown only regular polygons. Thus, among the shapes shown here, a child sees only the first as a hexagon, instead of realizing they are all hexagons.

Children should be encouraged to think of real objects that are shaped like these.

The names *heptagon, nonagon,* and *decagon* are not widely used, so in doing activities you may have to remind children of these names. In the Classroom 14–13 uses the names as well as other properties; students are asked to see shapes within other shapes, a task that is difficult for some.

A Glance at Where We've Been

Geometry is a topic that is often neglected in elementary school, yet it has many benefits for children if it is presented in an intuitive, informal manner.

This chapter presented a variety of examples of activities that provide this type of informal experience. These activities can be modified in many ways to suit the topic and the level of your students. They can also be modified to emphasize coordinate geometry on a rectangular grid. In the section on solid geometry we looked at processes that you can use with plane figures. The solid figures can be considered in terms of their properties, relationships among them, and classification schemes, as was emphasized in the plane geometry section.

We have touched on only a few things you can do to help children build concepts and skills in geometry, as well as only a few ways to present problems and apply geometry. There are many other fascinating topics and activities that you can use. Begin collecting and using them in your teaching.

Things to Do: From What You've Read

1. Give four reasons why geometry should be included in an elementary mathematics program. Explain, in your own words, what one of these reasons means to you.

2. Construct three solids using at least two of the different methods suggested in this chapter.

3. Name three properties of solids that children should learn at each of these levels: beginning, intermediate, and advanced.

4. Defend spending time on constructing models of solids.

5. List eight geometric properties of plane shapes that children can describe.

6. Try the Logo activity on In the Classroom 14–10. What did you discover?

7. Give the reason for including each example and nonexample of a triangle on In the Classroom 14–11.

8. Design a classifying activity for intermediate students based on one of the ideas in the beginning activities.

9. Explain how quadrilaterals can be classified. Why are squares a type of rectangle? How could rectangles be defined so that squares would not be rectangles?

10. A fellow teacher says that he cannot start to teach any geometry until the students know all the terms and definitions and that his fifth graders just cannot learn them, so he does not do any geometry. What misconceptions about teaching geometry does this teacher hold?

Things to Do: Going Beyond This Book

field Additional activities, suggestions, and questions are provided in *Teaching Elementary Mathematics: A Resource for Field Experiences.*

1. Find an art project that deals with symmetry for elementary students.

2. Design an investigative lesson for one of the properties of angles of triangles or quadrilaterals listed in the section on angles.

3. *field* *Solid Activity.* Try one of the activities with solids described in the section on describing and classifying objects.

4. Suppose you have a student in your class who cannot manipulate a compass. Describe materials you could have him or her work with to make geometric figures.

5. Try some of the Logo activities for yourself. Write a lesson plan for children to use Logo.

6. Look at the geometry in a textbook at a given grade level. Make a list of the activities from this chapter that would complement the text.

7. Read about the use of geometry in everyday life in another country or culture. Describe how it is different and how you could use this in your teaching.

8. *field* *Classifying.* In the Classroom 14–11 provides examples and nonexamples of triangles. Ask young children to tell which of the mixed examples are not triangles and to justify their selections. Or use In the Classroom 14–12 with older children to see what they understand about the classification of quadrilaterals.

9. *field* *Compare Shapes.* Interview a range of students from K–8 asking them to compare the two shapes in Figure 14–7. Compare the responses you receive with those in the text.

10. *field* *3-D.* In the Classroom 14–4 is one of the activities with building three-dimensional shapes. As you try this with children, observe which shapes children make and whether they can tell the number of edges and verticies. Can they make shapes with a given number of edges and verticies?

11. *field* *Number of Sides.* In the Classroom 14–6 is a game for younger children, and In the Classroom 14–8 has challenging puzzles. Try one of these with students and observe how they react to games or puzzles.

12. Find a vignette involving geometry in *Professional Standards for Teaching Mathematics* (NCTM 1991). Share and discuss it with your classmates.

BOOK NOOK FOR CHILDREN

Ada, Alma Flor. *El Reino de la Geometria*. Laredo, Tex.: Laredo Publishing Co, 1993.

Ayture-Scheele, Zulal. *Beautiful Origami*. New York: Sterling, 1990.

Brown, Ruth. *If at First You Do Not See*. New York: Henry Holt, 1982.

Dorros, Arthur. *This is My House*. New York: Scholastic, 1992.

Ehlert, Lois. *Color Zoo*. New York: Lippincott, 1989.

Ernst, Lisa, and Ernst, Lee. *The Tangram Magician*. New York: Harry N. Abrams, 1990.

Esterl, Arnica. *The Fine Round Cake*. New York: Four Winds Press, 1991.

Feldman, Judy. *Shapes in Nature*. Chicago: Children's Press, 1991.

Flournoy, Valerie. *The Patchwork Quilt*. New York: Dial Books, 1985.

Hoban, Tana. *Shadows and Reflections*. New York: Greenwillow Books, 1990.

Hoban, Tana. *Spirals, Curves, Fanshapes and Lines*. New York: Greenwillow Books, 1992.

Hutchins, Pat. *Changes, Changes*. New York: Macmillan, 1987.

Isaacson, Philip M. *Round Buildings, Square Buildings, and Buildings That Wiggle Like a Fish*. New York: Knopf, 1988.

Jonas, Ann. *Reflections*. New York: Greenwillow Books, 1987.

Keller, Wallace. *The Wrong Side of Bed*. New York: Rizzoli, 1992.

Morris, Ann. *Houses and Homes*. New York: Lothrop, Lee & Shepard, 1992.

Murphy, Pat. *By Nature's Design. An Exploratorium Book*. San Francisco: Chronicle, 1993.

Rogers, Paul. *The Shapes Game*. New York: Holt, 1989.

Tompert, Ann. *Grandfather Tang's Story*. New York: Crown Publishers, 1990.

Selected References

Bartels, Bobbye Hoffman. "Truss(t)ing Triangles." *Mathematics Teaching in the Middle School,* 3 (March-April 1998), pp. 394–396.

Battista, Michael T., and Clements, Douglas H. "Research into Practice: Constructing Geometric Concepts from Logo." *Arithmetic Teacher,* 38 (November 1990), pp. 15–17.

Battista, Michael T., and Clements, Douglas H. "Using Spatial Imagery in Geometric Reasoning." *Arithmetic Teacher,* 39 (November 1991), pp. 18–21.

Bradley, Claudette. "Making a Navajo Blanket Design with Logo." *Arithmetic Teacher,* 40 (May 1993), pp. 520–523.

Carroll, William M. "Middle School Students' Reasoning about Geometric Situaions." *Mathematics Teaching in the Middle School,* 1 (March-April 1998), pp. 398–403.

Clements, Douglas H.; Russell, Susan Jo; Tierney, Cornelia; Battista, Michael T.; and Meredith, Julie Sarama. *Investigations in Number, Data, and Space: Flips, Turns, and Area*. Palo Alto, Calif.: Dale Seymour, 1995.

Confer, Chris. *Math by All Means: Geometry Grade 2*. Sausalito, Calif.: Math Solutions Publications, 1994.

Craig, Bill. "Polygons, Stars, Circles, and Logo." *Arithmetic Teacher,* 33 (May 1986), pp. 6–14.

Crowley, Mary L. "The van Hiele Model of the Development of Geometric Thought." In *Learning and Teaching Geometry, K–12,* 1987 Yearbook (ed. Mary Montgomery Lindquist). Reston, Va.: NCTM, 1987, pp. 1–16.

Dana, Marcia E., and Lindquist, Mary Montgomery. "The Surprising Circle." *Arithmetic Teacher,* 25 (January 1978), pp. 4–11.

Dana, Marcia E., and Lindquist, Mary Montgomery. "Let's Try Triangles." *Arithmetic Teacher,* 26 (September 1978), pp. 2–9.

Evered, Lisa J. "Folded Fashions: Symmetry in Clothing Designs." *Arithmetic Teacher,* 40 (December 1992), pp. 204–206.

Fosnaugh, Linda S., and Marvin E. Harrell. "Covering the Plane with Rep-Tiles." *Mathematics Teaching in the Middle School,* 1 (January–February 1996), pp. 666–670.

Friedlander, Alex, and Lappan, Glenda. "Similarity: Investigations at the Middle School Level." In *Learning and Teaching Geometry, K–12,* 1987 Yearbook (ed. Mary Montgomery Lindquist). Reston, Va.: NCTM, 1987, pp. 136–145.

Germain-McCarthy, Yvelyne. "The Decorative Ornamental Ironwork of New Orleans: Connections to Geometry and Haiti." *Mathematics Teaching in the Middle School,* 4 (April 1999), pp. 430–436.

Giganti, Paul, Jr., and Cittadino, Mary Jo. "The Art of Tessellation." *Arithmetic Teacher,* 37 (March 1990), pp. 6–16.

Heukerott, Pamela Beth. "Origami: Paper Folding—the Algorithmic Way." *Arithmetic Teacher,* 35 (January 1988), pp. 4–9.

Jacobson, Cathy, and Lehrer, Richard. "Teacher Appropriation and Student Learning of Geometry Through Design. *Journal for Research in Mathematics Education,* 31 (January 2000), pp. 71–88.

Lehrer, Richard, and Curtis, Carmen L. "Why Are Some Solids Perfect? Conjectures and Experiments by Third Graders. *Teaching Children Mathematics,* 6 (January 2000), pp. 324–329

Leidtke, Walter W. "Developing Spatial Abilities in the Early Grades." *Teaching Children Mathematics,* 2 (September 1995), pp. 12–18.

Lindquist, Mary Montgomery; Brown, Catherine A.; Carpenter, Thomas P.; Kouba, Vicky L.; Silver, Edward A.; and Swafford, Jane O. *Results from the Fourth Mathematics Assessment of the National Assessment of Educational Progress*. Reston, Va.: NCTM, 1989.

Lindquist, Mary Montgomery, and Dana, Marcia E. "Strip Tease." *Arithmetic Teacher,* 25 (March 1980), pp. 4–9.

Martin, W. Gary, and Strutchens, Marilyn E. "Geometry and Measurement." In *Results from the Seventh Mathematics Assessment of the National Assessment of Educational Progress*. (eds. E. A. Silver and P. A. Kenney). Reston, Va.: NCTM, 2000.

Manouchehri, Azita; Enderson, Mary C.; and Pugnucco, Lyle A. "Exploring Geometry with Technology." *Mathematics*

Teaching in the Middle School, 3 (March–April 1998), pp. 436–442.

Morrow, Lorna J. *"Geometry through the Standards." Arithmetic Teacher,* 38 (April 1991), pp. 21–25.

National Council of Teachers of Mathematics. *Principles and Standards for School Mathematics.* Reston, Va.: NCTM, 2000.

National Council of Teachers of Mathematics. *Professional Standards for Teaching Mathematics.* Reston, Va.: NCTM, 1991.

Pohl, Victoria. "Visualizing Three Dimensions by Constructing Polyhedra." In *Learning and Teaching Geometry, K–12,* 1987 Yearbook (ed. Mary Montgomery Lindquist). Reston, Va.: NCTM, 1987, pp. 144–154.

Sconyers, James M. "On My Mind: Proof and the Middle School Mathematics Student." *Mathematics Teaching in the Middle School.* 1 (November–December 1995), pp. 516–518.

Sundberg, Sue E. "A Plethora of Polyhedra." *Mathematics Teaching in the Middle School,* 3 (March–April 1998), pp. 388–391.

Taylor, Lyn. "Activities to Introduce Your Class to Logo." *Arithmetic Teacher,* 39 (November 1991), pp. 52–54.

U.S. Department of Education. *Pursing Excellence: A Study of U.S. Eight-Grade Mathematics and Science Teaching, Learning, Curriculum, and Achievement in International Context.* Washington, D.C.: U.S. Government Printing Office, 1996.

Williams, Carol. "Sorting Activities for Polygons." *Mathematics Teaching in the Middle School,* 3 (March–April 1998), pp. 445–446.

Zaslavsky, Claudia. "People Who Live in Round Houses." *Arithmetic Teacher,* 37 (September 1989), pp. 18–21.

Zaslavsky, Claudia. "Symmetry in American Folk Art." *Arithmetic Teacher,* 38 (September 1990), pp. 6–13.

Zilliox, Joseph T., and Lowrey, Shannon G. "Faces Many Have I." *Mathematics Teaching in the Middle School,* 3 (November–December 1998), pp. 180–183.

15 *Measurement*

Snapshot of a Lesson

Orientation

A sixth-grade class of 29 students is studying area of rectangles. In the previous lesson, the class learned to use the base and the altitude to find areas of rectangles. In this lesson, small groups of three or four will find the area of rectangular objects in the room. Mr. Katz circulates to help groups or to ask questions of those who need challenging.

PAT: This card wants us to find which is larger, the desk top or the top of the bookcase? That's easy. The bookcase is much longer.

KIM: But it says "area," Pat. We need to find the area, and I think the desk is larger.

WES: I think it's the bookcase. Let's see.

MR. KATZ: Well, what did you find?

PAT: The desk was larger in area even though the bookcase was longer. When we covered them with squares the other day, the desk took more squares.

KIM: Unless I remember that I'm trying to find how many squares, I forget why I'm measuring the lengths and whether to add or multiply.

WES: It really helps me to think of the number of rows and the number of squares in each row. All you have to do is to count the number of squares, and multiplying is an easy way to count.

MR. KATZ: Why don't you try a challenge card instead of the next task card?

KIM: Oh, let's try this one. I've always wanted to cover the science table with a rug!

AREA   TASK C-11

Which is larger in area?

Rug   Science table

Draw a picture to show how your group decided.

WES: These aren't rectangles.

PAT: Look, we can make them into two rectangles. Remember when we cut those shapes apart? Let's cut the rug!

WES: Funny, but you're right. Let's mark where we would cut them. Then we can find the area of each rectangle and add them.

MR. KATZ: (Approaching another group) What's the problem?

SASHA: We don't know where to begin.

MR. KATZ: What are you trying to do?

SASHA: We have to find something in the room that is about 150 square centimeters. That's awfully large. Are you sure there is something?

SUE: No, it isn't. A square centimeter is awfully small.

JANE: Well, I just can't imagine 150 square centimeters. What can we do?

MR. KATZ: Do you know how large your name card is?

SUE: Let me measure. It's about 7 centimeters by 11 centimeters. That means it's about 77 square centimeters. We need something larger.

SASHA: How about this sheet of paper?

JANE: That's way too much. It's about four times larger. We need something in between.

Across the room, a group of students seems to be struggling with another problem.

MAUREEN: Mr. Katz, can you help us?

MR. KATZ: We'll see. What are you doing?

TOMAS: Well, we were talking and Maureen said the reading table was larger than this table. How can we tell?

Note that the reading table is trapezoidal.

MR. KATZ: Is the reading table a rectangle?

TOMAS: No, but can't we just measure the length and width?

MR. KATZ: What would be the length?

MAUREEN: Isn't it the longest side?

As students are working, Mr. Katz has many decisions to make. For example, should he answer Maureen's question or let the group proceed? He made a note that when the whole class looked at trapezoids he would have to address the "longest side" issue.

MR. KATZ: Let's get back together and see what you have found.

SUE: We found three things that were about 150 square centimeters. One was the task card itself—that was pretty sneaky.

KIM: The science table is larger than the rug. Even if we could cut the rug, it wouldn't cover the table. Guess we won't have an easy-on-your-elbows table after all.

TOMAS: We finally figured out the reading table. How about other shapes? How do you find the areas without covering them with squares?

MR. KATZ: Tomas, what do you mean you "figured out" the reading table?

TOMAS: Well, it isn't a rectangle, so we had to do some cutting. We cut off this triangle and put it there to make a rectangle.

MR. KATZ: Right. When things aren't rectangles, we need other ways to find the area. Tomorrow, we'll look at shapes other than rectangles. We will begin to develop formulas for some other common shapes from what we already know.

Introduction

The Snapshot of a Lesson gave us a glance into a sixth-grade classroom. What experiences should the children have before this lesson? What concepts and skills are important for the children to learn? How do you help children to have these experiences? Before examining these and other questions that we should consider as teachers, we will discuss why measuring should be taught.

Stop and think about how you have used numbers in the past few days. Did you tell someone how long it took you to drive to school, how many calories are in a piece of chocolate cake, how far it is to the nearest store, or how many cups of coffee you drank? All of these are measurements. Measurement is the topic from the elementary curriculum that we use the most in our daily lives. Thus, one of the main reasons to include measuring is that it has many practical applications. Measurement is desig-

nated as one of the ten standards in the *Principles and Standards for School Mathematics* (NCTM 2000) because of its power to help students see the usefulness of mathematics in everyday life.

A second reason is that measurement can be used in learning other topics in mathematics. It is apparent that children need many of the other topics of mathematics to help them with measuring. For example, they may count the number of grams it takes to balance an object on a scale, multiply to find a volume, divide to change minutes to hours, subtract to see how close an estimate was, or add to find the perimeter of a triangle. To report the number of units, children may use whole numbers, common fractions, decimals, and negative numbers.

Although not quite as apparent, measurement can help teach about numbers and operations. Many of the numeration models we use have a measurement base. For example, the number line is based on length. One model for multiplication is an area of a rectangle. Also, there are concepts and procedures that underlie both measurement and number ideas. As shown in Figure 15–1, measuring to the nearest unit is similar to rounding to a given unit. Thus, measurement ideas may be used to complement numerical ideas.

Not only is measurement useful in everyday life, but it also is useful in other areas of the curriculum. If you are trying to think of ways to connect mathematics with other subjects, think of measurement and consider the ways in which measurement is used in art, music, science, social studies, and language arts.

Another reason why measurement is an important part of the mathematics curriculum is not so much mathematical as pedagogical. Measurement is an effective way to involve students in activities that are often a change of pace from other mathematics topics. Look again at the Snapshot of a Lesson at the beginning of this chapter. Were you fortunate enough to have such lively math classes when you were in sixth grade?

Measurement provides an excellent way to present problem-solving experiences at every level. Lesson Idea 15–1 gives samples of some problems at various grade levels. Each could be used at the grade level suggested or could be modified for use with students at another grade level.

Research from international studies has often shown that measurement and geometry are the two topics on which students in the United States perform less well than their counterparts in other countries. This is particularly evident in the *Third International Mathematics and Science Study* (U.S. Department of Education 1996, 1997). Through the years, the data from the mathematics assessments of the National Assessment of Educational Progress (NAEP) have given reason for concern about students' performance on measurement items. As you read about these results in this chapter, think about your responsibility to help students develop better understanding of measurement and measuring skills.

In summary, measurement should be an integral part of the mathematics curriculum for several important reasons:

- It provides many applications to everyday life.
- It can be used to help learn other mathematics.
- It can be related to other areas of the school curriculum.
- It involves the students in active learning.
- It can be approached through problem solving.

The NCTM *Principles and Standards* call for measurement to be a continuing part of the mathematics program, rather than being presented in a few isolated lessons. You will find many ways to include measurement activities for children as you are teaching many mathematical ideas and other subject areas.

Figure 15–1 • **The similarity between measuring and rounding**

Lesson Idea 15–1

Problem? Solve It!

Length   **Grade 2**

▼ Cut a strip of paper:

30 cm | 2 cm

▼ Measure 5 cm from one end and fold:

5 cm

fold

▼ Put away the ruler.
▼ Fold the whole strip to make a rectangle with the 5 cm as one side.

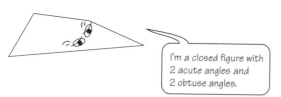

5 cm

▼ Tell how you know it is a rectangle.

Area   **Grade 4**

▼ Take 4 squares of the same size.

How many rectangles can you make?

▼ Make as many other figures with area of 4 squares as you can by putting the squares side by side like

this   not this

▼ How many different shapes can you make? How can you convince a friend that there are no others?

Angles   **Grade 6**

I'm a closed figure with 2 acute angles and 2 obtuse angles.

Can you draw a closed figure with

• 2 right angles, 1 acute angle, and 1 obtuse angle?
• 3 right angles and 2 other angles?
• 2 right angles and 2 acute angles?
• 1 right angle, 1 acute angle, and 1 obtuse angle?

▼ Which shapes are impossible? Explain why.

Volume   **Grade 8**

8 cm

4 cm

3 cm

You can change one dimension of this rectangular solid by 1 cm.

• Which dimension would you change to change the volume

the most? _____   the least? _____

Try another rectangular solid.

• What is your hypothesis? Justify your hypothesis through several examples and an explanation.

TEACHING MEASUREMENT

Most of the research about how children measure and think about measurement does not indicate specifically and directly how the teacher should plan for instruction. Rather, research has focused on what children can do and understand. For example, Wilson and Osborne (1988, p. 109) suggest the following based on their study:

• Children must measure frequently and often, preferably on real problems rather than on textbook exercises.

• Children should encounter activity-oriented measurement situations by doing and experimenting rather than passively observing. The activities should encourage discussion to stimulate the refinement and testing of ideas and concepts.

• Instructional planning should emphasize the important ideas of measurement that transfer or work across measurement systems.

Measuring is a process by which a number is assigned to an attribute of an object or event. Length, capacity, weight, area, volume, time, and temperature are the measurable attributes considered in most elementary mathematics programs. Although each of these attributes is different, there are some overall commonalities in how to help children learn about measuring them. The following outline is based on the measuring process and can be used to plan instruction:

I. Identify the attribute by comparing objects
  A. Perceptually
  B. Directly
  C. Indirectly through a reference

II. Choose a unit
  A. Arbitrary
  B. Standard

III. Compare the object to the unit

IV. Find the number of units
  A. Counting
  B. Using instruments
  C. Using formulas

V. Report the number of units

If a new attribute is being introduced, one recommended approach is to cycle through the outline several times: the first time using only arbitrary units and counting, the next time using standard units and counting, and only after this introducing instruments or formulas. This cycling may take place over several years for the first attributes studied, but after several attributes have been introduced, the length of the cycle should be shortened.

Identifying Attributes

To measure with understanding, children should know what attribute they are measuring. Take, for example, a measure of attitude. What are we actually measuring? Because we do not fully understand the attribute being measured, scores on attitude tests are often difficult to interpret. For young children, measuring the area of an object also can be difficult if they do not understand the concept of area. Thus, one of our first tasks is to build an understanding of measurable attributes.

Children's literature provides excellent sources for developing understanding of attributes. For example, the book *More Spaghetti, I Say!* (Gelman 1977) can be used to help develop an understanding of length and weight by using pasta as a unit of measurement. We also encourage comparing and estimating lengths as a way to build understanding of length concepts.

Three types of comparisons can build understanding of attributes: comparing objects perceptually, comparing them directly, and comparing them

indirectly. As children make these types of comparisons, not only are they gaining an understanding of the particular attribute and the associated vocabulary, but they are also learning procedures that will help them in assigning a number to a measurement. We will examine each attribute separately because of the importance of having children participate in such experiences. As you read, see if you can tell the differences among the three types of comparison, and how each can be used to develop an understanding of that attribute.

Length Length is one of the most easily perceived attributes of objects. Children come to school with some concept of length and some vocabulary associated with it. However, they often have what adults may consider misconceptions about length. For example, they may say that a belt is shorter when it is curled up than when it is straight. These misconceptions disappear as children develop cognitively and are given constructive experiences.

Lesson Ideas 15–2, 15–3, and 15–4 illustrate comparison activities that are appropriate for kindergarteners, first graders, or older children who need a review. Lesson Idea 15–2 involves comparisons made perceptually. In the beginning of this activity, all irrelevant perceptual attributes have been masked—

Lesson Idea 15–2

Perceptual Comparison of Lengths

Materials: Collections of long, thin objects such as rods, spaghetti, pencils, and crayons

Description: ▼ Hold up two long objects and one short object.

- Ask children to tell which is different.
- Use vocabulary of *shorter, taller,* and *longer.*
- Repeat with other objects that differ *only* on length and are obviously different in length.

▼ Hold up a long pencil and a short crayon.

- Ask how they are different. Expect answers such as color, type of object, paper wrapper, eraser.
- If no one says the crayon is shorter or the pencil is longer ask "Which is longer?"

Lesson Idea 15–3

Direct Comparison of Length

Materials: A box of long, thin objects, some of which are about the same length, and sheets of construction paper (one of each labeled "shorter," "same," and "longer"):

Description:

Place a box of long, thin objects that children can sort at a center individually or in pairs. Let a child choose one object to be the reference, and compare the other objects to that one, putting the objects on the sheets marked shorter, same, or longer.

Baseline

SHORTER	SAME	LONGER

Lesson Idea 15–4

Indirect Comparison of Length

Objective: To indirectly compare two objects on length.

Materials: String or connecting links, index cards, tape, and objects in the room selected for children to represent.

Description: Choose two lengths that are about the same on objects that cannot easily be moved to compare directly. For example, the height of your desk with the width of your desk. Ask the children which is longer, and let them pose a solution of how they can tell.

Discuss the ways they propose and then show them how you would use the links (or string) to represent each of the lengths and then compare.

After this discussion and demonstration, give each pair of children a string and have them represent one of the objects you have marked.

Make a "graph" of all the lengths for easy comparison.

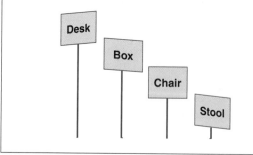

that is, the objects are the same except for length. This allows children to build the concept of length as an attribute of long, thin things. As the activity progresses and vocabulary is reviewed and extended, the objects to be compared differ on several attributes, but the focus remains on length.

Lesson Idea 15–3 uses the procedure of making direct comparisons. This type of comparison of length involves taking two objects and placing them side by side on a common baseline. This activity may be extended to seriating objects by length—that is, arranging them from shortest to tallest. For the young child, this task is more difficult because multiple comparisons must be made.

Lesson Idea 15–4 presents the problem of indirectly comparing two objects when they cannot be placed side by side. Children must use a third object to help them make the comparison. When we use a ruler to assign measurements, it is the third object that assists us in making a comparison. Young children can work with string, strips of paper, erasers, or other items as the third object.

Through activities such as these, children begin to develop an understanding of length as an attribute of long, thin objects. However, length is used

in other ways. For example, length is the distance around your waist. Young children can use string to compare their waists or to compare their wrists with their ankles. Older children can guess whether the height or the distance around a variety of cylindrical cans is longer and then check their guess by using string.

The distance between two points is also measured by length. In this case, words such as *nearer* and *farther* may be used when comparing two distances. Distance is often more difficult to perceive than the length of a long, thin object, so it should be introduced later.

Perimeter—the distance around a region—is a special type of length. Children should be given the opportunity to measure the distance around a region with string or a measuring tape. Later, they can add the lengths of the various sides of the region to find the perimeter.

Capacity Capacity is an attribute of containers that can be introduced to young children by asking, "Which holds more?"

Although perceptual comparisons can be made between two containers, young children often make the comparisons based on length (height) rather than on capacity. When asked which holds more—a tall container or a short container—most children will choose the taller container even if the shorter one may actually hold more. Thus, it is probably best to begin the study of capacity by using direct comparisons.

Some type of filler is needed to make direct comparisons. Water and sand are easy for young children to use. Given a variety of containers, children can fill one and pour it into the other to see which holds more. After children have done some experimenting with direct comparison, activities involving perceptual comparisons are possible. For example, children greatly enjoy guessing contests in which they guess which container holds more, and then you can check the results together.

Indirect comparisons are used when two containers cannot be compared perceptually or directly. For example, suppose you have two containers with small openings that make it difficult to pour from one into another. By pouring each into a pair of identical large-mouth containers, the capacities can be compared. Note that this activity is similar to what we do when we use graduated cylinders.

Weight To compare weights perceptually, we need to be able to lift the two objects. Children should be given a variety of pairs of objects (one of which is much heavier than the other) and asked to hold one in each hand. Children often think that a larger object weighs more. Thus, some of the objects should be small and heavy and others large and light. For children to understand that to find which is heavier, they must do more than look at the object; they may need experiences in comparing two objects that look the same but weigh different amounts. An easy way to provide this experience is by having children compare identical containers with lids (such as cottage-cheese containers) filled to weigh a different amount.

When you cannot feel the difference between the weight of two objects, you need a balance scale to assist in the comparison. To introduce the balance, choose two objects that differ greatly in weight so children can see that the heavier object "goes down" on the balance.

Many activities may be set up in which children compare the weights of two objects. One challenging activity is to compare five identical containers, with lids secured and filled with different amounts of weight, and put them in order from lightest to heaviest.

Indirect comparisons are not necessary until units of weight are introduced because, whenever each of two objects could be compared to a third on the balance, it would be much simpler to compare the two directly.

Area Area is an attribute of plane regions that can be compared by sight if the differences are large enough and the shapes similar enough. That is, it is easy to tell this page is larger than a driver's license, but it may be difficult to compare the areas of the three regions A, B, and C.

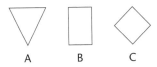

If the regions can be cut out, it is fairly easy to compare regions B and C by placing one on top of the other. It is more difficult to compare either B or C with A. Only when children have some idea of *conservation of area*—that a region can be cut and rearranged without changing the area—can this experience be meaningful. Thus, the first direct comparisons should be made with two regions, one of which fits within the other.

If objects cannot be moved to place one on top of the other, children can trace one object and use this representation to make an indirect comparison. For example, to compare the area of a desk to the area of a bulletin board, you could ask them to cut a piece of paper the size of the desk and put it on the bulletin board.

To help children understand that regions can be rearranged and not affect the area, geometry activities, such as the shape search in In the Classroom 15–1, are helpful. Notice that the children are asked to discuss the area of the shapes; this type of discussion will help focus on the objective of comparing shapes indirectly.

Volume If volume is considered as "how much space a three-dimensional object takes up," then it is difficult to make anything but perceptual comparisons before units are introduced. Thus, volume should receive little attention until fourth or fifth grade. However, because there is a close connection between volume and capacity, some background can be provided if containers are filled with nonliquids, such as blocks, balls, or other objects.

In The Classroom 15–1

Are We the Same Size?

Objective: To indirectly compare areas.

Materials: Cut out the four right, isosceles triangles below.

Name _____

Are We the Same Size?

1. Draw a line to show how you placed two triangles to make each of the shapes A, B, and C.

　　A.　　　　B.　　　　C.

2. Which of shapes A, B, or C looks the smallest to you? Explain to your classmates why each shape actually is the same size in terms of area. What is different?

3. What shapes can you make from three of the triangles? Draw a sketch of each.

4. What is area (use the triangle as the unit) of each shape you made? What would be the area if the unit was the square shown in B above?

Temperature We can certainly sense great differences in temperatures. Before introducing thermometers, you can have children compare to see which of two objects is colder (or hotter). You can also talk about things (or times) that are hot or cold; however, there are few other comparisons you can make without an instrument to help.

Time There are two attributes of events that can be measured: *time of occurrence* and *length of duration*. You can begin describing the time of occurrence by giving a time span: It happened today, in the morning, in October. Young children need to develop the vocabulary of days, months, and seasons of the year.

Children can tell which of two events takes longer (duration) if their lengths are greatly different. Does it take longer to brush your teeth or read a story? If the events are similar in duration, children can tell which lasts longer if they both begin at the same time (note the similarity to deciding which object is longer when both are placed on a baseline). You can think of many contests that use this idea:

whose paper plane flew longer; whose eyes were shut longer; who hopped for a longer time.

Units of Measure

After children have begun to develop a firm concept of an attribute through comparison activities, it is important to help them move through the remaining steps of the measurement process (steps II–V) described on page 323. Before instruments or formulas are introduced, children should be able to count the number of units that describe a given attribute.

To answer the question, "How long is the pencil?" we can say, "It's longer than my thumb" or "It's shorter than my arm." These are relative statements that give a range of possibilities for length but do not do a very accurate job of describing it. To be accurate, we need to compare the pencil to a unit. We can use an arbitrary unit such as a paper clip and say that the pencil is 7 paper clips long, or we can use a standard unit and say it is 16 centimeters long. Once we have described the length, we can compare it to other lengths. That is, we use the symbolic description to assist us in indirectly comparing. The unit of measurement gives us much power; we can communicate with others and we can make comparisons that were previously difficult to make.

Concepts Related to Units There are many concepts related to units of measurement that teachers need to help children develop. The concepts described here are developed over time. A single activity will not suffice; you need to be aware of the concepts, include similar activities with other attributes, and look for opportunities within any measurement activity to further the development of the concepts.

1. *A measurement must include both a number and the unit.* How many times do you remember a teacher telling you to be certain to write inches? And how many times did you not see the necessity—probably because you were only measuring in inches for the entire lesson? When children measure the same object with many different arbitrary units, research indicates that they are more likely to see the need to report the unit. Having children measure the length of a book with paper strips, erasers, or cubes, or weigh an object with washers, pennies, or paper clips, is the type of task that will encourage younger children to write (or draw) the unit. In the Classroom 15–2 provides an activity that encourages children to focus on the importance of reporting the unit.

2. *Two measurements may be easily compared if the same unit is used.* Young children often rely on only the number or possibly only the unit to make a

In The Classroom 15–2

Measuring Length with Arbitrary Units

Objective: To measure lengths with different arbitrary units; to compare those measurements.

Materials: Erasers, paper clips, books, boxes, and other objects that can be used as arbitrary units of measure.

Description:

▼ Give each pair of children an arbitrary unit and the name of what they are to measure.

▼ Have the children record their measurements at a place everyone can see. Observe to see whether they record the unit (if they do not, it will lead to the discussion below).

▼ Ask children to use the information about the lengths to compare the lengths of the different objects.

▼ Ask children why the unit is necessary. Ask the children which comparisons are easy to make (ones measured with the same unit) and what they can tell about those made with different units.

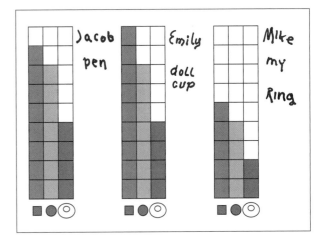

Figure 15–2 ● **Children's graphs of weights of objects**

comparison. For example, if one pencil is 6 paper clips long and another pencil is 2 strips long, some children will say that the one that measures 6 is longer. They have not yet reached the stage where they can coordinate the number with unit. The activity in In the Classroom 15–2 addresses this concept along with the need to report both the number and the unit.

3. *One unit may be more appropriate than another to measure an object.* The size of the unit chosen depends on the size of the object and on the degree of accuracy desired. If children are allowed to choose the unit, the idea of the unit's size depending on the size of the object will be clearer. To encourage this, ask questions such as "Should we use the edge of a book or a paper clip to find out how tall the door is? Should we use a thimble or a coffee mug to find out how much water the big bucket will hold? Should we use a paper clip or a pencil to find out the length of the book?

4. *There is an inverse relationship between the number of units and the size of the unit.* When measuring the same object with three different units, children soon realize that the larger the unit, the fewer are required. For example, you could ask each child to weigh an object with pennies, washers, and cubes. If

each child makes a graph of the results, a pattern becomes apparent when all the graphs are compared. In Figure 15–2, one can see that it always takes more cubes than washers to weigh each object. So cubes are lighter than washers.

5. *Standard units are needed to communicate effectively.* Many concepts about units can be developed with arbitrary units. At the same time you will be teaching procedures of measuring with units (how to line up units, use a balance, cover a region, keep track of how many units, and so on).

At some point, depending on the attribute, you will begin using standard units. Standard units are either customary (inch, pint, pound, etc.) or metric (meter, gram, liter, etc.). Most children already have heard of standard units but may not realize why we use them. Unfortunately, in the United States we still use both types of units. It is clear from the recent national assessments that children have a better understanding of customary units. On the 1996 assessment, although approximately three-fourths of the fourth-grade students selected an appropriate customary unit for length, only about one-third selected an appropriate metric unit to measure length (Martin and Strutchens 2000).

Stories and activities that demonstrate the difficulty in communicating sizes when there is no standard of measurement are one way to present the necessity of a standard unit. The book *How Big Is a Foot?* (Myller 1991) is an interesting and amusing source to use in helping children see the necessity for a standard unit. Another enjoyable activity for children is making a recipe of powdered drink such as lemonade—using a very large cup for the water and a very small spoon for the powder. (Be sure to have enough of the powder so the children can make it tasty.)

6. *A smaller unit will give a more exact measurement.* First, children need to realize that all measurements are approximate. If you have had them do a lot of measuring of real objects, they will have been reporting approximate measurements but perhaps without being fully aware of it. A practice of saying "about 6 inches," "more than 6 inches," or "between 6 and 7 inches" will help.

To set up the need for a more precise measurement, give one child a strip of paper that is 27 centimeters long and another child, sitting across the room, a strip that is 29 centimeters long. Give each decimeter strips to measure the paper. After they report the measurement, ask the class which strip is longer (no fair comparing the strips directly). Next, have them measure with centimeters. Discuss with the class why a smaller unit was needed.

Measuring in Units Length is the first attribute that most children measure. They take an arbitrary unit and copies of that unit and put them end to end until the units are as long as the object they are measuring. From previous direct comparisons of two objects, children should know when the lengths are the same. However, they have not lined up the units in a straight line with no gaps in between and no overlaps, nor have they counted the units. Units that connect, such as connecting cubes or links, are good to begin with because they are easy to handle and line up readily without gaps or overlaps.

After an example or two, you need only set up objects to be measured and supply the units, then observe and help. Later, children can take one unit and move it (an *iteration*). This more advanced skill is needed for proper use of a ruler when measuring objects longer than the ruler. It is a skill that should not be pushed too early. If you find children who cannot move, mark, and count, postpone introducing it until later.

If children have been measuring with arbitrary units, then using standard units should be easy. They will have a good understanding of the process of measuring, so the purpose should be to give them a feel for the standard unit. Let us take the decimeter as an example and consider some ways to build the feel for it as a standard unit.

Give each child a paper strip that is 10 centimeters by 2 centimeters. Do a variety of activities that have the children compare things to the decimeter strip. Some are suggested here.

- *Decimeter list-up:* Put a list on the board of objects children can find in the room that are the same

length as a decimeter. Be sure to include things on them such as fingers, pockets, soles of shoes.

- *Decimeter hold-up:* Pair the children and have one child try to hold two forefingers a decimeter apart, vertically, horizontally, and obliquely. The partner should check each time; then roles should be reversed.

- *Decimeter stack-up:* Set up stations with pennies, chips, clips, beans, cubes, and the like. At one station, children should try to stack the chips a decimeter high. At another station they should try to make a line of chips a decimeter long. Then they should use their decimeter strip to see how close they were.

After children are somewhat familiar with the length of a decimeter, they can begin to measure with decimeters. A good way to begin is by asking them to estimate the lengths of objects and then measure. As children are measuring with decimeter strips, they (and you) should notice that putting down strip after strip is not the easiest way to measure. Have them tape their strips together, end to end as below, alternating colors if two colors are available.

Now they have a "decimeter ruler," except they still have to count the units. After they have done some counting, see if anyone suggests numbering the strips. This activity will help children understand how rulers are made and that they are counting units.

Once children are familiar with the decimeter measurement of small objects, the next stage is measuring something very long. Have each child make a 10-decimeter ruler. Tell the children that this unit is called a *meter* and is used to measure longer distances. Activities similar to those suggested with decimeters will help them become familiar with meters. New units should be related to those children have already used to help them understand the new unit and to assist them in making conversions from one unit to another.

Children become familiar with standard units through comparing, measuring, estimating, and constructing. The experiences you provide should include all these processes. It is also important that not too many standard units are introduced at one time, that the unit is not too small or too large for a child of that age to handle, and that the numbers generated are not too large. Table 15–1 is a guide to the most common standard units used in elemen-

Table 15–1 • Standard units for elementary students (with approximate grade level)

Attribute	Metric Units	Customary Units
Length	Decimeter (1–2)	Inch (1–2)
	Centimeter (2–3)	Foot (2–3)
	Meter (2–3)	Yard (2–3)
	Millimeter (3–4)	Mile (4–5)
	Kilometer (4–5)	
Weight	Kilogram (2–3)	Ounce (2–3)
	Gram (4–5)	Pound (2–3)
Capacity	Liter (1–2)	Quart (2–3)
	Milliliter (4–5)	Cup (1–2)
		Gallon (2–3)
Area	Square centimeter (4–5)	Square inch (4–5)
	Square meter (5–6)	Square foot (4–5)
		Square yard (4–5)
Volume	Cubic centimeter (5–6)	Cubic inch (5–6)
	Cubic meter (5–6)	Cubic foot (5–6)
		Cubic yard (5–6)
Temperature	Celsius degree (2–3)	Fahrenheit degree (2–3)
Time		Hour (1–2)
		Minute (1–2)
		Second (3–4)
		Day (K–1)
		Week (1–2)
		Month (K–1)

tary school and the approximate grade levels at which it is appropriate to introduce them.

Instruments for Measuring

Instruments are used to measure some attributes. In elementary school, the more common instruments are rulers, scales, graduated containers, thermometers, protractors, and clocks. Other attributes (such as area and volume) are assigned a measurement by the use of a formula after an instrument has been used to measure some dimensions. Later, other attributes are derived from measurements of more than one attribute (for example, speed is derived from distance and time).

Much of the emphasis in the elementary curriculum is on instruments and formulas, and some children encounter difficulty with both. One probable source of difficulty is that the children do not understand what they are measuring and what it means to measure. The activities and suggestions presented so far in this chapter have dealt with building this understanding. Here we will look at some common problems children have with particular instruments and some ways to assist in developing the correct skills.

Ruler A ruler automatically counts the number of units, but children must realize what unit they are using and line up the ruler properly. Children will focus on the unit being used if the scale on the ruler has only that unit. For example, if the unit is centimeters, choose a ruler marked in centimeters, not in centimeters and millimeters. Or if the unit is inches, choose a ruler without the markings of fourths or eighths.

It is important that children measure real objects with the ruler. Make certain that you include activities in which children measure objects longer than one ruler. Can they move the ruler (iterate), and do they have the addition skills to add the units? For example, suppose the children have a 25-centimeter ruler and they are to measure something that is 43 centimeters long. Can they add 25 and 18? Of course, they could use counting or techniques that rely on their place value and counting background: 25, 35, 36, 37, . . . , 43. Let them try; they will surprise you if they are given a problem to solve. Your role is to ask questions to assist.

Children may have difficulty in measuring to the nearest fourth, eighth, or sixteenth of a unit. One cause of this difficulty may be the smallness of the unit (there is more room for error), but more probably it is their lack of confidence and understanding of fractions, their lack of understanding of the unit (fourths), and their lack of consciousness of how to measure to the nearest unit. In measuring to a unit, they tend to decide by simply looking at the nearest larger unit. The example of measuring in Figure 15–1 gives you some idea of how to make this process more explicit. The rulers in Appendix B marked in halves, fourths, and eighths provide a good intermediate step before moving to a standard ruler marked in sixteenths. It also is helpful to emphasize the units by asking, "What two units is the nail between—two-fourths and three-fourths or three-fourths and four-fourths?" Children must be able to answer this question before deciding which it is nearer. A firm foundation of fractions, especially fractions as they relate to length, will help with measuring to the nearest unit.

Figure 15–3 illustrates an exercise for using a ruler similar to a question from national mathematics assessment. What do you think was the most common answer of fourth-grade students? Most said the segment was 5 inches long.

Children begin counting with one, so it is natural that they often begin measuring at one. Activities like making a ruler and seeing that the 1 is placed at the end of the first unit are helpful. If children are having difficulty, return to directly comparing the object with the ruler (use a baseline as

Figure 15–3 • An exercise assessing understanding of a ruler

described in the section on direct comparison). You also could use separate units or just mark the inches on the segment and count the units.

Although we have concentrated on the difficulties some children have in learning to use a ruler, do not be discouraged. Children love to use rulers, and overall they do quite well with them. Make certain you have children not only measuring objects but also constructing line segments or objects of a given length. Research shows that children have more difficulty drawing a line segment of a given length than in measuring. Part of this may be the lack of experience.

Scaled Instruments Instruments such as bathroom scales, graduated cylinders, and thermometers cause children some trouble because each unit is not marked. On national assessments, students have always had difficulty reading thermometers on which the markings represent 2 degrees. Over half of the fourth-grade students on the sixth national mathematics assessment chose a distractor based on thinking the marking represented one rather than two units (Kenney and Kouba 1997).

One way to help children become more aware of the markings on a scale is to show to them and read with them many scales with different markings, but a more powerful way is to have them make their own instruments. They can make graphs, for example, using different scales, or they can mark their own graduated cylinders. Lesson Idea 15–5 gives instructions on how to make the "cylinder." Children can make such a measurement instrument and then use it to measure the amounts other containers hold. Note that this activity is also good practice for finding multiples of a number; in this case, children are working with multiples of six since it took six spoons to fill the small container.

Clocks The ordinary dial clock or watch is one of the most complicated instruments to read—and yet it is often one of the first to be taught. Not only are

there two or more ways to read the scale on it (hour, minute, and second), but the hands (indicators of the measures) move in a circular fashion. There is no set age at which children appear ready to learn how to tell time; you will often notice a wide range of ability within a class. The following list of skills associated with telling time is not necessarily in the order in which children may develop them.

- Identify the hour hand and the minute hand and the direction they move.
- Orally tell time by the hour (noting that the minute hand is on the 15) and moving the hands of a clock to show the hourly times.
- Identify the hour that a time is "after" (for example, it's after 4 o'clock).
- Count by fives to tell time to the nearest 5 minutes and report it orally (for example, as 4 o'clock and 20 minutes after).
- Count on by ones from multiples of 5 to tell time to the nearest minute (for example, 25, 26, 27).
- Identify the hour that a time is "before" (for example, it's before 10) and count by fives and ones to tell about how many minutes before the hour.
- Write the time in digital notation (4:20).
- Match the time on a digital clock to a regular clock.

These skills need to be developed over a long period of time, and children need to have clocks with movable hands.

You can begin problem solving with young children if they have clocks or watches. For example, as soon as children can tell time on the hour, you can ask questions such as, "What time will it be in 2 hours?" As the children become more familiar with the clock, you can give more challenging questions, such as those on Lesson Idea 15–6.

Although reading digital clocks is easier than reading regular clocks, solving the types of problems

Lesson Idea 15–5

Make Your Own

▼ You need these materials:

- Large glass
- Masking tape
- Spoon
- Water
- Small container
- Felt-tip pen

▼ Now follow these directions:

1. Put a piece of tape on the side of the glass.

2. Fill the small container with spoonfuls of water. Count how many it takes. Empty the small container into the glass. Mark the level of the water and the number of spoonfuls on the tape.

3. Fill the small container again. Empty into glass and mark.

4. Continue to the top of the glass.

Now that you have your own measure, use it to see how much other containers hold!

Lesson Idea 15–6

How Time Flies!

Fill in these blanks.

| | NOW | 2 hr., 20 min. LATER |
| | ____ : ____ | ____ : ____ |

| | NOW | 15 min. BEFORE |
| | ____ : ____ | ____ : ____ |

| | NOW | 5 hr. LATER |
| | ____ : ____ | ____ : ____ |

| 12:05 | NOW | 20 min. BEFORE |
| | ____ : ____ | ____ : ____ |

given in Lesson Idea 15–6 is more difficult with a digital clock. In learning to read a regular clock, a child learns the relationship of the minutes and hours and has a model to use in solving such problems. If all clocks were digital, teachers would need to spend less time on reading time but more on how our time system works.

To integrate math and history, an interdisciplinary unit on the history of time and clocks could prove to be interesting to older students. Students might enjoy seeing how the measurement of time has evolved through the years.

Students could make sand clocks or other primitive instruments.

Formulas for Measuring

Formulas for area, perimeter, volume, and surface area usually are introduced in the upper grades. Although formulas are necessary in many measurement situations, they should not take the place of careful development of measurement attributes and the measuring process. The skill of using formulas needs to be developed—but not at the expense of helping students see how formulas are derived. The main emphasis in this section will be on ways to build meaning of the area formulas. The formulas for the other attributes may be developed similarly.

Before formulas are considered, students should be given the opportunity to compare regions of area with and without units. We have already discussed comparing areas without the aid of units by placing one region on top of the other and by cutting one region in order to make the comparison.

When introducing units of area, provide students with experiences in covering a region with a variety of types of units—squares, triangles, rectangles. To find the area of a region, they should count the number of units. Covering many different shapes will help students see the need to approximate and to use smaller units. For example, this region was first covered by one size of squares and then by smaller squares:

When students are thoroughly familiar with counting units covering different shapes, especially rectangles, it is time to introduce the formula for area

In The Classroom 15–3

Areas, Areas, Areas

Objective: Find the area of irregular shapes using familiar shapes.

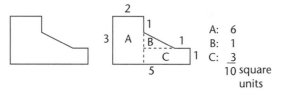

A: 6
B: 1
C: <u>3</u>
10 square units

"Rectangle A is a 2 by 3 so its area is 6 square units. Rectangle C has a base of 3 and a altitude of 1, so its area is 3 square units. The base of triangle C is 2 and its altitude is 1, so its area is 1 square unit. The total area is 10 square units."

▼ Find the area of each of these shapes. The shading indicates that part is missing.

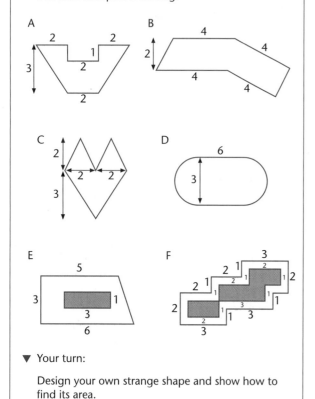

▼ Your turn:

Design your own strange shape and show how to find its area.

the shape into different smaller shapes for which they can use area formulas that they know. There are many different ways to subdivide the shapes. If you try this with students, have them show the different ways they subdivided the shapes.

Rectangle The formula for the area of a rectangle is often the first formula children encounter. Use of the rectangle is appropriate because it can be developed easily, building on models that children may have used for multiplication.

Figure 15–4 shows a sequence of steps that can be used to develop instructional activities that lead to the formula for the area of a rectangle, $A = ba$ (where A is area, b is base, and a is altitude). This form of the formula generalizes better than $A = lw$. Recall in the Snapshot of a Lesson at the beginning of this chapter that the length-and-width interpretation led to initial confusion with the trapezoidal table.

When children measure with square units, the base and altitude will not be an exact number of units. You may have them begin by estimating how many squares it would take to cover the shape. Later, you can develop the idea of using smaller units or fractional parts of the unit.

6 units

4 units

Think

It takes $4 \times 6 = 24$ and about 2 more squares, so the area is 26 square units.

We are not suggesting that you teach the steps as listed in Figure 15–4. It is given as an outline to help you sequence experiences and assess students' understandings. Although some of the steps could be combined into a single activity, step 3 should not be done until children have the experiences listed in step 1. In addition, problems may arise when children are doing step 7 if they have not had prior experience in covering real objects.

One difficulty that children often have with area of a rectangle is that they may learn, by rote, that the area is the length times the width (or base times altitude) but not develop the underlying concepts. Thus, when they are faced with finding the area of a square, they run into difficulty. (It has no side that is longer than the others!) The results of the fourth national assessment (Kouba et al. 1988) showed that seventh-grade performance dropped from 50 percent correct for rectangles to 10 percent correct for squares.

of a rectangle. In this section, we examine steps for developing this formula and then show how to use it to develop the formulas for parallelograms, triangles, trapezoids, and other figures. After learning how to use these formulas, children need experiences such as those on In the Classroom 15–3, in which they cut

Figure 15–4 • One sequence for developing the area formula for a rectangle

Parallelogram After children have worked with the area formula for a rectangle, the area formula for a parallelogram can be developed. Children need background in geometric experiences in which they have compared parallelograms with rectangles and have tried to cut the parallelograms to rearrange them into rectangles. Next, they should identify the base and altitude of parallelograms. Note that any side can be designated as a base, and the altitude depends on what side was chosen.

The next stage in developing the formula is seeing the relationship of the area of a parallelogram with base *b* and altitude *a* and the corresponding rectangle. From exercises such as those on In the Classroom 15–4, children should see the area of a parallelogram is the same as the corresponding rectangle:

$$A = b \times a$$

Triangle Children's understanding of the area of a triangle can be developed from the realization that a triangle is always half of a parallelogram. This development depends on a strong background of geometry, experiences like those described in Chapter 14 and activities such as In the Classroom 15–5. Even when students see that the area of a triangle is half that of a corresponding parallelogram, or

$$A = \frac{1}{2}(b \times a)$$

they have difficulty identifying the altitude, especially in triangles like E in In the Classroom 15–5.

Trapezoid There are many ways to develop the formula for the area of a trapezoid. One of the easiest is to rely again on the area of a parallelogram. Consider the example of finding the area of the following trapezoid.

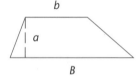

Students can be instructed to make a copy of the trapezoid and place it adjacent to the original:

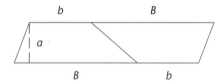

The area formula can now be developed through a series of questions.

What figure have you formed? [a parallelogram]

What is its base? [*B* + *b*]

What is its altitude? [*a*]

What is its area? [*A* = *a*(*B* + *b*)]

How does the area of the trapezoid compare to the area of the parallelogram? [half as much]

Therefore, how might we write a formula for area of a trapezoid? [*A* = ½*a*(*B* + *b*)]

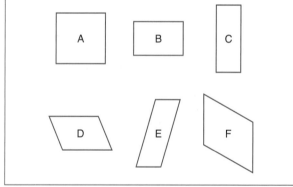
Circle The circle is the one common geometric figure whose area is not directly related to the previous procedures. Students may discover that the formula is logical by cutting a circle into segments and rearranging them to form a pseudo-parallelogram, as shown in Figure 15–5. This interpretation depends on their knowledge of the circumference of a circle being 2p*r*.

COMPARING MEASUREMENTS

After making a measurement, we often use it to solve a problem involving a comparison or an arithmetic operation. In so doing, we may need to change from

In the Classroom 15-5

Make Two of Me!

Objective: Find the area of a triangle.

Materials: Scissors, ruler, and tape.

Directions: Work with a partner. Cut out the triangles below from each of your sheets. Tape them together to make a parallelogram. Use what you know about finding the area of a parallelogram to find the area.

	Base	Altitude	Area of parallelogram	Area of triangle
A				
B				
C				
D				
E				
F				

▼ Describe how you found the area of a triangle?

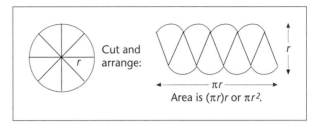

Figure 15–5 • **Picture relating the area of a parallelogram to the area of a circle**

one unit to another *(conversion),* which relies on the *equivalence* relation of the two units.

In this section, we will examine equivalences and conversions within the customary or the metric system. Students should become conversant in each system and not rely on converting between systems.

Equivalences

As you introduce new standard units, you should relate them to the others. For example, suppose you are introducing the millimeter; you should relate it to a centimeter by showing that it is smaller and that it is one-tenth of a centimeter.

After using different units and being given the equivalences, children should learn certain equivalences. Some of these, such as 7 days = 1 week, 60 minutes = 1 hour, and 12 inches = 1 foot, will become known through repeated use. Children need to know that they are expected to know other equivalences.

Although children are no longer required to memorize long tables of equivalences, you should expect them to memorize the ones that are commonly used. The task is easier with metric system because of the standard prefixes and tens relationship between units as indicated in Table 15-2. The table shows the relationship between metric measurements of different units of length, capacity, and mass (or weight). For example, the meter (m) is the base unit for length. A kilometer (km) is 1000 times as long as a meter. A decimeter (dm) is one-tenth of a meter.

Because not all equivalences will be memorized, children must become familiar with using a table of

Table 15–2 • **Most commonly used metric units**

	kilo (k) *1000*	*hecto (h)* *100*	*deka (da)* *10*	Base unit	*deci (d)* *0.1*	*centi (c)* *0.01*	*milli (m)* *0.001*
Length	kilometer (km)			meter (m)		centimeter (cm)	millimeter (mm)
Capacity				liter (l)			milliliter (ml)
Mass	kilogram (kg)			gram (g)			

equivalences. You will need to help them develop the different skills related to equivalences.

The following table and questions illustrate these skills:

Unit	Equivalent
1 day	24 hours
1 hour	60 minutes
1 minute	60 seconds

How many hours in a day?

(This answer is a straightforward reading from the table.)

What part of a day is 1 hour?

(This answer involves knowledge of fractional relations of the units in the table.)

How many seconds in an hour?

(This answer involves conversion of units in the table.)

Area and volume equivalences can be difficult for many children because they are often derived from the linear equivalences. For example, knowing that 1 m = 10 dm allows you to derive 1 m^2 = 100 dm^2 and 1 m^3 = 1000 dm^3. Children need experiences in seeing these basic relationships through models, drawings, and questions such as in Lesson Idea 15–7.

Conversions

To change from one unit to another, children must know the equivalence or relation between the two units. However, by itself, this information is not sufficient to make conversions. Let's look at an example of a class discussion.

MR. BANE: It seems that several of you are stumped on the assignment. Devon, please read the first exercise and let's look at it together.

DEVON: Blank dm equals 5 m.

Mr. Bane writes on the board: _____ dm = 5 m.

MR. BANE: Who can tell me what we are looking for?

GEORGE: How many decimeters there are in 5 meters.

MR. BANE: What do you know about decimeters and meters?

ALANA: A decimeter is about this big and a meter is about this big.

MR. BANE: That's right. Could everyone see Alana's hands? Which unit is larger, the meter or the decimeter?. .. Right, so will it take more than 5 decimeters or less than 5 to make 5 meters?

Lesson Idea 15–7

Solving Conversion Problems with Square Units

▼ Ask students how many square decimeters (dm^2) are in one square meter (m^2). A representation of the relationship is shown below.

1 dm^2

1 m^2

▼ Establish that it would take 100 square or 1 m^2 = 100 dm^2. Show that each row would have 10 and that there would be 10 rows.

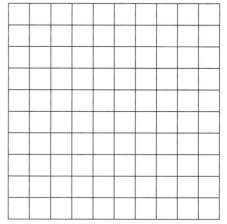

10 × 10 = 100 squares

▼ Use sketches and the model above to answer the following questions.

• Conrad has a piece of cloth that is 3m^2 or 3 m × 1 m. How many dm^2 is that?

• Maria has a blanket that is 15 dm × 10 dm. How many m^2 is it?

KARINA: It'll take more. It takes 10 decimeters to make 1 meter.

Mr. Bane draws this on the board:

MR. BANE: If 1 meter is 10 decimeters, then what would 5 meters be?

DEVON: I see, it's 5 groups of the 10 decimeters or 50 decimeters.

MR. BANE: Good. Let's try another:

$$20 \text{ cm} = \underline{\hspace{1cm}} \text{ dm.}$$

LEON: Centimeters are smaller, they take more; so it won't be as many as 20 decimeters.

MR. BANE: Good. We know our answer must be less than 20.

RANDY: Let's draw a picture like this. Oh, there's no use drawing in all 20 marks. We know 10 centimeters makes 1 decimeter. So we want to know how many tens in 20.

MR. BANE: Right, in this case we can just look at the picture and see that it is 2 decimeters. But what if it was 184 centimeters?

DAVE: We still need to know how many tens in 184—we divide.

JIM: There are 18 decimeters.

MR. BANE: What about the 4 left over?

PAULA: Those are centimeters. We have 18 full decimeters and 4 left-over centimeters.

MR. BANE: Let's write that down:

$$184 \text{ cm} = 18 \text{ dm } 4 \text{ cm}$$

Okay. Try some on your own, and I'll help you if you have questions.

This discussion, although not an initial presentation to the class, points out many good techniques to use in developing conversions. First, Mr. Bane had the children decide whether their answer would be larger or smaller than the number given. This relies on children's knowing the relative sizes of the units and their understanding that the smaller the unit, the more it takes. Second, Mr. Bane tried to have the children visualize the relationship between the units. Third, he related the operation to be used to their understanding of what multiplication and division mean.

If one is doing a lot of metric conversions, there are shortcuts. These depend on the facility to estimate and to multiply and divide by powers of ten. These shortcuts are helpful but should not replace a careful building of the process.

ESTIMATING MEASUREMENTS

Estimating is the mental process of arriving at a measurement without the aid of measurement instruments. There are many reasons to include estimating in the development of measurement. It helps to reinforce the size of units and the relationships among units. It is a practical application—think of all the times you want to know approximately how long, how heavy, or how much something holds.

There are two main types of estimation. In the most common type, the attribute and object are named, and the measurement is unknown. For example, about how long is your arm? In the other type, the measurement is known and the object is to be chosen. For example, what piece of furniture in your room is about one meter long?

By keeping the two classes of estimation in mind, you will be able to expand your repertoire of estimation activities. Several common strategies can be used with either type. You can help children develop these strategies by talking through the various methods that different children use to make an estimation and by presenting the following strategies.

One strategy is to *compare to a referent.* If you know that you are 1 meter 70 centimeters tall, then you can estimate the height of a child who comes up to your waist. Or, if you have to choose a board that is 2 meters long, you will have some idea of the size.

Another strategy is that of *chunking.* In this process, you break the object into subparts and estimate each part. For example, you want to know about how far you walked from your home to the library and the store and then back to your home. If you know that from your home to the library is about a mile, that it's about that same distance from the library to the store, and twice as far from the store back to your home, you walked about four miles altogether.

A refinement of chunking is *unitizing.* In this case, you estimate one part and see how many parts are in the whole. For example, someone asks you to cut a piece of string that is about three meters long. You estimate 1 meter and take three of these. This strategy is a good one to emphasize when you are teaching multiplication because it provides an application of multiplication.

When including estimation in your program, you should try to make it a natural part of measurement activities.

1. Encourage children to see if they can tell about how long or heavy the object before they measure.

2. Look for ways to include estimation in other subject areas:

   About how far did you jump?

   What size paper do you need for your art project?

   About how long did it take you to read the book?

3. Plan estimating activities for their own sake or use brief ones as daily openers for several weeks throughout the year.

The suggestions in on Lesson Idea 15–8 give some ideas to get you started. Once you begin thinking about the things in your room, you will be able to come up with a lot of variations.

Lesson Idea 15–8

About how many centimeters long?

	Estimate	Measure
Little finger	_____	_____
Nose	_____	_____
Foot	_____	_____

Which holds about 2 cups?

A   B   C

Make a decimeter

Draw a snake that you think is a decimeter long.

Draw a tree that you think is a decimeter high.

CONTEST FOR WEDNESDAY

About how much does the wonderful watermelon weigh?

Name	Guess
____	____
____	____

Winner gets the largest piece at Ho-Ho's picnic.

Guess which of the boxes will hold 60 sugar cubes.

x   y   z

About how many squares?

The floor _____

Your desk _____

The bulletin board _____

We'll collect your estimates on Friday.

HUNT   HUNT

There is something in the room that weighs a kilogram.

Can you find it?

One thing to remember: do not call an estimate right or wrong. Help children develop ways to make better estimates, but do not discourage them. Let them check their estimates by measuring. They will know whether they were close or not. You may be surprised to find out who are the good estimators in your class.

CONNECTING ATTRIBUTES

Activities involving two attributes can help children see how the attributes are related or how one attribute is not dependent on the other. For example, by doubling the dimensions of a rectangle, children may see how the area is changed. By examining figures with the same area but different shape, children may see that area is independent of shape. We have included sample activities with suggestions of other variations or extensions. If you do not know the answer, you will be able to find it by doing the activity.

Area and Shape

In the Classroom 15–6 encourages children in grades two through four to investigate the different shapes they can make using two to four squares. For older children, you can extend this activity to more squares and place the restrictions that the squares must have touching sides (not corners) and that two shapes are the same if one is a reflection or rotation (see Chapter 14) of the other. A variation is to use triangular graph paper rather than the square. You also can have children look at figures with the same shapes but different areas.

Volume and Shape

An activity such as the one in In the Classroom 15–6 can be done with cubes. For older children, In the Classroom 15–7, not only has them examine different shapes with constant volume but also ties their investigation to number theory (primes and composites).

Perimeter and Area

Children are often confused about perimeter and area. This confusion may be due partly to a lack of understanding of area and partly to premature introduction of the formulas. There are many activities that can help children see that a figure with a given perimeter may have many different areas. One is found in In the Classroom 15–8. Children also should realize that figures with the same area can have different perimeters. You can modify In the Classroom 15–6 for older children by asking them to find the perimeter of each of the shapes or by challenging them to take five squares and see

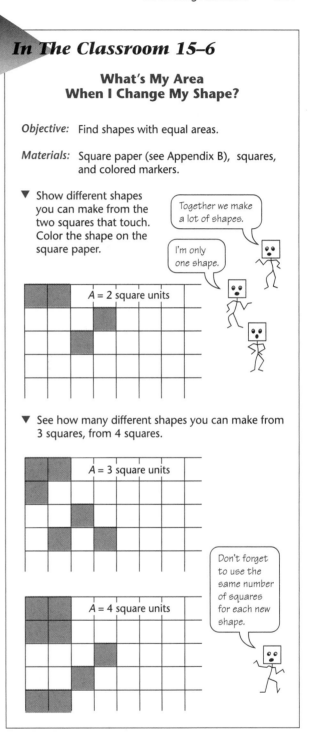

In The Classroom 15–6

**What's My Area
When I Change My Shape?**

Objective: Find shapes with equal areas.

Materials: Square paper (see Appendix B), squares, and colored markers.

▼ Show different shapes you can make from the two squares that touch. Color the shape on the square paper.

Together we make a lot of shapes.

I'm only one shape.

A = 2 square units

▼ See how many different shapes you can make from 3 squares, from 4 squares.

A = 3 square units

A = 4 square units

Don't forget to use the same number of squares for each new shape.

what shape they can make that has the largest perimeter or the smallest perimeter.

Volume and Surface Area

Just as the area of a figure does not depend on the perimeter, the volume does not depend on the surface area. The experiment in In the Classroom 15–9 looks at the relation of lateral surface area to volume. You can vary this activity by having children fold the

In The Classroom 15–7

Same Volume, Different Shape

Objective: Exploring the different shapes of solids that can be made with a given volume.

Materials: Cubes.

I'm 8 cubes — 8 by 1 by 1.
My volume is
8 square units.

I'm 8 cubes — 2 by 2 by 2.
My volume is
8 square units, too!

▼ See how many different rectangular solids you can make with 12 cubes. Record the dimensions and volume of each.

▼ Now try some of these:

7, 9, 16, 11, 13, 18, 15 cubes

▼ How many different solids can you make if the number of cubes is

• prime? _____

• a product of two primes? _____

• a perfect square? _____

▼ How many solids can you make with

24 cubes? _____

In The Classroom 15–8

Do You Know How to Connect Perimeter and Area?

Objective: Explore different areas that can be made from a given perimeter.

Materials: Square paper (1 cm in Appendix B) and pencil.

▼ How many different rectangles can you make with a perimeter of 14 cm? Find the area of each.

I see you followed the rules and made each side a whole number.

Here's one that I made.

$P = 14$ cm
$A = 10$ cm^2

▼ With three other students, try each of the following perimeters: 8 cm, 9 cm, 10 cm, 11 cm, 12 cm, and 13 cm. Make a table of the number of different rectangles you can make from each perimeter.

▼ How many different rectangles do you think you could make if the perimeter were 52 cm? What is your conjecture?

---

papers into thirds (sixths) both ways or make cylinders (a long, thin one and a short, fat one). In middle school, after developing the formula for rectangular solid, students could calculate the volume of each of the tubes in In the Classroom 15–9.

Perimeter and Dimensions

On In the Classroom 15–10, children may expect the pattern that emerges relating the length of each side to the number of sides, but be surprised by the pattern of the number of sides and the height. See if they can describe the pattern and have any explanation.

Metric Relations

In the Classroom 15–11 helps children find some of the important relationships among different metric units. These relationships make the metric system

convenient to use because it gives an easy translation from solid measures to liquid measures.

A Glance at Where We've Been

Measuring is a process that may be used for many attributes. Basically, each attribute is measured in the same way, but the unique characteristics of each make the actual steps differ. Most important in these steps is knowing the attribute that is being measured.

In The Classroom 15–9

What Is the Connection between Volume and Area?

Objective: Exploring the volume of prisms and cylinders with the same lateral area.

Materials: Construction paper (9 in. by 12 in.), tape, and dry filler.

▼ Use construction paper to make two tubes:

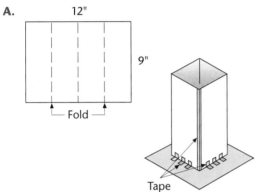

A. 12"
9"
Fold
Tape

B. 12"
9"
Fold
Tape

▼ Guess which tube holds more, or do they hold the same? _____

▼ Fill and see.

▼ Try the same with triangular prisms, hexagonal prisms, octagonal prisms, and cylinders.

▼ Do you have a conjecture about which shape, the shorter or the taller of each pair, will hold the most?

In The Classroom 15–10

What Is the Connection between Perimeter and Height?

Objective: Explore the relationship between polygons with the same perimeter and their height.

Materials: Stiff paper such as file folders.

▼ Cut 6 strips (2 cm by 21 cm) from stiff paper.

▼ Fold one strip into thirds, and tape together to make a fence triangle:

Tape

▼ Fold the other strips into fourths, fifths, sixths, sevenths, and eighths to make additional fences.

▼ Fill it in the chart:

Number of sides	Length of each side in mm	Height (stand it on one side and see how tall)
3	_____ mm	_____ mm
4	_____	_____
5	_____	_____
6	_____	_____
7	_____	_____
8	_____	_____

• Which has the largest area?
• Which has the smallest area?

ment. Children may first assign a number by counting and later by using instruments or formulas. Other suggested ways to help children learn about measuring are estimating and relating two attributes.

By including measuring in your classroom, you have the opportunity to show how mathematics is practical, to develop problem-solving skills, to develop other mathematical ideas, to relate mathematics to other topics, and to make mathematics fun for many children.

This chapter has given many suggestions about ways to develop premeasurement ideas by comparing perceptually, directly, and indirectly. Children should build on these ideas as they use units of measure-

In The Classroom 15–11

Metric to Metric

Objective: Examine the relationship between metric measures of different metric units.

Materials: Liter measuring container, plastic model of a decimeter cube, scales, and a kilogram weight.

1 dm^3 1 liter (l)

Capacity and Volume

▼ Fill the liter measure with water, and pour it into the cubic decimeter.

What did you find?

1 liter = _____ cubic decimeters

Remember: 1 liter = 1000 milliliters (ml)

1 cubic decimeter (dm^3) =
1000 cubic meter (cm^3)

Therefore, 1 ml has a volume of _____ cm^3

Weight and Capacity

▼ Weigh the liter of water.

What did you find?

1 liter = _____ kg of water

Remember: 1 liter = 1000 milliliters (ml)

1 kilogram = 1000 grams (g)

Therefore, 1 ml has a volume of _____ g of water

Weight and Volume

▼ Use your findings:

1 cubic decimeter = _____ kg of water

1 cubic centimeter = _____ g of water

Things to Do:
From What You've Read

1. What are the five steps in the measuring process?
2. What attributes, units, and instruments are included in most elementary mathematics programs?

3. Why should you include measurement in your mathematics program? Choose one reason and give examples of how measurement fulfills that reason.

4. What concepts related to units need to be developed as children have experiences with measurements?

5. List three difficulties children have with measuring instruments.

6. Why do students need to be able to convert from one unit to another?

7. Show how you would find the areas of each of the figures in In the Classroom 15–3.

8. Give three examples of connections that can be made between different attributes. Include at least one connection between time and another attribute.

Things to Do:
Going Beyond This Book

field Additional activities, suggestions, and questions are provided in *Teaching Elementary Mathematics: A Resource for Field Experiences.*

1. You have a child in your class who physically cannot handle a ruler. What would you do in this situation? Give at least two solutions.

2. Describe a set of activities that you could use to introduce a centimeter, a kilogram, a liter, or a square decimeter.

3. Design an activity card that investigates a fixed area to varying perimeters; for example, a fixed area of four square units made with four square tiles. Include the answer to the investigation.

4. Describe how you could help convince a student that these triangles have the same area.

5. Design three task cards for the Snapshot of a Lesson that opened this chapter, one of which is an extension for students who need to be challenged.

6. Critique the video, "Pencil Box Staining," from the series: *Teaching Math: A Video Library, K–4.* What strategies did the students use to find the area?

7. Check the scope-and-sequence chart of a textbook series to see how the introduction of units corresponds to Table 15–1.

8. *field* Units. Develop and teach the lesson described in In the Classroom 15–2. What ideas about units of measurement do children grasp?

9. *field* Discovery. Try the activities in In the Classroom 15–4 or 15–5 with students. What difficul-

ties did they encounter? How did you help them? How would you change the activity?

10. Examine upper-level textbooks to see how they introduce the formula for the area of a rectangle. Contrast this with the sequence suggested in Figure 15–4.

11. For a grade level of your choice, design five estimation activities that include both types of estimation (estimating measurement for a known object and choosing an object that fits a known measurement).

12. *field* Connections. Try the activity in In the Classroom 15–9 or 15–10 with students. Describe your experience, including whether or not the children could make the connections expected.

13. Outline a series of steps for developing the volume formula for rectangular solids, similar to those for developing the area formula for a rectangle.

BOOK NOOK FOR CHILDREN

Allen, Pamela. *Who Sank the Boat?* New York: Putnam, 1990.

Anno, Mitsumasa. *All in a Day.* New York: Putnam, 1990.

Gelman, Rita Golden. *More Spaghetti, I Say!* New York: Scholastic, 1977.

Hutchins, Pat. *Happy Birthday, Sam.* New York: Penguin, 1985.

Myller, Rolf. *How Big Is a Foot?* New York: Dell Publishing, 1991.

Pluckrose, Henry. *Capacity.* New York: Franklin Watts, 1982.

Youldon, Gillian. *Sizes.* New York: Franklin Watts, 1982.

Selected References

Battista, Michael T. "How Many Blocks?" *Mathematics Teaching in the Middle School,* 3 (March–April 1998), pp. 404–411.

Burns, Marilyn. *Math and Literature (K–4).* Sausilito, Calif.: Math Solutions Publications, 1992.

Carpenter, Thomas P.; Corbitt, Mary Kay; Kepner, Henry S., Jr.; Lindquist, Mary Montgomery; and Reys, Robert E. *Results from the Second Mathematics Assessment of the National Assessment of Educational Progress.* Reston, Va.: NCTM, 1981.

Duke, Charlotte. "Tangrams and Area." *Mathematics Teaching in the Middle School,* 3 (May 1998), pp. 485–487.

Fry, Nancy, and Tsarides, Catherine. "Metric Mall." *Arithmetic Teacher,* 37 (September 1989), pp. 6–11.

Harrison, William R. "What Lies Behind Measurement?" *Arithmetic Teacher,* 34 (March 1987), pp. 22–23.

Jensen, Robert J. (ed.). *Research Ideas for the Classroom: Early Childhood Mathematics.* Reston, Va.: NCTM, and New York: Macmillan, 1993.

Johnson, Gretchen L. "Using a Metric Unit to Help Preservice Teachers Appreciate the Value of Manipulative Materials." *Arithmetic Teacher,* 35 (October 1988), pp. 14–20.

Kenney, Patricia Ann, and Kouba, Vicky L. "What Do Students Know about Measurement"? In *Results from the Sixth Mathematics Assessment of the National Assessment of Educational Progress* (eds. Patricia Ann Kenney and Edward A. Silver). Reston Va.: NCTM, 1997, pp. 141–163.

Kliman, Marlene. "Integrating Mathematics and Literature in the Elementary Classroom." *Arithmetic Teacher,* 40 (February 1993), pp. 318–321.

Kouba, Vicky L.; Brown, Catherine A.; Carpenter, Thomas P.; Lindquist, Mary Montgomery; Silver, Edward A.; and Swafford, Jane O. "Results of the Fourth NAEP Assessment of Mathematics: Measurement, Geometry Data Interpretation, Attitudes, and Other Topics." *Arithmetic Teacher,* 35 (May 1988), pp. 10–16.

Lindquist, Mary Montgomery. "Estimation and Mental Computation." *Arithmetic Teacher,* 34 (January 1987), pp. 16–17.

Lindquist, Mary Montgomery. "Implementing the Standards: The Measurement Standards." *Arithmetic Teacher,* 37 (October 1989), pp. 22–26.

Lindquist, Mary Montgomery, and Dana, Marcia E. "The Neglected Decimeter." *Arithmetic Teacher,* 25 (October 1977), pp. 10–17.

Martin, W. Gary, and Strutchens, Marilyn E. "Geometry and Measurement." In *Results from the Seventh Mathematics Assessment of the National Assessment of Educational Progress* (eds. Edward A. Silver and Patricia Ann Kenney). Reston Va.: NCTM, 2000.

National Council of Teachers of Mathematics. *Principles and Standards for School Mathematics.* Reston, Va.: NCTM, 2000.

Owens, Douglas T. (ed.). *Research Ideas for the Classroom: Middle Grades Mathematics.* Reston, Va.: NCTM, and New York: Macmillan, 1993.

Payne, Joseph N. (ed.). *Mathematics for the Young Child.* Reston, Va.: NCTM, 1990.

Silverman, Helene. "Ideas." *Arithmetic Teacher,* 37 (March 1990), pp. 26–32.

Teaching Math: A Video Library, K–4. South Burlington, VT.: The Annenberg/CPB Math and Science Collection, 1995.

U.S. Department of Education. *Pursuing Excellence: A Study of U.S. Eighth-Grade Mathematics and Science Teaching, Learning, Curriculum, and Achievement in International Context.* Washington, D.C.: U.S. Government Printing Office, 1996.

U.S. Department of Education. *Pursuing Excellence: A Study of U.S. Fourth-Grade Mathematics and Science Achievement in International Context.* Washington, D.C.: U.S. Government Printing Office, 1997.

Wilson, Patricia S., and Osborne, Alan. "Foundational Ideas in Teaching about Measure." In *Teaching Mathematics in Grades K–8* (ed. Thomas R. Post). Toronto: Allyn and Bacon, 1988, pp. 78–110.

Young, Sharon, "Ideas." *Arithmetic Teacher,* 38 (September 1990), pp. 23–34.

Data Analysis, Statistics, and Probability

First graders are gathered on the rug at the front of the classroom with their teacher. For several weeks, they have been rinsing and saving their lunch drink cartons for a science project. Children need opportunities to build and construct graphs. This first-grade lesson provides some valuable experiences and, while doing so, moves naturally from concrete toward symbolic representation of data. Graphs help us organize and analyze data. Once constructed, they trigger many questions that help develop graph-reading skills and lead to better understanding of data. The teacher knows that involving students in collecting data and formulating questions is an important part of problem solving.

TEACHER: We have been keeping track of the drink cartons saved from our lunches. Yesterday, one of

you wondered how many people have been drinking chocolate milk. Here are the chocolate milk cartons we collected day last week. We can answer our question more easily if we make a graph.

The teacher spreads out a vinyl tablecloth that has been marked in a grid of 5-inch boxes. A column of boxes for each day of the week has already been labeled. The children place one milk carton in each box under the day of the week, forming a real graph.

TEACHER: Now let's graph this information on grid paper.

Look at our graph carefully. I want you to ask a question that could be answered from this graph. Bob, your hand was up first.

BOB: How many students drank milk in our school?

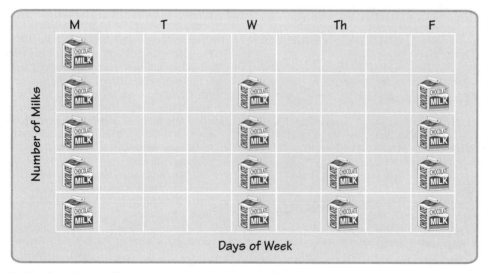

Daily chocolate milk counts in our class last week

GLORIA (AFTER A LONG WAIT): The graph doesn't answer that question. It only shows information about our room.

TEACHER: That's right, Gloria. This graph only shows what happened in our room. Also, it doesn't tell us how many drank milk, only how many drank chocolate milk. That reminds us to read the title of the graph so that everyone will know what it represents. Now, let's hear another question. Aaron?

AARON: How many people drank chocolate milk Wednesday?

SHARON: Four.

TEACHER: Doug, let's hear your question.

DOUG: On which day did no one drink chocolate milk?

SHARON: Tuesday.

DOUG: That's right, because the cafeteria was out of chocolate milk that day.

TEACHER: Do you have a question, Kelly?

KELLY: On which day did we drink the most chocolate milk?

SHARON: Monday had the most. There were five cartons that day.

JANE: Would next week look like this?

Other questions are posed and discussed. A bit later in the lesson, the teacher continues.

TEACHER: Let's look at the chocolate milk we drank for the last two weeks. Here are tallies of the cartons for each day.

Let's make a graph of them on this paper.

SANDY: Our graph paper isn't tall enough!

TEACHER: What do you mean?

SANDY: We can only show six cartons on the paper, but there were eight cartons on Monday.

TEACHER: Could we do any trading here?

SANDY: What do you mean?

TEACHER: In place value, when we get ten ones we trade for one ten.

SANDY: But we don't have ten.

TEACHER: Maybe we can make other trades. For example, we trade five pennies for a nickel or. . . .

SANDY: Two nickels for a dime.

SHARON I got it—we can trade two cartons for one square on the grid.

TEACHER: That's a nice idea, let's try it. We would color four squares for Monday. How many for Tuesday?

SHARON: One. And two for Wednesday.

SANDY: Two and one-half for Thursday and five for Friday.

Daily chocolate milk counts in our class for the last two weeks

TEACHER: This graph is almost finished.

SANDY: It looks done to me . . . what else could we do?

TEACHER: We need to show on the graph what each box represents.

The code is recorded in a highly visible place beside the graph:

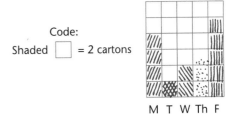

Daily chocolate milk counts in our class for the last two weeks

Later, in the computer lab, a couple of children used a graphing program to display their milk carton data in a picture graph and then a circle graph.

Introduction

Statistics and probability provide a meaningful context for promoting problem solving and critical thinking, communication, developing number sense, and applying computation. The study of these topics supports a problem-solving or investigative approach to learning and doing mathematics. Students are engaged in doing real mathematics. Statistics and probability are now highly visible topics in elementary school mathematics programs. Therefore, NCTM's *Principles and Standards for School Mathematics* recommend increased attention to data analysis (NCTM 2000). The shift of attention to these areas has been dramatic and reflects the growing importance of analyzing data in our daily lives.

Increased attention to statistics and probability in elementary mathematics programs has increased student performance in these areas. For example, the National Assessment of Educational Progress (NAEP) indicates that although there are areas that still need improvement, student progress levels have increased significantly from the fifth assessment to the sixth (Kenney and Silver 1997).

Let's look at some reasons for including the study of statistics and probability in elementary and middle school.

- **Children encounter ideas of statistics and probability outside of school every day.**

Communication media rely on statistical techniques for summarizing information. Radio, television, newspapers, and the Internet bombard us with information. For example, news reports present national economic and social statistics, opinion polls, weather reports, and medical, business, and financial data.

The current demand for information-processing skills is much greater than it was twenty-five years ago, and technological advances will place a far greater premium on such skills in the years ahead. Many consumer and business decisions are based on market research and sales projections. However, statistics about issues or the quality of commercial products can be misleading to the public. If these data are to be understood and used widely, every educated person must be able to process such information effectively and efficiently. An intelligent consumer, able to make informed decisions, must be able to understand and use statistics and probability.

The data students encounter outside of school are often presented in a graphical, statistical, or probabilistic form:

Graphical: Where are the jobs?

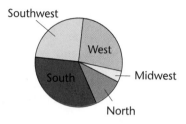

Statistical: The mean salary of professional baseball players is $2,350,000 a year.

Probabilistic: The probability of rain today is 0.35.

Each of these statements needs to be understood if meaningful interpretations are to be made.

The context and format of the way such information is presented vary greatly, but correct interpretation of the information often requires the application of a variety of mathematics. Consider, for example, the mathematical concepts involved in weather reports (decimals, percents, and probability), public opinion polls (sampling techniques and errors of measurement), advertising claims (hypothesis testing), and monthly government reports involving unemployment, inflation, and energy supplies (percents, prediction, and extrapolation).

- **Statistics and probability provide connections to other mathematics topics or school subjects.**

The study of data provides an excellent opportunity for curriculum integration. As mentioned earlier, a variety of mathematics topics are often included in statistical formats. In addition, statistics and probability are often used as tools during the study of other mathematics topics. For example, each day kindergarten children create a picture graph with their photos to show who is present and absent. In doing so, they practice basic counting skills. A third-grade lesson involves estimating. The children may graph their estimates for the number of candies in single-serving packages. After counting the actual number of candies, a second graph may be created, displaying the actual number of candies in each package. The children are able to compare their estimates with the actual results. Fourth graders are studying measurement in centimeters. After measuring the height of each student in the class, the students may decide to find the mean, median, mode, and range so they can better understand their data. As sixth graders conduct a probability simulation with dice, they use fractions, decimals, and percents to report their results.

Statistics and probability are also easily integrated into other school subjects. For example, second graders might use graphs in reading to keep track of numbers and types of books they have read. Fifth-grade students conducting a science experiment on rolling a car down ramps of various heights may calculate the mean distance for the number of trials at each height. In social studies, graphs and charts are frequently used to display information about populations or geographic areas. In physical education class, students often graph pretest data from physical fitness tests and compare it with posttest results at the end of the year. First graders, reading folk tales in language arts may develop a chart listing which events from the stories are possible and which are impossible. Effective teachers should look for ways to make data analysis an integral part of the elementary and middle school curriculum. It can be useful in many contexts and students will have greater success if they use statistical techniques all year long rather than in a single unit.

- **Statistics and probability provide opportunities for computational activity in a meaningful setting.**

Data are not merely numbers but numbers with a context. The number 12 in the absence of a context carries no information, but saying that a baby weighed twelve pounds at birth makes it easy to comment about its size! Data provide many opportunities to think, use, understand, and interpret numbers, rather than simply carrying out arithmetical operations. Using data helps further develop number sense. Working with real data requires judgment in choosing methods and interpreting results. Thus, statistics and probability are not taught in elementary school for their own sake but because they provide an effective way to develop quantitative understanding and mathematical thinking.

For example, calculating the mean price of six CDs is a routine exercise in arithmetic. However, noticing that the prices of six CDs vary, deciding which is the best buy, and determining how much can be saved help develop mathematical thinking, as well as further promoting respect for the power and usefulness of mathematics.

Graphing, statistics, and probability should not be viewed or treated in isolation. Their study provides numerous opportunities to review and apply much mathematics in a variety of real-world situations. For example, understanding of whole numbers, fractions, decimals, percents, ratios, and proportion is essential and often called upon. Many computational skills are reviewed and polished as they are applied in graphing or doing statistics and probability.

The content standard, Data Analysis, Statistics, and Probability, in the *Principles and Standards for School Mathematics* (NCTM 2000), highlights key expectations. As you can see from this standard, the study of statistics and probability should engage students actively. Students need to go beyond examining preformed graphs and results from experiments. They need to be involved asking questions, collecting data, organizing and displaying their data, making conjectures, and reporting their results. In this chapter we will discuss how to involve students with statistics, which includes using data collection, display, and analysis as well as probability, which allows us to predict what is likely to happen and how often it might occur.

DATA ANALYSIS

A statistical investigation typically is completed in several steps, which include posing a question and collecting data to answer the question, displaying the collected data, and analyzing and communicating results. We will examine each of these steps.

Posing a Question and Collecting Data

We must begin with a good question or problem that interests students and where the answer is not immediately obvious. The question should also clearly give students a reason for gathering, analyzing, and presenting data. Allow students to brainstorm questions they would like to answer or problems they have observed. There is a real benefit to having students identify their own questions or problems as they will take ownership of the investigation and motivation will be high (Borhan et al. 1995). Questions may come from a variety of sources. In the Classroom 16–1, Let's Find Out, gives a few examples. These ideas may be shared with children to help them brainstorm the kind of questions they might ask as they plan their survey.

Once a suitable question has been identified, students will need to plan how to collect the data needed to answer the question. Communication skills are very important during this stage. To be successful, students must be able to develop clear survey questions and logical steps for their experiments or

In The Classroom 16–1

Let's Find Out

Objective: Planning and conducting a survey

Steps

1. Think of a question you would like to answer. Here are some ideas to get you started.

   • **Questions about ourselves:** Who can tie our shoes? How far can we throw a softball? What is our class's typical height, eye color, shoe size, number in family, amount of allowance, pets . . . ?

   • **Questions about opinions or feelings:** How do you feel about fractions? Does life exist on other planets? What should be done about pollution? What country do you want to study in social studies? What is your favorite television show, song, book, sport, color, food . . . ?

   • **Questions about the world:** Which month has the most birthdays? What is the most popular color of car in the school parking lot? Which brand of cookie has the most chocolate chips? How many paper towels do we use in one day? What is the effect of fertilizer on bean plant growth? What type of paper airplane will fly the farthest?

   My Question: _____

   _____

2. Plan the survey by answering these questions.

   a. Where or from whom will I collect the data?

   b. How will I collect the data?

   c. How much data will I collect?

   d. When will I collect the data?

   e. How will I record the data as I collect them?

   f. What else do I need to do before I start collecting data?

3. Collect your data!

Surveys

Survey data result from collecting information. These data may range from a national public opinion poll or observing cars pass the window, to simply tallying the ages of students in a class. The actual data used depends on student interest and maturity, but survey data collected by students provides a freshness that increases student interest and sustains persistence in related problem-solving activities. A good source of data is the U.S. Census Bureau. Their Web address is http://www.census.gov/. Computer software is also available that allows students to design a survey and have the persons surveyed enter their responses directly into the computer. Once the data have been collected, the program can display results in a table or in several types of graphs.

Each question from In the Classroom 16–1 gives students the opportunity to collect data themselves. A lesson built around Lesson Idea 16–1 will sharpen data-collecting techniques, and a host of other idea starters is available (Bamberger and Hughes 1995, Freeman 1986, Lindquist et al. 1992, Zawojewski et al. 1991). In planning a survey like the one in Lesson Idea 16–1, students are required to refine and polish their questions to get whatever information they are seeking, which in itself is an important and valuable experience.

Lesson Idea 16–1

Counting Cars

Let's find how many cars, buses, and trucks pass by our school.

Before beginning this survey, we need to agree on some things.

• What streets will we survey?

• What day will the survey be conducted?

• What time will the survey start?

• How long will the survey last?

▼ Why do these questions need to be answered before starting the survey?

▼ Name two other important questions that need to be answered before beginning.

simulations. They must communicate with others to negotiate the details of the investigation. They must find a clear and efficient method of recording their data. Students may collect data from surveys, experiments, and simulations (Zawojewski 1991), all of which typically involve counting or measuring. Data may be recorded in a variety of ways such as using tally marks or placing information in a table. Computer software may also be used for recording data.

Experiments

Experiments may be somewhat more advanced than surveys. When students conduct experiments, in addition to using observation and recording skills, they often incorporate the use of the scientific method (Zawojewski et al. 1991). For example, students may design an experiment to measure the effect of applying different types of fertilizer on plant growth or compare flight times of different paper airplanes. They may try to determine which brand of tissue is the most absorbent. Students may play a spinner game to determine if it is fair to all players.

Simulations

Although a simulation is similar to an experiment, random number devices such as coins, dice, spinners, or computer programs are also used to model real-world occurrences (Zawojewski et al. 1991). Students may start with a probability question such as "If I flip a coin twenty times, how many times will it land on heads?" Then they carry out the simulation and record data as they are generated. We will discuss more about probability simulations later in this chapter.

Sampling is another method of data collection that students can simulate. In statistics, the whole group you are studying is called the *population*. In real-life data collection, there are times when it is impossible or impractical to collect data from a complete population. A *sample* is a subset of a population. Samples are often collected to learn more about public health issues or the public's buying habits, or to predict election results. It is important for students to realize that the use of a particular sample may make a survey biased and to discuss ways to reduce bias. For example, let's say some students are surveying the students in their room in order to purchase some new games to be used during recess. The population to be surveyed is Ms. Smith's fifth-grade class. However, if the students interview only the girls in the class (a sample) their results will probably not reflect the wishes of both boys and girls. Students to be interviewed could be randomly selected by drawing names out of a hat, and that would more likely reflect the total population.

Researchers have developed a method of collecting samples so they may learn more about a population that would be impossible to survey completely. For example, when wildlife biologists want to count the number and types of fish in a lake they use a mark-recapture technique. The biologist captures a number of fish, counts them, marks them, and releases them. More samples are collected and the number of marked fish in the sample are compared in a ratio to the unmarked fish in the sample. The biologist may then use the data from the samples collected to estimate the total population of fish and the ratio of marked and unmarked fish. These techniques and how they can be simulated with elementary and middle school students using beans, crackers, or games are explained further in Hitch and Armstrong (1994), Morita (1999), and Quinn and Wiest (1999).

DISPLAYING DATA

After data have been collected, graphs are often used to display data and help others digest the results. Tables, tallies, or pictures are also sometimes used to present data. Many different types of graphs exist. Knowledge related to constructing and interpreting the various types of graphs is an important part of mathematics instruction and should begin in the primary grades. Children gain competence with age and experience. The National Assessment of Educational Progress (NAEP) shows that although only about half of fourth-grade students can read and use tables, picture graphs, and bar graphs, most eighth-grade students can do so (Kenney and Silver 1997).

For young children, initial work with data means they will begin by working with concrete objects in their environment. Collecting and counting objects, sorting them into categories, and then displaying them in an organized fashion is a good introduction. For example, the children may each bring a favorite book then collaborate to organize their collection. A *real graph* or concrete graph is developed as the actual books are arranged in rows. As students work with their "data," counting skills are also practiced. Older students may work with larger collections of objects, and by grouping the objects into groups of tens, place value may be reinforced. The teacher must also find ways to help children move from the concrete, real-graph representations to more symbolic representations.

Here is a way to get started. First, ask each child to choose one piece of his or her favorite fruit from a basket and position this piece of fruit on a table, as shown in Figure 16–1A. The resulting rows of fruit represent the children's preferences in a concrete fashion as a real graph. Next, ask each child to draw the fruit he or she chose on an index card, then have the children use the cards to build a picture-bar graph, as in Figure 16–1B. Although this graph is a less concrete means of showing the information, most children still find it a very meaningful way to represent their preferences.

Finally, this same information can be expressed more symbolically in the bar graph in Figure 16–1C.

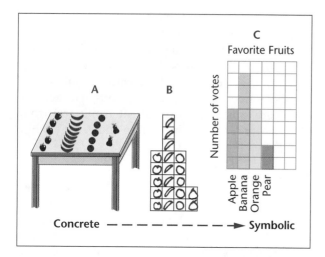

Figure 16–1 • One method for introducing graphs

Children can also be given blank paper and encouraged to organize and report their data on the page in a way that makes sense to them. In this way, children learn to communicate their information in ways that are meaningful both to themselves and others (Folkson 1996). Regardless of how the data are presented, pertinent questions can be asked to encourage thoughtful interpretation of the graphs. Such questions might include the following:

How many children prefer apples?

What is the favorite fruit?

How many different fruits are shown?

How many children contributed to the graph?

These types of questions result naturally from the data and provide valuable opportunities for students to ask as well as answer questions.

We will examine the most common types of graphs used in elementary and middle school. We'll also show some examples typical of those found in elementary programs as well as those that demonstrate how the same graphical form is used in real life.

A *graph* is a type of diagram that may be used to visually present or illustrate data. At the elementary and middle school level, students frequently encounter and create real, picture, bar, and circle graphs. As they move through school, the types of graphs they read and create will increase and become more complex. For elementary children, the process of construction of a graph helps them learn about its critical features and is a valuable activity. However, some graphs are more difficult to create than others, and construction may develop into a

lengthy process. If the main purpose of visually displaying the data is simply to learn more about the data and easily examine results, several alternatives exist to having students create complete publication-quality graphs by hand. By using some of the materials mentioned below and illustrated in Figure 16–2, data may be displayed immediately as it is being collected. Russell and Corwin (1989) call these quick graphs "sketch graphs" or "working" graphs. Sketch graphs can be created quickly and provide a visual representation of the shape of the data. They should be clear, but they may not be neat and may not ever be displayed for public view. Sketch graphs don't require labels or titles and don't require time-consuming attention to construction. Sketch graphs may be made with concrete materials such as those listed below or with paper and pencil.

Quick and Easy Graphing Materials

- *Connecting cubes or blocks* may be stacked in towers on a desk or in the chalk tray.
- *Counters* such as beans or plastic bears may be placed on a grid or in cups or bowls. Ice cube trays may also be used to hold the counters, placing one counter in each ice cube slot.
- *Plastic links* or *paper clips* may be hung from push pins.
- *Self-stick notes* may be arranged on the chalkboard or posterboard grid.
- *Technology* Computer graphing programs are available that are simple enough for even young children to use. As an added benefit, once the data have been entered, students can quickly and easily see their data displayed and printed in more than one type of graph or with a different scale. The graphing calculator is another tool that may be used for making graphs. Graphing calculators designed for middle grades allow students to create picture graphs, bar graphs, and pie graphs.

Line Plots and Stem-and-Leaf Plots

A *plot* is another type of graph used to visually display data. In recent years, plots have been used frequently in magazines and newspapers because they provide efficient ways of showing information, as well as comparing different sets of data. Some plots, such as line plots and stem-and-leaf plots, are quick and easy to make and can be used as sketch graphs to get an initial look at the shape of the data.

Line Plots A line plot may be used to quickly display numerical data with a small range. The range and distribution of the data may be clearly seen in the display. Line plots may be successfully used at all levels. Young children can more easily create a line plot than a bar graph, and older students will enjoy the quick feedback they receive when sketching a line plot.

Let's say at a class party, some third-grade students receive candy in single-serving packages. The children open the packs and someone suggests they count to see how many candies they each received. The class begins counting, and soon each child begins calling out his or her total. The teacher writes the totals on the chalkboard as they are called out:

17, 19, 21, 20, 15, 18, 22, 17,
20, 18, 17, 18, 22, 17, 20

Discussion continues as students try to draw conclusions from the data. The teacher suggests putting the data into a line graph so it will be easier to see and understand. The children notice that the smallest value is 15 and the largest is 22, so they direct the teacher to draw a horizontal number line beginning with 15 and ending with 22. Next, an *x* is placed above each number to mark its frequency in the set of data. Figure 16–3 shows the completed line plot. The students are easily able to see that 17 occurred most often, followed by 18 and 20. The student who had only 15 in the package felt cheated, and those who had 22 felt lucky. The class talked about why there might not always be the same amount in each package.

Stem-and-Leaf Plots A stem-and-leaf plot is another quick way to display data and provides a quite different representation than when the data are arranged in a line plot or bar graph. It works best

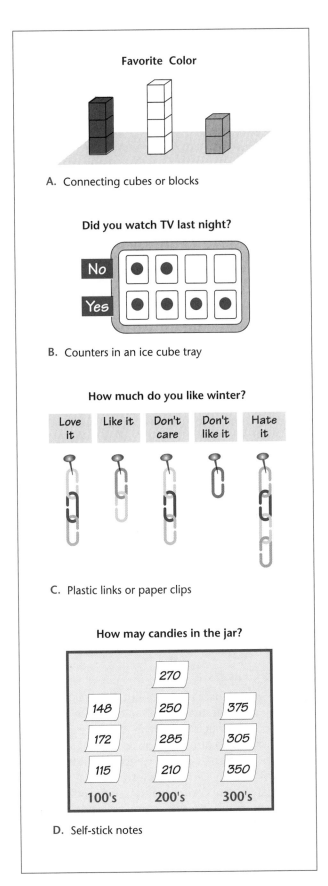

Figure 16–2 • Quick and easy graphing materials

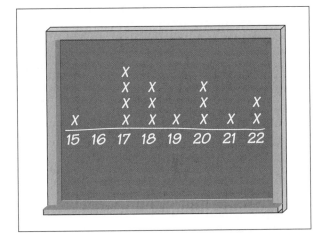

Figure 16–3 • Line plot of number of candies per package

Figure 16–4 • Stem-and-leaf plot of number of candies per package

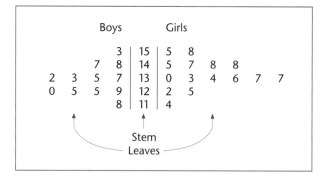

Figure 16–5 • Stem-and-leaf plot of heights of boys and girls

Boys				Girls			
118	132	135	137	122	155	114	125
120	125	147	129	155	137	136	137
133	148	153	125	134	130	133	145
				148	148	147	

with data which span over several decades since the plot is usually organized by tens. This plot is a little more abstract than the line plot, but it may be successfully used with students in the intermediate grades.

It is often useful to display data in more than one way. Let's take the candy data we just displayed in a line plot and arrange it in a stem-and-leaf plot (Figure 16–4). To begin, we divide each value into tens and ones. The tens become the "stem," and the ones will be the "leaves." We notice that the data fall into two decades, the tens and twenties. A vertical line is drawn with the tens values (1 and 2) on the left of the line. The ones values are placed on the right side. By examining the plot, it is easy to see that 17 occurred most often in this set of data. From this arrangement we can also see that more packages contained candy amounts in the tens than in the twenties. Now all those students who had twenty or more feel lucky.

Stem-and-leaf plots may also be used to compare two sets of data in the same plot. In the intermediate grades, students can successfully compare more than one data set. Suppose you wanted to explore some questions related to the height of students in a fourth-grade class. Comparing the heights of the boys and girls will generate some interesting discussion. Questions such as "Which group is tallest?" and "Which group has the most variability?" are naturals. After some conjectures have been made, it is time to have students measure their heights and begin to analyze those data. Here are some steps that lead to stem-and-leaf plots. The heights of the twenty-seven fourth-grade students (fifteen girls and twelve boys) are reported in centimeters in the following table:

Rather than use a traditional frequency distribution, the values are organized in a stem-and-leaf plot, shown in Figure 16–5. The stem represents the hundreds and tens places of the data on student height, and the leaves represent the ones place. Thus, in the last row of Figure 16–5, 8/11/4 means one girl has a height of 114 cm and one boy is 118 cm tall. The stem-and-leaf plot preserves the individual measures while revealing the general shape of the organized data. Thus, it presents all of the information, in this case for both groups, and provides a clear visual picture of it.

In addition to the quick graphs and plots mentioned previously, students should also be involved with graphs that require more construction time and effort.

Picture Graphs

In *picture graphs*, data are represented by pictures. For example, children may graph pictures of their favorite food or the pets they own. A picture can represent one object (Figure 16–6) or several (Figure 16–7). To properly interpret picture graphs, children must know how much each object represents. Research shows that students often ignored such coding information when interpreting graphs (Bright and Hoeffner 1993). This is why coding was highlighted in the opening Snapshot of a Lesson. Creating and reading picture graphs is a logical transition for young children as they move from real graphs to more abstract displays.

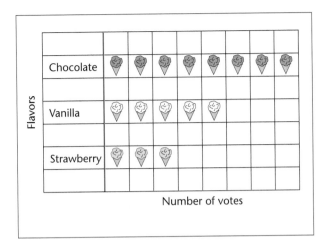

Figure 16–6 • A picture graph in which each picture represents one object

Estimated school retention rates in the United States, 1982 to 2000

Each figure represents 10 persons:

For every 100 pupils in the 5th grade in Fall 1982,

77 graduated from high school in Fall 1990,

and 25 are likely to earn bachelor's degrees in 2000.

Figure 16–7 • A picture graph in which each picture represents several objects (From surveys, estimates, and projections of the National Center for Education Statistics.)

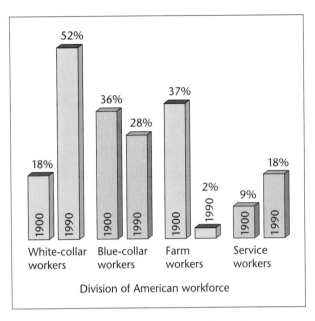

Figure 16–8 • A bar graph with values shown directly on the bars

Bar Graphs

As you saw in the Snapshot of a Lesson, even young children can move from making real and picture graphs to making *bar graphs*. Bar graphs are used mostly for discrete or separate and distinct data; the bars represent these data. For example, they might graph the number of birthdays in each month or the number of students who travel to school by bus, car, or foot. Figure 16–1 showed that values can be read from the axis. Figure 16–8 shows that other times the values are reported directly on the graph. Bar

graphs are often used for quick visual comparisons of categories of data and are appropriate for all ages.

Pie Graphs

A *pie graph* is a circle representing the whole, with wedges reporting percents of the whole, as illustrated in Figure 16–9. The pie graph is popular because it is easy to interpret. It has major limitations in that it represents only a fixed moment in time, and it cannot exceed 100 percent. For example, students may graph how they spend their weekly allowance or the favorite colors of the class. While students in the upper elementary grades can read and interpret pie graphs, effective construction may require the use of fractions, percents, proportions, and measurement

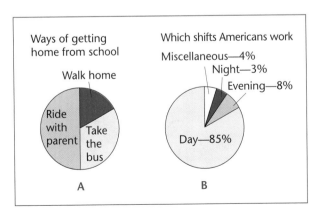

Figure 16–9 • Pie graphs

of angles. Pie graph construction is more appropriate for middle school students. However, there is an effective, concrete method of connecting pie graphs to bar graphs, which elementary students may successfully complete.

As we illustrated with the line and stem-and-leaf plots, showing the same data in different displays can be both useful and effective. For example, the data shown in the bar graph in Figure 16–1 can be easily shown in a pie graph. Cubes of different colors to match the fruits could be strung together as shown here:

Then the string can be placed in a circle:

This experience helps make a connection between bar and pie graphs. It also provides a natural context for fractions and percents. For example, the pie graph suggests that $1/4$ of the fruits are oranges.

This model can be extended by placing a meter tape, or a 100-centimeter strip of paper marked with similar units, around the circle of blocks to form concentric circles, as shown in Figure 16–10A. Comparing the sections suggested by the different groups of colored blocks with the markers on the strip or meter tape will identify percents that can be easily read.

As a more concrete visualization, twenty children can be arranged in a circle, and the "wedges" of a circle graph duplicated with string, as is illustrated in Figure 16–10B. Both of the models in Figure 16–10 make it easy to estimate or read the percents and conclude, for example, that more than 50 percent of the children chose apples or bananas.

Similar observations might have been made directly from the bar graph in Figure 16–1, but conclusions involving fractions and percents are much more obvious from the pie graph. The process of moving from a bar graph to a pie graph also provides different perspectives for the same set of data, and research suggests that developing such multiple perspectives helps promote greater understanding (Shaughnessy 1992).

Line Graphs

Line graphs are effective for showing trends over time. In line graphs, points on a grid are used to represent continuous or uninterrupted data. Each axis is clearly labeled, so the data shown can be interpreted properly. A wide variety of line graphs exist and are used, but two basic assumptions are inherent:

1. The data are continuous rather than discrete.
2. Change is accurately represented with linear functions (that is, by lines) rather than some other curve.

As Figure 16–11 shows, line graphs are particularly good for showing variations or changes over time, such as hours of daylight, temperatures, rainfall, and so on. For example, students could graph

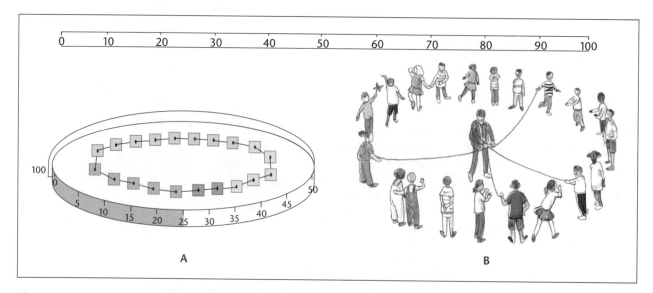

Figure 16–10 • Models for interpreting circle graph data

Figure 16–11 • A line graph of a single set of varying data

plant growth in a science experiment. Line graphs are also an effective visual means of comparing several sets of data, as illustrated in Figure 16–12. Constructing or interpreting line graphs requires students to examine both horizontal and vertical axes, which is good preparation for coordinates. Line graphs are used most often at the middle school level.

Box Plots

A *box plot* summarizes data and provides a visual means of showing variability, that is, the spread of

data. The box plot shown in Figure 16–13 summarizes the student height data previously used very succinctly. The median is a key reference point; more will be said about the median in the next section. The lower hinge is the median of the lower half of the data, and the upper hinge is the median of the upper half. These are found by computing the medians of the data in the lower and upper halves, respectively. The midspread is a measure of variability and is the difference between the upper and lower hinges. In Figure 16–13, the midspread for the boys is 17 (142 – 125) and that for the girls is 16.5 (148 – 131.5). The smallest and largest heights represent the lower extreme and the upper extreme. The lines (also called "whiskers") extending from the top of the upper hinge to the largest value and then from the bottom of the lower hinge to the smallest value provide another visual indication of variability.

The box plot shows many things. For example, it shows the median height for the girls is greater than that for the boys. Although the groups have about the same midspread, the boys are a bit more evenly distributed throughout the box than the girls are. (Why? Because the median of the boys is closer to the middle of the box than is the median of the girls.) The box plot is derived naturally from a stem-and-leaf plot. The box plot shows many important characteristics of a group visually and, when two or more groups are shown on the same graph, it allows comparisons to be made easily. The box plot is an appropriate display for middle school students to construct. It provides a nice connection to descriptive statistics such as median and range. The scatter plot is another graphical representation that can be introduced in middle school and is often used when examining data for trends. The scatter plot also has connections to coordinate graphing in geometry and algebraic thinking, discussed in Chapters 13 and 14.

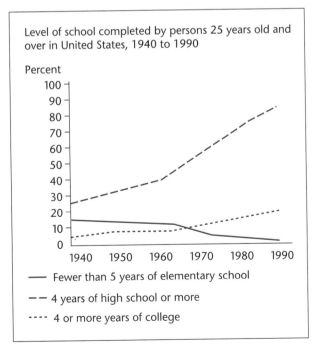

Figure 16–12 • A line graph comparing several sets of data

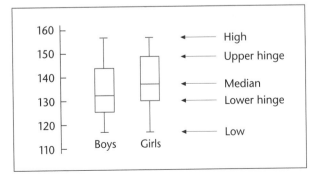

Figure 16–13 • Box plot for heights of boys and girls

Graphical Roundup

Each of these graphs deserves instructional attention as students examine ways to display their data. Children need experience constructing them and interpreting information that is represented. In the children's book *The Best Vacation Ever* (Murphy 1997), a little girl collects and displays data for her family so they can plan a vacation. Lesson Idea 16–2

Lesson Idea 16–2

More Counting Cars

Now that we've collected our data, we need to display and present it. Let's make a graph and report on it.

Before graphing and presenting our data, we need to agree on some things.

Graphing

- Shall we start with a sketch graph?
- What kind of graph will best display our data?
- Can we show our data in more than one way?
- How shall we label our graph?

Reporting Results

- What questions can we answer with our data?
- How might we describe the shape of our data?
- What descriptive statistics shall we report?
- How will we report our findings?
- Who might be interested in our results?

▼ Why do these questions need to be answered before graphing and planning our report?

▼ Name two other important questions that need to be answered before beginning.

1. _____

2. _____

guides students to think about how to display the Counting Car data collected in Lesson Idea 16–1.

The availability of graphing calculators and graphing programs allows for the construction of a variety of graphs easily. This availability of different graphs via technology places a greater premium on interpreting and understanding the graphs that are so easily produced. As children become familiar with different graphs, they should recognize some characteristics associated with them. Figure 16–14 highlights specific characteristics of graphs that are encountered in elementary and middle school. The focus here is not on memorizing characteristics of these graphs, but rather on becoming aware that each type has strengths and the selection of a particular graph should capitalize on these strengths, while recognizing any of its limitations.

ANALYZING AND COMMUNICATING RESULTS

Data Sense

Once data have been collected and displayed, they should be examined and analyzed. Just as children develop a knowledge about numbers or number sense, they can also develop knowledge about statistics or *data sense*. Data sense is gradually developed as students pose questions, collect data, construct graphs, and interpret them in a variety of contexts. Students with data sense are able to determine how data should be analyzed. They are able to read and evaluate statistical information being presented such as material presented by the media. Students also display data sense when they are able use statistical language when reasoning about data. It should be our goal for students to develop both procedural knowledge (how to construct a graph or calculate a statistic) and conceptual knowledge (understanding what a graph or statistic is communicating; Friel 1998).

Analysis

One way to analyze data is through the use of questions. Like our opening Snapshot of a Lesson, students should be encouraged to examine their results and discuss questions that may be answered by the data. Curcio, cited in Friel et al. (1997), identifies three levels of graph comprehension, which progress from lower-level to higher-level questions. Our goal should be to teach students to move beyond lower-level thinking and to ask and answer higher-level questions.

1. *Reading the data*. The student is able to answer specific questions for which the answer is promi-

Type of Graph	Characteristics
Real	Used by young children Actual objects are placed on a graph
Line Plot	Provides a quick way to examine the shape and variation or spread of data Gives a bar-graph-like representation
Stem-and-Leaf Plot	Efficient way to show detailed data Provides similar visual patterns as a bar graph but more detailed information Uses stem and leaf coding that needs to be understood Technology has facilitated its use
Picture	Frequently encountered in newspapers and reports Generally easy to use and interpret but visuals may be misleading Codes/keys which accompany graph need to be understood
Bar	Mostly used for discrete data Frequently encountered in newspapers and reports Easy to interpret Uses scales/codes that need to be understood
Pie	Frequently encountered in newspapers and reports Shows fractional parts, which are based on a whole or 100% Easy to use and interpret Difficult to construct by hand, easy with technology
Line	Frequently encountered in newspapers and reports Used for continuous data Effective to show patterns, trends, comparisons and change over time Uses vertical and horizontal scales that need to be understood Provides good readiness for coordinate graphs
Box Plot	Provides useful information about the variability of data Requires knowledge of range, median and quartiles to interpret Technology has facilitated its use

Figure 16–14 • **Characteristics of graphs**

nently displayed. For example, "Which player scored the most points?"

2. *Reading between the data.* The student is able to find relationships in the data such as comparison and is able to operate on the data. For example, "How many players earned more points than John?" "How many points did Steve earn in games 1 and 2?"

3. *Reading beyond the data.* The student is able to predict or make inferences. For example, "In game 3, how many points would you expect Steve to score? Why do you think so?"

Data may also be analyzed by describing the shape of the data in the graph. Corwin and Friel (1990) suggest first having students use informal language such as "clumps, holes, and spread out" to describe features of the data. Second, students should attempt to develop theories about why the

data look the way they do. This second step encourages students to read beyond the data.

Another beneficial graph analysis task is to give students mystery graphs that are missing some of their labels and have students predict what the data might be. For example, groups of students may have each measured a body part such as arms, legs, or distance around heads. A graph that contains measurements from 18 to 24 inches is displayed. Students would be asked to hypothesize which body parts might be illustrated on the graph. This activity also reinforces the importance of using labels on graphs. A variation of the mystery graph activity involves the use of a graphing calculator and a calculator-based laboratory (CBL). With a CBL motion detector, graphs may be created to show movements. Students may be given a CBL graph, and the challenge is to move so they can duplicate the previous graph. For example, Figure 16–15 shows the graphs of three different people walking. Time is shown on

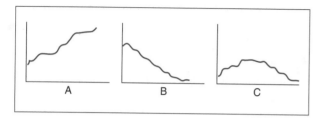

Figure 16–15 ● Graphs showing distance and time

the horizontal axis and the distance from a motion detector is shown on the vertical axis. Examine Parts A, B, and C, and decide which of these graphs shows movement toward the motion detector. Part C is different because, instead of showing continuous movement away or toward, it shows a person leaving and then returning. These sorts of activities encourage students to consider the axes of the graphs and think carefully about how data are placed on a graph.

Misleading Graphs

Another important component in developing data sense is the ability to critically examine graphs and correctly interpret the data presented. Sometimes even simple graphs may be misleading. For example, consider the graph shown in Figure 16–16. Eighth-graders were asked to explain why this graph was misleading.

Although the data in the graph indicate that the amount of trash has doubled in two decades, the visual elements reflect a doubling of both the width and height to produce a figure whose area is four

times greater. People may focus on the visual graph and ignore the numerical data that accompany the graph. In fact, less than ten percent of eighth graders identified the critical problem associated with the graph in Figure 16–16, which suggests that instructional attention needs to be given to helping children examine graphs with a careful and suspecting eye.

Graphs also may be deceptive in other ways. For example, the graph in Figure 16–17A reports changes in allowances for three children. It shows that Ann's allowance was doubled, Bill's tripled, and Chris's increased by one-half. Based on this information, we may imagine Bill feeling philanthropic and Chris complaining of hard times. What is wrong with the graph? Technically, it is correct, but it doesn't tell the entire story because the original allowances were not the same.

Let's look at the data:

	Size of Increase	Amount of Increase	New Allowance
Ann	Double	$6.00	$12.00
Bill	Triple	6.00	9.00
Chris	Half	4.00	12.00

As Figure 16–17B shows, a graph with a labeled vertical axis reflects the situation more accurately. These

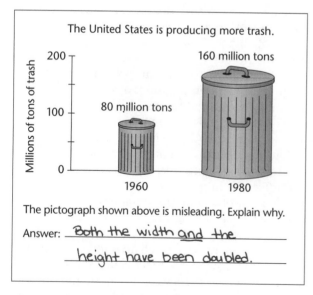

Figure 16–16 ● Eighth-grade national assessment question on interpreting graphs

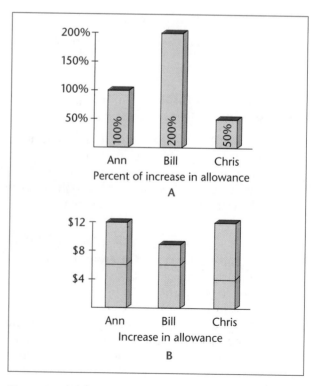

Figure 16–17 ● Example of distortion of data in graphs

different graphs of the same data demonstrate how graphs can distort and sometimes misrepresent information. Developing a healthy skepticism of graphical displays is an important part of developing graphing skills.

Communicating Results

Once data have been collected, displayed, and analyzed, it is appropriate for students to communicate their findings. Just as in problem solving, students should be encouraged to look back at their results (Bohan et al. 1995). Communication can help students clarify their ideas during this process. For example, students might complete regular journal entries throughout their project. It is also useful to have large or small group discussions about the data.

When analyzing data, Friel et al. (1992) suggest having students go through a writing process similar to one used in language arts. First, the students are involved in planning or prewriting. Second, a rough draft is created. Third, students revise their work, and finally the work is published and shared with others. Lesson Idea 16–2 shows how you can probe students to analyze their Counting Cars data.

It is valuable for students to learn to communicate their results with others. Their final presentation may include oral or written communication or both. They must learn to clearly report the answers to their original questions and hypotheses and select the most appropriate way to communicate their findings in a graphic format or by using other statistical measures. Some projects may be interesting to share with local media. The presentation may be for other classmates or a presentation for someone outside of the classroom can be particularly meaningful. For example, one class calculated the area of classrooms in their building and compared the average area of the fifth-grade classrooms to the sixth-grade classrooms. Their findings were presented to the principal who made room assignments for the building (Scavo and Petraroja 1998). Another group of students collected data to find out which school lunches were the most and least popular. Once their findings were collected and displayed, they presented their findings to the director of food services who planned the monthly menus.

DESCRIPTIVE STATISTICS

Another way to analyze data is to use descriptive statistics. So much information exists today that it must often be simplified or reduced in ways other than by graphs. The organization and summarization of data is called *descriptive statistics*. Descriptive

statistics are in common use. They are introduced in the primary grades through data collection and graphs, and then extended with further exploration and practice activities in the intermediate and middle school grades. Here are some familiar examples:

> "Most children in the fifth grade are twelve years old."
>
> "The median family income is $35250."
>
> "The average temperature today was 29°."

Each of these statements uses a number to summarize what is typical for a current situation or condition. Two of the most common types of descriptive statistics include measures of variation and measures of central tendency. For each of the descriptive statistics that follow, we will show a concrete example using cubes and an example using numbers. For some children, manipulating the physical model not only helps them understand the formula but promotes retention.

Measure of Variation

The Range The *range* is a simple measure that is used to describe the variation of a set of data or how spread out the data are. The variation in a data set is easily examined in a line plot or graph. Figure 16–18 shows the ages of five children, 2, 3, 7, 9, and 9, illustrated with cubes. Students may find the range by comparing the tallest tower to see how much taller it is than the shortest tower. We see that the tallest tower is 7 cubes taller than the shortest. Thus the range is calculated by subtracting the smallest value in the set from the largest. For the age data we would subtract 2 from 9 to get a range of 7. Once the range has been introduced in the elementary grades,

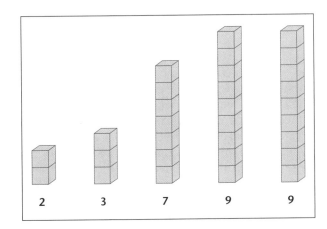

Figure 16–18 • Ages of children

middle school students often learn to measure variability with variance or standard deviations.

Measures of Central Tendency or Averages

The word average is a popular statistical term that many children have heard. It is used to report such things as average temperature, average family income, test averages, batting averages, and average life expectancy.

Any number that is used to describe the center or middle of a set of values is called an *average* of those values. Many different averages exist, but three—mode, median, and mean—are commonly encountered in elementary and middle school. Simply being able to state the algorithm for finding these statistics is not enough. To support the development of data sense, each of these should be developed meaningfully through concrete activities before computation is introduced. Such experiences will provide greater conceptual knowledge or understanding of the concept of average. Furthermore, they will help the later acquisition and development of symbolic formulas in secondary school. Wilson and Krapfl (1995) describe how students can develop some of these conceptual understandings through explorations with a computer spreadsheet program. The program allows them to investigate what happens to various descriptive statistics when different values are used.

The Mode The *mode* is the value that occurs most frequently in a collection of data. Using concrete materials such as cubes, the mode is easily identified as the tower height that occurs the most. In Figure 16–18 it is easy to see that 9 is the mode. In graphical terms, this is also the largest portion; the tallest column in a bar graph, for example. In Figure 16–19A the most frequently occurring test score is 90 (it occurred twice), so the mode is 90. The mode is a versatile average in that it may be used with both numeric and nonnumeric data. The mode is easy to find and is affected very little by extreme scores. Young children are often interested in which item on the graph received the most votes. Therefore, their initial experience with average begins with mode. The children are comfortable using the mathematical term, mode, as the teacher introduces it to them.

Students' ages within a class provide an excellent application of mode, because, within a given class, a large number of children will be the "same" age. Businesses also frequently rely on the mode to select merchandise. Suppose, for example, that you own a shoe store. The mean and/or median size of shoe you sell has no practical value for restocking, but the

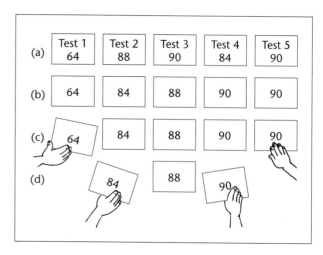

Figure 16–19 • **Model for finding the median of five test scores**

modal shoe size holds clear implications because you want to stock the sizes most people wear.

The Median The *median* is another type of average that can easily be identified without the need for computation. It is used with numeric data and is the middle value in a data set. The median divides the data into two equal subsets. Thus the same number of values are above as below the median. The median is easy to illustrate. Let's look again at the children's ages in Figure 16–18. Before looking for the median, we must always be sure the data have been ordered. For example, these towers are arranged smallest to largest. Once that has been done, the outside towers can be removed, one at a time, until the middle value remains. It is easy to see that the middle age or median tower is 7 years. Reference to a highway median will remind students that a median in statistics is a middle position. Notice that the median is not the middle of the range of data because data aren't always spread symmetrically over the range. In the children's age example, the median simply tells us that there are as many children in the group from ages 2–7 as there are in the group containing ages 7–9.

The median too, can be modeled with numbers. For example, consider the five test scores shown on cards in Figure 16–19A. Ordering them from lowest to highest, as in Figure 16–19B provides practice in using greater than, less than, and ordering skills. To find the middle score, or median, simply remove the highest and lowest cards simultaneously, as shown in Figures 16–19C and D. Continue this process until the middle card remains. This score, 88, is the median.

There are five scores in Figure 16–19. Suppose a sixth score of 17 was made. A new arrangement could be made by ordering the six test scores, as shown in Figure 16–20A. Again, remove the highest and lowest cards simultaneously until two cards remain. In this case, as shown in Figure 16–20B the median is the middle point between these two scores, or 86.

The Mean The *mean,* is called the arithmetic average because it is determined by adding all the values involved and dividing by the number of addends. The mean is the most difficult to compute although it can be understood by children beginning in the upper elementary grades. It is used with numeric data. Often, when people talk about finding the average of a set of data, they are referring to calculating the mean.

Simply being able to state or use the algorithm does not indicate understanding of the mean. Difficulties in interpreting the mean were shown on a national assessment (Educational Testing Service 1992). Figure 16–21 shows a question that required eighth graders to determine what data would be reasonable for a given mean. Less than 40 percent answered all four choices correctly. These assessment results illustrate the findings from research that many middle-grade students are able to calculate averages when asked to do so, but the depth of their understanding of the concept of average is shallow (Shaughnessy 1992).

Uccellini (1996) describes two conceptual interpretations for the mean that are helpful in developing understanding of this average. Let's say that four students have 9, 5, 3, and 7 trading cards (Figure 16–22). The cubes in Figure 16–22A show the number of cards each child has. The first interpretation involves the concept of equal distribution or sharing, an idea very familiar to students. In this interpretation, the mean is identified as the number that describes the data if

Akira read from a book on Monday, Tuesday, and Wednesday. He read an average of 10 pages per day. Circle whether each of the following is possible or not possible.

Possible	Not Possible		Monday	Pages Read Tuesday	Wednesday
A	(A)	(a)	4 pages	4 pages	2 pages
(B)	B	(b)	9 pages	10 pages	11 pages
(C)	C	(c)	5 pages	10 pages	15 pages
D	(D)	(d)	10 pages	15 pages	20 pages

Figure 16–21 • **Eighth-grade national assessment question on interpreting an average (correct responses are circled)**

each piece of data were evened out or the same as all others. We often think of this as what is "typical" for the data. If children are asked to "even out" or share the cards so that each student has a fair or equal share of cards, this evening-out process produces a mean of six cards per student (Figure 16–22B). As students gain

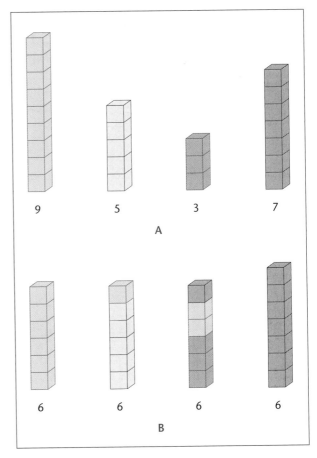

Figure 16–22 • **Equal distribution or sharing model for the mean**

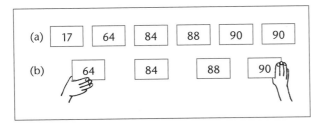

Figure 16–20 • **Model for finding the median of six test scores**

experience and become comfortable with the equal distribution interpretation, they will also realize that with large data sets such as whole class data, trying to share equally will become cumbersome. Students often discover the add-then-divide algorithm on their own, or the teacher can introduce it with concrete materials. The mean also could have been determined by computing:

$$\text{mean} = \frac{9 + 5 + 3 + 7}{4}$$

$$\frac{24}{4} = 6$$

Figure 16–23 shows a way to model the add-then-divide algorithm for the mean. Test scores are returned to children on pieces of adding machine tape, and the length of each strip is determined by the score. That is, a score of 88 is 88 cm long, and a score of 64 is 64 cm long. Scores can be physically compared using the tapes; for example, it is clear that the score on Test 2 was higher. To show the mean score, simply tape the two strips of paper together (add) and then fold the resulting strip in half (divide by 2). This technique is very appealing and enlightening.

Not all data sets will divide evenly, and once students are comfortable with the concept of evening out, they can discuss what to do with leftovers which makes a natural connection to fractions. They can also discuss how some data cannot be divided and some averages that we calculate are not realistic. For example, in one data set the mean indicated that the

average number of children per family was 2.5. Children will be quick to point out that you can't have five-tenths or one-half of a child.

The second interpretation involves the idea of mean as being a "balancing point" for a set of data. You can see the trading card data have been placed on a line plot.

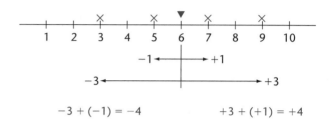

We previously determined that the mean for the data set was 6, and by examining how far away from the balance point of 6, each of the numbers is, we see that 6 is the middle of the data. The total distance numbers are above the mean will be the same as the total distance numbers are below the mean. Students can be given a mean and encouraged to develop sets of data that would balance to create that mean.

These types of experiences help students understand some fundamental notions related to the mean; namely, that the mean must be somewhere between the values averaged and that it is the typical value or balancing point for a set of data.

Choosing Averages

As students use these averages, they must also be aware of the effects certain sizes of data may have on them. The following table provides a summary of the test scores reported in Figures 16–19 and 16–20:

	Mean	*Median*
Five tests	83	88
Six tests	72	86

This summary illustrates that the median was affected very little by the extremely low score on the last test, but the mean dropped greatly (from 83 to 72). One negative characteristic of the mean is that its value is affected by extreme scores.

Suppose you are preparing a report of average incomes and you want to present the fairest picture. Should the mean—which would be affected by the extremely high salaries of movie stars, professional athletes, and corporate heads—be used? Many governmental agencies handle this problem by reporting median family incomes.

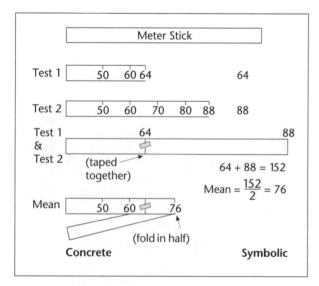

Figure 16–23 • **Model for finding the mean using lengths of adding machine tape to indicate test scores**

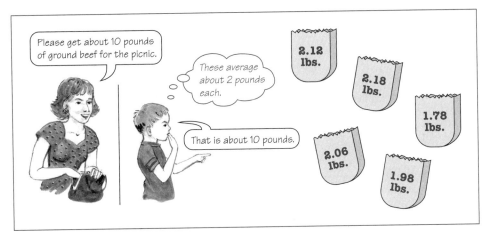

Figure 16–24 ● Example problem for developing averaging and estimating skills

Grasp of "average" is a powerful tool in estimation and problem solving. Problems such as the one in Figure 16–24 provide opportunities to apply averages and estimation in everyday situations.

Finding the mean, median, and mode for the same data can generate discussion about when certain averages should be used. You can use In the

Classroom 16–2 to allow children to calculate averages with concrete materials or numbers and to discuss how one might select a particular average to describe the data. For another example, look at Lesson Idea 16–3. Calculating the mean, median, and mode provides practice in computational skills. More important, however, is deciding which of these

---

In The Classroom 16–2

Peanuts

Objective: Choosing the best average.

Suppose you have opened some Nutty Bars to check the company's claim of an "average" of 8 peanuts per bar. Here is what you found after opening ten bars.

Bar	1st	2nd	3rd	4th	5th	6th	7th	8th	9th	10th
Number of Peanuts	5	8	8	8	11	7	8	6	6	6

▼ Create some different sketch graphs so you can examine the shape of the data. Which graph would the company probably use to promote their product? Why?

▼ Calculate the averages. You may use counters such as beans and grid paper to represent the peanuts if you wish.

  • What is the mean number of nuts?

  • What is the median number of nuts?

  • What is the modal number of nuts?

  • Which average did the company probably use? Why?

▼ Write at least three questions that can be answered by your graphs and statistics.

  1. _____

  2. _____

  3. _____

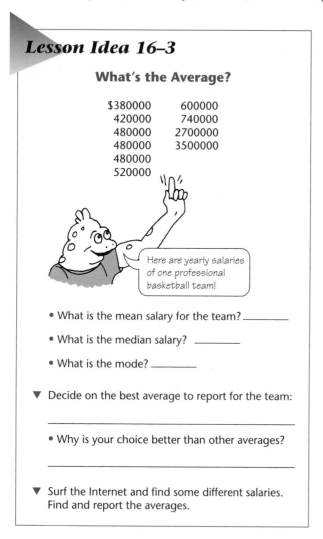

Lesson Idea 16–3

What's the Average?

$380000	600000
420000	740000
480000	2700000
480000	3500000
480000	
520000	

Here are yearly salaries of one professional basketball team!

• What is the mean salary for the team? _____

• What is the median salary? _____

• What is the mode? _____

▼ Decide on the best average to report for the team:

_____

• Why is your choice better than other averages?

_____

▼ Surf the Internet and find some different salaries. Find and report the averages.

averages to report. The median salary of $500000 or the modal salary of $480000 seems more representative than the mean salary of $1030000. If salary negotiations were taking place, the players might cite one "average" and the owners a very different "average." Discussing which averages are appropriate for what purpose helps students better understand why different ones exist and are used. Once children have collected their own data, they should determine which averages will be calculated and reported. For an amusing example of this type of activity, in the children's book *What Do You Mean by "Average"?* (James and Barker 1978) Jill is running for student council. To convince the school she will best represent them, she decides to show she is the most average person in the school.

Each of the averages can be modeled and developed in ways that are appealing, interesting, and meaningful. No new mathematics is required, yet learning about averages provides a vehicle for ap-

plying many mathematical concepts and skills that students are developing.

Care must be taken to ensure that statistics is viewed as more than a series of skills or techniques. For example, how to find an average is an important skill that should be developed. However, the teaching of statistics must not stop with the "how to"; rather, it must raise questions such as, "When is an average useful?"

For example, the ice cream survey in Figure 16–7 reports eight students like chocolate, five like vanilla, and three like strawberry. This picture graph clearly and accurately shows student ice cream preferences. These preferences are an example of nonnumeric data. A mean or median of these data could be computed, but would be inappropriate. In fact, a mean or median is meaningless for these data! Before any statistics are computed, challenge students to decide what questions are to be answered and discuss what statistics, if any, are needed to answer them. Nonnumeric data such as ice cream flavors are better analyzed with frequency tables or graphs. If an average is desired, the mode would be the appropriate average to use.

Additional questions might include "Why should the average be reported?" "What average is most appropriate?" "Why?" "What degree of precision is needed?" These questions are essential and must be asked regularly. This sort of discussion will support students as they develop their data sense. The teaching of statistics in elementary school must aim higher than skill development. Students should know how to "get" a statistic, but they must also know what they have "gotten."

PROBABILITY

Probability is used to predict the chance of something happening. It is encountered daily. Here are some examples of common probabilistic statements:

"The chance of rain today is 40 percent."

"The Cards are a 3-to-1 favorite to win."

"The probability of an accident on the job is less than 1 in 100."

"The patient has a 50–50 chance of recovering."

"If I study, I will probably pass the test."

"I am sure we will have a test Friday."

"We will have milk in the cafeteria today."

The first three statements are commonly heard and relate directly to probability. The last four illustrate a subtle but frequent use of probability in many everyday situations. In all these cases it is the utilitarian role of probability that makes it an important basic skill. One way to increase awareness that probability surrounds us is to have students make a daily or weekly list of probability statements they have seen (in newspapers, magazines, or on television) or heard (on radio and television).

Probability will not and should not be learned from formal definitions; rather, the presentation of varied examples will help illustrate and clarify its important concepts. At all stages of instruction, teachers must use correct language to describe what is happening. This language serves as a model for children as they begin developing probability concepts and simultaneously add new probabilistic terms to their vocabulary. Let's look at appropriate ways for elementary students to experience some key concepts and terms.

Probability of an Event

Look at these statements that involve probability:

The probability of tossing a head is $\frac{1}{2}$.
The probability of rolling a four on a die is $\frac{1}{6}$.
The probability of having a birthday on February 30 is 0.

In these examples, tossing a head, rolling a four, and having a birthday on February 30 are *events*, or *outcomes*. Probability assigns a number (from zero to one) to an event. The more likely an event is to occur, the larger the number assigned to it, and so the probability is 1.0 when something is certain to happen. For example, the probability of students in an elementary class having been born is 1. On the other hand, the probability of something impossible happening is zero. For example, the probability of students in the class having been born in the nineteenth century is zero.

Long before probabilities of specific events are calculated, it is important that terms such as *certain, uncertain, impossible, likely,* and *unlikely* be introduced and discussed. Most students, even in primary grades, are familiar with the terms *impossible* and *certain* and can give meaningful examples. Although *likely* and *unlikely* will be less familiar and will require more careful development, using In the Classroom 16–3 with children provides a good start. As each card is sorted, an explanation or argument for placing it in the specific box should be given. This rationale is essential in refining and developing a clear understanding of these important terms.

An excellent extension at the bottom of In the Classroom 16–3 is to have students write statements

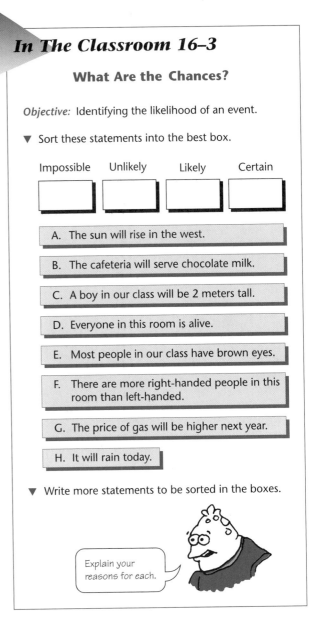

In The Classroom 16–3

What Are the Chances?

Objective: Identifying the likelihood of an event.

▼ Sort these statements into the best box.

Impossible   Unlikely   Likely   Certain

A. The sun will rise in the west.
B. The cafeteria will serve chocolate milk.
C. A boy in our class will be 2 meters tall.
D. Everyone in this room is alive.
E. Most people in our class have brown eyes.
F. There are more right-handed people in this room than left-handed.
G. The price of gas will be higher next year.
H. It will rain today.

▼ Write more statements to be sorted in the boxes.

Explain your reasons for each.

to be sorted into the same categories. Each should write several original statements and then exchange papers so that someone else classifies them. Once these general probabilistic terms become familiar, more specific probabilities can be determined.

Sample space is a fundamental concept that must be established or at least understood before the probabilities of specific events can be determined. The sample space for a probability problem represents all possible outcomes.

Lesson Idea 16–4 suggests ways to help children think about what outcomes are possible for a particular event. Consider, for example, the situation in which a coin is tossed. Some children may realize that a coin will not land on its edge, nor will it float. Thus

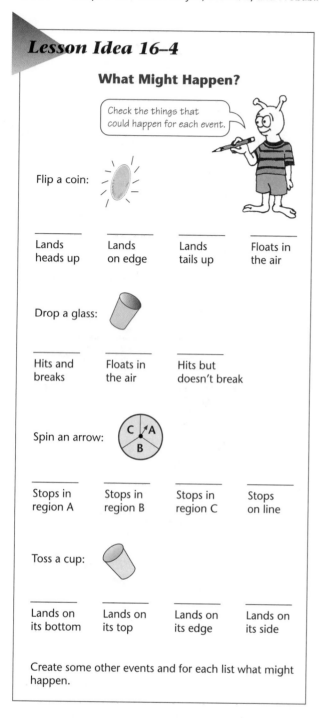

Lesson Idea 16–4

What Might Happen?

Check the things that could happen for each event.

Flip a coin:

——————— ——————— ——————— ———————
Lands   Lands   Lands   Floats in
heads up   on edge   tails up   the air

Drop a glass:

——————— ——————— ———————
Hits and   Floats in   Hits but
breaks   the air   doesn't break

Spin an arrow:

C | A
B

——————— ——————— ——————— ———————
Stops in   Stops in   Stops in   Stops
region A   region B   region C   on line

Toss a cup:

——————— ——————— ——————— ———————
Lands on   Lands on   Lands on   Lands on
its bottom its top   its edge   its side

Create some other events and for each list what might happen.

---

head can occur divided by the total number of outcomes (head or tail), or $\frac{1}{2}$. Specific probabilities rest heavily on fractions, which provide a direct and convenient means of reporting and interpreting probabilities.

Discussion of possible outcomes helps identify the sample space and clarify notions of probability. Questions along these lines might get the discussion started:

> Can the spinner shown in Lesson Idea 16–4 stop in region C if there is no area marked C?
>
> Can the spinner stop on a line?

Even though this outcome is unlikely, it can happen, and a plan of action should be specified if it does. (Maybe you spin again.) See Appendix B for spinner masters.

Consider the sample space for tossing cups, as shown in Lesson Idea 16–5. Is a cup equally likely to land on its top, its side, or its bottom? Without additional information, it would be foolhardy to decide.

Lesson Idea 16–5 provides suggestions for a possible start. In addition to helping children decide which outcomes are more or less likely, this exploration may lead to more precise statements. For example, one reasonable conclusion from Lesson Idea 16–5 is that the probability of the cup landing on its side is about one-half.

In the Classroom 16–4 involves collecting data, graphing results, and exploring patterns. It uses several valuable ideas of probability (sample space and probability of an event) in a natural and interesting setting. As children are involved in this process, they are developing and practicing basic facts, as was shown earlier in Chapter 8. Such an activity further illustrates how mathematical topics are interrelated and how important connections can be made.

Once you have tried In the Classroom 16–4 with children, another perspective can be obtained by examining Table 16–2, which summarizes the results when two dice are added. The diagonal of Table 16–2A shows all the ways that a sum of 7 can be obtained. Table 16–2 also shows the different ways that each of the other sums can result. Is the sum of two dice more likely to be even or odd? An examination of Table 16–2A shows the even sums will occur 18 out of 36 times, or half the time.

Is the product of two dice more likely to be even or odd? The shaded cells in Table 16–2B show the even products much more likely. In fact, an even product would be expected to occur 27 times out of 36, or three-fourths of the time. Analyzing and discussing why this happens helps connect probability

---

only two outcomes can happen, and these possible outcomes comprise the sample space. Likewise, when a coin is being flipped, it will neither float nor land on its edge, so only two outcomes are possible. Having children create their own events and determine possible outcomes is also a beneficial experience.

Once the sample space is known, the calculation of specific probabilities usually follows naturally. When a coin is flipped, as described in Table 16–1, the probability of a head is the number of ways a

Table 16–1 ● Sample spaces of some events and their probabilities

Questions	Sample space	Number of successes	Probability
What is the probability of getting a head on a single toss of a coin?	H,T	1	½
What is the probability of getting two heads when two coins are tossed?	HH, HT, TH, TT	1	¼
What is the probability of getting a five on a single roll of a die?	1, 2, 3, 4, 5, 6	1	⅙
What is the probability of drawing a spade from a deck of 52 playing cards?	52 cards	13	¹³⁄₅₂ or ¼
If each letter of the alphabet is written on a piece of paper, what is the probability of drawing a vowel?	26 letters of the alphabet	5 (a, e, i, o, u)	⁵⁄₂₆

to properties and relationships between numbers and operations.

Randomness

Randomness is an important concept underlying all learning in probability. When something is random, it means that it is not influenced by any factors other than chance. Lesson Idea 16–6 could be used to build on In the Classroom 16–3 and provides an opportunity to discuss randomness in a specific context. Here students are encouraged to think about events based on their classmates and decide about where these events would be placed on a probability number line that shows 0 and 1. Here are some starter questions:

> Why is it important that the "name will be randomly picked"?
>
> Should the names be seen by the person doing the drawing?
>
> Would it matter if some people wrote their names on large pieces of paper and others on small pieces of paper?

If the names are seen or if people don't all write their name on the same size of paper, the drawing might not be random. When this happens, some people would have an advantage and the notions of *fair* and *unfair* become important.

The term *fair* is often used in describing a situation. For example, to say "a fair coin" or "fair dice" makes it clear that no inherent biases exist that

would affect randomness. A person may be asked to toss (not scoot) a die to ensure that one face is not favored. If ping-pong balls are drawn from a bowl, it is important that the balls be thoroughly mixed and the person doing the drawing be blindfolded to ensure both randomness and fairness. The children's book *No Fair!* (Holtzman 1997) describes two children who are trying to determine when activities such as drawing an item from a bag are fair.

Discussions on the consequences of unfairness and absence of randomness should be a regular part of developing probability. For example, would it be fair if two dice are rolled and player A wins if the product is even and player B wins if the product is odd? Table 16–2B shows that A will win much more than B, so this game is not fair. On the other hand, if the game is based on the sum of two dice (Table 16–2A), each player has an equal chance of winning and the game is fair. Suppose you modify the sum-of-two-dice game to play with three players:

> Player A wins if the sum is 1, 2, 3, or 4.
>
> Player B wins if the sum is 5, 6, 7, or 8.
>
> Player C wins if the sum is 9, 10, 11, or 12.

Is this game fair for each of the players? Does each player have the same chance of winning? An analysis of Table 16–2A suggests that Player B will win more often than either of the other players. As children explore this game, you might challenge them to tell how the game might be modified to make it fair for everyone.

Lesson Idea 16–5

What's the Probability?

▼ Toss a cup to see how it lands:

▼ Before you toss it again, circle how you think it will land:

▼ Toss your cup 20 more times, and tally how it lands!

Bottom	Top	Side

• I have decided that _____ is most likely.

• I have decided that _____ is least likely.

> You can make some more tosses if it will help.

▼ Here are some results from tossing the cup:

A. | 2 | 0 | 3 | B. | 15 | 10 | 25 |

C. | 32 | 17 | 51 |

• Is it possible that all these tallies are results of tossing the same cup?_____ Explain.

• Which of these tables would you feel best about using?_____ Explain.

Decision time:

The probability of landing on the side is about _____ .

In The Classroom 16–4

Rolling and Recording

Objective: Conducting a probability experiment.

▼ Try this:

1. Choose a partner, and each of you make a chart like the one shown. Predict which sum of two dice will come up most often.

2. Each of you take turns rolling two dice.

3. On a turn, find the sum of the spots on the two dice, and place a tally mark in that column on your chart.

4. Continue rolling and recording until one of you has 10 tally marks in one column. Compare your prediction with the actual result.

2	3	4	5	6	7	8	9	10	11	12
			/							

Putting it together:

• Why doesn't the chart need a ones column? A thirteens column?

• In which column did you or your partner reach 10?

• Compare your results, and tell how they are similar. Different.

• Tell why you would expect more sums of 7 than 2.

• Complete the following: "I would expect about the same number of sums of 4 as . . . ."

• Would you expect to get about the same number of even sums as odd sums? Tell why.

Extending this activity:

Suppose you multiplied the numbers on the dice instead of adding them.

• How would the values along the top of the chart change?

• How many values (that is, different products) would be needed?

• Which values would be least likely?

• Would you expect to get about the same number of even values as odd values? Tell why.

Independence of Events

Independence of events is an important concept in probability, but one that does not develop naturally from intuition. If two events are independent, one event in no way affects the outcome of the other. Thus if a coin is tossed, lands heads, and then is tossed again, it is still equally likely to land heads or tails. This sounds simple enough, but consider this question: Suppose four consecutive sixes have occurred on four rolls of a fair die. What is the probability of getting a six on the next roll?

Table 16–2 • Results of operations with two dice

+	1	2	3	4	5	6
1	2	3	4	5	6	7
2	3	4	5	6	7	8
3	4	5	6	7	8	9
4	5	6	7	8	9	10
5	6	7	8	9	10	11
6	7	8	9	10	11	12

A

×	1	2	3	4	5	6
1	1	2	3	4	5	6
2	2	4	6	8	10	12
3	3	6	9	12	15	18
4	4	8	12	16	20	24
5	5	10	15	20	25	30
6	6	12	18	24	30	36

B

Lesson Idea 16–6

Are You a Winner?

Our class is having a drawing. Each person gets to place their name in the drawing one time. One name will be randomly picked, and that person will be the winner.

▼ Read each of the following statements.

▼ Think about the people in our class.

▼ Then, check the number line below and decide about where the following statements should be placed:

A. The winner will be left-handed.

B. The winner will be a girl.

C. The winner will be someone in our class.

D. The number of letters in the first name of the winner will be less than the number of letters in their last name.

E. The winner's first name will begin with a vowel.

F. The winner will wear glasses.

G. You will be the winner.

H. The winner will be wearing socks.

I. You will not be the winner.

```
0                    .5 or 1/2              1
Impossible                              Certain
                                        to happen
```

Research shows that a majority of middle-grade students miss this question (Shaughnessy 1992). Many students suggested that the die had a "memory," and things would "even out." Most did not conclude that the probability was unchanged, regardless of what had already happened. If an event has occurred a number of times in a row, most people falsely presume that the "law of averages" makes it unlikely that the event will occur on the next trial. This basic misunderstanding contradicts the notion of independence of certain events.

Having children collect data and discuss the results can help dispel some of this erroneous thinking. When you use In the Classroom 16–5 with children, different students will produce different results, yet the answers to the questions will be very similar. Why? Because these events, the rolls of a die, are independent of one another.

Tossing a coin and recording the outcomes in sequence will likely generate some long runs of an occurrence even though each outcome is independent of the others. Although the probability of a head is

$\frac{1}{2}$, children might flip a coin ten times and get eight, nine, or even ten heads in a row. Consider this record of twenty tosses of a coin:

There are two sequences of four consecutive heads and one of five consecutive tails. Overall, eleven heads appeared. Such analysis and discussion helps children understand that things don't even out on each flip. However, as the number of flips gets very large, the ratio of heads to the total number of flips will get closer and closer to the theoretical expected value of $\frac{1}{2}$. This latter point is very important, but it often baffles elementary students. Using simulation programs to repeat an event many times helps

In The Classroom 16–5

Can You Make Predictions?

Objective: Identifying independence of events.

▼ Roll a die six times and record the results:

1	2	3	4	5	6

- Did each face appear once? _____

- Does knowing what happened on the first roll

  help predict the second? _____

  the third? _____

▼ Roll a die 24 times and record the results.

1	2	3	4	5	6	7	8	9	10	11	12

13 14 15 16 17 18 19 20 21 22 23 24

- Did each face appear once? _____

  the same number of times? _____

- What face appeared most? _____

- Does this mean the die is unfair? _____

- Does this record tell you
  what will occur on the next roll? _____

children better understand the notion of the expression, *in the long run.*

There are, of course, times where one event may depend on another. For example, suppose you wanted to roll two dice and obtain a sum of 8. If a 1 is shown on the first die, it is impossible to get a sum of 8. This leads toward notions of *conditional probability.*

Instruction is needed to develop the necessary techniques to solve simple probability problems. There are, of course, other very complicated situations for which probabilities are difficult to calculate. What is the probability of New York winning the World Series? Of a woman being elected president? Such questions do not lend themselves to simple solutions, but their probabilities can be approximated by experts. Regardless of who determines the numerical probabilities, the knowledge and interpretative skills developed in simpler probability situations can be successfully applied.

A Glance at Where We've Been

Collecting data and then using it to organize, analyze, and interpret information develops critical thinking. In addition, using data provides many opportunities to apply fractions, decimals, and ratios as well as practice computational skills and problem solving. Also, the elements of uncertainty inherent in working with probability and statistics present situations that require critical thinking skills.

Meaningful learning is always important. It is difficult to imagine any mathematical topic that allows for more involvement and stimulates more enthusiasm than probability and statistics. The importance of probability and statistics is unchallenged, yet performance on these topics still leaves much to be desired. Contemporary elementary school mathematics programs are giving much more attention and emphasis to all forms of data analysis at all grade levels. The NCTM *Standards 2000* have made a strong push toward relating school mathematics to real-world mathematics, and no area lends itself better to this linkage than using data.

Things to Do: From What You've Read

1. Here are the results on three tests: 68, 78, 88. What are the mean and the median? Explain why the mode is of little value. What score would be needed on the next test to get an average of 81? Describe two different ways this could be done.

2. Arrange interlocking cubes together in lengths of 3, 6, 6, and 9.

   a. Describe how you could use the blocks to find the mean, median, and mode.
   b. Suppose you introduce another length of ten cubes. Has the mean changed? The median? The mode?

3. Answer each of the following questions, and tell why you answered as you did.

   a. Is it possible for a set of data to have more than one mode? Give an example.
   b. Is it easier to find the median of 25 or 24 student scores?
   c. Could the mean be as large as the largest value in a set of data? Tell how.

4. Describe how the activities in Lesson Idea 16–4 could be used to discuss probabilities of zero and one.

5. Ten cards are marked 0, 1, 2, 3, . . . , 9 and placed face down. If the cards are shuffled and then one card is drawn, tell why the following statements are true:

   a. The sample space has 10 events.

   b. The probability of drawing the 6 is $\frac{1}{10}$.

   c. The probability of drawing the 3 is the same as the probability of drawing the 7.

6. Many state lotteries advertise with a slogan, "If you don't play, you can't win." Does that mean if you do play, you will win? Explain.

7. The chances of picking six numbers correctly in a state lottery depends on the numbers from which you select. Explain why you would rather pick from the set of numbers 1 through 10 than from the set of numbers 1 through 20. About how much better are your chances of winning with the smaller set of numbers than with the larger set of numbers?

Things to Do: Going Beyond This Book

field Additional activities, suggestions, and questions are provided in *Teaching Elementary Mathematics: A Resource for Field Experiences.*

1. *field* *Let's Find Out.* Use In the Classroom 16–1 with a small group of children as they plan and conduct a survey. Describe how it went.

2. Review the NCTM books *Making Sense of Data* (Lindquist et al. 1992) and *Dealing with Data and Chance* (Zawojewski et al. 1991). Select an activity. Decide where and how you would use it in teaching a lesson.

3. Examine newspapers or magazines. Start a file of graphs students can examine. Make a list of the different kinds of graphs used. Select a few and tell why you think a particular graph (picture graph, pie graph, bar graph) was used in each situation.

4. Examine the scope-and-sequence chart for an elementary textbook series. At what level is graphing first introduced? What kinds of graphing skills are highlighted? What important statistical topics are included? At what levels are they taught? Do the same for probability.

5. Review the *Wonderful World of Mathematics* (Thiessen et al. 1998). Find a book related to statistics or probability that is highly recommended. Read the book with some children and describe how they reacted.

6. *field* *Peanuts.* Use In the Classroom 16–2 with some children in grades 4–8. Which key features of various graphs and statistics did you discuss

with the children? Write several questions about the graphs using the levels described by Curcio (1997). How did you guide the children to create higher-level questions?

7. Select one of the activities from *Probability* (Phillips et al. 1986 or Burns 1995). Develop the materials needed and demonstrate the lesson.

8. Examine the March 1999 issue of *Mathematics Teaching in the Middle School,* which was a focus issue on data and chance. Select an article to read and use as a basis for preparing a lesson plan.

9. *field* Working with children, use In the Classroom ideas 16-3, 16–4, or 16–5 to teach a hands-on lesson on probability. Reflect on how the lesson went.

10. Games are fun and can help develop a better understanding of probability. Play the game Montana Red Dog, described in *Dealing with Data and Chance* (Zawojewski et al. 1991), play one of the games from "Fair Games, Unfair Games" (Bright et al. 1981), *What Are My Chances?* (Shulte and Choate 1996) or the "Cover Up Game" from *Chance Encounters: Probability in Games and Simulation* (Brutlag 1996). Identify some of the mathematics learned in these games. Tell how you might use these games with students.

11. Read one of the research articles related to probability or statistics listed in Bright and Hoeffner (1993), Shaughnessy (1992), or Friel et al. (1997). Discuss the nature of the research. Also identify an instructional idea or activity suggested by the research that you think would be effective in helping children learn a particular concept.

12. Examine one of the following books from the *Used Numbers: Real Data in the Classroom* series, published by Dale Seymour Publications:

   Counting: Ourselves and Our Families (K–1)
   Sorting: Groups and Graphs (2–3)
   Measuring: From Paces to Feet (3–4)
   Statistics: The Shape of the Data (4–6)
   Statistics: Prediction and Sampling (5–6)
   Statistics: Middles, Means, and In-Betweens (5–6)

   Choose an activity and discuss how it might be presented to a group of students. Better yet, present it to an appropriate group of students. Discuss what happened.

13. *field* Select a middle school student and use In the Classroom 16–2 to conduct the interview for statistics and probability. What did you learn about the child's thinking?

14. Use technology such as spreadsheet, graphing or survey software or a graphing calculator to display and analyze data. Evaluate how these might be used with children. Better yet, try it out with children and then evaluate.

BOOK NOOK FOR CHILDREN

Arnold, Caroline. *Charts and Graphs: Fun, Facts, and Activities.* New York: Franklin Watts, 1984.

Cushman, Jean. *Do You Wanna Bet? Your Chance to Find Out about Probability.* New York: Clarion Books, 1991.

Diagram Group. *Comparisons.* New York: St. Martin's Press, 1980.

Gardner, Beau. *Can You Imagine . . . ? A Counting Book.* New York: Dodd, Mead and Co., 1987.

Holtzman, Caren. *No Fair!* New York: Scholastic, 1997.

James, Elizabeth and Barkin, Carol. *What Do You Mean By Average?* New York: Lothrop, Lee, and Shepard, 1978.

Linn, Charles F. *Probability.* New York: Thomas Y. Crowell Publishers, 1972.

McGrath, Barbara Barbieri. *More M+M's Math.* Watertown, Mass.: Charlesbridge, 1998.

Mori, Tuyosi. *Socrates and the Three Pigs.* New York: Philomel Books, 1986.

Murphy, Stuart J. *The Best Vacation Ever.* New York: HarperCollins, 1997.

Parker, Tom. *In One Day.* Boston: Houghton Mifflin, 1984.

Spier, Peter. *People.* New York: Thomas Y. Crowell Publishers, 1975.

Srivastava, Jane Jonas. *Averages.* New York: Thomas Y. Crowell Publishers, 1975.

Winthrop, Elizabeth. *Shoes.* New York: Harper & Row, 1986.

Ziefert, Harriet. *Where's the Halloween Treat?* New York: Puffit Books, 1985.

Selected References

Bamberger, Honi, and Hughes, Patricia. *Super Graphs, Venns, and Glyphs.* New York: Scholastic, 1995.

Bohan, Harry; Irby, Beverly; and Vogel, Dolly. "Problem Solving: Dealing with Data in the Elementary School." *Teaching Children Mathematics,* 1 (January 1995), pp. 256–260.

Bright, George W., and Hoeffner, Karl. "Measurement, Probability, Statistics and Graphing." In *Research Ideas for the Classroom: Middle Grades Mathematics* (ed. Douglas T. Owens). Reston, Va.: NCTM, and New York: Macmillan, 1993, pp. 78–98.

Bright, George W.; Harvey, John G.; and Wheeler, Margarette Montague. "Fair Games, Unfair Games." In *Teaching Statistics and Probability,* 1981 Yearbook (ed. Albert Shulte). Reston, Va.: NCTM, 1981, pp. 49–59.

Browning, Christine A., and Channell, Dwayne E. "A 'Handy' Database Activity for the Middle School Classroom." *Arithmetic Teacher,* 40 (December 1992), pp. 235–238.

Brutlag, Dan. "Choice and Chance in Life: The Game of 'Skunk.' " *Mathematics Teaching in the Middle School,* 1 (1), (April 1994), pp. 28–33.

Brutlag, Dan. *Chance Encounters: Probability in Games and Simulation.* Palo Alto, Calif.: Creative Publications, 1996.

Burns, Marilyn. *Math By All Means: Probability Grades 3–4.* Sausalito, Calif.: Math Solutions Publications, 1995.

Burrill, Gail. "Implementing the Standards: Statistics and Probability." *Mathematics Teacher,* 83 (February 1990), pp. 113–118.

Corwin, Rebecca, and Friel, Susan. *Used Numbers—Statistics: Prediction and Sampling, Grades 5–6.* Menlo Park, Calif.: Dale Seymour Publications, 1990.

Curcio, Frances R. *Developing Graph Comprehension: Elementary and Middle School Activities.* Reston, Va.: NCTM, 1989.

Dixon, Juli K., and Falba, Christy J. "Graphing in the Information Age: Using Data from the Worldwide Web." *Mathematics Teaching in the Middle School,* 2 (March-April 1997), pp. 298–304.

Educational Testing Service. *NAEP 1992 Mathematics Report Card for the Nation and the States.* Princeton, N.J.: ETS, 1992.

Folkson, Susan. "Meaningful Communication among Children: Data Collection". In *Communication in Mathematics* (ed. Portia Elliott), 1996 Yearbook. Reston, Va.: NCTM, 1996, pp. 29–34.

Freeman, Marji. *Creative Graphing.* White Plains, N.Y.: Cuisenaire Co., 1986.

Friel, Susan. "Teaching Statistics: What's Average?". In *The Teaching and Learning of Algorithms in School Mathematics* (ed. Lorna J. Morrow) 1998 Yearbook. Reston, Va.: NCTM, 1998, pp. 208–217.

Friel, Susan; Bright, George; and Curcio, Frances. "Understanding Students' Understanding of Graphs." *Mathematics Teaching in the Middle School,* 3 (November–December 1997), pp. 224–227.

Friel, Susan N., and Corwin, Rebecca B. "Implementing the Standards: The Statistics Standards in K–8 Mathematics." *Arithmetic Teacher,* 38 (October 1990), pp. 35–39.

Friel, Susan; Mokros, Janice; and Russell, Susan Jo. *Used Numbers—Middles, Means, and In-Betweens, Grades 5, 6.* Palo Alto, Calif.: Dale Seymour Publications, 1992.

Hitch, Chris and Armstrong, Georganna. "Daily Activities for Data Analysis." *Arithmetic Teacher,* 41 (January 1994), pp. 242–245.

Hofstetter, Elaine B., and Sgroi, Laura A. "Data with Snap, Crackle, and Pop." *Mathematics Teaching in the Middle School,* 1 (4), (March-April 1996), pp. 760–764.

Ihor, Charischak, and Berkman, Robert. "Looking at Random Events with Logo Software." *Mathematics Teaching in the Middle School,* 1 (4), (January-March 1995), pp. 318–322.

Kader, Gary, and Perry, Mike. "Learning Statistics with Technology" *Mathematics Teaching in the Middle School,* 1 (2), (September-October 1994), pp. 130–136.

Kenney, Patricia Ann, and Silver, Edward A. (eds.) *Results from the Sixth Mathematics Assessment of the National Assessment of Educational Progress.* Reston, Va.: NCTM, 1997.

Landwehr, James M., and Watkins, Ann E. *Exploring Data and Exploring Probability.* Palo Alto, Calif.: Dale Seymour Publications, 1986.

Landwehr, James M., and Watkins, Ann E. "Stem and Leaf Plots." *Mathematics Teacher,* 78 (October 1985), pp. 528–538.

Lindquist, Mary M.; Brown, Catherine A.; Carpenter, Thomas P.; Kouba, Vicky L.; Silver, Edward A.; and Swafford, Jane O.

Results from the Fourth Mathematics Assessment of the National Assessment of Educational Progress. Reston, Va.: NCTM, 1989.

Lindquist, Mary M.; Lauquire, J.; Gardner, A.; and Shekaramiz, S. *Making Sense of Data.* Reston, Va.: NCTM, 1992.

Morita, June. "Capture and Recapture Your Students' Interest in Statistics." *Mathematics Teaching in the Middle School,* 4 (March 1999), pp. 412–418.

National Council of Teachers of Mathematics. *Curriculum and Evaluation Standards for School Mathematics.* Reston, Va.: NCTM, 1989.

National Council of Teachers of Mathematics. *Mathematics Teaching in the Middle School Focus Issue: Data and Chance in the Middle School Curriculum* 4 (March 1999).

National Council of Teachers of Mathematics. *Principles and Standards for School Mathematics* Reston, Va.: NCTM 2000.

Paull, Sandra. "Not Just an Average Unit." *Arithmetic Teacher,* 38 (December 1990), pp. 54–58.

Paulos, John Allen. *Innumeracy.* New York: Hill and Wang, 1989.

Phillips, Elizabeth; Lappan, Glenda; Winter, Mary Jane; and Fitzgerald, William. *Probability.* Menlo Park, Calif.: Addison-Wesley, 1986.

Quinn, Robert J. "Having Fun with Baseball Statistics." *Mathematics Teaching in the Middle School,* 1 (10), (May 1996), pp. 780–785.

Quinn, Robert, and Wiest, Lynda. "Reinventing Scrabble with Middle School Students." *Mathematics Teaching in the Middle School,* 5 (December 1999), pp. 210–213.

Russell, Susan Jo, and Corwin, Rebecca B. *Used Numbers—Statistics: The Shape of the Data, Grades 4–6.* Palo Alto, Calif.: Dale Seymour Publications, 1989.

Sakshaug, Lynae. "Which Graph is Which?" *Teaching Children Mathematics,* 6 (March 2000), pp. 454–455.

Scavo, Thomas R., and Petraroja, Byron. "Adventures in Statistics." *Teaching Children Mathematics,* 4 (March 1998), pp. 394–400.

Shaughnessy, J. Michael. "Research in Probability and Statistics: Reflections and Directions." In *Handbook of Research on Mathematics Teaching and Learning* (ed. Douglas Grouws). New York: Macmillan, 1992, pp. 495–514.

Shulte, Albert P. (ed.) *Teaching Statistics and Probability,* 1981 Yearbook. Reston, Va.: NCTM, 1981.

Shulte, Albert P., and Choate, Stuart A. *What Are My Chances?* Palo Alto, Calif.: Creative Publications, 1996.

Thiessan, Diane; Matthias, Margaret; and Smith, Jacquelin. *The Wonderful World of Mathematics: A Critically Annotated List of Children's Books in Mathematics.* Reston, Va.: NCTM, 1998.

Uccellini, John C. Teaching the Mean Meaningfully. *Mathematics Teaching in the Middle School,* 2 (2), (November–December 1996), pp. 112–115.

Wilson, Melvin R. (Skip), and Krapfl, Carol M. "Exploring Mean, Median, and Mode with a Spreadsheet" *Mathematics Teaching in the Middle School,* 1 (6), (September–October 1995), pp. 490–495.

Zawojewski, Judith S. "Research into Practice: Teaching Statistics: Mode." *Arithmetic Teacher,* 35 (March 1988), pp. 25–27.

Zawojewski, Judith S.; Brooks, G.; Dinkelkamp, L.; Goldberg, E.; Goldberg, H.; Hyde, A.; Jackson, T.; Landau, M.; Martin, H.; Nowakowski, J.; Paull, S.; Shulte, A.; Wagreich, P.; and Wilmot, B. *Dealing with Data and Chance.* Reston, Va.: NCTM, 1991.

Zawojewski, Judith and Heckman, David. "What Do Students Know about Data Analysis, Statistics, and Probability?" In *Results from the Sixth Mathematics Assessment of the National Assessment of Educational Progress* (eds. Patricia Kenney and Edward Silver). Reston, Va.: NCTM, 1997, pp. 195–223.

Zawojewski, Judith, and Shaughnessy, J. Michael. "Mean and Median: Are They Really So Easy?" *Mathematics Teaching in the Middle Grades,* 5 (March 2000), pp. 436–440.

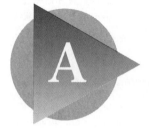

Standards and Expectations National Council of Teachers of Mathematics, 2000

Number and Operations

Standard	Pre-K–2	Grades 3–5	Grades 6–8
Instructional programs from prekindergarten through grade 12 should enable all students to—	**Expectations** In prekindergarten through grade 2 all students should—	**Expectations** In grades 3–5 all students should—	**Expectations** In grades 6–8 all students should—
Understand numbers, ways of representing numbers, relationships among numbers, and number systems	• count with understanding and recognize "how many" in sets of objects; • use multiple models to develop initial understandings of place value and the base-ten number system; • develop understanding of the relative position and magnitude of whole numbers and of ordinal and cardinal numbers and their connections; • develop a sense of whole numbers and represent and use them in flexible ways, including relating, composing, and decomposing numbers; • connect number words and numerals to the quantities they represent, using various physical models and representations; • understand and represent commonly used fractions, such as 1/4, 1/3, and 1/2.	• understand the place-value structure of the base-ten number system and be able to represent and compare whole numbers and decimals; • recognize equivalent representations for the same number and generate them by decomposing and composing numbers; • develop understanding of fractions as parts of unit wholes, as parts of a collection, as locations on number lines, and as divisions of whole numbers; • use models, benchmarks, and equivalent forms to judge the size of fractions; • recognize and generate equivalent forms of commonly used fractions, decimals, and percents; • explore numbers less than 0 by extending the number line and through familiar applications; • describe classes of numbers according to characteristics such as the nature of their factors.	• work flexibly with fractions, decimals, and percents to solve problems; • compare and order fractions, decimals, and percents efficiently and find their approximate locations on a number line; • develop meaning for percents greater than 100 and less than 1; • understand and use ratios and proportions to represent quantitative relationships; • develop an understanding of large numbers and recognize and appropriately use exponential, scientific, and calculator notation; • use factors, multiples, prime factorization, and relatively prime numbers to solve problems; • develop meaning for integers and represent and compare quantities with them.
Understand meanings of operations and how they relate to one another	• understand various meanings of addition and subtraction of whole numbers and the relationship between the two operations; • understand the effects of adding and subtracting whole numbers; • understand situations that entail multiplication and division, such as equal groupings of objects and sharing equally.	• understand various meanings of multiplication and division; • understand the effects of multiplying and dividing whole numbers; • identify and use relationships between operations, such as division as the inverse of multiplication, to solve problems; • understand and use properties of operations, such as the distributivity of multiplication over addition.	• understand the meaning and effects of arithmetic operations with fractions, decimals, and integers; • use the associative and commutative properties of addition and multiplication and the distributive property of multiplication over addition to simplify computations with integers, fractions, and decimals; • understand and use the inverse relationships of addition and subtraction, multiplication and division, and squaring and finding square roots to simplify computations and solve problems.
Compute fluently and make reasonable estimates	• develop and use strategies for whole-number computations, with a focus on addition and subtraction; • develop fluency with basic number combinations for addition and subtraction; • use a variety of methods and tools to compute, including objects, mental computation, estimation, paper and pencil, and calculators.	• develop fluency with basic number combinations for multiplication and division and use these combinations to mentally compute related problems, such as 30 × 50; • develop fluency in adding, subtracting, multiplying, and dividing whole numbers; • develop and use strategies to estimate the results of whole-number computations and to judge the reasonableness of such results; • develop and use strategies to estimate computations involving fractions and decimals in situations relevant to students' experience; • use visual models, benchmarks, and equivalent forms to add and subtract commonly used fractions and decimals; • select appropriate methods and tools for computing with whole numbers from among mental computation, estimation, calculators, and paper and pencil according to the context and nature of the computation and use the selected method or tool.	• select appropriate methods and tools for computing with fractions and decimals from among mental computation, estimation, calculators or computers, and paper and pencil, depending on the situation, and apply the selected methods; • develop and analyze algorithms for computing with fractions, decimals, and integers and develop fluency in their use; • develop and use strategies to estimate the results of rational-number computations and judge the reasonableness of the results; • develop, analyze, and explain methods for solving problems involving proportions, such as scaling and finding equivalent ratios.

Algebra

Standard	Pre-K–2	Grades 3–5	Grades 6–8
Instructional programs from prekindergarten through grade 12 should enable all students to—	**Expectations** In prekindergarten through grade 2 all students should—	**Expectations** In grades 3–5 all students should—	**Expectations** In grades 6–8 all students should—
Understand patterns, relations, and functions	• sort, classify, and order objects by size, number, and other properties; • recognize, describe, and extend patterns such as sequences of sounds and shapes or simple numeric patterns and translate from one representation to another; • analyze how both repeating and growing patterns are generated.	• describe, extend, and make generalizations about geometric and numeric patterns; • represent and analyze patterns and functions, using words, tables, and graphs.	• represent, analyze, and generalize a variety of patterns with tables, graphs, words, and, when possible, symbolic rules; • relate and compare different forms of representation for a relationship; • identify functions as linear or nonlinear and contrast their properties from tables, graphs, or equations.
Represent and analyze mathematical situations and structures using algebraic symbols	• illustrate general principles and properties of operations, such as commutativity, using specific numbers; • use concrete, pictorial, and verbal representations to develop an understanding of invented and conventional symbolic notations.	• identify such properties as commutativity, associativity, and distributivity and use them to compute with whole numbers; • represent the idea of a variable as an unknown quantity using a letter or symbol; • express mathematical relationships using equations.	• develop an initial conceptual understanding of different uses of variables; • explore relationships between symbolic expressions and graphs of lines, paying particular attention to the meaning of intercept and slope; • use symbolic algebra to represent situations and to solve problems, especially those that involve linear relationships; • recognize and generate equivalent forms for simple algebraic expressions and solve linear equations.
Use mathematical models to represent and understand quantitative relationships	• model situations that involve the addition and subtraction of whole numbers, using objects, pictures, and symbols.	• model problem situations with objects and use representations such as graphs, tables, and equations to draw conclusions.	• model and solve contextualized problems using various representations, such as graphs, tables, and equations.
Analyze change in various contexts	• describe qualitative change, such as a student's growing taller; • describe quantitative change, such as a student's growing two inches in one year.	• investigate how a change in one variable relates to a change in a second variable; • identify and describe situations with constant or varying rates of change and compare them.	• use graphs to analyze the nature of changes in quantities in linear relationships.

Geometry

Standard	Pre-K–2	Grades 3–5	Grades 6–8
Instructional programs from prekindergarten through grade 12 should enable all students to—	**Expectations** In prekindergarten through grade 2 all students should—	**Expectations** In grades 3–5 all students should—	**Expectations** In grades 6–8 all students should—
Analyze characteristics and properties of two- and three-dimensional geometric shapes and develop mathematical arguments about geometric relationships	• recognize, name, build, draw, compare, and sort two- and three-dimensional shapes; • describe attributes and parts of two- and three-dimensional shapes; • investigate and predict the results of putting together and taking apart two- and three-dimensional shapes.	• identify, compare, and analyze attributes of two- and three-dimensional shapes and develop vocabulary to describe the attributes; • classify two- and three-dimensional shapes according to their properties and develop definitions of classes of shapes such as triangles and pyramids; • investigate, describe, and reason about the results of subdividing, combining, and transforming shapes; • explore congruence and similarity; • make and test conjectures about geometric properties and relationships and develop logical arguments to justify conclusions.	• precisely describe, classify, and understand relationships among types of two- and three-dimensional objects using their defining properties; • understand relationships among the angles, side lengths, perimeters, areas, and volumes of similar objects; • create and critique inductive and deductive arguments concerning geometric ideas and relationships, such as congruence, similarity, and the Pythagorean relationship.
Specify locations and describe spatial relationships using coordinate geometry and other representational systems	• describe, name, and interpret relative positions in space and apply ideas about relative position; • describe, name, and interpret direction and distance in navigating space and apply ideas about direction and distance; • find and name locations with simple relationships such as "near to" and in coordinate systems such as maps.	• describe location and movement using common language and geometric vocabulary; • make and use coordinate systems to specify locations and to describe paths; • find the distance between points along horizontal and vertical lines of a coordinate system.	• use coordinate geometry to represent and examine the properties of geometric shapes; • use coordinate geometry to examine special geometric shapes, such as regular polygons or those with pairs or parallel or perpendicular sides.
Apply transformations and use symmetry to analyze mathematical situations	• recognize and apply slides, flips, and turns; • recognize and create shapes that have symmetry.	• predict and describe the results of sliding, flipping, and turning two-dimensional shapes; • describe a motion or a series of motions that will show that two shapes are congruent; • identify and describe line and rotational symmetry in two- and three-dimensional shapes and designs.	• describe sizes, positions, and orientations of shapes under informal transformations such as flips, turns, slides, and scaling; • examine the congruence, similarity, and line or rotational symmetry of objects using transformations.
Use visualization, spatial reasoning, and geometric modeling to solve problems	• create mental images of geometric shapes using spatial memory and spatial visualization; • recognize and represent shapes from different perspectives; • relate ideas in geometry to ideas in number and measurement; • recognize geometric shapes and structures in the environment and specify their location.	• build and draw geometric objects; • create and describe mental images of objects, patterns, and paths; • identify and build a three-dimensional object from two-dimensional representations of that object; • identify and build a two-dimensional representation of a three-dimensional object; • use geometric models to solve problems in other areas of mathematics, such as number and measurement; • recognize geometric ideas and relationships and apply them to other disciplines and to problems that arise in the classroom or in everyday life.	• draw geometric objects with specified properties, such as side lengths or angle measures; • use two-dimensional representations of three-dimensional objects to visualize and solve problems such as those involving surface area and volume; • use visual tools such as networks to represent and solve problems; • use geometric models to represent and explain numerical and algebraic relationships; • recognize and apply geometric ideas and relationships in areas outside the mathematical classroom, such as art, science, and everyday life.

Measurement

Standard	Pre-K–2	Grades 3–5	Grades 6–8
Instructional programs from prekindergarten through grade 12 should enable all students to—	**Expectations** In prekindergarten through grade 2 all students should—	**Expectations** In grades 3–5 all students should—	**Expectations** In grades 6–8 all students should—
Understand measurable attributes of objects and the units, systems, and processes of measurement	• recognize the attributes of length, volume, weight, area, and time; • compare and order objects according to these attributes; • understand how to measure using nonstandard and standard units; • select an appropriate unit and tool for the attribute being measured.	• understand such attributes as length, area, weight, volume, and size of angle and select the appropriate type of unit for measuring each attribute; • understand the need for measuring with standard units and become familiar with standard units in the customary and metric systems; • carry out simple unit conversions, such as from centimeters to meters, within a system of measurement; • understand that measurements are approximations and understand how differences in units affect precision; • explore what happens to measurements of a two-dimensional shape such as its perimeter and area when the shape is changed in some way.	• understand both metric and customary systems of measurement; • understand relationships among units and convert from one unit to another within the same system; • understand, select, and use units of appropriate size and type to measure angles, perimeter, area, surface area, and volume.
Apply appropriate techniques, tools, and formulas to determine measurements	• measure with multiple copies of units of the same size, such as paper clips laid end to end; • use repetition of a single unit to measure something larger than the unit, for instance, measuring the length of a room with a single meterstick; • use tools to measure; • develop common referents for measures to make comparisons and estimates.	• develop strategies for estimating the perimeters, areas, and volumes of irregular shapes; • select and apply appropriate standard units and tools to measure length, area, volume, weight, time, temperature, and the size of angles; • select and use benchmarks to estimate measurements; • develop, understand, and use formulas to find the area of rectangles and related triangles and parallelograms; • develop strategies to determine the surface areas and volumes of rectangular solids.	• use common benchmarks to select appropriate methods for estimating measurements; • select and apply techniques and tools to accurately find length, area, volume, and angle measures to appropriate levels of precision; • develop and use formulas to determine the circumference of circles and the area of triangles, parallelograms, trapezoids, and circles and develop strategies to find the areas of more-complex shapes; • develop strategies to determine the surface area and volume of selected prisms, pyramids, and cylinders; • solve problems involving scale factors, using ratio and proportion; • solve simple problems involving rates and derived measurements for such attributes as velocity and density.

Data Analysis and Probability

Standard	Pre-K–2	Grades 3–5	Grades 6–8
Instructional programs from prekindergarten through grade 12 should enable all students to—	**Expectations** In prekindergarten through grade 2 all students should—	**Expectations** In grades 3–5 all students should—	**Expectations** In grades 6–8 all students should—
Formulate questions that can be addressed with data and collect, organize, and display relevant data to answer them	• pose questions and gather data about themselves and their surroundings; • sort and classify objects according to their attributes and organize data about the objects; • represent data using concrete objects, pictures, and graphs.	• design investigations to address a question and consider how data-collection methods affect the nature of the data set; • collect data using observations, surveys, and experiments; • represent data using tables and graphs such as line plots, bar graphs, and line graphs; • recognize the differences in representing categorical and numerical data.	• formulate questions, design studies, and collect data about a characteristic shared by two populations or different characteristics within one population; • select, create, and use appropriate graphical representations of data, including histograms, box plots, and scatterplots.
Select and use appropriate statistical methods to analyze data	• describe parts of the data and the set of data as a whole to determine what the data show.	• describe the shape and important features of a set of data and compare related data sets, with an emphasis on how the data are distributed; • use measures of center, focusing on the median, and understand what each does and does not indicate about the data set; • compare different representations of the same data and evaluate how well each representation shows important aspects of the data.	• find, use, and interpret measures of center and spread, including mean and interquartile range; • discuss and understand the correspondence between data sets and their graphical representations, especially histograms, stem-and-leaf plots, box plots, and scatterplots.
Develop and evaluate inferences and predictions that are based on data	• discuss events related to students' experiences as likely or unlikely.	• propose and justify conclusions and predictions that are based on data and design studies to further investigate the conclusions or predictions.	• use observations about differences between two or more samples to make conjectures about the populations from which the samples were taken; • make conjectures about possible relationships between two characteristics of a sample on the basis of scatterplots of the data and approximate lines of fit; • use conjectures to formulate new questions and plan new studies to answer them.
Understand and apply basic concepts of probability		• describe events as likely or unlikely and discuss the degree of likelihood using such words as *certain*, *equally likely*, and *impossible*; • predict the probability of outcomes of simple experiments and test the predictions; • understand that the measure of the likelihood of an event can be represented by a number from 0 to 1.	• understand and use appropriate terminology to describe complementary and mutually exclusive events; • use proportionality and a basic understanding of probability to make and test conjectures about the results of experiments and simulations; • compute probabilities for simple compound events, using such methods as organized lists, tree diagrams, and area methods.

Problem Solving

Standard

Instructional programs from prekindergarten through grade 12 should enable all students to—

- Build new mathematical knowledge through problem solving
- Solve problems that arise in mathematics and in other contexts
- Apply and adapt a variety of appropriate strategies to solve problems
- Monitor and reflect on the process of mathematical problem solving

Reasoning and Proof

Standard

Instructional programs from prekindergarten through grade 12 should enable all students to—

- Recognize reasoning and proof as fundamental aspects of mathematics
- Make and investigate mathematical conjectures
- Develop and evaluate mathematical arguments and proofs
- Select and use various types of reasoning and methods of proof

Communication

Standard

Instructional programs from prekindergarten through grade 12 should enable all students to—

- Organize and consolidate their mathematical thinking through communication
- Communicate their mathematical thinking coherently and clearly to peers, teachers, and others
- Analyze and evaluate the mathematical thinking and strategies of others
- Use the language of mathematics to express mathematical ideas precisely

Connections

Standard

Instructional programs from prekindergarten through grade 12 should enable all students to—

- Recognize and use connections among mathematical ideas
- Understand how mathematical ideas interconnect and build on one another to produce a coherent whole
- Recognize and apply mathematics in contexts outside of mathematics

Representation

Standard

Instructional programs from prekindergarten through grade 12 should enable all students to—

- Create and use representations to organize, record, and communicate mathematical ideas
- Select, apply, and translate among mathematical representations to solve problems
- Use representations to model and interpret physical, social, and mathematical phenomena

Blackline Masters

B–1 Five and Ten Frames

Reys et al., *Helping Children Learn Mathematics*, 6E, copyright © 2001 John Wiley & Sons, Inc.

B–2 Hundred Charts

1	2	3	4	5	6	7	8	9	10
11	12	13	14	15	16	17	18	19	20
21	22	23	24	25	26	27	28	29	30
31	32	33	34	35	36	37	38	39	40
41	42	43	44	45	46	47	48	49	50
51	52	53	54	55	56	57	58	59	60
61	62	63	64	65	66	67	68	69	70
71	72	73	74	75	76	77	78	79	80
81	82	83	84	85	86	87	88	89	90
91	92	93	94	95	96	97	98	99	100

0	1	2	3	4	5	6	7	8	9
10	11	12	13	14	15	16	17	18	19
20	21	22	23	24	25	26	27	28	29
30	31	32	33	34	35	36	37	38	39
40	41	42	43	44	45	46	47	48	49
50	51	52	53	54	55	56	57	58	59
60	61	62	63	64	65	66	67	68	69
70	71	72	73	74	75	76	77	78	79
80	81	82	83	84	85	86	87	88	89
90	91	92	93	94	95	96	97	98	99

B-3 Variations of Hundreds Charts: A

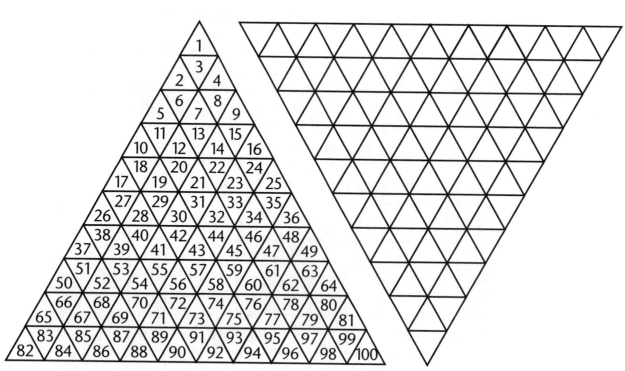

Reys et al., *Helping Children Learn Mathematics*, 6E, copyright © 2001 John Wiley & Sons, Inc.

.01	.02	.03	.04	.05	.06	.07	.08	.09	.10
.11	.12	.13	.14	.15	.16	.17	.18	.19	.20
.21	.22	.23	.24	.25	.26	.27	.28	.29	.30
.31	.32	.33	.34	.35	.36	.37	.38	.39	.40
.41	.42	.43	.44	.45	.46	.47	.48	.49	.50
.51	.52	.53	.54	.55	.56	.57	.58	.59	.60
.61	.62	.63	.64	.65	.66	.67	.68	.69	.70
.71	.72	.73	.74	.75	.76	.77	.78	.79	.80
.81	.82	.83	.84	.85	.86	.87	.88	.89	.90
.91	.92	.93	.94	.95	.96	.97	.98	.99	1.00

10	20	30	40	50	60	70	80	90	100
110	120	130	140	150	160	170	180	190	200
210	220	230	240	250	260	270	280	290	300
310	320	330	340	350	360	370	380	390	400
410	420	430	440	450	460	470	480	490	500
510	520	530	540	550	560	570	580	590	600
610	620	630	640	650	660	670	680	690	700
710	720	730	740	750	760	770	780	790	800
810	820	830	840	850	860	870	880	890	900
910	920	930	940	950	960	970	980	990	1000

B–4 Basic Addition and Multiplication Facts

+	0	1	2	3	4	5	6	7	8	9
0	0	1	2	3	4	5	6	7	8	9
1	1	2	3	4	5	6	7	8	9	10
2	2	3	4	5	6	7	8	9	10	11
3	3	4	5	6	7	8	9	10	11	12
4	4	5	6	7	8	9	10	11	12	13
5	5	6	7	8	9	10	11	12	13	14
6	6	7	8	9	10	11	12	13	14	15
7	7	8	9	10	11	12	13	14	15	16
8	8	9	10	11	12	13	14	15	16	17
9	9	10	11	12	13	14	15	16	17	18

☐ Commutativity
☐ Using 0 and 1
☐ Doubles, Doubles + or −1
☐ Counting On (1,2,3)
☐ Adding to 10

X	0	1	2	3	4	5	6	7	8	9
0	0	0	0	0	0	0	0	0	0	0
1	0	1	2	3	4	5	6	7	8	9
2	0	2	4	6	8	10	12	14	18	18
3	0	3	6	9	12	15	18	21	24	27
4	0	4	8	12	16	20	24	28	32	36
5	0	5	10	15	20	25	30	35	40	45
6	0	6	12	18	24	30	36	42	48	54
7	0	7	14	21	28	35	42	49	56	63
8	0	8	16	24	32	40	48	56	64	72
9	0	9	18	27	36	45	54	63	72	81

☐ Commutativity
☐ Using 0 and 1
☐ Skip Counting
☐ Repeated Addition
☐ Splitting Product into Known Parts
☐ Patterns

4	9
3	8
2	7
1	6
0	5

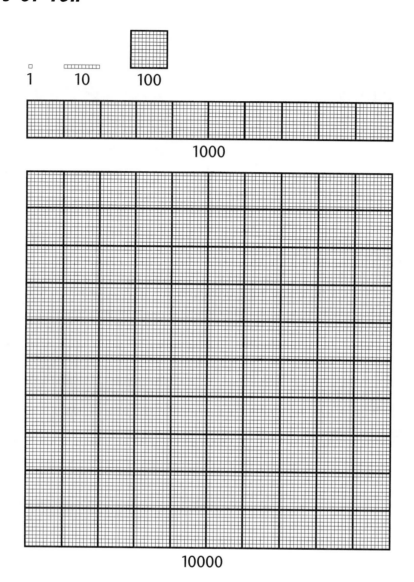

1   10   100

1000

10000

Reys et al., *Helping Children Learn Mathematics*, 6E, copyright © 2001 John Wiley & Sons, Inc.

B–7 Decimal or Percent Paper

B-8 Fraction Bars

one	1										
halves	$\dfrac{1}{2}$					$\dfrac{2}{2}$					
thirds	$\dfrac{1}{3}$			$\dfrac{2}{3}$			$\dfrac{3}{3}$				
fourths	$\dfrac{1}{4}$		$\dfrac{2}{4}$		$\dfrac{3}{4}$		$\dfrac{4}{4}$				
fifths	$\dfrac{1}{5}$	$\dfrac{2}{5}$		$\dfrac{3}{5}$		$\dfrac{4}{5}$		$\dfrac{5}{5}$			
sixths	$\dfrac{1}{6}$	$\dfrac{2}{6}$	$\dfrac{3}{6}$		$\dfrac{4}{6}$		$\dfrac{5}{6}$		$\dfrac{6}{6}$		
eighths	$\dfrac{1}{8}$	$\dfrac{2}{8}$	$\dfrac{3}{8}$	$\dfrac{4}{8}$	$\dfrac{5}{8}$	$\dfrac{6}{8}$		$\dfrac{7}{8}$	$\dfrac{8}{8}$		
ninths	$\dfrac{1}{9}$	$\dfrac{2}{9}$	$\dfrac{3}{9}$	$\dfrac{4}{9}$	$\dfrac{5}{9}$	$\dfrac{6}{9}$	$\dfrac{7}{9}$	$\dfrac{8}{9}$	$\dfrac{9}{9}$		
tenths	$\dfrac{1}{10}$	$\dfrac{2}{10}$	$\dfrac{3}{10}$	$\dfrac{4}{10}$	$\dfrac{5}{10}$	$\dfrac{6}{10}$	$\dfrac{7}{10}$	$\dfrac{8}{10}$	$\dfrac{9}{10}$	$\dfrac{10}{10}$	
twelfths	$\dfrac{1}{12}$	$\dfrac{2}{12}$	$\dfrac{3}{12}$	$\dfrac{4}{12}$	$\dfrac{5}{12}$	$\dfrac{6}{12}$	$\dfrac{7}{12}$	$\dfrac{8}{12}$	$\dfrac{9}{12}$	$\dfrac{10}{12}$	$\dfrac{11}{12}$ ... $\dfrac{12}{12}$

Reys et al., *Helping Children Learn Mathematics*, 6E, copyright © 2001 John Wiley & Sons, Inc.

B–9 Fraction Models

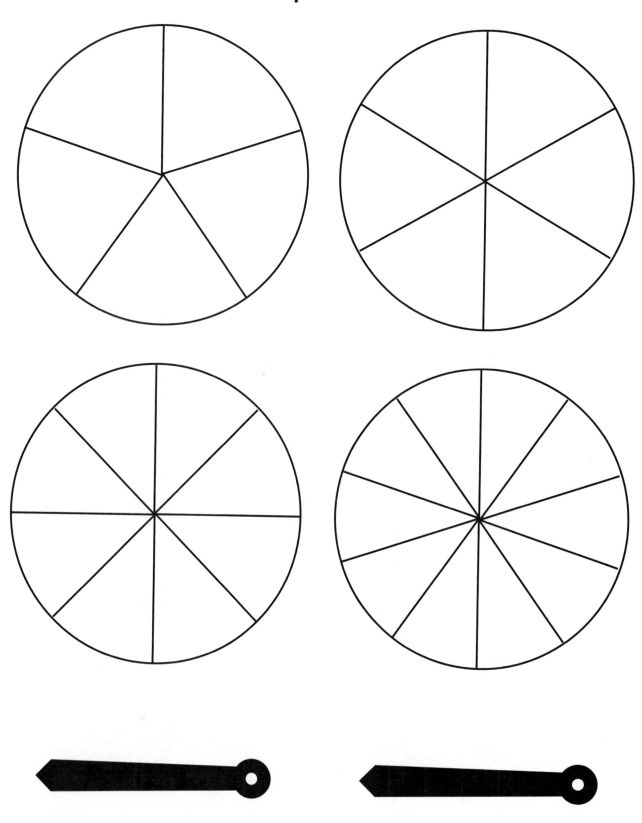

Reys et al., *Helping Children Learn Mathematics*, 6E, copyright © 2001 John Wiley & Sons, Inc.

B–11 Rulers

Primary inch ruler

Half-inch ruler

Fourth-inch ruler

Eighth-inch ruler

Primary centimeter ruler

Millimeter ruler

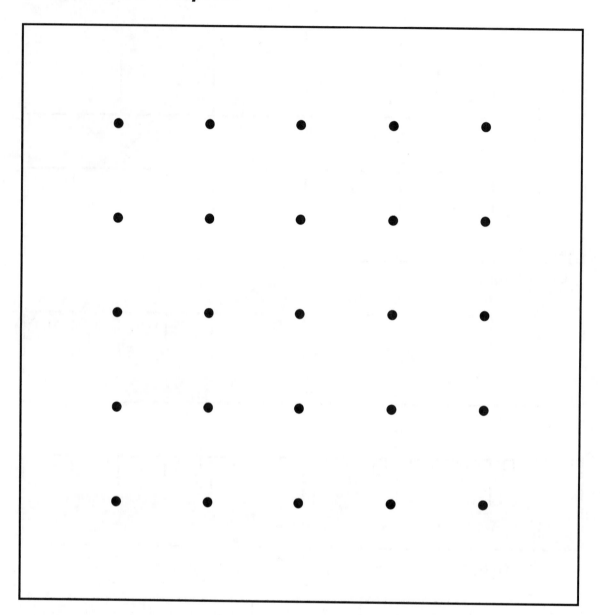

B–13 Geoboard Recording Paper

B–14 Centimeter Dot Paper

Reys et al., *Helping Children Learn Mathematics*, 6E, copyright © 2001 John Wiley & Sons, Inc.

B-15 Isometric Paper

B–16 Centimeter Grid Paper

B-17 Inch Grid Paper

B–18 Half-Inch Grid Paper

B-19 Quarter-Inch Grid Paper

B–22 Attribute Pieces

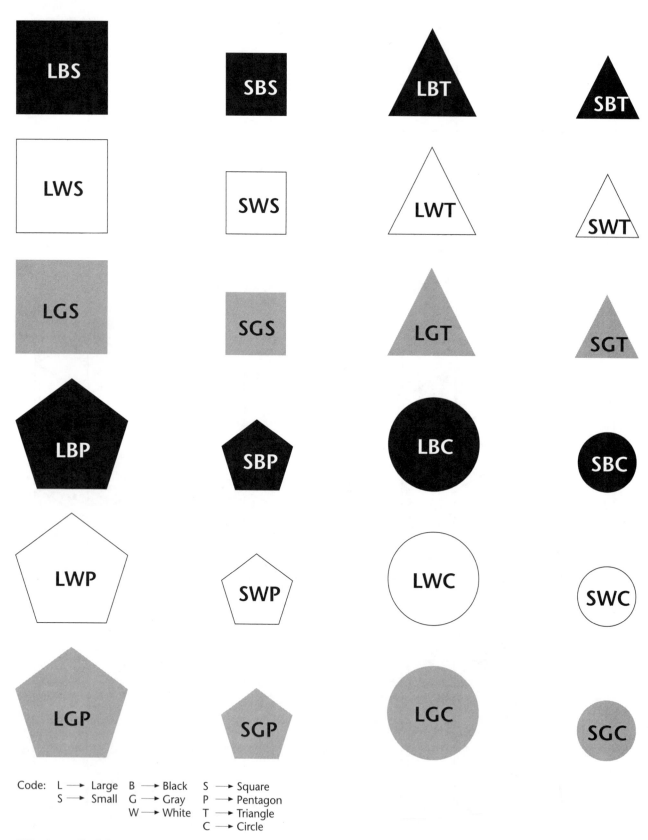

Code: L → Large   B → Black   S → Square
      S → Small   G → Gray   P → Pentagon
                  W → White   T → Triangle
                              C → Circle

LBS = Large Black Square

Publishers and Distributors

Instructional Materials

Creative Publications
5623 W. 115th St.
Alsip, IL 60803
800-624-0822
creativeinfo@tribune.com
www.creativepublications.com

Dale Seymour Publications
Pearson Learning
299 Jefferson Road
P.O. Box 480
Parsippany, NJ 07054
800-321-3106
pearson-learning2@prenhall.com
www.pearsonlearning.com

Delta Education, Inc.
P.O. Box 3000
Nashua, NH 03061-3000
800-442-5444
abacon@delta-edu.com

Didax, Inc.
Education Resources
395 Main Street
Rowley, MA 01969-3785
800-458-0024
webmaster@didaxinc.com
www.Didaxinc.com

ETA/Cuisenaire
500 Greenview Court
Vernon Hills, IL 60061-1862
800-445-5985
info@etauniverse.com
www.etauniverse.com

GEMS
Lawrence Hall of Science #5200
University of California
Berkeley, CA 94720-5200
510-642-5132
gems@uclink4.berkeley.edu
www.lhs.berkeley.edu/GEMS/

Heinemann
88 Post Road West
Westport, CT 06881
800-793-2154
custserv@heinemann.com
www.heinemann.com

Ideal School Supply Company
Instructional Fair Group
3195 Wilson Drive NW
P.O. Box 250
Grand Rapids, MI 49544
    or 49502-0334
800-443-2976
ifcomments@tribune.com
www.instructionalfair.com

Key Curriculum Press
1150 65th St.
Emeryville, CA 94608
800-995-MATH
www.keypress.com

National Council of Teachers
    of Mathematics
1906 Association Drive
Reston, VA 22091-9988
800-235-7566
nctm@nctm.org
www.nctm.org

NASCO Math
901 Janesville Avenue
Fort Atkinson, WI 53538-0901
800-558-9595
info@nascofa.com
www.enasco.com

Scott Resources
P.O. Box 2121
Ft. Collins, CO 80522
800-446-8767
www.hubbardscientific.com

Summit Learning
P.O. Box 493
Ft. Collins, CO 80522
800-777-8817
info@summitlearning.com
www.summitlearning.com

Tricon Publishing
6400 South Crawford Road
Mt. Pleasant, MI 48858
888-224-8053
www.triconpub.com

USA Today Teaching Guides
1000 Wilson Blvd.
Arlington, VA 22229
800-757-TEACH
www.usatoday.com

Index